Marketing
and
Society

HOLT, RINEHART AND WINSTON MARKETING SERIES

Paul E. Green, Adviser
Wharton School, University of Pennsylvania

Philip Kotler, Adviser
Northwestern University

James F. Engel, David T. Kollat, Roger D. Blackwell
All of the Ohio State University
CONSUMER BEHAVIOR
CASES IN CONSUMER BEHAVIOR
RESEARCH IN CONSUMER BEHAVIOR

Ronald R. Gist
University of Denver
MARKETING AND SOCIETY: A CONCEPTUAL INTRODUCTION
READINGS: MARKETING AND SOCIETY

Charles S. Goodman
University of Pennsylvania
MANAGEMENT OF THE PERSONAL SELLING FUNCTION

Philip Kotler
Northwestern University
MARKETING DECISION MAKING: A MODEL BUILDING APPROACH

John C. Narver, *University of Washington*
Ronald Savitt, *Boston University*
THE MARKETING ECONOMY: AN ANALYTICAL APPROACH
CONCEPTUAL READINGS IN THE MARKETING ECONOMY

Thomas R. Wotruba
San Diego State College
SALES MANAGEMENT: PLANNING, ACCOMPLISHMENT, AND EVALUATION

Thomas R. Wotruba, *San Diego State College*
Robert M. Olsen, *California State College, Fullerton*
READINGS IN SALES MANAGEMENT: CONCEPTS AND VIEWPOINTS

Marketing and Society

A Conceptual Introduction

Ronald R. Gist

University of Denver

Holt, Rinehart and Winston, Inc.
New York   Chicago   San Francisco   Atlanta
Dallas   Montreal   Toronto   London   Sydney

The cover painting is by
Leon Polk Smith, *Correspondence Red-Black*.
Oil on canvas. *Courtesy* Galerie Chalette, New York.

Copyright © 1971 by Holt, Rinehart and Winston, Inc.

All rights reserved

Library of Congress Catalog Card Number: 72-124538

ISBN: 0-03-081280-1

Printed in the United States of America

1 2 3 4 074 9 8 7 6 5 4 3 2

Editors' Foreword

The Advisory Editors of the Holt, Rinehart and Winston Marketing Series are pleased to publish this highly interesting and relevant new text in marketing. It is the first introductory marketing text in recent times to emphasize a *societal* approach to marketing. In this age, when concerned people are searching for meaningful values to guide their life style, it is most appropriate that students be introduced to the subject of marketing in terms of the social and public policy questions raised by the marketing system. Professor Gist presents the criticisms and the praises of the marketing system in a most articulate and open way, so that the students can reflect on public policy questions as citizens and future executives.

The book is also notable for its conceptual treatment of the marketing system, markets, and managerial issues. Rather than describing things only as they appear, the author introduces a host of concepts that throw much light on surface phenomena. A good concept is worth a thousand words and here the author's text excels.

Finally the book is well-written and enjoyable to read. This should be true of all books, but unfortunately is not. When an author is an especially able communicator, it should be noted. Altogether, we look forward to Professor Gist's book becoming a pacesetter in introductory marketing courses, as instructors and students search for a meaningful societal and conceptually based text.

Philadelphia, Pennsylvania   —Paul E. Green
Evanston, Illinois   —Philip Kotler
January 1971

Preface

In the last several years, there has been increasing unrest with a purely managerial emphasis in the introductory course in marketing. The reasons for this unrest appear to center around three basic points:

a. An intensive managerial exposure at the introductory level can serve to weaken the marketing curriculum. This may seem a curious remark. But while the use of the management approach at the introductory level has unquestionably served to strengthen the first course, it has also probably tended to weaken the senior level "problems" or "case" course. Too often, one result of an intensive exposure to managerial marketing at the introductory level is that little is left that is truly new or fresh in concept for the senior course that follows. The senior level marketing management course today is frequently different from the introductory course only in that the latter uses cases extensively rather than a lecture/discussion format. Both the perspective and the principal concepts utilized in the senior course are often essentially the same as in the basic course.
b. An intensive managerial exposure at the introductory level seems to assume that most students in the basic course will go on for further course work in marketing. The managerial approach is, pedagogically, a foundation which, for maximum value, must be built upon. The fact is that for about 80 percent of all students enrolled, the introductory course in marketing is the terminal marketing exposure.
c. It is apparent that marketing teachers at all levels of work are increasingly concerned with the inability of many managerial texts to deal effectively with issues that relate to the social responsibility of our marketing system. Moreover, a sound theoretical basis is an extremely important foundation for the most meaningful study of almost any discipline. An important element in attracting good students and in

properly conveying the challenge of a career in marketing is the logic of a conceptual or theoretical type of exposure. Understandably, most managerial texts deal principally with techniques and processes and not with the societal issues that may attend business activity.

The approach most often mentioned as a logical alternative to a purely management oriented introduction utilizes an environmental or societal perspective. This book emphasizes, to a greater degree than the current group of managerial texts, a societal perspective. The point of view held through substantial portions of the book is more nearly that of an individual or a household being served by our system of markets. The book is not, however, exclusively societal in perspective. Indeed, many of the materials that teachers of a managerial course in marketing have become accustomed to working with are developed in the book. Where possible, the social importance of these managerial actions is emphasized.

But this book is distinctive in still another way. It is largely conceptual in the sense that there is little description of any kind in it. Each chapter is developed around some basic concept or set of related concepts. It is believed that this use of conceptual subject matter encourages the use by students of logic and formal reasoning processes rather than recitation and description. The book is written at a level that should permit its use either as an undergraduate first course in marketing or as a first course at the graduate level. The book should be particularly well adapted to the needs of the graduate student in marketing who has undergraduate work in a field of study other than business.

In summary then, and contrasted to most current introductory texts, this book:

a. Gives relatively more consideration to societal issues in marketing.
b. Explores "managerial" subject matter, but where possible from a social consequences point of view.
c. Embodies an extensive use of conceptual and analytical materials.

While it is popular to identify oneself and one's books as being either behavioral or mathematical, I will resist that temptation. Such dichotomous nomenclature is often misleading, and sometimes fraudulent. This book includes, I believe, a discussion of every major behavioral concept with relevance in marketing: It introduces the student to most of the significant mathematical techniques. Though in both cases, the emphasis is always on marketing. That is, care has been exercised not to let the technique or the concept dominate the discipline. More specifically, such behavioral concepts as learning theory, formal principles of persuasion, social stratification, occupational profiling, perception, the "self" concept and subception* are included. The book includes a discussion of the possible

*Subception is a syllable acronym constructed from the phrase *subliminal perception.*

role of queueing theory, linear programming, brand switching, and many other concepts founded in mathematics. It is important enough to repeat, however, that mathematics does not dominate the discussion—nor is the math developed in a cryptic manner. An effort has been made throughout to answer rather than raise questions. The basic analytical concepts are introduced; it is essentially up to the individual teacher to determine how far to develop the mathematical processes. In order to work with the book, the student needs no more than college algebra, and can survive with less than that.

The book is organized around four major parts. Part One defines the scope of the marketing discipline, explores briefly the historical status of marketing, and explores at greater length some current attitudes toward the field of marketing. The last chapter in Part One defines the social and economic foundations upon which marketing is founded.

Part Two identifies the major dimensions in which marketing activities are formally regulated. But these chapters are not the customary recitation of the relevant state and federal law. Regulation is prompted by one or more of several basic business activities—deception, expansion or discrimination. And Part Two is developed around the motives underlying these three types of business activity. The teacher who has come to have a warm spot in his heart for the law and the specific provisions of the law will find these materials in evidence, though in a different organizational scheme.

Part Three is concerned with markets and market behavior. Accordingly, three basic topics are treated: (a) consumer behavior, (b) marketing research and (c) sales forecasting. Three chapters are devoted to consumer behavior. The first of these chapters defines such major consumption patterns as income allocation patterns, brand loyalty patterns and time-of-adoption patterns. The remaining two chapters explore the theoretical foundations that are evolving as explanations of these three types of consumption patterns.

In general, Part Four introduces the analytical elements that are a part of the general strategy of marketing behavior. Of the thirteen chapters that constitute this part of the book, two are concerned with the nature of modern competition. These two chapters quarrel with the traditional, or economic, view of competition—they identify the concepts of vertical competition, innovistic competition and competition with the marketing mix. The concern in these chapters is with the impact of such competition upon society, as well as with the strategy of the individual firm. Two chapters are devoted to a consideration of some of the social and economic results of our commercial system of mass communications. These two chapters center on attitudes toward and responsibilities of the mass communications media.

One chapter is developed around the consequences, both social and economic, of a market system that produces a continuous panorama of new products and services. The conceptual device of the product life cycle and the notion of planned product obsolescence constitute the nucleus of this latter discussion. Four chapters deal with dealer-distributor networks, the theory of institutional change in marketing, and the basic concepts of physical distribution. Three chapters are concerned with the role of price in modern competition. The last chapter in the price series introduces some problems in the arithmetic of pricing. This placement of pricing problems makes it convenient to omit that chapter if the teacher does not wish to work with that material.

Two types of questions are provided at the end of each chapter. There are *review questions* that examine the reader in a factual sense over the materials in each chapter; there are *discussion questions* that encourage the student to go beyond the factual content of the corresponding chapter and relate his own experiences and observations to the text material. A summary for each chapter is provided. These summaries provide an overview of the basic points made in each chapter and should serve effectively as a quick review device for the student.

Several persons have been very helpful to me in the development of this book. First, I want to thank Professor Philip McVey, Professor of Marketing and Chairman of the Department of Marketing at the University of Nebraska. Professor McVey provided much of the clerical assistance required for the typing of the first eight chapters of the book. I wish also to thank Philip Kotler, A. Montgomery Ward Professor of Management, Northwestern University, and Professor Paul Green of the Wharton School, both of whom provided a careful and helpful critical reading of the manuscript. I acknowledge also the encouragement given me by Dean Arthur Mason, Jr., of the College of Business Administration, University of Denver. Finally, I would be remiss if I did not recognize the indispensible assistance provided by Mrs. Natalie Hermansen. Mrs. Hermansen typed virtually all of the manuscript, and made all deadlines, however short the notice, however difficult the copy to work from.

−R.R.G.

Denver, Colorado
December 1970

Contents

Marketing
and
Society

Part I

A BACKGROUND FOR THE STUDY OF MARKETING

Chapter 1

WHAT MARKETING IS

In 1964 the IBM Corporation obtained the patent rights on something called a "vacuum wand." This device may one day greatly expedite the checkout process in supermarkets. Briefly, this mysterious wand will pull special perforated price tabs from the items of merchandise being purchased and total the value of each order. Prices are printed on these price tabs in an electromagnetic type font, which can be read and summed electronically.

An experiment designed to explore both the process through which consumers develop loyalty to particular brands of products and the strength of such brand loyalty revealed the following tendencies:

1 Consumers develop loyalty to particular brands even where competing products are identical. That is, even when there are no discernible product differences, preferences for particular brands will develop. If this fact is not particularly startling, consider that this is apparently true even in the complete absence of advertising of any kind.
2 Consumers may pay as much as 7 cents more for a loaf of bread which is a preferred brand, even though the rejected brands came from the same bakery batch and are, effectively, identical to the preferred brand.[1] Note again that none of the brands in the experiment were ever promoted or advertised in any way.

In the late fall of 1968 General Motors Research Laboratories announced that experiments were under way that would help to determine the feasi-

[1] W. T. Tucker, "The Development of Brand Loyalty," *Journal of Marketing Research,* August 1964, pp. 32–35; reprinted in Harold H. Kassarjian and Thomas S. Robertson, editors, *Perspectives in Consumer Behavior,* Glenview, Ill.: Scott, Foresman and Company, 1968, pp. 114–120.

bility of a type of hybrid car which operates on batteries—batteries which are recharged during use by a small internal combustion motor. Note that the roles of battery and internal combustion engine are reversed in this concept: The principle power source is a battery driven electric motor and the supplementary power source is the internal combustion engine. This electric/gasoline hybrid may point the way to smogless urban areas and low cost, short range, commuter transportation.[2]

Research conducted in underdeveloped countries suggests that the low-margin high-turnover retail prototype which we call a supermarket may prove to be an extremely important part of the standard prescription for economic growth and development. Evidence suggests that the supermarket concept, when introduced into a developing country, may stimulate both the level of consumption and the willingness of manufacturers to invest in capital goods.[3]

A marketing research experiment conducted in a New Jersey movie theater exposed a total of about 45,000 patrons to the messages "eat popcorn" and "drink Coca-Cola." These messages were shown on the movie screen at *subliminal* speeds and at a lower intensity of light than that of the film being shown. Popcorn sales increased almost 60 percent over previous comparable periods, and sales of the soft drink increased almost 20 percent over comparable periods.[4]

A national advertiser had the alternative of using either a four-color, full-page advertisement or a page and two-fifths in black and white. The cost of the two was approximately the same. An analysis of the eye movements (with ophthalmographic equipment) of panel subjects indicated that the black and white advertisement was not only scrutinized more closely, but also produced better recall.[5]

[2] One detailed description of this research may be seen in *Popular Science,* December 1968, pp. 116–119.
[3] See, for example, Charles C. Slater, "Marketing Processes in the Development of Latin American Societies," *Journal of Marketing,* July 1968, p. 53.
[4] Subliminal means, literally, below the threshold of conscious perception. A report of the scare of subliminal perception may be seen in *Consumer Reports,* January 1958, p. 8. A good statement of the available evidence relating to subliminal impressions may be seen in Edward L. Brink and William T. Kelley, *The Management of Promotion,* Englewood Cliffs, N.J.: Prentice-Hall, Inc., 1963, pp. 140–143.
[5] See D. B. Lucas and S. H. Britt, *Measuring Advertising Effectiveness,* New York: McGraw-Hill Book Co., 1963, pp. 162–163.

All the anecdotes above have one thing in common. Each involved some facet of a business discipline that is called marketing. And, although the subject matter of these several anecdotes ranges widely from essentially psychological phenomena (brand loyalty formation and subliminal perception) to technological matters (vacuum "wand" checkout and hybrid electric cars) and the identification of the critical factors underlying economic growth and development, each is nonetheless closely related to some aspect of the study of marketing.

On the basis of the clues in these introductory anecdotes, we may conclude that marketing is an area of study with diverse subject matter which deals with both business and economic issues. For this reason marketing is somewhat more difficult to define than other fields of study.[6] Indeed, most of the remainder of this chapter is devoted to identifying and illustrating various aspects and dimensions of the study of marketing. More specifically, the remainder of the chapter is divided into four major sections. First, "market" is formally defined. Then "marketing" is defined—with special attention being given to (a) the economic dimensions, (b) the managerial dimensions, and (c) the societal and cultural dimensions of the discipline. Another section is devoted to a careful identification of the interdisciplinary character of marketing. Finally, the current economic importance of marketing is established briefly.

Market defined

The term "marketing" evolved from the root word "market." By first considering this linguistic ancestor of the word "marketing," it is possible for us to discover something about the term marketing itself. The term *market* is used in essentially three different ways: (a) a verb sense, (b) a place sense and (c) a people sense.

It is not uncommon to find the word market used as a verb to suggest the action of dealing in or exposing for sale. This usage is undoubtedly one reason why many people interpret the term marketing as synonymous with selling. Another verb usage occurs when, for example, a housewife uses the word in the sentence, "I'm going marketing." Although it is popular lay usage to consider the word market as a verb, we will find relatively little value in doing so.[7]

[6] One effort to reduce this diversity of subject matter is discussed in Kenneth D. MacKenzie and Francesco M. Nicosia, "Marketing Systems: Toward Formal Descriptions and Structural Properties," in Robert L. King, editor, *1968 Fall Conference Proceedings,* American Marketing Association, p. 14.

[7] The various meanings of the word "market" are explored at length in Roland S. Vaile, "Some Concepts of Markets and Marketing Strategy," in Robert V. Mitchell, editor, *Changing Structure and Strategy in Marketing,* Urbana, Ill.: University of Illinois Press, 1958, pp. 18–19. See also Cyril S. Belshaw, *Traditional Exchange and Modern Markets,* Englewood Cliffs, N.J.: Prentice-Hall, Inc., 1965, pp. 7–9.

A second rather common use of the term market is as a place or a sphere. When one speaks of a market for mutual funds or corporate stocks and bonds, the term is being used in the sphere or place sense. That is, when we say a market for mutual funds exists, we usually mean that some organized facility or organization exists whose function it is to expedite the purchase and sale of such shares. Sometimes a market is a precisely defined physical place, as in the statement, "He went to the market." On occasion it is a broader and more nebulous place, as in the sentence, "There is a world market for wheat." Although both are encountered, neither the verb sense nor the place sense of the word market are used extensively in the study of marketing.

But the word market carries one other denotation: it can refer to groups of people. It is this meaning that we are presently most interested in. Thus, when we may say that the market for sports cars is greatest among the young and the young-at-heart, we are using the term to suggest a group of persons having similar preferences for particular automotive styling. The sentence, "The product failed because there was no market for it," further illustrates the use of the word in this people sense. But we need to introduce one further refinement to this people concept of a market. Using the term somewhat more selectively, we will define a market as: (a) *people with* (b) *purchasing power and with* (c) *either a felt or quiescent need for some product or service.* It is very much worth our time now to examine the nature of this definitional refinement.

First, we have specified that people without *purchasing power* do not comprise a market. This does not mean that people necessarily need money to be considered a market; for example, in embryonic economic systems, formal markets may exist in which real goods are exchanged for other real goods. Thus, purchasing power may assume either a *monetary* or a *real* form. Moreover, purchasing power may also be *credit,* or some negotiable promise to pay.

Second, we have specified that either a felt or a quiescent need was a further requisite for a market in a people sense. We need to specify this additional condition in order to establish an extremely important (and, as we shall see later, controversial) point. This stipulation, that a market may be either aware or unaware of its needs for products or services, means, in effect, that a market may be developed or expanded through what we will now simply call promotional activities.

When we say that markets are people with purchasing power and with either felt or quiescent needs, we are suggesting that there is an important relationship between the concept of a market and people as they perform in their role as *consumers* of goods and services. It is a point that should be emphasized that modern marketing is (or should be) consumer (or market) oriented—that is, modern marketing endeavors to understand consumer demand in order that such demand, either felt or quiescent, might be more precisely fulfilled.[8] With these brief comments in mind, we are now ready to develop a preliminary definition of the term marketing.

Marketing defined

Largely as a point of departure, we will define *marketing activities* as those human activities which are directed toward the satisfaction of either a felt or a latent demand for goods and services. Although this general definition is superficially satisfactory, upon more careful scrutiny it raises an important additional question: What human activities are directed toward the satisfaction of felt or latent demand? In order to answer this, we will identify three additional dimensions of the term marketing:

1 The economic dimension.
2 The managerial dimension.
3 The societal dimension.[9]

Marketing—its economic dimension

Economics is a field of study whose principal concern is the identification of the processes through which scarce means of production (land, labor and capital) are ideally allocated among endless aternative uses. The economic process of allocating resources among alternative ends includes four basic types of human activities: (a) *extractive* and *agrarian* activities, such as mining, farming and fishing; (b) *manufacturing, assembling* and *fabricating* activities; (c) *distributive* activities, such as wholesaling and retailing and transportation; and (d) *consumption* activities. These four classes also represent the *basic stages of economic allocation*. And, even though it involves some oversimplification, it will be of some value to us initially to think of marketing as most closely associated with the

---

[8] We shall see in a later chapter that the word "consumer" is not completely satisfactory as it is used here. We shall see, for example, that individuals act as consumers, that businesses act as consumers, and that the government also acts as a consumer. We will refine the concept of the consumer, especially in Chapter 7.

[9] There is another definitional perspective of marketing which can still be found in the recent literature and which has what might be called a "legalistic" thrust. This point of view tends to emphasize the relationship between marketing activities and the transfer of legal title to goods (or services). A relatively recent use of this type of definition may be seen in Rayburn D. Tousley and others, *Principles of Marketing,* New York: The Macmillan Company, 1962, p. 4. That text, for example, defines marketing as those efforts that effect transfers in the ownership of goods and services which provide for their physical distribution. It is highly probable that the earlier popularity of this legalistic type of definition has given encouragement to the tendency to think of marketing as synonymous with selling, partly because selling activities are perhaps the most obvious cause of title transfer—though other activities also contribute to such transfer. The legalistic definition of marketing was most popular in the 1940's and 1950's.

distributive stage of this allocation process.[10] As a means of positioning this diverse set of human activities, we may thus visualize marketing as occurring, in general, after the extractive and manufacturing processes are complete but before consumption begins. The schematic representation (Figure 1.1) suggests this sequential relationship.

Figure 1.1 The Allocation Process

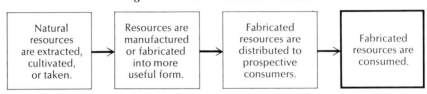

But, specifically, what human activities are included in the distributive stage? In order to answer this question, we need to explore one further facet of this general allocation process.

It is quite normal that as a natural resource moves from its natural habitat into the manufacturing/fabricating stage of economic allocation and then into the distributive stage of allocation it undergoes step-like increases in value.[11] For example, a quantity of iron ore is normally worth more to people when it is shaped into a screwdriver than when it is a lump of ore. This difference in value is referred to as *form utility*.[12] Concentrating for a moment upon the nature of these step-like increases in value will lead us closer to an important means of distinguishing marketing activities from other kinds of economic activities. Consider the simplified representation of the sequential nature of the economic allocation process in Figure 1.2.

Figure 1.2

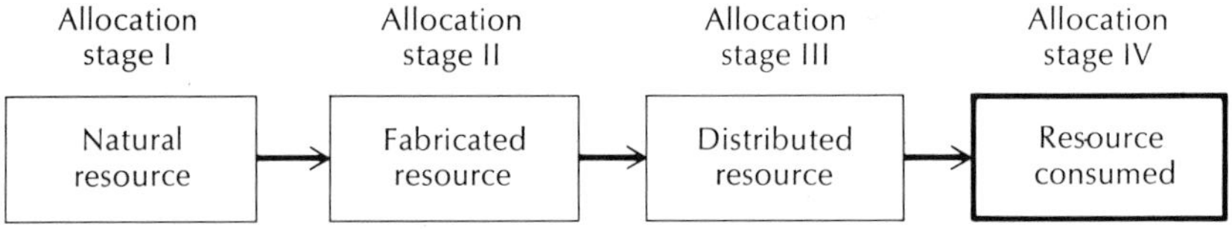

Allocation stage I	Allocation stage II	Allocation stage III	Allocation stage IV
Natural resource	Fabricated resource	Distributed resource	Resource consumed

[10] The oversimplification here stems from the unavoidable fact that some marketing activities occur at each of the several stages of allocation. Thus, producers of raw materials seek markets (and thus engage in marketing), as do manufacturers and fabricators.

[11] This step-like increase in value is normal, but not necessary. That is, value is not created by the allocation process alone—consumers or intermediate buyers must recognize such enhancement in value and be willing to pay for it.

[12] Form utility may be man-made or made by nature. A change in physical or chemical composition occasioned by the efforts of man may thus increase the value of an item—and a change in physical or chemical composition occasioned by nature (pearls in oyster shells, for example) may likewise increase the value of an item.

We have suggested that value increases as a natural resource moves from Stage I to Stages II and III. But what accounts for the increase in economic value that occurs during Stage III? The answer is that activities performed in Allocation Stage III may result in the creation of time, place and possession utility. And the human activities that produce time, place and possession utilities are, in general, the human activities that accomplish the third stage of economic allocation—distribution.

We will define *time utility* as the difference between what a product can be sold for at the instant of its manufacture and what it can be sold for at a later, more favorable time. An example will help to clarify this idea. Consider the temporal nature of the business that a paint manufacturer confronts. Suppose, for purposes of illustration, that this paint manufacturer operates the year round—accumulating inventories in anticipation of the house painting season. What would a gallon of paint be worth in the dead of winter—would it be worth more or less than during the painting season? The answer is that the gallon of paint would normally tend to be less valuable during the off-season than during the peak season. Let's assume a simple set of data and see if we can measure this thing we call time utility more precisely.

Suppose that a gallon of top grade paint will sell for $6 in December. Suppose, however, that the same gallon of paint will sell for $7 in the late spring months. This difference of one dollar is a value increment traceable solely to the fact that the product is offered for sale at a more favorable time. Note also that time utility may be decreased by holding the product too long. That is, should our judgment of the market for paint be poor, we might hold it into late September and then be able to get only less than $7 for our hypothetical gallon of paint. Indeed, it should be apparent that the most propitious moment to offer something for sale is not always easy to forecast. But we will have more to say about time utility in the next chapter. For the moment we are primarily concerned with making the basic point that *time itself can create economic value.*

We will similarly define *place utility* as the difference between what a product can be sold for at its place of manufacture and what it can be sold for at some more favorable place. Consider the spatial nature of the business confronting a processor of orange juice. Assume that the processor is located in some part of the world in which oranges grow in great abundance. In order to make our concept of place utility more concrete, suppose further that a can of processed orange juice in the processor's home city will sell for $.20. Place utility is created and its value measured by the increase in price which would result from selling that same can of orange juice in an area in which demand conditions are more favorable.

Finally, we will define *possession utility* as the difference between the price at which a particular product will sell when no explanation is given of the uses to which it may be put and the manner in which it is to be used, and the price which that product will bring if prospective buyers are informed regarding these issues. This idea is perhaps the most difficult to convey of the several intangible utilities we have thus far considered. The difficulty is in part attributable to the fact that the word "possession" is not entirely descriptive of the meaning we wish to impart. There is longstanding convention, however, for the use of this term. It may be helpful at the moment to think of possession utility as that increment in economic value which results from making prospective buyers fully and correctly *informed* regarding some product or service.

We have now outlined the concepts of form, time, place and possession utility in sufficient detail to attempt a systematic definition of marketing from an economic point of view. *Marketing, in its economic dimension, includes all those human activities which result in the creation of time, place and possession utility.* More specifically, *storage* creates time utility, *transportation* creates place utility and *informative promotional efforts* create what we have called possession utility. Thus, when retail outlets hold merchandise until we demand it, they are, in the terminology of economics, engaged in the creation of time utility. Likewise, when the various modes of transportation (including rail, pipeline, airline, truck and steamship) move merchandise from some point of assembly-fabrication-manufacture to a point of consumption, they are engaged in the creation of place utility. And similarly, when advertising agencies and promotion departments of businesses inform prospects regarding the relative merits of their products and services, they are said to be creating possession utility.

Figure 1.3 Economic Value and Basic Utility

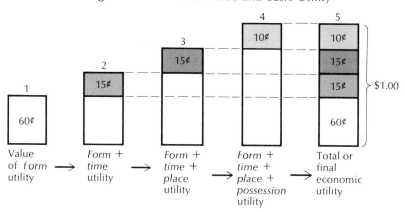

Before we leave the subject of the economic dimensions of marketing, we should note that all *economic value* is created by one of the four basic utilities we have now identified. Figure 1.3 will both summarize what we have said and clarify this latter idea. Let the value of some object which embodies only form utility be represented by the area in column one. In order to make our example as concrete as possible, assume that this area represents a value of $.60. Observe further that the final or total economic value (what you and I pay as consumers) is $1.00 (the area in Column 5). This $.40 difference (final value minus form value) is the value created by time, place and possession utility, and the people creating those utilities are engaged in marketing activities. Note particularly that these numbers are illustrative and do not represent actual values. We shall have occasion later to examine the actual value of form, time, place and possession utility. At the moment, there is another dimension of marketing which we need to explore.

Marketing—its managerial dimension

Thus far we have examined marketing from an economic perspective. We have observed that marketing activities are a part of the general process of economic allocation, and that marketing activities create a special kind of value—a value which we have identified with the terms time, place and possession utility. But there is another helpful way for us to view the activities of marketing. This second view of marketing embodies the perspective of a businessman who we shall assume is functioning as an important marketing executive in a medium-sized to large corporate organization. This business-oriented view of marketing activities we shall call the management, or managerial, dimension of marketing.[13]

When marketing is studied as a management activity in business, it is conventional to begin with an identification of the important areas of decision making that are normally the concern of the chief marketing executive. We shall identify four such areas:

1 Products and services, including quality, warranty, design and packaging.
2 Prices, including suggested prices, distribution margins and credit.
3 Promotion, including personal selling, advertising and sales promotion.
4 Physical distribution, including transportation, warehousing and distributor/dealer networks.[14]

Using these four basic areas of decision making as the nucleus of our definition, we may now define marketing in its managerial dimension as *the purposeful management*[15] *of the products and services, the prices and the promotional and distribution activities of a business organization*

[13] We shall understand the term "management" to include the planning, organizing and controlling of business activities.
[14] This list is adapted from one suggested by Jehiel Zif in "Marketing Research as a System of Information with Application to the Introduction of New Products," in M. S. Moyer and R. E. Vosburgh, editors, *Marketing for Tomorrow—Today*, 1967 June Conference Proceedings, American Marketing Association, p. 60.
[15] Including the creation of product and service concepts.

according to the preferences of some market or market segment and in a manner calculated to achieve the objectives of the business. This definition has three distinct and important elements in it:

1 To manage products or services, prices, promotion, and distribution.
2 To effectively serve some market or part of a market.
3 To achieve some defined business objectives.

These "defined business objectives" may include efforts to achieve some specified minimum level of profit, some target percentage of the total market (market share), some specified level of sales or any of many other possible goals. Note also that the firm may elect to serve either a general market or some small part of that general market—the small part of the market normally being distinguished by its individual tastes and preferences. We will have occasion to explore this latter point in greater detail later.[16]

We may now also define the related idea of a *marketing strategy.* We will use this latter term to describe the specific plan of action that identifies the competitive role to be played by the product or service offered, by prices, by promotion and by distribution. The marketing strategy of a firm will also necessarily include an identification of the market or markets to which the plan will be directed—we will call these *target markets.* Stated in slightly different language, the task of the chief marketing executive is to devise and implement a marketing strategy which is carefully aligned with target market preferences and which has a high probability of achieving the basic goals of the firm.

We might now summarize our remarks about the managerial dimension of marketing in schematic form. Figure 1.4 depicts in three stages the elements that we have emphasized.

Economic and managerial dimensions of marketing compared

We have now explored in a preliminary manner both the economic dimension of marketing and the managerial dimension of marketing. It may seem that these two perspectives yield totally different concepts of what marketing is. Such is not the case at all—indeed these two definitions have a great deal in common. It should be apparent, for example, that the managerial activity which we have called "promotion" corresponds closely to the economic activity which we have identified with the term "possession utility." Moreover, the managerial activity which we identify with the term "distribution" encompasses to some extent both the economic concepts of time and place utility. That is, distribution planning from a managerial point of view would necessarily involve the creation of time and place

---

[16] The concepts of, and distinctions between, "local" markets, "mass" markets, and "segmented" markets are carefully developed in Chapter 12, which also presents the usual distinction between market segmentation and product differentiation.

Figure 1.4 Managerial Dimensions of Marketing

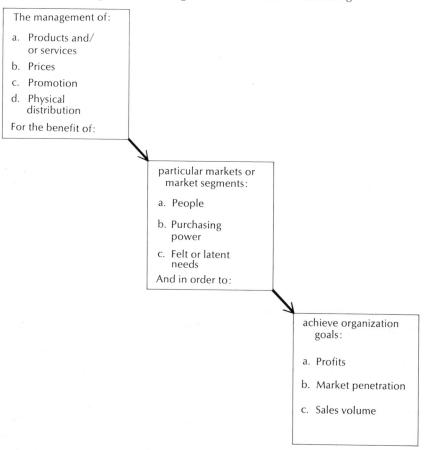

The management of:

a. Products and/
   or services
b. Prices
c. Promotion
d. Physical
   distribution

For the benefit of:

particular markets or
market segments:

a. People

b. Purchasing
   power

c. Felt or latent
   needs

And in order to:

achieve organization
goals:

a. Profits

b. Market penetration

c. Sales volume

utilities. The economic view differs from the managerial view in that (a) the *product* is assumed to be given (remember that the creation of form utility was definitionally excluded from marketing activities) and (b) *price* is assumed to be determined by the market and not by executive judgment. Thus, when compared to the economic definition, the managerial definition explicitly increases the scope of marketing to include both product and price decisions.

Marketing—its societal dimension

We have seen, thus far, that marketing may be viewed as either or both an economic phenomenon and a managerial activity. Marketing also has important societal dimensions. Because marketing activities lead to the creation of new products and services, because marketing activities promote new ideas to the society which is being served, and because marketing, activities involve an important persuasive role in the formation of public opinion, marketing is unavoidably a social concern. Because prices influence the purchasing power of the incomes we earn, and because distribution influences buying convenience, marketing has pervasive and profound societal dimensions. Marketing practitioners have not always wanted to admit this societal dimension of their activities, and indeed marketing has not always been taught as though it included important societal considerations. Events of recent years make it completely clear, however, that societal responsibility in the performance of marketing activities may be even more forcefully defined in the future than it has been to date. But we need to be even more specific about what these societal dimensions of marketing are. In order to be more systematic in our consideration of the societal aspects of marketing, we need to introduce two basic concepts. These two ideas are "social balance" and something called the "dependence effect."

SOCIAL BALANCE

The notion of social balance is suggested in the following words:

The final problem of the productive society is what it produces. This [problem] manifests itself in an implacable tendency to provide an opulent supply of some things and a niggardly yield of others. This disparity carries to the point where it is a cause of social discomfort and social unhealth. The line which divides our area of wealth from our area of poverty is roughly that which divides privately produced and marketed goods and services from publicly rendered services.[17]

"Balance" in this social sense thus relates to the proportion of total productive effort that a society gives to private interests and the proportion that is devoted to public interests. That is, social balance is achieved when the level of activities in the private sector of the economy is correct or proper relative to the level of activity in the public sector of the economy. To be perfectly candid then, much of the concern today is with imbalance in the relationship between social (governmental) spending and individual (private) spending. The following quotation suggests more precisely both the form and, to some extent, the degree of social imbalance that is felt by some persons to prevail in the United States today.

The family which takes its mauve and cerise, air-conditioned, power-steered, and power-braked automobile out for a tour passes through cities that are badly paved, made hideous by litter, blighted buildings, and posts for wires that should long since have been put underground. They pass on into a countryside that has been rendered largely invisible by commercial art. They picnic on exquisitely packaged food from a portable icebox by a polluted stream and go on to spend the night at a park which is a menace to public health and morals. Just before dozing

[17]John K. Galbraith, "The Theory of Social Balance," in Lee E. Preston, editor, *Social Issues in Marketing*, Glenview, Ill.: Scott, Foresman and Company, 1968, p. 247.

off on an air mattress, beneath a nylon tent, amid the stench of decaying refuse, they may vaguely reflect on the curious unevenness of their blessings. Is this, indeed, the American genius?[18]

THE DEPENDENCE EFFECT

Before we explore the relationship between social imbalance of the kind suggested above and marketing activities, it will be helpful for us to identify one other and a related concept, namely, the idea of the dependence effect. Underlying the notion of social imbalance is the idea that as an economic system matures and grows in affluence, it turns an increasing amount of attention to the satisfaction of less urgent wants. That is, those who believe that social imbalance exists would contend that as economic affluence progresses, the productive machinery of the system is diverted more and more to the satisfaction of trivial or inconsequential wants. Indeed, it is often asserted that the "wants which are satisfied by increasing production are themselves increasingly created by the increase in production itself, through the passive social process of emulation and envy of one's neighbors, and the active commercial process of creation and stimulation of wants through advertising and salesmanship."[19] The nature of the dependence effect is clearly suggested in this last sentence. This effect alleges that material wants in an increasingly affluent society are likely to be contrived or created by essentially the same productive process which created the goods themselves. And it is further alleged that the productive process is embodied in the form of private business interests.

Figure 1.5 Social Balance and Economic Maturity

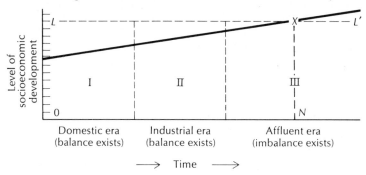

| | Domestic era (balance exists) | Industrial era (balance exists) | Affluent era (imbalance exists) |

$\longrightarrow$ Time $\longrightarrow$

Briefly, then, social balance (or more correctly imbalance) and the dependence effect evolve as characteristics of a socioeconomic system as it matures and undergoes an increasing standard and level of living. Figure 1.5, summarizes the essence of the argument. Note in Figure 1.5, for example, that social imbalance is felt by some critics of our market system to be most pronounced during Era III, the Affluent Era. Note as well that

[18] *Ibid.,* p. 248.
[19] Harry G. Johnson, "The Consumer and Madison Avenue," in Preston, *op. cit.,* p. 254.

the dependence effect is thought of as a kind of unavoidable symptom of social imbalance and it, too, is most pronounced during the affluent stages of economic development. Figure 1.5 suggests that as economic development increases progressively past some threshold level (in this instance, OL) such affluence typically produces imbalance and that such imbalance is in turn attended by an undesirable dependence of demand upon supply. The point at which social imbalance besets the socioeconomic system depicted in Figure 1.5 is defined by the values ON on the time axis, and OL on the vertical axis.

We should note that the roles of supply and demand are allegedly reversed during this condition of social imbalance. That is, we would normally expect supply to depend upon demand, but social imbalance brings with it a dependence of demand upon supply. At this point in our discussion no special effort is being made to deny or to support the idea of social imbalance; our concern for the moment is only to define the idea as clearly and precisely as possible. We shall see later, however, that the notion of social imbalance is not entirely unassailable.[20]

Why, allegedly, does social imbalance exist? Why, allegedly, does the dependence effect occur? We are told that imbalance exists because the private economic sector is overemphasized and the public sector underemphasized. Whether or not we agree with this particular value judgment, it is clear that marketing activities, inasmuch as they often underlie the creation of new product concepts and because they actively persuade (mold public opinion) through promotional activities, could have a significant role in the development of imbalance of this social kind. Indeed, marketing activities (and especially selling efforts) may well be viewed as the principal catalytic agent in the alleged dependence effect. That is, the argument is often advanced that inconsequential or trivial supply is demanded largely because of marketing efforts. This view holds that were it not for marketing activities, the productive skills of society might be turned to less trivial—more consequential—matters. It is largely because marketing activities impinge upon the social order in this way that we assert here that marketing has some very important societal dimensions. Indeed, to put it in somewhat plainer language, marketing activities are undoubtedly viewed by some critics as an important cause of the materialistic preoccupation with which our socioeconomic order is so often supposed to be afflicted. Again, it is not our purpose at this time to agree or deny that this relationship exists or to resolve whether the result is harmful; we shall consider those related issues in the next two chapters. Let it suffice for now that we have defined the concepts of social balance and the dependence effect and an important relationship between marketing activities and our social or societal well-being.

[20] See, for example, F. A. Von Hayek, "The Non-Sequitur of the Dependence Effect," *Southern Economic Journal,* April 1961, pp. 346–348.

Marketing, society, and American culture

We have now seen that there are important societal implications that relate to the manner in which marketing activities are performed. We have noted, for example, that social balance is, to some extent, influenced by marketing activities. When we say that there are societal implications that relate to marketing, we mean that our marketing system does some things to us collectively, as groups of persons having some common interest. It is in this manner that the societal influences of marketing are generally distinguished from the influence which marketing activities may have upon us as *individuals*. But there is still another aspect of marketing that is of growing concern to many people. This latter dimension we will identify as the *cultural influences* of marketing.

Culture is an elusive concept at best and, wishing not at all to get into the semantic quagmire that the term can produce, we will define culture simply as "enlightenment and excellence of taste acquired by intellectual and aesthetic training." Note that taste is an extremely important element in this concept of culture. Indeed many writers on the cultural aspects of American life use expressions such as "high cultural levels" and "low cultural levels" as virtually synonymous with good and bad taste. It should also be noted that culture is a variable concept; that is, it can be purposefully altered, although slowly. Thus if properly nourished, the cultural levels of a society may be elevated. If improperly attended, these cultural levels may deteriorate.

Moreover, culture is rarely meaningful as a singular concept—that is, at any given time many subcultures exist within a society as several layers, or levels. It is quite common, for example, to encounter discussions in sociology and anthropology of the various levels of culture which comprise a given society. Students of the cultural aspects of our lives identify such cultural levels with special names, such as (a) "superior" or refined culture, (b) "mediocre" culture and (c) "brutal" culture.[21] Figure 1.6 illustrates several hypothetical cultural *profiles*. These profiles will serve to illustrate both the layer, or level, aspect of culture and the variability of the concept. In System A, for example, the superior culture dominates and the brutal culture is of minor significance. If the three systems are considered *sequentially*, then System C is one in which cultural deterioration has proceeded to an extreme degree.

But how are changes in culture effected? And how is such change related to marketing? Culture is influenced primarily by such forces as education, the church and the mass communications media. The argument is that as these forces set the example, so will the culture be: these several forces

---

[21] See Edward A. Shils, "Mass Society and Its Culture," in Bernard Berelson and Morris Janowitz, editors, *Reader in Public Opinion and Communication,* Second Edition, New York: The Free Press, 1966, p. 508.

are thus seen as playing an important role in the determination of our collective tastes. And, as one might anticipate, some writers on American culture are very much concerned with the directions that such collective tastes may be taking. One respected writer notes, for example that there is, in general, growing pessimism about the direction of American taste.[22] This same author believes that it is a mere avoidance of the issue to dismiss such pessimism as the viewpoint of the intellectual snob, who automatically defines that which is popular as necessarily bad. American culture is often described as *kitsch*—as a mass society alloy—and while it reflects everybody's taste to some extent, it is not likely to represent anyone's taste exactly.[23] And the tendency, the argument continues, is that such mass culture tends to overwhelm us with its quantity and push collective tastes "to that of the least sensitive and most ignorant."

Figure 1.6 Cultural Profiles

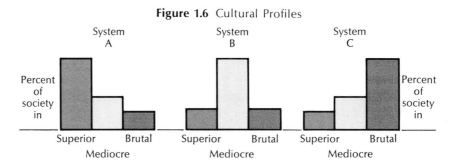

All of this maintains, though perhaps in less than straightforward terms, that we are, increasingly, a beer, chewing gum, and Western movies society; that we are inextricably in the grip of a special kind of Gresham's law—a Gresham's law in a cultural context. Gresham's law is a proposition in the field of monetary economics that maintains that within an economic system, the weaker currency will tend to displace that which is stronger.[24] The parallel *principle of kitsch culture* holds that the brutal culture tends to displace the higher cultures. Moreover, this process of cultural deprecia-tion is thought by some to be actively aided and abetted by the business community in general and by marketing activities in particular.

There are at least four major forces working to influence American taste: (a) changes in real income, (b) more education, both formal and informal, (c) the efforts of tastemakers to spread their own gospel and (4) the American striving for self-betterment.[25] The potential influence of marketing

[22] See Gilbert Burch, "How American Taste Is Changing," in H. C. Barksdale, editor, *Marketing: Change and Exchange*, New York: Holt, Rinehart and Winston, Inc., 1964, p. 48.
[23] *Ibid.*, p. 49.
[24] Gresham's law is discussed, for example, in E. Shapiro and others, *Money and Banking*, Fifth Edition, New York: Holt, Rinehart and Winston, Inc., 1968, p. 23.
[25] See Gilbert Burch, *op. cit.*, p. 40.

upon American culture is most immediately suggested by the third item. "Tastemakers," as the term is employed in this instance, refers to "writers, corporate managers and their designers, and merchandisers," a grouping that clearly includes some marketing activities. It is likewise clear that the mass communications media, prompted largely as they are by enterprise motives, are potentially a profound influence upon this thing we are calling culture. And although the relationship is perhaps less clearly defined, the striving for "self-betterment" is partially actuated by some marketing activities, and some marketing activities involve what might be called informal educational processes.

Thus, marketing activities play, both directly and indirectly, a pivotal role in tastemaking. Because marketing has this potential for tastemaking and because abuse of this power influences all of us, marketing practitioners may inherit a much more complex hierarchy of responsibilities than is casually apparent.

A societal viewpoint is emphasized

We have now briefly identified the economic, the managerial and the societal/cultural dimensions of marketing. An introduction to the study of marketing might reasonably emphasize any or all of these three basic perspectives. The basic content of the marketing discipline is accessible, as it were, from any of these three perspectives. The principle thrust of this book, however, is a societal viewpoint. That is, the viewpoint we wish to emphasize is primarily, though not exclusively, that of a society being served by a marketing system. This societal perspective permits us to criticize our marketing system when criticism seems in order; it permits us to commend the system when commendation seems appropriate. The result of this societal viewpoint should be not only to develop an awareness and understanding of the issues, questions and problems which comprise the discipline of marketing, but also to impart a respect for social responsibility in the performance of marketing activities.

It is important to note that a societal perspective does not replace a managerial viewpoint. Indeed, though it may seem a curious statement, it is our intent to study many of the managerial aspects of a firm from a societal perspective. It is a point worth great emphasis that every action of a business firm has, unavoidably, some economic and social consequences. When a firm changes its prices, when a firm develops a better product, when a firm alters its system of distribution, when a firm alters its promotional efforts, our social and economic system is, unavoidably, altered. For example, when a firm such as the United States Steel Corporation raises its prices, a substantial portion of society is influenced; when general increases in transportation rates are effected, a substantial portion of society is likewise influenced.

In the years ahead, it will be increasingly necessary that business management take cognizance of both the social and the economic results of their actions. Social responsibility will be a necessary consideration in business decision making. The decade of the 1970's is very likely to be a decade during which no tradition of our enterprise system will be able to avoid increasingly articulate criticism. It is now clear that no institution, social or economic, is unalterable. The threat of change of a fundamental kind is virtually everywhere. Our market system is likely to have many more vocal critics than vocal defenders in the next ten years. The nature of the interface between society and our market system must be understood by every student of business administration.

Marketing is an interdisciplinary study

When we say that marketing is interdisciplinary, we mean that it is not an insular or selfcontained body of knowledge. Marketing is eclectic: its interdisciplinary character stems from the fact that it utilizes concepts, principles and ideas from many other fields of knowledge. More specifically, the discipline of marketing incorporates and uses ideas from such areas as economics, psychology, social psychology, sociology, anthropology, law, mathematics and many others. And although the extent and nature of the use of these supporting disciplines is reflected throughout this book, some brief indication of the manner in which these supplementary disciplines will affect our study of marketing is in order now.

In an earlier section we defined markets as people, with purchasing power, and either a felt or quiescent need for some product or service. Markets are the principal concern of a well conceived marketing program—that is, attention to the particular and perhaps unique character of market preferences in products and services is the prime ingredient of a successful marketing program.[26] Because markets are people and because the behavior of markets must be understood in order that they be well served, the discipline of marketing makes extensive use of the behavioral sciences. The behavioral sciences endeavor to understand human behavior and are normally defined to include economics, psychology, social psychology, sociology and cultural anthropology. The behavioral science of economics has long been concerned with consumer behavior—indeed the concept of the "economic man" is a kind of monadic theory of consumer behavior.[27] Economics has attempted to develop means for predicting consumer behavior, and in later chapters we shall have some interest in progress that economists may be making toward that goal.

There is increasing evidence that the interpersonal, or social, relationships

[26] The term "marketing program" is used here to suggest the total complex of efforts exerted by a firm to serve a market or a market segment.

[27] A monadic theory is one that concentrates, perhaps excessively, upon a single factor of influence. This argument is elaborated in Philip Kotler, "Behavioral Models for Analyzing Buyers," *Journal of Marketing*, October 1965, pp. 37–45.

of individuals influence their behavior as consumers. Because of this relationship between social behavior and consumer behavior, students of marketing have been especially interested in the work of sociologists—particularly those concerned with social stratification (social class) and sociometry (interpersonal influence). Both the quality of markets and market behavior are also influenced by the changing demographic character of the US population. Demography is the study of human populations; it is especially concerned with population size, density and distribution. Accordingly, marketing teachers and practitioners have an interest in the fundamental concepts of the field of demography—birth rates, death rates, net rates of reproduction and so forth.

There is also an aspect of consumer behavior (or market behavior) which is individually determined rather than socially determined. Psychology and social psychology are two behavioral sciences that have provided valuable insight into these individually oriented aspects of market behavior.

Because we are necessarily interested in the problems confronted by marketing practitioners, we are also necessarily interested in the means used to resolve those problems. More particularly, we will find that a study of marketing research will require some use of fundamental concepts from statistics, including sampling theory. Our interest in marketing research will likewise require that we be conversant with special measurement devices, many of which originate in the social sciences. We will find that the evolving field of operations research will suggest several relevant analytical and problem solving techniques, including linear programming and queueing theory.

Our interest in the societal dimensions of marketing will dictate that we explore the battery of federal and state laws that may influence marketing activities. As a necessary part of this exploration we will consider interpretive legal doctrine of several types and will find it useful to acquaint ourselves with some specialized legal concepts.

Although there are other examples that would serve to further illustrate the interdisciplinary nature of marketing, the basic eclectic nature of the discipline has been sufficiently indicated for now.

Marketing—its economic importance

Marketing is an extremely important form of human endeavor; it is clearly important in terms of its ability to influence our lives. Marketing plays a significant role in determining the type and number of products and services that we buy and when and where we buy them. Marketing includes the commercial uses of the mass media and has, therefore, an almost daily influence upon our lives.

Marketing is important also in the sense that it represents one of the few fields of enterprise that is effectively open to individuals with limited amounts of investment capital. In an age when bigness in business seems to be a prerequisite of success, a career in marketing is still possible for the individual who can afford to make only a relatively modest investment. This is particularly true in the fields of retailing and wholesaling.

Another reason for the importance of marketing is the number of persons who are employed in it. The 1968 estimate of the size of the adult civilian labor force was almost 75 million persons. Of this figure it is perhaps conservative to estimate that at least 19 million persons were engaged in some aspect of marketing and that that figure would be even greater today.[28]

Although the data developed by the US Bureau of the Census often make precise interpretation difficult,[29] it is possible to make some estimates of the total number of persons actually engaged in marketing activities. There are, in fact, two census employment classifications that contain virtually no human activities other than those that we have defined as a part of marketing. First, the Bureau of the Census identifies employment in "wholesale and retail trade." It is significant to note that almost 14 million persons were employed in this category in 1967, and that this figure is exceeded only by the number employed in manufacturing. It is likewise important to note that of the major employment classifications in current use by the United States Bureau of the Census, only those employed in manufacturing exceed this number. Moreover, in 1967, over 4 million persons found gainful employment in the category "transportation and public utilities." Note carefully, however, that it is not being suggested that all these 4 million persons were engaged in what we have defined as marketing activities; there are obviously some job descriptions included in the "transportation and public utilities" category which are not closely associated with the marketing process.[30]

In spite of many problems of interpreting census data and the difficulties of applying them in a specific context, it is apparent that the group of human endeavors which we have called marketing are, collectively, extremely important.

Consider the enormous importance of marketing from one other per-

---

[28] Indeed, some authorities estimate the figure as higher, and that "one out of every four persons gainfully employed is in some manner engaged in marketing." See Charles F. Phillips and Delbert J. Duncan, *Marketing: Principles and Practices*, Sixth Edition, Homewood, Ill.: Richard D. Irwin, Inc., 1968, p. 13.

[29] These difficulties trace, for the most part, to the census definitions currently employed. The US Bureau of the Census develops categories of employment in such a way that details are often lost. For example, in 1967, there were over 19 million persons employed in "manufacturing." Clearly some of those people are involved in marketing activities as we have defined that term. How many we do not know. Likewise, the employment category which the Bureau of the Census defines as "services" unquestionably includes some human endeavors which fall within the general scope of marketing activities. It is effectively impossible to tell just what that proportion would be.

[30] See *Statistical Abstract of the United States 1968*, Washington, D. C.: U. S. Government Printing Office, 1968, pp. 221–223.

spective. There are over 1.7 million retail stores in the United States.[31] There are over 300,000 wholesale establishments. There is, therefore, one marketing institution for every hundred persons. This statistic serves not only to illustrate the size of the marketing system in the United States, but may suggest important public policy questions to many persons.[32] Let it suffice to say that marketing activities are both numerous and important.

SUMMARY

Our purpose in the present chapter has been to identify the scope and the nature of the human activity called marketing. Pursuant to that purpose, we have developed our discussion around four basic points.

First, we examined various meanings of the word "market." We observed that the word is sometimes used in a verb sense, sometimes in a place sense, and sometimes in a people sense. We noted that the term market, used in the context of the study of marketing, is most frequently used to indicate people with purchasing power and a felt or quiescent need for some product or service.

Second, we explored three basic dimensions of the field of study called marketing: economic, managerial and societal/cultural. We developed an economic definition of marketing around the concepts of time, place and possession utility. We developed a managerial definition of marketing that emphasized business decision making that centers on products and services, prices, promotion and physical distribution. We then identified what we referred to as the societal/cultural dimensions of marketing, emphasizing that business activities unavoidably have social and cultural ramifications. (When a business firm sets a price, develops a promotional plan, develops a new product or service or evolves a new plan for physical distribution, that firm necessarily influences the society and the cultural patterns of that society.) We also identified the concepts of "social balance," and the "dependence effect" and noted that important cultural questions are often related to marketing activities.

Third, in order to suggest some additional characteristics of the field of marketing, we identified what we called its interdisciplinary character. We observed that the field of marketing employs analytical concepts from economics, sociology, psychology, social psychology, cultural anthropology, law, statistics, operations research and many other disciplines.

Finally, we briefly established the importance of marketing from an economic point of view. In this latter connection, we noted that very nearly one out of every four persons in the active labor force is employed in some aspect of marketing.

[31] Ibid., p. 762.
[32] See, for example, Reavis Cox and others, Distribution in a High-Level Economy, Englewood Cliffs, N.J.: Prentice-Hall, Inc., 1965, Chapter 12. The issue treated in this chapter is, among other things, how many retailers and wholesalers are too many?

1 Carefully define and indicate the relevance of each of the following concepts to the study of marketing:
   a. Market
   b. Time utility
   c. Place utility
   d. Possession utility
   e. Marketing strategy
   f. The four basic stages of economic allocation
   g. Social balance
   h. Cultural profiles
2 Distinguish carefully between each element in the following pairs of terms:
   a. A felt need *and* a quiescent need
   b. Monetary purchasing power *and* real purchasing power
   c. The dependence effect *and* the level of economic development
   d. High culture *and* kitsch culture
   e. Form utility *and* possession utility
3 In what way does Gresham's law in monetary economics parallel a phenomenon observed by students of American culture?
4 In what specific ways is marketing an eclectic or interdisciplinary field of study?
5 In what specific ways can it be argued that marketing is an important form of human endeavor?

DISCUSSION QUESTIONS

6 In what specific ways is a sponsor of a prime-time television show able to influence his audience? Be as complete as you can.
7 Specifically, what areas of social responsibility do you believe a manufacturing enterprise should honor?
8 What do you believe would be the most effective way to encourage a socially responsible point of view among businessmen?
9 Cite several examples of actions by businessmen that you believe run counter to the public interest. What is the probable motive for these actions?

Chapter 2
MARKETING: A STEREOTYPE?

In the preceding chapter we developed some basic definitional concepts of marketing. We identified very briefly the economic, the managerial and the societal/cultural aspects of the discipline. We observed that marketing activities influence virtually all our lives—often in a very profound way. We noted, for example, that the public character of our society is shaped to some extent by our private behavior and that private behavior is influenced by marketing activities. The degree of social balance we achieve is determined in part by marketing activities. We have suggested that the mass media and marketing activities are a powerful, persuasive team—one which may influence the cultural levels we attain and the levels to which we aspire. It should now be clear that marketing activities are both ubiquitous and, on occasion, controversial. It is our purpose in the present chapter to identify more systematically the nature of the controversy which may be generated by the performance of our marketing system.

More specifically, we will examine some of the arguments that are most often advanced in criticism of marketing activities.[1] The arguments we will consider are:

1 That marketing is, in an economic sense, unproductive.
2 That the costs of marketing activities are excessive.
3 That the marketing system is often unresponsive to consumer wants.
4 That marketing practitioners are often unscrupulous.
5 That marketing is an imprecise and unscientific discipline.
6 That marketing activities are among the prime forces behind a materialistic society.

Since one of our concerns throughout this book is with the societal

[1] An article that recognizes many of the basic issues in a criticism of marketing activities is D. Beryl Manischewitz and John A. Stuart, "Marketing Under Attack," *Journal of Marketing*, July 1962, pp. 1–6.

aspects of marketing, an awareness of the various criticisms leveled at our marketing system is important to us. An examination of these criticisms will not only provide additional insight into the nature of marketing activities but will also encourage us to begin to prepare answers to such criticisms.

The stature of marketing—historical perspective

The human activities which we refer to collectively as marketing have never enjoyed great social prestige. With the exception of some relatively short periods of time, marketing activities have historically been viewed, as they say, with alarm. Indeed it would seem essentially correct to argue that alarm over, and therefore concern with, marketing practices has gained some momentum in recent years. At least, the voice of the critic of our marketing system seems more articulate and perhaps more systematized than it has been in the past. The interest of the executive branch of our federal government in consumer affairs, the vigilance of people like Ralph Nader, and the concern of state legislatures with various marketing activities all seem to support this viewpoint. In a recent article directed to both marketing teachers and marketing practitioners, an academic critic argued that "many aspects of the field of marketing are both irrelevant and unethical."[2] To quote that same source more fully:

For the past 6,000 years the field of marketing has been thought of as made up of fast-buck artists, con-men, wheeler-dealers, and shoddy-goods distributors. Too many of us have been "taken" by the tout or con-man; and all of us at times have been prodded into buying all sorts of "things" we really did not need, and which we found later on we did not even want.[3]

This particular critic singles out advertising, promotion and other "techniques and studies calculated to push goods on uninterested individuals" as the real villains. Indeed, he commends the physical distribution aspects of marketing because they "offer a great deal to the human race which has never been efficient enough to give all persons their material due." The point is at least established that any image problem which marketing may have had in the past has not been substantially improved in recent times. But we are getting ahead of ourselves—we need to examine each of the basic criticisms of our marketing system more carefully.

Criticism one: marketing is unproductive

We have seen earlier that marketing activities create intangible utilities—utilities which we designate with the terms time utility, place utility and

[2] Richard N. Farmer, "Would You Want Your Daughter to Marry a Marketing Man?" *Journal of Marketing,* January 1967, p. 1.
[3] *Ibid.*

possession utility. These utilities are intangible in the sense that they produce no visible change in form; that is, in chemical structure or physical appearance. This is an important distinction for us to draw, for there is some evidence that activities which apparently bring nothing new into existence have historically been viewed as suspect or in some cases simply condemned as unworthy. It is but one of several crosses which marketing must bear that the product of its efforts is essentially intangible.[4] The early Greek philosophers observed the intangible nature of some human activities and reacted accordingly: The various occupations of man were ranked into those which were productive and those which were merely acquisitive. Productive enterprise included manufacture, agriculture and the fine arts; those which were acquisitive brought nothing new into existence, but simply helped men to procure that which was extant.[5] But to make matters worse, there was a subclassification of acquisitive occupations. There were acquisitive activities which were relatively good and others which were deplorable. This is illustrated by the fact that the acquisition of the "science of learning" was a human undertaking which ranked among the highest, but the acquisition of worldly goods (material things) was among the least respectable occupations. No lesser light than Plato classified the various occupations of man into a superordinate-subordinate hierarchy which assigned the lowest status to "those who sell but did not *produce the good.*" Resting firmly and without question at the bottom of this status hierarchy is the market specialist.[6] It is important to note that "produce the good" means alter the form of the good. We shall have occasion to return to this narrow interpretation of the concept of production later. But let's look briefly at some other philosophical perspectives of marketing activities.

Aristotle, another Greek philosopher of great repute, felt that some marketing activities were exploitive. His reasoning involved the premise that "the services for which the traders charged added nothing to the life-sustaining qualities of the goods handled."[7] Thus, it is apparent that this philospher was misled, to some extent, by the fact that no *visible* changes occur as a result of marketing activities. It might also be noted that if nothing new is created by the actions of a person, then any gain that person realizes must be realized to the detriment of the other party

[4] "Essentially intangible" because there are instances in which marketing influences form utility. Thus, for example, storage may create a chemical change in spirits, in cheese, in fresh fruit, and so forth. Moreover, marketing normally "breaks bulk"—that is, resells in successively smaller units or quantities—sometimes this breaking of bulk is closely akin to a change in form, for example ice cream dips in cones rather than in bulk.

[5] This is essentially the position taken by Plato, one of the classic Greek philosophers. For a more complete discussion, see James Bonar, *Philosophy and Political Economy*, Second Edition, London: George Allen & Unwin, Ltd., 1909, p. 19.

[6] A similar discussion may be seen in J. M. Cassels, "The Significance of Early Economic Thought on Marketing," *Journal of Marketing*, October 1936, p. 130.

[7] *Ibid.*

to exchange: At least this is the kind of logic which these early critics of marketing specialization employed. Enough has been said now to establish our basic point—that marketing activities have been suspect because, among other things, they often do not produce tangible changes in the goods being handled. We will hold our rebuttal to that argument for the next chapter. For now let us consider a second major criticism of our marketing system—that the economic resources devoted to the performance of marketing activities are excessive.

Criticism two: the costs of marketing activities are excessive

It is a significant economic fact that nearly fifty cents of every dollar we spend as final consumers goes ultimately to compensate someone engaged in marketing activities.[8] That is, on the average, half of every dollar we spend pays the margins or fees charged by various marketing specialists—wholesalers, retailers, transportation agencies, advertising agencies, and many others. This fact places marketing, inextricably, in the middle of the *income distribution controversy*. That is, the fact that marketing activities are costly from the consumer's point of view means that the income of marketing specialists is, relatively speaking, large. We noted earlier that one of the reasons for societal concern with the performance of marketing activities was the high cost of performing such activities. We are now in a position to amplify that earlier view. The general allegation that marketing activities cost too much is often reduced to a closely related charge: the income received by those performing marketing activities is relatively large not because those activities are indispensible to us all but because they are performed in an inefficient manner. This latter articulation of the problem has been referred to as the "mediocrity hypothesis." Just to be sure that the idea here is clear, this mediocrity hypothesis suggests that we (society) pay a large collective marketing bill because the marketing industry is, to a significant degree, composed of small, poorly managed and therefore inefficient firms. But how do we know that aggregate marketing costs are high? What indications of inefficiency are there in the performance of marketing activities?

[8] Several significant studies have undertaken to estimate the percentage of the final consumer dollar going to compensate marketing activities. Perhaps the most careful and complete discussion of those studies is Paul D. Converse and others, *Elements of Marketing*, Seventh Edition, Englewood Cliffs, N.J.: Prentice-Hall, Inc., 1965, pp. 622–625. Another work which is primarily concerned with the issue of aggregate marketing costs is Reavis Cox and others, *Distribution in a High-Level Economy*, Englewood Cliffs, N.J.: Prentice-Hall, Inc., 1965, see especially Chapters 8, 9 and 10. See also Stanley Hollander, "Measuring the Cost and Value of Marketing," *Business Topics*, Summer 1961, pp. 17–27; reprinted in Perry Bliss, editor, *Marketing and the Behavioral Sciences*, Second Edition, Boston: Allyn and Bacon, Inc., 1967, pp. 493–512 (see especially the section beginning on p. 506).

MEASURING THE COST OF MARKETING

Efforts to establish definitive measurements of the cost of our marketing system have met with only limited success. Such measurement is inherently difficult to accomplish. If we define aggregate marketing costs as that portion of national income which is income to persons engaged in the creation of time, place and possession utility, the procedures required for the estimation of these costs would be very complex. The magnitude of the problem is increased as data are not always available in the most usable form. There are, however, two methods with which total marketing costs have been estimated. These two methods are (a) the sum-of-marketing-margins method and (b) the total-value-minus-form-costs method.[9]

The sum-of-marketing-margins method develops aggregate marketing costs estimates by adding the gross margins (expenses plus net profits) of firms engaged essentially in marketing activities. Thus, if a retailer pays a manufacturer $1.00 for some item of merchandise and the retailer resells it to us for $1.50, the gross margin of the retailer is $.50. That $.50 is income to the retailer, but it is an element of marketing cost to us. Similarly, if a manufacturer sells to a wholesaler who, in turn, sells to a retailer who then sells to a final consumer, the sum-of-marketing-margins involved might be determined as follows:

Manufacturers selling price (cost to wholesaler)	$1.00	
		+$.30
Wholesalers selling price (cost to retailer)	1.30	
		+ .40
Retailers selling price (cost to consumer)	1.70	
Sum of marketing margins		$ .70

In the hypothetical situation above, the final consumer paid $1.70 for an item of merchandise of which $1.00 went to compensate the manufacturer and $.70 cents went to pay for marketing activitites. The sum-of-marketing-margins method of estimating aggregate marketing costs for the United States simply applies this or a similar approach to all marketing agencies.

The total-value-minus-form-costs method of estimating aggregate marketing costs is a somewhat simpler concept, although it is potentially complex in use. The total-value-minus-form-costs method subtracts the sales income of manufacturers from the final value of manufactured goods (price paid by final consumers) in order to estimate marketing costs. An example will clarify this approach. Using the same data as in the previous example, the manufacturer's selling price for an item is $1.00 and the final selling price $1.70; the difference, $.70, is then the estimated cost of mar-

[9] Perhaps the most lucid discussion of the problems involved in estimating aggregate marketing costs may be seen in Theodore H. Beckman and William R. Davidson, *Marketing*, Eighth Edition, New York: The Ronald Press Company, 1967, pp. 794–803.

keting. Note that an important difference between these two methods is that individual intermediate margins need not be collected and summed when the total-value-minus-form-costs technique is employed.

The reader should note that the foregoing discussion of marketing cost measurement is purposely oversimplified; the actual calculations involved in such measurement raise many very difficult problems. This liberty is taken at this time in order to provide an understanding of the basic nature of aggregate marketing costs; the purpose has not been to provide statistical tools to estimate such costs.

MARKETING COSTS AND MARKETING EFFICIENCY

We have now seen that the aggregate cost of our marketing system is relatively high. But high marketing costs are not necessarily indicative of inefficiency in the performance of marketing activities. Such costs may simply reflect the fact that more complex tasks must be performed. What evidence is there of general inefficiency in our marketing system? The evidence usually offered by critics of the marketing system falls into one of four basic categories: (a) marketing mortality rates, (b) quality and cost of marketing services, (c) relative changes in marketing costs and (d) productivity analysis. Each of these categories deserves brief elaboration.

The mortality rate of firms engaged in the performance of marketing activities is high. It is presumed that "a high rate of mortality wastes . . . resources in the sense that it uses larger quantities (of them) than would be required by a more stable trade population."[10] One reputable source estimates that there were well over 11,000 business failures in 1966, over 10,500 such failures in 1967, and well over 8,500 failures in 1968—with this latter figure representing incomplete returns on the year.[11] Although these figures are conservative (for many very small firms elude the data collecting procedures), it should be made clear that not all the firms included in the statistics cited above are exclusively marketing firms. The majority of them are, however. Indeed, over 6000 of the 1967 business failures were retail firms. It is partially because of this great number of visible failures in marketing enterprise that marketing is often perceived as a relatively inefficient part of our total economic system. "Visible" because such failures are most apparent to us when they occur at the retail level of distribution. Failure and instability are thus often judged as a symptom of general inefficiency.

The quality of services rendered and the popular conception of the size of gross margins enjoyed by marketing enterprise is another cause

[10] See Reavis Cox and others, op. cit., p. 180.
[11] The data are from Duns Review, December 1967, page 93, and December 1968, page 91 respectively. A "failure" is defined as having occurred when "a concern is involved in court proceedings or voluntary action likely to end in loss to creditors." This same source also publishes a "failure index," which reflects the annual failures per 10,000 enterprises listed in the Dun and Bradstreet Reference Manual.

for the general notion that our marketing system is inefficient. We have all been treated brusquely or impolitely by some inarticulate and perhaps poorly informed salesperson; we have all seen salespersons congregate for what are apparently purely social reasons to the utter neglect of eager customers; we can all recall the promise of merchandise delivery which was not properly fulfilled; and we may also remember the embarrassment of having a personal check challenged. We probably tend to remember the more offensive and inefficient encounters with salespeople more vividly than the more pleasant and efficient ones. This negative recall forms a kind of mental stereotype which we may tend to associate with all marketing activities. Dissatisfaction with the marketing system is even more pronounced among those who believe that market specialists receive extremely large margins of profit for the questionable quality of service they provide. Thus, to those who believe that profits in marketing are at exploitative levels, the quality of the service given seems all the more inadequate. A related complaint is that there are too many of certain types of marketing institutions—for example, that the number of gasoline stations now serving us is excessive.[12] This charge is related to marketing efficiency in the following way: if there are too many institutions of a particular type, then some of the economic resources devoted to the operation of those institutions might profitably be diverted to other, more useful, human endeavors. To the extent that marketing institutions exist in excess, then, they introduce an element of inefficiency into the economic process of allocation.

A third major source of dissatisfaction with the efficiency of our marketing system can be traced to relative changes in marketing costs. But changes relative to what? There is a long-standing tradition of comparing relative marketing costs with relative manufacturing costs. The relationship between aggregate marketing costs and aggregate manufacturing costs is then often used (or misused) to draw some inference regarding the efficiency of one or the other of these broad economic sectors. It is in the process of inferring efficiency from relative marketing and manufacturing costs that an important fallacy in logic may occur. This fallacy is called the *fallacy of complementary percentages,* and the following hypothetical figures will illustrate the error in logic that it involves.

Percentage of average consumer dollar spent for	1950	1960	1970
Manufacturing Cost	60%	50%	40%
Marketing Cost	40%	50%	60%

[12] An effort to identify the optimum number of marketing institutions, prompted by this kind of allegation, may be seen in Reavis Cox and Wroe Alderson, editors, *Theory in Marketing,* Homewood, Ill.: Richard D. Irwin, Inc., 1950, pp. 321–333.

Consider the relationship between marketing costs and manufacturing costs in this data. Note that the figures represent a complementary and, from the view of marketing costs, an ascending series. That is, marketing costs account for a progressively larger portion of the total consumer dollar. Exactly what would a series of figures such as these indicate about efficiency if they were actual data? The temptation of some critics has been to infer that the marketing system grew less efficient during the 20-year span represented in the figures. This interpretation of the figures is incorrect. Indeed it is quite impossible to infer changes in efficiency from complementary percentages.

As an example, consider the following analogy. Two distance runners each race one mile at different times on different tracks. The distance each has to run is one mile and, to get a more reliable basis for comparing their performances, two separate heats are run.[13] The results of these races are indicated in tabular form below:

	Percentage of total time required for first heat	Percentage of total time required for second heat
Runner "A"	44.8%	49.0%
Runner "B"	55.2%	51 %

Now, which of our two runners improved the most between the running of the first and second races? Indeed, do we know that either of our two runners improved at all? The complementary percentages provided above leave us uncomfortably ignorant about what actually transpired in the running of the two heats of the race. The truth is that there is an infinite number of absolute numerical combinations which are consistent with the complementary percentages in the table. For example, if the total time elapsed in heat one was nine minutes and five seconds and if the total time elapsed in heat two was eight minutes and thirty seconds then both our runners were more efficient. If, on the other hand, the total time elapsed in heat one was nine minutes and five seconds, and the total time elapsed in heat two was ten minutes, then both our runners became less efficient. Let it suffice to say that inferences drawn from complementary percentages and concerning efficiency are often dangerous and usually untenable.

Criticism three: the marketing system is often unresponsive to consumer wants

The allegation that our marketing system is often unresponsive to our wants as consumers may be divided into two subordinate types of criticism: first,

[13] A "heat" is one of several preliminary races held to eliminate less competent contenders.

that marketing institutions do not adjust readily to changes in consumer demand; and, second, that products and services provided by the marketing system do not accurately reflect consumer preferences. In the present section we will examine these criticisms more carefully.

A fundamental tenet of our economic system is that scarce economic resources are ultimately allocated by the preference patterns of final consumers; that is, we as consumers vote, as it were, for particular types of institutions and for particular types of products and services. We vote by purchasing things we wish to encourage in institutions we wish to encourage. We vote by not buying things we wish to discourage. If the system is working properly, we collectively encourage some institutional forms, bring about the modification of some and the demise of still others. What exactly does it mean, then, to say that the institutions which comprise our marketing system respond imperfectly to our economic urgings. An illustration of a criticism of this kind might be made for one of our best known marketing institutions—the department store. It has been charged, for example, that the department store was excessively service-oriented in the years following World War II. This excessive concern with service took the form of offering costly, non-goods services presumably on the basis of the belief that large numbers of consumers wanted such services. The critic would thus contend that the continued operation of the department store on an intensive service basis is evidence that our marketing system is, on occasion, effectively deaf to our wants. There are many other instances in which the institutions of our marketing system are asked to adjust; but for the moment it is enough that we appreciate the fact that the marketing system has an institutional character which is, ideally, modified by preferences of final consumers.

The charge that our marketing system does not provide the products and services we desire has been aired frequently and vigorously in recent years. We shall see in a subsequent chapter that concern with this problem has already produced legislation and will likely produce even more. Our concern here is with defining more precisely the nature of this charge. There seem to be two types of criticism involved: (a) that product quality is poor and declining (against the wishes of the consumer) and (b) that there are specific instances in which the preferences of consumers are ignored altogether. The first of these two views is exemplified by the following quotation from a popular news magazine:

There are times when the United States consumer seems doomed to constant annoyance from the things he buys and the people who sell them to him. If he somehow escapes rattles, pings, loose buttons or missing knobs, there probably will be dents, mismatched sizes, static fluttering, leaking or creaking. Worse yet from the standpoint of life and limb, there can be exposed electrical terminals with near lethal voltages, faulty steering columns, room heaters that emit carbon monoxide and wringer washers that await their owners erring fingers. The customer can complain but very often his complaint will end up in a computer, which will analyze, quantify and correlate it before shooting back a form reply that never quite touches on the original problem.[14]

The reader should note that not all the ills suggested in the foregoing quotation are directly traceable to corporate marketing policy. Indeed, many of the problems cited are more nearly engineering matters. The final consumer may nonetheless associate these problems with marketing because the faulty product, whatever it may be, was purchased through a marketing specialist. But the critic may insist that there is another reason why marketing policy may be suspected of encouraging, tacitly or otherwise, minimum quality standards: Since products with a short life expectancy normally mean greater opportunity for subsequent sales, marketing has a vested interest in poor quality. This viewpoint is, of course, the "planned failure" argument, and it is a specific genre of the more popular phrase, "planned obsolescence."

An additional and a closely related instance in which the marketing system may be accused of reacting imperfectly to customer demands is suggested by the phrase "controlled engineering progress." The thrust of this criticism is that, left alone, products and services will take on characteristics which are profitable but are not necessarily in the best interests of consumers. Unsafe but aesthetically magnificent cars, drugs and remedies not fully and carefully tested, and many similar examples are cited. Thus the system is alleged to be not only unresponsive to consumer wants, but also insensitive to real needs. Another very closely related argument is that product characteristics are virtually dictated to consumers in some instances. One especially popular view, for example, is that particular fashions are thrust upon a docile public, which has little recourse but to accept them.[15] One writer, for example, challenges the view that consumers alone establish fashion and argues that relative to a particular automotive design feature the consumer was "the somewhat inattentive auditor of a conversation among professional automobile stylists."[16] The true role and influence of the consumer has been argued for years and will be argued for many more. Let it be sufficient for now that we identify that longstanding argument as yet another instance in which the critic may assert that the free working of the market is more or less thwarted

---

[14] "Rattles, Pings, Dents, Leaks—Creaks—And Costs," *Newsweek*, November 25, 1968, p. 92.

[15] See, for example, William H. Reynolds, "The Wide C-Post and the Fashion Process," *Journal of Marketing*, January 1965, pp. 49–54. In this piece, Reynolds argues that the consumer "was at best a participant" in the evolvement of the wide C-post, and auto design characteristic. Reynolds' position is challenged, in turn, by D. E. Robinson in the *Journal of Marketing*, April 1965, p. 114.

[16] Reynolds, *op. cit.*, p. 49. The reader is directed also to Chester R. Wasson, "How Predictable Are Fashion and Other Product Cycles?" *Journal of Marketing*, July 1968, pp. 36–43. See especially, Wasson's comment "that fashion is a synthetic creation of the seller is an idea so entrenched that even marketing professionals are often blind to the observably low batting average of those who attempt such 'creation.' "

by commercial interests and that the result is that consumers get, not what they want, but what some diabolical group wants them to want.

Criticism four: marketing practitioners are often unscrupulous

If we are to believe recorded history, marketing practitioners have always been thought of as persons with an eye for a quick dollar and little regard for the ethics of how it was earned. Writers on early English trading have described "unscrupulous dealers who took advantage of their fellow traders at every chance,"[17] and "dealers in foodstuffs and innkeepers making profits of 200 percent and more."[18] Writers about the Middle Ages also suggest that the shopkeepers of London were not above using the attractions of their womenfolk to lure customers. Thus, historical descriptions of trade often identify the early marketing specialist as at least a rascal and quite probably something worse. Is the marketing man of today haunted in any way by this wretched past? Is he thought to be a person of questionable ethics and flaccid moral fiber? The best answer to the question is probably that, while today's marketing specialist is not thought to be as bold and brazen in his disregard for the truth as his precursors, he is felt to be, at very best, devious.

How is the devious character of the marketing specialist allegedly evident? Though the following taxonomy is by no means complete, the ensuing discussion will be developed around three general classes of alleged malpractice: (a) manipulation, (b) exploitation and (c) deception.

MANIPULATION

The critics' notion that marketing practitioners are not above the use of manipulative methods is best exemplified by the popular thesis that special research methods are often used to "get inside the consumers' subconscious in order to discover the 'psychological hook' which will impel consumers by the millions to buy a certain product."[19] But this subtle type of manipulation is allegedly accompanied by another type of manipulation—manipulation by brute force. This second type of manipulation is alleged to occur as a result of the use of the mass media by commercial persuaders to batter the consumer into "a state of dazed acceptance of whatever goods and services were put before them." A concomitant of this brute force manipulation is that "a stunting and withering of the independent personality" was produced, and "the consumer was turning

[17] H. G. Selfridge, *The Romance of Commerce*, London: John Lane, The Bodley Head, Ltd., 1923, p. 174.
[18] S. Trupp, "The Grocers of London: A Study of Distributive Trade," in Eileen Power and M. M. Postan, editors, *Studies in English Trade in the 15th Century*, London: G. Bell & Sons, Ltd., 1925, p. 261.
[19] Vance Packard, "The Growing Power of Admen," in C. H. Sandage and Vernon Fryburger, editors, *The Role of Advertising*, Homewood, Ill.: Richard D. Irwin, Inc., 1960, pp. 268–269.

into a virtual automaton."[20] The view of the critic, then, is that subtle research methods and domination of the mass communications media may serve business interests in a manipulative way.

These subtle methods of research are normally collected in the term *motivation research,* a term which involves "the application of techniques from clinical psychology" and related fields to the solution of marketing problems.[21] The indictment of motivation researchers, if such an indictment has indeed been accomplished, was aided and abetted by the widely circulated book *The Hidden Persuaders,* by Vance Packard. But there are other ways in which subtle manipulation is alleged to occur. Motivation research is evil, in the eyes of critics, because the researcher learns too much about what motivates buyers. The seller, thus armed, is in a position to play on emotional themes and interfere with the rational process of judgment which the buyer might otherwise employ.

Another class of manipulative methods are alleged to work in even more subtle ways—upon the subconscious of an individual. This discussion suggests that there are at least three different levels on which the communications specialist might appeal to the buyer-prospect. These levels are: (a) the conscious-rational, (b) the conscious-emotional and (c) the subconscious. The value system of the critics of mass communications and marketing persuasion would seem to hold that appeals directed to the conscious-rational level are "fair," that appeals directed to the conscious-emotional are "unfair" and that appeals directed to the subconscious are deplorable. But how are these subconscious sales appeals accomplished?

Psychologists recognize the concept of *subliminal influence.* If something is subliminal it is below (*sub*) the threshold of perception (*liminal*). Thus, for example, a very high-pitched whistle may be subliminal for most humans, but may be perceived by other animals with more sensitive hearing. In the terminology of the psychologist, the stimulus of the whistle is thus subliminal for many human beings. So it is with our other senses; that is, stimuli may either be perceived by or avoid (subliminate) our senses of sight, smell, taste and feeling. We may thus experience a particular phenomenon either consciously (within our conscious range of perception) or subconsciously (subliminally). Equipped with this succinct definition of the concept of subliminal perception, we are in a better position to understand the allegation that consumer manipulation may occur as a result of using subliminal techniques of communication. But how is this subliminal type of communication alleged to influence buyers or prospects? One student of the subject describes the process as follows:

[20] Edward L. Brink and William T. Kelley, *The Management of Promotion,* Englewood Cliffs, N.J.: Prentice-Hall, Inc., 1963, pp. 352–353.
[21] Robert V. Williams, "Is It True What They Say About Motivation Research," *Journal of Marketing,* October 1957, p. 125.

(It is) the process whereby the name or picture of a product is flashed on a motion picture or television screen so rapidly that it cannot be seen by the conscious eye. The message is registered in the fringes of the viewer's attention and, it is claimed, may thus motivate him to buy.[22]

The alleged power of the subliminal message was publicized and popularized by an experiment in a New Jersey movie theater. That experiment exposed moviegoers to the subliminal cues, "eat popcorn," and "drink Coca-Cola," at an exposure speed of approximately 1/3000 of a second. The results were that sales were substantially above those previously achieved. A result of that experiment was that the popular press identified subliminal cues, among other things, as "the latest weapon in the arsenal of the psychological manipulator."[23] We should note here that a careful survey of findings on the use of subliminal messages—a survey conducted by reputable professional psychologists—concludes that the research evidence is "still quite insufficient to warrant such claims."[24] The findings of this research team, however, achieved but a fraction of the public exposure that the New Jersey experiment did. But we shall have later occasion to develop this point more carefully. We have made our basic point that the marketing practitioner has been, and is, held in some disrepute because of his alleged use of manipulative tactics.

EXPLOITATION

Exploitation is another charge which the critic of marketing activities has made. During 1968, United Press International news service revealed that the House Government Operations Committee felt that "the poor have been sold inferior food at possibly higher prices at ghetto supermarkets." In a book titled *The Poor Pay More*,[25] findings are disclosed which suggest that "New York poor families paid higher prices than the well-to-do for consumer durables." Certainly, if this charge is true, it is a serious indictment. It may be an indication of the social irresponsibility of some marketing organizations. In the aftermath of most urban riots, two charges are common enough to be predictable: police brutality and consumer exploitation. And as is often the case, the public seems to hear the charge more clearly than the rebuttal. The U.S. Department of Agriculture, for example, concluded on the basis of "an exhaustive six city investigation" that "food chains do not now and never have discriminated against any groups or class of customers and fully recognize their obligations to deal fairly and honestly with everyone they serve." Similarly, "recent studies attempting

[22] Franklin S. Haiman, "Democratic Ethics and the Hidden Persuaders," *Quarterly Journal of Speech,* December 1958, p. 385.
[23] The theater experiment and other similar evidence is reviewed in *Consumer Reports,* January 1958, p. 8.
[24] See James V. McConnel and others, "Subliminal Stimulation: An Overview," *The American Psychologist,* May 1958, pp. 229–242.
[25] David Kaplovitz, New York: The Free Press, 1963.

to determine if food chains were charging higher prices in low-income areas than in other parts of the same city found that this frequent allegation was not supported by evidence in any of the several cities studied."[26]

DECEPTION

Finally, the poor image which marketing practitioners often have is aggravated by the widespread notion that they regularly employ techniques which are at best deceptive and often border on fraud. Because a major portion of a subsequent chapter is devoted to an examination of deceptive acts and the law which attempts to regulate them, we will not at this time attempt to identify the various types of deception one may encounter. Instead, we will cite one recent evidence of marketing fraud as a concrete instance of the type of practices which adversely influence the image of the marketing specialist.

During the fall and winter of 1967, most of the major petroleum companies were using promotional games of various kinds. In most cases, the customer was given a chance for some kind of prize with a purchase, though some of the games required no actual purchase in order to play. The prizes were of various cash and merchandise types. That is, some prizes were small immediate cash payments, some involved portable TV sets and similar household items and some involved substantial amounts of cash and valuable merchandise. The games were apparently based on chance—that is, the customer could draw a valuable prize on any particular transaction. The element of chance was an important part of these games, for if the station operator knew which envelopes contained substantial prizes, he would be in a position to manipulate the contest to his own advantage. Some of the games were cumulative, or "addictive," in the sense that the customer had to fill a card with some number of pictured stamps in order to qualify for more valuable prizes. This addictive characteristic in the contests produced, it was hoped, at least temporary brand loyalty.

Several news items cast serious doubt on the basic integrity of the game administrators and further weakened the public's conception of the marketing practitioner. One of these news items revealed that station operators could tell in advance which envelopes contained cash prizes and which were of no immediate value. This meant that in some cases the element of chance was replaced by the station operator's whim. In another instance, in a type of promotional game in which auto license plate numbers determined the contest winners, the winning license plate numbers were leaked. In at least one instance, a car bearing a winning license plate number was bought cheaply from its unsuspecting owner and the cash prize was claimed by the new owner. (This manipulation of the contest was possible because in that particular state a license plate stayed with a car regardless

[26] Charles S. Goodman, "Do the Poor Pay More," *Journal of Marketing*, January 1968, p. 18.

of its owner.) Indeed, the public sentiment against these promotional games has been so strong that a Federal Trade Commission study was conducted into both supermarket games and gasoline station promotional games. The results of that study were a shock. *The National Observer* carried an article in January 1969 which revealed that one southern supermarket chain "continued to advertise $1000 prizes for eight weeks after they all had been given away." One large chain claimed that customers had one chance in three of being a winner when, in fact, the promoter that supplied the games said shoppers faced odds of 15,373 to 1 against winning a cash prize and odds of 33 to 1 against winning minor prizes of stamps or products. The FTC survey found odds of about 300 to 1 against winning cash prizes and 80 to 1 against winning anything at all in the average supermarket contest.[27]

Criticism five: marketing is an imprecise and unscientific discipline

The criticisms of marketing that we have identified so far are charges that are largely social or economic in their origin; that is, the critics are likely to be social or economic "protectionists." But the marketing *discipline* (that body of related knowledge which deals with the subject of marketing) is, on occasion, subject to criticism from other academic disciplines. The foundations for this academic form of criticism are often related to what we will identify here as *academic weaknesses* of marketing as a professional field of study. These academic weaknesses in various degrees often influence the student who is seeking an area of study in which to major. We shall concentrate here on what are, essentially, two academic criticisms: (a) that marketing is not a scientific discipline and (b) that marketing has no truly professional standards of membership.

Marketing is relatively young as an academic discipline. The first courses in marketing were taught in the 1920's and 1930's. This fact makes marketing a mere infant compared to, say, economics, law, medicine and other studies. Because marketing is a young discipline, it does not display the traits usually associated with more mature disciplines.[28] Marketing, for example, does not now have a well defined nucleus of formal principles, or laws, which explain or identify relationships between variables which, are, in turn, crucial to an understanding of some marketing phenomena. Physics, in contrast, is a mature physical science; it has evolved as an integrated body of principles or laws. Physics has academic stature in part because of its degree of scientific maturation—marketing lacks academic

---

[27] See also *Marketing Insights*, October 30, 1967, p. 8.
[28] An extremely good discussion bearing on the process of epistemological maturation of an academic discipline may be seen in Dwight P. Flanders, *Science and Social Science*, Champaign, Ill.: Stripes Publishing Co., 1959, pp. 10–17.

stature in part because it is young. But there is another aspect of this same point which should be emphasized. When we say that the discipline of marketing has not yet evolved a nucleus of fundamental principles—principles which enhance our understanding of marketing phenomena—we are also admitting that marketing is, to a degree, a *subjective* area of study. For our purposes, we will take the word subjective to mean that there are significant problems within the discipline of marketing which are partly *judgmental*—that is, they depend to some extent upon particular opinion. This condition makes for some frustration because there is, on occasion, no unique answer to a particular marketing problem. For the beginning student of marketing, however, this judgmental characteristic of the discipline may properly be viewed as a meaningful challenge. Because some of the most difficult, most important and unresolved problems confronting business today are in the marketing area, it follows that talented young people will, with hard work, help to shape an evolving discipline.

But the relative immaturity of the discipline itself is not the only academic weakness of marketing. There is impressive evidence that the perception of the marketing field as a relatively unscientific discipline has a distinct influence on college students in their selection of career objectives. Students often tend to equate marketing with selling, and having done so, conclude that marketing is not for them because selling is, or can be, a disagreeable task. It is fairly common to see studies that indicate that college students dislike the prospect of a career in marketing, and particularly in selling, because the field is thought to be full of people with relatively little formal education. This view, in effect, emphasizes the relatively low occupational prestige of selling activities.[29] Sociologists who have an interest in social class (or sometimes "social stratification") and the determinants of social class position argue that the principal factors that serve to determine occupational prestige include (a) income, (b) freedom of action, (c) education and training and (d) power.[30] For the most part, these factors are self-evident. Since the education factor is very much to the point we are considering here, some brief explanation may be in order. It has been observed elsewhere that "to say that a man is a physician or a lawyer implies a specific, formalized educational experience; but to say that a man is a salesman makes no educational implication whatsoever."[31] This tendency to judge various occupations in terms of educational prerequisites unquestionably contributes to the inability of some college-age youth to develop enthusiasm for the field of marketing.

[29] See, in this vein, John L. Mason, "The Low Prestige of Personal Selling," *Journal of Marketing,* October 1965, pp. 7–10.
[30] See Theodore Caplow, *The Sociology of Work,* Minneapolis: University of Minnesota Press, 1954, p. 39.
[31] Mason, *op. cit.,* p. 9.

Criticism six: marketing is the father of materialism

There is one final criticism of marketing which we have hinted at but have not yet stated boldly. In the view of some critics, marketing is at the base of the materialistic rat race which is felt by some to characterize our socioeconomic system today. We observed in Chapter 1 that marketing activities have societal implications because they persuade and, in so doing, influence the allocation of scarce economic resources among alternative ends. A slight modification of that same process of reasoning suggests that marketing activities create discontent among those whom they influence by creating an awareness of new material things. Stated in a different manner, it is charged that children are taught to refine and sharpen their acquisitive instincts almost from the cradle stage—and that this encouragement comes primarily from marketing interests.

These critics are, in effect, arguing that our social and economic character would be improved—there would be less frustration and unhappiness—if the marketing-inspired acquisitive rat race were less intensive. They are suggesting that without marketing, greater efforts could and would be exerted in the nonmaterial, spiritual aspects of living—that there would be more attention given to the individual and less homage paid to the hardtop V-eight. Indeed we have all heard some form of these arguments in recent years. The hippies, yippies, and their ideological offspring all to some degree lament the materialistic nature of our system. Critics who explicitly identify marketing activities as an important contributor to the urban race riots of recent years tend to agree that the widespread looting of stores during those riots indicates one of the results that can occur when people are *tempted* with elaborate artifacts but not given the *means* to acquire them. Though this brief statement of the materialism problem does not give recognition to all the nuances of the argument, it will suffice for our purposes.

SUMMARY

The purpose of the present chapter has been to identify some of the forms of criticism that underlie attitudes toward the field of marketing. It has not been our purpose to systematically challenge these forms of criticism; that kind of challenge is the central purpose of the following chapter. Our examination has been developed around six basic points. First, we explored the notion that marketing is economically unproductive and observed that the intangible "product" of marketing is probably related to this viewpoint. We also examined briefly the idea that the economic resources that are devoted to the performance of marketing activities are excessive. This view contends that marketing is to a significant degree an inefficient activity.

We noted that there is some feeling that marketing is unresponsive to consumer wants—that it does not serve us faithfully, although it may claim that it does. We suggested that some negative attitudes toward marketing stem from the view that marketing practitioners are, on occasion, unscrupulous. It is probable that marketing has a weak academic reputation because it is relatively young and is felt to be to some extent an immature discipline. Students tend to give less than complete consideration to marketing as a career choice, in part, because they tend to equate marketing with selling, and selling may have many negative connotations. Finally, we noted that marketing and materialism are often thought of as partners in social discontent—this kind of connection further contributes to the general suspicion with which marketing is, on occasion, viewed.

REVIEW QUESTIONS
1 Carefully define and indicate the relevance of each of the following concepts to the study of marketing:
   a. Intangible utility
   b. Income distribution controversy
   c. Mediocrity hypothesis
   d. Inferred efficiency and complementary percentages
   e. Planned failure argument
   f. Motivation research
   g. Subliminal influence
   h. Addictive forms of promotion
   i. Occupational prestige of selling
2 Distinguish carefully between each element in the following pairs of terms:
   a. The sum-of-margins method of measuring marketing costs *and* the total-value-minus-form-costs method of measuring marketing costs
   b. Marketing *and* selling
   c. Marketing costs *and* manufacturing costs
   d. Consumer manipulation *and* consumer deception
   e. The conscious-rational level *and* the conscious-emotional level
   f. The conscious-emotional level *and* the subconscious level
3 The argument that marketing is inefficient usually develops around any of four basic points. What are these points?
4 What is a specific example of the argument that marketing practitioners are often given to the use of exploitative methods?
5 This chapter is organized around six basic criticisms of marketing. What are these basic criticisms?

DISCUSSION QUESTIONS
6 As you reflect on the definitions of marketing provided in Chapter 1, what are the most visible aspects of marketing? What are the least visible aspects of marketing?
7 Develop a narrative description of the kind of person who would elect to specialize in marketing. Be as complete as you can.
8 Develop a narrative description of the kind of person who would elect to specialize in medicine or law.

Chapter 3

THE SOCIAL AND ECONOMIC
FOUNDATIONS OF MARKETING

It was the purpose of the preceding chapter to examine the stature of marketing from a critical perspective. Toward that end we identified and briefly explored six of the most frequently encountered and most effectively articulated criticisms of our marketing system. There was no special effort exerted in that chapter to answer these criticisms—though the sympathetic reader may have observed some points of vulnerability in the arguments. It is the principal purpose of this chapter to identify and examine the social and economic foundations upon which our marketing system rests. The view taken here is that marketing activities are not evidence of a grand commercial conspiracy that has been thrust forcibly upon the consumer, but that such activities are a natural form of human endeavor. Marketing activities are, in fact, to be fully expected as a part of the process which we call economic development.

More specifically, the present chapter explores seven issues that relate to the social and economic foundations upon which marketing activities rest: (a) a consideration of the true nature of production and value; (b) a more systematic consideration of the economic value created by information, by spatial convenience and by time; (c) an analysis of the relationship between the process of economic maturation and marketing activities, including an identification of the Clark-Fisher Hypothesis; (d) a discussion of the relationships between our actions as consumers and the aggregate costs of our marketing system; (e) an examination of the issue of dynamic consumption; (f) a discussion of the relationship between ease of entry in our enterprise system and the performance of that system; and (g) the role of scientific method in marketing.

The nature of "production" and "value"

We have noted in an earlier discussion that, historically speaking, some kinds of human endeavor have been thought more productive than others.

We observed that because marketing activities do not generally alter the physical nature of products, the true nature of the contribution of the marketing specialist may be underestimated. We need to return briefly to that issue and to formally define two especially important terms—"production" and "value."

Clearly, productive human activity is not necessarily evidenced by tangible physical output. That is, there are trades and human activities besides marketing which are held in generally high esteem but which do not produce tangible units of output. Thus, there is no physical stock of output when a brilliant trial lawyer argues a case and wins—yet he may willingly be paid thousands of dollars for the quality of his argument. It should be clear that our hypothetical trial lawyer is productive, and because he is, he creates economic value. A professional psychiatrist may successfully handle the mental, emotional or other behavioral disorders of his clients, yet when he is through there will be no physical product to which he might point and claim as his product. And so it is with many service activities—they cannot be packed, stacked or stored, but they are valuable in the sense that people willingly part with purchasing power to acquire them. Services thus have economic value, and those who provide them are *economically productive.*

This may all seem manifestly evident, but the explicit identification of this idea seems impelled by a semantic trap which the word "production" may embody. This trap traces to a weakness in the human psyche which produces a tendency to dichotomize or polarize events as a means of simplifying complex matters. Thus, the manufacture of goods, say automobiles, is referred to as "production," and it may be convenient to some to infer that services are therefore a form of "nonproduction." Those engaged in manufacturing may be thought of as "productive"; those in ancillary service activities as "nonproductive." The convenience of the dichotomy is compelling, even if illogical.

A *productive* human activity is one, then, which gives rise to value. We shall not concern ourselves with the nature of the output of that human activity, except to note that tangible and intangible outputs may both reasonably have economic value, and the human activities which gave rise to them are therefore productive. As has been observed elsewhere, "while the creation of form utility is what we generally think of as 'production,' there are also time, place and possession utilities, and these are created through marketing."[1] Our concept of production is in general agreement with the national income accounting concept of gross national product. The gross national product is defined as the value in dollars of all goods and services produced in a given time period. The student should note that our definition of production does not define all creative human

---

[1] D. Maynard Phelps and J. Howard Westing, *Marketing Management,* Revised Edition, Homewood, Ill.: Richard D. Irwin, Inc., 1960, p. 1.

activity as productive. Indeed, one might labor mightily by driving nails into a board and thus "manufacture" a board full of nails, but our hypothetical "manufacturer" is not productive until someone willingly parts with purchasing power in order to acquire the board full of nails. Similarly, a retailer may provide a service of some type for his clientele, but the activities of making that service available are not productive until someone willingly parts with money or its equivalent to avail himself of that service.

There is one other small semantic difficulty which we should anticipate. This problem centers around the word "value," a word which we will have frequent occasion to use in the discussion which follows. One frequent criticism of our marketing system—a criticism which is akin to one we noted earlier—is that marketing specialists prefer to compete on nonprice terms.[2] This criticism alleges that while consumers want lower prices, the marketing system gives them, instead, nonprice amenities or services. These nonprice amenities or services are not, this criticism holds, as valuable as are lower prices. The theoretical economist, in particular, often reflects this preference for price competition over nonprice competition. An alternative view, and a preferred one, is that value may be thought of as a simple equation or ratio as follows:[3]

$$\frac{\text{Perceived Quality}}{\text{Perceived Price}} = \text{Perceived } \textit{Value} \text{ (by the consumer or buyer)}$$

This "value equation," though very simple, will help us keep an important perspective in the face of critical challenge. Note that there are two essential ways in which perceived value may be increased: one may decrease price or one may increase quality.[4] Either of these actions can logically produce an increase in perceived value. Note that we say *can* rather than

[2] This is a specialized form of the argument that the marketing system is insensitive to or unresponsive to the wants of consumers. See the relevant discussion on pages 32 to 35 of Chapter 2.

[3] Though this ratio will prove valuable to us for the problem at hand, it should be noted that there is some argument regarding its universal validity. One well qualified student of consumer behavior argues, for example, that the quality-price ratio does not have operational meaning in some instances. This is true "where the consumer finds her own self-worth elevated through the act of purchase. In such diverse product categories as automobiles, cosmetics, detergents, clothing, appliances, and homes, we have consistent evidence that consumers decide on the basis of a *gestalt* or pattern of virtues that far transcend either 'quality' or 'price.' " It is, of course, possible to define quality to include that *gestalt*—indeed this is frequently implied. See Irving S. White, "The Perception of Value in Products," in Joseph W. Newman, editor, *On Knowing the Consumer,* New York: John Wiley & Sons, Inc., 1966, pp. 92–93.

[4] The perceived quality of the product or service is determined by three essential factors: (a) the cultural importance of the product or service, (b) the brand image of customer .stereotype of the product or service and (c) the physical-sensory aspects of the product itself. These factors are suggested by Irving S. White, *op. cit.,* p. 101. The application of this set of factors is, however, modified.

must, for it is possible that lower prices may actually connote lower value.[5] Note especially that there is no a priori reason why a lowering of price should better serve to increase value as perceived by the consumer than would an increase in quality. Indeed, it should also be noted that a substantial increase in quality accompanied by a small price increase can produce an increase in the customer's perceived value. Finally, it should be noted that the value actually perceived by a consumer is a highly personal thing—value is in fact determined in the mind of the consumer. This is an important point, for it suggests that where aesthetic and psychological product properties are concerned, few people are qualified to determine preferences in behalf of others. That is, we would expect to find relatively little agreement among consumers as to the precise value of a particular good or service: Such value is ultimately determined by the interaction of such a complex group of conditions that no two persons are likely to behold a given item as having precisely the same value. Indeed we may state this position more assertively: Products and services may reasonably be completely worthless to one consumer or household and have substantial value to others; because one does not smoke, and because one therefore may not have use for a cigarette lighter, one cannot logically conclude that cigarette lighters are overpriced for someone else.

The economic values created by marketing activities

We have had several occasions to refer to the intangible utilities created by marketing activities. We are now in a position to explore some additional dimensions of time, place and possession utility. In the discussion which follows we will explore some determinants of (a) the economic value of information, (b) the economic value of spatial convenience and (c) the economic value of time.

THE ECONOMIC VALUE OF INFORMATION [6]

Suppose that you are returning to your home after an evening of scholarly endeavor at the library, and, as you pass the corner of the library, a man

[5] We shall explore this notion at greater length later, but for now the reader is invited to examine "Some Consequences of the Habit of Judging Quality by Price," Tibor Scitovsky, in *Marketing and the Behavioral Sciences,* Second Edition, Perry Bliss (Editor), Boston: Allyn and Bacon, Inc., 1967, at pages 442–450.

[6] Though the discussion which follows is primarily concerned with the way in which information influences the values of goods and services as perceived by consumers and users, there are a number of recent experiments which endeavor to scrutinize the value of information to business decision makers. There are some obvious parallels between these two perspectives, and some of the ideas expressed in the discussion in this section are suggested by those experiments. The reader is directed to Paul E. Green and others, *Experiments on the Value of Information in Simulated Marketing Environments,* Boston: Allyn and Bacon, Inc., 1967. Note especially the systematic variation in reliability of information described in "Exercise 2." See also Paul E. Green, "Consumer Use of Information," in Newman, *op. cit.,* pp. 67–80.

steps out from the shadows and says, "Hey buddy—wanna buy a good recent model used Cadillac for five hundred bucks?" What is your first reaction to this curious offer? You might reasonably disclaim any interest and continue hurriedly on your way. You might, on the other hand, have your interest sufficiently piqued to attempt to have some of the now ambiguous aspects of the proposition clarified. Our concern with this hypothetical case is with the changes in your perceived value of the Cadillac as information is made available to you. In order that we may clarify the relationship between perceived value and information, let us assume that you begin to quiz the mysterious nocturnal salesman. Suppose, to be specific, that your principal concern centers around two points. First, you need to know if the man who confronts you has legal title to the car he wishes to sell or, conversely if the car is "hot." Second, you need to know if the car has been abused in some way which is not immediately apparent; that is, you need assurance that the car is physically what it appears to be. Accordingly, you attempt to clarify these two points. The man insists he has title to the car, and that it is in a good state of repair. If you could be sure that the man had answered truthfully, his testimony might well prompt you to part with $500.

But our anecdote has suggested two important points for us. Customer perceptions of value in goods and services depend significantly upon (a) acquiring *information* about such goods and services and (b) a kind of *credibility coefficient* that serves to temper the degree to which particular items of information influence our perceived value and therefore how much money we will part with to acquire the goods or services in question.[7] That is, information, when credible, has the ability to increase the economic value which consumers are willing to part with. This is not to say that advertising, because it informs with various degrees of credibility, necessarily drives actual consumer prices up; indeed there are cases where continued advertising tends to reduce both costs and prices. The statement above properly emphasizes the *willingness* of consumers to part with increased economic value rather than the *necessity* to part with increased economic value.[8] But we need to make one further refinement.

Information may assume any of several different forms, and evidence suggests that different types of information have different degrees of

---

[7] This credibility coefficient may simply be some probabilistic evaluation of the truthfulness of the person responsible for the testimony being given. Thus, one source may be a .9 source (meaning that the probability that the information is accurate is 90 percent) and another may be a .2 source (meaning that there is only one chance in five that the information given is accurate).

[8] See, for example, Jules Backman, *Advertising and Competition,* New York: New York University Press, 1967, p. 143. Backman comments to this point "the assumption that relatively high advertising costs necessarily must lead to higher prices reflects a misunderstanding of the pricing process. Although cost is one factor influencing prices, cost alone does not determine prices. It follows that a small component of total costs, such as advertising, usually will not play an influential role in setting prices."

influence upon perceived values. It will further the present argument if we now distinguish four basic classes of informative appeals.[9] The basic classes are as follows:

1 Economic-Relevant Appeals
2 Economic-Irrelevant Appeals
3 Noneconomic-Relevant Appeals
4 Noneconomic-Irrelevant Appeals

There is long tradition in the literature of marketing for distinguishing between rational actions and emotional actions by consumers. As one text puts it, "If one reasons out logically that he needs and should have an article, he arrives rationally at the decision to buy. On the other hand, if he decides to buy without thinking the matter out logically and carefully, his decision is emotional."[10] Because of the tradition for these two classes of behavior, there has been some tendency to transfer this terminology to the context of promotional appeals. Thus, an appeal is thought of as rational if it presents serious, hard evidence about price or performance of a product or service. Conversely, an appeal is thought of as emotional if it is based on such judgmental matters as aesthetics, self-esteem, peer acceptance and similar bases. But these terms, when used to identify communications appeals, often carry a connotative implication of quality differences; that is, the rational appeal is good, the emotional appeal is bad. For this reason, the terms "economic" and "non-economic" appeals are used instead here.[11]

An *economic-relevant* informative appeal is one which endeavors to inform about some aspect of price or performance which is clearly germane to the product or service. For example, an automobile advertisement which

[9] The classes of informative appeals which follow may seem to imply that each appeal is insular in the sense that it occurs in a pure or unadulterated form. This is rarely true. The appeals are nearly always mixed in complex ways; that is, each of these appeals may be present in some degree.

[10] Paul D. Converse, *Elements of Marketing,* Seventh Edition, Englewood Cliffs, N.J.: Prentice-Hall, Inc., 1965, p. 74.

[11] These terms are suggested in Raymond A. Bauer, "The Limits of Persuasion," *Harvard Business Review,* September-October 1958, pp. 105–110; reprinted in C. H. Sandage and Vernon Fryburger, *The Role of Advertising,* Homewood, Ill.: Richard D. Irwin, Inc., 1960, pp. 228–237 (see especially p. 231). To this same point, see Malcolm P. McNair, "Marketing and the Social Challenge of Our Times," in Keith Cox and Ben M. Enis, editors, *A New Measure of Responsibility for Marketing,* 1968 June Conference Proceedings, American Marketing Association, pp. 1–8. On p. 3, McNair says, "the distinction between rational and emotional appeal is mostly a false dichotomy. If you could analyze a purchase to know all the considerations that entered into it—it would be a logical purchase. 'Rational versus emotional' is a distinction that belongs to the realm of ideas on how people *should* behave. According to a rational view, i.e., what 'somebody' thinks is 'good' for them."

specifies price and miles per gallon under normal city driving conditions utilizes an economic-relevant basis of appeal.

An informative appeal which is *economic-irrelevant* presents evidence about price or performance, but it is irrelevant from the point of view of the average prospect. Thus, an automobile advertisement which focuses on mileage performance under competitive circumstances may not be germane. Advertisements which claim economy records but fail to state the peculiar adjustments made to the car and the unusual driving techniques employed by the driver are economic-irrelevant in the sense which we intend here.

We will define *noneconomic* informative appeals to include all appeals which are not price and performance appeals. These noneconomic appeals tend to be socially or psychologically based. An advertisement which stresses design beauty, pride of ownership, the social acceptability of the product or service and similar appeals is noneconomic. But what is the distinction between noneconomic-relevancy and noneconomic-irrelevancy? A *noneconomic-irrelevant* informative appeal is one which is effectively sterile—upon close examination it says virtually nothing, but it often leads the reader or viewer to infer that something is being said. Advertisements that claim a product is best—with no point of particular reference—fall into this noneconomic-irrelevant classification.

The position held throughout this text is that informative appeals which are relevant—be they basically economic or basically noneconomic—have the potential to increase perceived values. This view is in contrast to that held by some critics who would prefer that only economic information be permitted in advertisements. These critics feel that the noneconomic type of informative appeal, which emphasizes an emotional sales premise, is socially undesirable. The realistic view is that emotional reasons underlie the desire for some types of products and services—it has always been that way, and it shall always be that way. No inherent fault is found here with informative appeals which are socially or psychologically based solely because they are appeals to the human emotions. Fault is found, however, with the informative appeal which we have designated irrelevant. This type of appeal cannot, as a long-run matter, increase consumer perceptions of value. It is essentially sterile; it only appears to inform.

THE ECONOMIC VALUE OF SPATIAL CONVENIENCE

We have suggested that marketing activities may produce place utility. We have suggested that place utility is a legitimate economic value (though it does not result in physical change), and those who produce place convenience are deserving of remuneration. But this view may seem more a value judgment than a truth. What evidence can we now muster to support this view? The discussion which follows will outline the geometric principle of place utility. And although the illustrative anecdote is developed in the context of a retailing enterprise, the basic principle involved is applicable on a broader geographical basis. To demonstrate this principle of place utility, we need to resort to a highly oversimplified socioeconomic system. But this "unreal" assumption does not alter our essential conclusions.[12]

Assume that we have under our scrutiny a minature economic system that comprises three craftsmen, each of whom specializes in the fabrication or cultivation of one product. Each of our craftsmen produces an amount of his specialty sufficient not only to meet his own requirements, but also to trade for the specialties of each of the other craftsmen. In order that we might examine the role of location policy and distance in the process of distribution, assume that each of these craftsmen lives at the angles of an equilateral triangle; that is, lines connecting each of our craftsmen would form such a simple geometrical pattern.[13] Figure 3.1 represents our highly simplified system.

Figure 3.1 Spatial Convenience

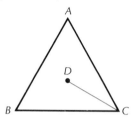

To deal more precisely with the influence of distance in the exchange process, we must assign actual dimensions to Figure 3.1. For simplicity, assume that the distance from the geometric center of the triangle (DC) is 1, or unity. Using simple trigonometric relationships, it can be demonstrated that the value of any external element (AB, BC or AC) is 1.732.[14] Since our three craftsmen must travel along routes AB, AC, and BC during

---

[12] The model which follows is from Ronald R. Gist, *Retailing: Concepts and Decisions,* New York: John Wiley & Sons, Inc., 1968, pp. 22–29.

[13] The classic statement of central place theory is given in W. Christaller, *Die zentralen Orte in Süddeutschland: Eine ökonomischgeographische Untersuchung über die Gestzmass igkelt der Verbreitung und Entwicklung der Siedlungen mit städtischen Funktionen,* Jena: Gustav Fisher Verlag, 1933. For an abstract of the theoretical parts of Christaller's argument, see Brian J. L. Berry and Allen Pred, *Central Place Studies: A Bibliography of Theory and Applications,* Philadelphia: Regional Science Research Institute, 1961, pp. 15–18. Notice particularly Christaller's argument that central markets, at least in the early stages of their development, are likely to assume geometric patterns similar to those postulated in the present argument.

[14] Let r equal the distance from the geometric center of the triangle to any angle; in our case this distance is 1. Let K represent the value of any outside line segment (AB or BC or AC). Let Θ equal the angle between any outside line segment and any line as DC above. In the case of Figure 3.1, Θ equals 30°; cos 30° equals 0.866, and where r is 1, K equals 2 × cos 30° or 1.732.

the process of exchange, the distances represented in our triangle may be conceived as a kind of resistance that must be overcome in order that the exchange process be completed.

As an illustration, then, if Producer A undertakes a trip to the residence of Producer B in order to exchange specialties, Producer A would expend an effort represented by 3.464 units of distance (2 × 1.732); this would include, of course, the effort required for A to return to his own residence. Clearly, this concept of "distance units" can be used to reflect the total distance that must be overcome in the process of effecting *complete exchange*; that is, exchange in which each craftsman in the system has acquired the specialty of each of the other specialists.

We now need answers to these three questions:

1 What is the minimum aggregate distance in Figure 3.1 that must be traversed in order that each of our craftsmen acquire the specialty of each of the others in the absence of a marketing functionary?
2 What is the minimum aggregate distance in Figure 3.1 that must be traversed in order that each of our craftsmen acquire the specialty of each of the others where a marketing specialist serves the system?
3 What is the difference between the minimum aggregate distance required to effect complete exchange without the marketing specialist and that required with the marketing specialist? In other words, what is the difference between the answers to Questions 1 and 2 above?

SPATIAL INCONVENIENCE WITHOUT MARKETING SPECIALIZATION
With reference to Figure 3.1, assume that Craftsman A desires some of the specialty of Craftsmen B and C. Craftsman A would presumably undertake a journey around the system; that is, he would follow a path described by the sides of our equilateral triangle. In so doing, Craftsman A will, of necessity, expend an effort represented by 5.196 (3 × 1.732) distance units. This journey complete, Craftsman A will have acquired the specialties of Craftsmen B and C—naturally, B and C will have received some of the specialty of A in exchange. As things would then stand, Craftsmen B and C would not have exchanged specialties. Since an exchange must take place between these two producers in order that our requirement of complete exchange of specialties be fulfilled, it is necessary that another trip, one involving 3.464 (2 x 1.732) distance units, be undertaken. We may thus conclude that, in Figure 3.1, where there is no marketing specialist, a total of 8.66 (5.196 + 3.464) distance units must be traversed in order that each of our craftsmen acquire the specialties of each of the others.

SPATIAL CONVENIENCE WITH MARKETING SPECIALIZATION What, then, would be the minimum aggregate distance that our craftsmen would have to overcome in order to effect complete exchange where a market specialist exists? This question raises two additional questions:

Where is the marketing specialist located, and what kind of business does he conduct?

Obviously, his location will influence aggregate distances which must be traveled in the process of exchange. Let us assume that the specialist will be in the geometric center of the system he serves, since this location results in the greatest convenience to the system being served.[15]

The kind of business the marketing specialist conducts also influences our illustration. Clearly, our specialist could run a catalog service, which could conceivably require two trips to the market for each of our producers: one trip to order, another to pickup. Or, our marketing specialist could carry stocks sufficient in size to fill the consumption needs of all the members of our system for several months in advance. In this latter instance, only one trip to market would be necessary. Naturally, the market intermediary, at periodic intervals, would have to replenish his supply of stocks. We assume here that the specialist is a full-inventory operation, and not simply an order service.

Assuming that our specialist has accumulated stocks from all the producers in the system, and assuming further that the intermediary locates at the geometric center of our system, only 6 (or 3 × 2) distance units need be overcome to effect complete exchange.[16] A trip to the geometric center of our system and a return trip home on the part of each of our craftsmen would result in complete exchange.

THE GAIN IN SPATIAL CONVENIENCE   Now we can determine with greater precision the value of the location policy of our specialist from the point of view of the system that he serves. Since we have observed that our miniature system must exert an aggregate effort sufficient to overcome 8.66 distance units where there is no marketing specialist, and that an aggregate effort of only 6.00 distance units need to be overcome to effect complete exchange where the specialist is operative, we might reasonably argue that our specialist could charge up to 2.66 distance units (or the equivalent in terms of real goods or some money measure) for his services. Our specialist, then, represents the potential for reducing the distance units which must be traversed to effect complete exchange by 30.7 percent (2.66 ÷ 8.66) below the distance units which must be traversed to effect a similar exchange in his absence. This percentage advantage is *general* in the sense that it remains the same regardless of the absolute dimensions assigned to our three-producer system as long as the geometrical properties which we have assumed prevail.

Table 3.1 indicates the potential increase in place convenience resulting from the specialist's location policy in systems having a larger number

[15] In general, a tendency of this sort exists.
[16] This is a reasonable assumption. The vast majority of marketing enterprises are stock points, not simply order-taking enterprises.

Table 3.1 *

	Distance units required to effect complete exchange		Potential gain in place convenience from market specialist	
Number craftsmen	Without market specialist	With market specialist	Units	Percent
3 (Triangle)	8,660	6,000	2,660	30.70
4 (Square)	13,312	8,000	5,312	39.90
5 (Pentagon)	18,116	10,000	8,116	44.80
6 (Hexagon)	23,000	12,000	11,000	47.82
7 (Heptagon)	27,740	14,000	13,740	49.53
8 (Octagon)	32,050	16,000	16,050	50.08
10	41,226	20,000	21,226	51.48
12	50,372	24,000	26,372	52.35
50	221,125	100,000	121,125	54.27
100	447,150	200,000	247,150	55.27

* All calculations assign a constant value of 1 to the distance between the geometric center of the system and any angle. In effect, as the number of craftsmen in the system approaches infinity, the system assumes the configuration of a circle of craftsmen, each of whom is equidistant from the retailer.

of craftsmen or specialists. The table reflects, to some extent, what common sense would lead us to suspect. As an economic system becomes increasingly complex, the aggregate distance which must be traversed in order to effect a complete exchange of the specialties of each of the craftsmen constituting the system increases rapidly.[17] In our model system, complete exchange between 100 craftsmen would necessitate travel of 447,150 distance units. In the absence of a market specialist the system becomes literally a honeycomb of paths connecting each of our craftsmen. It should be noted that any additional service the market specialist might offer which reduces the distance each of us must overcome in order to exchange economic specialties increases the claim that the specialist can legitimately make of his clientele. If, for example, the market specialist decided to modify his operations in such a way that he developed branch operations,

[17] The detailed solution to the four-craftsmen case is presented in Appendix 3.A at the end of this chapter.

or in such a way that he sold door to door, further gains in place convenience occur, and to the extent that his new policy reduces the effort that we (as consumers) must expend, we may be willing to increase his remuneration.

One final comment is in order. Obviously, this highly simplified model of place convenience is not a faithful reproduction of the world in which we live. However, our model is like the real world in some important respects. We are all economic specialists of some kind; and through the medium of a monetary system, we exchange our specialty for those of others around us. Moreover, marketing facilities do tend to serve a clientele which surrounds them, and this circular type of trade-area pattern would tend to prevail in our model where the number of craftsmen was extremely large.

THE ECONOMIC VALUE OF TIME

Up to this point in our discussion, we have explored some aspects of the value-creating potential of information and of space. Of the three intangible utilities of principal concern to us, time utility is the focus of this section. More specifically, we are interested in developing a logical argument that *time has demonstrable value,* and that, therefore, the time convenience offered to a socioeconomic system by market specialization is a legitimate activity, one which creates true economic value. In order to demonstrate this point we need to introduce the concepts of market *duration* and market *frequency.*

Consider, as a point of departure, the present situation in many large cities and urban areas: service stations operate around the clock, seven days a week; similarly, some drug and prescription services operate on a virtually continuous basis. Indeed, one of the limiting cases in terms of market duration and frequency is the *continuous* case: where this circumstance prevails, the marketing system stands ready to meet the needs of consumers at all times. Where the continuous market exists, the consuming unit need not plan carefully ahead for an out-of-stock condition, because the market is definitionally always ready to correct such a deficiency. It must be noted, however, that the continuous market places great demands upon the resources engaged in marketing activity—indeed it diverts some resources to marketing activity that might otherwise occupy themselves in other ways.

The opposite limiting case, in terms of market duration and frequency, is the no-market-at-all case. Indeed this case would produce a barter system in which each manufacturer/fabricator/grower traded directly with some other manufacturer/fabricator/grower. Such a circumstance, strictly speaking, would not involve marketing—at least not in a specialized sense. But if there was a formal market open on, say, the first Tuesday of every other month, then we would have some measurable degree of market duration and frequency.

Consider for a moment the impact of a market which stands ready to serve your needs on one day every other month. In what ways, profound or unimportant, would your life be altered? Clearly, consumption planning would have to be substantially refined as contrasted to the way it is practiced today. It is also clear that the normal household would practice some *stockpiling*—that is, households would be storehouses to a greater extent than is now true. For some highly perishable goods the household would have to lay in stocks which would make the present concepts of refrigeration and home freezing seem woefully inadequate. The possible ramifications of the intermittent market are both profound and numerous. Let it suffice now to say that a continuous type of market is one which makes it easier for us in some respects, although we pay for the ease which it represents to us. Thus time influences economic value through what we will call market duration and frequency.

Market specialization is a sympton of economic maturation

It is a fundamental fact that the need for specialization in the performance of marketing activities is directly related to the level of economic development of a socioeconomic system. Consider the foregoing statement carefully; it suggests that marketing specialization is not needed in some economic environments and, conversely, that marketing specialization is quite natural in other economic circumstances. In general, the rule to observe is that *as an economic system matures—as greater specialization and division of labor occurs—the need for marketing specialization increases.*

In order to clarify any ambiguities attending this point, consider an economic circumstance in which each household produces only the goods and services required for its own use. This state of affairs (sometimes called a domestic economic system) obviates the need for exchange between households. If each household produces only for its own requirements, then there are no exchangeable surpluses; indeed it follows that there is no compelling reason for any economic interaction between the household units which constitute the system. Each household is defined as self-sufficient. How much and what kinds of marketing activity will occur in this domestic economic environment? It should be clear that there is no collective or societal need whatever for physical movement of goods between households; there is no societal need for one household to inform another about the characteristics of its handiwork; there is no strong societal need for storage of the productive output of several households which make up the system. In short, there is no societal need for most of the activities which we have called marketing activities.

But suppose that specialization and division of labor proceeds to the point where households produce only a portion of their total consumption requirements, but they produce surpluses of their specialty—surpluses which are in turn traded for those items of consumption which they are not well suited to produce for themselves. This type of economic system may be called an incipient industrial system. Note that in this system the degree of household specialization necessitates economic interchange. But what kinds of marketing activity will occur in this emerging industrial economic system? Certainly, a collective need for physical distribution now exists. Natural geographical specialization inevitably produces regional surpluses and regional dearths; these surpluses and dearths produce, just as inevitably, the need for physical distribution. And, because specialization in production makes one an expert on his own line of products or services but ignorant about lines which others produce, there is clearly an evolving collective need for the dissemination of commercial information. We might, therefore, reasonably expect a system of mass communications to evolve in this incipient industrial economy. Moreover, because production and consumption are often temporally separated, that is, because rates of production and rates of consumption are rarely the same, storage facilities are likely to be a societal requirement. Indeed, the industrial economy brings with it a collective or societal need for all the major classes of marketing activity which we have previously identified. But we might gainfully attempt to distinguish one other state of economic development.

Suppose that specialization and division of labor proceeds to the point where a package of goods and services sufficient to meet all minimum requirements for survival and security is made available to all members of the society. Some of the exchange which would now take place between members of the system would involve products and services which are not clearly required but which require persuasive as well as informative sales efforts. We will refer to this state of economic development as the "affluent" stage, and it should be clear that marketing activities under these conditions are not precisely the same as we have depicted in less advanced socioeconomic systems.[18] The crux of the difference between marketing in an industrial economy and marketing in an affluent economy is that consumers *needs* are likely to be the focus of attention in the former and that consumer *wants* are likely to be the focus of attention in the latter. This distinction between needs and wants requires clarification, and in this instance clarification is not easy.

True *needs*, we are told, are both obvious and felt. As the originator of the concept of the affluent economy has suggested, "It is not necessary to advertise food to hungry people, fuel to cold people or houses to the homeless."[19] But wants are another concept altogether. The *want* is contrived by marketing activities—especially, persuasive communications. Galbraith put it this way:

[18] The concept of an affluent economy is elaborated in John Kenneth Galbraith, *The Affluent Society,* Boston: Houghton Mifflin Company, 1958.
[19] Jean Boddewyn, "Galbraith's Wicked Wants," *Journal of Marketing,* October 1961, p. 15.

The fact that wants can be synthesized by advertising, catalyzed by salesmanship, and shaped by the discreet manipulations of the persuaders shows that they are not very urgent. A man who is hungry need never be told of his need for food. If he is inspired by his appetite, he is immune to the influence of Messrs. Batten, Barton, Durstine and Osborn. The latter are effective only with those who are so far removed from physical want that they do not already know what they want. In this state alone men are open to persuasion.[20]

The Galbraithian want is one which is not a requirement for physical survival; that is, it is more nearly in the realm of a creature comfort or perhaps a luxury. The demand for the Galbraithian want is not spontaneous; the demand for the Galbraithian want is created by the sweet-talking of "Madison Avenue." If one subscribes to all of this argument, it then follows that one must believe that marketing in an affluent economy must act in the role of first creating a want and then filling that want—a process that is both endless and sterile: endless because there is presumably no effective limit to the number of such contrived needs, sterile because there can be no meaningful fulfillment in satisfying a contrived need.

But are needs and wants as distinctive as we are led to believe? When does a want in the Galbraithian sense become a need? Did the average American family in 1900 *need* an automobile? Does the average American family in 1970 *need* an automobile? It is apparent that the concept of need is both a highly personal and a very elastic concept. The history of man records, in an endless repetitive pattern, the opposition of society to some new product (a wicked want) and the subsequent and complete integration of that product into its cultural patterns (a genuine need?). But still another point obscures our thinking about wants, needs and marketing activities. The Galbraithian need is largely biological—it seems exclusively a life sustaining thing. Is it not possible and meaningful to think of social, psychological and cultural needs?

The view held here is that man is quite properly concerned not only with his physical well-being, but also with the social, psychological and cultural aspects of his well-being. Nor is this broader concept a convenient escape hatch from the impeccable logic of the Galbraithian argument. Social, psychological and cultural needs are much more difficult to define than physical needs. Indeed, the continual quest for new products is in a very real sense a quest for the means of a more precise satisfaction of social, psychological and cultural needs. How then is marketing different in the affluent economy? Our answer is that a more important problem in the affluent system is the identification and satisfaction of the non-biological needs.[21] Or, as one student of the subject words it:

Producers (are) no longer trying merely to use advertising as a coupling device between existing market demand and their own supply; rather they (are) trying

[20] Quoted in Boddewyn, *op. cit.,* p. 14.
[21] Boddewyn, *op. cit.,* p. 18.

to create a demand. Since the function of advertising (has) become one of exerting influence (as well as) providing information, the older factual prosy notice which focused upon the specifications of the commodity now gives way to a more lyrical type of appeal which focusses upon the desires of the consumer.[22]

THE CLARK-FISHER HYPOTHESIS

In the preceding discussion, we traced the societal need for marketing specialization through the domestic-industrial-affluent stages of economic development. A different perspective on the relationship between marketing activities and this process of maturation, one which affords a somewhat different insight, is suggested by the "Clark-Fisher Hypothesis." This hypothesis identifies three fundamental stages of economic development through which economies evolve. These stages are the primary, secondary and tertiary. They are characterized as follows.[23]

PRIMARY STAGE The essential problem confronting the economy during this stage is biological—provisions for food and protection from the rigors of nature are immediate problems. The preoccupation of the economy is, accordingly, with extractive and agrarian pursuits. The fundamental problem confronting the system is physical survival. Marketing activities are likely to be limited to physical distribution and storage—with little compelling need for a mass communications network. An economy which is fundamentally extractive/agrarian exchanges *commodities*—or items of produce which are very similar, perhaps even standardized. The similarity of commodities reduces the societal need for a very elaborate system of marketing. A relative shortage of want satisfying goods means that relatively little selling effort is required. A ready and unsophisticated market exists for that which is produced. It follows that marketing costs are, in the aggregate, relatively unimportant.

SECONDARY STAGE During this stage of economic development, the foremost problem confronting the economic system lies in discovering the *most efficient means* of production. Note that the problem is no longer simply one of survival, but one of using nature and its resources to *greatest advantage*. This stage is usually one in which demand, in the aggregate, exceeds supply. That is, relative shortage still exists. The emphasis is, moreover, on manufacturer, fabrication and assembly. This secondary stage is certainly akin to the stage of economic development which we often identify with the term "industrial revolution." The principal problems

[22] David M. Potter, "Advertising: The Institution of Abundance," *Yale Law Review*, Autumn 1953; reprinted in Hiram C. Barksdale, editor, *Marketing in Progress: Patterns and Potentials*, New York: Holt, Rinehart and Winston, Inc., 1964, pp. 561–576.
[23] Stanley Hollander, editor, *Explorations in Retailing*, East Lansing, Mich.: Michigan State University Press, 1959, pp. 52–59.

confronting the economy are inside the factory, as it were—not agrarian as they were in the preceding phase. It should be noted that the role of marketing is still not fully matured. Though the means of distributing mass produced goods and services are now developing, the emphasis and concern is with industrial processes.

TERTIARY STAGE   This stage might correctly be called the distributive stage of economic development. Problems in agriculture and manufacturing still exist—indeed they always will—but the problem area most requiring immediate societal attention is an inadequate and inefficient distribution system. The state of affairs which prevails early in this tertiary stage of development may be depicted as an incongruity—an incongruity between manufacturing and distribution. For while manufacturing has achieved semi- or fully-automated status, distribution continues through relatively archaic means. The crucial problem confronting the economy is now the expedient distribution of great quantities of mass produced goods and services. And expedient distribution may be taken to include the means for mass communications as well as distributive institutions (wholesalers and retailers) with low cost operating capabilities. But before truly efficient distribution can be achieved the relative costs of distribution are likely to climb. Indeed, relatively higher costs in marketing are, to an extent, caused by tremendous efficiencies in the manufacturing processes. One might correctly view the problem as a *disparity in capacities,* in which the capacity to manufacture is very great, and the capacity to distribute is something less. As a *pipeline concept,* the manufacturing capability exceeds the ability of the pipeline to purvey goods and services. The tertiary stage embodies, in this sense, a grand bottleneck or logjam problem.

The Clark-Fisher hypothesis thus suggests several points which are relevant to our concern with why marketing specialization occurs and with why marketing costs behave as they do. Certainly, the societal need for physical distribution is felt in all three stages of the Clark-Fisher sequence. The societal need for mass communications is minimal in the primary stage of development, but that need emerges as maturation proceeds, and the need is absolutely unavoidable in the tertiary stage. We should observe too that we may logically expect marketing costs to be substantial during the logjam period. Indeed, relatively high marketing costs are, in a broad sense, one result of economies of scale in production.

A note of warning is in order. The Clark-Fisher hypothesis is a *reasonably* accurate description of a sequence of economic conditions which are universal. Note that while the sequence of stages does not describe any single economy perfectly, neither is it completely inapplicable in any system. The process of growth may be accelerated in evolving economies, and acceleration itself may tend to blur the several stages so that they overlap. Assisted economic growth may accelerate the process in some countries so that each stage, though distinguishable, is not of great longevity. The reader is cautioned not to apply Clark-Fisher in a literal sense—it is a composite which can be analytically valuable, but which may not be clearly defined in any particular circumstance.

The costs of marketing are democratically self-inflicted

We need now to amplify an idea which has been suggested in an inferential way at several points in our earlier discussion. This point is that *marketing costs are what we ask them to be*—with two basic imperfections. These two imperfections are (a) a lagged response and (b) the natural inequity of a democratic system. This idea needs to be amplified and illustrated. First, let us examine the notion that marketing costs are self-inflicted (or, what is the same point, that such costs are what we ask them to be).

One of the aspects of our marketing system which is apparent to us all is that it offers us choice. Indeed, it often gives us so many brands and styles to select from that we may be hard put to effect a decision. Choice is the means to a degree of individual fulfillment. Suppose, for example, that we had a system in which choice was restricted to some arbitrary number of styles in each product category. Suppose, in other words, that instead of the choice we now have, we operated on an *issue* system (in some respects like a military supply room). The choice then exercised would be a size choice, rather than a style choice. Let us visualize a full choice system at one end of a spectrum and an issue system at the other. In a very real sense, we encourage our system to provide greater choice by displaying individualistic preferences as consumers. We would, by the same token, encourage a restriction of choice if we displayed collective instead of individualistic preferences. In effect, we encourage great choice by patronizing it, and discourage great choice by not responding to it. We also decide through such patronage whether the costs of marketing are to be relatively great or relatively low; for is it not clear that a system characterized by great choice is more costly than one which borders on "issue" circumstances? But perhaps this argument seems too lofty to be concrete. Is there a way to illustrate the same point in less esoteric terms?

Consider the more immediate matter of store hours as just one example. If we are concerned with reducing marketing costs, we might simply legislate a maximum number of hours during which stores could be open. If we set that legislative maximum at a very low level, say two hours per day, six days per week, we could doubtlessly reduce the societal costs of marketing. It would be true, would it not, that fewer people would be engaged in retailing and those who left that trade could do other things?

But the popularity of weekend and late-night openings suggests that an important element among our population wants a system which stands ready to serve us virtually all the time. Again, we might sharpen the argument by visualizing the ends of a spectrum—this time however the ends are labeled with terms like "continuous operation" and "infrequent operation." Clearly, when we patronize stores evenings, during the day and on weekends we encourage longer hours and induce an increase in the societal costs of marketing.

As noted earlier, this self-inflicted character of many marketing costs is not a perfect cause-and-effect relationship. We noted that there were essentially two imperfections in the relationship. We need to clarify these two points of weakness in the responsiveness of our marketing system to our preferences.

First, the market system responds to our wishes only after a *time lag.* As an example, consider the matter of services offered by retail stores. There is evidence that some retail stores have, in the past, offered more exotic services than consumers actually wanted; at least there was no significant body of consumers interested in the services. If these stores had immediately sensed the lack of consumer interest, they would have ceased to offer those particular types of services. But the mechanism through which such matters are sensed is imperfect itself, so that some extended period of time may elapse before conditions can be rectified.

Second, the market system responds with what might be called a *democratic inequity.* That is, those casting the greatest number of votes are heard, and those in the minority may be slighted. A specific case to this latter point might be the American supermarket—a self-service retail institution familiar to us all. During the 1930's, the approximate time of the birth of the supermarket, there were critics of "impersonal" retailing who genuinely felt that there was no real place for such an institution. It was cold (in an impersonal sense), stark, barren and many other undesirable things—yet the supermarket is inextricably a part of our marketing system today. In retrospect then, those who disliked the institutional concept of the supermarket were cast in the minority role, those who saw the potential of the institution proved to be the majority. Thus, the market system may at times seem totally unresponsive to our *personal* preferences when in fact it is responding to the opposite view of some larger group.

Marketing and the issue of dynamic consumption

In Chapter 1 we noted that there are profound social and cultural ramifications to what our marketing system does. In order to conceptualize that relationship we identified the concepts of social balance and the dependence effect. We need now to confront that form of criticism more explicitly. Briefly, the Galbraithian concept of social balance calls attention to the *quality* of wants at different stages of economic development. A condition of economic affluence produces wants which are contrived by social and commercial pressures on consumers. The commercial pressures are primarily marketing activities. But the wants thus "contrived" are "valueless and even contemptible."[24] Because these marginal wants are effectively valueless, the argument goes, economic resources devoted to their production ought more properly be devoted to other things—things usually in the public area. Is there a logical answer to this kind of challenge? Wherein, if at all, does the argument err?

Consider the notion that "marginal wants are effectively valueless." What the candid critic should say is that given *his* value structure the wants *seem* valueless. That is, the notion that social imbalance exists involves, as a pivotal assumption, a value judgment on the part of the critic. The Galbraithian argument presumes that social imbalance can be detected and that, in turn, assumes:

That it is possible to judge the quality of other people's wants and satisfactions in a communicable and authoritative way. But it is not possible, contrary to what Galbraith assumes, to dismiss wants as valueless simply because they have been acquired under the pressures of social emulation and advertising. All economically relevant wants are learned. Moreover all standards of taste are learned. It is therefore both arrogant and inconsistent to assume that those who have acquired their standards from general culture and advanced education can choose and pass judgments according to standards possessing independent validity, while those who have acquired their standards from social pressures and advertising can neither understand nor learn to understand the difference between good and bad taste.[25]

Indeed a fundamental task of a marketing system is to assist in the process of maintaining private aggregate consumption at desirable levels.[26] Marketing is an important means of producing cultural change; it is an important means for increasing both levels and standards of living. Nor is this role an evil role. It appears that modern capitalism in a mature state of development is inherently beset with problems of unemployment. It is an undeniable fact that changing levels of aspiration are as important as any other single factor in maintaining tolerable levels of unemployment in such a modern economy. The quarrel with this role of marketing seems always to appear when a critic sees a significant level of consumer interest developing in something which seems to him to be silly, wasteful or in

[24] Harry G. Johnson, "The Consumer and Madison Avenue," in Lee E. Preston, editor, *Social Issues in Marketing: Readings for Analysis,* Glenview, Ill.: Scott, Foresman and Co., 1968, pp. 253-259, particularly p. 256.

[25] *Ibid.,* p. 257.

[26] This task of marketing is identified in Roland S. Vaile and others, *Marketing in the American Economy,* New York: The Ronald Press Company, 1952, pp. 28-31.

"bad taste." The critic has, unwittingly or otherwise, set his own tastes and preferences up as a standard which he believes all of us should share and enjoy with him.

A weakness of our marketing system

We have, to this point in the present chapter, answered several of the criticisms raised in the preceding chapter. We have addressed ourselves thus far to (a) the economically unproductive argument, (b) the excessive cost of marketing argument, (c) the unresponsive to consumer wants argument, and (d) the catalyst for materialism charge. We have not yet considered the charges that marketing practitioners are often unscrupulous and that marketing is an imprecise and unscientific discipline. Our concern in the present section and in the one which follows is with these issues.

Our market system of enterprise is one which makes it relatively easy to enter business. Not business on a national or even regional basis to be sure, but some kind of business. It has been said that the one inalienable right that everyone exercises at one time or another is his right to lose some important part of his shirt in a business venture. Considering leasing arrangements, franchises, modest retail establishments, motels, eating and entertainment facilities, thousands of people move into and out of our market system every year. And although there is a high rate of mortality with new businesses, those that do succeed provide the inspiration for another try by those who fail. Like hamburgers, apple pie and hot dogs, entrepreneurship is American.

It is an inherent part of our market system that relative ease of entry attracts many persons who are not adequately prepared for management roles in a business enterprise. Not only are such persons often totally unfamiliar with modern methods of business management, but they also fail to fully appreciate the social responsibility with which American business is necessarily charged. Inadequate financing often means that the essential problem confronting the firm is never to "maximize profits," but rather, from the beginning, to survive and preserve what one can of invested funds. A business enterprise that is constantly threatened with demise is one that is willing to employ short-term competitive expedients even though they are known to be improper and, indeed, irresponsible. A man threatened with death may momentarily abandon his normal value system—the end may, in other words, temporarily justify the means.

But we should not imply that irresponsible action is alone the behavior of the small enterprise; that is clearly not the case. But death can come within the organization as well as to the organization—and a copywriter who is told to see that merchandise moves (or to seek employment elsewhere) may confront a death of a special but very real type.

What does all this prose have to do with the issues before us now?

The charge that marketing practitioners are on occasion guilty of unprofessional conduct is true.[27] The cases with which the Better Business Bureaus and the Federal Trade Commission deal attest more than adequately to this fact. And in the chapter which follows, we shall see that the malpractices of business are not only virtually endless in number but often ingenious in application. But such practices are not new—that is, this particular character trait of our market system is not a sympton of modern marketing alone. Indeed the entire history of trade reflects malpractices of one kind or another.[28] This is an important point, for many critics seem to be suggesting that current marketing practices are not just bad but rapidly degenerating as well. Though the point is essentially one of opinion, it is probable that there are, in general, more responsible persons in important policy making positions in business today than ever before. Social irresponsibility in business practice is probably not more widespread than ever before—but evidence of such irresponsibility is infinitely more apparent. The information gathering facilities which disseminate news in this country are efficient, and the powers of those facilities are staggering; the general focus of the news facilities can highlight a social problem more quickly and more searchingly than ever before possible. The result is often a cumulative and perhaps unwitting overstatement which suggests imminent doom. Note carefully that this is not a charge of irresponsibility in news reporting—but it is a charge that particular subjects are journalistically fashionable, and that antibusiness is from time to time highly readable news.

But there is more than just an illusion of unscrupulous practices in business. Consumers themselves are better able to sense when they have been abused in some business dealing. Consumers are more sophisticated today than ever before, and the complexity of decisions confronting consumers clearly requires greater sophistication. This growing alertness to exploitive or abusive practices in business is perhaps the most significant long-run deterrent to such practices—more significant even than existing "consumer" legislation

It is clearly one of the most perplexing social problems of our time whether a free market system such as ours can continue to admit virtually

[27] An interesting perspective is suggested in "Marketing and Ethics: Comments," Joseph W. McGuire, in *Marketing and the New Science of Planning*, Robert L. King, editor, American Marketing Association, Chicago, 1968, at pages 556–557. McGuire argues that the "traditional market system" may be efficient, but that there is no a priori reason to expect it to be ethical. Indeed, the very forces that tend to make it efficient may tend to produce actions of questionable ethics.

[28] There are many graphic descriptions of these malpractices. The reader is directed to E. S. Turner, *The Shocking History of Advertising*, Baltimore: Penguin Books, Inc., 1965. This short treatise provides a historical panorama of advertising from the fifteenth century through the subliminal scare of the 1950's.

all persons who wish to conduct a business of their own and at the same time expect that system to act in a professional and socially responsible manner. Is a system which endeavors to encourage the smaller entrepreneurial effort a system which is comfortably consistent with socially responsible actions? Does relative freedom of entry necessarily mean some degree of unprofessional membership? The answer, though not a particularly satisfying one, is *no*. It is possible to have both relative freedom of entry and an acceptable level of professional conduct by membership; but a *more general* sense of social responsibility will have to prevail than presently.

What kinds of solutions are there to the problem of unethical or unprofessional practices in business? There are two general approaches: (a) selective membership and (b) a punitive system. Solutions which would seek control through selection of membership either attempt through screening to eliminate those who are not likely to conduct themselves with a professional demeanor or to regulate the number of firms of particular types. Presumably, the regulation of the number of firms would be done in such a way as to preserve a desirable element of competition but to avoid the forms of panic competition which often produce conduct of the kind we wish to minimize. Punitive systems of regulating business practices are those in which rules of conduct are delineated and in which a violation of those rules leads to some form of punishment. The antitrust system we have now is punitive—it may punish the deviate firm by fine, jail sentence or with some combination of those things. Though we do not often encounter the idea, a punitive system could also mete out banishment or excommunication. Under this latter scheme, a person would simply lose his rights to participate as a business owner. As a practical matter commercial banishment, as it were, would be an extremely difficult concept to implement, although some professional organizations do just that.

But schemes which select membership and plans which result in banishment seem foreign to our economic philosophy.[29] Such schemes—although they may be feasible—do not simply modify the existing system, they in effect produce a new system. Consider, for example, the kind of administrative paraphernalia that would be required to effectively screen or select budding entrepreneurial candidates. For this and other reasons, we have, since 1890, endeavored to develop an effective punitive system, one that would regulate business practices in the social interest. Whether or not the resultant system is effective is the subject of endless debate. Our task in the next three chapters is to define that punitive system more carefully and to show more clearly the cause for it.

---

[29] Licenses to do business, such as those issued by state and local governments, are in fact selective membership systems.

Marketing and scientific methods

We have noted that marketing has, at times, been criticized for its lack of intellectual rigor. Our answer to this criticism is, in effect, developed in the remainder of this book. The reader may conclude for himself—having completed a careful consideration of the issues, concepts and methods identified in this text—whether such a charge is properly made. In the chapters that follow, the reader will encounter an extremely broad scope of subject matter requiring facility with concepts from many fields of study. A true mastery of marketing involves an ability to understand and interpret legal doctrine, an ability to analyze and interpret human behavior in terms of concepts from the behavioral sciences, an ability to choose and use research methods that represent scientific method, and an ability to reason within the framework of models of complex phenomena. Few academic disciplines demand more than that.

But in addition to this general answer to the charge that marketing is a weak academic discipline, we should also note that such criticism most often comes from what have been called "institutional educational forces." These critical forces are often (a) teachers of the liberal arts who are interested in maintaining the inherent status of the liberal arts, (b) teachers of liberal arts who, for reasons of their own, do not believe that professional curricula belong in a university and (c) those who oppose the profit system as a basic economic regulator.[30] Placed in this perspective, it is perhaps more easily understood why marketing has been criticized as an academic discipline.

SUMMARY

We have now examined seven issues that relate to the social and economic foundations upon which marketing activities rest. We have identified the nature of production, and we have considered the components of value. We noted that productive human activities are those for which people willingly pay, whether such activities produce tangible or intangible results. We noted that information can produce economic value; we classified information into some types that are productive; we identified some unproductive forms of mass communications.

We developed a simple model of place convenience. This model helped us illustrate the nature of the value created by place. We noted that the spatial convenience that is produced by the market specialist is greater as the number of specialized members of the society is larger. Time has economic value. We illustrated this point by considering the influence upon our lives of changes in our present market system. We noted that

---

[30] This argument is effectively presented in William Lazer, "The Development of Marketing as a Discipline," in Peter D. Bennett, editor, *Marketing and Economic Development*, Chicago: American Management Association, 1965, pp. 788–802, see especially p. 789.

a system that serves our needs infrequently costs us less, but leaves much more for us to do for ourselves.

Marketing costs more and occupies a greater percentage of the resources of an economic system as that system grows in maturity and complexity. This point was illustrated with the assistance of the Clark-Fisher hypothesis. We emphasized that marketing costs are to an important degree self-inflicted—but with two important imperfections. First, the market system does not react instantly to our individual wishes. Second, the market system does not react to all minority views; that is, we may as individuals have preference patterns that are not economically feasible to serve. Marketing is charged with the task of keeping the level of consumption at proper levels. The fulfillment of this task requires that human want patterns be in a regular pattern of change and modification.

Our marketing system does not always act in a manner that is socially responsible. We seek, largely through punitive measures, to control the harmful actions of our business enterprise system. The chapters that follow explore the nature of these punitive measures more completely.

REVIEW QUESTIONS
1 Carefully define and indicate the relevance of each of the following concepts to the study of marketing:
   a. Production
   b. Value
   c. The value equation
   d. Economic value and information
   e. A credibility coefficient, information, and economic value
   f. Distance units
   g. The Clark-Fisher tertiary stage
   h. A "democratic inequity"
2 Distinguish carefully between each element in the following pairs of terms:
   a. Rational *and* emotional appeals
   b. Economic-relevant *and* economic-irrelevant informative appeal
   c. Market duration *and* market frequency
   d. A domestic economic system *and* an industrial economic system
   e. An industrial economic system *and* an affluent economic system
   f. Human wants *and* human needs
   g. The Clark-Fisher primary stage *and* the Clark-Fisher secondary stage
   h. A choice system *and* an issue system
3 What similarities do you see between the world in which we live and the world depicted in the spatial convenience model? In what specific ways is the model of spatial convenience unrealistic?
4 Provide examples of the idea that marketing costs are self-inflicted. Considering your own behavior, what demands do you place on the marketing system?

DISCUSSION QUESTIONS
5 Is it possible to infer the value of choice? That is, is it possible to determine in some deductive way how important choice is to a society?

6 How does economic waste occur when an advertisement is irrelevant?

7 Who is the final arbiter regarding the value of particular goods and services? That is who can say whether a good or service is valuable or valueless?

APPENDIX 3.A THE MEASUREMENT OF SPATIAL CONVENIENCE IN A MORE COMPLEX ECONOMY Earlier in Chapter 3, we developed a simple model of place convenience. That model permitted us to demonstrate the nature of the contribution of the marketing specialist in the place, or locational, dimension with some precision. We might now ask: Does the magnitude of the contribution of the specialist change with the complexity of the system he serves? In other words, if we increase the number of craftsmen in the system, what change is accomplished in terms of the specialist's contribution to place convenience?

Consider a system in which there are four craftsmen. Moreover, assume that our four-producer system has a configuration such as that in Figure 3A1. What aggregate distance must be overcome in order to effect complete exchange where there is no retailer in our four-producer system?

With reference to Figure 3A1, Craftsman A would undertake a trip to B, D and C, respectively. Including the return home, A would expend an effort measured by 5.656 (or 4 × 1.414) distance units. Second, a trip from B to D, D to C, and back to B would be required to place the specialty of B in the hands of both D and C, respectively. In this case, B would return home from C diagonally, because this alternative would involve less distance. This second trip would involve a total of 4.828 distance units.* As yet, Craftsmen D and C have not exchanged their respective specialties. Regardless of whether D or C initiates this last exchange, 2.828 distance units must be overcome. In total, then, 13.312 (5.656 + 4.828 + 2.828) aggregate distance units must be overcome in completing the exchange process in our four-producer system when there is *no* marketing specialization.

What aggregate distance must be overcome in order to effect complete exchange where the marketing specialist serves the system? Assuming, as we did earlier, that the specialist locates at the geometric center of the system and a return trip home would put the specialty of each of the craftsmen into the hands of each of the others. In this instance, the minimum number of distance units which must be completed is simply 8.00 (4 × 2).

---

* As in our example of a three-producer system, any line segment connecting the center of the square with an angle is assumed to have a value of unity. The value of any line segment (AC, AB, BD, CD) is simply 2 cos 45°, or 1.414.

Notice that in the process of acquiring the specialty of each of the other producers, any given producer must proceed along a course described by some combination of external or radial elements. This assumption, necessary in order that our system permit simple mathematical determination, results in a slight overstatement of the total distance to be traversed, in the absence of a retailer, as the number of craftsmen approaches infinity. There is however, no such overstatement in the three- and four-craftsmen systems.

Figure 3.A1

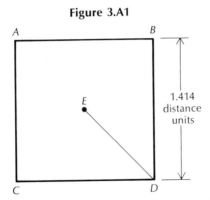

Again, we are prepared to assert, with some precision, the actual saving in place convenience which our market specialist may pass along to the system he serves. Where the specialist makes no charge for this spatial convenience, the participants in our four-member system would gain 5.312 distance units (13.312 − 8.00 distance units). In general, the market specialist will offer the four-craftsmen system the potential for reducing efforts to overcome distance 39.90 percent below the effort that would be required in his absence.

SUGGESTED SUPPLEMENTARY READINGS IN GENERAL MARKETING

I.   GENERAL TEXT AND READING SOURCES

Beckman, Theodore N., and William R. Davidson, *Marketing,* Eighth Edition, New York: The Ronald Press Company, 1967.

Bell, Martin L., *Marketing: Concepts and Strategy,* Boston: Houghton Mifflin Company, 1966.

Boyd, Harper W., Jr., and Richard M. Clewett, *Contemporary American Marketing,* Homewood, Ill.: Richard D. Irwin, Inc., 1962.

Buskirk, Richard, *Principles of Marketing,* New York: Holt, Rinehart and Winston, Inc., 1966.

Cateora, Phillip R., and Lee Richardson, editors, *Readings in Marketing,* New York: Appleton-Century-Crofts, 1967.

Converse, Paul D., Harvey W. Huegy, and Robert V. Mitchell, *Elements of Marketing,* Englewood Cliffs, N.J.: Prentice-Hall, Inc., 1965.

Cox, Keith, and Ben M. Enis, editors, *A New Measure of Responsibility for Marketing,* Chicago: American Marketing Association, 1968.

Cox, Reavis, Charles S. Goodman, and Thomas C. Fichandler, *Distribution in a High-Level Economy,* Englewood Cliffs, N.J.: Prentice-Hall, Inc., 1965.

Cundiff, E. W., and R. R. Still, *Basic Marketing,* Englewood Cliffs, N.J.: Prentice-Hall, Inc., 1964.

Day, Ralph L., editor, *Concepts for Modern Marketing,* Scranton, Pa.: International Textbook Company, 1968.

Dirksen, Charles J., Arthur Kroger, and Lawrence C. Lockly, editors, *Readings in Marketing,* Homewood, Ill.: Richard D. Irwin, Inc., 1968.

Elling, Karl A., *Introduction to Modern Marketing*, New York: Crowell-Collier and Macmillan, Inc., 1969.

Enis, Ben M., and Keith K. Cox, *Marketing Classics*, Boston: Allyn and Bacon, Inc., 1969.

Fisk, George, *Marketing Systems: An Introductory Analysis*, New York: Harper & Row, Publishers, 1966.

Holloway, Robert J., and Robert S. Hancock, *Marketing in a Changing Environment*, New York: John Wiley & Sons, Inc., 1968.

Matthews, John B., Jr., Robert D. Buzzell, Theodore Levitt, and Ronald E. Frank, *Marketing: An Introductory Analysis*, New York: McGraw-Hill Book Company, 1964.

Phillips, Charles F., and Delbert J. Duncan, *Marketing: Principles and Methods*, Homewood, Ill.: Richard D. Irwin, Inc., 1968.

Raymond, Robert S., *Basic Marketing*, Cleveland: The World Publishing Company, 1967.

Rodger, Leslie W., *Marketing in a Competitive Economy*, London: Hutchinson & Co. (Publishers), Ltd., 1965.

Shapiro, Stanley J. and Alton F. Doody, *Readings in the History of American Marketing: Settlement to Civil War*, Homewood, Ill.: Richard D. Irwin, Inc., 1968.

Smith, L. George, editor, *Reflections on Progress in Marketing*, Chicago: American Marketing Association, 1965.

Walters, S. George, Max D. Snider, and Morris L. Sweet, *Readings in Marketing*, Cincinnati: South-Western Publishing Company, 1962.

Warner, Daniel S., *Marketing and Distribution: An Overview*, New York: McGraw-Hill Book Company, 1969.

Westing, J. Howard, and Gerald Albaum, *Modern Marketing Thought*, Second Edition, New York: Crowell-Collier and Macmillan, Inc., 1969.

II.   MARKETING MANAGEMENT SOURCES

Adler, Lee, editor, *Plotting Marketing Strategy: A New Orientation*, New York: Simon and Schuster, Inc., 1967.

Alderson, Wroe, and Paul E. Green, *Planning and Problem Solving in Marketing*, Homewood, Ill.: Richard D. Irwin, Inc., 1964.

Alexander, Ralph S., and Thomas L. Berg, *Dynamic Management in Marketing*, Homewood, Ill.: Richard D. Irwin, Inc., 1965.

Britt, Steuart H., and Harper W. Boyd, Jr., *Marketing Management and Administration Action*, New York: McGraw-Hill Book Company, 1968.

Cox, Keith K., editor, *Analytical Viewpoints in Marketing Management*, Englewood Cliffs, N.J.: Prentice-Hall, Inc., 1968.

Davis, Kenneth R., *Marketing Management*, New York: The Ronald Press Company, 1966.

Kelley, Eugene J., editor, *Marketing: Strategy and Functions*, Englewood Cliffs, N.J.: Prentice-Hall, Inc., 1965.

———, and William Lazar, *Managerial Marketing*, Homewood, Ill.: Richard D. Irwin, Inc., 1967.

King, Robert L., editor, *Marketing and the New Science of Planning*, Chicago: American Marketing Association, 1968.

Kotler, Phillip, *Marketing Management: Analysis, Planning and Control*, Englewood Cliffs, N.J.: Prentice-Hall, Inc., 1967.

Lazo, Hector, and Arnold Corbin, *Management in Marketing,* New York: McGraw-Hill Book Company, 1961.

Mayer, M. S. and R. E. Vasburgh, editors, *Marketing for Tomorrow—Today,* Chicago: American Marketing Association, 1967.

McCarthy, E. Jerome, *Basic Marketing,* Homewood, Ill.: Richard D. Irwin, Inc., 1968.

Newman, Joseph W., *Marketing Management and Information: A New Case Approach,* Homewood, Ill.: Richard D. Irwin, Inc., 1967.

O'Dell, William F., *The Marketing Decision,* New York: American Management Association, 1968.

Oxenfeldt, Alfred R., *Executive Action in Marketing,* Belmont, Calif.: Wadsworth Publishing Company, Inc., 1966.

Phelps, D. Maynard, and J. Howard Westing, *Marketing Management,* Homewood, Ill.: Richard D. Irwin, Inc., 1968.

Rathmell, John M., *Managing the Marketing Function,* New York: John Wiley & Sons, Inc., 1969.

Rewoldt, Stewart H., James D. Scott, and Martin R. Warshaw, *Introduction to Marketing Management,* Homewood, Ill.: Richard D. Irwin, Inc., 1969.

Scranton, William J., *Fundamentals of Marketing,* New York: McGraw-Hill Book Company, 1967.

Stern, Mark E., *Marketing Planning: A Systems Approach,* New York: McGraw-Hill Book Company, 1966.

Weiss, E. B., *Management and the Marketing Revolution,* New York: McGraw-Hill Book Company, 1964.

III. MARKETING THEORY SOURCES

Alderson, Wroe, *Marketing Behavior and Executive Action,* Homewood, Ill.: Richard D. Irwin, Inc., 1957.

Cox, Reavis, and Wroe Alderson, editors, *Theory in Marketing,* Homewood, Ill.: Richard D. Irwin, Inc., 1950.

Howard, John A., *Marketing Theory,* Boston: Allyn and Bacon, Inc., 1965.

Kernan, Jerome B., and Montrose S. Sommers, *Perspectives in Marketing Theory,* New York: Appleton-Century-Crofts, 1968.

Schwartz, George, *Science in Marketing,* New York: John Wiley & Sons, Inc., 1965.

IV. INTERNATIONAL MARKETING SOURCES

Carson, David, *International Marketing: A Comparative Systems Approach,* New York: John Wiley & Sons, Inc., 1967.

Hess, John M., and Phillip R. Cateora, *International Marketing,* Homewood, Ill.: Richard D. Irwin, Inc., 1966.

Kramer, Roland L., *International Marketing,* Cincinnati: South-Western Publishing Company, 1964.

Leighton, David S. R., *International Marketing: Text and Cases,* New York: McGraw-Hill Book Company, 1966.

Liander, Bertil, Vern Terpstra, Michael Y. Yoshino, and A. A. Sherbini, *Comparative Analysis for International Marketing,* Boston: Allyn and Bacon, Inc., 1967.

Patty, C. Robert, and Harvey L. Vredenburg, editors, *Readings in Global Marketing Management,* New York: Appleton-Century-Crofts, 1969.

Ryans, John K., Jr., and James C. Baker, *World Marketing,* New York: John Wiley & Sons, Inc., 1967.

Sommers, Montrose, and Jerome B. Kernan, *Comparative Marketing Systems,* New York: Appleton-Century-Crofts, 1968.

Stewart, Charles F., editor, *The Global Businessman,* New York: Holt, Rinehart and Winston, Inc., 1966.

Thomas, Michael J., *International Marketing Management,* Boston: Houghton Mifflin Company, 1969.

Part II

MARKETING AND FORMAL REGULATION

Our task in Part Two is to develop a better understanding of the business actions which give rise to legislative restrictions on marketing activities. We are concerned with identifying the existing legal constraints upon marketing activities, but we are equally concerned with examining types of business actions which have produced these legal constraints. In the three chapters which follow, three general classes of business activity are examined. Each of these three basic classes of business activity represents an important area of legislative regulation and an important aspect of marketing from what we have called a managerial point of view. That is, each of these chapters focuses on an important decision area for marketing management. We shall also see that each area has important societal implications.

We are concerned in Chapter 4 with *deception*—with deceptive acts in business and with legislative restrictions upon them. Chapter 5 focuses on *expansion*—with business efforts to expand (largely through acquisition of other firms) and with legislative restrictions upon expansion. Chapter 6 deals with *discrimination*—with business actions which produce discriminatory circumstances and legislative efforts to curb such actions. When we have completed Part Two, we will have examined the bulk of existing federal and state legislation that is relevant to marketing activities. We will, hopefully, understand why, how and to whom a particular business action is harmful, what the specific nature of such harmful actions are, and how we collectively attempt to regulate such actions.

Chapter 4

DECEPTIVE COMMUNICATIONS AND SOCIETY

In one section of the preceding chapter, it was observed that our collective efforts to resolve the problem of socially irresponsible acts in business have taken the form, principally, of punitive measures. That is, we have attempted to define rules of conduct to serve as guides to the businessman and to the judiciary through state and federal legislation.[1]

Our purpose in the present chapter is to explore the underlying need for one particular type of legislation—legislation which attempts to control deceptive acts of all types. Deceptive practices in business have obvious and far-reaching societal implications—indeed if there is a single word which identifies a most profound regulatory problem in business today it is perhaps deception.

More specifically, we are concerned in the present chapter with four aspects of deception: (a) what it is—that is, how deception is defined, (b) how deception is injurious to the competitive environment in which it occurs, (c) the particular forms deception assumes and (d) the nature and character of the law which attempts to control deceptive practices.

What is deception?

In order for deception to occur, it is necessary that some kind of communication occur. Communication is inextricably a part of all deception.[2] Communication may be verbal (either personal or impersonal) or visual, direct or symbolic. And each of these forms of communication has the potential to deceive. Direct communication involves spoken or printed words. Symbolic communication does not utilize the body of words that

---

[1] And, to some extent, local ordinances.

[2] The term "communication" as used here is defined to exclude inter- and intra-company correspondence; that is, it includes only personal and impersonal selling efforts and public relations activities.

comprise a formal language. And because symbolic communication is often more subtle than direct forms, it can be an effective vehicle for deceit.

Symbols are an important form of human communication—perhaps more important than any of us would at first imagine. For example, for many people snow is the symbol of Christmas, and a snowscape may, if used correctly, impart the idea of Christmas more quickly and clearly than hundreds of words. Symbolic communication is especially important in business, for it is often important to be able to communicate the concept of an entire company to both customers and prospects with a minimum usage of words. Company symbols (for the moment we will call them "brands") are developed to facilitate this and other communications needs. Our point here, however, is that because we often tend to draw extensive inferences from simple business symbols, such symbols are often an effective means of deceit. Suppose, for example, that you are confronted by three brands of a small appliance in a discount store. The products appear very similar but they have three different marks on them. These three marks are reproduced below:

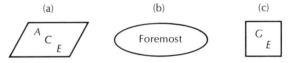

Which of these marks do you know? That is, with which of these three business symbols do you feel most familiar? If your answer is C, then you have reacted to a facsimile of a well known business symbol. Indeed, should you have been prompted to purchase Brand C because of your greater familiarity with it, you would have been symbolically deceived.

As a first approximation, we will define deception as *the communication, verbally or visually, directly or symbolically, of a message that has the reasonable capability of misleading, deluding or beguiling the audience to whom the communication is directed.* The usual audience to whom communication is directed includes (a) final consumers, (b) industrial buyers or users and (c) institutional buyers or users.

But there are also legal dimensions to the concept of deception. The Federal Trade Commission has suggested the following guidelines to assist in the identification of potentially deceptive communications:

1 In order to be harmful, a particular message need only tend to deceive—there is no requirement that the Commission prove that a particular customer was actually deceived.
2 Ignorance is not an acceptable defense. The fact that the sponsor of a message does not know that his message deceives is irrelevant. The crucial legal question is whether those to whom the message is directed are *generally* deceived.
3 An *esoteric message* is dangerous—especially if the esoterica has distinctive lay meaning. A relatively low level of expertise on the part of the

reader/listener/viewer is assumed. The public is not assumed to be familiar with idiosyncratic trade terms or trade practices.

4 The sum of the parts does not necessarily equal the whole. That is, while every part of the message may be literally correct and accurate, the impression created by *the whole* may deceive. Significant omission or nondisclosure is a near-classic way to create a deceptive whole with parts which are, individually, correct.

5 The rule of *multiple-entendre* messages suggests that when several possible interpretations of a message are possible, any one of which has the capacity to mislead, then the advertisement is potentially unlawful.[3]

These rules clearly place the burden upon the businessman—they require that the communications planner *anticipate* the likely perception by customers of a particular message. This kind of requirement may seem unfair, but it is an operational fact of life with which most large businesses must contend.

The foregoing definition of deception, when coupled with the FTC guidelines, provides an initial delineation of the concept of deception as it relates to certain marketing activities. Although this definitional preface will not anticipate all the particular types of deception with which we will ultimately deal, we will not add any refinements to it for now. We turn now to the task of clarifying the potentially harmful nature of deception.

How is deception harmful?

An answer to this question may seem obvious, but there is more to it than initially meets the eye. There are, in fact, three different potentially harmful effects of deceptive communications. These potentially harmful effects can be felt: (a) among business competitors, (b) among final consumers or institutional and industrial buyers and (c) by business in general.

If there were no deception of any kind in external business communications, all parties to a particular business transaction would act, at least, on the basis of accurate information. Note that there is a difference between complete information and accurate information. It is an extremely ambitious social goal to hope to achieve a competitive environment in which all parties to a business transaction are *completely* informed.[4] It is, in contrast, a feasible goal to hope to achieve a condition in which all parties are *accurately* informed. At the very least, we have attempted to regulate against the wanton competitive use of misinformation. In effect,

---

[3] These rules are adapted from a longer list in Earl W. Kintner, *An Antitrust Primer: A Guide to Antitrust and Trade Regulation Laws for Businessmen*, New York: Crowell-Collier and Macmillan, Inc., 1964, pp. 172–173.

[4] We are, however, clearly moving in this direction. Labeling acts of various kinds, packaging requirements and other legal requirements tend to produce fuller disclosure.

our philosophy with respect to external business communications has been this: To the extent that buyers make their selection among alternative and competing offerings on the basis of incomplete information, an undesirable, but to some extent unavoidable, situation exists; to the extent that buyers make their selection among alternative and competing offerings on the basis of inaccurate information, an inequitable but remediable situation exists. Fundamentally, all our societal concern with deception and our legislative efforts to control deception are related to the possibility of this latter state of affairs.

The specific nature of the competitive inequity that would characterize a market system shot through with inaccurate information is most easily demonstrated among business competitors. Most obviously, misinformation may produce an inequitable division of sales and profits within an industry. A frequently encountered measure of the division of trade among the firms in an industry is market share. The *market share* for a particular firm is defined as the proportion of total industry sales accounted for by that firm. A firm may thus suffer a declining market share as a result of misinformation purposely circulated by a competitor. Indeed, market share, or more precisely shifts in market share, may be used by regulatory authorities to identify the point of impact, as it were, of such misinformation. Deceptive communications can, as a result of diverting trade from one seller to another inflict estimable financial harm.[5]

The socially harmful effect of deceptive communications directed to final consumers is more difficult to demonstrate. Indeed, we can deal with the problem only in a supra-empirical way. We can demonstrate the harm of deception in a logical manner, but we cannot actually measure the result of the harmful act. For the most part, deceptive communication produces a less-than-maximizing allocation of disposable income among all the goods and services which consumers may buy. In less stilted terms, the total actual satisfaction realized by final consumers where some deception is involved is less than it would be if all the information upon which those consumers acted had been accurate. Deception may lead a buyer to think that a product will perform in excess of its actual capability—the consumers expectations, alas, are not realized. This result produces a kind of *consumer deficit*, the algebraic opposite of *consumer surplus*—the latter being a benefit which accrues to consumers when the value of the goods or services they acquire exceeds the value, to them, of the money with which they part.

The potentially harmful effect of deceptive communications directed

[5] The harm is "estimable" rather than determinable in a definitive way. This is but one kind of a causal relationship problem; that is, the problem is to establish in a positive way that the act of circulating misinformation actually precipitated the shift in market shares. The problem is to prove causality. The problem is complicated by the continuous movement of other variables any one of which, or any combination of which, may have *caused* the change in market shares.

to institutional and industrial buyers is only a little easier to define than for final consumers. In order to proceed we need to distinguish between final consumers, industrial buyers and institutional buyers. We will use the term *institutional buyer* to mean an employee of an organization such as government, schools, hospitals, and other similar service oriented operations; that is, organizations that are normally concerned primarily with the production of services rather than with the production of physical products.[6] We will use the term *industrial buyer* to designate an employee of an organization that manufactures, forms, fabricates, assembles and performs other similar functions. Both "institutions" and "industries" are markets for goods and services, and, as such, are buyers of the goods and services produced by other firms.

Institutional and industrial buyers differ from final consumers in as much as the latter are not employees of the organization for which they may act as buyer. Institutional and industrial buyers act in behalf of a formal business or governmental organization—the *final consumer* acts in behalf of either a household or himself. Because institutional and industrial buyers act in behalf of some formal organization, purchases made by them on the basis of deceptive communications may influence, in turn, the quality of the goods and services produced by those organizations. Because final consumers are usually the ultimate beneficiary of such goods and services, any deficiencies which those goods and services embody may ultimately accrue to final consumers.

Finally, deception in business communications has a harmful effect which is felt by everyone in business, no matter what the specific nature of that business might be. Besides the short-term effect of deceiving the reader/viewer/listener, the influence of deceptive advertising over the longer term is probably to diminish the general effectiveness of such forms of communications. Lie to me once and I'll forgive you; lie to me twice and I'll doubt you; lie to me again and I'll pay no attention at all to you. A widening credibility gap must develop when communications prove, over and over, to be unreliable. And this general result of deceptive advertising is a burden the entire business community must bear. That is, those firms guilty of deceptive practices as well as those not guilty of such practices all pay the price of such practices. Mass commercial communication is potentially a most efficient and formidable means of disseminating information. Indeed there is no more efficient means of communications yet devised by man.[7] All forms of business, profit or "nonprofit," as long as they have a commercial message to convey have a vested interest in maintaining

[6] We will later employ the term "intermediate markets" to identify firms who sell physical products but do not produce them. Examples of these markets include retailers and wholesalers.

[7] At least on a cost-per-exposure basis there is not known a method which will approach the performance of our mass media. Person-to-person communication may be more effective but not more efficient; the cost of person-to-person communication is very high.

the integrity of the mass communications media. In this view, then, one extremely important and potentially harmful effect of deceptive practices in business communications is the general, gradual erosion of the effectiveness of all such communications.

Deceptive marketing practices

It is an extremely difficult task to define clear-cut classes of deceptive marketing practices. The nature and number of such schemes seems limited only by the ingenuity of a cornered man—which has virtually no limit at all.[8] It is possible, however, to establish rather general classes of deceptive practices, and in so doing achieve a better understanding of the precise motivations which may underlie such practices. More for purposes of exposition than because these classes are definitive or exhaustive, three basic types of deceptive practices will be identified in the following discussion.[9] These general classes of deceptive schemes are:

Type 1 Schemes. These schemes involve deceptive efforts to enhance the value of a product or service in the eyes of a prospective buyer. This kind of scheme falls, basically, into two subordinate classes: (a) those which are directly or blatantly deceptive and (b) those which deceive in a subtle or inferential manner.

Type II Schemes. These are schemes which are prompted basically by the desire to enhance the credibility of the communicator. These schemes are often distinguished by the fact that an authority, or an apparent authority, presents the sales message.

Type III Schemes. These are business practices which may be construed as efforts to deceive, but which may reasonably be prompted by higher motives. These apparent schemes, in other words, seem as if they involve some element of deceptive hanky-panky when they may not.

DECEPTIVE SCHEMES—TYPE I

Deceptive schemes which endeavor to increase the value of the product or service (Type I) are by far the most numerous of the three classes identified here. These schemes include hundreds of variations on several basic themes. Perhaps the most frequent of these is simply a *gross overstatement* of the benefits of a product or service. Note that the overstatement of product or service benefits must be *gross*, for the body of interpretive law which governs these matters recognizes what has been termed *permissible puffery*. As that term perhaps suggests, a seller is per-

---

[8] Earl W. Kintner who served first as general counsel and then as chairman of the Federal Trade Commission and had, therefore, a ringside seat to observe some of the deceptive schemes which are produced by "savagely competitive advertisers" makes this same point in a book which describes his experiences. See his *An Antitrust Primer,* pp. 171–172.

[9] The following discussion does not include instances of outright fraud. Contests that promise prizes and do not deliver, real estate swindles and mail-order companies that send no merchandise fall into the category of outright fraud.

mitted some degree of pardonable pride in the object of his selling efforts.[10] The exact point where a pardonable overstatement of product benefits becomes a gross overstatement, and therefore unlawful, is a question which must be determined by quasi-judicial or judicial processes. The FTC has held that legal "puffery is considered to be offered and understood as an expression of the sellers opinion only, which is to be discounted as such by the buyer, and on which no reasonable man would rely."[11] This guide suggests at least one base upon which permissible puffery might be distinguished from unlawful puffery: whether the "reasonable man" construes the puffery to be the seller's opinion or whether it is offered as something more powerful than that.

In recent years, physical fitness equipment, weight-reducing schemes, and cure-all medicines have been disproportionately involved in these gross overstatement cases. These overstatement-of-benefits cases include some which deceive in a visual way as well as a verbal or printed way. One of the most often cited cases involving a visual overstatement of product benefits has been called "the great sandpaper shave." And the reasoning of the Federal Trade Commission in that case is representative. *Fortune* described the circumstance in this case in the following way:

The commercial showed a football player, either Frank Gifford or Kyle Rote of the New York Giants (there were different versions of the commercial), who was proclaimed by an unseen announcer to be "a man with a problem just like yours . . . a beard as tough as sandpaper . . . a beard that needs Palmolive Rapid Shave . . . super moisturized for the fastest, smoothest shave possible." A few seconds later the viewer saw some Rapid Shave lather spread upon sandpaper, immediately afterwards a hand appeared with a razor and shaved a clean path through the lather and the gritty surface of the sandpaper; during this action the announcer was saying, "to prove Rapid Shave's super-moisturizing power, we put it right from the can onto this tough dry sandpaper. It was apply . . . soak . . . and off in a stroke." A little later, a "split screen" showed Rapid Shave again being applied to sandpaper while Gifford or Rote applied some to his own face: and immediately afterward the viewer saw razors easily shave both the sandpaper and the face. The commercial ended conventionally, with Gifford or Rote looking pleased with himself and an off-camera male chorus singing a rousing jingle about Rapid Shave. All of this took exactly sixty seconds.[12]

The Commission subsequently demonstrated that even after prolonged

[10] An instance in which permissible puffery is involved is the Rapid-Shave case in which the Colgate-Palmolive Company and their advertising agency were charged with an overstatement of product benefits. See *Federal Trade Commission Complaints, Orders, Stipulations,* December 29, 1961. In the 1800's, before the Federal Trade Commission existed, the law of torts recognized "dealing talk" as essentially the parallel of permissible puffery. See John A. Larson, editor, *The Regulated Businessman,* New York: Holt, Rinehart and Winston, Inc., 1966, p. 172.

[11] Larson, *loc. cit.*

[12] Daniel Seligman, "Great Sandpaper Shave," *Fortune,* December 1964; reprinted in Larson, *op. cit.,* pp. 173-174.

soaking, Rapid Shave could not "shave" real sandpaper. What had, in fact, been done was to shave Plexiglass and sand, a surface which could by its nature be shaved wholly clean without the aid of moisture. This was held to amount to a visual overstatement of the product's ability to perform. Both Colgate-Palmolive and its advertising agency were found guilty.[13]

A more recent case involving a possible visual overstatement of the benefits of the product or service involved the J. B. Williams Company's Geritol. The circumstances which led to FTC action in this instance were described as follows:

Five of eight recent Geritol TV commercials screened during the hearing were 40 second dramas featuring an eager-beaver husband and a tired wife, who is dramatically rejuvenated by Geritol. The soundtrack, identical in all five ads, says "a great majority of the people who are tired don't feel that way because of iron-poor blood, and Geritol won't help them, but it is a medical fact that millions of people who have iron-poor blood are tired and need Geritol.[14]

Although the soundtrack carried a statement of the limitations of the product, the question was whether the pictures conveyed a quite different, indeed a contradictory message. "In the pictures, the Geritol-rejuvenated woman throws her arms around the man, bends him backwards, (and) kisses him passionately."[15] In this instance, the Commission was concerned with the overall impression created by the ad. The Commission acknowledged that a disclaimer was on the soundtrack, but said that the total impression of the advertisement might well negate the desired effect of the disclaimer.

A second general theme for Type I schemes is suggested by the phrase *fictitious prices*. The fictitious price scheme includes the overstatement of former prices to enhance the apparent value of a product or service now. The reasoning is obvious: if one suggests that a product formerly sold for a relatively high price but can now be had for a relatively low price, the attractiveness of the proposition is presumably all the greater. A variation of that scheme is the *bait-switch* price quotation. This technique involves advertising an item of merchandise at a price which is suggestive of a real bargain. When prospects appear they discover that the extraordinary bargain suggested in the advertisement has just been sold or they find the "bargain" in an abused state of repair. In either case they are directed to other merchandise, and an effort is made to sell them something else. The bait-switch technique uses a low price (bargain value) to attract traffic—it is a traffic building form of deceit.

Another twist which may be used in conjunction with fictitious prices is the *obscure-footnote* technique. This system *prominently* promotes a bargain but qualifies the particulars of the offer inconspicuously. A case

---

[13] See Richard M. Clewett and others, *Cases in Marketing Strategy,* Homewood, Ill.: Richard D. Irwin, Inc., 1964, pp. 257–258.
[14] *Marketing Insights,* November 25, 1968, p. 8.
[15] *Ibid.*

to this point involved a sale of carpeting in which truly fabulous bargains were offered. The advertisement had noted in almost illegibly small print that all carpet sizes were "approximate"; but further investigation showed that all sizes were indeed approximate—some by a substantial margin—and that in all cases they were "approximately" *under* the stated size.[16]

A second basic type of deceptive practice which endeavors to enhance the perceived value of a product or service attempts to do so in what may be thought of as an inferential way. This particular kind of deceit does not normally involve an outright falsehood but deceives with subtle suggestion. There are instances however, and we shall note some of them, in which these methods of deceit are not at all subtle. We will examine three basic types of *inferentially deceptive* practices: (a) euphemistic nomenclature, (b) brand emulation and (c) some form of preticketing.

The dictionary tells us that a "euphemism" is "the substitution of an agreeable expression for one which is less auspicious." The enhancement of a product or service through the use of a euphemism is an interesting facet of deception in marketing practice. Sometimes the use of the euphemism is harmless; sometimes it is clearly a kind of trickery. Consider, for example, the use of a phrase like "white-tailed mink" to describe a fur coat made of rabbit pelts. The innocent buyer may not know that in the trade the term "white-tailed mink" means rabbit.[17] Thus, the uninformed buyer is mislead initially regarding the thing he has bought but, to make matters worse, he may be made to feel stupid because he was unaware of the trade meaning of the euphemistic phrase. The use of euphemistic nomenclature is often defended as being common trade terminology—but we have observed earlier that such esoteric nomenclature is generally an inadequate defense.

Consider another circumstance in which an incorrect aura of quality is implied by a term used to describe the product. A large manufacturer of sunglasses described some of its glasses with, what the Commission felt, was a strong suggestion that the glasses met the standards of the US Air Force. An excerpt from a typical description of the glasses follows: [18]

One Pair Glasses, Flying Personnel
High Speed Clear Vision
Specification No. 8306-21200
Contract No. 290412

[16] An extremely complete examination of fictitious pricing methods may be seen in Carlton A. Horkrader, "Fictitious Pricing and the F.T.C.: A New Look at an Old Dodge," *St. John's Law Review*, December 1962; reprinted in Ronald R. Gist, editor, *Management Perspectives in Retailing*, New York: John Wiley & Sons, Inc., 1967, pp. 276–289.

[17] This example is purely illustrative; that is rabbit fur has not been called white-tailed mink. There are, however, many cases in which similar terms have been used. Hudson dyed muskrat was, at one time, used to describe rabbit fur.

[18] See *Federal Trade Commission Complaints, Orders, Stipulations,* April 16, 1962, pp. 15 and 823.

Note that it is the very nature of this kind of deception that there is no specific statement that these glasses *are* built to military specifications. The buyer must complete the illusion by inferring that such is the case. And this necessary assist on the part of the buyer permits the seller to argue that he cannot be responsible for inferences buyers may draw. The fact was, in the sunglasses case, that the glasses did not meet military specifications. As is common in these cases, the trade-terminology defense was ultimately advanced.

A second type of inferentially deceptive scheme is accomplished with the assistance of *brand emulation*. The trick here is to make your brand appear to be that of some other, better known and highly regarded manufacturer or service organization. The brand emulation scheme is an effort to ride on the reputation of some well-known product or service. Several examples will clarify this tactic. Several years ago a Finnish minnow—a floating fish lure with remarkably realistic action—was introduced in the United States. The lure was made by the Rapala family on almost a hand production basis, and the success of the lure was phenomenal. There was an understandably acute shortage of the lures in this country—so acute in fact that they were rented for as much as $5 per day in some sections of the country. The lure had not been promoted effectively (although a story about it appeared in *Life*), but it was an overnight success. Now consider the salient elements of this situation:

1 The brand (Rapala) is an unusual word—indeed it is a Finnish surname.
2 The promotion had been largely word-of-mouth, as a result of publicity.

What would you expect to occur now? The obvious part of the answer is that similar lures soon appeared. The part of the answer in which we are primarily concerned here is that lures with similar *names* soon appeared. Lures having such names as Rip-ola and Rap-ola were on the market quickly. Now, consider the situation in a tackle shop where a man wants this revolutionary Finnish minnow. How is the brand name pronounced? Our fisherman is not sure, but it's Rap something. The rest of the story is free ride—and history. The customer is sold the available sound-a-like.

The legal test used to determine whether or not such a tactic is unlawful or not has come to be called the *free-ride doctrine*.[19] The question to be resolved in free-ride cases is whether the prospective buyer is led to believe, because of the similarity of the brands, that a riding brand is produced by or is the same as some stronger brand. We will have more to say about the test of free-ride in a later chapter. For now we want

[19] See American Association of Advertising Agencies, *Trademarks: Orientation for Advertising People*, 1964, p. 10. This short monograph was compiled and written by the late Charles A. Holcomb with assistance in revision by the United States Trademark Association and Sidney A. Diamond, editor of *The Trademark Reporter*.

simply to establish the basic concept in a definitional way. The US Patent Office has declined to permit the use of many proposed brands because they involved some degree of free ride. Examples of riding brands include:

Lemon-Up (a soda)—held to sound too much like Seven-Up.
Nidol (an analgesic)—held to conflict with Midol.
Jantina (shoes)—held to ride on Jantzen beach wear.

A third type of inferential deception employs a practice which has been called *preticketing*. It is especially important to note that preticketing is not necessarily unlawful, it is potentially unlawful only under particular circumstances. *Preticketing* may be defined as the practice under which manufacturers place prices on their products before they are distributed to wholesalers and retail outlets. It is worth repeating that this action is not, in itself, harmful. The practice may well have originated to assist the retailer with the pricing decision. Such prepricing may also save the retailer the expense of such pricing activities. If the pricing can be done less expensively at the factory, then there may even be good economic reasons for the practice. But the practice can be modified slightly and its result changed substantially.

Suppose that a price is preticketed, but that the price is purposely overstated—indeed it is not even expected that sales take place at the preticketed price. Suppose, moreover, that the preticketed price is always crossed out by the retail dealer and a lower price substituted; but in the process of crossing out care is exercised not to completely obliterate the preticketed price. When this is done, and when the manufacturer knows that it is done, the practice falls within the test of *joint-connivance*. The effect of preticketing in these cases is to produce a situation in which merchandise appears to be marked down and therefore a better value when, in fact, the merchandise may never have been sold for the partially obliterated price. There is, once again, a subtle suggestion of value which is possibly misleading.[20] The reader should note that there is no explicit statement made to the effect that the merchandise has ever been sold at the preticketed price. It is held that the prospect might, however, reasonably draw that inference. It is also important to note that proof of joint connivance makes the offense all the more harmful. Joint connivance occurs when it can be established that both the manufacturer

---

[20] In the case of *Baltimore Luggage Co. v. Federal Trade Commission,* for example, the luggage company sold its products to 1276 dealers located in 46 states and the District of Columbia. "The record indicated that 70 percent, or 889, of its retailer-customers, located in 34 states, sold the luggage at the preticketed price, the remaining 30 percent, or 387 retailers, located in 12 states including the metropolitan trade areas of New York, Philadelphia and Washington, D.C., sold the luggage for approximately $2.00 less." The Commission, nonetheless, held that "the preticketed price could mislead customers in the trade areas in which it did not correspond with the usual and regular retail price." See Harkrader, *op. cit.*

and the dealer knew that the preticketed price was not the "usual and customary price" in the recent regular course of business and in the dealer's trading area.

DECEPTIVE SCHEMES—TYPE II

Deceptive schemes of Type II are those which are prompted by a desire to enhance the credibility of the sponsor of the commercial message. These schemes may assume both obvious and subtle forms. In their most obvious form, these schemes simply make claims that are supported by elaborate research facilities—facilities that may not, in fact, exist. In more subtle form, they may take any of several basic forms which we will examine momentarily. But before we do that it seems proper to establish that credibility is in fact an important element in successful persuasive efforts. That fact is, after all, the foundation upon which deceptive efforts to enhance credibility must rest.

There is a growing body of experimental evidence which suggests that credibility and the ability to change opinions are related matters. Social psychologists, notably Hovland, have systematically explored this relationship, and the evidence seems clear that where a witness is perceived as highly credible, he is able to persuade a greater number of his listeners. In one experiment, for example, a tape recording of a speech that advocated lenient treatment of juvenile delinquents was played to three different groups of subjects. The experimental design was such, however, that the speaker on the tape was introduced to one group as a judge, to another group as a person having a criminal record, and to the third group as a person from the studio audience. The subjects were carefully selected so that the three groups were comparable in terms of such usual socio-economic and demographic traits as age, income, education and so forth. Note that the actual speech was identical for each group, only the introduction of the speaker was different. Because the speech was taped, such subtle things as voice inflection were held constant. One result of the experiment was that the speech was evaluated as a "fair presentation" (that is, unbiased) over twice as many times by the group that thought the speaker was a judge as by those who thought he was an ex-criminal.[21]

A follow-up experiment using the same group of subjects suggests that the persuasive advantage of using highly credible witnesses may be less important in some circumstances than in others. The three groups in the preceding experiment were tested after three or four weeks had elapsed, and there was less difference in the persuasive ability of the several speakers. The rule seems, therefore, that high credibility is most important if the persuasion is to get immediate results, such as petition signing, vote

[21] See Herbert I. Abelson, *Persuasion: How Opinions and Attitudes Are Changed,* New York: Springer Publishing Co., 1959, p. 73.

taking or immediate purchasing.[22] This kind of evidence, while not as definitive as one might like, certainly bears out the notion that high credibility in communications can be a significant persuasive advantage.

What specific forms of deception attempt to use this persuasive advantage? Although there are certainly more, three such techniques are frequently encountered: (a) the use of editorial typography, (b) the false authority and (c) the false certification.

The first of these three methods utilizes the fundamental tendency of magazine and newspaper readers to read editorial matter somewhat more carefully than commercial matter.[23] Perhaps these terms need to be clarified. Editorial matter includes featured matter such as letters to the editors and the gossip columns, as well as the articles and serials which comprise the principal content of the magazine or newspaper. Commercial matter has an identified sponsor and endeavors to persuade in some way. It is generally accepted that readership of editorial matter is much more careful than readership of commercial matter. We tend to skim commercial matter. It seems therefore to follow that commercial matter that could be made to look like editorial content might be read more seriously. Such matter would be treated as a more credible information source.

The distinguishing mark of these editorial imposters is that the layout of the piece and the type font used in setting the piece for printing is virtually the same as the true editorial portions of the magazine or newspaper. These advertisements are often all type—there is no art or illustration and they look remarkably like editorial matter in the magazine in which they appear. Note carefully that these advertisements are not unlawful; they normally appear with the word "advertisement" at the top. They do however deceive in a most subtle way, and they may enjoy the status of a more highly credible witness in so doing. Some of these editorial facsimiles enhance their authenticity even more by including the name of an apparent author of the article. An advertisement for Black Flag ant and roach killer that appeared in *Reader's Digest* carried a headline which made it appear historically and scientifically oriented, the name of the author who was reporting the scientific breakthrough was provided and the ad was set in a type font indistinguishable from that of the true editorial portion of the magazine. The lightest type on the page was that which stated "advertisement" at the top of the page.

The *false authority* is another means to impart to the communicator greater credibility than might otherwise be achieved. This method, as the

---

[22] *Ibid.,* p. 75. See also Joseph T. Klapper, *The Effects of Mass Communication,* New York: The Free Press, 1960, pp. 99–103. This later discussion identifies additional research with supporting and conflicting findings.

[23] See Darrell B. Lucas and Steuart Henderson Britt, *Measuring Advertising Effectiveness,* New York: McGraw-Hill Book Co., 1963, p. 221. To this point, Lucas and Britt argue that "the popular consumer magazine attracts a reading audience with very little conscious motivation to read or look at advertising."

name implies, utilizes an apparent authority or sometimes simply the paraphernalia we associate with an authority. Thus a white coat or a thermometer or a stethoscope may suggest medical authority. An impressive library behind an actor may enhance the credibility of the testimony being given. In one case which came before the Federal Trade Commission, a man in a white coat, called "Doctor," recommended a certain digestive aid. In that case the doctor was not real, and the cease and desist order specified that the advertiser no longer suggest "by the use of a white coat or any other object, device or words indicative of the medical profession, that doctors or the medical profession recommend (the product) unless the representation is limited to numbers of doctors not greater than had been ascertained to be the fact."[24] Though much validating research remains to be done, it is clear that the subtle use of props of various kinds to achieve greater credibility has some fascinating possibilities. Indeed, do horn-rimmed glasses enhance credibility?

False certification is the last scheme that we will examine here that attempts to enhance the credibility of the communicator. As necessary background material, we should note that in the context of the advertising business the word certification often refers to testimony by an independent, and therefore presumably more objective, party that a product or service meets some standard or standards devised by the certifying party. The American Medical Association, for example will grant such a seal of certification for products meeting their standards.[25] A certification mark that is well known to virtually everyone is the Good Housekeeping Seal. That seal has come to represent a dependable buying aid to many people. The certification mark thus is a formal means of conveying information. But note that its distinctive character is that it testifies objectively—it supposedly tells it like it is. A mark or seal of this kind can have real integrity and may therefore serve to improve the quality of the information upon which consumer decisions are based. Because such a seal may have an audience of persons who depend upon it for guidance, it is a valuable business property. It is perhaps now apparent how a false certification scheme may work.

Basically two types of false certification plans occur. One of these plans is to include a seal—virtually any kind of seal—near the product or sponsor's name in a printed advertisement. The seal may have no real meaning; it may not, in fact, be a registered mark of an actual company. It may be no more than meaningless words (for example, A-B-C Testing Company Seal), it may be adorned with such symbols of integrity as eagles, the scales of justice and so forth. It lends an air of authenticity to the testimony in the copy of the advertisement. The second basic form in which these plans occur involves the use of a good replica of an actual certification

[24] Kintner, *An Antitrust Primer*, pp. 196–197.
[25] See Otto Kleppner, *Advertising Procedure*, Fifth Edition, Englewood Cliffs, N.J.: Prentice-Hall, Inc., 1966, pp. 348–349.

mark. This plan endeavors to use the prestige which a legitimate seal enjoys—it attempts to capitalize on the esteem in which consumers actually hold a particular seal or mark. This kind of scheme is obviously a special kind of free ride; instead of riding the brand, it rides a certification mark.

DECEPTIVE SCHEMES—TYPE III

Type III schemes involve business practices which may be construed as deceptive plans but which *may* reasonably be prompted by higher motives. Such schemes may be unjustly accused, but they may also involve an element of deception. We will examine three of these plans: (a) full-line pricing, (b) the multiple-brand, single-product strategy and (c) the fake survey.

The policy of *full-line pricing* involves two essential steps. First, the merchandise lines of a retailer (or the product line of a manufacturer) are split into several parts. Second, each of these parts is priced to produce a different target contribution to profits. One of the parts of the line may be priced in such a way that little if any profit is produced by it. Another part may be priced to yield a good profit. It is important to note that the overall target profit sought by our hypothetical retailer is a *weighted average* rate of profit of the several parts into which his total merchandise line is divided. An illustration will clarify this latter point. Assume that the following data are obtained from a supermarket:

	Target Profit Percent	Percent of total Sales Volume
Merchandise Line A	0	10
Merchandise Line B	5	50
Merchandise Line C	10	40

The data above indicate three basic lines of merchandise, each with different target rates of profit and each accounting for a different percent of total sales volume. The *overall target* profit for the store is 6.5%.[26] Line A carries no profit for the retailer, it is used as a traffic builder. Though we will have reason to refine this idea later, for now think of the merchandise in Line A as a leader; that line is low priced to attract shoppers.[27]

---

[26] Determined as follows:

A	0% × 10% =	0%
B	5% × 50% =	2.5%
C	10% × 40% =	4.0%
		6.5%

[27] This discussion is purposely developed at a superficial level. The intricacies of leader pricing and the lexicon which has evolved to express those intricacies is explored more fully in a later chapter.

Merchandise Line C, in contrast, carries a good target rate of profit. *Full-line pricing* is the term used when a conscious pricing effort is made to achieve a target profit based on the performance of the full merchandise line.

In what way, then, is full-line pricing deceptive? The concept of full-line pricing in the hands of a critic emerges as an evil thing. The allegation is made, for example, that the customer is attracted, as a moth to flame, by the promise of low prices on the items in Line A, only to be sold other items of merchandise on which exorbitant profits are made. The sacrificial line, or the leader as it is more popularly called, is the alleged villain of the piece. Indeed the real tragedy of this interpretation is the implicit suggestion that all the merchandise should be offered at profit levels like those of Line A. The fact is that the use of a sacrificial line leaves the retailer vulnerable to those customers who shop store-to-store and buy only the leader items.

The *multiple-brand, single-product* strategy is another practice which may stem from legitimate motives and, nonetheless, be interpreted as some form of trickery. A multiple-brand policy is one in which several different brands are promoted by a single company. The multiple-brand policy is contrasted to the single-brand strategy wherein a single or "blanket" brand is used for all the products of a particular company.[28] The General Electric Company uses the GE brand on almost all its products from electric motors to light bulbs to jet engines. A company like General Foods or Proctor and Gamble, on the other hand, has a different brand for virtually each of the different products which it sells. Thus, General Foods makes several different brands of coffee and several different cereals; Proctor and Gamble makes many different brands of cleaning and detergent products. Thus Proctor and Gamble and General Foods employ a multiple-branding policy. When the policy of selling under several different brand names is combined with that of a single product, the motives of the seller may indeed be suspect. To define this point for clarity: The practice is one in which a single product is sold under more than one brand name. Thus, a production run of 100,000 identical golf balls may ultimately be sold under several different brand names. What motives prompt such a policy, and is a desire to deceive the buyer a likely part of those motives?

Two very good reasons for the multiple-brand, single-product policy exist, neither of which has a particularly disgraceful underlying motivation; indeed the final consumer may actually be better off as a result of the practice. First, a single product may be sold under several different brands through several different types of retail stores in order to increase the total volume of sales. That is, the product when bearing Brand A may be sold to department stores, when bearing Brand B sold to jewelry stores,

---

[28] The discussion here is purposely simplified. In a subsequent chapter, the definitional nuances of brands, brand names and legal marks of several types are established.

when bearing Brand C sold to some other type of retail outlet. The larger total volume of sales now possible may permit production economies and lower prices to both intermediate and final consumers. If anyone is deceived by this practice, it is the retail dealer because he is now confronted by more numerous competitors selling what he may believe to be different products. Consider the example of General Electric and Hotpoint. These brands are both well known and have different dealership organizations, but they are made by the same parent organization, the General Electric Company. Similarly, the Outboard Marine Corporation manufactures both Evinrude and Johnson outboard motors. Thus, within any given market GE and Hotpoint dealers may compete vigorously and Evinrude and Johnson dealers may likewise find themselves trying to sell to the same customer. A desire to increase distribution may underlie such a practice. But we observed that there were two plausible reasons for the multiple-brand, single-product policy.

The second important reason for the multiple-brand, single-product policy stems from the demand characteristics of final consumers. There are some types of customers who are experimentally inclined with respect to brand usage. That is, some customers do not develop strong or loyal attachments to a particular brand or even just a few brands.[29] An appropriate strategy in such circumstances is to emphasize variety in the product line—to offer several competing brands. The cost of such a policy would be very high if the several products were vastly different; thus the products tend to be similar in order to maintain relatively low costs of production. This second explanation of the multiple-brand, single-product policy suggests that there are *apparently* deceptive business activities which may, in fact, be done to accommodate peculiarities in consumer demand rather than to trick, cheat or deceive.

The last of our Type III schemes is the *fake survey*. This type of survey may require that some member of the household fill out a questionnaire or answer a series of questions about almost anything. The sponsor of the survey will insist that no selling is being done, that one can't buy from the people handling the survey. In its most obviously deceitful form, the fake survey is a simple pretext for developing a prospect list for a sales organization, which will follow the survey team in a second-wave action. How can a scheme such as this be innocent?

Even the fake survey, however, does have its innocent counterpart. A research and consumer oriented business community uses the legitimate survey method extensively. Indeed in a market system such as ours, it is essential that those who produce goods and services both seek and get feedback from consumers on a regular and candid basis. Unfortunately, the legitimate research effort is often thwarted by the growing reputation

[29] Proctor and Gamble, in a series of cases made available to marketing teachers, offers this idea.

of the fake survey team. Moreover, it is not necessarily correct to assume that because your name (or family name) appears on a growing list of questionable direct-mail firms that a survey team put it there. The mailing list business is big business, and compilers of those lists secure their information from many sources, including sometimes local, state and federal governments.[30] All of us like to be sought out for our views; it is flattering to believe that our views are important. It is this flattery which may open the door for the high pressure sales organization acting in a phony research capacity.

Efforts to control deceptive marketing practices

We have now examined some of the most frequently encountered forms of deceptive marketing practices and seen that these deceptive practices assume diverse forms and often owe their success to some human foible. We have also seen that some schemes only appear to be evil—that they may, at times, be prompted by legitimate motives. In this, the final section of this chapter, our task is to examine the major societal efforts taken to control the use of deceptive marketing schemes. For the most part, efforts to control such practices have been through statute, though we will also examine some such efforts of a nonlegislative type. In the discussion that follows legislative efforts will be examined on a chronological basis. Relevant federal legislation is considered first; significant state legislation, where some similarity exists among the various states, is then considered; and an examination of nonlegislative efforts to control deceptive marketing practices concludes the present chapter.

FEDERAL EFFORTS TO CONTROL DECEPTIVE PRACTICES

We should emphasize that our concern here is with federal legislative efforts to control deceptive marketing practices; we are not at this time concerned with the general body of antitrust laws. Efforts to control deceptive marketing practices at the federal level have proceeded along two basically different lines. There are those laws which (a) attempt to regulate deceptive practices specifically associated with particular products (or services) or related classes of products (or services) and (b) those laws which attempt to regulate deceptive practices generally. Our principal concern is with the latter of these two basic types of control. The federal laws that endeavor to control deception in the marketing of specific products or product classes is a veritable labyrinth, the more exact nature of which is suggested by the following partial list of such laws.[31] We

[30] Indeed, mailing list brokers exist who can provide very specialized mailing list requirements with hundreds of different occupational, industrial and institutional list classes. See, for example, *United States and Canadian Mailing Lists,* dated yearly, Fritz S. Hofhomer Inc., 29 East 22nd St., New York, 10010.

[31] See Marshall C. Howard, *Legal Aspects of Marketing,* New York: McGraw-Hill Book Co., 1964, pp. 10–11.

should note in passing that each of the specific laws listed does not deal exclusively with the problem of deception; indeed in many instances a consideration of deception is a relatively minor aspect of these laws.

Attempts to Control Deceptive Practices in the Marketing of:	Year Law Passed
Imported Articles	1930
Perishable Agricultural Goods	1930
Securities	1933
Alcoholic Beverages	1935
Air Service	1958
Automobiles	1958
Hazardous Substances	1960
Garments:	
Wool Labeling	1939
Fur Labeling	1951
Flammable Fabrics	1953

The body of general laws which attempts to control deceptive marketing practices had its beginning with the creation of the Food and Drug Administration (FDA) in 1906. Originally, the regulatory province of the Food and Drug Administration was defined to include problems of misbranding as well as problems of adulteration for two classes of products: foods and drugs. With the passage of the Federal Food, Drug and Cosmetic Act of 1938, the FDA was further empowered to regulate not only questions relating to foods and drugs but those involving cosmetics and devices as well. "Devices" include products which relate to health and hygiene, such as medical and dental equipment, exercise and reducing paraphernalia and similar products. The number and type of products that fall within the potential influence of the FDA thus include all foods, drugs, cosmetics and devices traded in interstate commerce. And that clearly includes an extremely large number of products. Most of the day-to-day work of the FDA falls into one of the two general problem areas of (a) adulteration or (b) misbranding. Our principal interest here is with misbranding, because that general term includes many deceptive marketing practices.

More specifically, *misbranding* refers to false or misleading labeling or packaging as well as omissions of salient information relating to harmful conditions of product use.[32] Note carefully that this is not regulatory power

[32] See Howard, *op. cit.,* p. 10. There are important ambiguities concerning problems which fall within the jurisdiction of the FDA and those which fall within the province of the Federal Trade Commission. Exactly when "labeling" ceases to be labeling and becomes "advertising" is a question which has concerned these two regulatory organizations. A discussion of the rules in these cases may be seen in Kleppner, *op. cit.,* p. 526.

over the advertising of foods, drugs, cosmetics and devices, but only over those aspects of advertising which relate to the label and the package. We shall see momentarily that other types of false advertising are covered by another piece of legislation. Problems of misbranding that have come most frequently before the FDA include deceptive containers and short weights. Before the passage in 1966 of more specific legislation dealing with deceptive packaging, the FDA considered such problems under the general powers it possessed.

The problem of package fill—the case in which the package was much larger than seemed actually required for the contents—was among the most frequently encountered. The charge of the FDA was, often, that consumers were buying an undue amount of cardboard and paying cookie prices at that. The retort of the accused was usually that "normal settling" produced the unfilled portion of the container and was necessary in packing to insure that the contents not be damaged. We shall soon see that the problem of package fill, and a host of other packaging ills, formed the nucleus of a proposed truth-in-packaging law. The problem of short weights is another form of deception with which the FDA has often dealt. Short weights, as the name implies, designates the case where contents does not weigh what the package claims. The Food and Drug Administration can recommend jail terms and fines up to $10,000 where evidence suggests an intent to defraud or mislead.

A second major legislative effort to control deceptive practices in business began in 1914 with the creation of the Federal Trade Commission (FTC). This Commission was originally conceived as a body of specialists who might best be able to handle the economic and technical questions in antitrust matters. Accordingly, the FTC was given:

> (a) investigatory power, (b) quasi-judicial power in cases involving "unfair methods of competition in commerce" (Section 5) and (c) power to issue cease and desist orders.[33]

The chapter in the history of the FTC that is most pointedly concerned with deceptive practices, however, began in 1938 with the passage of the Wheeler-Lea Amendments. Note the plural form, amendments, for there are two distinct and important ways that the Wheeler-Lea Amendments amend the original Federal Trade Commission Act. The first of these two amendments gave the FTC additional expressed powers to prohibit practices that mislead the general public.[34] The Commission had, since its creation, been able to move to prohibit unfair practices that injure competitors. This first change introduced by the Wheeler-Lea Act declared "unfair

[33] See Howard, *op. cit.,* p. 6.
[34] The argument which seriously questioned the ability of the FTC to move against such cases, as it was then empowered, was *Federal Trade Commission v. Raladam Company.* See some of the details of this case in Kintner, *An Antitrust Primer,* p. 166.

or deceptive acts or practices in commerce" unlawful. It is this amendment to Section 5 which, in effect, recognized that deceptive practices may harm final consumers as well as business organizations.

The second of these two amendments served to clarify a question of jurisdiction. It will be recalled that the FDA has powers over misbranding of foods, drugs, cosmetics and devices and that "misbranding" here means, essentially, labeling and packaging. The Wheeler-Lea Amendment to Section 12 of the Federal Trade Commission Act expressly gives the FTC the power to proceed against false advertising (excluding that involving the label or package) of foods, drugs, cosmetics, and devices. Thus, if an advertiser should develop an advertising campaign in popular magazines and that campaign should contain some deceptive elements, the case would come under the jurisdiction of the FTC. Conversely should the same advertiser use the package to promote his product in a deceptive way, the problem would come under the jurisdiction of the FDA.

How does the FTC proceed against a deceptive practice? The Division of Investigation audits all major communications media.[35] Magazines and newspapers having a reputation for deceptive practices are examined continuously. Most other magazines and newspapers are examined several times a year. Fifty mail-order catalogs are examined for misleading material. Small radio and TV stations submit samples of commercial programming once yearly, the sample being all commercial material on seven specific dates. Larger city radio and TV stations are audited twice yearly, and the networks undergo continuous scrutiny. In addition to such questionable practices as the Division of Investigation may discover, complaints from the public and from business interests bring other issues to the Commission.

If the Division of Investigation identifies a case of misleading or deceptive communication, they may issue to the offending party what is called a stipulation. Upon receipt of the stipulation, the party responsible for the malpractice may elect to discontinue the objectionable part of the advertisement. In that case the FTC will act no further. Should the party responsible for the malpractice continue to employ the same technique however, the FTC may issue a cease and desist order. Failure to comply with a cease and desist order may be punished by fine or imprisonment or both.

In addition to its power to move against deceptive practices, the FTC plays an important educational role. Many persons who have been associated with the FTC believe that many of the malpractices which come before it are perpetrated unwittingly. Not all the schemes are unwitting,

---

[35] The FTC, in addition to its Washington offices had 11 field offices throughout the country in 1964. The Commission is made up of six basic bureaus: the Bureau of Deceptive Practices, the Bureau of Industry Guidance, the Bureau of Economics, the Bureau of Field Operations, the Bureau of Restraint of Trade and the Bureau of Textiles and Furs.

but many are. Because of this belief, the FTC has organized "trade practices conferences." In some instances, these conferences have as their basic purpose the education of various institutional and industrial groups regarding deceptive practices, including the development of guides and rules which will assist in minimizing their occurrence.

Still other federal organizations are empowered to move against deceptive marketing practices, although the FDA and the FTC are the most important regulatory bodies. The Federal Communications Commission (FCC) can, for example, through its power to decline renewal of radio and TV station licenses, exercise an influence on the quality of commercial material.[36] Although the FCC has not, in fact, used its licensing powers extensively in recent years, it may fail to renew a license if a particular station engages in the "persistent dissemination of false or misleading advertising or commercial material in bad taste."[37] In addition, the Post Office Department has the power to deny use of the mails for misleading or fraudulent purposes, and can prosecute any such offender.[38]

An important and relatively recent addition to the body of federal law that attempts to regulate deceptive business practices is the Fair Packaging and Labeling Act. This piece of legislation sponsored by Senator Philip A. Hart was, before its passage, also known popularly as the truth-in-packaging bill. This bill is directed to the more effective control of four basic packaging problems:

1 The "fill" problem (excessive "settling").
2 Illustrations on packages which have little actual similarity to the package contents. This problem is exemplified by the package picture of a slice of cherry pie stuffed full of cherries, whereas the entire pie in the package may have fewer cherries in total than the number depicted on the pictured slice.
3 The combination of odd prices, irregular package shapes and fractional content or volume expressions in such a way as to greatly complicate

[36] The Federal Communications Commission was created on July 11, 1934 from its predecessor organization, the Federal Radio Commission, which was created in 1927. For details, see G. F. Seehafer and J. W. Laemmer, *Successful Television and Radio Advertising*, New York: McGraw-Hill Book Co., 1959, p. 8.

[37] Over 7000 broadcasting stations are licensed in the US. Since the middle 1930's, only about 50 of them have lost licenses. There is, from time to time, an indication that this may change, however. A decision by the FCC in early 1969 stripped one Boston TV station of its license and in a "simultaneous order" gave a construction permit to a new licensee. The deprived station operators were "given a minor demerit for failure to editorialize, but the decision turned on 'diversification' of communications in the community and on 'integration of ownership with management,'" according to the Washington Post News Service.

[38] The Alcohol and Tobacco Tax Division of the Internal Revenue Service and the Securities and Exchange Commission can also exert some regulatory influence over advertising. These powers are not explored in the text because they are limited to rather narrowly defined instances.

comparisons of values offered. This malpractice requires some clarification. Consider the following two containers of hand lotion:

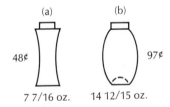

(a) 48¢   7 7/16 oz.   (b) 97¢   14 12/15 oz.

Note that Lotion B is packaged in a false bottom. That is, the container bottom actually goes up inside the container, as depicted by the dotted line. Which of these two offers is the greater value? Suppose that, to make the problem more challenging we make the lotions of different consistencies. Thus, one would require less per application than the other. The point is hopefully made that one can, through a systematic manipulation of prices, package styles and content measurement make value comparison very difficult.[39]

4 The excessive and confusing use of package nomenclature such as "jumbo," "king size," "tall quart" and other poorly defined size designations.

The Fair Packaging and Labeling Act, as it was finally passed in 1966, actually achieved effective control over few of these problems. The Act provides for mandatory regulation of none of the problems identified above. It does, however, give administrative agencies (FDA and FTC) discretionary authority to regulate some of the foregoing ills.[40] These discretionary promulgating powers enable the FDA and the FTC to develop rules for industry conduct which may have the effect of law.[41]

STATE-LEVEL EFFORTS TO CONTROL DECEPTIVE PRACTICES

State legislatures have obviously been very much aware of the problems of deceptive marketing practices. Law making bodies at the state level have, in recent years, entertained many bills to restrict such practices.

---

[39] In 1963, a test shopping experiment using college educated women was performed. The group of women, when instructed to select the largest quantity for the lowest price, failed 34 out of 70 times to identify the best buy. The conclusion was that packaging trickery accounted in part for this performance. See "What's in the Package? Lessons in Practical Detective Work for Supermarket Shoppers," *Harpers*, August 1963, p. 12.

[40] See Dik Warren Twedt, "What Effect Will The 'Fair Packaging and Labeling Act' Have on Marketing Practices," *Journal of Marketing*, April 1967, pp. 58–59.

[41] See Charles S. Moyer, "Requiem for the Truth in Packaging Bill?" *Journal of Marketing*, April 1966, p. 2. A delay was granted in the implementation of this law in order to "draft detailed specifications" of the law. The bill finally went into effect on September 10, 1969. Apparently all "durable" products are exempt from the law as it was finally implemented.

State-level truth-in-lending laws were a popular legislative proposal in the early 1960's. But our concern here is primarily with state laws that influence marketing practitioners generally rather than those which concern specific institutional or industrial groups. One such general law is the truth-in-advertising statute, which can be found in some form in over 45 of our 50 states. These statutes, sometimes called *Printers' Ink* statutes, usually make an advertisement which "contains assertions, representation, or statement of fact which is untrue, deceptive or misleading" a misdemeanor. It is of interest to note that these state statutes are called *Printers' Ink* statutes because the business publication bearing that name worked diligently for the passage of the laws.[42] This is only one instance among many in which the advertising industry itself has pressed for more professional conduct among its members. In many states, the number of cases successfully brought under these truth-in-advertising statutes is severely limited by the onerous requirement that the state prove that any alleged malpractice was knowingly done—that simple requirement effectively sterilizes the law.

NONSTATUTORY EFFORTS TO CONTROL DECEPTIVE PRACTICES

We have now seen that the federal and the various state governments have sought throughout most of the present century to develop some means of control of misleading and deceptive marketing practices. Our attention is now directed to efforts to control such practices through means other than legislative statutes. Included in this nonstatutory type of control are three basic regulatory efforts: (a) business self-regulation, (b) the "consumer movement" and (c) government suasion. The discussion which follows examines these three regulatory efforts in order.

We had occasion earlier to note that the state-level truth-in-advertising laws were popularized in part by business journalism. We also noted that there were many other instances in which business itself has sought to clean its own house, as it were. Exactly what is the nature of these business efforts to self-regulate against the deceptive practices which we have identified? Such self-regulation is effected through (a) the Better Business Bureaus, (b) industry communications codes and (c) written company policy.

Better Business Bureaus (BBB) are organizations supported financially by business interests such as chambers of commerce and having as one important purpose the disclosure of fraudulent and deceptive business practices. There is a national BBB, and there are hundreds of local chapters. The national organization publishes a "Service Bulletin" which often discloses not only fashionable deceptive schemes but also the names of

---

[42] *Printers' Ink* was for many years a business magazine serving the interests of advertising professionals. That publication was renamed *Marketing/Communications* in 1966, and is now published monthly by Decker Communications Incorporated, New York.

those using the schemes. In large metropolitan areas, the BBB may also sponsor a weekly radio or TV program given to the disclosure of fraudulent schemes. Many of the local chapters of the BBB also publish similar bulletins.[43] The BBB is an excellent example of business efforts to preserve the integrity of mass communications.

Codes of behavior have been developed and enforced by many industries, trade associations and advertising media. A study published in 1964 by the US Department of Commerce indicated that more than 40 separate industries—ranging from air-conditioning and appliances to dance studios and jewelry stores to pest controls and vending machines—have entered into communications codes of some kind.[44] In a similar vein, the American Association of Advertising Agencies (4A's) has a comprehensive creative code intended to self-regulate that very important group of communications specialists.[45] Further, the various media also endeavor to regulate against deceptive advertising. Organizations such as the National Association of Broadcasters, the American Newspaper Publishers Association, the Magazine Publishers Association (and many others) have long been concerned with abuses of all kinds in the use of the mass media.

Finally, individual company policy may represent another means of self-regulation. Revlon, a large cosmetic advertiser, claims that "any statement we make must bear scientific verification. In matters of advertising and/or labeling our lawyers seek clearances, or at least an opinion, from the various functionaries in Washington." At General Foods, as a further example, "all product claims of performance, quality and value must be approved by an advertising policy committee composed of representatives from the advertising, merchandising, product control, public relations and legal departments."[46]

A second nonstatutory class of efforts to control deceptive practices is suggested by the phrase "the consumer movement." This consumer movement may be thought of as the threatened possibility of collective remedial action by consumers or, what is the same thing, the threat of an active consumers' union. A popular business magazine recently made

[43] The National Better Business Bureau, Inc., is located at 230 Park Avenue, New York, New York, 10017. The BBB identifies nine basic classes of deception. These classes are:
1 Misdescription of seconds, irregulars or imperfects.
2 Unsupported superlative statements.
3 Misstatements of material content.
4 Incorrect description.
5 Misleading trade names.
6 Misleading use of trademark names.
7 Not on sale (bait advertising).
8 Misstatement of sizes and colors.
9 Abuse of comparative prices.
[44] *Self-Regulation in Advertising,* p. 24.
[45] *Ibid.,* p. 39.
[46] *Ibid.,* p. 16.

the following comment: "It is now quite clear where the consumer movement is going."[47] In this instance the consumer movement was proceeding under the urging of Mrs. Esther Peterson a special assistant for consumer affairs working at the direction of the President of the United States. Mrs. Peterson conducted several consumer conferences to identify consumer problem areas. Later, Betty Furness was appointed as a special assistant to the President for consumer affairs. In an address made before the 4A's, Miss Furness indicated that she felt that her job was to "find out what is troubling the consumer" and to "anticipate his needs."[48]

In effect then, the consumer movement is the publicized threat that efforts will be devoted to the development of an aggressive consumer organization through which corrective action of many kinds will be taken.[49] There seems little doubt that this threat is substantial enough to be of concern to the business community—indeed some heated exchanges between business and "consumerists" have been recorded by the press.[50] Nor is there any real doubt that a general consumer movement could be started. Canada has long had an active organization through which consumer problems could be identified. Great Britain recently placed into operation the most comprehensive consumer protection law ever passed in any country. Under this new law (The Trade Description Act), oral as well as written statements are included so that no salesman may misrepresent the merchandise he is offering.

Finally, government suasion is employed as a nonstatutory means of combating deceptive marketing practices. The FTC, largely through the activities of its Bureau of Industry Guidance, plays an important suasive role. The FTC conducts trade practices conferences, develops trade practice rules and publishes a series of guides which "make clear to businessmen those practices which the law prohibits and which should be avoided." While the trade practice rules deal with specific industry problems, the "Guides" series "may deal with practices common to many industries."[51] An FTC publication titled "Guides Against Deceptive Pricing," for example, is of potential value to any businessman making and quoting price decisions. The "Cigarette Advertising Guide" and the "Tire Advertising and Labeling Guides" are developed for more specialized business audiences. To the extent that deceptive practices occur unwittingly, the circulation

[47] *Printers' Ink*, August 13, 1965, p. 11.
[48] See Papers From the 1967 Region Conventions, the AAAA Eastern Annual Conference, New York City, October 10-11, 1967.
[49] These corrective actions might include picketing of firms that persist in questionable practices, the development of punitive measures to control such practices, and many others.
[50] See, for example, the series of anti-Peterson editorials in *Printers' Ink*; particularly December 4, 1964, p. 75, November 13, 1964, p. 9, and September 11, 1964, cover story.
[51] Kintner, *op. cit.*, p. 144.

of these materials are a positive influence in the battle against such practices.

An appraisal of efforts to control deceptive practices

We have now identified the principal efforts to regulate or control deceptive business practices. We have seen that such efforts are both numerous and diverse. It remains for us to consider briefly the success, or lack thereof, of these regulatory efforts. Unfortunately, the *existence* of laws is no a priori reason for the aggressive enforcement of those laws. And it is entirely possible that much "self-regulation" is generally ineffective window dressing—a convenient answer to those critics who claim that nothing is being done. What is the actual impact or effectiveness of regulatory attempts? All the relevant evidence is not yet in, but the prognosis is felt by some to be generally negative.

In many instances the state-level truth-in-advertising laws are simply not enforced. Nor is this properly construed as a criticism of state authorities; the simple fact is that there are in many instances no budgets available for such work. The problem of deceptive communications is thus recognized by virtually all our states, but the problem is not yet felt to be serious enough to hold much priority in money-spending matters. A frequent argument heard when the Hart-sponsored, truth-in-packaging bill was under congressional consideration was that what we needed was not another law, but the budgets to enforce existing law. The FDA, it was argued, was particularly limited by budgetary constraints.

There may be some truth in the notion that we need now to turn with greater concern to the problem of making the law work. Both President Kennedy and President Johnson displayed concern for the plight, real or imagined, of the American consumer. More recently, the FTC has come under serious criticism for the manner in which it perceives its own role and for the manner in which its responsibilities have been discharged.[52] A long report, completed in early 1969, concludes that the FTC has failed in its mission to protect the American consumer. More specifically, that report accuses the FTC of (a) "feeding and serving" those who threaten it (largely big business interests), (b) monitoring advertising only haphazardly and occasionally, (c) a regional imbalance in prosecuting cases, (d) a poor order of priorities, (e) a general reluctance to "go after" big companies and (f) assorted other shortcomings. The elusive truth is probably somewhere between the position of the FTC and that of such critical

---

[52] A "research team" headed by Ralph Nader and comprised of young lawyers and law students accused the FTC of "incompetence, lassitude, indolence, political cronyism, absenteeism, fear of big business, discriminatory hiring, delaying tactics, illegal secrecy and misrepresentation, a fixation on trivia, and a pervasive desire to avoid rocking the boat."

reports as this "Nader Report." It is axiomatic that if the accusations outlined in this report are essentially correct, business interests would be better served by a stronger Commission. A demonstrably weak Commission can only work in the direction of more onerous regulation.

The affluence of many consumers works to reduce the impact of deceptive activities: the wealthy man can be "taken" once and the experience will not kill him. This tendency may explain the apparent apathy of many people regarding such issues. But real integrity cannot be legislated; it must come from within the business community itself. And the apparent apathy vis-à-vis consumer problems today may not hold up when today's college-age population assumes leadership positions. The young are, in many instances, antibusiness in their leanings. As one student of the subject recently expressed it, "if business managers want to avoid new government regulations (with the attendant possibilities of excessive and punitive legislation), they will have to take positive action to demonstrate that the business interest is in more general accord with consumers' needs and wants."[53]

SUMMARY

Our purpose in this chapter has been to identify the nature of deceptive communications, to examine the harmful effects of such deception and to identify the efforts of our society to control such actions. Accordingly, we defined deception as communication, verbal or visual, direct or symbolic, of a message that has the reasonable capability of misleading, deluding or beguiling the audience to which it is directed. We noted that the FTC has developed guides that identify more specific forms of deceptive communications.

Deception was shown to be harmful at four different levels: (a) among business competitors, (b) among consumers, (c) among institutional and industrial buyers and (d) among businesses generally. We identified three types of deceptive schemes: Type I schemes tend to overstate the value of a product or service either directly or inferentially, Type II schemes tend to enhance the credibility of the communicator and Type III schemes may only appear to be motivated by a desire to deceive.

Finally, we explored federal and state efforts to control deceptive practices. The role of the FDA and the FTC were emphasized. The Wheeler-Lea Amendments were discussed. The recent Fair Packaging and Labeling Act was considered. State-level efforts to control deceptive business practices are exemplified by the *Printers' Ink* statutes. Nonstatutory efforts to control deceptive practices include self-regulation by business, efforts by consumers, and suasion by government. We concluded with a brief discussion of the effectiveness of efforts to control deception in commerce.

[53] Tom M. Hopkinson, "New Battleground—Consumer Interest," in Lee E. Preston, editor, *Social Issues in Marketing: Readings for Analysis,* Glenview, Ill.: Scott, Foresman and Co., 1968, p. 308.

1 Carefully define and indicate the relevance of each of the following concepts to the study of marketing:
   a. Symbolic deception
   b. Esoteric deception
   c. Deception through multiple-entendre messages
   d. Type III deceptive schemes
   e. Permissible puffery
   f. Deception with fictitious prices
   g. Bait-switch deception
   h. Inferential deception
   i. The free-ride doctrine
   j. Preticketing
   k. The doctrine of joint-connivance
   l. Credibility bias
   m. A weighted average target rate of profit

2 Distinguish carefully between each element in the following pairs of terms:
   a. Institutional buyers *and* industrial buyers
   b. Consumer surplus *and* consumer deficit
   c. Final consumers *and* industrial buyers
   d. Type I deceptive schemes *and* Type II deceptive schemes
   e. Euphemistic nomenclature *and* brand emulation
   f. Deception with editorial typography *and* deception with false certification
   g. Sacrificial lines *and* full-line pricing
   h. Misbranding *and* deceptive or false advertising

3 Discuss the comparative roles of the Food and Drug Administration and the Federal Trade Commission in controlling deceptive business practices.

4 What principal problems or abuses prompted the Fair Packaging and Labeling Act?

5 What are the so-called *Printers' Ink* statutes? Why do they have that name?

6 Identify and evaluate the principal nonstatutory efforts to control deceptive business practices.

7 Specifically, what weaknesses in the Federal Trade Commission did the "Nader Report" identify?

DISCUSSION QUESTIONS

8 If you were empowered to start all over again, what measures would you use to control deception in communications?

9 How would you make the existing state-level legislation that attempts to curb deceptive business practices more effective?

10 What are some Type I and Type II deceptive acts not specifically mentioned in the text?

Chapter 5

BUSINESS EXPANSION, MARKETING AND SOCIETY

In the preceding chapter, we identified some of the forms of deception that may be encountered in business, explored briefly the harmful effects of those deceptive practices, and identified the body of regulatory and control devices that have evolved to restrain such practices. In the present chapter, our principal concern is with business expansion and with the impact of such expansion upon the competitive environment. More specifically, our task is to: (a) define more exactly the nature of business expansion, (b) identify the various forms that business expansion may assume, (c) identify the principal reasons that underlie the practice of business expansion, (d) examine the influence of business expansion upon the strength or vigor of competition and (e) to examine the existing body of regulatory means through which control over business expansion may be exercised.

What is business expansion?

In order that we may define business expansion in the most meaningful way, it will be helpful to recall an idea that we encountered in Chapter 1: that the general economic process of allocation might be viewed as a sequence of events or stages that include the processes of extraction, manufacturing, distribution and consumption. We need now to understand the distributive aspects of that allocation process more carefully, for such an understanding is fundamental to understanding business expansion. But what are the "distributive aspects" of marketing?

When we refer to the *distributive aspects* of marketing, we shall understand that term to mean a set of specialized marketing institutions through which products and services are distributed to final consumers as well as those through which goods and services are distributed to industrial and institutional users.[1] We commonly refer to this set of institutions as a *channel of distribution*. This channel of distribution acts in the same way as a pipeline, and specialized terms have evolved to identify particular points or stages of that pipeline. Thus, retailing is one stage in a channel of distribution, wholesaling is another. The parallel nature of the channel of distribution and the pipeline is evident in Figure 5.1, which will also serve to further clarify the particular points, or stages, which the channel of distribution may possess.

Simply as a point of departure, consider what the view of a manufacturer might be as he contemplates the various ways in which he might place his product into the hands of consumers. In Figure 5.1, such a manufacturer would look down through three pipelines (labeled A, B and C). Should our manufacturer utilize Channel A, he would distribute directly (with no intermediate stops) to consumers. Should our manufacturer utilize Channel B, he would utilize a distribution specialist at Stage 2. Note that Figure 5.1 is not meant to imply that a manufacturer would use all three of these channels: a manufacturer is more likely to settle on one of these channels as being best for his particular circumstance. Three channels are depicted in Figure 5.1 simply to establish the channel concept as a pipeline comprised of various types of distributive specialists. This is not an especially rigorous definition of a channel—indeed we will have to sharpen this definition in a later chapter. But this preliminary concept of a channel of distribution will serve us effectively here. It should also be noted that many more stages of distribution may evolve than those depicted in Figure 5.1. That is, the number of different and relevant pipelines confronting the manufacturer may be great, but channels like A, B and C are frequently encountered. Channel B is a manufacturer-retailer-consumer sequence.

Figure 5.1 Channels of Distribution

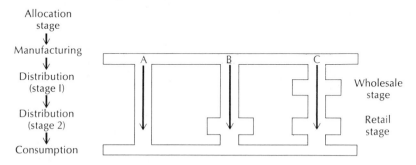

[1] The subject of channels of distribution is considered more completely in a later chapter. At the moment, our principal concern is with introducing the basic concept of the channel, not with exploring the intricacies of the idea.

Figure 5.2 Multiple Channels of Distribution

Stage of allocation

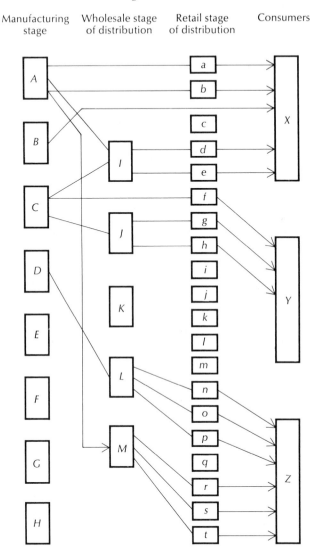

| Manufacturing stage | Wholesale stage of distribution | Retail stage of distribution | Consumers |

We need now to introduce one further factor, and then we will be equipped to provide a definition of business expansion. In Figure 5.1, we depicted a single manufacturing enterprise selling to a single group of consumers. In the interest of greater realism, we would have to introduce many manufacturers confronting many channels of distribution and serving many consumer groups. Figure 5.2 introduces this greater element of realism.

Observe the complexities of the channels of distribution utilized by

Manufacturer A. Note that he sells to Consumer Group Z through a whole-saler (M) and three retailers (r, s and t). Manufacturer A sells to Consumer Group X through a *dual channel system;* that is, he sells direct to Retailers a and b who, in turn sell to Consumer Group X *and* he sells through Wholesaler I to Retailers d and e, who sell, in turn, to Consumer Group X.[2] Manufacturer A does not sell to Consumer Group Y at all. Observe also the complex nature of the channels of distribution employed by Manufacturer C. Manufacturer A utilizes three channels of distribution. Manufacturer D utilizes one channel of distribution. Manufacturer B sells directly to consumers and uses only one channel of distribution.

We are now equipped with a sufficient understanding of the distributive aspects of marketing to develop a formal definition of business expansion. *Expansion,* as we will use that term, includes *the acquisition of control, through ownership or other means, of more than one firm at a given stage of allocation, and also acquisition of control, through ownership or other means, of firms at different stages of allocation.* A firm may be said to expand *horizontally* if it acquires control of another firm at the same stage of allocation as its own. A firm is said to expand *vertically* if it acquires control of another firm operating at a different stage of allocation than its own. Note that our definition of expansion does not require that a firm *buy* another firm in order that expansion occur: a firm need only gain an important degree of control over another firm in order to practice expansion as we employ that term. Indeed, as we shall see, much recent business expansion has been achieved without change in ownership inter-ests.

To be more specific, the three basic types of expansion are (a) expansion through ownership, (b) expansion through contractual agreement and (c) expansion through intimidation or the exercise of economic power. The distinctive character of these three forms of expansion will become clear in the discussion which follows. Note too, that expansion may be forward or backward; that is, a firm that functions principally at the retail stage of distribution may *expand backward* by acquiring control over some firm or firms at an earlier stage of distribution. Conversely, a firm may *expand forward* by acquiring control over some firm that operates at a subsequent stage of distribution. Expansion forward is a downstream acquisition of control; expansion backward is an upstream acquisition of control.

Now that we have defined business expansion and explored briefly some of the more obvious types of expansion, the reader may wonder why the subject is of particular interest in the study of marketing. At first blush, the subject of business expansion would seem more appropriate in a

[2] See, for example, Lee E. Preston and Arthur E. Schramm, Jr., "Dual Distribution and Its Impact on Marketing Organization," *Management Review,* Winter 1965, pp. 59–70; reprinted in Lee E. Preston, editor, *Social Issues in Marketing,* Glenview, Ill.: Scott, Foresman and Co., 1968, pp. 205–220.

finance course, or perhaps in one in general business policy. There are, however, two essential reasons for our interest in business expansion.

First, virtually all vertical expansion involves some kind of marketing institution, and even horizontal expansion which does not occur at a distributive stage may have a profound influence on marketing institutions. This latter point will be elaborated in a later section of the present chapter. Second, and most important, the marketing goals of a business may prompt expansion; that is, managerial marketing decisions relating both to distribution and to the product line frequently involve some type of business expansion. Thus, for example, the marketing management goal of securing adequate product distribution may logically lead to vertical expansion. Similarly, the desire to offer a more complete product line may logically lead to horizontal expansion. But we are anticipating to some extent the discussion of the next section. Suffice it to say that expansion, as we have defined that term, is of concern to us because it impinges upon the study of marketing in several significant ways.

The motivation for business expansion

There are at least two major classes of motives for business expansion. Some such motives are essentially psychological—the desire to claim large size or the desire to control a large organization for example. Most motives for business expansion are, however, probably economic. Three of these economic motives for expansion which concern us particularly here are: (a) the desire for business stability, (b) the desire for enhanced competitive effectiveness (larger profits) and (c) the desire to suppress competitors or prospective competitors. These motives are not mutually exclusive; an act of business expansion might reasonably be prompted by any one or indeed all of them. Their identification will nonetheless be useful to us because in any given instance one or another of these motives may be foremost.

BUSINESS STABILITY

The desire for business stability may prompt expansion. A firm that sells a limited line of products or services, particularly a line which is subject to seasonal or cyclical fluctuations in demand, confronts an unstable environment. Stability may be sought through the acquisition of existing firms—perhaps firms that specialize in the production of complementary products or services with the selling of the new and broader line of products producing a seasonally or cyclically stable volume of sales. Conglomerate mergers are of special interest to us here, largely because they are a type of merger which may reasonably be prompted by a desire for seasonal or cyclical stability. The term *conglomerate* suggests dissimilarity, and a conglomerate merger brings together dissimilar firms. The exact nature of the dissimilarity between the acquiring firm and the firm being acquired has given rise to three basic subordinate types of conglomerate mergers: (a) the pure conglomerate, (b) the market-extension conglomerate and (c) the product-extension conglomerate.[3]

The *pure conglomerate* unites two firms which have no meaningful economic relationship to each other. That is, the major parties to a pure conglomerate merger serve neither the same markets nor do they utilize similar technology in production.

The *market-extension conglomerate,* in contrast involves two firms that are dissimilar in some respects and similar in others. More specifically, the market-extension conglomerate is defined formally as an acquisition of the kind where a company operating in given geographic markets acquires a company manufacturing or selling the same or related products or services in other geographic markets.[4]

The *product-extension* conglomerate presents greater problems in definition. A product-extension conglomerate merger occurs "when the products of the acquiring and acquired companies are functionally closely related."[5] An example of one of these product-extension mergers is the Proctor and Gamble and Clorox merger which was ultimately disallowed. Proctor and Gamble sold soaps, detergents and other cleansers, and Clorox sold household liquid bleach; the products were "functionally closely related" but not perfect substitutes. The stability of a business organization may reasonably be enhanced with any of these types of mergers—though, as we shall see, some may be more readily approved by the Department of Justice than others.[6]

COMPETITIVE EFFECTIVENESS

The desire to enhance competitive effectiveness may also prompt business expansion. This general class of motives for expansion is often much more closely related to marketing issues than the stability motive. Thus, a firm

[3] See John C. Narver, "Some Observations on the Impact of Anti-trust Merger Policy on Marketing," *Journal of Marketing,* January 1969, pp. 24–31, particularly p. 26.
[4] See Betty Bock, *Mergers and Markets: An Economic Analysis of the First Fifteen Years Under the Merger Act of 1950:* The Conference Board, 1966, p. 142. See also John C. Narver, "Marketing and the Controversy over Conglomerate Mergers," *Journal of Marketing,* July 1967, pp. 6–10, especially the discussion on pp. 8–9.
[5] Bock, *op. cit.,* p. 159.
[6] One of the difficulties with definitions such as these for product-extension conglomerates, market-extension conglomerates and pure conglomerates is that both the acquiring firm and the acquired firm normally have several different product lines, so that a single merger may actually involve some horizontal relationships, some vertical relationships and some conglomerate relationships. No term has evolved to suggest this complex set of relationships. For a discussion of this point, see John C. Narver, "Conglomerate Mergers and Market Competition," in Peter D. Bennett, editor, *Proceedings of the Fall Conference of the American Marketing Association,* 1965, pp. 558–561.

which already advertises its line of products extensively may find that it may achieve significant economies or savings in its advertising as a result of acquiring still other product lines. This apparent paradox is easy to explain. Advertising media (such as television networks, magazines, radio and so forth) usually sell time or space on a quantity discount basis. That is, the more time or space one buys, the lower the unit cost. It is therefore conceivable that one result of adding a new product to one's line of products would be the ability to buy more advertising space or time at a lower unit cost than before, or in other words, at an improved competitive circumstance.[7]

But there are still other ways in which expansion may enhance the competitive effectiveness of a firm. Consider the instance wherein a firm finds that it can no longer be sure that its products will be given adequate shelf space in the retail outlets through which it distributes. In recent years, shelf space in supermarkets has become extremely scarce, with new products and brands aggressively seeking to replace the most vulnerable of the old products. In a circumstance such as this it might make very good sense for a firm to expand forward in order to assure an outlet for its products. Such a firm might, for example, buy into a chain of supermarkets.[8] The competitive position of that firm is clearly improved when assurance of distribution or access to consumer markets is achieved. There are other instances in which forward expansion though the purchase of existing wholesale or retail outlets may be well advised. As one authority notes "a manufacturer may be attempting to market a new product and distribution outlets may be slow to accept it, or the flow of products through independent wholesale outlets may prove irregular."[9]

To this point, we have emphasized those instances in which expansion occurs through the acquisition of an ownership interest in an ongoing enterprise. But it is increasingly common to find one firm acquiring some degree of control over another firm through *contractual agreement*. It should be recalled that when we defined business expansion, we did it in a way which would permit us to recognize expansion by contractual agreement as well as expansion by ownership acquisition. A firm may expand in a very meaningful way if it acquires some significant degree of control over the manner in which some other firm conducts its business.

[7] See John C. Narver, "Some Observations on the Impact of Anti-trust Merger Policy on Marketing," in Bennett, *op. cit.*, p. 25.

[8] Indeed, this solution to the problem may not be as unlikely as it would seem. The Consolidation Packing Company, one of the largest food canning businesses in the United States, acquired, for essentially these same reasons, a chain of supermarkets in the Pacific Northwest. The full story of the Consolidation acquisition may be seen in Ralph Westfall and Harper W. Boyd, Jr., *Cases in Marketing Management*, Homewood, Ill.: Richard D. Irwin, Inc., 1961, pp. 178–181.

[9] Marshall C. Howard, *Legal Aspects of Marketing*, New York: McGraw-Hill Book Co., 1964, p. 84.

An example will serve to clarify this notion. Suppose that a particular manufacturer is dissatisfied with the sales efforts being exerted in behalf of his products by the independently owned dealers and distributors who sell his products. Our dissatisfied manufacturer could improve the sales efforts of his dealers and distributors by training their salespeople, by providing advertising mat services, by providing point-of-purchase display materials and in many other ways. If, in exchange for these services, our manufacturer receives an agreement from his dealers and distributors that they will conduct their businesses in a way deemed best by the manufacturer, an *expansion of influence* has clearly been achieved—and it has been achieved without an outright or ownership purchase. We need to recognize this kind of contractual expansion, for it is often regulated by the same statutes that attempt to control expansion through the acquisition of ownership rights.

There is one other contractual form of expansion that is prompted by a desire to enhance competitive effectiveness, an example of perhaps greater historical than contemporary importance but by no means a dead issue. We have seen that a desire to insure a higher quality of competitive performance may underlie the urge of some business firms to expand their realm of influence. One decision over which business firms may wish to retain control is that which determines final selling price. A manufacturer or other brand owner, although separated spatially and temporally from final buyers, may nonetheless feel that he has a distinct vested interest in the final price at which his product is sold. One view, often encountered, is that excessive price cutting at the retail level may ultimately tend to erode the quality connotations that consumers attach to a product. This argument assumes that final consumers tend to judge product quality on the basis of price levels, among other factors. Thus, a product that is sold regularly at a very low price may, in time, be damaged by that low price reputation. This kind of argument is the basis for the *goodwill doctrine,* a legal theory that was at "the heart of the Supreme Court's acceptance" of the concept of fair trade in 1936.[10]

This goodwill doctrine identifies a means through which a manufacturer's name and reputation may be damaged even though his products have long since been sold to marketing specialists and the manufacturer no longer holds legal title to them. This line of reasoning suggests that the manufacturer should be protected from the kind of price cutting that could harm his reputation and gives the manufacturer a particular reason for expanding his realm of influence to include pricing decisions made by his dealers. The means through which a manufacturer might achieve this kind of control over dealers' prices will be discussed in a later section of this chapter. For now it is sufficient that we have noted the vital interest of some manufacturers in controlling final selling prices, and that this

[10] See Howard, *op. cit.,* pp. 43–44.

interest may underlie efforts to expand the sphere of influence of such manufacturers over their dealers and distributors.

How is expansion potentially harmful?

Expansion may be prompted by less honorable motives than those we have identified thus far. Expansion may seem an attractive course of action because it can be used to inflict harm upon competitors. There are indeed several forms of business expansion which are generally felt to be unfair and, therefore, potentially unlawful means of competition. Our concern here is with the following types of business expansion:

1 Expansion through extinction.
2 Expansion through tying arrangements.
3 Expansion through exclusive dealing arrangements.
4 Expansion through vertical acquisition.
5 Expansion through coercive reciprocity.

We noted earlier our essential concern with three types of expansion. We noted that these three types of expansion were accomplished through (a) ownership, (b) contractual agreement and (c) intimidation. We have, to this point in our discussion, cited examples of the first two of these forms of expansion.

EXTINCTION

Expansion through extinction involves acquisition of control over other firms through intimidative means. But just what does *extinction* mean? We shall understand that term to include any competitive action which is motivated by a desire to inflict economic harm upon a competitor. Consider, for example, the practice of charging extremely low prices—prices so low that losses are certain. If such prices are charged in order to divert trade from competitors and thus inflict economic damage upon them, the practice embodies an element of extinction. (Note that this is especially significant if the extremely low prices are discontinued after any damage is done.) It is also entirely reasonable that the damaged firm may forever thereafter be relatively timid about the use of price as a competitive weapon. Indeed, the experience of the profit squeeze may make the weaker firm a willing price follower.[11]

In all fairness it should also be noted that the motivation for such a

[11] In the now famous case of the Great Atlantic and Pacific Tea Company, the Antitrust Division of the US Department of Justice provided that "Defendants are jointly and severally restrained and enjoined from assigning or approving the assignment of a gross profit rate for any Division, knowing that such an assigned gross profit rate will result in the operation of any such a Division at a loss, for the purpose of or with the intent of destroying or eliminating competition in the retail purchase, sale or distribution of food or food products." Without saying so in that specific term, A&P was being accused of extinction practices. See Kenneth R. Davis, *Marketing Management*, New York: The Ronald Press Co., 1961, p. 737.

practice may *not* be extinction. It is possible that low prices on some items of merchandise may be used aggressively to build traffic for other items that offer a better profit potential. We will return to that point in a later chapter; for now, we have seen how extinction may be implemented, and we have seen how a degree of control over the damaged firm through economic intimidation may be effected. It is possible that the tacit threat of prolonged and severe price cutting by firms of relatively great financial strength can create a largely ineffective kind of competition. The influence of the firm practicing extinction is clearly expanded.

TYING ARRANGEMENTS

Another potentially harmful type of business expansion may occur as a result of a tying arrangement. A *tying* arrangement exists when a seller requires that relatively weak or undesirable parts of his line of products be purchased along with the stronger or more desirable elements in that line. The weaker products in the line are thus said to be *tied* to the stronger products. If, for example, a distributor of phonograph records requires that a package of recordings featuring relatively obscure artists be ordered along with several currently popular recordings, he is using a tying strategy. Similarly, the practice of "block booking" in the distribution of motion pictures has tying implications. Block booking refers to the practice of requiring television stations to accept a complete package of Grade A and Grade B motion pictures and, in effect, charging a single price for the package on a take-it-or-leave-it basis. The Grade B movies are tied to the Grade A movies.[12]

Tying agreements may assume still other forms. For example, a company that rents equipment may specify that only its supplies be used with that equipment. A firm which franchises retail outlets may effect a tying agreement if it specifies in great detail what its franchisees can and cannot do. Another particular type of tying arrangement is called "full-line forcing"— and it is perhaps easiest for us to see just why a tying agreement represents a form of business expansion with the full-line forcing case.

Full-line forcing identifies the instance in which a seller requires that his dealers carry all of his product line if they wish to carry any of it at all. Thus, a seller of vacuum cleaners may not permit his dealers to skim the cream off his line by carrying only the most popular models. The seller may argue that without the more complete assortments the dealers will be unable to properly satisfy the customers' desire for comparison. Whatever the seller's justification may be, full-line forcing is a particular type of tying agreement. And clearly, the use of a full-line strategy expands the realm of influence or control of the seller. A dealer stocking a full line of one seller's products is clearly more dependent upon that supplier than is one stocking

[12] See Lester G. Telser, "Abusive Trade Practices: An Economic Analysis," in Lee E. Preston, editor, *Social Issues in Marketing*, Glenview, Ill.: Scott, Foresman and Co., 1968, pp. 180–194, particularly p. 184.

parts of the lines of many sellers. Full-line forcing is a relatively subtle means of expansion.

No matter what the specific character of the tying agreement, the buyer who is subjected to the provisions of the arrangement is forced to forego some of the choices which he might otherwise have exercised. The buyer who is not bound by the tying agreement might reasonably purchase the tied portion of the line from other suppliers—the tied buyer has lost some freedom of choice.

EXCLUSIVE DEALING

Another type of potentially harmful business expansion may be effected through the practice of exclusive dealing. *Exclusive dealing* is best defined with the assistance of an illustration. Consider Figure 5.3.

Suppose that Figure 5.3 depicts a geographical market area in which there are six different retail shoe stores. Each of the stores is numbered, and each is symbolized by a rectangle. Suppose further that each of our six stores handles three brands of shoes. Store 1 sells Brands A, B and C, and store 5 sells Brands A, Y and M. The letter designations within each of the rectangles specifies the particular brands sold by each of the stores. In total, 13 different brands of shoes are represented in the market area. Several brands of shoes in our illustration are sold exclusively—that is, there is only one retail outlet in the market area through which those particular brands may be purchased. Brands P, H, M, E, R, B, C and Z exemplify exclusive selling. Note that exclusive selling is not the same as exclusive dealing—the latter being the practice which we wish to define carefully here.

Figure 5.3 Exclusive Selling

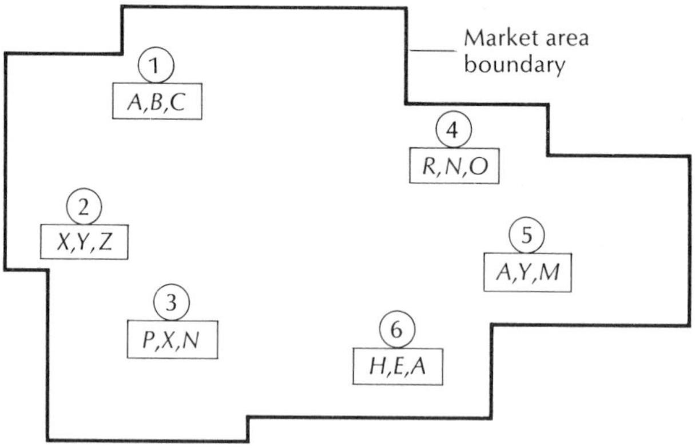

Exclusive selling occurs when only one dealer for a particular brand exists in a given market area; this is not held to be a harmful practice. But suppose that the seller of a new brand of shoes (Brand F) enters our hypothetical market seeking to gain dealers for his brand. If the seller of this new brand approaches one of the six stores in our small system and offers his brand of merchandise only if that store ceases to sell the brands it now sells, we have the essense of an *exclusive dealing* arrangement. Note that the seller of Brand F must require that the new dealer relinquish his other brands—thus the justification for calling this an exclusive dealing arrangement. The new dealer in Brand F would "deal exclusively" in Brand F if, in fact, he accepted the proposal.

If we make one further supposition, we can demonstrate clearly the potentially harmful nature of an exclusive dealing arrangement. Suppose that the seller of Brand F approaches Store 4 with his exclusive dealing proposition. What would be the competitive impact of the fulfillment of that proposition? The resulting competitive conditions are summarized in Figure 5.4. Brands R, N and O have been displaced as a result of the arrangement. But note also that there are now only 12 brands represented in our hypothetical market. Both Brands R and O were, prior to the exclusive dealing arrangement, sold exclusively. Thus, Brands R and O are no longer available in the market, although Brand F is. It is this tendency for exclusive dealing arrangements to reduce the number of competitors in a given market which makes it potentially harmful.

Figure 5.4 · Exclusive Dealing

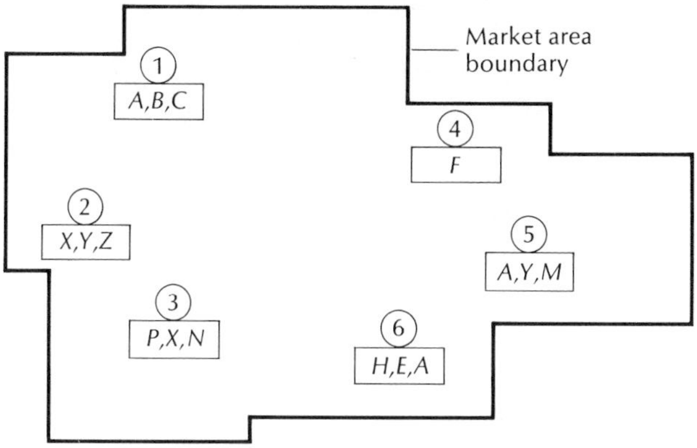

We say that this reduction in the number of competitors is a tendency rather than an absolute certainty because we can envision circumstances in which this harmful effect would not occur. We need to note also that an exclusive dealing arrangement may be accomplished in what appears to be a perfectly innocent way. Consider the instance in which the seller of Brand F is not so naïve as to expressly specify that all competing brands must be abandoned by his new dealers. Suppose that the seller of Brand F is much more sophisticated about harmful business practices and simply tells his new dealers that they should quietly abandon competing lines, as though such abandonment were dictated by quite normal business circumstances. In this case it would be much more difficult to establish in a definitive way that the seller of Brand F had actually effected a harmful exclusive dealing arrangement. "Quiet" exclusive dealing arrangements such as this example undoubtedly occur.

Still another potentially harmful means of achieving a type of business expansion is through the requirements contract. *Requirements contracts* are similar in effect to both tying agreements and exclusive dealing arrangements. This is particularly true if the percentage specified in the requirements contract is very high. A 100 percent requirements contract, for example, specifies that all of a particular buyer's needs be bought from a particular seller; the effect is to reduce the buyer's latitude of choice. The requirements contract can thus have the same harmful influence upon the strength of competition as the other methods of expansion that we have considered.

VERTICAL ACQUISITION

Earlier in our discussion we recognized the basic distinction between vertical and horizontal expansion. Under particular circumstances, either or both of these forms of expansion can be harmful. Horizontal expansion within the same industry reduces the number of competitors and may reduce the vigor of the competition within that industry, although there may be cases in which a recombination of the smaller firms within an industry into fewer firms may strengthen rather than weaken competition. This is virtually the argument advanced in the 1954 mergers of Studebaker with Packard and of Hudson with American Motors.[13] A horizontal merger proposal that would substantially strengthen an already strong firm would likely not be permitted because of its probable harmful effect on the strength of competition.

It is less immediately clear, however, how a vertical merger may have an adverse effect on the strength of competition. In order to understand this potential result of vertical merger, consider the Figure 5.5, which depicts two manufacturers, A and B. These two manufacturers are competitors in the sense that they serve the same final markets and do so through the same channels of distribution. The products of Manufacturer A find their way into ten retail stores labeled a through j. The products of manufacturer B find their way into these same ten retail outlets. Now consider the changes which might occur within this competitive situation if Manufacturer A acquires the ten retail outlets. Manufacturer A might continue to operate the retail outlets in a manner similar to the past. On the other hand, the situation may give rise to a kind of "foreclosure effect." Should foreclosure occur, the ten retail outlets (or some fraction of them) would no longer handle the products of Manufacturer B, and the strength of com-

---

[13] See Howard, *Legal Aspects of Marketing*, p. 80.

petition would clearly have been reduced.[14] It is in circumstances similar to these that vertical expansion may require careful regulation.

Figure 5.5 Foreclosure Effect

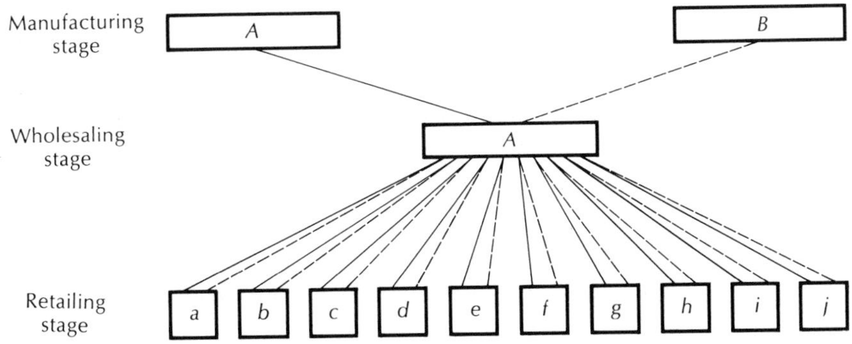

COERCIVE RECIPROCITY

One final form of expansion which may produce harmful effects is suggested by the impressive phrase coercive reciprocity. Although the phrase may connote a complex notion, it is really a fairly simple concept. The US Supreme Court has identified three basic types of reciprocity agreements: (a) consensual agreements, (b) accommodative agreements and (c) coercive agreements.[15] In general, reciprocity agreements exist when one firm purchases some of its requirements from another firm which, in turn, purchases some of its requirements from the former firm. Thus a tire manufacturer may exchange tires reciprocally with an automobile manufacturer. The automobile manufacturer gets tires and the tire manufacturer get automobiles. *Consensual reciprocity* exists when neither overt or covert pressure is applied by either of the parties to the reciprocity agreement and the agreement is mutually beneficial. *Accommodative reciprocity* involves no prior agreement; it occurs "when the purchases by one party flow either from the devout hope that the seller will return the favor or from a seller's thankful response in voluntarily placing return orders with

[14] This "foreclosure" argument was an important part of the now landmark *Brown Shoe Co. v. United States* case. In that case, the court felt that the foreclosure effect was not sufficient to make the proposed merger illegal. It has been generally true, however, that vertical integration has been viewed as a type of "exclusionary practice, since it is always possible that the manufacturing level will sell to the retail level of the same firm and thereby 'foreclose' a share of the retail market otherwise open to competing manufacturers." See Robert H. Bork and Ward S. Bowman, Jr., "The Crisis In Anti-trust," in John A. Larson, editor, *The Regulated Businessman: Readings From Fortune,* New York: Holt, Rinehart and Winston, Inc., 1966, pp. 87–88.
[15] See Ray O. Werner, "Marketing and the United States Supreme Court," *Journal of Marketing,* January 1967, p. 5.

a purchaser."[16] *Coercive reciprocity* forces one purchaser to deal with another, and is therefore clearly capable of restricting the choice that might otherwise be exercised by the restrained party. Coercive reciprocity interferes with the ability of a buyer to select freely from among alternative sources of supply. In this regard it is like tying agreements, requirements contracts, and exclusive dealing.

Legislative regulation of business expansion

We have now seen how some forms of business expansion may have a deleterious effect upon the strength of competition. It remains for us to explore the existing body of federal and state legislation that has evolved as a means of restraining such potentially harmful practices. We shall order our discussion as we have in earlier chapters, chronologically with federal legislation being first.

There are three federal laws that hold the capability of restraining harmful business expansion. These three laws are:

1 Sherman Antitrust Act of 1890
2 Clayton Act of 1914
3 Celler-Kefauver Amendment of 1950

The Sherman Act might correctly be described as omnibus legislation; it endeavored to establish the legal basis for preventing or correcting (a) monopoly, (b) actions which tend to restrain trade and (c) combinations or conspiracies that produce the effect of monopolization.[17] The Sherman Act does not explicitly identify the specific actions which will produce these undesirable conditions; it requires rather that each case be judged on its merits. In effect, the legislative branch of our government produced the law and asked that the courts, through the application of the general tenor of the law, develop more specific guides or criteria for implementing the law. It is, however, reasonable that any or all of the harmful forms of business expansion that we have considered could be found unlawful under the general terminology of the Sherman Act. Coercive reciprocity, foreclosure, exclusive dealing, tying arrangements and even extinction pricing have the capability of restraining trade. Thus, the Sherman Act might be used generally to correct many different forms of harmful business practices.

However, dissatisfaction with variations in interpretation of the Sherman

[16] *Ibid.*
[17] Today there are some notable exceptions to the kinds of firms that fall within the purview of the Sherman Act. The Capper-Volstead Act of 1922 exempts corporate or noncorporate agricultural associations, the Norris-LaGuardia Act of 1932 exempts (in some circumstances) organized labor, the Webb-Pomerene Act of 1918 exempts firms engaged in import-export activities, and the Small Business Act of 1953 exempts some types of small business.

Act and a lack of uniformity in adjudication under that statute augured for a law with a more specific identification of harmful and therefore undesirable business practices. A legislative effort to create this new and improved antitrust instrument was the Clayton Act of 1914.

The Clayton Act left much less room for interpretive judgment than the Sherman Act. The Clayton Act identified several business practices that were potentially harmful—and it is useful to emphasize that these actions were only potentially harmful. That is, the business actions or practices identified by the Clayton Act were not illegal per se; it was necessary that they have a harmful effect before they could be declared illegal. More specifically, the Clayton Act identifies five potentially harmful business practices that are of particular concern to the careful student of marketing. These five practices are (a) price discrimination, (b) mergers, (c) tying agreements, (d) exclusive dealing and (e) extinction pricing. The subject of price discrimination is an important part of the next chapter and we will defer further discussion of that subject until then.

Regarding mergers, the Clayton Act specified that an acquisition "of the stock or other share capital of another corporation engaged in commerce, where the effect of such acquisition may be to substantially lessen competition between the corporation whose stock is so acquired and the corporation making the acquisition" be declared illegal.[18] These exact words are important to us because, as we shall see, they were modified in a significant way in a 1950 amendment to the Clayton Act.

Section 3 of the Clayton Act attempts to prevent harmful tying agreements and exclusive dealing arrangements by prohibiting the "condition, agreement or understanding that a buyer shall not use or deal in the goods, wares, merchandise, machinery, supplies, or other commodities of a competitor or competitors." Note, again, that such a "condition, agreement or understanding" is not illegal per se; in order for it to be illegal it must "substantially lessen competition or tend to create a monopoly in any line of commerce." It is also important to note that practices such as coercive reciprocity and foreclosure tactics clearly fall within the purview of the Clayton Act. Extinction pricing is potentially illegal under the Clayton Act as it was later amended by the Robinson-Patman Act.

The Celler-Kefauver Act of 1950, an amendment to Section 7 of the Clayton Act, has been called the Antimerger Act.[19] And this amendment represents two important changes in the manner of dealing with proposed mergers. First, under the original wording of the Clayton Act it had been possible for a firm to purchase the assets rather than the stock of another business and thereby avoid the apparent intent of the law. The Celler-Kefauver Amendment expressly provides that the acquisition of another

[18] Howard, *Legal Aspects of Marketing*, p. 8.
[19] *Ibid.*

firm's assets, as well as the purchase of its stock, may be illegal. Second, the Celler-Kefauver Amendment incorporates a change in wording that makes it easier for the regulatory authorities to deny a merger proposal. This change in wording involves an application of the legal *doctrine of incipiency*. Incipient means, literally, just beginning—and the doctrine of incipiency permits the denial of a merger proposal on the grounds that it *may* have an adverse effect on the strength of competition. Before the passage of the Celler-Kefauver Act, denial of a proposed merger would have to be based on evidence that competition between the acquiring and the acquired companies or to that in any community would be injured. With the passage of Celler-Kefauver, it was now possible to deny a proposed merger if competition would be weakened in any line of commerce in any section of the country.[20] The use of this broader realm of influence of the proposed merger makes it considerably easier to establish incipient damage from the proposed merger.

Fair trade

We have now seen, briefly, that the Sherman Act, the Clayton Act, and the Celler-Kefauver Amendment to the Clayton Act all permit a degree of societal control over harmful forms of business expansion. There is one other related group of federal laws that relates to the issue of business expansion, but in a substantially different way. The laws we have considered thus far in this section have attempted to restrain acts of expansion; the laws we have yet to consider expressly permit a particular type of contractual expansion. These remaining laws are the fair trade laws, which are concerned with the issue of resale price maintenance.

We observed in an earlier section that a manufacturer or brand owner might desire to expand his influence to include a role in the determination of the final selling prices of his products. We noted that his rationale might be the goodwill argument—an argument that relates price and preceived quality. We need now to explore the issue of resale price maintenance more completely.

The phrase *fair trade laws* serves to identify the legislative means through which manufacturers and other brand owners may seek to maintain or support, the prices at which their products are resold. The phrase *resale price maintenance* identifies the issue of whether resale price maintenance should, in the interest of maintaining strong competition, be permitted. And the issue of resale price maintenance has been a controversial one. The effect of resale price maintenance contracts is to hold retail prices at a higher level than they might otherwise reach. Were this not true, there would indeed be no reason for such maintenance efforts. This ar-

---

[20] *Ibid.*, p. 9.

tificially high level of prices is presumably not in the best interest of final consumers.[21]

The artificially high level of prices which resale price maintenance would produce does, however, work to the distinct advantage of some types of retailers. It is, in fact, historically true that the real pressure for the passage of the fair trade laws came not from manufacturers concerned with the adverse price-quality association, but from retailers who were concerned with the price competition they were encountering from multiunit retail organizations we call chains. Thus fair trade was essentially retailer inspired, although such retailers often pressed through their manufacturing source for the passage of these laws.

There are two laws at the federal level that are an integral part of the resale price maintenance issue. The first of these laws, the Miller-Tydings Act, was passed in 1937. This Act embodied two provisions that have proven to be of considerable consequence relative to the resale price maintenance movement. First, this federal law gave the individual states the power to determine whether they wanted this legislative form of resale price maintenance. If a particular state was in sympathy with the resale price maintenance cause, they were to signify so by passing a law to that effect. If a particular state was not in sympathy with the resale price maintenance cause, they declined to pass such enabling legislation. Second, the Miller-Tydings Act provided that in those states having enabling legislation, only one dealer's signature on an agreement to maintain prices was sufficient to bind all other dealers in that state to the agreement, even though they had not individually signed it. This latter provision—an obvious legislative effort to simplify the implementation of resale price maintenance—is known as the nonsigner clause of the act.

In order to make an otherwise long story succinct, we will note here only that the nonsigner provision of the law was tested for its constitutionality (it did seem to usurp the rights of dissenting dealers) and the provision was ultimately found to be constitutional. Ultimately, an interpretive amendment, the McQuire-Keogh Act of 1952, was required to define more clearly the actual intent of the legislature and of the nonsigner provision in the earlier Act. Once the constitutionality of the federal nonsigner provision was established, the interest of the states in resale price maintenance began to wane. Many states then repealed the fair trade laws they had passed earlier (signifying their dissent from the clause) and some of the other states declared the nonsigner provision

---

[21] The argument that the final consumer actually does not profit from aggressive price competition has also been advanced. This seeming contradiction in terms can be resolved if one subscribes to the view that product quality ultimately declines in the face of rigorous price competition. The pending Quality Stabilization Bill, indeed, promises stabilized product quality through a renewal of fair trade legislation.

in their own statutes unconstitutional. The collective result was that fewer states were now equipped legislatively in such a way that a manufacturer or other brand owner could easily and inexpensively enforce a desire he might have to maintain resale prices through existing legal prerogatives.[22]

STATE-LEVEL LEGISLATION

Although the various state legislative provisions that are intended to restrain harmful acts of expansion are quite diverse, we will simplify our task and consider only one type of state law. More than thirty states have enacted legislation that is clearly intended to assist in the restraint of predatory practices, practices prompted by the motive that we have called extinction. These laws are variously referred to as unfair trade practices acts, sales below cost laws and, minimum markup laws. Whichever name is applied to the statute, the intent is the same: to prevent extinction pricing practices. In order to accomplish this purpose, such laws normally specify a *floor* expressed in terms of a markup percentage below which specified products are not to be sold. Thus, a particular state may have a 6 percent minimum markup law that would prohibit the resale of specified items of merchandise for margins lower than 6 percent of the selling price. Another state may have a statute that specifies a minimum markup of "landed cost plus 5 percent." In this latter case, *landed cost* is the cost of the merchandise plus the cost of inward transportation. A minimum 5 percent margin would have to be added to this landed cost in order to comply with the intent of the law. The rationale for such laws is simple and seemingly reasonable. They are based on the assumption that there is no good reason why a firm would attempt to sell something at less than cost unless it is to inflict harm upon a competitor. Such laws usually ·exempt distress merchandise, which a retailer must sell at a very low price in order to make a sale at all. There is, however, one pricing strategy requiring the use of loss leaders that may not be prompted by extinction motives, and yet may be unlawful in states having these unfair trade practices acts. We will consider this possible impediment to competition in a later chapter.

How do the fair trade laws differ from the unfair trade practices acts? This is a question that entangles beginning students of marketing more, perhaps, than any other. In order to assure minimum confusion about these two types of laws the following summary device may be helpful:

[22] There are many ways, other than those afforded by statute, for a manufacturer or brand owner to maintain resale prices. Examples include consignment selling, leasing and selective distribution.

	Fair Trade Laws	Unfair Trade Practices Acts
The law is	permissive	mandatory
The price floor is specified by	manufacturer or brand owner	state statute
The price floor is usually specified in	dollar amounts	percentage markups
Such laws exist at	both federal and state level	only at state level

Note first that the fair trade laws are not mandatory—a manufacturer may seek the protection from dealer price cutting afforded by such laws if he so wishes. The unfair trade practices acts, in contrast, must be complied with (unless the class or classes of merchandise in which a particular seller deals are specifically exempted). Note also that the decision regarding the actual floor price is statutory in the case of the minimum markup laws but subject to the discretion of the manufacturer or brand owner in the case of the fair trade laws. The laws also differ in the manner in which floors are specified. Thus, the fair trade laws contemplate a floor expressed in dollar terms (for example, $7.95). The unfair trade practices acts contemplate a floor expressed as a markup percentage (for example, cost plus 4 percent). Finally, the unfair trade practices acts are state-level legislation only; the fair trade laws may exist at both the state and federal level.

SUMMARY

In this chapter, we have been concerned with what business expansion is, why business seeks expansion, and some of the possibly harmful forms of business expansion. We defined expansion in a special way to include "the acquisition of control, through ownership or other means, of firms at different stages of distribution." This definition permitted us to explore three types of expansion: through purchase of an ownership interest, through contractual agreement and through various intimidative means.

We observed that the motivation for business expansion might be any or all of several basic reasons: the desire for stability, the desire to enhance competitive effectiveness and the desire to inflict harm upon competitors. We noted in the case of this third motive that extinction pricing, tying arrangements, exclusive dealing agreements, some forms of vertical expansion and coercive reciprocity all hold the potential for reducing the vigor of competition,

Finally, we considered the federal and state laws that attempt to regulate business expansion in its potentially harmful forms. More specifically, we discussed the Sherman Act of 1890, the Clayton Act of 1914 and the Celler-Kefauver Amendment of 1950. We noted that the Clayton Act, as amended by Celler-Kefauver, dealt with the possibly harmful effects of price discrimination (the subject of the next chapter), mergers, tying agreements, exclusive dealing and extinction pricing. We also noted one type of law that encouraged contractual expansion—the fair trade laws, both state and federal. The chapter was concluded with a discussion of the distinction between the fair trade laws and the state unfair trade practices acts, a common source of confusion.

REVIEW QUESTIONS

1 Carefully define and indicate the relevance of each of the following concepts to the study of marketing:
   a. Channel of distribution
   b. Stages of distribution or allocation
   c. Business expansion
   d. Dual or multiple channels of distribution
   e. Conglomerate expansion
   f. Product-extension conglomerates
   g. The goodwill doctrine
   h. Contractual business expansion
   i. Expansion through extinction
   j. Expansion through exclusive dealing agreements
   k. The foreclosure effect
   l. The doctrine of incipiency
   m. The nonsigner clause

2 Distinguish carefully between each element in the following pairs of terms:
   a. Forward expansion *and* backward expansion
   b. Pure conglomerates *and* market-extension conglomerates
   c. The goodwill doctrine *and* business expansion
   d. Expansion through tying arrangements *and* expansion through coercive reciprocity
   e. Exclusive selling *and* exclusive dealing
   f. Accommodative reciprocity *and* coercive reciprocity
   g. Fair trade laws *and* unfair trade practices acts

3 What are the major provisions of the Clayton Act?

4 How does the Celler-Kefauver Amendment amend the Clayton Act? Why was this type of amendment felt necessary?

5 How do the fair trade laws "permit a particular kind of contractual expansion"?

DISCUSSION QUESTIONS

6 If you were thus empowered, how would you regulate business expansion? That is, what rules or guides would you establish to assure that adequate levels of competitive vigor obtained?

7 Explain, in your own words, what expansion by intimidation means.

8 Do you believe it best to try to regulate business activities through a broad, omnibus bill (like Sherman) or through a series of more pointed provisions, such as those in Clayton? Why?

Chapter 6
PRICE DISCRIMINATION, MARKETING AND SOCIETY

We have now completed a consideration of deception in communications and of business expansion. We have examined some of the specific forms that these business practices assume, and we have seen how they may have a harmful effect on the strength of competition. Our third and final area of legislative consideration is that relating to discrimination. We shall see presently that discrimination can occur in many contexts and can have many results—some harmful to competition and some not. Our principal concern in this chapter is with discrimination effected through the manipulation of prices, although we will give very brief consideration to discrimination with nonprice vehicles. When we have carefully identified the most important form of discrimination and have examined the impact of such discrimination upon the vigor of competition, we will consider the battery of statutes that has evolved to control demonstrably harmful forms of discrimination. More specifically, the order of our concern in the present chapter is directed to answering the following questions: (a) what is price discrimination? (b) what forms of price discrimination are unlawful? and (c) what statutory guides exist to protect business and society against the harmful effects of price discrimination?

What is price discrimination?

In its most obvious form, price discrimination occurs when one person pays a different price than some other person for an identical good or service. Thus, price discrimination involves certain inescapable elements. Since there is often confusion among business students about the concept of price discrimination, we may profitably enumerate those elements. In order for price discrimination to occur, a minimum of two buyers, one seller, and a quantity of goods or services of specified quality are required. Consider the case of a bald man who pays standard prices for haircuts.

The elements to establish discrimination would be the barber (seller), the bald customer and a customer with a complete head of hair (two buyers), and a haircut of the same quality performed upon each of the two buyers (service). Our hypothetical bald man pays the same price but receives less service—at least one could reasonably argue that fewer hairs are severed in his behalf—and therefore our example has all the prerequisites of price discrimination. It is clear that price discrimination involves a particular type of inequity, but beginning students of the subject often err by equating all forms of inequity involving prices with price discrimination. A simple hypothetical example will identify one source of such confusion.

Assume that a physician charges Customer A $60 for a physical examination and charges Customer B $50 for an identical examination. Discrimination has occurred, but an important ambiguity exists. Who is discriminated against? Most would conclude that the customer paying the higher price is necessarily the party discriminated against. But it is possible, is it not, that $60 is a *correct* price for the service rendered and that the $50 price is, in effect, a subsidy for Customer B. The doctor who is charging the two prices may be the party discriminated against in the sense that the lower price is inequitable. It is clear that we have mixed price discrimination with some other kind of pricing inequity so that analytical confusion is possible if not likely. We can, however, clarify the issue if we consider the following hypothetical pricing situations:

Situation I

Equitable price	$5.00
Price charged Customer A	6.00
Price charged Customer B	6.00

Situation II

Equitable price	5.00
Price charged Customer A	4.00
Price charged Customer B	4.00

Situation III

Equitable price	5.00
Price charged Customer A	5.00
Price charged Customer B	4.00

Situation IV

Equitable price	5.00
Price charged Customer A	5.00
Price charged Customer B	6.00

These four pricing situations embody two important assumptions. First, it is assumed that an equitable or "right" price exists and can be determined. This equitable price is one which yields a reasonable profit to the seller—it is neither too high nor too low. (The equitable price is used here simply as a point of reference; it is not of great consequence that we might not be able to actually determine such a price.) Second, these four situations presume, as we noted above, that an identical good or service is delivered under identical conditions to both Customers A and B. The point we wish to make, with the assistance of these four hypothetical situations, is that discrimination is but one particular form of pricing inequity—that is, inequitable circumstances may obtain as a result of pricing practices, but not all such inequitable circumstances involve discrimination as that term will be employed here.

Consider Situations I and II. In both these cases, a type of inequitable condition exists. In Situation I a seller charges prices that are "too high" to two customers; in Situation II the seller is either philanthropically inclined or uninformed, for he charges prices that are "too low." It is important to note that in both situations he charges his inequitable prices *uniformly* to Customers A and B. Neither of these two cases embody discrimination as that term is employed here. Inequity of the kind suggested in Situation I and Situation II is, however, often confused with price discrimination. Situations I and II do not embody all the necessary conditions for price discrimination.

Contrast conditions in Situations III and IV with those just examined. They involve discrimination, though it may not, for one reason or another, be unlawful discrimination. This is an important distinction for us to emphasize, for much price discrimination occurs that is not unlawful.[1] Price discrimination is inherent in Situations III and IV not because of the relationship of the prices charged to the equitable price of $5, but because in both these instances different customers pay different amounts for identical goods or services. The significant character of price discrimination, then, is not that prices are higher or lower than they should be (that is, whether the pricing company takes too much or too little profit). The significant character of price discrimination is that one customer pays a different amount for identical goods and services than does another, competing customer.

With these preliminary remarks in mind, we are prepared to examine some additional aspects of price discrimination. We will distinguish between several basic forms of price competition: (a) a first-line price discrimination, (b) second-line price discrimination, (c) third-line price discrimination and (d) conspiratorial price discrimination.[2] We will also dis-

---

[1] We will distinguish lawful from unlawful price discrimination in the next section of the present chapter.

[2] The first three of these classes are suggested in Earl W. Kintner, *An Antitrust Primer: A Guide to Antitrust and Trade Regulation Laws for Businessmen,* New York: Crowell-Collier and Macmillan, Inc., 1964, pp. 65–68.

tinguish between direct and indirect price discrimination. In order to structure this discussion it will be helpful to employ some of the ideas that we encountered in our discussion of business expansion. Consider the components and stages of distribution in Figure 6.1.

Figure 6.1 First Line Price Discrimination

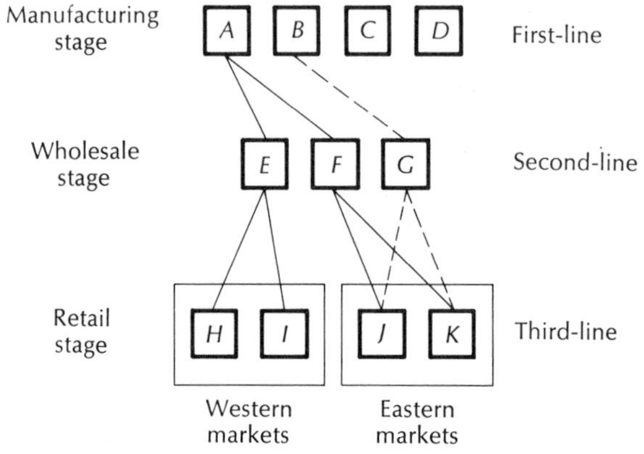

FIRST-LINE PRICE DISCRIMINATION

First-line price discrimination occurs within the manufacturing stage of distribution, and it involves pricing in more than one market. In order to illustrate this idea, assume that Manufacturer A sells through Wholesaler E to western markets and through Wholesaler F to eastern markets. Assume further that Manufacturer B, a smaller firm manufacturing the same basic product line as A, sells to eastern markets through Wholesaler G. These relationships are depicted in Figure 6.1. If Manufacturer A should seek to eliminate or weaken Manufacturer B, he might do so by selling at drastically low prices in eastern markets and at normal prices in western markets. That is, Manufacturer A might sell to Wholesaler F at prices substantially below cost and sell to Wholesaler E at normal profit margins. Such a tactic could easily reduce the strength of Manufacturer B. Note that this tactic is a special form of what we earlier called extinction pricing, except that the target of the extinction is the original seller rather than a retailer. This is called first-line discrimination because it ultimately works against the first-line, or original, seller (manufacturer). The student may wonder why this type of first-line discrimination would not also work against the retailers and wholesalers in eastern markets. It is possible, though not necessary, that such a result could be felt. The relatively lower prices of A's products, however, would simply divert trade to that line, and there is no particular reason to expect great injury. Clearly the retailer or wholesaler that stocked both the A line and the B line would be relatively protected; the retailer or wholesaler that dealt only in the B line would feel some of the impact of this form of discrimination.

SECOND-LINE PRICE DISCRIMINATION

Second-line price discrimination occurs within the same market, and the impact of the discrimination is felt at the wholesale stage of distribution. Consider the distribution components depicted in Figure 6.2.

Figure 6.2 Second Line Price Discrimination

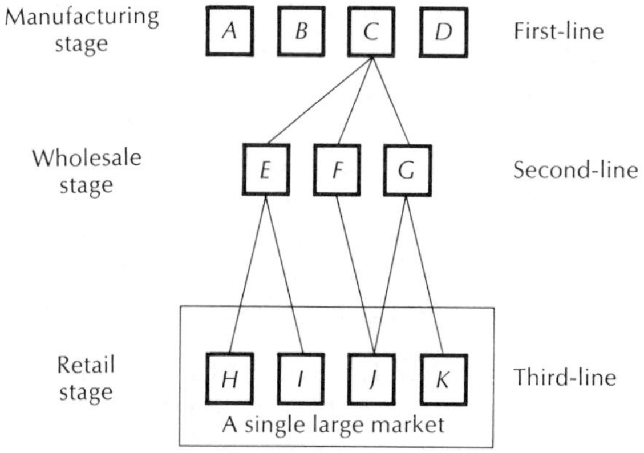

Assume that Manufacturer C sells his production specialty to Wholesalers E, F and G. These three wholesalers are competing with each other in the sense that they subsequently resell to Retailers H, I, J and K. Assume further that Manufacturer C charges Wholesaler F a higher price for a similar quantity of goods of identical quality than he charges either Wholesaler E or G. Where does the brunt of this type of price discrimination fall? The best answer is that the impact of the discriminatory action falls at the second-line, and more specifically upon Wholesaler F. F simply finds himself unable to compete for retail outlets because of his higher costs and the higher price possibly necessitated by those costs. Retailers J and K will, in this case, simply exercise their option to buy from Wholesaler G rather than from F. It is also possible that C, the manufacturer, could be hurt because of a restricted flow of his products through F. It follows logically that second-line price discrimination rarely occurs unless alternative channels of distribution exist. That is, the manufacturer practicing second-line discrimination must be assured of a continuing outlet for his goods before such discriminatory action is taken. This type of discrimination produces injury at the buyer level, rather than at the seller level as in the previous case.

THIRD-LINE PRICE DISCRIMINATION

A third and important type of price discrimination occurs at the third-line of distribution: the retail stage. Consider the components of distribution depicted in Figure 6.3. Third-line price discrimination contemplates a circumstance in which the original seller sells directly to some retail outlets and also indirectly, through wholesalers, to other retailers. Note also that the retailers who are supplied directly and those supplied through whole-salers must be serving the same market. How does third-line price discrim-ination occur? Suppose that Manufacturer C in Figure 6.3 sells directly to retailers I and J. He also sells to Retailers F, G and H, but in this case through Wholesalers D and E. If Manufacturer C should charge Retailers I and J a price significantly lower for goods of like grade and quality than Retailers F, G and H can buy them for from Wholesalers D and E, the situation may be discriminatory. Note that in this instance Manufacturer C would not be expected to sell to Retailers I and J at the same price as he sold to wholesalers D and E because D and E are not directly competitive with I and J. But, if the price to D and E is so high that, with the wholesaler's normal margin added, the resulting retail price is noncom-petitive, then a third-line case of price discrimination may exist. The poten-tial injury from such discriminatory action occurs at the third line of distribution: Retailers F, G, and H absorb the brunt of the price inequity.

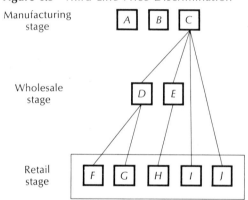

Figure 6.3 Third Line Price Discrimination

CONSPIRATORIAL PRICE DISCRIMINATION

Finally, there is the case of conspiratorial discrimination. We can illustrate the manner in which this type of discrimination occurs with the aid of two hypothetical circumstances. Observe the relationships depicted in Figure 6.4. Case One depicts an instance that is only slightly different from some we have encountered before. The slight difference may, how-ever, be significant. Case One summarizes the important facts surrounding two sales made by Seller A to competing Buyers I and II. Note that the transaction between Seller A and Buyer I is direct; there are no interme-diaries used. Goods and services having a price of $1000 are exchanged for $1000. The transaction between Seller A and Buyer II is accomplished with the assistance of a selling broker. This simply means that Seller A employs a sales specialist in this transaction. Goods of the same quantity and quality are sold, through the selling broker, to Buyer II. Buyer II parts with $1000, and there is no price discrimination here. It may be that the

$1000 that Buyer II parts with will go in part to the selling broker and in part to Seller A, but that fact does not produce a discriminatory circumstance.

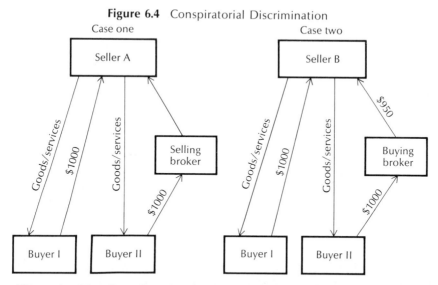

Figure 6.4 Conspiratorial Discrimination

Now, consider Case Two in Figure 6.4. The transaction between Seller B and Buyer II is only a little different from that depicted in Case One. Note that in Case Two the assistance of a broker is sought by the buyer. Note also that the seller enjoys net receipts of $950, with $50 being retained by the buying broker. The reason Seller B will accept $950 rather than $1,000 in this latter transaction is because the buying broker's efforts are substituted for his (the seller's). Again, there is no discrimination—at least our two competing buyers have parted with $1,000 each and have both received a like quantity of goods of identical quality.

How then does all this lead to conspiratorial discrimination? Suppose that the buying broker in Case Two is not wholly independent; suppose that he is a subsidiary of Buyer II, or that Buyer II has some other ownership interest in the buying brokerage office. If we make this one adjustment, the situation may change abruptly. If the buying broker is actually an instrument of Buyer II, it is possible that the profits of the brokerage represent a discriminatory price advantage for Buyer II. Consider once again the $50 that the buying broker received for his part in the transaction. Suppose that $20 of that $50 covers the actual cost of assisting in the transaction. Suppose further that the $30 of profit are returned to Buyer II, either directly as a rebate or in some convoluted accounting arrangement. In either event, it might reasonably be argued that Buyer II is, effectively, out only $970 while Buyer I has parted with $1000. In short, a condition of price discrimination may exist. This is conspiratorial price discrimination. Note that its distinctive mark is that *rebating* of some type is required. Note also that it is not the use of a broker per se that is potentially harmful; it is the conspiratorial relationship between the buyer and the broker that is at the base of the problem.

DIRECT VS. INDIRECT PRICE DISCRIMINATION

We now need to make one further distinction; a distinction that will serve to identify another basic source of potentially discriminatory pricing practices. Up to this point we have discussed *direct* price discrimination—that is, the ultimate cause of discrimination was produced by differences in prices. But it is possible to effect a discriminatory circumstance even though prices to competing buyers are identical. This is possible when competing buyers are provided with services in a discriminatory manner. Consider, for example, an instance where two competing buyers pay identical prices, but one receives promotional assistance of various types and the other does not. If the favored buyer receives window display materials, point-of-purchase sales materials and more expeditious delivery service than the nonfavored buyer, it should be clear that this form of discrimination may be an *indirect* form of price discrimination. The relationship between a discriminatory use of services and price discrimination might be reasoned as follows: The sales assistance provided the favored buyer but not provided the nonfavored buyer has an *opportunity cost* value—that is, it would cost some determinable number of dollars to duplicate the discriminatory services received. Since the nonfavored buyer would have to spend at least that amount to establish a condition of competitive equality, the discriminatory action is tantamount to charging him a higher price. We shall see, in a subsequent section, that this type of indirect price discrimination has been one concern of the legislative and judicial branches of our government.

When is price discrimination illegal?

We have observed earlier that price discrimination is not necessarily unlawful; it always involves some form of inequity, but it is not always illegal. This point is easily forgotten because the word "discrimination" carries a strong negative connotation, and students often conclude that all price discrimination is illegal. The fact is that as a society we necessarily tolerate many forms of price discrimination. The reasons for this tolerant attitude will become clear as the discussion proceeds. Specifically, there are five basic circumstances in which price discrimination may occur without being unlawful. These five circumstances are: (a) when there is no harm to competition, (b) when cost differences justify actual price differences, (c) when price differences are a response to equally low competitors' prices, (d) when market conditions have changed between the times the two sales in the discriminatory transaction occurred and (e) when the transaction does not meet the commerce requirement. Each of these circumstances is examined in the discussion that follows.

Price discrimination, including all the requisite conditions we have identified, may be perfectly legal because it does not result in a demonstrable reduction in the strength of competition. Indeed, no case of price discrimination in which the two buyers are final consumers is illegal. Thus, if a retailer sells an item of merchandise to one customer for $3 and another and identical item of merchandise to another customer for $2, the conditions for price discrimination exist, but the action is not illegal because there can be no injury to competition among final consumers; at least we do not normally consider final consumers as competitors. If we did not have this particular class of "legal" discrimination, the courts would be perpetually filled with customers seeking redress. It is well to emphasize this first requirement of *illegal price discrimination*. It is not the action of price discrimination itself that is harmful, it is the possible harmful effect of the action that we endeavor to control; and, since discrimination may occur without producing the required harm, we need to demonstrate harm to establish a particular action as unlawful.

Price discrimination, again with all the requisite conditions we have noted, may nonetheless be legal because such price differences as are involved may be justified by differences in the cost of serving the competing buyers. This point requires some elaboration. Suppose that the situation shown in Figure 6.5 occurs:

Figure 6.5 Legal Price Discrimination

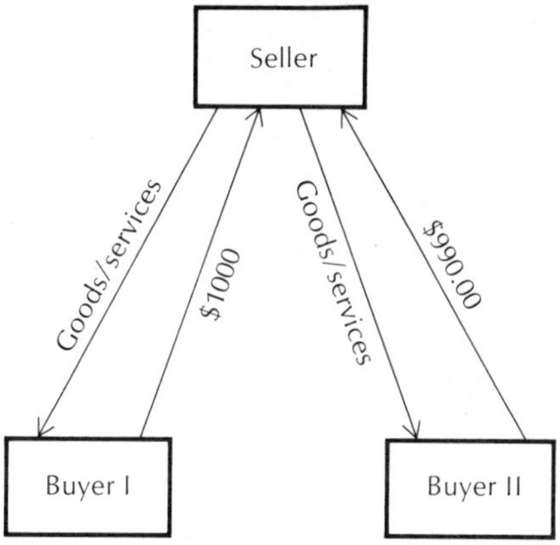

The quantity and quality of goods and services purveyed to Buyer I and Buyer II in Figure 6.5 is assumed to be identical. The difference in price ($10) may be legal even though Buyer I and Buyer II are competitors and even though Buyer I is demonstrably harmed by the price differential if the seller can show that the actual cost of serving Buyer II warrants the lower price.[3] We shall have more to say about this form of legal price discrimination in a subsequent section.

Still another instance in which conditions meeting the definitional requirements of price discrimination may not be prohibited by law occurs when such conditions are brought about by the prices being charged by a competitor. This situation may arise in several different circumstances. Figure 6.6 is representative. Figure 6.6 depicts a situation in which legal price discrimination is practiced by Seller I in the market served by Buyers I and II in order to prevent Seller II from selling to Buyer II at the low price charged Buyer III. Note that Buyers I and II are competitors and that Buyers II and III are competitors, but that Buyers I and III are not competitors. Buyer II is a firm that is thus common to both Market I and Market II.[4] We can perhaps make this condition clearer if we reason through what might result if price discrimination in Market I were prohibited. Should Seller I be forced to sell to Buyer II at the $1,000 price, then the business of Buyer II would go to Seller II. Seller I is, therefore, legally permitted to sell to Buyer II in order to meet the "equally low price of competition."

Figure 6.6 Good Faith Discrimination

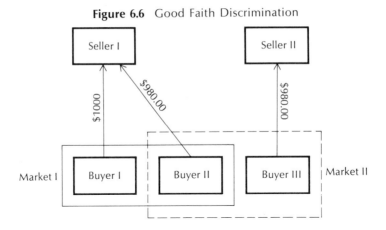

Interim changes in market conditions may produce a situation in which price discrimination is not unlawful.[5] This class of exemption normally occurs when there has been some passage of time between the two sales

---

[3] The ease with which this defense may be implemented may be decreasing. See, for example, Robert A. Lynn, "Is the Cost Defense Workable?" *Journal of Marketing*, January 1965, pp.37–42. See especially the discussion on p. 39 concerning the cost of the cost defense.

[4] The law is actually quite difficult to interpret in cases involving the "good-faith" defense. For a more complete discussion of some of these problems, See Lawrence X. Tarpey, "What About the Good-Faith Defense?" *Journal of Marketing*, July 1960, pp. 62–65. See also Robert C. Brooks, Jr., "Price Cutting and Monopoly Power," *Journal of Marketing*, July 1961, p. 48.

[5] This point is discussed briefly in Frederick D. Buggie, "Lawful Discrimination in Marketing," *Journal of Marketing*, April 1962, pages 1–8, particularly page 3 under the section head "timing."

transactions which produced the discriminatory condition. That is, the two transactions involving different prices (and, therefore, discriminatory prices) occur at different times. During the time between the two transactions some change in market conditions occurs and this interim change in conditions gives rise to the price differential. The later of the two prices may be either lower or higher than the earlier price. Changes in market conditions that might give rise to such price differentials as this include changes in demand occasioned by unexpected shortages of competing products, new forms or brands of competing products and similar events. This exemption recognizes the fundamental point that a particular price is right only for a particular environmental condition: A change in environmental conditions, when it occurs between two transactions that are otherwise discriminatory, may provide the rationale for legal price discrimination.

Finally, price discrimination may be perfectly legal because the transactions that embody the discrimination fall outside the jurisdiction of the existing law. Thus, for example, if the discriminatory action occurs in local commerce and in a state in which there is no statutory provision prohibiting price discrimination, the action may be lawful. As one authority suggests, "if a seller, such as a corporation, is engaged in purely local commerce within one state," prohibitive legislation may not exist.[6] We shall see momentarily that there are still other instances in which discriminatory conditions may be legal. For now, however we will turn to a brief consideration of price fixing—a practice related to, and often confused with, price discrimination.[7]

Price fixing and price discrimination contrasted

Earlier we noted that diverse types of pricing inequities are often confused with price discrimination. We saw that prices that are felt to be too high, for example, are sometimes described as discriminatory, although such an inequity does not involve the salient characteristics of price discrimination. Another type of pricing practice, one that is often harmful to society and often confused with price discrimination, is identified by the term *price fixing*. The essence of a price fixing agreement is conspiracy;

---

[6] See Kintner, *An Antitrust Primer,* p. 61.

[7] Price fixing is also occasionally confused with the practice of "administered pricing." This latter practice refers to those circumstances in which pricing is done by executive decision—those instances, in other words, in which the market does not provide a pricing guide. For a further discussion of this point of confusion, see P. D. Converse and others, *Elements of Marketing,* Seventh Edition, Englewood Cliffs, N.J.: Prentice-Hall, Inc., 1965, p. 170. Note that these authors prefer the term "judgment pricing" rather than "administered pricing," but the concept is the same. See also D. M. Phelps and J. H. Westing, *Marketing Management,* Third Edition, Homewood, Ill.: Richard D. Irwin, Inc., 1968, pp. 342–344. Note especially the authors' critical evaluation of the word "administered" and their historical perspective on the term.

that is, several business enterprises act collectively to determine selling prices. There are two basic types of price fixing: horizontal and vertical. When several competing sellers operating at the same stage or stages of distribution determine selling prices collectively, *horizontal* price fixing is involved. When several sellers doing business at different and subsequent stages of distribution determine selling prices collectively, *vertical* price fixing is practiced. Note the important difference between price fixing and price discrimination. In price fixing several sellers set prices collectively at a level that is presumably agreeable to them. The crux of price discrimination is that competing buyers are charged different prices for goods or services of the same quantity and quality. But the distinction between horizontal price fixing and vertical price fixing may not be clear. Consider the familiar components of distribution depicted in Figure 6.7.

Should Manufacturers B, C and D agree among themselves to sell at a particular price to (say) Wholesalers G and H, the actionable harm would be a horizontal price fixing conspiracy. Should Manufacturer A, Wholesaler F, and Retailer J agree regarding the prices at which particular products are to be resold, then the conspiracy would be one involving vertical price fixing. We have observed earlier that, in some instances, the law permits vertical price fixing agreements. Indeed, the use by a manufacturer or brand owner of the legal prerogatives provided under the Miller-Tydings Act, the McGuire-Keogh Act and the various state-level fair trade laws is clearly akin to a vertical price fixing arrangement. A significant difference between the two concepts may be that the resale price maintenance contract is unilaterally determined (by the manufacturer?) and that a price fixing arrangement is collectively determined by the several sellers implicated. At any rate, the resale price maintenance movement did make particular types of vertical pricing agreements legal.[8]

The harmful effect of a horizontal price fixing agreement should be apparent. Such an agreement, in effect, eliminates price as a form of competition. Indeed, horizontal price fixing is one of the few competitive actions that is illegal per se: There need not be a demonstrated harmful effect from such action. A former general counsel to the Federal Trade Commission contends that:

The government enforcement agencies have always regarded price fixing as the most serious of the various antitrust violations. The vast majority of criminal convictions for violations of the antitrust laws have been upon charges of price fixing.[9]

One of the most widely publicized antitrust cases in recent decades was the Electrical Conspiracy of 1961. In this celebrated case of price fixing,

[8] It is also true that the state-level unfair trade practices acts prevent the completely free use of price as a competitive weapon. Such laws, however, provide a lower price floor than the fair trade laws and, therefore, interfere less with the pricing mechanism.
[9] Kintner, *op. cit.*, p. 31.

the object was to fix prices (sealed bids in this instance) so that the contracts were rotated "on a fixed percentage basis among four participating companies. GE got 45 percent, Westinghouse 35 percent, Allis-Chalmers 10 percent and Federal Pacific 10 percent".[10] This case had more than all of the usual fictional embellishments. The meetings of the conspirators were conducted in a classically sinister way; meetings were coded as "choir practice"; and the companies had coded numbers GE 1, Westinghouse 2, Allis-Chalmers 3, and Federal Pacific 7: These numbers were used when exchanging bid information. In this instance, seven executives received jail sentences, twenty-three others were placed on probation and $2 million in fines were levied.

Figure 6.7 Horizontal Price Fixing

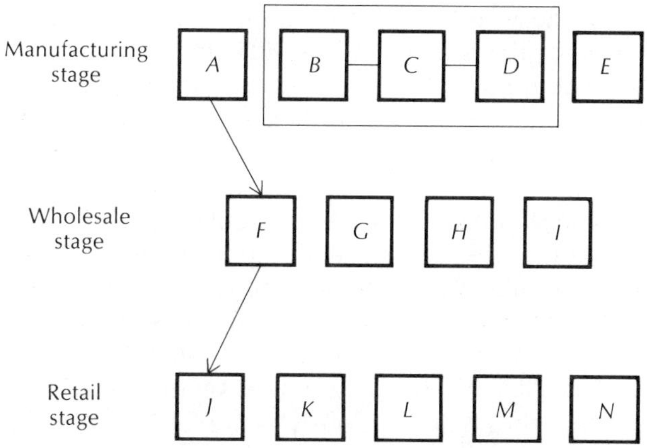

It is of interest here to note that the Justice Department need not have explicit evidence that a pricing conspiracy exists—it may bring action on the basis of the doctrine of *conscious parallel action*.[11] This legal doctrine permits the use of inferential evidence that horizontal agreement exists; thus, for example, a simple contract rotation pattern may suggest conscious parallelism.[12] If the rotational pattern is apparently related to firm size, the chance is greater that a type of conscious parallelism may be inferred. This kind of guilt by inference may identify a tacit price fixing agreement

[10] Richard Austin Smith, "The Incredible Electrical Conspiracy," in John A. Larson, editor, *The Regulated Businessman: Readings from Fortune*, New York: Holt, Rinehart and Winston, Inc., 1966, p. 116.

[11] See Marshall C. Howard, *Legal Aspects of Marketing*, New York: McGraw-Hill Book Co., 1964, p. 34.

[12] Conscious parallelism is much more easily defined as a concept than identified as an actual practice. As one student asserts, "Conscious parallelism is elusive for two reasons: (1) no lawyer is exactly certain what it is; (2) lawyers seem to have a great deal of difficulty distinguishing it from cut throat competition." See this tongue-in-check view continued in John Q. Lawyer, "How to Conspire to Fix Prices," *Harvard Business Review*, March-April 1963, pp. 95–103.

in which there is no formal spoken agreement, but rather an unspoken meeting of the minds not to disturb the status quo.

The regulation of harmful pricing practices

Price discrimination, in particular instances, may have a deleterious effect upon competition. We have identified some of the more important instances in which this may occur. Price fixing is likewise harmful—indeed we have seen that it has traditionally been viewed as the most serious of all the offenses regulated by our antitrust laws. Our purpose in this section is to examine existing legislative efforts that attempt to restrain illegal price discrimination and price fixing. Our task here is simpler than in previous chapters; indeed, we have only three relevant federal laws to consider. (Because of the great variation in the way the various states attempt to restrain pricing practices we will identify no particular legislation at that level.) The three federal statutes are (a) the Sherman Act, (b) the Clayton Act and (c) the Robinson-Patman Amendment to the Clayton Act. Our task is even further simplified because we will not have to dwell long on either the Sherman Act or the Clayton Act.

Section 1 of the Sherman Act makes particular types of price fixing illegal. We should note that there are several important exemptions to this legal provision. We have already mentioned the vertical price fixing exemption, permitted by both federal and state laws, but there are other groups which have the right to "bargain collectively in their best interests," although these groups are "fixing" the price either of their services or the price of the goods that they sell. Obviously some labor "collectively" fixes its prices; but less obviously, the Capper-Volstead Act permits producers of agricultural commodities to determine prices collectively, and the Webb-Pomerene Act permits businesses engaged in an import-export enterprise a degree of exemption from the Sherman Act.

For most businesses in the United States, however, price fixing, especially of the horizontal type, is illegal.[13] The general purpose of the Sherman Act is to thwart actions that represent conspiracy to restrain trade. And, as one author notes, such conspiracy "has been detected in the meeting of minds through informal agreement and through mutual adherence to pricing formulas, as well as in the more overt types of agreement." Circumstantial evidence, such as parallel price movements, may be sufficient proof of conspiracy under today's interpretation of the Sherman Act.[14]

In the preceding chapter, we noted that one of the provisions of the Clayton Act of 1914 attempted to restrain price discrimination. We can

[13] See the excellent article, Robert H. Bork, "The Rule of Reason and the Per Se Concept: Price Fixing and Market Division," Yale Law Review, 1965, p. 775.
[14] See Corwin D. Edwards, "The Influence of Government on Decision Making in Marketing," in J. Howard Westing and Gerald Albaum, Modern Marketing Thought: An Environmental Approach to Marketing, New York: Crowell-Collier and Macmillan, 1964, pp. 88–96.

now pick that story up and see why it was necessary to amend the original (Clayton Act) legislative effort at regulating price discrimination. The primary weakness in the Clayton Act as an effective deterrent to price discrimination lay in the fact that price differences charged to competing buyers were justifiable when the quantities supplied were different. It was permissible, in other words, to charge higher unit prices to a small buyer than to a large buyer because the economies associated with large scale transactions were assumed to be operative. This characteristic of the Clayton Act simply encouraged what was already a tendency: the larger buyer got a lower unit price than the smaller buyer. Note that the actual magnitude of such economies of larger scale purchases was often not known—that is, how much less one could charge a larger buyer than a smaller buyer was not specified in the Act. This flaw in the Clayton Act led to the passage in 1936 of the Robinson-Patman Amendment.

The Robinson-Patman Amendment dealt more specifically with the problem of price discrimination than the Clayton Act had. There are, in fact five important points about this Amendment we will do well to remember:

1 The Robinson-Patman Amendment specified that such differences in price as may be charged to competing buyers (grade and quantity the same) should not exceed actual differences in the cost of doing business with such buyers. Now, under this Amendment, larger buyers could lawfully be charged lower prices than competing and smaller buyers, but the price differential could not exceed the actual savings associated with the larger order.[15]

2 The Robinson-Patman Amendment added the *quantity limits provision,* which set an upper limit on the price concessions that larger buyers could receive. It provided that the Federal Trade Commission could set discount limits in those cases where only a very few buyers could qualify for the greatest quantity discounts.[16]

3 The Robinson-Patman Amendment forbade the giving of brokerage allowances except to independent brokerages; this provision was necessary to prevent conspiratorial discrimination of the kind we identified earlier.[17]

[15] Contrast this state of affairs with that under Clayton. One careful discussion of this difference may be seen in Robert A. Lynn, *Price Policies and Marketing Management,* Homewood, Ill.: Richard D. Irwin, Inc., 1967, pp. 252–253. Lynn argues that under Clayon, "any discount, however large, was legal if it was accompanied by the sale of a larger quantity, however small the quantity difference might be."

[16] See Frederick D. Buggie, "Lawful Discrimination in Marketing," *Journal of Marketing,* April 1962, pp. 4–5.

[17] This provision was prompted by the relationship that existed between ACCO and the Great Atlantic and Pacific Tea Company. The significant portions of this issue are discussed in Kenneth R. Davis, *Marketing Management,* New York: The Ronald Press Company, 1961, pp. 731–738. Note especially the discussion of ACCO, the Atlantic Commission Company, and its relationship to the Robinson-Patman Amendment on p. 733.

4 The Robinson-Patman Act specified that promotional allowances were illegal unless offered and given to all competing buyers on "proportionately equal terms." These promotional allowances are, in particular instances, an example of indirect price discrimination. Thus, if one buyer was given promotional assistance in the form of services but another (competing) buyer was not, the discrimination would be indirect. Since promotional discounts are sometimes given as a reduction in price, this provision also made it unlawful for such discounts to be given on anything but proportionately equal terms.

What are "proportionately equal terms"? Consider Figure 6.8 as a hypothetical example:

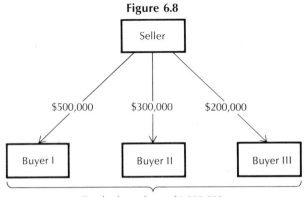

Figure 6.8

The seller in Figure 6.8 sells only to three buyers. If his total sales volume is $1,000,000, and he realizes that volume 50 percent from Buyer I, 30 percent from Buyer II and 20 percent from Buyer III, then he would be required to allocate any promotional allowances among these three buyers on a 50–30–20 percent basis. Thus, if our seller allowed a total of $20,000 for promotional purposes through his three customers, Buyer I should get $10,000, Buyer II $6,000 and Buyer III $4,000.

5 The Robinson-Patman Amendment provided that persons convicted of violating the provisions of the Act may be fined not more than $5,000 and may be imprisoned for a period of time not to exceed one year.[18]

SUMMARY

Price discrimination occurs when competing buyers are charged different prices for goods or services of like grade and quantity. Price discrimination is the term used to designate a particular kind of pricing inequity. Prices that are too low or too high do not necessarily mean that discrimination exists, although some form of price inequity clearly does exist.

---

[18] See Gilman G. Udell, "Antitrust Laws with Amendments," in Westing and Albaum, *op. cit.,* pp. 96–104. This article includes extracts from the major antitrust laws.

More specifically, there are five types of price discrimination that we should recognize. First-line price discrimination involves injury at the manufacturer level of distribution; second-line discrimination involves injury at the wholesale level; third-line discrimination is the case where the injury is felt at the retail level; conspiratorial discrimination occurs when a buyer and a broker conspire to effect a rebate to the buyer. These four types of price discrimination are direct. Indirect price discrimination occurs when services are provided to competing buyers in a discriminatory manner.

Price discrimination is not illegal per se. Indeed, there are five instances in which price discrimination may be entirely legal: (a) when there has been no harm to competition, (b) when cost differences justify price differences, (c) when different prices are charged to meet the equally low price of competition, (d) when interim market conditions have changed and (e) when the commerce requirement is not met. Price fixing is not the same thing as price discrimination. Price fixing of the horizontal type is illegal per se.

The important laws that regulate price discrimination are the Sherman Act, the Clayton Act and the Robinson-Patman Amendment to Clayton. The Robinson-Patman Amendment deals specifically with: (a) the cost justification for different prices to competing buyers, (b) the quantity limits provision, (c) conspiratorial discrimination, (d) promotional allowances, and (e) fines and imprisonment for pricing in a discriminatory manner.

REVIEW QUESTIONS

1 Carefully define and indicate the relevance of each of the following concepts to the study of marketing:
   a. Price discrimination
   b. Illegal price discrimination
   c. Third-line price discrimination
   d. Conspiratorial discrimination
   e. The doctrine of conscious action
   f. The quantity limits provision
2 Distinguish carefully between each element in the following pairs of terms:
   a. A discriminatory price and an inequitable but nondiscriminatory price
   b. Direct price discrimination and indirect price discrimination
   c. First-line price discrimination and second-line price discrimination
   d. Price fixing and price discrimination
   e. Horizontal price fixing and vertical price fixing
3 Specifically, under what circumstances can a seller charge competing buyers different prices for goods of like grade and quantity without such discrimination being illegal?
4 Explain the meaning of the phrase "proportionately equal terms" as it is used in connection with the competitive use of promotional allowances.
5 Why is it necessary to exclude from the definition of illegal discrimination all transactions in which final consumers are the buyers?

6 What would be the logical result of a total abandonment of efforts to regulate discriminatory activities in pricing? Why?

7 What specific forms of price discrimination can you identify that are not explicitly covered under the provisions of the Robinson-Patman Amendment to Clayton?

8 Would there be any advantage to permitting the small firms within an industry to act collusively? That is, might it make economic sense to permit relatively small firms to join forces in terms of competitive actions? Why?

SUGGESTED SUPPLEMENTARY READINGS IN THE LEGAL ENVIRONMENT OF MARKETING

Blumner, Sidney M., and D. L. Hefner, *Readings in the Regulation of Business* Scranton, Pa.: International Textbook Company, 1968.

Bock, Betty, *Mergers and Markets: An Economic Analysis of the First Fifteen Years Under the Merger Act of 1950*, New York: National Industrial Conference Board, 1965.

_____, *Mergers and Markets: An Economic Analysis of the 1964 Supreme Court Merger Decisions*, New York: National Industrial Conference Board, 1965.

Cook, Paul W., Jr., *Cases in Antitrust Policy*, New York: Holt, Rinehart and Winston, Inc., 1964.

Grether, E. T., *Marketing and Public Policy*, Englewood Cliffs, N.J.: Prentice-Hall, Inc., 1966.

Houser, Theodore V., *Big Business and Human Values*, New York: McGraw-Hill Book Co., 1957.

Howard, Marshall C., *Legal Aspects of Marketing*, New York: McGraw-Hill Book Co., 1964.

King, Robert L., editor, *Conferences, '55/'65*, Chicago: American Marketing Association, 1966 (especially Chap. I, Pt. 4).

Kintner, Earl W., *An Antitrust Primer: A Guide to Antitrust and Trade Regulation Laws for Businessmen*, New York: Crowell-Collier and Macmillan, 1964.

Larson, John A., editor, *The Regulated Businessman: Readings from Fortune*, New York: Holt, Rinehart and Winston, Inc., 1966.

_____, editor, *The Responsible Businessman: Readings from Fortune*, New York: Holt, Rinehart and Winston, Inc., 1966.

Preston, Lee E., *Social Issues in Marketing*, Glenview, Ill.: Scott, Foresman and Company, 1968.

Singer, E., *Antitrust Economics: Selected Legal Cases and Economic Models*, Englewood Cliffs, N.J.: Prentice-Hall, Inc., 1968.

Part III

MARKETS AND
MARKET BEHAVIOR

Two important preliminary issues have now been examined. In Part I we identified the nature of marketing from several perspectives: We examined, from a critical point of view, the status of the human activity we call marketing and, in the interest of hearing both sides of the story, we identified the fundamental factors that are the economic rationale for the particular kind of specialization and division of labor that is marketing. In Part II we identified three types of marketing activity that demand an important degree of social responsibility of the practitioner. Our concern was with deceptive practices, business expansion and discrimination; we were concerned in particular with the potentially harmful effects of particular forms of these activities. As a necessary part of that concern, we identified the battery of legislative efforts that we summarize in the term antitrust law and explored, in a preliminary way, the relationship of these laws to marketing practices.

Our task in Part III is to establish the special importance of the market as a focal point for both a responsible and a responsive market system. The "market"—that group of particular customers being served—is the highest priority consideration for a socially responsible business entity. More specifically, Part III comprises four chapters; each is concerned with a particular aspect of market behavior. Chapter 7 identifies the basic concept of the consumption pattern: several types of consumption patterns of special interest to the market oriented enterprise are examined. Chapter 8 is concerned with the identification of the causes that underlie variations in consumption patterns; it is devoted to an examination of various theories of consumer behavior. Chapter 9 emphasizes the notion of market appraisal as a means of measuring business opportunity; it considers some important means of estimating market opportunity. Chapter 10 considers the research techniques employed in the process of assessing business opportunity and appraising market strength.

Chapter 7

THE NATURE OF CONSUMPTION PATTERNS

Our principal concern in the present chapter is to identify and develop the basic concept of *consumption patterns.* By this term, we will mean any of several observable features or characteristics of consumer behavior. More specifically, these observable features of consumer behavior include: (a) patterns of consumer income allocation, (b) patterns of brand loyalty or disloyalty and (c) the time-of-adoption pattern of goods and services. Note that consumption patterns thus describe *how* consumers act: how they allocate income among alternatives; how loyal they are to various brands; and how they react to new goods or services. The consumption pattern is an overt act. Consumption patterns are measurable as an occurrence of some kind. A consumption pattern is, moreover, a symptom of the attitudes, values, beliefs and motives of a consumer or group of consumers; it is a sympton as distinct from a cause of consumer behavior. In the present chapter we focus on the nature of consumption patterns—the how. In the following two chapters we will explore the theories and factors that underlie distinctive consumption patterns—the why.

In order to avoid a possible ambiguity, we need to clarify one special detail. Exactly what do we mean by "consumer behavior"? This phrase embodies at least two disconcerting ambiguities. First, when we say "consumer" do we mean the actual consumer or do we mean the buyer?[1] It should be clear that buyers are not always consumers and that consumers are not always buyers. We shall mean by the term *consumer behavior* the actions of *both buying and using* useful goods or services.[2] Second,

---

[1] See Wroe Alderson, *Dynamic Marketing Behavior,* Homewood, Ill.: Richard D. Irwin, Inc., 1965, pp. 144–145, for a discussion of this ambiguity. An earlier perspective on this distinction can be seen in Wroe Alderson, *Marketing Behavior and Executive Action,* Homewood, Ill.: Richard D. Irwin, Inc., 1957, pp. 163–164.

[2] One widely respected scholar in the academic field of marketing uses the term "buyer behavior" almost exclusively. We actually know substantially more about buyer behavior than we do about consumption behavior. See, for example, John A. Howard, *Marketing Theory,* Boston: Allyn and Bacon, Inc., 1965, Chapter 4. Precedent for the broader use of the term can be seen in James E. Engel and others, *Consumer Behavior,* New York: Holt, Rinehart and Winston, Inc., 1968, p. 5.

exactly what kinds of consumers do we include in the phrase "consumer behavior"? We recognize that both final consumers and intermediate consumers are important to the efficient operation of our market system. We will mean by "consumers" *every person who acts in the capacity of a consumer, whether they consume in their own behalf (final consumer) or consume as a necessary part of their employment in institutions or industry (intermediate consumers).*[3] Thus, we will include the behavioral patterns of individuals buying or consuming in their own interests and institutional/industrial buyers acting in the interests of their employers. We shall see that the fundamental character of the consumption patterns that we will examine are revelant in both these contexts.

But before we turn to a more careful consideration of consumption patterns, we need to answer a very important and related question; namely, why should we have an interest in consumption patterns? Our answer is emphatic: The actions of consumers are the most important events business enterprise can study. "Consumer behavior is the principal a *priori* of business."[4] The efficiency with which a free market system of enterprise operates is, in the last analysis, dependent upon the extent of consumer understanding possessed by the business community. A business community that is ignorant of the nuances of consumer preferences cannot possibly fulfill its obligations in a meaningful and responsive manner. A business community that is carefully attuned to the subtleties of consumer preferences and acts responsibly to meet those preferences cannot fail to fulfill its social obligations. It is essentially for this reason that consumption patterns are an important early focus of attention in the study of marketing.

Income allocation as a consumption pattern

A pattern of consumer income allocation is a complex and revealing summary of many economic events. An income allocation pattern is a summary of the manner in which a particular consumer, or consuming unit (such as a household), allocates its expenditures for all the goods and services that are acquired for some specified period of time. Such a summary is complex because it may embody many hundreds of different classes of goods and services; it is revealing because it is a spending record that can indicate the attitudes and values of those whose actions it summarizes. Consider the following spider-web configuration.[5]

---

[3] The word "consumer" as used here is admittedly awkward. It is, however, most difficult to choose a good term for both buying and using. We will use the word with this recognized weakness.

[4] W. T. Tucker, *Foundations for a Theory of Consumer Behavior,* New York: Holt, Rinehart and Winston, Inc., 1967, p. 1.

[5] This disbursement summary is suggested in Warren J. Bilkey, "The Vector Hypothesis of Consumer Behavior," *Journal of Marketing,* October 1951, p. 139.

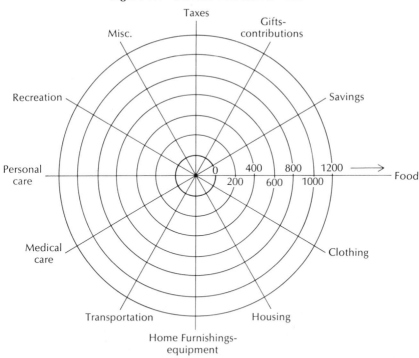

Figure 7.1 Income Allocation Pattern

Figure 7.1 suggests a means through which we can depict the complexities of a consumer or household income allocation pattern. This spider-web allocation pattern has several characteristics we should note. There are only 12 expenditure categories, admittedly a number that does not permit as careful scrutiny of particular classes of expenditures as we might prefer. It would be no great problem for us to increase this expenditure detail; we will however, in the interest of simplicity, develop our discussion around these 12 basic expenditure classes. Note also that there are dollar values represented on each vector. The values outside the innermost circle are positive, those inside this circle are negative. The reason for this algebraic arrangement will be evident momentarily. If we now represent some hypothetical data on this web-like apparatus, we will be able to better understand the value of understanding income allocation consumption patterns. Toward this end, observe Figure 7.2.

Figure 7.2 summarizes the income allocation pattern for two hypothetical persons, each earning about $6500 per year. Each of these persons spends about $1800 each year on food; each pays taxes of about $1200. But observe that the similarity ends there. The expenditure pattern depicted for B is clearly an embodiment of different values and attitudes than those suggested by the A pattern. The B pattern is, relatively speaking, *present oriented*; expenditures for recreation and transportation are an extremely important part of the economic dimensions of this person's life. The A pattern, on the other hand, embodies a degree of *future orientation*. Note the savings level for A; note also the substantially greater expenditure for housing and medical care. Which of these two persons is more likely to rent rather than buy his home?[6]

Figure 7.2 Allocation Patterns—Two Consumers

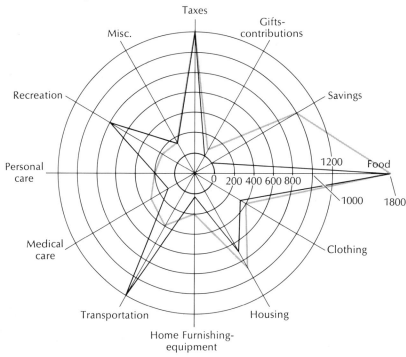

It should be emphasized that no one of these two patterns is better than the other; there is no intended judgment of that type at all. Our essential point is that different values and attitudes are, to a degree, visible in consumer income allocation patterns and that these patterns may therefore be helpful in developing an appreciation and understanding of markets. Such an understanding is fundamental to the study of marketing.

A consumption pattern may be distinctive in many ways not suggested by either of our examples here. Some patterns may embody greater emphasis on goods and services of status-symbolic quality. But, with some adjust-

[6] Although the intent here is not to examine these concepts rigorously, it should be noted that some types of durable goods purchases (homes, for example) are reasonable substitutes for savings. Thus, future orientation might reasonably be inferred from particular types of durable goods expenditures. This notion is developed in Thomas F. Juster, *Expectations Data and Short-Term Forecasting: An Analysis of the Saving-Income Ratio with Specific Reference for Consumer Durable Goods,* New York: Columbia University Press, 1955.

ment in terms of the classes of goods and services utilized, we could develop a particular web that would reflect that trait.

Figure 7.3 Allocation Patterns—Intermediate Buyers

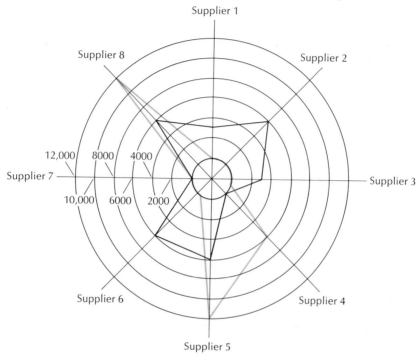

We have suggested earlier that the notion of an income allocation pattern is as applicable in the context of intermediate consumers as for final consumers. The preceding example, particularly the expenditure categories, are clearly relevant in the context of final consumers. How would one of these allocation patterns be modified if it were developed for an intermediate buyer? Observe Figure 7.3. Note that the dollar values on this web are larger than on our earlier example. Note also that we may be interested in which of several suppliers our intermediate buyers do business with, as well as in what types of supplies are purchased.

The web in Figure 7.3 has eight suppliers indicated. Although it may seem strange at first, a person concerned with intermediate markets may be very much concerned with the type of allocation patterns that are reflected in Figure 7.3. We have, as before, depicted allocation patterns of two different and hypothetical intermediate buyers. These allocation patterns are, as before, reflective of the different attitudes and values of these buyers. Both these buyers are confronted by similar supply conditions, each has a choice of eight different suppliers; but the expenditure patterns for the two are fundamentally different. Each buyer is assumed to have a budget of $30,000. Buyer A displays a "concentrated" pattern—indeed all his requirements are purchased from only three suppliers. This buyer may be prompted by the lower unit costs of relatively large purchases; he may believe he gets preferred treatment with larger orders than with small orders. And there are many other motives that may underlie an allocation pattern such as A.

The B pattern involves purchases from six different suppliers. This allocation pattern may reflect a desire on the part of the Buyer B to maintain an active account with a large number of suppliers so that he does not develop excessive dependence upon any one. Such a pattern may have evolved from the past—it may not make particularly good sense *today*. Our point is, again, that this allocation pattern is potentially a fundamental reflection of buyer attitudes.

Consumption patterns, aspirational levels and the treadmill effect

There is another characteristic of the income allocation pattern that requires elaboration. One may get the incorrect impression that income allocation patterns such as those we have examined are static descriptions. If this were true, the task of classifying such patterns and relating them to particular types of consumers would, at its worst, be manageable. But such consumption patterns are not static. The task of a market specialist is inestimably complicated by the fact that such patterns are constantly changing; they reflect, instead, a kind of constant movement toward a moving goal. They embody the worst kind of analytical circumstance—a change within a change.

We have already briefly noted that consumption patterns represent the aspirations of the individuals and consuming groups whose actions they summarize. Inasmuch as the aspirations of each of us undergo modification with changes in age, income, geographical location and many other factors, the life process itself may alter the nature of these allocation patterns.

There is another type of change embodied in these consumption patterns—a change that is perhaps not so obvious. Changes in the level of individual consumption aspirations can combine with changes in technology to produce an economic treadmill effect. Consider, for example, Figure 7.4.

Four basic dimensions are summarized in Figure 7.4: (a) several levels of consumption aspirations, labeled Patterns I through IV in descending order of costliness; (b) two time periods, t and t+1; (c) Consumers X, Y and Z; and (d) changing technology. The direction of the aspirations of each of these consumers is indicated by an arrow. The several consumption patterns at the left (I through IV) are effective during time period t. The several consumption patterns at the right (I+ through IV) are effective during time period t+1.

Figure 7.4 The Treadmill Effect

Aspirational level	Time period t	Time period $t + 1$	Aspirational level
			Consumption pattern I + (most sophisticated)
Consumption pattern I (most sophisticated)		X	Consumption pattern I
Consumption pattern II	X ↗		Consumption pattern II
Consumption pattern III	Y →	Y, Z	Consumption pattern III
Consumption pattern IV (least sophisticated)	Z ↗		Consumption pattern IV (least sophisticated)

⟶ Changing technology ⟶

The information summarized in Figure 7.4 is read as follows. Consumer X aspires to the more elaborate Consumption Pattern I in t+1. Y aspires to consume in the same basic Pattern in t+1. Z aspires to achieve Consumption Pattern III in t+1. Note that the plans of our consumers are made in Period t for Period t+1. Thus, when X makes his plans, Consumption Pattern I is the highest attainable pattern—but when t+1 arrives, a new standard of consumption also arrives, namely Pattern I+. X has been upwardly mobile; he has gained in an absolute sense, but he is still confronted by a package of goods and services superior to those he possesses. And, alas, this new and elusive package was not even in existence when his original plans were drawn. This *treadmill effect* is made possible, in part, because a constantly changing technology produces a never-ending variety of new goods and services—goods and services that become incorporated, as it were, into a new consumption pattern.

This treadmill is at once a source of both frustration and incentive. And for us, now, it serves to emphasize the essentially double-dynamic nature of this allocation type of consumption pattern. It is "double dynamic" because both personal aspirations and available patterns of consumption change.

The study of consumer behavior necessarily includes an understanding of particular types of income allocation patterns, but it also includes an appreciation of the forces that work to effect change in these allocation patterns. As we shall see in the next chapter, explanations for both these aspects of consumer behavior are evolving. But two other types of consumption patterns remain for us to examine.

Brand loyalty as a consumption pattern

We noted at the beginning of this chapter that patterns of brand loyalty (or disloyalty) are particular types of consumption patterns in which we have an interest. In some instances, consumers appear to develop strong attachments to particular brands—they would "rather fight than switch." In other instances, consumers develop little brand loyalty or preference. Thus, an understanding of loyalty patterns and of why such patterns develop is an important aspect of understanding consumer behavior in general. But how do we measure the strength of loyalty that exists between consumers and particular brands? Consider the following summary of buying behavior.[7]

Figure 7.5 Brand Switching Matrix

	Period t + 1			
Period t	**Brand A**	**Brand B**	**Brand C**	**Brand D**
Brand A (1000)	600	200	100	100
Brand B (1000)	200	400	200	200
Brand D (1000)	200	300	200	300
Brand E (1000)	200	500	300	0

Figure 7.5 depicts a brand-switching matrix. Brand-switching is a behavioral action of consumers that is thought to be very closely related to brand loyalty patterns. The strength of brand loyalty is, presumably, inversely related to the frequency of brand switching. Strong loyalty patterns exist, in other words, where little brand switching occurs. The famous "walk-a-mile" claim of Camel cigarettes is clearly a suggestion of strong brand loyalty. Interest in the brand-switching phenomenon has grown in recent years, and much of the modern language of brand-switching analysis

[7] The literature on brand switching has grown rapidly. An excellent statement of the basic concepts involved in brand loyalty analysis may be seen in Benjamin Lipstein, "The Dynamics of Brand Loyalty and Brand Switching," in *Better Measurements of Advertising Effectiveness: The Challenge of the 1960's*, Proceedings of the Fifth Annual Conference of the Advertising Research Foundation, 1959, pp. 101–108; reprinted in Steuart H. Britt and Harper W. Boyd, Jr., *Marketing Management and Administrative Action*, New York: McGraw-Hill Book Co., 1963, pp. 276–289.

is an extension of the ideas of A. A. Markov.[8] For this reason, the analysis of brand-switching patterns is often identified as "Markov chain" analysis. The term "chain" refers to the sequential nature of the events considered in switching analysis. Thus, for example, the following chain, or sequences, of brand usage may illustrate the actions of different groups of consumers:

Chain 1   A A A A A B A A A A C . . . .
Chain 2   A B C D E A B D G E F G A C . . . .

Chain 1 reflects a basic loyalty to Brand A with an intermittent experimentation with other brands (B and C).[9] Chain 2 embodies no particular pattern of loyalty—indeed it seems almost a rotating usage pattern. But let us now return to our brand-switching matrix.

Data for two time periods are represented in Figure 7.5. The information summarized vertically in the first column depicts a brand usage pattern in Time Period t. The next four columns refer to Period $t + 1$. Note that the sum of the values in any row of cells to the right of the first column equals 1000, the same number as is indicated parenthetically in the first column. This matrix is interpreted as follows: Of 1000 buyers of Brand A in Period t, 600 bought Brand A again in Period t+1, 200 switched to Brand B in t+1, 100 switched to Brand C in t+1, and 100 switched to Brand D in t+1. We might restate the information in that row as follows: Of 1000 buyers of Brand A, 60 percent remained loyal in the second purchase period and 40 percent switched to one of three competing brands. We may, in this manner, express the values in this matrix either as absolute numbers or as relative frequencies. Indeed the following matrix embodies exactly the same information as our original, although we have now converted the values to relative frequencies, or a kind of loose probability.[10]

[8] See, for example, George H. Styan and Harry Smith, Jr., "Markov Chains Applied to Marketing," *Journal of Marketing Research,* February 1964, pp. 50–55.

[9] If we wanted to find out more specifically, how strong this loyalty to Brand A is, we could do so experimentally. Tucker, for example, taped small amounts of change to competing brands increasing the amounts slowly to determine the point of consumer indifference between the two brands. He thus developed a monetary measure of brand loyalty. See W. T. Tucker, "The Development of Brand Loyalty," in the *Journal of Marketing Research,* August 1964, pp. 32–35. We should also note that some "loyalty" patterns may not be felt as such. That loyalty may appear where one buys on the basis of a conveniently located store—a store that may offer only one brand.

[10] This matrix is, strictly speaking, a first-order, stationary probability matrix. If we had brand usage information for three successive use periods, we could develop a refinement in the form of second-order probabilities. A classic experiment in which five use periods were involved is reported in Alfred A. Kuehn, "Consumer Brand Choice as a Learning Process," *Journal of Marketing Research,* December 1962, pp. 14–15. This matrix is "stationary" in the sense that the same proportions of buyers are assumed to switch (say) from Brand A to Brand B "in each successive pair of time periods I/II, II/III, III/IV, and so on for each proportion in the matrix." See A. S. C. Ehrenberg, "An Appraisal of Markov Brand Switching Models," *Journal of Marketing Research,* November 1965, pp. 348–349. Ehrenberg also notes (p. 361) that the values in the cells of a matrix such as ours are, strictly speaking, proportions that may be probabilities.

A Probabilistic Brand-Switching Matrix

	Period t + 1			
Period t	**Brand A**	**Brand B**	**Brand C**	**Brand D**
Brand A (1000)	.6	.2	.1	.1
Brand B (1000)	.2	.4	.2	.2
Brand C (1000)	.2	.3	.2	.3
Brand D (1000)	.2	.5	.3	-0-

This simple probability matrix tells us that the probability that an average person using Brand A in Period t will switch to Brand C in Period t+1 is .1, or one in ten. Similarly the probability that a buyer of Brand C in Period t will switch to Brand D in period t+1 is .3. Note particularly that the cells that relate the same brand, are, themselves, a measure of brand loyalty. Thus, the level of loyalty to Brand A is .6, the level of loyalty to Brand B is .4, and buyers of Brand D are perfectly *disloyal:* none of these latter buyers buy Brand D in Period t+1. In general, then, the main diagonal in a probabilistic brand-switching matrix provides us with a type of measure of brand loyalty.

Note too that the sum of the cells in any row excluding the main diagonal cell is the *cumulative switching-out rate* for a particular brand. The cumulative switching-out rate for Brand C is .8; the cumulative switching-out rate for Brand D is 1.0. It was, in part, an excessive cumulative switching-out rate that prompted the Ford Motor Company to introduce the now defunct Edsel. The following brief quotation reflects this thinking:

Let's look for a moment at the relatively common behavior of trading up one step from a low-price car to a medium-price car. Each year approximately one out of five trades of a low-price car buys up to the medium-price range. As Chevrolet traders buy-up—and have three GM medium price makes from which to choose—87 per cent stay with GM. As Plymouth traders buy up—and have two Chrysler products from which to choose—47 per cent stay with Chrysler Corporation. But as Ford traders buy-up—and have but one Ford Motor Company product available to them—only 26 per cent stay with Ford Motor Company. And in total volume, we can estimate quickly that Ford uptraders contribute almost as much to GM's medium price penetration as GM, through Chevrolet, is able to generate for itself. This has been one of the greatest philanthropies of modern business.[11]

[11] Henry G. Baker, "Sales and Marketing Planning of the Edsel," in Robert J. Holloway and Robert S. Hancock, editors, *The Environment of Marketing Behavior: Selections from the Literature,* New York: John Wiley & Sons, Inc., 1964, pp. 308–309.

Observe also in the matrix that the sum of the values in any column, again excluding the value in the main diagonal cell, is a *cumulative switching-in rate*. Note, for example, the relatively strong cumulative switching-in rate for Brand B. It is particularly noticeable, for example, that buyers of Brand D later switch into Brand B.

A closely related concept provides a measure of the *average staying time* of an average buyer of a particular brand. Such data can be inferred from a probabilistic brand-switching matrix like the one we have here. Consider, as an example, the average staying time for users of a brand with a loyalty rate of .5. This rate of loyalty suggests that, on the average, buyers of that brand would stay with it for two use periods. That is, it would require two use periods to achieve turnover of all original (first period) users. The average staying time, thus determined, for Brand B in our probability matrix is 2.5. In general, average staying time (AST) is defined as $1 \div 1 -$ loyalty rate, or what is the same thing, $1 \div$ cumulative switching-out rate. Thus, for example:

$$AST_A = \frac{1}{1 - \text{loyalty rate}} = \frac{1}{1 - .6} = 2.5$$

or

$$AST_A = \frac{1}{\text{cumulative switching-out rate}} = \frac{1}{.4} = 2.5$$

We need to introduce one further concept that is related to brand loyalty. This concept is the *directed graph* and is more in the nature of a different perspective than an altogether new concept for us. A directed graph is a means of representing the same information that we have seen embodied in a probabilistic switching matrix, though the directed graph focuses on an aspect of the data that was not readily apparent in that earlier form. Consider the directed graph in Figure 7.6.

Figure 7.6 The Directed Graph

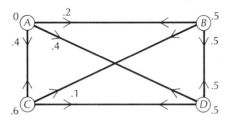

Four brands are represented in Figure 7.6, and the switching-out, switching-in rates are quite obvious. Note that for Brand C, for example, the loyalty rate is .6, the switching-out rate to D is .2, and the switching-out rate to B is .2. This type of graph not only highlights the significant rates in which we have had an interest, but it also indicates where consumer movements between brands are relatively large and where they are relatively light. Note, for example, that Brand D is an important beneficiary of dissatisfied previous users of Brand A. Brand A is, in fact, a curious case. It is a *transient* brand: no buyer stays with it beyond one period. Buyers who are new in the market may try Brand A, but they quickly abandon it. Moreover, the switching-in rate to A from Brands B, C and D is zero.

Brands B and D represent a particularly interesting switching arrangement. Note that B and D exchange buyers in equal proportions and that no buyers move from Brands B or D to Brands A or C. From the consumers' point of view, a *dual loyalty* exists.[12] The average staying time for both Brands B and D is 2. An average buyer uses Brand B for two periods, then uses Brand D for two periods, and so forth. We might also note that from the brand owners' (manufacturers') point of view it would be desirable to own both brands. If such were the case, the two brands would constitute what is known as a *closed set* of brands. Consumers would apparently satisfy their experimental proclivities by alternating between B and D, but they would be doing business with the same firm—perhaps not aware of the common origin of the brands.

Most of the basic concepts used in the analysis of brand loyalty have now been introduced. In brief recapitulation, we have identified:

1 The basic form of the brand-switching matrix.
2 The probabilistic form of the brand-switching matrix.
3 The basic brand loyalty rate.
4 Switching-in and switching-out rates (both simple and cumulative).
5 The average staying time of the brand.
6 The directed graph.
7 The transient brand concept.
8 The dual loyalty pattern.

Our particular concern here has been with some of the patterns of brand loyalty or disloyalty. Because of this basic concern, we have not attempted to consider why these brand loyalty patterns evolve. As mentioned earlier, we shall examine the reasons that underlie this particular form of consumer behavior in the next chapter.

The time-of-adoption pattern as a type of consumer behavior

There is one other consumption pattern in which we have a particular interest. This pattern relates to the time of adoption of new product concepts by consumers. An important aspect of understanding the working

---

[12] We shall have more to say about this in the next chapter, but this notion of dual loyalty is empirically based. See, for example, W. T. Tucker, "The Development of Brand Loyalty," *Journal of Marketing Research*, August 1964, pp. 32–35.

of our economic system relates to the process of integrating new products and services into American cultural and subcultural patterns.[13]

This process of acceptance of new products is more fundamental, and therefore more important, than might be casually apparent. The continued economic growth of an already affluent economic system depends importantly upon our ability to periodically renew the vigor of consumption expenditures. Without such a renewal, an economic stagnation can persist. The planning of product obsolescence is one means of accomplishing this renewal—a means with which we are all familiar. Planned obsolescence is, at very best, an imperfect solution to the problem of sustaining appropriately high levels of consumption. The great promise of a more complete understanding of the time-pattern of consumer adoption of new products and services is that we will, in the process, develop new insights into the working of our market system.

This time-of-adoption consumption pattern involves two basic components: innovation (in product or service) and the diffusion, or acceptance, of that innovation by consumers. This process of diffusion is a particular type of consumer behavior and is the principal focus of our interest here. We are, of course, concerned with the processes that give rise to innovation, but for now we will take them as given.[14] Initially, it will be useful for us to think of this process of diffusion as occurring coincidentally with the *life cycle* of each particular product or service innovation. Figure 7.7 suggests this relationship.

Figure 7.7 depicts the life cycle of a product innovation. The bold curved line depicts the *maturation process* for a new product concept from its initial appearance to its ultimate decline.[15] Note especially the several stages of this product life cycle. In the horizontal dimension, we have delineated six time zones or eras: Innovation, Early Growth, Market Growth, Market Maturity, Saturation and Decline. Virtually every product (not each individual brand) goes through a process of maturation approximated by this kind of sequence.[16] It follows that at any given time different classes of

[13] This point is the basic thrust of H. G. Barnett, *Innovation: The Basis of Cultural Change*, New York: McGraw-Hill Book Co., 1953.

[14] For a useful bibliography in the area of concepts of innovation, innovation as a process and its importance to business, see Thomas S. Robertson, "The Process of Innovation and the Diffusion of Innovation," *Journal of Marketing*, January 1967, pp. 14–15.

[15] This idea of a product life cycle is one that we will find very useful in later chapters. We will, at that time, amplify this preliminary statement of the concept.

[16] The exact number of stages or phases involved in this cycle varies depending upon the expected use of the life cycle concept. There are almost always at least four basic stages, however. These stages are introduction, growth, maturity and decline. Where more than four stages are employed, a split of one or more of these four basic classes is usually involved. The stages used in Figure 7.6 for example, involve such a split in the Introduction stage and another in the Decline stage. A good general reference on the product life-cycle concept is Arch Patton, "Top Management's Stake in the Product Life Cycle," in Britt and Boyd, *op. cit.*, pp. 254–264.

products may exist in different stages of their respective life cycles. Consider for example, the position of facial saunas on the cycle above; do they exist at a different relative position on the cycle than (say) soft drinks?

We will see in later chapters that because different classes of products are at different stages of maturation, correspondingly different marketing strategies will be developed for them. Our principal concern here, however, is with relating the behavior of consumers to this product life cycle notion.

The vertical dimension of Figure 7.7 relates to consumer behavior: it is a depiction of the process of consumer acceptance, or diffusion. This diffusion process is the aspect of consumer behavior that we have referred to as the time-of-adoption pattern.

Figure 7.7 Diffusion and the Product Life Cycle

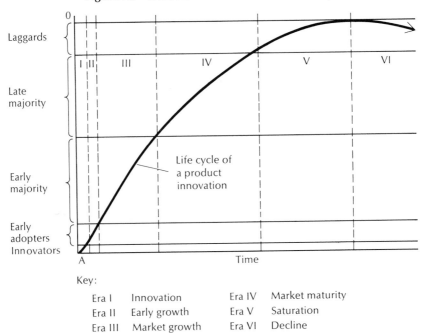

Key:

Era I	Innovation	Era IV	Market maturity
Era II	Early growth	Era V	Saturation
Era III	Market growth	Era VI	Decline

Note in Figure 7.7 that when classified by the time-of-adoption pattern there are five basic categories of consumers: innovators, early adopters, early majority, late majority and laggards.[17] These five categories have been the subject of much recent interest, particularly relating to the identification of distinguishing characteristics of the early adopters and the late adopters.

[17] These particular classes are those suggested by Everett M. Rogers in *Diffusion of Innovation,* New York: The Free Press, 1962, p. 162. Some recent research has focused on just two classes: innovators and all other consumers. See, for example, Charles W. King, "Communicating with the Innovator in the Fashion Adoption Process," in Ronald R. Gist, editor, *Management Perspectives in Retailing,* New York: John Wiley & Sons, Inc., 1967, pp. 133–136.

More particularly, there is interest in defining the exact nature of the innovator class—this class is thought by some to be pivotal in the adoption process. That is, these innovators are believed to wield influence disproportionate to their numbers; they are believed to act in a kind of "gatekeeper" capacity. For reasons that are not now fully understood, innovators:

> . . . take calculated risks on new products. They are respected for being successful, but ordinarily do not enjoy the highest prestige in the community. Because innovators adopt new ideas so much sooner than the average (consumer), they are sometimes ridiculed by their conservative neighbors.[18]

Although we are getting a bit ahead of ourselves, there are some similarities between the diffusion of new product/service concepts and the contagion models used in medicine. That is, after innovators have taken the first step, more and more adopters follow suit. To this basic point, it has been suggested that "for some products the social-pressure on non-adopters becomes overpowering. As more and more of one's neighbors obtain power mowers, for example, the owner of a hand mower feels increasingly isolated if he is without benefits of this new product."[19]

It is believed that an understanding of innovative consumers lies at the base of an improved understanding of the process of innovation diffusion generally. We shall see in the next chapter that early adopters differ from late adopters in other important ways, including age, education, gregariousness and other traits. But there are two important points concerning Figure 7.7 that need to be made explicit before we leave this combination product life cycle and consumer adoption curve.

First, it might seem that this curve of innovative diffusion is simply a lifetime sales curve for the innovation. This is not quite true. It is a *first-purchase* industry sales curve—that is, it excludes all repeat purchases of the product or service innovation. Thus, while an industry sales curve would normally include both first-time and repeat purchases for any particular consumer, this curve, because of our special interest in time-of-adoption, depicts only first-time purchases. The *initial* purchase of an innovative product or service necessarily occurs at the *time-of-adoption;* subsequent purchases necessarily occur after adoption.[20] The vertical line AO represents the total number of different buyers of the innovative

[18] *The Adoption of New Products: Process and Influence,* Ann Arbor, Mich.: The Foundation for Research on Human Behavior, 1959, p. 5.

[19] Frank M. Bass and Charles W. King, "The Theory of First Purchase of New Products," in Keith Cox and Ben M. Enis, editors, *A New Measure of Responsibility for Marketing,* 1968 June Conference Proceedings, American Marketing Association, pp. 263–264.

[20] Some writers identify pre-adoption actions that involve some trial of the product or idea on a small scale to determine its suitability. No argument is made against this notion—except that it is an unnecessary complication in a text such as this. The interested reader, however, is directed to Harper W. Boyd, Jr., and Sidney J. Levy, *Promotion: A Behavioral View,* Englewood Cliffs, N.J.: Prentice-Hall, Inc., 1967, pp. 98–99.

product or service but not the total number of units of the product or service sold.

Note also the symmetry of the classes of consumer-adopters depicted.[21] Those who lead in the adoption of new ideas (innovators + early adopters) constitute about the same percent as those who adopt after everyone else has. These laggards, or slow adopters, are not necessarily the economically underprivileged. They lag in adoption patterns for what may be much more complex sociopsychological reasons. Let it suffice at the moment to say that an improved understanding of these adopter categories is important to the continued success of our market system.

We should note also that time as depicted on the horizontal axis in Figure 7.7 is analytical time rather than clock time. Thus, the calendar time required for a particular product or service innovation to move completely through its life cycle is different from that required for some other innovations.[22] In some instances the new product or service may move quickly from introduction to maturity; in other instances the process may require much more time. We do not pretend to foretell the rate at which technology or consumer demand may render particular products or services obsolete; the demise of particular products or services ultimately depends upon both changing technology and waning consumer interest. This flexible characteristic of time, however, does not represent an insurmountable conceptual difficulty—we do it simply as an analytical convenience.

SUMMARY

Our purpose in the present chapter has been to identify the concept of a consumption pattern. We developed the discussion around three types of consumption patterns: (a) the income allocation pattern, (b) the brand loyalty (or disloyalty) pattern and (c) the time-of-adoption pattern. We defined income allocation patterns in terms of a web-like apparatus that permitted us to summarize the manner in which a consuming unit (individual or household or business) allocated its income to the various consumption alternatives that exist. We noted that these allocation patterns

[21] Rogers suggests that these categories are present in proportion reasonably close to a normal distribution. That is, the innovators comprise 2.5% of the general population, the early adopters 13.5%, early majority 34%, late majority 34% and laggards 16%. See Thomas S. Robertson, "The Process of Innovation and the Diffusion of Innovation," *Journal of Marketing*, January 1967, pp. 16–17.

[22] One study indicates, "Fifteen years elapsed between the introduction of hybrid seed corn and its adoption by almost 98 percent of the farmers. Other changes take longer. The adoption of new education practices by school systems took 50 years." See, "The Adoption Process: Foundation for Research on Human Behavior," in Britt and Boyd, *op. cit.*, p. 249. This article identifies several relatively obscure studies that bear on the adoption process. An interesting recent effort to identify the rate of innovation diffusion among food chains can be seen in Fred C. Allvine, "Diffusion of a Competitive Innovation," in Robert L. King, editor, *Marketing and the New Science of Planning*, 1968 Fall Conference Proceedings, American Marketing Association, pp. 341–351. Some useful insights are provided by the summary statement on pp. 350–351.

reflect to some extent the values, attitudes and preferences of the consuming unit whose actions they summarize. We also noted the double-dynamic nature of these allocation patterns. We observed that both the consumption aspirations of the consuming unit and the consumption alternatives confronting the consuming unit change. The problem of understanding consumer behavior is further complicated by this double-dynamic character of the allocation pattern.

Brand loyalty was identified as a second type of consumption pattern. We developed the brand-switching matrix as a basic means of focusing on this issue. Our principal task here was to introduce some of the analytical concepts that are a part of loyalty analysis. Toward this goal, we developed the ideas of switching-out rates, switching-in rates, average staying time, the directed graph, transient brands, dual loyalty and a closed set of brands.

Finally, we considered time-of-adoption consumption patterns. Our interest was in the process of diffusion of innovative ideas in products or services. To assist in our examination of this diffusion process, we introduced the notion of the product life cycle and the idea of innovative consumers. We noted that innovative consumers are thought to play a pivotal role in the innovation diffusion process. We purposely avoided a consideration of why consumption patterns are what they are. That subject comprises Chapters Eight and Nine.

REVIEW QUESTIONS

1 Carefully define and indicate the relevance of each of the following concepts to the study of marketing:
   a. Consumer behavior
   b. Income allocation patterns
   c. Present oriented consumption
   d. Future oriented consumption
   e. A concentrated purchase pattern
   f. A brand-switching matrix
   g. Probabilistic brand-switching matrix
   h. Average staying time for a brand user
   i. A directed graph
   j. Dual loyalty patterns
   k. Brand loyalty rate
   l. Innovation diffusion

2 Distinguish carefully between each element in the following pairs of terms:
   a. Aspiration levels *and* the treadmill effect
   b. Brand loyalty *and* brand switching
   c. The cumulative switching-out rate *and* the cumulative switching-in rate
   d. A transient brand *and* a closed set of brands
   e. The time-of-adoption pattern *and* the life cycle of a product innovation

3 What is a time-of-adoption consumption pattern? What major components are there in such a pattern?

4 What are the basic stages in the product innovation maturation process? What time-of-adoption classes correspond to each of these basic stages of product innovation maturation?

DISCUSSION QUESTIONS
5 How would the income allocation pattern for a student differ from that of a serviceman? Why? (Assume that both have an income of only $2,000.)
6 How would the income allocation pattern of a young intern earning $6,000 yearly compare with that of a retired couple with a similar income? Why?
7 Have you ever had your consumption plans interfered with by the treadmill effect depicted in Figure 7.4? Specifically, what products were involved?
8 What products do you seem to develop the greatest brand loyalty to? What types of products do you have little brand loyalty for?

Chapter 8

DETERMINANTS OF CONSUMER BEHAVIOR
—PART ONE

In the previous chapter, three basic types of consumption patterns were identified: (a) patterns of income allocation, (b) patterns of brand loyalty and (c) time-of-adoption patterns. Care was exercised in Chapter 7 not to dwell on matters relating to *why* different patterns of income allocation, various levels of brand loyalty, and distinctive time-of-adoption patterns evolve. Our concern in that chapter was primarily with the identification of the nature of these patterns; our purpose in the present chapter is to examine a growing body of theory that endeavors to explain *why* different people or different consuming units (such as households) adopt different patterns of consumption.

With one minor exception, we will develop our discussion around the same three basic patterns of consumption discussed in Chapter 7. More specifically, Chapters 8 and 9 are comprised of the following major sections: (a) a brief identification and discussion of the principal areas from which theories of consumer behavior are evolving, (b) an examination of some efforts to explain variations in consumer income allocation patterns, (c) a consideration of theories that endeavor to explain variations in patterns of brand loyalty and (d) an identification of some theoretical explanations of variations in consumer time-of-adoption patterns.

General approaches to understanding consumer behavior

The task of understanding consumer behavior is perhaps the most formidable of all the intellectual challenges in the study of marketing. Every human experience and some genetic traits can reasonably have a bearing on the actions of consumers. This fact alone suggests that the reasons underlying variations in consumer behavior are both numerous and complex. The task of isolating and identifying the interrelationships among the principal

determinants of consumer behavior is, at best, the work for several generations of students. At present, the study of variations in consumer behavior
is proceeding along four principal lines. These four approaches emphasize:
(a) the economic aspects of consumer behavior, (b) the social or sociological dimensions of consumer behavior, (c) the psychological aspects of
consumer behavior and (d) the social-psychological dimensions of consumer behavior.[1]

Because each of these four fields of study can have very broad and
general meaning, we need to indicate explicitly what we will include when
we refer to each one.

When we refer to "the economic aspects of consumer behavior," we
have in mind those aspects of consumer behavior that are influenced by
income or purchasing power. Thus, if a particular purchase was made
because the money required for the purchase was available, and for no
other reason, the behavior would be an economic phenomenon. Similarly,
if a person bought a particular car because of its low price or economy
of operation, the purchase was economically motivated.

When we refer to "social or sociological dimensions of consumer behavior," we have in mind consumer actions that are either related to demographic matters or are reference-group determined. Demography is the
study of populations—particularly the age and geographical density characteristics of populations. Demography is normally considered a subordinate
part of the broader discipline of sociology. It is for this reason that we
will consider consumer actions that are influenced or determined by age
or geography as a sociological dimension of consumer behavior. A second
type of social dimension in consumer behavior is suggested by the term

[1] This list may seem incomplete in a significant way because of the omission of cultural
anthropology as a fundamental source of theory relating to consumer behavior. The omission
is, however, intentional and is done for two reasons. First, cultural anthropology is concerned
with issues and questions that transcend the usual boundaries of the several social sciences;
in a sense, cultural anthropology is common to all social science. Second, cultural anthropology
utilizes, for the most part, the analytical tools and conceptual devices of related social sciences.
The field has not, to my knowledge, produced distinctive theoretical or explanatory apparatus
that can be focused sharply on a particular problem of human behavior. It seems only to
tell us, generally, that consumer behavior has some foundation in culture. The doubtful reader
is invited to see S. H. Britt, editor, Consumer Behavior and the Behavioral Sciences: Theories
and Applications, New York: John Wiley & Sons, Inc., 1966, pp. 57–72. See also Charles Winick,
"Anthropology's Contributions to Marketing," Journal of Marketing, July 1961, pp. 53–60. This
article indicates some of the ways in which the cultural anthropologist can be helpful in
the resolution of marketing problems but offers no conceptual framework for cultural analysis.
Another, and articulate, argument of the case for cultural anthropology may be seen in W.
T. Tucker, The Social Context of Economic Behavior, New York: Holt, Rinehart and Winston,
Inc., 1964, pp. 35–41. Again, the discussion is essentially devoid of significant analytical
concepts. A discussion of culture that begins to identify analytical notions of merit may
be seen in Gerald Zaltman, Marketing: Contributions from the Behavioral Sciences, New
York: Harcourt, Brace & World, Inc., 1965, Chapter 2.

reference group. A purchase that is made in order to stay abreast of one's neighbors, for example, has distinctive social overtones and is group influenced. If you feel the need for a car because your campus acquaintances have them, the pressure is distinctly of a social type. The family is normally an important reference group in buying behavior.

"Psychological aspects of consumer behavior" include those consumer actions that are influenced importantly either by the learning process or by the self-concept. Learning is a phenomenon that necessarily involves the psyche; and it is believed that some types of consumer behavior are learned processes. We therefore have an interest in the psychological process of learning as it bears on consumer behavior. The relationship between mass communications, learning and consumer behavior is apparent. In addition, a consumer may buy a product because, among other things, he feels that the product enhances his self-image. Similarly, a consumer may decide not to buy a product or not to shop at a particular store if he feels that these actions are not consistent with his own perceptions of himself. The person who buys a Plymouth Roadrunner, for example, because it displays for him his own concept of his personality is acting or reacting to what is called *self-concept.*[2] Such a purchase motivation has important psychological dimensions.

Finally, when reference is made to the "social-psychological aspects of consumer behavior" we will have in mind those aspects of consumer behavior that are determined importantly by *influential personages.*[3] Though we will have much more to say about this later, we should note now that the distinctive character of those kinds of consumer actions that are influenced by influential personages is that an individual influences masses or groups; the relationship therefore has both social and psychological aspects. This circumstance differs from the earlier reference group determined behavior inasmuch as the latter involves a flow of influence from the group to the individual. If you and many other persons bought a set of aluminum-shaft golf clubs because Arnie Palmer or some other influential personage suggested it was wise to do so, the purchase has a social-psychological character. Concern with the role of *influentials* in the analysis of consumer behavior is essentially a concern with the interrelationships between persons in some group and particularly with the flow of influence from some persons to others. The measurement of these

[2] See S. H. Britt, *op. cit.,* pp. 186–195.

[3] Whether this facet of consumer behavior should "belong" to social psychology, sociometry or, indeed, "psychological sociology" is not always clear. Steuart Henderson Britt, would include studies of leadership or influentiality as a part of psychological sociology. See "Social Psychologists of Psychological Sociologist—Which?" *The Journal of Abnormal and Social Psychology,* October-December 1937, pp. 314–318. For a discussion of the ambiguities of similar terms used to describe subordinate fields in the social sciences, see S. H. Britt, *op. cit.,* pp. 17–19.

interrelationships is the task of a subscience called sociometry. Literally, sociometry means the measurement of social interaction.[4]

A word of warning is in order. We have discussed, very briefly, each of four different approaches to understanding variations in consumer behavior as though each approach were insular. That is, we have perhaps left the reader with the incorrect impression that a particular consumer action is often either economic or social or psychological or social-psychological. It should be emphasized that any particular consumer action probably embodies, perhaps simultaneously, all of these considerations. It is simply a convenience in exposition to identify each of these dimensions of consumer behavior separately. It is, in fact, the realization that consumer behavior is often the simultaneous embodiment of all of these economic-social-psychological considerations that underlies our earlier statement that understanding the reasons for variations in consumer behavior is an immensely complex assignment. It is, moreover, our realization that a consumer action often depends upon both an ability to buy and a willingness to buy that prompts us to consider economic matters (ability to buy) as well as social-psychological matters (willingness to buy). It is in understanding the willingness of consumers to buy that we will find psychology, sociology and social psychology most helpful.

Consumer Behavior Determinants	Concept from the field of:
1. Income or purchasing power	Economics
2. Demographic traits	Sociology
3. Reference groups	
4. Learning process	Psychology
5. Self-concept	
6. Persuasive or influential personages	Social psychology

Before we turn to a more detailed examination of these ideas, it will be valuable for us to summarize what we have thus far suggested about consumer behavior. We have said that consumer behavior is determined to an important degree by the influence of six behavioral determinants. We have noted also that these six determinants represent concepts from

[4] There are two types of interpersonal relationships in which we will later have an interest. There are those that are (a) face-to-face and (b) separated by great distance (either spatial or temporal). These latter relationships usually involve public personages as the influential. Both these types of interpersonal relationships embody social-psychological characteristics. It is, to be quite accurate, the face-to-face circumstance that is the nucleus of the subscience of sociometry.

four fields of study. These observations may be summarized as follows: In the discussion that follows, each of these behavioral determinants is amplified and related to one of our three basic types of consumption patterns.

Determinants of income allocation patterns

Among the important determinants of the income allocation patterns of consumers and households are: (a) the absolute level of their incomes, (b) changes in their incomes and (c) the expected distribution of their incomes through time. Each of these influences on income allocation patterns is considered in the following discussion.

ABSOLUTE LEVELS OF CONSUMER INCOME

It is perhaps perfectly obvious that the level of income influences consumer expenditure patterns. But for all the obviousness of the statement, there are some subtleties in the relationship. There is also a great deal that is not well understood about income levels and expenditure patterns. Indeed, there are instances in which identical incomes produce basically different patterns of income allocation. The study of income levels and expenditure patterns has, however, produced some valuable concepts and some helpful insights into aggregate consumer behavior. Two income allocation patterns are particularly fundamental to the study of consumer income allocation patterns. These patterns are (a) the nondiscretionary pattern of allocation and (b) the discretionary pattern of allocation.

The nondiscretionary pattern of expenditures is characterized by an emphasis upon money outlays that are of three types: contractual, necessary and habitual.[5] Contractual expenditures are exemplified by mortgage payments, installment debt and life insurance premiums. Necessary expenditures are basically for food, clothing and medical expenses. Although the term "necessaries," or "necessities," is unfortunately ambiguous, it is in frequent usage to designate those expenditures that are life sustaining.[6] Habitual expenditures are those involving product categories that are frequently purchased and tend to have relatively low unit value. Examples of habitual outlays include cigarettes, beer and liquor. The nondiscretionary income allocation pattern is dominated by expenditures of these three types and occurs primarily among the lowest income levels. Indeed, we may formalize what we have suggested here by the statement of a formal principle: *the proportion of income spent for nondiscretionary goods and*

---

[5] This classification scheme is suggested in the classic work, George Katona, *The Powerful Consumer: Psychological Studies of the American Economy,* New York: McGraw-Hill Book Co., 1960, pp. 14–15.

[6] The courts hold, for example, that what is necessary is in part determined by what one is accustomed to. This legal interpretation suggests a subjective or judgmental kind of concept.

services decreases as income increases. If we now recall the spider-web income allocation pattern that was introduced in the previous chapter, we can modify that web-like pattern slightly and depict this general rule as follows.

Figure 8.1 Income Allocation Patterns

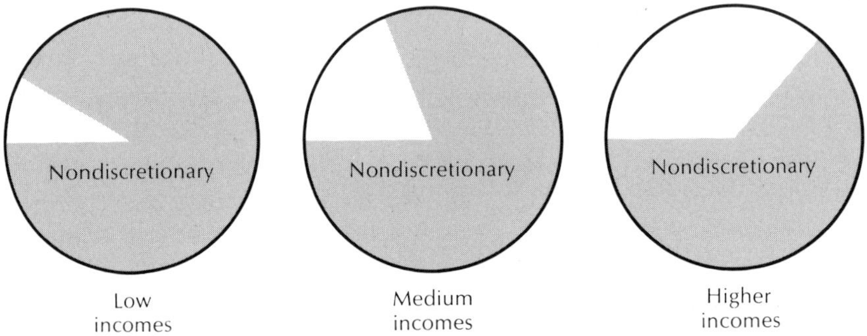

| Low | Medium | Higher |
| incomes | incomes | incomes |

The shaded portion of each of the three figures represents the proportion of consumer expenditures for nondiscretionary goods and services. The remainder of the area in each of the figures represents the proportion of discretionary expenditures.

By definition, *discretionary* expenditures are those that: (a) are not motivated by a compelling need, (b) are not generally governed by habit and (c) normally entail some deliberation prior to purchase.[7] But how is the concept of discretionary income (or supernumerary income) meaningful in marketing? The existence of adequate aggregate supernumerary income is virtually a requirement for some kinds of marketing enterprise. Stated in another way, many business firms depend upon these discretionary types of expenditures for their livelihoods. It is therefore not uncommon to encounter firms planning their growth around estimates of supernumerary income. To meet this need, several sources provide estimates of aggregate discretionary income or similar data. One authority estimates, for example, that in 1944 about 12 million families had supernumerary income (over $4000) and that in 1957 about 20 million families had some amount of supernumerary income (over $6000). A simple extension of these data indicates aggregate national supernumerary income in 1944 of about $84 billion; in 1957 the comparable figure would be $220 billion.[8] Let it suffice for now to note that an extremely important market—the market for discretionary goods and services—depends upon the absolute level of consumer incomes. But the notion of nondiscretionary and discretionary expenditures leaves a great deal of consumer behavior unex-

[7] See Katona, *op. cit.*, pp. 11–12.
[8] *Ibid.*, p. 12.

plained. We need to explore other aspects of the relationship between purchasing power and consumer allocation patterns.

CHANGES IN CONSUMER INCOME

Another idea that has analytical value is the notion that changes in the level of consumer income are related to changes in income allocation patterns. The history of our economy since 1940 has been one of virtually uninterrupted growth in real incomes. It has been observed that during that period some types of expenditures have come to occupy a relatively more important role in many household budgets. We have, conversely, seen some expenditure classes grow relatively less important. We have seen passenger rail travel decline. We have been told, by almost everyone, that leisure expenditures are booming. All this suggests the possibility of relating, in some more precise manner, changes in consumer incomes to changes in consumer expenditure patterns. The first such systematic attempt was made by an early student of consumer behavior named Ernst Engel.

Engel's early efforts to relate income changes to changes in expenditure patterns earned him, among other things, textbook immortality. The summary of Engel's findings is often referred to, charitably, as Engel's laws.[9] These laws, four in number, suggested that (a) as income increases the percentage spent for food declines, (b) as income increases the percentage spent for clothing remains approximately the same, (c) as income increases the percentage spent for household operations remains unchanged and (d) as income increases the percentage spent for all other goods and services increases. There are two specific points about these laws that we should note carefully.

First, note that the laws do not predict amounts spent for particular classes of goods: the "percentage spent" is the statistic that Engel highlighted. Thus, while the percentage spent for food may decline as incomes increase, the amount spent for food can (and does) increase with increasing incomes. It is a common misstatement of these laws to make the phrase "amount spent" interchangeable with "percentage spent." Second, not all of Engel's original laws are true today.[10] Recent evidence indicates that Engel's second law (the one dealing with clothing) is inaccurate. Expenditures for clothing tend to increase in percentage as incomes increase. In other words, clothing expenditures behave like his "all other goods and services" category.

[9] There is some indication that Engel may generally be given more credit for these laws than is due him. The evidence suggests that one Carrol D. Wright, a government statistician, may have played a more important role in the formulation of these laws than has been widely recognized. The curious reader is directed to the *Sixth Annual Report of the Massachusetts Bureau of Statistics of Labor*, 1875, p. 438.

[10] Though they may have been at the time his studies were conducted.

Even with this latter shortcoming, it is clear that Engel pointed the way to fruitful analysis. One can, alas only in a broad and general way, predict growth industries and industries with limited growth potential with Engel's original laws. But analysis of income change and consumer expenditure patterns would be substantially more useful if it related income changes to many, more specific, product classes. That is, we would be much better able to anticipate variations in consumer income allocation patterns if we had reliable rules like those of Engel, but rules which dealt with more specific groups of products and services. And indeed, such a refinement of Engel's laws exists. Engel's laws were the very early forerunner of what has been called a coefficient of income sensitivity.

These *coefficients of income sensitivity* relate a percentage change in consumer incomes to a percentage change in consumer expenditures for particular types of products or services. An example will help us define these coefficients. Suppose that a family having earnings of $10,000 in 1969 spent $500 for clothing. Suppose further that this same family earned $11,000 in 1970 and with that higher income spent $600 for clothing. What is the coefficient of income sensitivity for clothing? The coefficient is 2, determined as follows:[11]

$$\frac{\% \text{ change in dependent variable}}{\% \text{ change in independent variable}} = \frac{\% \text{ change clothing expenditures}}{\% \text{ change in income}}$$

$$= \frac{\dfrac{\$100}{\$500}}{\dfrac{1{,}000}{10{,}000}} = \frac{20\%}{10\%} = 2.$$

Note that these coefficients define changing income as the dependent (causal) variable and expenditures for some class of good or service as the dependent (caused) variable. Note also that these coefficients may have a positive value or a negative value. What conditions would be required to produce a negative coefficient of income sensitivity? If you say that an increase in income must produce an absolute decrease in expenditures for a particular type of product or service, you are correct. Thus, if the same family as in the illustration above spent $100 for personal railroad travel in 1969, but spent $50 for the same mode of travel in 1970, the coefficient would be calculated as follows:

$$\frac{\% \text{ change in rail travel expenditures}}{\% \text{ change in income}} = \frac{\dfrac{-\$50}{\$100}}{\dfrac{1{,}000}{10{,}000}} = \frac{-50\%}{10\%} = -5.$$

We have now said enough about this idea of a coefficient of income

[11] This calculation uses the last year's clothing expenditures and last year's income as the basis for calculating percentage change.

sensitivity to see that it could be a valuable device for predicting income allocation patterns if we knew (a) how income would change in the future and (b) exactly what these coefficients were for particular classes of goods and services. We are moving toward a fulfillment of both these requirements.

Table 8.1 Coefficients of Income Sensitivity for Selected Expenditures—Urban Families

Expenditure Category	Income Level (in dollars)						
	1513 to 2508	2508 to 3516	3516 to 4506	4506 to 5495	5495 to 6710	6710 to 8573	8573 to 11724
1. Food at Home	1.20	0.62	0.70	0.82	0.55	0.51	0.35
2. Food Away from Home	1.60	0.90	0.32	*	1.50	1.32	1.11
3. Tobacco	1.25	1.00	0.59	0.55	0.55	0.32	*
4. Alcoholic Beverages	1.08	1.82	1.05	1.40	1.23	0.90	0.86
5. Housing	0.53	0.67	0.56	0.54	0.47	0.51	0.70
6. Clothing	1.70	1.35	1.00	0.82	1.10	1.10	1.03
7. Personal Care	1.15	0.82	0.44	0.50	0.55	0.76	0.60
8. Medical Care	0.90	0.62	0.20	0.90	0.86	0.64	0.83
9. Recreation	1.60	0.78	1.15	0.55	1.64	1.05	1.19
10. Reading	0.73	2.08	0.70	0.55	1.08	0.64	0.83
11. Education	1.70	2.07	0.66	2.30	2.30	1.57	3.54
12. Transportation	1.90	2.75	1.50	0.80	0.82	0.95	0.86

*No change in level of expenditure.
Source: *Contrast in Spending by Urban Families,* United States Department of Labor, Bureau of Labor Statistics, Report No. 238-8, February 1965, p. 1409.

Economic forecasting techniques are now refined to the point that it is possible to anticipate changes in national income accounting aggregates on the basis of changes in "lead" variables. Lead variables change before, and therefore foretell, later change in these economic aggregates. The numerical value of these coefficients, for particular types of goods and services, is also known.[12] One recent study included 12 expenditure cate-

[12] Originally, the concept of the coefficient of income sensitivity was developed by a statistician for the United States Bureau of Labor Statistics. Some early coefficients may be seen in the September 1955 *Survey of Current Business.* More recently, Bureau of Labor Statistics data for urban families were utilized to develop such coefficients for different income levels. See, for example, Richard D. Millican, "A Re-examination of Engel's Laws Using BLS Data (1960-61)," *Journal of Marketing,* October 1967, pp. 18–21.

gories. Table 8.1 summarizes the coefficients developed in that study. The data in Table 8.1 are useful not only because they identify more specific expenditure categories, but also because they indicate differences in these coefficients of income sensitivity at different income levels. Observe, for example, the coefficients for educational expenditures for different income groups. Make sure that you can "read" the cell values in this table. For example, the value 1.20 in the first row, first column. That value indicates that a 1 percent increase in income among urban families reporting an income between $1513 and $2508 produced a 1.2 percent increase in expenditures for "food at home." Does this value (that is, the 1.2) confirm or deny Engel's law relating to food expenditures? Consider the value 0.35 in the first row, last column. This value indicates that among urban families reporting an income between $8,573 and $11,724, a 1 percent increase in income produced an increase in expenditures for "food at home" of 0.35 percent. Coefficients such as these hold the promise of increasing the accuracy of predictions of consumer income allocation patterns.

INCOME EXPECTATIONS

We have seen that both absolute levels of income and changes in income play a role in determining consumer income allocation patterns. Still another aspect of income that may be influential in determining consumer expenditure patterns is expected changes in income. Income expectations vary in three basic respects: (a) the probability that a change in income will occur, (b) the direction of the expected change (increase or decrease) and (c) the permanency of the expected change. The cross classification device in Figure 8.2 suggests some of the possible combinations of income expectations that may exist.

Figure 8.2 Income Expectations

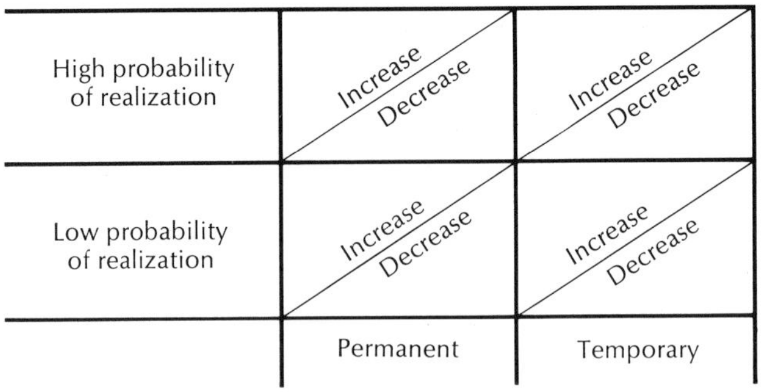

High probability of realization	Increase / Decrease	Increase / Decrease
Low probability of realization	Increase / Decrease	Increase / Decrease
	Permanent	Temporary

Figure 8.2 identifies eight types of income expectations. Consumers might have high probability expectations of a permanent income increase; they

may have low probability expectations of a temporary income decrease; and so forth. Although we cannot conveniently represent the possibility of stability as a further type of expectation, we should note that such a condition is entirely relevant. But why dissect the various types of income expectations in this manner? Our answer is that evidence suggests that some variation in consumer behavior is related to these specific types of expected changes in income.

Although we know relatively little about the patterns of consumer behavior that these various types of expectations may produce, a body of understanding is evolving. Consumers who expect temporary income declines apparently do not immediately adapt their expenditure patterns to a reduced level of income. This tendency to maintain expenditure patterns at high levels in the face of temporary declines produces a kind of *ratchet effect*. This effect is suggested in Figure 8.3.

The line ab traces the expenditures of (say) a household as its income increases. Note that the slope of line segment ab agrees with our earlier observation that the proportion of income spent for discretionary goods and services increases as income increases. But observe also that the process is not perfectly reversible; as income declines the consumption pattern is maintained at approximately the level that existed before the decline. Indeed, a general reluctance to admit that income declines are permanent could produce a series of steps down to more appropriate levels of consumption rather than a smooth return along line ba. Thus, where income declines are expected to be temporary, the consuming unit (for example a household) may adjust downward along a path like c-d-e.[13]

Figure 8.3 The Ratchet Effect

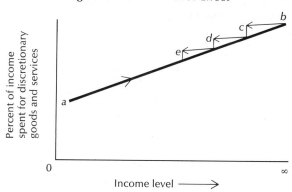

[13] The term "ratchet effect" is coined in the excellent book, James S. Duesenberry, *Income Saving and the Theory of Consumer Behavior*, Cambridge, Mass.: Harvard University Press, 1952, pp. 114–115.

Households with expectations of permanent income declines make significant reductions in expenditures for durable goods—one of the principal components of what we earlier called discretionary expenditures. These discretionary expenditures also "tend to increase more than proportionally when income increases and is expected to increase further."[14] Thus income allocation patterns may involve "dissaving"—a drawing down of past savings. There is some evidence that totally unexpected income (that having an extremely low level of realization probability) is quickly spent. For example, of a group of consumers who earlier stated that they did not intend to buy a new car, 63 percent of those who experienced unexpectedly large incomes actually bought new cars.[15]

But consumer income allocation patterns are related to income expectations in another way. The expectations we have discussed to this point are those of the near future. There are longer range aspects to income expectations, and these longer range expectations often relate to human occupations. Different persons have different long-term income expectations. Take the obvious case of a professional fighter who may have a negatively inclined income stream. He may earn $100,000 for a night's work today and find himself with no marketable skills in two years. Consider the case of the medical intern who currently earns $7,500 annually but who will soon find the world his economic oyster. The intern's income expectations form a positively inclined stream through time. Clearly, the expenditure patterns of these two individuals should be different. The intern might reasonably borrow against assured future earnings, the fighter might reasonably allocate a significant portion of his current earnings to savings.

The influence of demographic characteristics on income allocation patterns

Demography is the study of populations. And there are particular aspects of the demographic character of the United States that are related to the income allocation patterns of consumers and households. Our interest here is limited to three aspects of the demographic character of the United States: (a) population size and changes in population size, (b) the geographical distribution of populations (particularly their spatial density) and (c) the life-cycle composition of the population.

In a general sense, the population size of a country in relation to its natural wealth dictates the level of living enjoyed by that nation. Thus, chronic overpopulation produces a particular, and tragic, kind of income allocation pattern. There are, indeed, chronically overpopulated parts of the United States, and the income allocation patterns of the ghetto are just what one would expect. Population size and changes in population

[14]Both these conclusions are suggested in Katona, *op. cit.,* pp. 150–151.
[15] *Ibid.,* p. 152.

size thus relate in a general way to consumer expenditure patterns. The demographer uses special analytical devices to focus more sharply on the exact character of population changes. Birth rates, expressed in births per thousand of population, and death rates, expressed in deaths per thousand, provide special insights into population size. What may appear to us to be insignificant changes become, in the hands of the capable demographer, a change of special significance for particular business firms. Consider, for example, the following statistical fact: "During the population explosion of the 1950's, the birth rate averaged 24.8 births per 1000. In the twelve months ended last May (1967), the birth rate averaged 18.2, a record low."[16] What is the consequence of this change in the birth rate?

A sharp decline in the birth rate will produce an "implosion group"—a relative dearth of particular age groups as time goes by. This is just the reverse of the relatively high birth rates of the early post World War II years that produced an "explosion group" whose influence has been felt in every major market except perhaps homes and home furnishings. The implosion group will have attained teen status by the 1980's, and "their diminished ranks could mean a decrease in demand for such teen staples as phonograph records, cosmetics, fad clothing and motion pictures."[17]

The place where populations reside has an influence on income allocation patterns. The family that lives in a downtown apartment necessarily allocates its income among alternative goods and services in a different way from the suburban family. This is true even when incomes of the two families are identical. The rural family has an expenditure pattern that is different from that of the suburbanite. A young adult living in southern California spends his income in a different way from a person of similar age in Aspen, Colorado. Because consumer expenditure patterns are related to geography in the foregoing manner, we have an interest in the geographical aspects of populations. Both the warm climate of Los Angeles and the sprawl of that urban area have obvious implications for the automotive and petroleum markets. The severe winters of Minnesota and Maine have similar implications for insulated building materials; the proximity of skiing facilities makes Denver a good outdoor fashion market.

Finally, the life-cycle composition of a population influences consumer expenditure patterns. The *life-cycle composition* of a population refers to the proportion of a population falling into particular stages of the human life cycle. This human life cycle has at least six stages, as follows:[18]

---

[16] *Marketing Insights,* October 2, 1967, p. .4.

[17] *Ibid.*

[18] This classification is used in J. B. Lansing and J. H. Morgan, "Consumer Finances Over the Life Cycle," in L. H. Clark, editor, *Consumer Behavior,* New York: New York University Press, 1955, vol II, pp. 36–51. See also J. B. Lansing and Leslie Kish, "Family Life Cycle As an Independent Variable," *American Sociological Review,* 1957, pp. 512–519. These classes are not the only meaningful states in the life cycle. There may, for example, be several stages within the bachelor stage.

1 The bachelor stage: the young unmarried adult
2 The newlywed stage: the young with no children
3 The full nest stage, I: the young, married with dependent children
4 The full nest stage, II: the older, married with dependent children
5 The empty nest stage: the older, married, no dependent children
6 The solitary survivor stage: the older, unmarried

At any moment in time a population is characterized by what we have called life-cycle composition. The life-cycle composition of a population may conveniently be thought of as a profile of the proportions of households falling into each of these several life-cycle stages. Figure 8.4 depicts several such profiles.

Figure 8.4 Life-cycle Composition

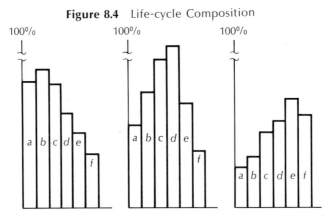

Profile A in Figure 8.4[19] shows a life-cycle composition skewed toward youth. This youthful life-cycle profile might characterize some vacation or resort areas—and a population of this kind would tend to be characterized by a distinctive type of income allocation pattern. Profile C, in contrast, has an older composition; it might exemplify a retirement city. It, too, would tend to have an average income allocation pattern of a distinctive character. But what kinds of purchases are influenced by the life-cycle composition of populations? Observe Figures 8.5 and 8.6.[20]

Each of these seven charts embodies four dimensions. The Roman numerals across the bottom of each chart represent the six stages of the human life cycle. I represents the bachelor stage, II represents the newlywed stage, III represents the full nest I stage, and so forth. The vertical

[19] The numbers 1 through 6 in Figure 8.4 correspond to the six stages of the family life cycle. That is, 1 represents the bachelor class, 2 the newlywed class, 3 the full nest I class and so forth.
[20] The data for these charts are from Table 15, "Differences in Durable Goods Purchases During the Life-Cycle (In 1956)," in George Katona, *op. cit.,* p. 166. The original source of the data is the 1956 Survey of Consumer Finances. Because the data are aging, the relationships depicted should be thought of as illustrative rather than definitive.

Figure 8.5

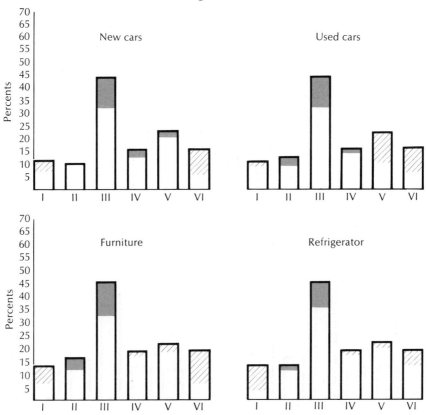

axis is expressed in percentage, which represents (a) the percentage of each life-cycle stage in the total population and (b) the percentage of purchases of selected durable goods each life-cycle group accounted for. Each chart also represents a particular class of durable goods. An example will clarify the process of interpreting these charts.

Consider new car purchases, the first of these seven charts. The bachelor stage represented 10 percent of the total population and accounted for only 6 percent of new car purchases. The newlywed group represented 8 percent of the population and made 8 percent of the purchases. The full nest I group made up 35 percent of the total population but accounted for about 45 percent of the total puchases of new cars. In order to simplify the reading of these data, the shaded areas designate disproportionately high consumption, and the hatched areas designate disproportionately low consumption. Where neither hatching or shading appears, that partic-ular class made purchases proportionate to their group size.

With that note of interpretation, observe generally in what stages of the life cycle disproportionately high and disproportionately low con-

Figure 8.6

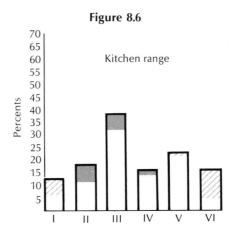

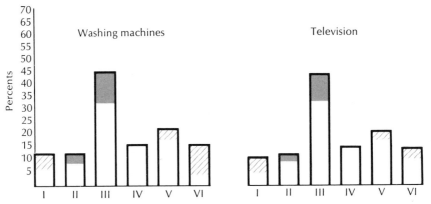

sumption occurs. In all seven classes of durable goods represented here, the heavy spenders are in Stages II, III, IV, and V. Moreover, Stages II and III represent the periods of greatest durable goods acquisition. It is clear then that the family formation years, a stage in the human life cycle, has a profound bearing on consumer income allocation patterns. It is likely also that other types of expenditures vary in importance throughout the life cycle. But we have shown enough to establish the basic notion that income allocation patterns are determined to some extent by the stage of the life cycle.

The influence of reference groups on income allocation patterns

Clearly, the style of our lives is influenced to an important degree by groups. A particular kind of group, the reference group, is of special importance to us here. The term *reference group* identifies *any group of persons, formal or informal, face-to-face or distant, that is capable of influencing the behavior of an individual.*[21] Any person may identify with several such reference groups at any point in time. Groups which may have at some earlier time been influential in a person's life may cease to wield such influence; reference group influence is, in this sense, transient. Reference groups may be small, as is generally the case with one's immediate family; they may be large, as is the case of (say) a national political party. Reference groups may be clearly defined (such as the senior class) or they may be perceived in a less definitive way (such as one's social class affiliation or an imagined and perhaps competitive social clique).

Reference groups may be those in which we now hold membership, or, they may be groups to which we aspire. Indeed, in this latter instance, it is often true that our aspirations to memberships in a particular group may cause us to affect some of the behavioral characteristics we see displayed prominently by current members of that group. We may identify *positively* with particular reference groups—we would eagerly adopt the distinctive behavioral traits of such a group. We may identify *negatively* with particular reference groups—we would just as eagerly avoid the distinctive behavioral traits of such a group.[22]

There is an impressive and growing body of evidence that reference groups do, in fact, influence human behavior. An early study dealing with group influence, one that utilized social class as a controlled variable, is of interest in this context. An experimental design was developed in which two basic objectives were to determine: (a) "whether pedestrians would violate the 'wait' (traffic) signal more often if they saw someone else violating it, than if there were no violators; and, (b) whether the social class that the violator apparently represented (by the way he was dressed) had any effect on other people's behavior."[23] In order to accomplish these objectives, the experiment made use of a confederate who dressed on some occasions as a higher-status person in "freshly pressed

---

[21] This is but one sense in which the term has been employed. The definition is, in spirit, the same as that utilized by T. M. Newcomb in *Social Psychology*, New York: Dryden Press, 1950. See also, T. M. Newcomb and W. W. Charters, Jr., "Some Attitudinal Effects of Experimentally Increased Salience of a Membership Group," in G. E. Swanson and other, editors, *Readings in Social Psychology*, New York: Holt, Rinehart and Winston, Inc., 1952, pp. 415–420. For a brief statement of historical perspective on reference group theory and an examination of evolving definitions of reference groups see James E. Stafford, "Reference Theory as a Conceptual Framework for Consumer Decisions," in Robert L. King, editor, *Marketing and the New Science of Planning*, 1968 Fall Conference Proceedings, American Marketing Association, pp. 280–284.

[22] Reference groups that involve a negative kind of identification have been called "dissociative" groups. See James E. Stafford, "Effects of Group Influence on Consumer Brand Preferences," *Journal of Marketing Research*, February 1966, p. 69.

[23] Herbert I. Abelson, *Persuasion: How Opinions and Attitudes Are Changed*, New York: Springer Publishing Co., Inc., 1959, pp. 20–21.

suit, shined shoes, white shirt, and tie," and on other occasions as a low status person with a costume consisting of "well worn scuffed shoes, soiled and patched trousers, and an unpressed blue denim shirt." This confederate on some occasions obeyed and on others disobeyed the traffic signal in both his high and low status attire. In addition, the traffic intersection was observed when the confederate was not there at all, as a control measurement. A total of 2103 pedestrians were observed. Under normal (control) conditions, approximately 99 percent of the pedestrians obeyed the traffic sign. The confederate was able to induce others to violate the signal, and his degree of success depended upon his apparent social class. "When he violated the signal in his low status clothes, 4% of the other pedestrians disobeyed. When he violated the signal in his high status clothes, 14% of the other pedestrians also violated it."[24] Many other similar experiments corroborate the basic notion that reference group identification can influence human behavior.

If the notion that reference groups play an important role in the determination of human behavior in general and consumer behavior in particular is correct, then the task before us might be posed as a question: "Which kinds of groups are likely to be referred to by which kinds of individuals under which kinds of circumstances in the process of making which decisions?"[25] Measuring the extent of reference group influence is, of course, an important part of this general task. And clearly, the recent literature of marketing reflects a movement toward the goals suggested by this quotation. To date, however, most work with reference groups has been directed toward an understanding of a general type of reference group—the reference group called "social class."

The nucleus of what might be called reference group theory has been developed by sociologists and social psychologists. One aspect of reference group theory is of particular interest to us here because of its assumed close relationship to distinctive patterns of consumer behavior. This special aspect is suggested by the phrase "social stratification."[26] Social stratification suggests a system characterized by social strata or classes. For our purposes, the terms "social stratification" and "social class" will be used synonymously. But how does the idea of social strata relate to

[24] Ibid., p. 21.

[25] See Francis S. Bourne, "Group Influence in Marketing and Public Relations," in Rensis Likert and Samuel P. Hays, Jr., editors, Some Applications of Behavioral Research, Paris: UNESCO, 1957.

[26] The notion that social class is properly conceived of as a special type of reference group is explored carefully in Elizabeth Bott, "The Concept of Class as a Reference Group," in Perry Bliss, editor, Marketing and the Behavioral Sciences, Second Edition, Boston: Allyn and Bacon, Inc., 1967, pp. 223-227. A divergent view may be seen in John A. Howard, Marketing Theory, Boston: Allyn and Bacon, Inc., 1965, p. 167. See also B. Barber, Social Stratification, New York: Harcourt, Brace & World, Inc., 1957, p. 7.

reference groups? Social strata are believed to be general kinds of reference group that are, in turn, assumed to influence the behavior of individuals in many ways, including consumer behavior. Before we proceed, we should be sure that our argument thus far has been clear. We have suggested that:

1 Reference groups influence our behavior.
2 Social strata, or social classes, represent a general form of reference group.
3 Individuals or households may belong to or identify (either positively or negatively) with such social classes.
4 Our behavior as consumers is influenced by such membership or identification (positive or negative).

THE NATURE OF SOCIAL STRATIFICATION

The word "stratification" implies a system of ranked (hierarchical) statuses. That hierarchy may be thought of as layers, or strata, of the total population as pictured in Figure 8.7. But layers or strata of what? Figure 8.7 depicts two oversimplified but initially useful societal models. Three classes have been identified in the model labeled A. This model is an open three-strata prestige representation of society. It is "open" rather than "closed" because we assume that persons have freedom to move from one class to another. A closed, or "caste," system would preclude such interclass movements. It is a "prestige" system because the division of the society into the three classes that are identified is not based on power conflict or opposition between the classes, but on prestige. This three-class prestige model is one that many people identify when asked to discuss their perceptions of the existing class structure.[27]

Figure 8.7 Social Classes

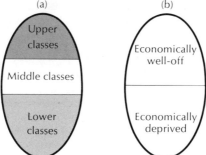

The model in Figure 8.7 labeled B represents a power model. This is a two-strata concept of class structure—a kind of hierarchy based on

[27] See, for example, Elizabeth Bott, *op. cit.,* pp. 233–234.

conflict and opposition between the "haves" and the "have-nots."[28] Again, this two-strata power model is a class structure that is perceived by large numbers of people in the United States. A society may be stratified by power, by prestige or even by some more complex combination of factors.[29] Any of these means of stratification may represent a means through which variations in consumer behavior may be better understood. That is, when we know how and with what groups various persons identify we know also what social position they assign themselves to, and we are, therefore, in a better position to understand why their behavior as consumers is what it is.

THE IDENTIFICATION OF SOCIAL STRATA

We have thus far been discussing class systems as though there were no question about their existence. The fact is that the existence of social classes is not accepted by some people. There are two basic reasons for this reluctance to admit freely to the existence of a social class system in the United States. To some critics, the basic thought of social classes is abrasive because such a system implies a hierarchy, and a hierarchy suggests inherent inequality. These doubters confuse "caste" and "class." Ours is a casteless society, but not a classless system. The difference between these two terms is admittedly one of degree. Caste systems are likely to be closed—absolutely inviolate; class systems are often very subtle in their workings. To a second group of critics, the concept of social class is dismissed because it is thought to represent the (angry?) moralizing of the social quasi-scientist. This latter view is based on the mistaken notion that the actual process of assigning individuals a position in the class hierarchy is purely judgmental and subjective—that the social "scientist" is moralizing about what is good-better-and-best. It is to this latter point that the following discussion is directed.

We want to emphasize the fact that many systems of social stratification

[28] Many other criteria for stratification have been considered important. Examples include: (a) ownership of property; (b) income; (c) consumption patterns and style of life; (d) occupation or skill and achievement in it; (e) education, wisdom and learning; (f) divinity or control over the supernatural; (g) altruism, public service and morality; and many others. See a more complete list in Bernard Berelson and Gary A. Steiner, *Human Behavior: An Inventory of Scientific Findings,* New York: Harcourt, Brace & World, Inc., 1964, p. 454.

[29] Three basic types of social class have been explored in the literature of social stratification. *Power* class, for example "economic power as measured by income and wealth is one such dimension of class." A second social class is *status* class and these groups or "castes are strata which are viewed as primarily oriented to a prestige hierarchy." More recently, stratification by *cultural* class is emerging as a distinct dimension of stratification. These three classes of class are distinguished in a scholarly work, James M. Carman, *The Application of Social Class in Market Segmentation,* Research Program in Marketing, Graduate School of Business Administration, University of California, Berkeley, IBER Special Publications, 1965, pp. 14–17.

have an objective and empirically based foundation. The concept of social class is empirically demonstrable; it is not an unreal product of the overactive imagination of unrealistic persons. How then are social classes identified? Through what method or technique is it possible to determine the class position of an individual or a household?

When we say that methods of determining the social class position of individuals may have an objective and empirical basis, we mean that such systems—at least the reputable ones—have been validated with a broadly based national sample. This process of validation involves two basic steps. The first such step is to identify such classes of society as representative elements of the total population may perceive. For example, in the validation of the North-Hatt occupational prestige scale, the National Opinion Research Center originally gathered "data through personal interviews with 2920 respondents."[30] It was the task of these interviewers to establish (or deny) the existence of a "rank-structure of the prestige status of occupations." When research indicates that people do feel the existence of such prestige rank and also agree where particular occupations rank relative to others, the prestige scale has been validated. It is this ordering process that constitutes the second step in the validation process. With such validation complete, it is then possible to make preliminary inferences about the relative prestige rank of an individual from information about his occupation.[31]

In much of the work that is done with social class, the respondent is assigned some final position in the class hierarchy according to several rather than a single socioeconomic or demographic characteristic. Illustrative of this multifactor approach is the Warnerian procedure in which place of residence, source of income, house type and occcupation are weighted to arrive at some numerical score that identifies the respondent as belonging in a specific status niche. This approach to class assignment has come to be identified as the ISC (Index of Social Class) method.[32] This index of social class is felt by some to be a much more powerful

---

[30] This scale—one that we will explore later in greater detail—is one of the most widely accepted as "affirming a rank-structure of the prestige status of occupations." See Albert J. Reiss, Jr., *Occupations and Social Status,* New York: The Free Press, 1961, pp. 3ff.

[31] The problem of possible discrepancies is recognized. A "status discrepancy" occurs when the occupational character of a person points to different status assignment than some other relevant social, economic or demographic characteristics. This point is discussed in Berelson and Steiner, *op. cit.,* p. 455.

[32] For a complete discussion of the ISC method, see W. Lloyd Warner and others, *Social Class in America,* Chicago: Science Research Associates, 1949. There are, of course, other multifactor indexes. See, for example, James F. Engel and others, *Consumer Behavior,* New York: Holt, Rinehart and Winston, Inc., 1968, pp. 280–282. Included in this reference is a brief discussion of: (a) Coleman's Index of Urban Status (IUS), (b) Carman's Index of Cultural Classes, (c) Hollingshead's Index of Social Position (ISP) and (d) the Index of Class Position developed by Ellis, Lane and Olesen.

device for understanding consumer actions than more conventional economic measures.[33]

The procedure for validating one of these multifactor class indicators is more complex than for a single-factor system. The procedure may begin with the placement of specific persons in a community into a status hierarchy by a representative group of persons from that community. The initial judgment is then collective rather than the opinion of the researcher. Having placed these specific persons into a status hierarchy, it is possible to study the social, economic and demographic characteristics of each one and determine by inference what factors combined in what way to give each person his rank. When these social, economic and demographic character traits have been identified, it becomes possible to make class assignments. The following hypothetical example will clarify this process:

Individual A	Scores
1. Occupation: Professional	10
2. Source of income: Salary, dividends, interest, capital gains	10
3. House type: X	8
4. Dwelling area: New residential	8
	36

Individual B	
1. Occupation: Clerk/kindred worker	5
2. Source of income: Salary	6
3. House type: Y	6
4. Dwelling area: Old residential	5
	22

Individual C	
1. Occupation: Farm laborer	3
2. Source of income: Wages	4
3. House type: Z	3
4. Dwelling area: Old industrial	2
	12

[33] See Pierre D. Martineau, "The Pattern of Social Classes," in Robert L. Clewett, editor, *Marketing's Role in Scientific Management,* Chicago: American Marketing Association, 1957, p. 133. It is also true that the multifactor method of identifying class strata is substantially more difficult to validate than the single-factor system. As Tucker notes, "since membership in a social class is not determined by commonly accepted criteria," it "becomes possible for the artist and the businessman to look down on one another, the one holding that creative achievement is the real measure of a man, the other equally certain that income is the valid measure." See W. T. Tucker, *The Social Context of Economic Behavior,* New York: Holt, Rinehart and Winston, Inc., 1964, p. 16.

Note that each of these three hypothetical individuals has been scored according to four socioeconomic-demographic traits.[34] In order to concentrate our attention on the process of class assignment we have purposely avoided some difficult problems—but we will return to that momentarily. Observe the differences in occupational traits of our three individuals. Individual A ranks at the top of most occupational prestige scales; Individual C ranks near the bottom. The numerical scores corresponding to each of these occupational classes are taken (arbitrarily) from a 0-10 point scale. A similar system is employed with each of the other traits. Note that a combined source of income such as "salary, dividends, capital gains and interests," ranks higher (in points scored) than either "salary" or "wages" alone.

It is with a class position scoring system such as this that most multiple factor class delineation procedures work. The most difficult conceptual problems with these systems are encountered in identifying and weighting the attributes that correlate best with collective judgments of social position. Note that we have given all four factors equal weight; but it would be relatively simple to give one or more of these four factors relatively more or less weight. Note especially the final scores for each of our hypothetical individuals. We need now only to place these scores in some social class hierarchy to identify each of these individuals by social class. Toward this end, consider Figure 8.8 on page 186.[35]

The combined effects of occupation, source of income, house type, and dwelling area places our first hypothetical individual at the top of the class index. Individual A is in the range of social class identified by the terms Upper-Upper or Lower-Upper—his score is 36. Individual B falls into the Lower-Middle stratum (22 points); and Individual C is Upper-Lower in class position (12 points). Before we explore what we know about differences in the consumer behavior of these various social classes, it will be worthwhile to summarize briefly what we have suggested about the procedure of social stratification:

---

[34] Categories of "house types" necessarily vary between communities. That is, the most revealing differences between house types is different in different communities. In one instance where these Warner classes were used, it was "necessary to provide the field investigators with photographs covering a wide range of dwelling types all the way from exclusive apartments to rooms over stores." See Pierre Martineau, "Social Class and Spending Behavior," *Journal of Marketing*, October 1958, p. 125.

[35] These social class divisions are those developed by W. Lloyd Warner and initially proposed in *The Social Life of a Modern Community*, New Haven, Conn.: Yale University Press, 1941. A more recent interpretation of these classes may be seen in Richard P. Coleman, "The Significance of Social Stratification in Selling," in Martin L. Bell, editor, *Marketing: A Maturing Discipline*, Chicago: American Marketing Association, 1961, pp. 171–184. It should be emphasized that this scoring system is not, in a numerical sense, like that used by Warner, but it is similar in its method of development. For an actual application of the Warner ISC system, see Pierre Martineau, "Social Classes and Spending Behavior," pp. 121–130. See particularly p. 125 for the weighting scheme and the ISC scores for the various social classes.

Figure 8.8 Social Class Scores

			Illustrative score or index
$1/2\%$	Upper-upper classes	Second or third generation wealth, gracious living, sense of community responsibility.	36
2%	Lower-upper or nouveau riche	New wealth, "executive elite," doctors, lawyers, pursuit of gracious living.	34
10%	Upper-middle	Junior executives, apprentice professionals educated in better colleges, career-oriented, social participation, home decor important.	32
$30-35\%$	Lower-middle	Nonmanagerial office workers, small business owners, higher-paid blue-collar workers, concerned with respectability. Striving and respectability are words of immense importance.	24
40%	Upper-lower	Semiskilled assembly-line workers, make "good money" but don't buy respectability with it. Present-oriented rather than future-oriented. Keeping up in a material sense is important.	14
15%	Lower-lower	Unskilled workers and "unassimilated" ethics, only 7-8 percent of total purchasing power.	6

1 Stratification procedures include those accomplished with single factor indicators (such as occupation) and those determined on the basis of multifactor indexes (such as the ISC).

2 It is most desirable that stratification procedures be based on classes that are actually perceived by representative samples of the population at large. This makes the resulting stratification scheme a societal phe-

nomenon rather than the sole (and perhaps biased) judgment of the researcher.

3 Multifactor indexes of social class are particularly well adapted to use because they prevent an overemphasis of the role of any single socio-economic or demographic characteristic of the person being classified. Multifactor indexes, however, are much more difficult to validate and to weight properly.

CONSUMER BEHAVIOR AND SOCIAL STRATIFICATION

The task of establishing definitive relationships between social class position and variations in consumer behavior is far from complete. Much of the work that has been done is more nearly exploratory than definitive. Social Research Incorporated, a Chicago-based organization is, in one way or another, responsible for much of the effort to better define the role of social class in consumer behavior. The findings of five or six people have contributed much of our present understanding.[36] These people have collectively provided the basis for a word picture of the distinctive dimensions of consumer behavior patterns of the largest of the Warnerian social classes. These three classes, Upper-Middle, Lower-Middle and Upper-Lower, are distinctive consumers in at least four basic respects. Pronounced differences are thought to exist between these classes in terms of:

1 The degree and kind of commitment they have to the home.
2 Their propensity to consume; that is, how much they spend and how much they save from a given income.
3 Their mass media usage patterns.
4 Their uses of leisure time.

The Upper-Middle, Lower-Middle and Upper-Lower classes have been studied to the relative neglect of the Upper-Upper, Lower-Upper and Lower-Lower because the latter categories represent either relatively few persons or because they are not strong markets in an economic sense.[37] In order to focus more closely on differences in consumer behavior attributable to social class differences, the discussion that follows will characterize three hypothetical families, one at each of the three majority classes enjoying a similar household income. Obviously there will normally be differences in the consumption patterns of households in different social strata—differences traceable to income differences that may exist. But we wish, here, to quiet the effect of such income differences and focus on consumption differences that are related to social class.

[36] Prominent roles have been played by Pierre Martineau, Burleigh Gardner, Richard P. Coleman, Lee Rainwater and Sidney Levy.
[37] Though in recent years, the Lower-Lower urban household has been a frequent focus of research.

UPPER-MIDDLE-CLASS HOUSEHOLD—A COMPOSITE OF CONSUMER VALUES

1 Commitment to the Home

The U-M household has a well defined preference for a particular neighborhood. The cost of the neighborhood as a percentage of the total value of the real property is relatively high. That is, the home site carries a premium price. The home must be smartly designed and the landscaping well planned; the home may not be the structural equal of a Lower-Middle-class family with a similar income. The home is tastefully decorated; the U-M housewife prides herself on her ability with aesthetically subtle decor.[38] Ideas about decor are likely to come from professional sources (interior decorators) rather than general shelter magazines.

2. Average Propensity to Consume

The savings ratio is relatively low in the young U-M household. The propensity to consume is high.[39] Organizational memberships are important, and "society" is a meaningful, reachable, concept. The upward mobility of this household promises better economic circumstances, and both brand and store patronage preferences are economically demanding. Stock and insurance are clearly distinguished as upper status investments.[40]

3. Mass Media Usage

Reading material is a much more important mass medium to the U-M household than to other classes of similar income. Editorialized analysis of current events is important, and nodding acquaintance with recent literary efforts is needed. Media should, for maximum value, inform, interpret and condense. The U-M household is part of what has been called the "issues and culture set." Ideas in the news are an important subject for discussion.

4. Leisure Usage

Such pastimes as club golf (rather than public), tennis, sailing—in general games and sports requiring finesse—are preferred. Evidence indicates that among the U-M household, canasta and bridge were favored over TV viewing.[41] The U-M household may see leisure as a time for fund raising and community betterment causes. Spending for memories is important, especially international travel.

---

[38] See Coleman, op. cit., reprinted in Hiram C. Barksdale, Marketing in Progress: Patterns and Potentials, New York: Holt, Rinehart and Winston, Inc., 1964, p. 361.
[39] Same source as immediately above, at page 360.
[40] See Pierre Martineau, "Spending Classes and Spending Behavior," p. 128.
[41] L. S. Graham, Selection and Social Stratification, unpublished Ph.D. dissertation, Yale University, 1951, pp. 134–187, 230. See also Howard, Marketing Theory, pp. 167–168.

LOWER-MIDDLE-CLASS HOUSEHOLD—A COMPOSITE OF CONSUMER VALUES

1. *Commitment to the Home*

From a similar income, the L-M household will spend relatively more for a house, substantially less for a neighborhood; the house is an important focal point for the L-M housewife. Decor in the L-M household is that being urged by general service and shelter magazines. The house design may be more fundamental; less attention is given to the lawn and landscaping. The L-M household is less mobile, both economically and geographically, than its U-M counterpart.

2. *Average Propensity to Consume*

The L-M household finds it easier to save (from a similar income) than the U-M household. There are fewer consumption demands on the L-M budget. Brands are less important. Aspirations to become a part of society are minimum—"society" is not a meaningful concept. Club memberships and the latest fashions in clothing are distinctly less urgent needs for the L-M housewife than the U-M housewife.

3. *Mass Media Usage*

Reading is relatively less important for the L-M household than for the U-M home. Popular and general appeal magazines are most often read. Less concern with editorialized versions of the news is an L-M trait. TV viewing is important, but criticism of the programming is an important subject of discussion.

4. *Leisure Usage*

Public or inexpensive club golf and college football are important male leisure uses for the L-M household head. This class is the "conforming, church-going, morally serious part of society." Church-related activities are an important part of leisure use patterns.[42]

UPPER-LOWER-CLASS HOUSEHOLD—COMPOSITION OF CONSUMER VALUES

1. *Commitment to the Home*

The home is, as Martineau puts it, "the anchor of the world," a symbol of security for the U-L household. But neighborhood is a very small part of the total value of the home. The U-L household is kitchen oriented in the sense that that room is fully equipped with modern laborsaving devices. They believe themselves to be "decent, hard-working people who don't 'put on airs.'" They want a house which is comfortable and in

---

[42] See Pierre Martineau, "The Pattern of Social Classes," pp. 233–249.

good shape, with enough room for the family; but they do not want to feel owned by it or feel that it out-ranks them in status.[43]

2. Average Propensity to Consume

Spending is important for display purposes—evidence that the U-L household is not only able to keep up with the Joneses but, on occasion, to surpass them is proudly exhibited.[44] The mass appeal media show the U-L household the standards to which they should aspire. "High society" is a distasteful concept, social appeals in selling are, per se, ineffective. Saving here tends to be a "noninvestment saving where there is almost no risk, funds can be quickly converted to spendable cash and returns are small."[45] The U-L household tends to use its credit cards for installment credit to a greater extent than upper classes.[46]

3. Mass Media Usage

Editorial interpretation is a relatively unimportant part of the U-L household's expectations from the mass media. Much of the most popular TV programming is rated highly by the U-L TV viewer; sporting events, Westerns and fantasy situations are popular. The romance magazines are important to the U-L housewife, as is TV soap opera.[47] Home decor is not in the least subtle—newspaper advertising may provide the guidance for home decoration. Little reading beyond the local newspaper is done. A distinctly local orientation is reflected; national and international affairs are not of great interest.[48] Media that dwell on such matters do not play a significant role.

4. Leisure Usage

The U-L man of the house is sports minded; hunting, fishing, baseball are all important. High School football is immensely important in the fall of the year. TV viewing is an important and relatively time-consuming pastime.[49] Social relationships tend to emphasize family and relatives. College football has little meaning.

[43] See Lee Rainwater and others, *Workingman's Wife: Her Personality, World and Life Style,* New York: MacFadden-Bartell Corp., 1962, p. 221.

[44] See Ronald R. Gist, *An Examination of the Influence of Education and Occupational Characteristics of the Household Head on Expenditure Patterns for Selected Classes of Consumer Durable Goods,* unpublished doctoral dissertation, University of Illinois, 1963, p. 29.

[45] See Pierre Martineau, "Social Class and Spending Behavior," p. 128.

[46] See H. Lee Mathews and John W. Slocum, Jr., "Social Class and Commercial Bank Credit Card Usage," *Journal of Marketing,* January 1969, pp. 72ff.

[47] See Lee Rainwater, *op. cit.,* Chap. 8.

[48] See Sidney J. Levy, "Social Class and Consumer Behavior," in Joseph W. Newman, editor, *On Knowing the Consumer,* New York: John Wiley & Sons, Inc., 1966, p. 155.

[49] See L. S. Graham, *op. cit.,* pp. 134, 187, 230. See also John A. Howard, *op. cit.,* pp. 167–168.

SUMMARY

The purpose of this chapter has been to examine some of the important factors that serve to determine the character of consumer income allocation patterns. More specifically, we have explored: (a) the influence of differences in absolute levels of income upon consumer expenditure patterns, (b) the influence of changes in the level of consumer income upon consumer expenditure patterns, (c) the influence of demographic characteristics upon consumer behavior and (d) the role of reference groups upon income allocation patterns.

Each of these areas we considered produced some analytical concept or concepts. For example, we developed the idea of discretionary and nondiscretionary patterns of income allocation and stated a formal principal that related nondiscretionary expenditures to the absolute level of consumer or household earnings. Likewise, we noted that the "laws" of one Ernst Engel represent an early effort to relate income allocation patterns to changes in the level of income. We observed that the coefficient of income sensitivity is a somewhat more precise means of relating consumer income allocation patterns to changes in household earnings. We also identified the ratchet effect—a phenomenon that relates consumer expenditure patterns to income expectations. This effect describes a slowness to adjust income allocation patterns to expected income decreases.

Demography is the study of population size and characteristics, and it plays an important role in the determination of consumer income allocation patterns. More particularly, the geographic distribution of populations and the age composition of populations are important determinative demographic variables. We were particularly interested in establishing the role of life-cycle composition as an important factor in consumer behavior. We found that of the six basic life-cycle stages, the newlywed, the full nest I, and the full nest II stages constitute the most important durable goods market.

Finally, we developed the idea that reference groups may play a significant role in the determination of income allocation patterns. We were especially interested in the general reference group we call social class. In order to identify the manner in which social class influences consumer behavior, we constructed three composites of consumer values. More specifically, we developed: (a) an Upper-Middle-class household composite of values, (b) a Lower-Middle-class household composite of values and (c) an Upper-Lower-class household composite of values. These three social strata differ importantly in terms of the kind and degree of commitment to the home, their average propensity to consume, their use of the mass media and their use of leisure.

REVIEW QUESTIONS

1 Carefully define and indicate the relevance of each of the following concepts to the study of marketing:

a. Demography
b. Reference group theory
c. Self-concept
d. Sociometry
e. The ratchet effect and income expectations
f. The family life cycle
g. The life-cycle composition of a population
h. Social stratification
i. A prestige model of society
j. A power model of society
k. Multifactor indicators of social class
l. Propensity to consume

2 Distinguish carefully between each element in the following pairs of terms:
a. Discretionary patterns of income allocation *and* nondiscretionary patterns of income allocation.
b. Engel's laws of consumption *and* the idea of a coefficient of income sensitivity.
c. A negatively inclined income stream *and* a positively inclined income stream.
d. The income allocation pattern of a full nest household *and* the income allocation pattern of an empty nest household.
e. An open class system *and* a closed class system.

3 What are Engel's laws? How are these laws related to consumer behavior? In what way(s) are his laws inaccurate today?

4 Discuss the relationship between durable goods purchases and the several stages of the family or household life cycle.

5 What are some reference groups that influence your life? Specifically, how is your own consumer behavior influenced by these groups?

6 What respondent traits are used to develop the ISC? What problems do you see in the use of this system?

DISCUSSION QUESTIONS

7 Develop a complete list of all the factors that played some role, important or otherwise, in the determination of the brand and the dealer from whom you made your last automobile purchase.

8 What important considerations are involved in a clothing purchase of more than $50? What important considerations are involved in a purchase of a food item with a cost of less than $.50?

9 What reference groups now wield some influence in your life? Be specific and complete; that is, identify present membership groups, aspirant groups, and negative groups. How is your consumption behavior influenced by these groups?

Chapter 9
DETERMINANTS OF CONSUMER BEHAVIOR
—PART TWO

In the preceding chapter, we identified and explored briefly several important determinants of consumer behavior. We explored the role of absolute levels of household income, the effects of changes in household income, and the influence of expectations of change in income distribution upon consumer expenditure patterns. We defined the concept of the family life cycle and identified some of the ways that the life cycle may influence consumer behavior. Chapter 8 concluded with a discussion of the role played by reference groups in the determination of consumer expenditure patterns. This discussion of reference groups placed particular emphasis upon social class as a reference group of fundamental importance. We observed that the basic value structure of different social strata is often distinctive. What one class may hold to be important, another may place little value upon. We noted that the degree and kind of commitment to the home, the household propensity to consume, the usage of mass media and leisure usage patterns differ among the various social classes. The fundamental premise throughout our discussion of consumer behavior has been that marketing can be a more efficient social and economic process when variations in human values (such as those between social classes) are recognized and honored.

Our immediate task in the present chapter is to conclude our discussion of social stratification and its relationship to consumer income allocation patterns. We will also consider two additional aspects of consumer behavior: (a) an examination of theories that endeavor to explain variations in patterns of consumer brand loyalty and (b) an examination of some theoretical explanations of variations in consumer time-of-adoption behavior patterns.

Social stratification—some concluding remarks

In our earlier discussion, we defined the concept of social class, we identified some means for the measurement of social class, and we considered how differences in social class may influence human values (and, therefore, consumption patterns). We may rightly conclude that social class is both an insightful and a practicable way to think of mass markets.[1] But there are two other ideas that relate to social class that we should consider. These two ideas are (a) stratification profiling techniques and (b) the notion of consumer "privilege."

Figure 9.1 Stratification Profiles

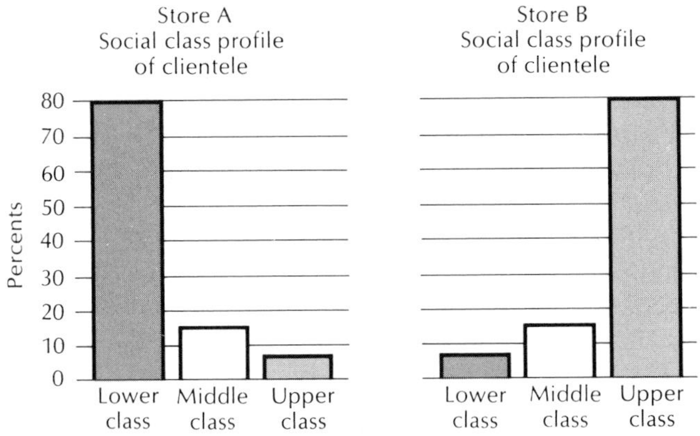

STRATIFICATION PROFILE

A useful analytical device, and one which may be developed with social class data, is the stratification profile. A *stratification profile* is a summary of the proportions of a particular population falling into each of several different social strata. Consider, for example, the following stratification profiles for two different retail stores.

The two stratification profiles in Figure 9.1 are hypothetical summaries of the social class membership constituting the clientele of two very different retail stores. Note that Store A deals primarily with a lower-class clientele and Store B caters to an upper-class customer group. The profiles are potentially helpful because of the insight they provide regarding the values and preferences of the customers of each of the stores. The management of Store A, when fully aware of the social class composition of its customers, is in a position to accommodate more exactly the preferences of that group. The actual process of "accommodating more exactly the preferences" of the clientele may have far-reaching implications.

[1] To this point, John Howard argues that "from the point of view of the marketing executive the scheme (division of populations into social classes) constitutes a meaningful set of categories which perhaps can aid him in designing the most effective marketing strategy for consumer markets. Knowledge of the categories is especially useful because consumer markets are typically heterogeneous to an extreme degree. Any device that will enable a marketing manager to look at market segments each of which is more homogeneous than the whole with respect to buyer motives, attitudes, and behavior will contribute to marketing effectiveness." See *Marketing Management: Analysis and Decision,* Homewood, Ill.: Richard D. Irwin, Inc., 1957.

Such accommodation may influence the kinds of merchandise carried, the specific brands carried, the credit plans offered, the media through which advertising is done, the language of the copy used in advertising and many other aspects of business operation. As a test of your own perceptiveness, which of the two stores above would most likely:

1 Utilize FM radio advertising?
2 Utilize installment sales contracts aggressively?
3 Have the least white space in printed advertisements?

But these profiles of social strata may have value in a context other than that of an individual retail store. It is possible to develop a kind of stratification profile for entire cities. Indeed, if one subscribes to the view that occupation of the household head is an important determinant of the social class position assigned to the household, stratification profiles already exist for many cities. This connection between occupation, social class and stratification profiles requires some elaboration.

To this point in our discussion of social stratification, we have placed greatest emphasis on the notion that the social class assigned to a particular household is the result of several socioeconomic characteristics of that household. The ISC that we demonstrated in the previous chapter was, in fact, developed around four such socioeconomic characteristics. There are, however, single-factor indicators of social class position—and one of the most frequently utilized factors is the occupation of the household head.[2] Lloyd Warner, one of the pioneers in the use of social class as a conceptual means of gaining insight into human behavior, has "found occupation (of the household head) the best single indicator of status."[3] Another highly regarded source also suggests a very close relationship between occupation and social class.[4] If occupation of the household head does correlate highly with social class position, then occupational profiles of entire cities are, to an extent, reflective of the social class composition of those cities. This reasoning suggests that we may be able to infer something about the type of market opportunities presented by different cities if we know the occupational profiles of those cities. In effect, then, we are suggesting a four-step argument, as follows:

1 Consumer behavior depends to an important degree upon social class.
2 Social class depends to an important degree upon the occupation of the household head.

---

[2] See L. Reissman, "Levels of Aspiration and Social Class," *American Sociological Review*, June 1953, pp. 233–241. See also Theodore Caplow, *The Sociology of Work*, Minneapolis: University of Minnesota Press, 1954, pp. 124–141.

[3] See Eric Larrabee and Rolf Mayersohn, *Mass Leisure*, The Free Press, Glencoe, Illinois, 1958, footnote page 213.

[4] See R. Bendix and S. M. Lipset, editors, *Class, Status and Power: A Reader in Social Stratification*, New York: The Free Press, 1953, p. 325. Bendix and Lipset identify the "social equation" as follows: Consumption depends upon occupational position, occupational position depends upon social class position and social class position, in turn, depends upon consumption.

3 Therefore, the occupation of the household head is an important determinant of the consumption behavior of the household.

4 Knowing the occupational profile of a city, we may be able to draw helpful inferences regarding the aggregate consumption patterns of the city under scrutiny.

Consider the city occupational profiles in Figure 9.2.

Figure 9.2 Occupational Profiles—Cities

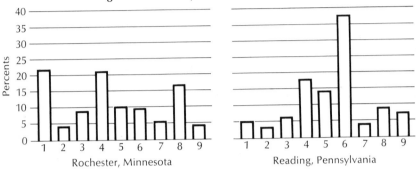

Note: The horizontal numbering system identifies occupational classes as follows:
1. Professional
2. Semiprofessional
3. Proprietors
4. Clerical
5. Crafts
6. Operatives
7. Domestic service
8. Service
9. Laborers

Observe that the occupational classes represented on the horizontal axis of Figure 9.2 are arranged in order of occupational prestige.[5] That is, the most prestigious occupations are coded 1, and the least prestigious occupations are coded 9. This scale of occupational prestige is virtually identical to the North-Hatt scale of occupational prestige—a widely used and carefully validated scaling device.[6] The North-Hatt scale is based on ratings of occupations by a cross-section of the American population as interviewed by the National Opinion Research Center.[7]

---

[5] The two occupational profiles in Figure 9.2 are from P. B. Gillen, *The Distribution of Occupations as a City Yardstick,* New York: Kings Crown Press, 1951.

[6] Albert J. Reiss, Jr., in his *Occupations and Social Status,* presents a complete discussion of the problems associated with construction of the North-Hatt continuum of occupational prestige. The reader is directed especially to Chapters 1–3. For an account of efforts prior to the NORC (North-Hatt) work to relate occupational types with social class the reader is directed to George S. Counts, "The Social Status of Occupations, A Problem in Vocational Guidance," *School Review,* January, 1925 pp. 16–27. See also Mapheus Smith, "An Empirical Scale of Prestige Status of Occupations," *American Sociological Review,* April 1943, pp. 185–192.

[7] The original report of this study by NORC appeared in *Opinion News,* Vol. 9, September, 1947.

But how might these city-wide, or aggregate, occupational profiles be valuable from a marketing point of view? In much the same way that we found stratification profiles potentially helpful to the individual retail establishment, these aggregate profiles tend to suggest the type of marketing opportunity represented by a particular city.[8] If, for example, the two cities represented in Figure 9.2 were alike in other aspects but had occupational compositions as depicted, substantial differences would exist in marketing opportunity of the two cities. Again, to test your own understanding, which of these two cities would probably represent the greater potential for:

1 The services of a travel bureau?
2 A family tavern?
3 A cocktail lounge?
4 Classes in investment planning?
5 Subscriptions to the *New Yorker* magazine?

Figure 9.3 Consumer Privilege

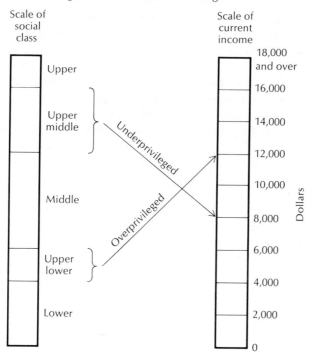

[8] Moreover, occupational data is readily available. As one sociologist states it, "occupation, next to size, is perhaps the most common criterion used in the classification of urban community." The reader is directed to Noel P. Gist and Sylvia F. Fava, *Urban Society,* Fifth Edition, New York: Thomas Y. Crowell Company, 1964, pp. 84–86.

SOCIAL STRATIFICATION AND CONSUMER PRIVILEGE

When we originally defined the concept of social class, we were careful to emphasize the point that income level alone does not, indeed cannot, buy class position.[9] It is generally agreed that the form in which income is earned is a better indication of social class than the level of such income. Thus, whether income is taken in the form of wages, salary, interest, royalties, dividends, capital gains or profits, correlates more highly with social class position than the amount of such earnings. It necessarily follows, then, that there are income differences within class strata—and these differences are obviously also important from a marketing point of view. Indeed, income differences within social class strata are the basis for the idea of "consumer privilege." But to make sure that the direction of our thought is clear, consider the following system of social class and income scales.

Any position on the scale of social class in Figure 9.3 may be thought of as representing a special type of economic demand. This economic demand is for a standard package of consumption—home, home furnishings, clothing, transportation, recreation, and other goods and services appropriate to each class level or social stratum. In general, this standard package of consumption is more elaborate (and therefore more expensive) at higher levels of social class. Because there are significant income differences within social classes, it necessarily follows that the consumption package appropriate to any particular stratum is more easily obtained and maintained by some class members than by others within the same class. A middle-class household with (say) a $25,000 per year income can acquire and maintain the package dictated by its class and enjoy a substantial income residue. Conversely, the upper-middle-class household with (say) an income of $12,000 is hard put to obtain and maintain the standard package of consumption dictated by that class. The term "overprivileged consumer" has been suggested to identify the consumer whose income exceeds the class demands placed upon it. The term "underprivileged consumer" has been suggested to identify the consumer whose income is inadequate relative to the class demands placed upon it.[10]

These terms—"overprivileged" and "underprivileged" consumers—do not represent a perfect selection of terms. Unfortunately, they carry some unintended connotative meaning. The overprivileged segments of any class

[9] See the discussion in the section titled "The Identification of Social Strata" (and especially the numerical illustration in that section) of Chapter Eight.

[10] The notion of consumer privilege was originally defined by Richard P. Coleman, "The Significance of Social Stratification in Selling," in Martin L. Bell, editor, *Marketing: A Maturing Discipline,* Chicago: American Marketing Association, 1961, pp. 171-184; reprinted in Steuart Henderson Britt and Harper W. Boyd, Jr., editors, *Marketing Management and Administrative Action,* New York: McGraw-Hill Book Co., 1968, pp. 232-242. The basic concept of consumer privilege is clearly set forth also in Harold H. Kassarjian and Thomas S. Robertson, editors, *Perspectives in Consumer Behavior,* Glenview, Ill.: Scott, Foresman and Company, 1968, pp. 375-376.

"are not overprivileged in the absolute sense," they are only overprivileged "relative to what is required or needed by families in their class."[11] Thus, the term "overprivileged" does not suggest that these families have more than they should—it only suggests that they have more than their class requirements specify. Similarly, an underprivileged household does not have an income that is inadequate in an absolute sense, it simply has less income than required by its social class requirements. In terms, then, of Figure 9.3, the overprivileged segments of a market may be depicted as those that combine any relatively low position on the social class scale with a relatively high income. The underprivileged segments of a market may be depicted as those that combine any relatively high position on the social class scale with a relatively low income.

These overprivileged and, to a lesser extent, underprivileged markets are of particular interest from a marketing point of view. For when overprivilege occurs at the upper-lower levels of social class, evidence suggests that the consumption pattern becomes "artifact oriented." Gadgetry, in the form of appliances, is an extremely important expenditure outlet for the lower-class overprivileged.[12] Research conducted by MacFadden Publications Incorporated tends to support the same conclusion. This MacFadden research created momentary overprivileged households out of wage-earner households (as opposed to salaried households) by asking them specifically how they would spend larger incomes. This research disclosed that the wives in wage-earner households would like to spend 30 percent more for laborsaving devices and home furnishings than did wives of salaried workers if both were at the $5000 level of income. At the $7000 level of income, the wage-earner wives expressed a desire to spend 50 percent more for these two classes of products than their salaried counterparts. This same research indicated that wage-earner wives were "innovation prone"—a point to which we shall return in a later section of the present chapter.[13]

It has been argued that the heart of the compact car market is to be found in the underprivileged segments of each class, at least in those instances in which the compact car is the first (or only) car. Richard P. Coleman, who introduced the concept of consumer privilege, argues that "it is not the really poor who are buying these cheapest, most economical cars—rather it is those who think of themselves as poor relative to their status aspirations and to their needs for a certain level of clothing, furniture, and housing, which they could not afford if they bought a more expensive car."[14]

[11] Richard P. Coleman, op. cit., p. 238.
[12] See, for example, Ken Rotzoll, "The Effect of Social Stratification on Market Behavior," Journal of Advertising Research, March 1967, pp. 22–27.
[13] For further detail regarding the MacFadden research, see Why Wage Earners Want More Appliances, Marketing Memo Number 61–4, MacFadden Publications, April 21, 1961.
[14] Britt and Boyd, op. cit., p. 240.

Regardless of the specific use to which the concept of privilege is applied, it seems clear that the refinement of social class through the use of the concept of privilege is a meaningful and useful refinement. It is equally clear that there is still as much or more that we do not know about the influence of "privilege" upon consumer behavior as we presently do know.

Some theoretical explanations of brand loyalty

We have noted previously that brand loyalty (or disloyalty) is an aspect of consumer behavior in which there is substantial current interest. The development of brand loyalty is a process about which relatively little is known, yet it is clear that a more complete understanding of this process can provide valuable insight into the actions of consumers. What we know now about brand loyalty is fragmented; we do not have a comprehensive, well integrated understanding. Some of the evidence that we have about brand loyalty formation seems to defy explanation. We know, for example, that strong brand loyalty can develop in circumstances in which there are no real differences among the various brands that the consumer can buy.

In one experiment, for example, housewives were asked to make 12 successive choices of bread from among four previously unknown brands lettered L, M, P and H. These women were told that the study "was designed to find out how women went about purchasing when they moved to a new location and were faced with unfamiliar brands."[15] When the housewives were making their brand selection, the position of the brands on the selection tray was varied so that locational convenience did not work to the special benefit of any one brand. The bread was wrapped in plain waxed paper, and all brands were taken from a single oven on the morning of delivery. Note that this experimental design effectively sterilizes the experience of the buyers. The subjects in the experiment did not know the brands, they were named in a way that did not give one brand any clear avenue of superiority, and their position on the selection tray was rotated so that position bias was controlled. Several results of this experiment are of particular interest to us here.

1 Strong brand loyalties did develop. When loyalty patterns began to evolve (loyalty was defined as three successive purchases of any one brand), a premium was placed on another brand. The strength of the evolving brand preference could thus be measured in terms of the value of the premium required to entice the buyer away from her preferred brand. A premium of 3½ cents was required, on the average, to interrupt a loyalty pattern.

2 The pattern of brand experimentation of the subjects is of interest. There

[15] See W. T. Tucker, "The Development of Brand Loyalty," in Kassarjian and Robertson, *op. cit.,* pp. 114–120. See p. 116 for a description of the research design.

was, for many subjects, a search period (during which all brands were being sampled) and a loyalty period. This loyalty period varied in intensity for different subjects—that is, some fell into uninterrupted patterns of brand preference, some developed what might be called dual loyalty patterns and others continued with some experimentation.

3 Even among those subjects that did not develop brand loyalty, one of the brands had been "essentially eliminated from further consideration" early in the search procedure. (Remember that the physical product was identical in all brands.)[16]

But there are compelling reasons for our concern with brand loyalty patterns besides the intrigue of the inexplicable. As final consumers, we are enticed both economically and socially to develop brand loyalties. To fight before we switch is depicted as the swinging thing to do; to walk a mile for *our* brand is a practice for the strong individualist; in general, to ask for products by brand name is a practice for the informed; to repeatedly buy Brand B will give us coupons that will, in turn, enable us to acquire premiums of all kinds. In a sense, to develop strong brand loyalties is a form of addiction. If enough of us become addicted, as it were, on one brand, it might be argued that the vigor of competition is inescapably altered. It might in this sense be argued that brand loyalty is a social issue.

What kinds of theories attempt to explain this phenomenon of brand loyalty? Three major theories of brand loyalty are evolving. These three theories emphasize respectively:

1 The process of learning brand preferences.
2 The consumer's perception of risk in brand switching.
3 The consumer's self-concept.

Each of these approaches to understanding brand loyalty is examined in the discussion that follows.

LEARNING THEORY AND BRAND LOYALTY

There are several different explanations of brand loyalty that, in effect, imply that learning is a fundamental cause of such loyalty. All these theories view learning as the result of an experience—an experience capable of changing human response to a particular situation. The phrase *learning theory* identifies a body of knowledge within psychology that endeavors to identify systematically conditions under which learning is most effective.

[16] Other experiments with brands reveal equally bizarre results. An extremely interesting study of brands is Ralph I. Allison and Kenneth P. Uhl, "Influence of Beer Brand Identification on Taste Perception," *Journal of Marketing Research*, August 1965, pp. 36–39. This study suggests the great value of the advertising image created for a particular brand. See also J. Douglas McConnell, "The Development of Brand Loyalty: An Experimental Study," *Journal of Marketing Research*, February 1968, pp. 13–19.

When we say that brand loyalty is a phenomenon that can be explained in terms of learning theory, we are thus utilizing a concept from the field of psychology to improve our understanding of a business phenomenon. But we are getting slightly ahead of ourselves. Before we explore in detail the insights that may be provided by learning theory, we need to identify the several different explanations of brand loyalty that utilize learning as the cause of such loyalty.

There are two basic explanations of brand loyalty that rest on a "learning" foundation. These basic explanations we will identify with the terms (a) nonprobabilistic explanations and (b) probabilistic explanations. Probabilistic learning explanations of brand loyalty divide, in turn, into two basic types—those that are linear and those that are nonlinear. If we now summarized these learning explanations of brand loyalty in outline form, our summary would appear as follows:

> Learning explanations of brand loyalty
> **1** Nonprobabilistic learning explanations
> **2** Probabilistic learning explanations
>   a. Linear (simple)
>   b. Nonlinear (simple)
>   c. Nonlinear with a built-in dislearning feature

Our task now is to examine briefly each of these explanations of brand loyalty.

NONPROBABILISTIC LEARNING EXPLANATIONS OF BRAND LOYALTY   Nonprobabilistic learning explanations of brand loyalty are the least rigorous (subject to the greatest degree of imprecision) of all the explanations we shall consider here. These nonprobabilistic explanations, at best, identify ordinal relationships rather than cardinal relationships. An example will make this clear. A nonprobabilistic learning explanation of brand loyalty is suggested by the psychological *principle of exercise*—a formal principle from the body of knowledge we called learning theory. This principle of exercise says that "the more a certain response to a situation is repeated, the more likely the same response will occur in the same situation later."[17] This learning principle says, in effect, that the more frequently we confront a problem of some kind, the more are we likely to develop routine ways of solving that problem. Note that the "exercise" in this principle may not be physical at all. Exercise may refer to any human action, physical or mental. Note also that the principle is loose in the sense that it does not specify how much more likely it is that a particular response will occur. The principle is, as we suggested, an ordinal concept. But how does this learning principle relate to brand loyalty?

This principle suggests that habitual patterns of buyer behavior are most

[17] See Edward L. Brink and William T. Kelley, *The Management of Promotion,* Englewood Cliffs, N.J.: Prentice-Hall, Inc., 1963, pp. 133–134.

likely to evolve for products that are purchased most frequently. The need or requirement of frequent purchase is the action that becomes routinized or habitualized, and this process of routinization is likely to mean that a decision on which brand to buy is not likely rendered with each purchase—the purchase of one brand becomes repetitive. Think for a moment about your own consumer behavior. When you make a purchase of some product very frequently are you more or less likely to develop loyalty patterns? With cigarettes, for example, do you explore different brands continuously, or do you habitualize a particular brand? This principle of learning theory says that, in general, we tend to routinize the buying procedure for those of our needs that occur most frequently. This principle also suggests that, other things being the same, brand loyalty is likely to be weakest in those circumstances in which a purchase need arises infrequently. That is, the need that arises infrequently constitutes less "exercise," and is, therefore, not as likely to be resolved through a routinization of behavior.

PROBABILISTIC LEARNING EXPLANATIONS OF BRAND LOYALTY
Probabilistic learning explanations of brand loyalty are an extension, or a refinement, of the nonprobabilistic explanations. The probabilistic explanations are more rigorous—they speak, as it were, with greater precision. We can best demonstrate the nature of these probabilistic learning models with the assistance of a brand purchase chain. Consider the two brand purchase chains below:

Chain A   Y N X X X X X
Chain B   Y N X Y Y Y Y Y Y Y

Chain A depicts seven purchase events, the last five being purchases of Brand X. Chain B depicts ten purchase events, the last seven being purchases of Brand Y. The goal of probabilistic learning explanations of brand loyalty is to enable us to predict what brand will be purchased with the next purchase event, given some historical purchase pattern.

The purchase chains above are viewed as distinctive learning experiences. This distinctive learning experience serves to determine in a probabilistic way what brand will be purchased in the next event. Thus, the fact that the buyer in Chain A has experimented with Brands Y, N and X and has purchased Brand X the last five times in succession, constitutes a learning experience for that buyer that will suggest to him what his next purchase should be. If we knew a great deal more about the learning that has taken place during the events depicted in Chain A, we might be able to assert that the probability that the buyer whose actions are summarized in Chain A will buy Brand X in the eighth purchase event is (say) .7. That is, the chances are 7 out of 10 that Brand X will be the brand selected in the next purchase. Similarly, we might, if we knew more about the learning that had taken place in the series of purchases summarized in Chain B, be able to predict probabilistically the likely outcome of the next purchase in the sequence.

Enough has now been said so that the basic nature of probabilistic learning explanations of brand loyalty should be clear. But we need to refine our thinking about these probabilistic models. Toward that end, we should distinguish three subordinate classes of probabilistic learning models of brand loyalty: (a) the linear model, (b) the nonlinear model and (c) the model that embodies a dislearning feature.

The simplest form of a probabilistic learning model of brand loyalty is the linear model. Both the essence of this linear model and the reason for calling it "linear" should be apparent in the following representation.

Figure 9.4 Linear Learning Model of Brand Loyalty

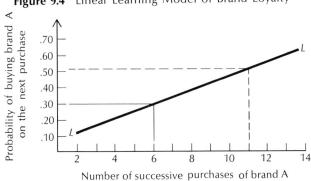

The line segment LL' represents a linear rate of learning brand loyalty for Brand A. Note that for the buyer who has purchased Brand A on six successive occasions, the probability that he will purchase Brand A on the next purchase is slightly over 30 percent. The buyer who has purchased Brand A on eleven successive occasions has a probability of purchasing brand A on the next purchase of over 50 percent. It should be emphasized that the data summarized in Figure 9.4 are hypothetical. The data are presented only to illustrate, not to define, the nature of a linear learning model of brand loyalty.

The distinctive characteristic of a *linear learning model* is that *each successive experience increases the probability of repurchase and does so by the same amount*. Note in this connection that every experience with Brand A in Figure 9.4 adds about .05 to the probability of a subsequent and successive purchase of the same brand; the slope of LL' is constant. In effect, then, this linear model increases the probability of repurchase by a constant amount for each purchase and cumulates the sum of these constant increments. The linear representation of learning brand loyalty is thus very simple—indeed overly simple. We need to modify it in order to make it reflect more accurately the actual learning process. But before we introduce this further modification, we should identify more specifically the shortcomings of this linear learning model.

There are two essential faults with the linear learning model of brand preference. First, this simple model does not tell us what happens if a buyer interrupts his chain of purchases of any particular brand. That is, suppose that a buyer purchased Brand A five successive times and then Brand M. What would be the probability that the buyer would revert to Brand A on the next purchase? Does he forget all that he ever knew about Brand A, or does he "remember" the experience of five successive previous uses of that brand? At.very best, the linear model is ambiguous regarding the effects of an interrupted chain. Second, the linear model seems unacceptable because it does not seem reasonable to assume that the first experience with a particular brand contributes the same increment of understanding about the brand as does, say, the tenth use experience with the brand. Yet that is precisely what this simple model would have us believe. Make sure that you understand this last point, for our first refinement of this learning model will endeavor to correct this particular shortcoming.

A nonlinear probabilistic learning model of brand loyalty is depicted in Figure 9.5 below.

Figure 9.5 Nonlinear Probabilistic Learning Model of Brand Loyalty

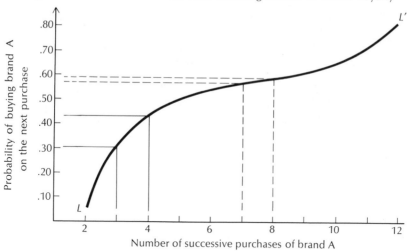

One important change has been made in LL' as it is now represented in Figure 9.5. We have now, with our wavy LL', anticipated the possibility that the rate of learning may be different at different points in a succession of purchases. Although the curve LL' depicted in Figure 9.5 is purely illustrative, it incorporates an element of realism that was lacking in the earlier, linear, model. Note carefully that the increase in probability of a repurchase of Brand A increases sharply with early purchase experience. Note also that the rate of increase in the probability of repurchase increases again with the habitual user—the buyer with 12, 13 or 14 successive purchases in his purchase chain. But the most important point about our nonlinear model is that it is nonlinear. Again, the particular shape of our LL' curve is illustrative, not definitive. Much current research is, in fact, being devoted to the definition of the exact shape of this and similar curves.[18]

But even when we introduce a nonlinear learning function, we still have a model of brand loyalty that has the "interruption ambiguity" that we mentioned earlier. The last of the probabilistic models that we will consider here explicitly accommodates the problem of the interrupted purchase sequence. Consider Figure 9.6.

Figure 9.6 A Nonlinear Learning Model of Brand Loyalty with a Dislearning Feature[19]

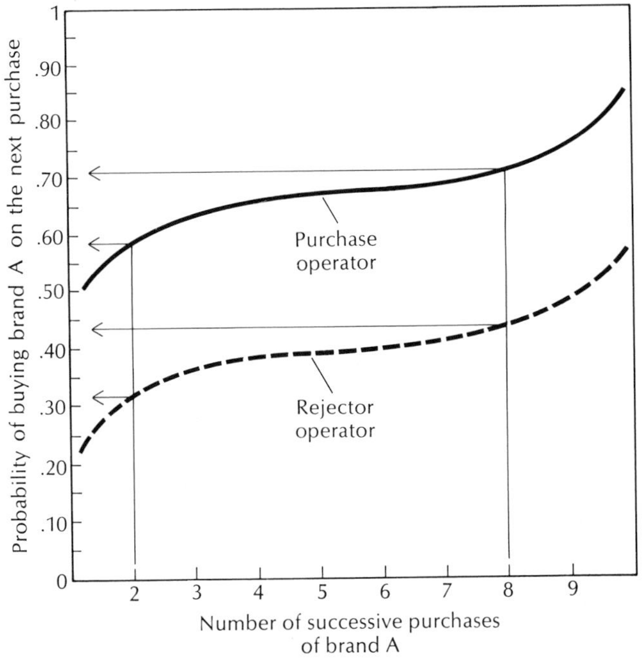

Although the nonlinear learning model in Figure 9.6 looks forbidding, it actually represents a rather simple modification of the models we have considered thus far. Note for example that both axes read as before. We

---

[18] See, for example, Alfred A. Kuehn, "Consumer Brand Choice as a Learning Process," *Journal of Advertising Research*, December 1962, pp. 10–17. See James M. Carman, "Brand Switching and Linear Learning Models," *Journal of Advertising Research*, June 1966, pp. 23–31. For a criticism of learning models, see Raymond J. Lawrence, "Patterns of Buyer Behavior: Time for a New Approach," *Journal of Marketing Research*, May 1969, pp. 137–144.

[19] This model is an adaptation of a model first suggested by Alfred A. Kuehn in his "Consumer Brand Choice as a Learning Process," *Journal of Advertising Research*, December 1962, pp. 10–17; reprinted in Kassarjian and Robertson, *op. cit.*, pp. 104–114. See especially p. 105.

have, however added a "rejector operator," and we have explicitly identified our old LL' as a "purchase operator." How does one read this new
model? Consider the buyer who has completed two successive purchases
of Brand A. If we read vertically to the purchase operator, we are told
that the probability that such a buyer will buy Brand A on the next purchase
is between 55 and 60 percent. So far, this model reads exactly like the
earlier forms. But suppose that the buyer has a purchase sequence of
two successive uses of Brand A and one use of some other brand. In
other words, the buyer's learning experience with Brand A is interrupted.
What, then, is the probability that the next purchase will be Brand A?

In order to read this model when the purchase sequence has been
interrupted, we read vertically to the rejector operator and thence to the
probability scale. This particular model tells us that a buyer with two
successive uses of Brand A and an intervening use of some other brand,
will revert to Brand A about three times out of ten (the .3 level of probability). Similarly, the probability that a buyer who has used Brand A on
eight successive occasions and then experimented with some other brand
on his last purchase will revert to Brand A on the next purchase is about
.425. The reader is again cautioned not to view the actual numerical values
in this model as definitive—the values are hypothetical and are for purposes
of illustrating the use of the model. This caution is worth repeating. The
actual position of the purchase operator and the rejector operator relative
to the probability scale will be different for different types of products;
and the task of defining both the position and the slope of these operators
remains, in large measure, to be accomplished.

Figure 9.7 Learning and Purchase Frequency

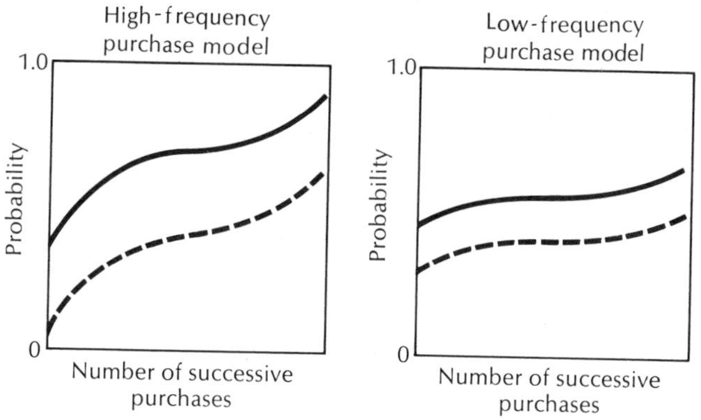

There are, however, some general comments we can make about both
the slope and the position of the purchase and rejector operators relative
to the probability scale. In general, it is believed that for high-frequency
purchases the slope of the purchase operator and the rejector operator
approaches a southwest-northeast diagonal through our model. This gen-

eral tendency seems consistent with the basic notion that the cumulative effects of learning would be "a more important factor for high-frequency purchases (small time interval between purchases) than for low-frequency purchases (large time interval between purchases)."[20] Similarly, it is believed that as the time interval between purchases is longer, the purchase operator and the rejector operator approach the horizontal. Figure 9.7 suggests this relationship.

Notice that the relationships suggested in Figure 9.7 are entirely consistent with the principle of exercise that we examined earlier. Observe that a higher probability of repurchase can be attained with the high-frequency purchase model than with the low-frequency model.[21] We shall return to this point later (when we discuss products), but for now we turn to a consideration of theories of brand loyalty that emphasize the consumer's perception of risk.

PERCEPTION OF RISK AND BRAND LOYALTY

Virtually every human action carries some risk with it. When we drive a car, when we work, when we eat, there is some element of risk. More to the point of our interest here, there is risk in consumer behavior—when we buy an unknown brand there is some risk that it will not perform in an acceptable manner.[22] There is, moreover, some evidence that different persons see (or perceive) greater risk in experimentation with new brands than others. These two points—(a) that there is risk in brand experimentation and (b) that some persons perceive greater risk in brand experimentation than others—represent the foundation for an evolving theory of brand loyalty.

The great promise of this risk-perception theory of brand loyalty is that we may be able, in some simple way, to measure and classify persons as (say) high, medium or low risk-perceivers and predict the degree of brand loyalty on the basis of that measurement. Those persons who perceive the greatest risk in a brand change would, presumably, tend to be the most loyal. Conversely, those who perceive little risk in change would tend to be least loyal to any one brand. Although the evidence is far from conclusive, there is some support for this theory of brand loyalty.[23]

---

[20] See James M. Carman, op. cit., p. 24.

[21] See Alfred A. Kuehn, op. cit., p. 106.

[22] The role of risk in consumer behavior was initially explored in Raymond A. Bauer, "Consumer Behavior as Risk Taking," in Robert S. Hancock, editor, Proceedings of the American Marketing Association, 1960, pp. 389–398.

[23] An interesting recent study in which the risk element in the experimental design was systematically controlled is described in Jagdish N. Sheth and M. Venkatesan, "Risk-Reduction Processes in Repetitive Consumer Behavior," Journal of Marketing Research, August 1968, pp. 307–310.

In a study conducted in a housing complex for married students in Cambridge, Massachusetts, only 36 percent of those housewives who were judged high risk-perceivers switched from their normal brand of coffee to a new brand that was being tested. In this same experiment, 55 percent of those judged to be low risk-perceivers tried the new brand.[24] This approach to understanding brand loyalty is an interesting one. Certainly the assumed relationship between risk perception and brand switching is logical. The most formidable problem associated with this approach lies in the method(s) used to classify consumers according to degree of risk perception.

SELF-CONCEPT AND BRAND LOYALTY

Within the field of psychology there is a school of thought that has developed as a "personal approach" to understanding human behavior. The central thrust of this school of thought is that all of human behavior has some purpose, "but to be understood, it must be observed not from the point of view of an outsider, but from the view of the behaver himself."[25] This self theory of human behavior holds, further, that our actions are, in important degree, determined not by what we are as seen by others, but by what we believe we are. This "totality of an individual's attitudes, feelings, perceptions, and evaluations of himself is his self-concept or his self-image."[26] This view suggests that if a person truly believes himself dull, he will affect the behavior of a dull person; if a person believes himself a bon vivant, he will affect behavior that he believes appropriate for such a person. To be more specific, the theory says that we may decide not to buy a psychedelic shirt because it does not match the austerity rating we give ourselves. But how does this theory find application in the problem of understanding brand loyalty?

There is some evidence that consumers tend to attribute to some brands personalities that have characteristics similar to those attributed to human personalities. Thus, one brand may be perceived by significant numbers of consumers as dull, old-fashioned, feminine, and so forth. Another brand may be perceived by a large number or people as aggressive, successful and exciting. Because people often attribute these human attributes to brands of products, it is possible to use a technique called "congruence

[24] See Johan Arndt, "Word-of-Mouth Advertising and Perceived Risk," in Kassarjian and Robertson, op. cit., p. 333 and Table 5.

[25] Joseph W. Newman, "The Concept of Self-Image," in Steuart Henderson Britt, editor, Consumer Behavior and the Behavioral Sciences, New York: John Wiley & Sons, Inc., 1966, p. 189.

[26] See Edward L. Grubb, "Consumer Perception of Self-Concept and Its Relation to Brand Choice of Selected Product Types," in Peter D. Bennett, editor, Marketing and Economic Development, Chicago: American Marketing Association, 1965, p. 419.

scaling" to further our understanding of self-concept and brand loyalty. But what are congruence scales?[27] The following illustration will clarify this idea.

As a person, I tend to be:

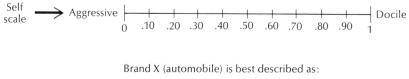

Brand X (automobile) is best described as:

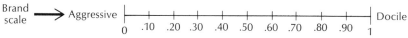

Consider the two scales above. Note that one scale is the "self scale" and that the other is a "brand scale." Note also the lead-in sentences for each of the scales. Congruence is said to exist when persons score themselves the same as they score a particular brand of product and also own that brand. For the sake of brevity, only one rating scale is illustrated. In actual practice, we might scale eight, ten or even more dimensions.[28] The important point now is that scaling devices such as these permit us to quantify both self-images and brand-images, and thus to explore any relationships which might exist between the two.

The fundamental notion underlying the use of self-concept in a brand loyalty context is that individuals tend to accept brands with images similar to their self-concept and tend to reject brands with images dissimilar to their self-concept. If this premise is true, it would be possible to reason back from self-image and brand-image data to brand purchases and loyalty. But what evidence is there that self-image and brand-image congruence exists?

A recent study of owners of the Pontiac GTO series and owners of the Volkswagen 1200–1300 series produced some interesting results.[29] In this particular study, Pontiac owners were asked to rate themselves (self-concept), the Pontiac image, and the Volkswagen image. Volkswagen owners were asked to rate themselves, the Pontiac image, and the Volks-wagen image. The following tabulation indicates some of the results of the study.

[27] This phrase is suggested by Ira J. Dolich in "Congruence Relationships Between Self-Images and Product Brands," *Journal of Marketing Research*, February 1969, pp. 20–34.
[28] For that matter, there is nothing sacred about the scales illustrated here. Any number of different approaches would be workable. See Edward L. Grubb and Gregg Hupp, "Perception of Self, Generalized Stereotypes, and Brand Selection," *Journal of Marketing Research*, February 1968, pp. 58–63 for a description of variation of the scaling device illustrated here.
[29] *Ibid.*, p. 59.

Table 9.1 Self-Concept and Automobile Images

Scale Items	Pontiac Owners		
	Self-Concept	**Pontiac Image**	**VW Image**
Adventurous	2.83	3.03	1.61
Fashionable	2.31	3.11	1.06
Flashy	1.31	2.75	.47
Interested in Opposite Sex	3.14	3.03	1.39
Pleasure-seeking	2.61	3.00	1.28
Sporty	2.42	3.39	.89
Status-conscious	2.42	2.97	.89
Style-conscious	2.61	3.36	.72

Scale Items	Volkswagen Owners		
	Self-Concept	**Pontiac Image**	**VW Image**
Conservative	2.19	.74	2.23
Creative	2.19	1.47	2.14
Economical	2.77	.86	3.42
Individualistic	2.60	1.26	2.44
Practical	2.74	.91	3.33
Quality-conscious	3.02	1.81	2.88
Sensible	2.79	1.35	3.97
Thrifty	2.56	.58	3.28

Each of the numbers in Table 9.1 is an average scale value similar to those we discussed as congruence scales. Each automobile owner in the study rated himself, Pontiac, and VW along a five-point scale for each of the scale items. For example, the self-concept value of the "adventurous" scale item resulted as follows:

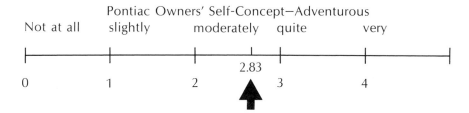

The mean value for "adventurous" for the Pontiac owners' self-concept means that most Pontiac owners rated themselves "moderately" to "quite" adventurous. Now consider the Pontiac owners' image of VW. The value of 1.61 in this case is developed as follows:

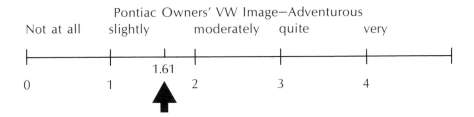

Pontiac Owners' VW Image—Adventurous

In order to be sure that you understand what each of the values in Table 9.1 signifies, what does the value .58 on the "thrifty" scale suggest about VW owners' perceptions of Pontiac owners? This study indicates the practicality of self-concept measurement and brand-image measurement. Congruence studies will undoubtedly be undertaken more frequently in the future. Much of the task of relating congruence data to brand switching and brand loyalty remains to be done. The basic notion that brand loyalty is closely related to congruence is, however, extremely promising.

Some theoretical explanations of consumer time-of-adoption patterns

It was noted in the previous chapter that an understanding of the process of diffusing a product innovation throughout a population is thought to be very important to a complete understanding of the functioning of our market system. We noted that the adoption of product innovations often works on the general economy as a boost to the level of economic activity. It is conceivable that the timing of the introduction of new product concepts could be a powerful supplementary means of controlling our market system. That is, in addition to traditional controls, such as the lending rates of financial institutions, the open market activities of the Federal Reserve, and adjustments in the reserve requirements of Federal Reserve member banks, the introduction of new product concepts might well be thought of as an additional means through which to achieve basic economic goals. But a more complete understanding of consumer time-of-adoption patterns is also of great potential value to the individual firm. For the moment, let it suffice to note that both the planning of promotion and the process of sales forecasting may be done with greater precision as a result of an increased understanding of consumer time-of-adoption patterns.

There are four aspects of consumer time-of-adoption patterns that will concern us here. In the discussion that follows, we will examine (a) the nature of innovators and early adopters and our reasons for special interest in them, (b) the trickle-down thesis of the diffusion process, (c) the horizontal influence thesis of the diffusion process and (d) the booster station (or two-step flow) theory of influence.

INNOVATORS AND EARLY ADOPTERS

In chapter 7 we defined consumer innovators as those who represent the first 2.5 percent to accept a new idea or a new product. We defined early adopters as the 13.5 percent of consumers who follow the innovators in the time-of-adoption process, but who lead the early majority, the late majority and the laggards. Concern with the nature of innovators and early adopters is an integral part of virtually all studies of the time-of-adoption process. Our concern with these consumption leaders stems from the belief that they function as catalysts in the diffusion/adoption process.

Much of the research of the diffusion process to date has been directed to a more precise definition of the characteristics of these innovators and early adopter households or consumers. The rationale for such an emphasis is simple. If we can define these innovators and early adopters in social, demographic, economic and psychological terms, it follows that we may then determine: (a) how they differ from less innovative households and consumers; (b) where they reside in the total population—that is, how they are distributed in the total population; and (c) how the acceptance of new ideas (including new products) is influenced by their actions.[30] This latter point is an important one because it is also thought that "innovators and early adopters tend to be inordinately influential in the sense that they either set trends by taking new courses of action" or are able to persuade others through their opinions.[31] For these reasons, a consideration of innovators and early adopters has been an unavoidable part of explorations of the diffusion process.

But what are these innovators and early adopters like? The following descriptions have been suggested:

Innovators are venturesome— . . . they are eager to try new ideas. This interest leads them out of a local circle of peers and into more cosmopolite social relationships. Communication patterns and friendships among a clique of innovators are common, even though the geographical distance between the innovators may be great. They travel in a circle of venturesomeness, like circuit riders who spread new ideas as their gospel. Being an innovator has several prerequisites. They include control of substantial financial resources to absorb the loss of an unprofitable innovation, and the ability to understand and apply complex technical knowledge.

The major value of the innovator is venturesomeness. He must desire the hazardous, the rash, the daring, and the risking. The innovator also must be willing

---

[30] Whether psychological attributes correlate with innovative behavior is open to dispute. One recent study, for example, concludes cautiously that "a marketer trying to reach innovative or influential individuals will find little help by identifying these people in terms of basic personality variables." See Thomas S. Robertson and James H. Myers, "Personality Correlates of Opinion Leadership and Innovative Buying Behavior," *Journal of Marketing Research,* May 1969, pp. 164–168.

[31] Britt, *Consumer Behavior,* p. 281.

to accept an occasional debacle when one of the new ideas he adopts proves unsuccessful.

Early Adopters are a more integrated part of the local social system than are innovators. While innovators are cosmopolites, early adopters are localites. This adopter category, more than any other, has the greatest degree of opinion leadership in most social systems. Potential adopters look to them for advice and information about the innovation. The early adopter is considered by many as "the man to check with" before using a new idea. This early adopter category is generally sought by change agents as a local missionary for speeding the diffusion process. Because early adopters are not "too far" ahead of the average individual in innovativeness, they serve as a role-model for many other members of a social system. The early adopter is respected by his peers. He is the embodiment of successful and discrete use of new ideas. And the early adopter knows that he must continue to earn this esteem of his colleagues if his position in the social structure is to be maintained.[32]

Some studies of innovators and early adopters suggest that the one word that best identifies these thought leaders is mobility. Studies conducted by the Opinion Research Corporation, Princeton, New Jersey, indicate that innovators and early adopters:

1 Travel more and change residences more often.
2 Move more through their occupational structure.
3 Are more likely to change their economic status.
4 Move in more diverse social circles—do not depend upon kinfolk for companionship.
5 Expose themselves to different intellectual influences (including the mass media).
6 Have more formal education and achieved it in more institutions.[33]

These mobile thought leaders were found by the Opinion Research Corporation to have been among the first to use credit cards, electric blankets, frozen soups, low-calorie beverages, hi-fi, foreign cars and clothes driers. They were likewise early users of freezers, colored sheets and blenders.[34]

THE TRICKLE-DOWN THESIS OF DIFFUSION

Another important aspect of time-of-adoption research relates to the manner in which opinions are diffused in the general population. This word

[32] Both these descriptions are from Everett M. Rogers, *Diffusion of Innovations,* New York: The Free Press, 1962, pp. 168–169. See also, however, Thomas S. Robertson and James N. Kennedy, "Prediction of Consumer Innovators: Application of Multiple Discriminant Analysis," *Journal of Marketing Research,* February 1968, pp. 64–69. Robertson and Kennedy conclude that "it appears that two variables, venturesomeness (willingness to take new product risks) and social mobility (movement up the social class hierarchy) account for most of the innovative behavior difference between innovators and non-innovators of new home appliances." See particularly page 69.
[33] See Britt, *Consumer Behavior,* p. 291.
[34] *Ibid.*

diffusion as we will employ it here may be defined as *a process of transmittal of ideas, points of view or preferences among some total population.* If we whispered an idea in the ear of one person in an auditorium full of people and asked that person to spread the idea, and to also ask those he thus contacted to likewise further spread the idea, we would create a kind of miniature diffusion sequence. The specific kind of diffusion process in which we are most interested is not forced in the sense that the members of the group are acting under instructions to spread an idea; we are more immediately concerned with a natural diffusion process, one in which the pass-along procedure is entirely voluntary.

A natural diffusion process is exemplified by the transmittal of awareness of new products, political issues, information about books and movies, and so forth. But we should further recognize and distinguish between diffusion that is occasioned by commercial sponsorship and diffusion that is occasioned by informal word of mouth. An advertisement that extols the virtues of a particular car certainly effects a "transmittal of ideas, points of view or preferences." But a man's word of praise about his new car directed to his neighbor in a casual conversation is also an element in an important kind of diffusion. Indeed, a classic study of influence suggests that this informal word-of-mouth transmittal is extremely potent. The data below suggests the role of various media in the diffusion process.

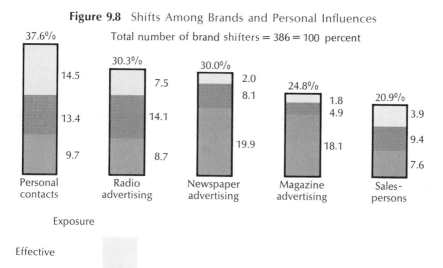

Figure 9.8 Shifts Among Brands and Personal Influences

Source: Elihu Katz and Paul Lazarefeld, *Personal Influence,* New York: The Free Press, 1955, Chart I, p. 176.

The data summarized in Figure 9.8 suggest that personal contacts—the force that we have referred to as word-of-mouth influence—is the single most important medium of influence. Note that 37.6 percent of respondents who had recently changed brands acknowledged that personal contacts were instrumental in making the decision to change. Note also that the data distinguish three degrees of influence: effective, ineffective and contributory. Personal contacts accounted for the highest incidence of effective influence. To summarize briefly, then, we are concerned primarily with improving our understanding of natural diffusion processes—both those that are commercially sponsored and those that are informal word of mouth.

Figure 9.9 The Trickle-Down Process

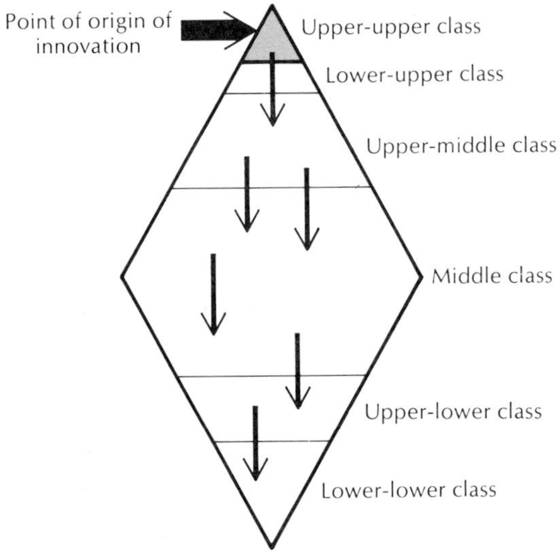

How does this diffusion process work? Perhaps the most frequently encountered theory of diffusion assumes that new ideas flow in an essentially vertical direction through a social system. This notion is suggested by the term "trickle-down thesis." The trickle-down thesis presumes a stratified, or layered, social system as suggested in Figure 9.9. The trickle-down thesis suggests that innovation in a social system normally begins at the upper levels of the social structure. The basic notion is that subordinate social strata look to levels above them for guidance in matters of taste. There are several reasons why this trickle-down argument seems plausible. First, hundreds of years ago royalty did act as style innovators, nobility copied royalty, and undoubtedly some of the middle classes copied nobility. Moreover, we still witness some trickle-down influence in matters of dress. We still see some tendency for new styles to appear first at the level of exclusive or high fashion shops, then at high quality ready to wear outlets and finally, at mass appeal stores. To the extent that each of these types of retail outlets caters to a clientele of descending social class, a kind of trickle-down phenomenon is suggested. The following quotation is directed to this point.

As the new styles, set by Paris and first imitated by the designers of expensive "limited editions," gain wider favor, the designers of each lower price range include the new "fashion" points as best they can in lines they create in response to actual or anticipated demand from those on lower class levels. As the fashion trickles down, fabrics become cheaper and mass production necessary. When a general style has trickled down through all levels, the "fashion" must change. The universalization of what started out as distinctive cheapens its symbolic value. A new change, a new "fashion" symbol is necessary.[35]

HORIZONTAL INFLUENCE AND THE DIFFUSION PROCESS

Although the trickle-down thesis is logical and seems operative in some contexts, there are critics of the theory. These critics argue that the trickle-down description of diffusion is of limited applicability today and that it errs because it assumes that opinion leadership necessarily originates at the top of the social hierarchy. A view often encountered is that such leadership may, and in fact does, originate at virtually all levels of the social system. In a now classic study, it was found that opinion leadership was not concentrated in any particular social stratum. A summary of that study notes that in matters of "marketing (brand choice), fashions, and movie going . . . there is no appreciable concentration of influentials in any of the three socioeconomic levels."[36] Another study also found "opinion leaders in similar proportions on every socioeconomic and occupational level" and found conversations of a persuasive content between people of similar age, occupation and political opinion.[37]

Still another study, one that explored the proportion of families adopting television, canasta and supermarkets, tends to refute the trickle-down concept. The tabulation below relates adoption of these three "ideas" to occupational prestige. These data suggest that acceptance of television and canasta were very different processes. Indeed, TV seems almost a "trickle-up" phenomenon. We should conclude that the trickle-down thesis is perhaps a useful initial generalization, but that it breaks down as one examines specific realms of influence.

[35] See Bernard Barber and Lyle S. Lobel, "Fashion For Women's Clothes and the American Social System," Social Forces, December 1952, p. 127.
[36] See Elihu Katz, "The Two-Step Flow of Communication: An Up-to-Date Report of An Hypothesis," in Ben M. Enis and Keith K. Cox, editors, Marketing Classics, Boston: Allyn and Bacon, Inc., 1969, pp. 195–196.
[37] Ibid., p. 196.

Table 9.2   The Acceptance of Television, Canasta and Supermarkets by Occupational Classes[38]

Occupational Class	Proportion Accepting		
	TV	**Canasta**	**Supermarkets**
I Mainly professional	24	72	52
II Proprietors, managers, officials	44	72	80
III Clerks and kindred	48	44	56
IV Skilled workers and foremen	52	20	80
V Semi-skilled workers	84	32	52
VI Unskilled workers	72	12	48

An opposing theory of the diffusion process is suggested by the phrase "horizontal influence thesis." This notion of the diffusion process is not as tidy as the trickle-down thesis—but it is probably much closer to the truth. The horizontal influence thesis assumes that opinion leaders, or influentials, reside at every social and economic stratum, and that such opinion leaders tend to specialize in terms of their realms of expertise. That is, "there is very little overlap of leadership: a leader in one sphere is not likely to be influential in another unrelated sphere as well." [39] Though all the evidence is not in, there is some suggestion that there is a slightly greater concentration of opinion leaders among the more educated people on each socioeconomic level.[40] The central thrust of the horizontal influence thesis is that influence moves essentially within socioeconomic classes.

Clearly, from a marketing point of view, the notion that opinion leadership resides throughout the social structure of the system is a complicating fact. The notion that opinion leaders are also specialists (rather than generally influential) tends further to complicate matters. For, if something like the trickle-down thesis were an accurate portrayal of the diffusion process, a new concept in products or services would first have to be sold only to the elite classes, and we could then stand back and wait for the "trickle." [41] If "trickle" was less than we desired, the mass media could be used to hasten the adoption process. But with potential opinion leaders virtually everywhere, each having a different field of competence,

[38] This table is from data in L. S. Graham, *Selection and Social Stratification,* unpublished Ph.D. dissertation, Yale University, 1951; the data are reprinted in John A. Howard, *Marketing Theory,* Boston: Allyn and Bacon, Inc., 1965, pp. 167–169.

[39] See Enis and Cox, *op. cit.,* p. 195.

[40] *Ibid.,* pp. 196–197.

[41] This is not to imply that the trickle-down notion does not have pragmatic value in the field of marketing management. Such is not the case at all. See, for example, the discussion of fashion cycles in Ronald R. Gist, *Retailing: Concepts and Decisions,* New York: John Wiley & Sons, Inc., 1968, pp. 288–293.

the task of harnessing the force of this interpersonal word-of-mouth influence is, at the very best, complex.

THE BOOSTER STATION THEORY OF INFLUENCE

Despite these complexities, it is possible to use the force of word-of-mouth influence in an intelligent way. It has been suggested that a commercial message may have a kind of pass-along value—that it may be part of a two-step flow of influence. To be more specific, a particular message may move from the commercial sponsor of the message to some listener/viewer/reader and from that listener/viewer/reader to some other person or persons. This two-step flow of influence is of greatest value when the second step of the communications process is an extremely persuasive or influential personage. As a means of clarifying and amplifying this idea, observe the relationships depicted in Figure 9.10.

Figure 9.10   Two-Step Influence

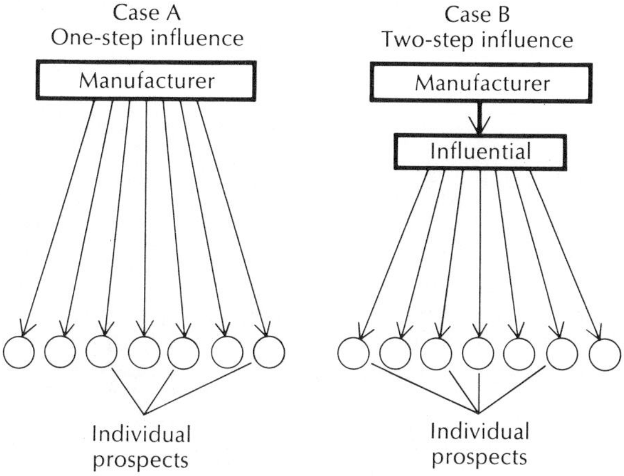

Case A depicts a "normal" one-step flow of influence—from commercial sponsor to prospect. Case B depicts a two-step system of influence—from manufacturer to influential and from influential to prospect. It should be emphasized that there might be distinct economic advantages in concentrating sales efforts on persons who act in a pass-along capacity. Thus this influential, if properly persuaded, may sell, in turn, whatever the manufacturer sells to him. But to designate this process "the two-step flow" of communications results in a deemphasis of an extremely important part of the process. Something happens in the second step of this process that can make it vastly superior to a direct, or one-step, type of communication.

To be of greatest value, the message being transmitted must have greater impact among prospects when it comes from the influential than when it comes directly from the sponsor of the message. Were this not true, there would be substantially less reason to use a two-step communications system. The heart of the two-step flow of influence lies in the relatively greater persuasiveness of the influential. This fact seems to argue for what is a better descriptive term—a *booster station theory of influence*. Consider the now modified paths of influence depicted in Figure 9.11.

Figure 9.11[42] Booster Station Effect

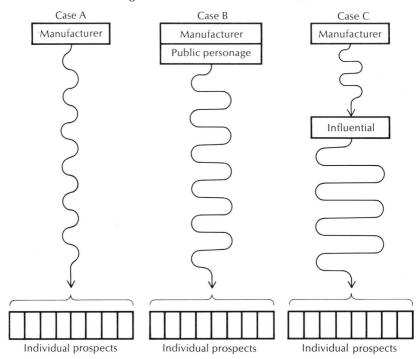

Case A in Figure 9.11 depicts the direct or one-step flow of influence. Note the amplitude of the signal transmitted by the sponsor of the message. We shall use this signal amplitude to suggest the impact of the message. By impact we mean persuasiveness and credibility. Observe the difference between Case A and Case B. The sponsor's message is sent through a public personage—a Lee Trevino, an Arne Johnson or some other public figure. Note, too, that the signal transmitted is of greater amplitude than in Case A. Were this not so there would be less reason to use the testimonial of the public personage. In effect, the public figure is more persuasive—he has greater impact upon prospects. Now consider Case C. Note that there are two distinct steps depicted here. The message from sponsor to influential is (relatively speaking) low impact communications; the message from influential to prospect is extremely persuasive. The influential is seen by prospects as "clean" (free of economic interest) and therefore

[42] There are obviously cases other than those depicted here. The sponsor of a commercial message might choose a particular magazine because of the impact it has with his audience.

much more likely to tell the whole truth. It is this amplification process that is the single reason for the use of two-step systems of influence.

SUMMARY

Our purpose in Chapter 9 has been: (a) to conclude our discussion of social stratification, (b) to examine some theories that represent explanations of patterns of consumer brand loyalty and (c) to examine some theories of consumer time-of-adoption behavior. The concept of the stratification profile was introduced—and the idea was found applicable to the clientele of a business, as well as to entire political subdivisions. The notion of consumer privilege was also defined, and its analytical value was explored. Consumer privilege provides a means through which social class position and income may logically combine to explain particular types of consumer behavior. Overprivileged and underprivileged market segments represent a helpful analytical refinement.

Our examination of explanations of brand loyalty patterns centered upon three types of theories. First, we considered those theories that rest upon a learning theory foundation. These learning explanations of brand loyalty included nonprobabilistic learning models ("exercise" explanations) and probabilistic models. Probabilistic models included three types: (a) simple linear, (b) simple nonlinear and (c) nonlinear with a dislearning feature.

We examined briefly the idea that the brand loyalty of consumers is related to their perception of risk in brand experimentation. We noted that evidence is accumulating that suggests that high risk-perceivers tend to be timid brand experimenters. Conversely, persons who see little risk in brand experimentation tend to develop less well defined patterns of loyalty. We noted that another promising concept in terms of understanding brand loyalty is suggested by the term self-concept. Again, there is some evidence that brand loyalty may relate to brand-image and self-image congruence.

Finally, we explored some aspects of consumer time-of-adoption patterns. In particular, we considered: (a) the nature and importance of innovators and early adopters, (b) the trickle-down thesis of the diffusion process, (c) the horizontal influence thesis of the diffusion process and (d) the booster station theory of influence.

REVIEW QUESTIONS

1 Carefully define and indicate the relevance of each of the following concepts to the study of marketing:
   a. City occupational profiles
   b. Social class profiles
   c. An overprivileged consumer
   d. An underprivileged consumer
   e. The psychological principle of exercise
   f. A dislearning feature in a brand loyalty model

g. A purchase operator in learning models of brand loyalty

h. A rejector operator in learning models of brand loyalty

i. The risk perception theory of brand loyalty

j. Self-concept

2 Distinguish carefully between each element in the following pairs of terms:

a. Nonprobabilistic *and* probabilistic learning explanations of brand loyalty.

b. A linear probabilistic learning model *and* nonlinear probabilistic learning model of brand loyalty.

c. Self-concept *and* congruence scales

d. The trickle-down thesis of diffusion *and* the horizontal influence thesis of diffusion

3 What is meant by the statement that linear and simple nonlinear models of learning embody an interrupted purchase ambiguity?

4 If you wanted to hasten the acceptance of a new product or a new idea, would you find innovators or early adopters the most helpful allies? Why?

5 What is meant by the term "booster station theory of communications"? How can this theory be applied in a practical way?

DISCUSSION QUESTIONS

6 Reflect upon your own actions as a consumer. What leads you to act in a brand-loyal manner? What leads you to act in a brand-experimental manner?

7 What sources of influence affect your own consumer behavior?

8 In general, does your own self-image agree with the apparel purchases you make?

9 Considering both Chapter 8 and Chapter 9, what are the most important determinants of your consumer behavior?

SUGGESTED SUPPLEMENTARY READINGS IN CONSUMER BEHAVIOR

Arndt, Johan, editor, *Insights into Consumer Behavior,* Boston: Allyn and Bacon, Inc., 1968.

Berelson, Bernard, and Gary A. Steiner, *Human Behavior: An Inventory of Scientific Findings,* New York: Harcourt, Brace and World, Inc., 1964.

Bliss, Perry, editor, *Marketing and the Behavioral Sciences,* Boston: Allyn and Bacon, Inc., 1967.

Britt, Steuart Henderson, editor, *Consumer Behavior and the Behavioral Sciences,* New York: John Wiley & Sons, Inc., 1966.

Carman, James M., *The Application of Social Class in Market Segmentation,* Berkeley, Calif.: School of Business Administration, University of California, 1965.

Cheskin, Louis, *Why People Buy,* New York: Liveright Publishing Corporation, 1959.

Cox, Donald F., editor, *Risk Taking and Information Handling in Consumer Behavior,* Boston: School of Business Administration, Harvard University, 1967.

Dickinson, Roger A., *Buyer Decision Making,* Berkeley, Calif.: School of Business Administration, University of California, 1967.

Engel, James F., David T. Kollat, and Roger D. Blackwell, *Consumer Behavior,* New York: Holt, Rinehart and Winston, Inc., 1968.

Hickman, C. Addison and Manford H. Kuhn, *Individuals, Groups and Economic Behavior,* New York: The Dryden Press, 1956.

Houthakker, H. S., and Lester D. Taylor, *Consumer Demand in the United States, 1929-1970,* Cambridge, Mass.: Harvard University Press, 1966.

Howard, John A., and Jagdish N. Sheth, *The Theory of Buyer Behavior,* New York: John Wiley & Sons, Inc., 1969.

Kassarjian, Harold H., and Thomas S. Robertson, *Perspectives in Consumer Behavior,* Glenview, Ill.: Scott, Foresman and Company, 1968.

Katona, George, *The Powerful Consumer: Psychological Studies of the American Economy,* New York: McGraw-Hill Book Company, 1960.

King, Robert L., editor, *Conferences, '55/'65,* Chicago: American Marketing Association, 1966 (especially Chap. V).

Markin, Rom J., *The Psychology of Consumer Behavior,* Englewood Cliffs, N.J.: Prentice-Hall, Inc., 1969.

Massy, William F., editor, *Marketing: Contributions from the Behavioral Sciences,* New York: Harcourt, Brace and World, Inc., 1965.

Myers, James H., and William H. Reynolds, *Consumer Behavior and Marketing Management,* Boston: Houghton Mifflin Company, 1967.

Myers, John B., *Consumer Image and Attitude,* Berkeley, Calif.: School of Business Administration, University of California, 1968.

Newman, Joseph W., editor, *On Knowing the Consumer,* New York: John Wiley & Sons, Inc., 1966.

Nicosia, Francesco M., *Consumer Decision Progress,* Englewood Cliffs, N.J.: Prentice-Hall, Inc., 1966.

Preston, Lee E., and Norman R. Collins, *Studies in a Simulated Market,* Berkeley, Calif.: School of Business Administration, University of California, 1966.

Rainwater, Lee, Richard P. Coleman, and Gerald Handel, *Workingman's Wife: Her Personality, World and Life Style,* New York: Macfadden-Bartell Corp., 1962.

Reiss, Albert J., Jr., Otis Dudley Duncan, Paul K. Hatt, and Cecil C. North, *Occupations and Social Status,* New York: The Free Press, 1961.

Tucker, W. T., editor, *Foundations for a Theory of Consumer Behavior,* New York: Holt, Rinehart and Winston, Inc., 1967.

———, *The Social Context of Economic Behavior,* New York: Holt, Rinehart and Winston, Inc., 1964.

Veblen, Thorstein, *The Theory of the Leisure Class,* New York: New American Library, 1953.

Wassen, Chester R., and David H. McConaughy, *Buyer Behavior and Marketing Decisions,* New York: Appleton-Century-Crofts, 1969.

Chapter 10

BUSINESS OPPORTUNITY AND MARKET APPRAISAL

Consumer behavior and market opportunity

The last three chapters have been concerned with a study of the behavior of consumers. We have purposely given careful and extended consideration to this question; an understanding of consumer behavior is surely the prime requisite to successful and efficient marketing. In the present chapter, our attention is focused on the appraisal of market opportunity. This is an extension rather than a change in subject matter, for when we appraise market opportunity, we are simply applying our understanding of consumer behavior on a collective rather than an individual basis. That is, when we appraise market opportunity we are, in effect, asking ourselves how many prospective buyers have value systems that will make particular products and services desirable. When any new product or service idea is conceived, the single question of greatest importance is whether consumers in sufficient numbers share the same enthusiasm for the idea as those who have conceived the product or service. Successful business enterprise ultimately rests upon *market opportunity,* and market opportunity is ultimately defined by consumer preferences.[1]

Some resounding product failures are traceable, at least in part, to an inability to apply this fundamental precept. Again, the Edsel experience of the Ford Motor Company is a case in point. There is evidence that the overwhelming reason for the introduction of the Edsel was that Ford needed it. Consider the following quotation:

Clearly, the economic climate favors a continued trend to medium-price cars. General Motors has three makes—Pontiac, Oldsmobile, and Buick—in the medium-price class (which together almost equal the penetration of Chevrolet).

---

[1] This priority of consumer preferences is the most important element in the business philosophy that is called the "marketing concept." See *The Marketing Concept: Its Meaning to Management* (Marketing Series No. 99), New York: American Management Association, 1957.

Chrysler has two makes in the medium-price field (Dodge and Desoto). But Ford Motor Company has only Mercury, which is responsible for less than 20 per cent of the company's current business.[2]

A reasonable inference from this quotation is that because both GM and Chrysler had intermediate offerings *Ford needed another car.* Research that was conducted seemed to take Ford's need as given and to focus instead on what kind of car it should be. The more relevant question was "Do consumers want another car from Ford?" Instead, the question asked was, "What kind of car should it be?"

Bristol-Myers' experience with Analoze reflects a similar, though perhaps less monumental, oversight. Analoze was a "combination analgesic (pain killer) and antacid." It was, moreover, waterless: to be taken as were Tums and Rolaids. "The executives who conceived the product a few years ago were impressed by the fact that Americans were gulping record quantities of analgesics such as Bufferin and Anacin. Since this was true, they reasoned, wouldn't an analgesic that could be taken without water have a ready market?"[3] Test markets showed this reasoning to be incorrect, and the product was withdrawn.[4] There are, of course, many other instances in which an inability to consider consumer preferences first has led to failure.

And such failure is costly—not just from the point of view of the individual company, but from the perspective of the economy as well. To the extent that better investment alternatives exist, expenditures for products and services for which there are no markets represent a misallocation of scarce economic resources. This is an extremely important point. For the more accurately we can detect and interpret market opportunity, the more efficient our market system can be. We all have a stake in encouraging a well-informed business community—one that truly understands and does not simply give lip service to the importance of recognizing market and consumer preferences. This chapter is directed to an examination of the means through which more accurate measurements of market opportunity may result. More specifically, the discussion that follows is developed around two basic tasks: (a) the development of some refinements in our concept of a market and (b) an examination of some methods of estimating market opportunity.

[2] Henry G. Baker, "Sales and Marketing Planning of the Edsel," *Marketing's Role in Scientific Management,* Proceedings of the 39th National Conference of the American Marketing Association, June 1957, pp. 128–144. This fascinating article is reprinted in R. J. Holloway and Robert S. Hancock, editors, *The Environment of Marketing Behavior,* New York: John Wiley & Sons, Inc., 1964, pp. 308–316.

[3] Harper W. Boyd, Jr., and Richard M. Clewett, editors, *Contemporary American Marketing: Readings on the Changing Market Structure,* Homewood, Ill.: Richard D. Irwin, Inc., 1962, p. 115.

[4] There was, apparently, real customer resistance to the idea of a painkiller without water. That is, aspirin and water are apparently thought of by many consumers as an inseparable pain-relieving team.

Markets: some refinements of the concept

In Chapter 1 we found it helpful to define the word "market" in order to further our definition of marketing itself. At that time we defined a market as "people, with purchasing power (money, credit or real goods), and a felt or latent inclination to buy." We now need to introduce some refinements in this concept of a market, for there are several different ways in which one may conceive of markets—all of which may be completely consistent with this basic definition. More specifically, we need to distinguish: (a) the local market concept, (b) the mass market concept, (c) the segmented market concept and (d) the global market concept. These four concepts of a market represent a historical transition—a sequence of perspectives, or viewpoints, through which many businesses have progressed. That is, the notions of local, mass, segmented and global markets have some relevancy in a historical context, as well as having an analytical or descriptive value.[5]

A *local market concept* is natural, and indeed unavoidable, in an economic system with limited transportation and communications media. At least one student of American markets believes that most corporate enterprise in this country held this local market concept, either explicitly or implicitly, until about the 1930's.[6] Because of severe limits on their ability to reach distant markets, it was reasonable for businesses to sell to those customers who: (a) were geographically close enough, (b) had the money and (c) preferred the product. This state of affairs is depicted in Figure 10.1. Note that the local market concept required either many small producers or inadequate coverage of the total market.

The evolution of efficient and extensive transportation systems and ubiquitous mass communication systems produced a corporate concept of the market that has been suggested by the term *mass market*. There are essentially two ways in which the mass market differs from the earlier, local market idea. First, the mass market included all persons in the United States who could be reached by transportation facilities and the mass media. Second (but certainly of no less importance), the mass market was often assumed to be comprised of people with want patterns that were remarkably similar from person to person. Market preferences were treated as though they were, to an important degree, homogeneous. This meant, in effect, that the product that was presented to the market was a compromise—it tended to be somewhat acceptable to everyone rather than precisely what was preferred by any part of the total market. Figure 10.2 depicts the mass market concept.

[5] The basic idea for this historical transition is suggested in Steven C. Brandt, "Dissecting the Segmentation Syndrome," *Journal of Marketing*, October 1966, pp. 22–27. Note, however, that the term "local market" is substituted for Brandt's term "open market." This minor change seems to avoid ambiguity in the student's mind between the open market as the Federal Reserve and Treasury Department use that term and the meaning suggested by Brandt.
[6] *Ibid.*, p. 23.

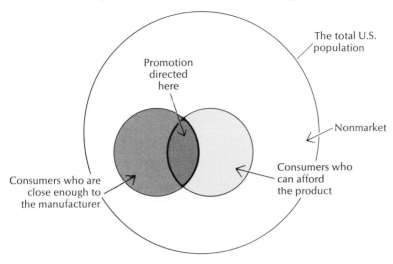

Figure 10.1 The Local Market Concept

The total U.S. population

Promotion directed here

Nonmarket

Consumers who are close enough to the manufacturer

Consumers who can afford the product

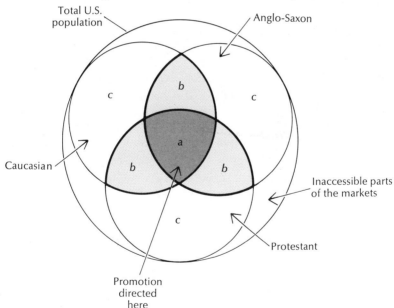

Figure 10.2 The Mass Market Concept

Total U.S. population

Anglo-Saxon

Caucasian

Inaccessible parts of the markets

Protestant

Promotion directed here

Note in Figure 10.2 that relatively little of the total United States population was inaccessible to the corporate enterprise serving the mass market concept. Note also the assumption of homogeneous market preferences. The product sold was a perfect fit to the preferences of (say) the white, Anglo-Saxon, Protestant. It was a combination of features that would appeal generally to everyone but would not appeal especially to anyone. In this latter regard, observe the area designated a. Promotional activities were directed to some average person—a statistical composite who was all the things that characterized the majority. Note that the areas designated b are the compromised part of the market. Persons falling into these areas possess two of the three mass characteristics. They used the product, but they found it less than a perfect reflection of their needs. The areas labeled c contain relatively fewer customers than b. Persons in c possess only one of the three majority traits, and were not, therefore, served with great care.

We should also observe that the state of affairs suggested by the mass market concept may be an ideal set of conditions for an economic system with limited wealth and purchasing power. The condition depicted in Figure 10.2 is one in which mass production and the attendant low unit costs obtain.[7] This point may require clarification. Producing a product that is intended for the majority of a population is, by definition, an opportunity to produce in the largest possible quantities. Long production runs permit economies of scale, and low unit costs of production are the possible result. We might even state the position in a somewhat bolder form: If low consumer prices are the most important economic goal, then the corporate mass market concept is appropriate; if producing goods and services that most precisely match consumer preferences is a legitimate economic goal, then some other concept of the market is appropriate.

The third stage in this evolution of corporate market concepts is suggested by the term *segmented market*. A segmented view of a market represents a partial abandonment of the mass market concept. Whereas attention was focused on the majority traits of a population in the mass market concept, the minority elements become the concern in a segmented market concept. The segmented market concept is a perspective of markets that is most likely to evolve with affluent conditions. Affluence is a condition in which many elements within the total population control some significant amount of purchasing power—virtually all elements can articulate and afford their own product and service preferences. Consider the market segments depicted in Figure 10.3.

A firm viewing markets as a segmented concept might serve any or all of the lettered areas in Figure 10.3 except a, the inaccessible part of the total market. Consider Area f, for example. If a firm elected to develop a special product for the requirements of this segment of the market, that firm would be electing to serve urban households, earning over $15,000 per year, renting their housing and speaking English. Similarly, Area i comprises urban dwellers with incomes of less than $15,000 per year who are home owners and who speak English. Another firm may elect to serve

[7] This idea is developed in Alan A. Roberts, "Applying the Strategy of Market Segmentation," *Business Horizons,* Fall 1961, pp. 65–72. Roberts identifies a "strategy of market aggregation" that is, in effect, closely parallel to the mass market concept as defined here.

market segment *m*. Segment *m* is made up of nonurban households with incomes of less than $15,000 annually who own their homes and are not English-speaking. Note especially that whatever segment or segments a firm may elect to serve, the promotion effort exerted in behalf of the product or service being offered is directed to the particular segment in question. The distinctive characteristic of the segmented market concept is the presumption of *heterogeneous want patterns* within each of the market segments.

Figure 10.3 The Segmented Market Concept

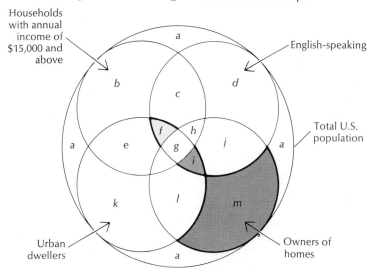

While the mass market concept was characterized by compromise, the segmented market concept is characterized by a more precise definition of the distinctive preferences of each of the segments being served. We should also note that the dimensions in which the total population is segmented in Figure 10.3 are purely illustrative. Segmentation may be accomplished on virtually any social, economic, demographic or psychological basis. Thus, markets may be divided by age categories, by family life cycle, by education of the household head, by religion, or by any other meaningful and measurable consumer trait.

A policy of market segmentation may be defined as one in which a firm consciously develops a product or a service that embodies attributes that are preferred by a small part of the total market for the product or service. When a firm makes a different shampoo for dry, for oily and for normal hair, it achieves a degree of market segmentation. When an automobile producer makes a two-seat supercharged racing sports car selling for over $10,000 and also offers a subcompact completely without ornamentation at less than $2,000, it is practicing market segmentation. Indeed, when an automobile producer develops a special heavy-duty suspension and transmission package for use in taxicab fleets, the market segment being recognized is an industrial segment.

Consider, for example, the number of market segments served by General Electric. That firm provides motors for clocks, for phonographs, for jet engines, for use in missiles, and for many other special uses. Segmentation in the beer market occurs along at least four basic dimensions. The emphasis on premium versus low price is a quality dimension; the emphasis on the "beer pro" in many advertisements suggests segmentation by consumption level; the emphasis on lightness suggests segmentation by taste preferences; and clearly, there is a distinction drawn between the on-premises beer drinker (tavern ads) and the home beer drinker (home entertainment appeals).[8]

There is an alternative policy that may appear to embody the basic characteristics of market segmentation but, in fact, does not. This policy we will call *product differentiation*.[9] Product differentiation often creates the illusion of segmentation. Product differentiation occurs when one physical product is sold to different market segments with different *sales appeals* emphasized to each segment. Thus, while the product offered to different segments is physically the same, the promotion featured to each of these segments is distinctive. The task of promotion is to differentiate the product between segments. A manufacturer of floor tile may, for example, make only one basic product in one basic pattern. But that tile may be promoted in exclusive home-decorator magazines, pictured in luxurious decor, and achieve a luxury image as a result. An identical tile may be featured in a general appeal magazine with copy emphasis on low cost, durability, and similar matters. The result with the reader audience of the general appeal magazine is that the tile is thought of as thrifty, tough, just right for the household with active children. Note that this strategy of product differentiation often tends to emphasize psychological product differences.

Although there is a similarity between the mass market concept and the strategy of product differentiation, they are not the same thing. The mass market concept featured promotion to the "average man," but there was no effort to direct different sales appeals to different parts of the total market. The mass market concept thus featured a single product and a single promotional target. Product differentiation may feature a single

[8] These and many other illustrations of segmentation dimensions are discussed in Daniel Kankelovich, "New Criteria for Market Segmentation," *Harvard Business Review*, March/April 1964, pp. 83–90.

[9] The distinction between "market segmentation" and "product differentiation" is made in Wendell R. Smith, "Product Differentiation and Market Segmentation as Alternative Marketing Strategies," *Journal of Marketing*, July 1956, pp. 3–8. This article has been influential in the recent literature of marketing in spite of semantic difficulties with the phrase "product differentiation." The term "market aggregation," as suggested by Roberts (*op. cit.*), is a far more effective term.

product and several different targets for promotion. These distinctions between the mass market concept, the strategy of product differentiation, and the segmented market concept are summarized in Figure 10.4.

Figure 10.4 Mass Market Concept

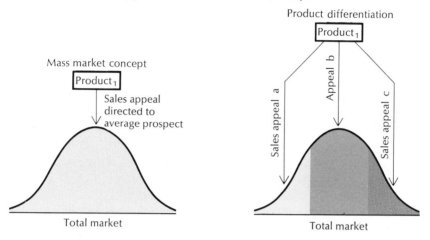

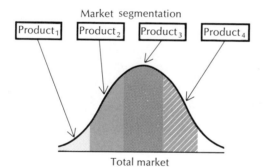

In the interest of completeness, we should also recognize one other stage in the corporate concept of a market. A market concept that has gained interest in recent years is the *global market concept*. This global view of a market is occasioned by improved international transportation and the existence of mass communications media in most modern economies.[10]

[10] See, for example, Charles F. Stewart, editor, *The Global Businessman*, New York: Holt, Rinehart and Winston, Inc., 1966. Another recent book that explores the multinational market concept is John K. Ryans, Jr., and James C. Baker, editors, *World Marketing*, New York: John Wiley & Sons, Inc., 1967. Recent text treatments of the subject include John M. Hess and Philip P. Cateora, *International Marketing*, Homewood, Ill.: Richard D. Irwin, Inc., 1966; and David Carson, *International Marketing: A Comparative Systems Approach*, New York: John Wiley & Sons, Inc., 1967.

Some methods of estimating market opportunity

Until this point we have used the term "market opportunity" in a very general sense to mean the ability and willingness of markets to spend money for the products and services that are sold by business organizations. There are two kinds of market opportunity appraisal in which we are primarily interested. We will distinguish between the terms "market potential" and "sales forecast." Estimates of *market potential* are defined as estimates of the maximum possible sales opportunities (in dollars or units) for all sellers of a particular good or service, usually during some stated period of time. The term *sales forecast* will be defined as an estimate of the sales (in either dollars or units) for (a) a particular product or service for (b) a specified period of time for (c) a particular combination of marketing efforts and for (d) a single firm.

For a company that produces several products, the "company sales forecast" would be the sum of the several product sales forecasts. The sales forecast may be expressed as a percentage either of market potential or of actual industry sales. The latter case we will refer to as a "market share forecast." The estimate of total industry sales is 100 percent, and the shares of all firms selling in the same product or service market sum to 100 percent.

In the discussion that follows, we will examine two basic approaches to estimating market potentials and sales forecasts. These two basic approaches are aggregative methods and disaggregative methods. The dictionary tells us that the process of aggregation involves the "collection of parts into a mass or whole." *Aggregative methods* of estimating sales volume, accordingly, all move from estimates of parts, by summation, to an estimate of the whole. *Disaggregative methods* begin with a grand total, or whole, and reason systematically down from that total until a residual approximating either market potential or the sales forecast is left. The distinction between aggregative methods and disaggregative methods of estimating market performances will be amplified and clarified in the sections that follow.

AGGREGATIVE METHODS OF ESTIMATING MARKET OPPORTUNITY

There are four principal aggregative methods of estimating market opportunities: (a) sales force/executive estimates, (b) sampling systems, (c) census systems and (d) survival coefficients (a special purpose technique). Each of these methods is examined in the discussion that follows.

SALES FORCE/EXECUTIVE ESTIMATES The use of sales force/executive estimates is a particularly good method to illustrate the basic nature of the aggregative method. This method is simple and inexpensive, but often not especially accurate. The procedure followed is to secure estimates of future sales from the man who is presumably most closely and regularly in contact with the market—the salesman. For a firm having (say) 30 salesmen in specified territories around the United States, the salesmen's territorial estimates for the specified future period are aggregated to produce the sales forecast. A sales forecast developed in this manner may prove to be conservative, especially if the performance of the sales personnel responsible for the forecast is also to be judged by sales quotas which are, in turn, based on the forecast. For this reason, the sales estimates of field sales personnel are rarely utilized without some executive consideration of their veracity. This method may be adapted so that dealers and distributors of the company's products play a role in the development of sales estimates.

SAMPLING SYSTEMS A second method that also clearly displays its aggregative nature is suggested by the term "sampling systems." Such systems either sample the attitudes of some market regarding purchase plans or use actual test market conditions. In the case in which the sales forecast is developed from expressed purchase plans of consumers, the procedure includes a selection of a representative sample of prospects and an "aggregation" of the plans disclosed by that group up to total market size.[11] Thus if 15 percent of a representative sample of consumers expresses a firm plan to purchase a particular product, then the sales forecast would be set at 15 percent of the total (not just the sample) number of prospects. In practice, these purchase plans sampling systems are likely to be very much more complicated than we have suggested here.[12] For example, the plans of consumers may be expressed in terms of probabilities rather than in a simple yes-or-no dimension. Thus, our sample may indicate that 7 percent of consumers plan a purchase with a 90 percent level of surety, that 14 percent plan a purchase with a 60 percent level of surety, and so forth. Even with this use of probabilities, the method is fundamentally the same.

A second use of sampling systems of sales forecasting is in an actual test market condition. A *test market* is one in which a product or service is actually introduced—either as a means of measuring the efficiency of the product or as a means of developing an effective combination of selling efforts. Thus, for example, in the case of Bristol-Myers Analoze (a waterless analgesic mentioned earlier), test markets for the product were established in Denver, Memphis, Phoenix and Omaha. Such test markets

---

[11] For now, we can think of a "representative sample" as one that approximates a small scale replica of the total population from which it was drawn. We shall have more to say about sample attributes in the next chapter.

[12] See, for example, Frederick E. May, "The Use of Consumer Survey Data in Forecasts of Domestic Demand for Consumer Durable Goods," *Proceedings of the American Marketing Association,* winter 1958, pp. 569–571.

provide actual sales feedback from which it may be possible to estimate sales in the total market area. It may already be apparent that both the use of consumer purchase plans and the use of test markets are methods of sales forecasting that are particularly well adapted to conditions in which relatively little history exists upon which to develop sales estimates.

Consider, for example, the plight of a company with a totally new product or service concept. There is no existing sales history that might be adjusted in light of the current environment, and there is no similar product that might serve as a yardstick. About the only source available is a sample of customer reaction—either in the form of intentions-to-buy studies or test markets. Clearly, the more nearly the test markets approximate the total population of which they are a part, the more justified a generalization of the results to the total population would be. If the test markets were thus representative of the total population, the sales forecast might be developed on the basis of market penetration achieved in the test circumstance.

CENSUS SYSTEMS   Another means of estimating market opportunities is with the use of census data. Although census data is potentially useful in sales forecasting in many different ways, our interest here is with the use of the Standard Industrial Classification (SIC) system as a means of aggregative sales forecasting. The census of the United States includes a coded classification system for all business establishments in the national economy. "The purpose of this Standard Industrial Classification and its codification is to provide a sound definitional basis for the collection of business statistics by government agencies" and to summarize a great mountain of economic data in relatively simple coded form. The SIC system "divides business activities into general divisions, subdivides each general division into major groups (2-digit code), breaks each major group into subgroups (3-digit code) and further separates each subgroup into detailed industry classes."[13] Thus, for example, the two-digit code number 26 designates a business involving paper and allied products; the three-digit code 263 identifies a paperboard mill; and the four-digit code 2643 designates a paper bag manufacturer. Similarly, 25 is the SIC code for furniture and fixtures; 251 designates household furniture; and 2511 identifies wood furniture, not upholstered. But how does all this assist in the development of sales estimates?

Since the customers of most large businesses are other businesses (very few large business firms sell directly to final consumers), it is possible to use the SIC system to define a firm's customers. Thus, for example, a building materials manufacturer may make virtually all his sales to the following SIC's:

[13] Richard M. Hill, *Techniques of Measuring Market Potential for Wholesalers,* Urbana, Ill.: University of Illinois Press, Bureau of Business Management, 1962, pp. 7–8.

174 masonry, stonework, tile setting and plastering contractors
175 carpentering and wood flooring contractors
176 roofing and sheet metal contractors
521 lumber and other building material dealers
523 paint, glass and wallpaper stores
5251 hardware stores

Since it is possible to define a manufacturer's market in terms of SIC code numbers (as we have just done), it would also be possible to develop estimates of potential for the manufacturer if we could estimate the volume of business that each of his customers has. Consider the hypothetical example in Figure 10.5.

Figure 10.5 County X—SIC Map of Selected Businesses

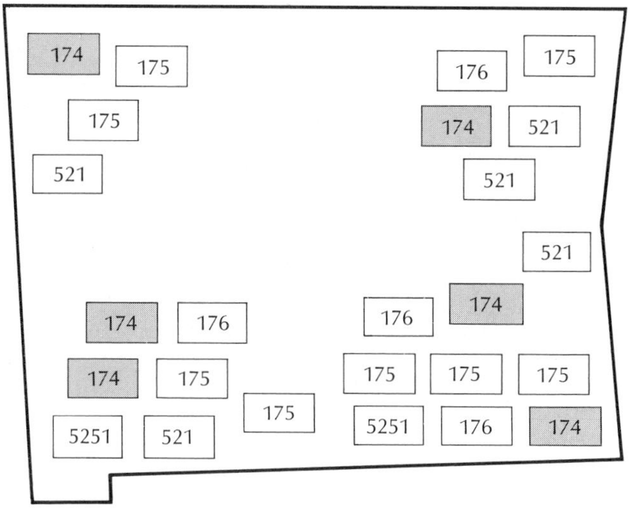

Figure 10.5 summarizes, for a building materials manufacturer, the business organizations in County X having SIC numbers to which he normally sells. (Note that no particular care has been exercised to make the distribution of businesses in Figure 10.5 realistic. It is the method of estimating potential that can be developed from information such as this that is of primary concern to us here.) If the building materials manufacturer knew the number of relevant SIC's in a given geographical area, and if he knew something about the size of each of the businesses, it would be possible to develop estimates of sales potential from that information. But are such maps as depicted in Figure 10.5 available? And is it possible to estimate the size of each of these businesses?

The answer to both these questions is yes. *County Business Patterns* is a "statistical tabulation based on information reported under the Federal Old Age and Survivors Insurance Program"[14] and can provide the kind of information required to convert SIC data into a useful basis for estimating market potential. Because *County Business Patterns* also provides detailed information about the number of employees in each of the businesses in every country, it may be possible to develop a statistical relationship between the number of employees in each firm and sales expectations for the building materials manufacturer. This procedure involves two steps: (a) identification of the average relationship between the size of a business (number of employees) and purchases made by that firm from the building materials manufacturer, and (b) the application of this statistical relationship in order to estimate sales expectations. This procedure is not as obscure as it might sound—Figure 10.6 will help to clarify it.

Figure 10.6 Number of Employees and Market Potential

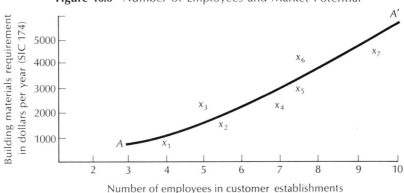

Number of employees in customer establishments

The curve AA' in Figure 10.6 summarizes the relationship between building materials requirements for SIC 174 and the size of the customer's business (expressed in number of employees).[15] Each of the points, X_1, X_2, X_3, and so forth, is a historical fact. That is, our experience with Customer X_2, who averages between five and six employees, indicates that we sell him about $2000 in building materials yearly. Similarly our experience with Customer X_3 (who employs between seven and eight persons) indicates annual sales expectations of about $3000. The curve AA' does not connect each point; it is, rather, a path that describes generally the position of all the points. Now, armed with an understanding of this relationship,

[14] Richard M. Hill, *op. cit.*, p. 15. Dunn and Bradstreet's financial rating manual is also coded by SIC numbers and may therefore be useful for this same purpose.

[15] *Ibid.*, p. 22. The description above is purposely quite superficial. In the next section of the present chapter we will deal much more carefully with regression analysis—and in particular univariate regression analysis. Technically, the line AA' is a regression line, the number of employees the independent variable and building materials requirements the dependent variable.

we can convert our census data into an estimate of market potential. Consider Figure 10.7—a more complete version of Figure 10.5.

Figure 10.7 County X—SIC Map of Selected Businesses, Including Number of Employees

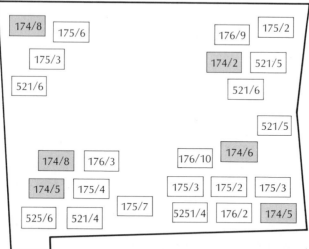

Note that Figure 10.7 provides two numbers for each business: the SIC number that identifies the type of business and the average number of employees in each business. The number 521/6 in the northwestern part of that county thus identifies a "lumber and other building material dealer" with six employees. If we want to estimate the potential for any one SIC category, we would combine the information in Figure 10.6 with that in Figure 10.7 as follows:

SIC Code/ No. of Empl.	Market Potential
174/8	$ 4,000
174/2	500
174/8	4,000
174/5	1,500
174/6	2,000
174/5	1,500
Total	$13,500

Note that curve AA' might very well be different for different SIC categories. It also might change with a change in the way each business is operated. Thus, a self-service lumber dealer would produce different potential than one offering full personal selling services. If we want to estimate the potential for any group of several counties, the process is simply aggregative.

SURVIVAL COEFFICIENTS The idea of a survival coefficient brings us to a particular problem in market analysis that we have not yet considered. For many businesses, there are at least two basic components to be estimated in a sales forecast or in a measure of market potential. These two components might be designated first-time buyers and replacement buyers. Survival coefficients are useful in estimating *replacement demand.* But, specifically, what are survival coefficients, and how are they used to estimate replacement demand?

A survival coefficient is a probabilistic estimate of the percentage of some defined universe of products, all sold initially within the same time period, that will "survive" until the next forecast period.[16] Consider, for example, the case of 1000 portable electric typewriters sold during a defined (say) three-month period. One means through which we might begin to define the level of replacement sales for typewriters would be to follow these typewriters through their useful life and observe the points in time when they cease to be useful. In order to keep the initial discussion as simple as possible, suppose that as we observe these 1000 typewriters, we witness the following actuarial phenomenon:

Number of typewriters surviving after 1 year: 950, or 95 percent
Number of typewriters surviving after 2 years: 900, or 90 percent
Number of typewriters surviving after 3 years: 800, or 80 percent
Number of typewriters surviving after 4 years: 700, or 70 percent
Number of typewriters surviving after 5 years: 600, or 60 percent
Number of typewriters surviving after 6 years: 500, or 50 percent

We might reasonably call the percentage of typewriters that survive at any point in time a *survival coefficient.* Thus the survival coefficient after one year is estimated at .95. And, if we were dealing with a much larger sampling base, such a coefficient might have inherent predictive value. This procedure would then become an actuarial phenomenon not unlike those underlying life insurance rate structures. But how does all this lead to a sales forecasting technique? In effect, the maximum replacement demand is defined by the difference between any pair of neighboring coefficients multiplied by the original number of typewriters sold. Maximum replacement sales during the second year would thus be (.95 − .90) × 1000, or 50 typewriters. Maximum replacement sales during the fourth year would be defined as (.80 − .70) × 1000, or 100 typewriters. But why do we call this *maximum* replacement demand?

If brand loyalty were 100 percent, we could expect every typewriter

[16] The idea of survival coefficients as a forecasting device is discussed in M. Spencer and others, *Business and Economic Forecasting,* Homewood, Ill.: Richard D. Irwin, Inc., 1961, pp. 256–257. See also Lee Gunlogsen, "Estimating Replacement Demand for Durable Goods," *Proceedings of the American Marketing Association,* Winter 1962, pp. 344–357.

owner to replace his fully spent machine with the same brand. Since brand loyalty is generally appreciably less than 100 percent, we can expect less than this maximum replacement value. Indeed, this matter of brand loyalty is not the only refinement we need to make in order that our simple typewriter example more nearly approximate an operational model. In the interest of increased realism, observe the data in Table 10.1.

Table 10.1 Survival coefficients—first three years of sales

End of Year	1st Year	2nd Year	3rd Year
1	1.000000		
2,(1)	.950000	1.000000	
3,(2),(1)	.850000	.950000	1.000000
4,(3),(2)	.750000	.850000	.950000
5,(4),(3)	.500000	.750000	.850000
6,(5),(4)	.300000	.500000	.750000
7,(6),(5)	.100000	.300000	.500000
8,(7),(6)	.005000	.100000	.300000
9,(8),(7)		.005000	.100000
10,(9),(8)			.005000

The data in Table 10.1 permit a determination of the maximum value of replacement demand where products of different ages are in service. (In order to introduce this element of realism, we have selected data only for the first three years of typewriter sales. We could increase the number of years of sales, but that would not alter the basic lesson with which we are concerned.) Note that the data represent a progression within a progression. The survival coefficients advance much as they did before (although a different rate of functional obsolescence is used) and each successive year's sales "progress" by starting at a later point relative to the original (first-year) series. How do we determine the maximum value of replacement demand from this data? The procedure is aggregative—and is defined as follows:

Maximum
Replacement
Demand in
the year to
be predicted. $= (SC_4 - SC_5) \times$ (1st year sales) +

$$(SC_3 - SC_4) \times \text{(2nd year sales)} +$$

$$(SC_2 - SC_3) \times \text{(3rd year sales)}$$

or, substituting actual values in the data and assuming that we sold 1,000 typewriters in each of the three years:

Maximum
Replacement
Demand, Year 5 = $(.75 - .50) \times (1000) + (.85 - .75) \times$

$$(1000) + (.95 - .85) \times (1000)$$

$$= 250 + 100 + 100$$

$$= 450$$

Or, if we wish to reflect a lower brand loyalty rate among buyers receiving shorter service, we might modify this aggregative procedure in one additional way.

Expected
Replacement
Demand, Year 5 = $250 \times .50 + 100 \times .25 + 100 \times .15$

$$= 125 + 25 + 15$$

$$= 165$$

This estimate of expected replacement demand assumes (arbitrarily, for purposes of illustration) that the brand loyalty rate is .50 among buyers who get four years of service from their typewriters, .25 among buyers who get three years of service and .15 among buyers who get only two years of service.

DISAGGREGATIVE METHODS OF ESTIMATING MARKET OPPORTUNITY

We have seen that aggregative methods of estimating market opportunity are usually built up as a summation of some logical set of components. Disaggregative methods have in common the characteristic that they begin with a grand total, or changes in a grand total, and proceed thence to an estimate of market opportunity. A very important means of developing these disaggregative methods is suggested by the word *regression*. A regression system is one that measures the degree of change in some dependent variable that is associated with changes in one or more independent variables.[17] For example, if we observe that when the gross national product increases by 3 percent our company sales increase by 4 percent, we can derive the very simple regression equation:

Company sales depend upon the level of gross national product
or

Company Sales = F(GNP)

[17] See an excellent discussion of regression analysis in Paul E. Green and Donald S. Tull, *Research for Marketing Decisions*, Englewood, N.J.: Prentice-Hall, Inc., 1966, pp. 318–322.

or

$$\frac{\text{\% Change in Company Sales}}{\text{\% Change in Gross National Product}} = \text{Regression Coefficient}$$

$$\frac{.04}{.03} = 1.333$$

Note that the change in company sales represents the dependent variable, that the change in gross national product represents the independent variable, and that 1.333 is a simple regression coefficient. This regression coefficient identifies the relationship of the dependent variable to the independent variable.

The 1.333 tells us that as the independent variable increases by 1 percent, we can expect a 1.333 percent increase in the dependent variable. There are several aspects of this simple example that are worth our careful consideration. It should be clear that if this 1.333 identifies a dependable relationship, the knowledge of the exact value of this regression coefficient could be a valuable sales forecasting device. That is, it could be valuable if changes in the independent variable *lead* changes in the dependent variable by a sufficient time interval. Indeed, if we knew that a 1 percent change now in the independent variable would produce a 1.333 percent change in the dependent variable one year from now, we would have discovered a valuable predictive device. We would simply develop our sales forecast in terms of changes in the current level of gross national product.

But seldom is the relationship so neat as this. The complications of regression analysis normally center around one or more of four basic problems:

1 The amount of lead time between the independent and the dependent variable. In general, the shorter the lead time, the less valuable is knowledge of the regression relationship for forecasting purposes.

2 The value of the regression coefficient at different values of the independent variable. That is, can we rely upon the regression coefficient to hold at any and all values of GNP? Normally the regression line that relates independent and dependent variables is curvilinear rather than linear—which suggests a regression coefficient that changes slightly at different levels of economic activity.

3 The reversibility of the regression coefficient. That is, does the relationship suggested by the 1.333 hold for decreases as well as increases in GNP? Will a 1 percent decrease in GNP produce a 1.333 percent decrease in company sales volume?

4 The number of independent variables required to accurately predict changes in the dependent variable. Normally, more than one independent variable is required to identify a predictable relationship to the dependent variable. The 1.333 regression coefficient that we have developed is, strictly speaking, the result of *univariate* regression analysis.

If the regression coefficient thus developed proves unreliable as a predictive device, we would probably explore the usefulness of a *multivariate* regression system—one utilizing two or more independent variables.[18]

Three procedures for estimating market opportunities that may employ some form of regression analysis are: (a) general purpose market indexes, (b) input-output techniques (I/O), and (c) a special "filter" technique. The discussion that ensues will consider each of these three procedures.

General purpose market indexes are exemplified by the *Sales Management* Buying Power Index (BPI). This particular market index is developed around three variables—population, effective buying income and retail sales. This Buying Power Index is, in effect, a general purpose independent variable to assist in the appraisal of market opportunity. But an illustration will reveal much more about the nature of this index.

Table 10.2 Buying Power Index—An Illustration

State of California

Population per cent of U.S.	Effective Buying Income per cent of U.S.	Retail Sales per cent of U.S.
9.7720	11.1725	10.9795

Buying Power Index:

$$9.7720 \times 2 = 19.5440$$
$$11.1725 \times 5 = 55.8625$$
$$10.9795 \times 3 = \underline{32.9385}$$
$$108.3450 / 10 = \underline{10.8345}$$

State of Alabama

Population per cent of U.S.	Effective Buying Income per cent of U.S.	Retail Sales per cent of U.S.
1.7760	1.2723	1.3080

Buying Power Index:

$$1.7760 \times 2 = 3.5520$$
$$1.2723 \times 5 = 6.3615$$
$$1.3080 \times 3 = \underline{3.9240}$$
$$13.8375 / 10 = \underline{1.3838}$$

---

[18] The reader is directed to Robert E. J. Snyder, "A Two-Group Discriminant Analysis to Predict Success for U.H.F. Television Stations in the Small Market," in L. George Smith, editor, *Reflections on Progress in Marketing,* Chicago: American Marketing Association, 1964, pp. 139–142. In this report, four independent variables were found to be significant in predicting success of the television stations.

This three-variable market index assumes that population, effective buying income and retail sales all reflect, in varying weights, the ability of an area to support business activity. Note especially the weighting procedure employed in the development of this index.[19] It should also be noted that although the data here are for entire states, similar data are available for individual counties and cities. Notice that the index tells us that although 9.7720 percent of the population in the United States resides in California, 10.8345 percent of the buying power is there. Similarly, the index tells us that although 1.7760 percent of the population resides in Alabama, only 1.3838 percent of the buying power is there. Whereas California is a relatively stronger market than population figures would lead us to believe, Alabama is relatively weaker.

This kind of analysis does not constitute evidence that California is necessarily a better opportunity for a new firm at all—indeed competition might be very strong in California and relatively weak in Alabama. This is an important point, for general purpose indexes such as the BPI do not include a built-in consideration of the strength of existing competition. This index, as well as others like it, may nonetheless be valuable indicators of changes in market opportunity.[20] The sales volume of a particular firm may correlate well with changes in an index such as this. Thus, an analysis of past sales may show that as buying power increases so does our own sales volume.[21]

A second basic approach to estimating market opportunity, one that should be included in a discussion of systems using regression techniques, is input-output analysis. Input-output analysis (I/O) proceeds from the basic premise that all economic output is dependent upon identifiable economic inputs. Input-output analysis thus rests on a premise of economic interdependence.[22] And because input-output analysis forces a careful consideration of the interdependence of economic activities, it holds the promise of becoming a useful and insightful supplement to sales forecasting techniques. In order to better understand the way in which I/O analysis may facilitate sales forecasting procedures, consider Table 10.3.

[19] These data are from "Survey of Buying Power," *Sales Management,* June 10, 1968, pp. C20–C26, C16–C17.

[20] See Albert Haring, "Establishing the Market Index for Your Company," *Winter Proceedings of the American Marketing Association,* 1958, pp. 417–420. Haring argues that a market index can greatly aid a company in forecasting, production planning, and in other ways.

[21] *Sales Management* data permit the development of additional means of evaluating the strength of a market area. Besides the Buying Power Index, a Quality Index and an Index of Sales Activity are calculated for virtually every state, city and county. For a definition of these two indexes, and a further discussion of the usefulness of such indexes, see Ronald R. Gist, *Retailing: Concepts and Decisions,* New York: John Wiley & Sons, Inc., 1968, pp. 182–184.

[22] For a good definition of the input-output approach, see Heinz Kohler, *Scarcity Challenged: An Introduction to Economics,* New York: Holt, Rinehart and Winston, Inc., 1968, pp. 265–272.

Table 10.3 Input-Output Table

A gross output of Requires an input of	500,000 automobiles	500,000 washing machines	1,000,000 TV sets
Plastic (million tons)	1/25	1/50	1/45
Aluminum (million tons)	1/25	1/100	1/60
Steel (million tons)	3/4	1/5	1/40
Rubber (million tons)	1/40	1/50	1/100
Man hours of labor (millions)	4	1	3

Table 10.3 identifies, in a precise way, the relationship between outputs of three different kinds—automobiles, washing machines and television sets—and some of the economic inputs required to effect those outputs. (The relationships suggested in Table 10.3 are purely illustrative, however they will serve to demonstrate the nature of input-output analysis.) The numbers in each cell of this table are called *technical coefficients*—and these coefficients are the heart of input-output techniques. They define the relationship between some specified total output and the amount of a specific input required. Consider the fraction "1/25" that relates the automobile output column and the plastic input row. This fraction indicates that 1/25 of a million tons of plastic products are required to produce an output of 500,000 finished automobiles. Similarly, the fraction "3/4" in the automobile output column and the steel input row indicates that three-quarters of a million tons of steel are required to effect output of half a million automobiles.

Strictly speaking, the cells in the bottom row in Table 10.3 contain *resource coefficients* rather than technical coefficients, but they are interpreted in a similar manner. The number "3" in that row relates the television sets output column to the man-hours-of-labor row, for example. And that number indicates that 3 million man-hours of labor are required to effect a total output of 1 million television sets. Note that the row data in Table 10.3 are incomplete. Many more inputs than plastics, aluminum, steel, rubber and labor are required to produce each of the three output categories. A complete and detailed input-output summary for automobile production would contain well over a hundred input categories; we have simplified our table for purposes of clarity. But how does input-output analysis assist in the task of sales forecasting?

Suppose that published industry estimates indicate that the 1971 model year will be a 10 million-units year for domestic automobile manufacturers. Firms who do a significant amount of business with automobile manufacturers can reason backward, as it were, to an estimate of the demand for (say) plastics, aluminum, steel or whatever. According to Table 10.3, for example, a total output of 10 million autos would require 800,000 tons of plastic (20 × 1/25 × 1,000,000). If estimates of the total number of units of washing machines, television sets and other final products were available, it would be possible to develop a workable estimate of the demand for any of the input items.[23] But note that input-output analysis is no better as a sales forecasting device than the technical coefficients which are a part of it. And dependable technical coefficients have not always been available when needed.[24]

National Steel Corporation has constructed an I/O model for the steel industry and is presently using it for both short-range and long-range forecasting. The following quotation indicates, in a general way, the procedure they use:

As our own basis for starting, we obtained matrices for the years 1947, '58, '60, '61, '62, '70, and 1975. Along with these matrices, we also gained the knowledge of why each projection for 1970 and 1975 was made and the growth curves for each cell. From this knowledge we were able to generate I/O matrices of the total economy for any year that we did not have up to 1975.[25]

One final method of estimating market opportunity—one that is in spirit a kind of regression system—has been called the "filter technique."[26] This filter technique uses statistical correlation and history, in a combined, systematic way, in order to project the future. More specifically, this approach includes three steps: (a) the selection of a logical independent test variable, (b) a plotting that will reveal the coincidence (or lack thereof) between the test variable being forecast and actual company (or industry) sales, and (c) a historical analysis of the points of least correlation between the independent test variable forecast and the actual sales volume achieved. Observe Figure 10.8.

Three dimensions are represented in Figure 10.8. Time is represented on the horizontal scale. Both the independent test variable (new housing starts in thousands) and the dependent variable (company sales) are represented on the vertical scales. By placing a dollar scale in juxtaposition with the housing starts scale, we are better able to identify visually any tendency to coincidence that may exist between the two variables. Note

---

[23] See, for example, André B. Celestin, "How National Steel Uses I/O to Forecast Annual Steel Opportunities to 1975," in Keith Cox and Ben M. Enis, editors, *A New Measure of Responsibility for Marketing,* Chicago: American Marketing Association, 1968, pp. 313–316. What National Steel does is "project already known coefficients—cell by cell—incorporating expert judgments and expected technological advancements of each industry to develop matrices for future years."

[24] See Anne P. Carter, "How to Handle Changing Technical Coefficients in Input-Output Tables," in Cox and Enis, *op. cit.,* pp. 306–309.

[25] Celestin, *op. cit.,* p. 313.

[26] See James H. Lorie, "Two Important Problems in Sales Forecasting," *Journal of Business,* July 1957, pp. 172–179.

that the time scale is both historical and projective. Figure 10.8 accomplishes the first two steps of the filter technique as those steps were just outlined. We have (a) selected a logical independent test variable (new housing starts), and we have (b) developed a plotting technique that can reveal any coincidence between the independent and the dependent variables. Note that the independent variable coincides well with company sales except for three time periods. The periods in which coincidence is lacking are labeled with roman numerals. It remains for us to subject these periods of least correlation to intensive study in an attempt to find explanatory variables.[27] This procedure permits us to refine our understanding of the causal relationship that may exist between the independent and dependent variables, and, as a result, to improve our predictive skills. For example, we might now use projected new housing starts as a predictive variable subject to the intervention of any or all of the factors that were operative during the atypical Periods I, II and III.

Figure 10.8 The Filter Technique

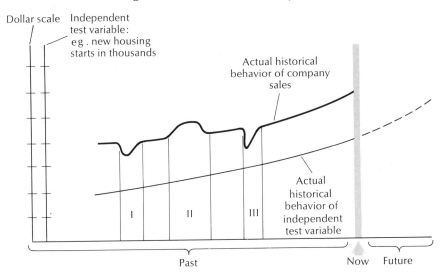

SUMMARY

Our purpose in the present chapter has been (a) to sharpen our understanding of the word "market" and (b) to examine some of the methods that are used by business to measure market opportunity. Toward the first of these two goals, we developed the ideas of the local market, the mass market, the segmented market and the global market. We noted that these four market concepts represent a historical transition in the

[27] *Ibid.,* pp. 176–177.

perspective of American businesses. We noted that market segmentation is like, though not identical with, the practice of product differentiation.

We examined two basic types of methods used in the estimation of market opportunity: (a) aggregative methods and (b) disaggregative methods. Among the aggregative methods we discussed were those that were developed from estimates made by the sales force or dealer-distributor networks and systems that were based on market samplings. These sampling techniques included the use of test markets and purchase planning by consumers. Aggregative census systems were exemplified by the use of SIC's to develop the sales forecast. Survival coefficients were defined, and their potential usefulness as estimators of replacement demand was noted.

Disaggregative methods of measuring market opportunity were defined as those methods that "begin with a grand total, or changes in a grand total, and proceed thence to an estimate of market opportunity." Regression or correlation techniques were found important to most disaggregative methods. We considered the Buying Power Index (BPI) of *Sales Management,* input-output analysis and a special filter technique of forecasting as representative of disaggregative methods of estimating market opportunity.

REVIEW QUESTIONS
1 Carefully define and indicate the relevance of each of the following concepts to the study of marketing:
   a. The local market concept
   b. The mass market concept
   c. A market-share forecast
   d. The sales force/executive estimate method of sales forecasting
   e. Sampling systems of sales forecasting
   f. An SIC system of sales forecasting
   g. Survival coefficients
   h. Regression methods of sales forecasting or estimating market potential
   i. General purpose market indexes
   j. An input-output technical coefficient
2 Distinguish carefully between each element in the following pairs of terms:
   a. Market segmentation *and* product differentiation
   b. Sales forecasts *and* market potentials
   c. Aggregative methods of forecasting *and* disaggregative methods of forecasting
   d. Univariate regression analysis *and* multivariate regression analysis
   e. The Buying Power Index *and* input-output analysis
   f. Technical coefficients *and* resource coefficients
3 Indicate (a) what a survival coefficient is, (b) what special purpose it has and (c) some complicating problems in its use.
4 Specifically, how does the filter technique of sales forecasting work? What steps are involved in its implementation?

5 In what specific ways could it be argued that an economic system is more efficient when precise tools of measuring market opportunity are employed?

6 Statistical methods of correlation are fundamental to most techniques of estimating market opportunity. Do you agree or disagree? Why?

7 Aside from the increased efficiency that may result, what very practical reasons are there for developing dependable methods of estimating market opportunity?

Chapter 11

MARKETING RESEARCH

Chapter 10 was concerned with two basic considerations: it identified several concepts of a market, and it identified several methods that may be used to estimate either market potentials or sales forecasts. Efforts to measure market potentials or to estimate future sales are a particular type of research activity—a kind of research activity that is a part of what we call *marketing research*. Marketing research is an extremely broad concept—it has been defined, for example, as "a systematic and objective search for and analysis of information relevant to the identification and solution of any problem in the field of marketing."[1] This omnibus definition, though accurate, is not especially explicit. Specifically, what is included in the term marketing research? Much of the current research interest in marketing is directed to the following specific problem areas:

1 Market Analysis
   a. *General market measurements,* such as economic forecasting, determination of market potential and sales forecasting (considered in the preceding chapter).
   b. *Analysis of specific market territories and trade areas, and sales analysis.* Sales analysis may include the development of market share estimates in various territories, a consideration of "batting averages" for salesmen, an evaluation of dealers or distributors, and other studies.
2 Advertising Research
   a. *Audience measurements* include research efforts that endeavor to identify the characteristics of media audiences, such as readers, listeners or viewers. Knowledge of audience characteristics is an extremely important prerequisite to effective mass communications.

[1] Paul E. Green and Donald S. Tull, *Research for Marketing Decisions,* Englewood Cliffs, N.J.: Prentice-Hall, Inc., 1966, p. 2.

b. *Effectiveness studies* include research efforts to identify the impact of particular media, of particular advertising vehicles (specific radio stations, television stations, magazines, newspapers, and so forth) and of particular advertisements upon consumer memory and consumer behavior.

c. *Allocation studies* are those that endeavor to identify the proper level of advertising effort. The problem to be resolved with this type of research is, "How much should we spend (a) to get a particular task accomplished with (b) a minimum waste in expenditure?"

3 Consumer Research

a. *Brand awareness and preference studies* are those that seek to identify the changing level of awareness of consumers of different brands and the strength of consumer brand loyalties.

b. *Motivation studies* are those that seek to identify the reasons underlying particular aspects of consumer behavior. Indeed, the term "motivation research" has become virtually synonymous with a particular type of research methodology—projective measurement methods. We will have reason later to consider this type of research much more fully.

c. *Allocation studies* of consumers include those that seek to gain insight into consumer behavior through a detailed examination of consumer expenditures. These studies often entail the use of diaries, or journals, of household expenditures. Such studies may, for example reveal the income allocation patterns of sample households.

d. *Product design and performance studies* seek to determine the aesthetic preferences of consumers, as well as the desired functional attributes of products or services.

Although the foregoing enumeration is not exhaustive, it serves to indicate the diversity of problems suggested by the phrase marketing research. In the discussion that follows, we will examine four basic aspects of marketing research. First, we will identify some terms that are fundamental to a study of research methodology and will consider briefly some particularly useful statistical concepts. Second, we will examine the concept of research design; we will identify several types of research plans and indicate the problems to which they are often applied. Third, we will identify some special problems in marketing research; this discussion will include consideration of measuring qualitative phenomena and of estimating types and amounts of research bias. Finally, we will examine briefly some uses of mathematical models in marketing research.

Statistical concepts and marketing research

The marketing research problem in which it is feasible to question or scrutinize the entire relevant population is rare. For economic reasons, most research efforts require a *sampling* of the population that seems to hold the required insight. Sampling procedures are, therefore, an unavoidable consideration in virtually all research undertakings. Although it might seem that this requirement is a compromise that must necessarily work to destroy the integrity of research efforts, such is not always the case. When particular sampling procedures are followed, it is possible to produce research results that have predictable accuracy. That is, if the correct sampling procedures are employed, results can be produced that are fully acceptable. What, then are these "correct sampling procedures"?

In order to have the greatest usefulness, samples need to embody (a) representativeness and (b) a known nonzero probabilistic element. In addition, the research procedure must have validity. When we specify that a sample should be "representative," we mean that in order that correct inferences may be drawn from the sample, it should be like the total population of which it is a part. A sample that is representative in this statistical sense is one that embodies, in correct proportion, all the salient properties of the larger group of which it is a part. The distinguishing characteristic of a representative sample is that it is a small scale replica of some total population. Consider the following representation of the racial composition of the student body of a large western university.

Figure 11.1 Sample Representativeness

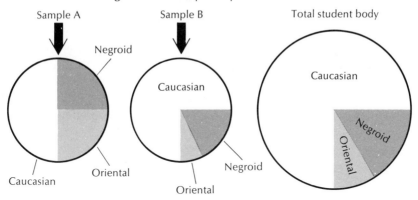

Sample A in Figure 11.1 is not representative; the results of this sample would tend to understate the Caucasian view—whatever that view might be. Sample B is a small scale likeness, or a proportional model, of the total student body—Sample B is representative in the sense that we will use that term. But we should note that Sample B is only representative in the dimension represented here—namely race. It is entirely possible that Sample B lacks representativeness in other dimensions; for example, it might include more older students, on the average, than those in the total student body. That is why we say that a truly representative sample embodies "all the salient properties" of the population of which it is a part.

A sample, to be of greatest value, should also embody a known nonzero probabilistic element. This second condition recognizes an extremely important aspect of sampling theory. When we say that a sample should have a known nonzero probabilistic element, we mean that each member, or element, of the sample should have a known and positive probability of having been represented in the sample. It is only when we know this probabilistic element that we can begin to establish what we referred to earlier as "predictable accuracy." When we know the probability that each element in the total population has of being a part of the sample, we can begin to be aware of the limitations of our sample and, therefore, are less apt to claim more for it than is warranted.

When we know the probability that any element in the population has of being included in the sample, and we know that that probability is the same for all such elements, a condition of randomness obtains. And when randomness in sampling is accomplished, we can scientifically determine the level of confidence that we may properly have in our sample results.[2] We say, then, that having a known probabilistic element in sampling is useful, and having randomness is an ideal condition.

But there are different types of random samples.[3] And these different types of random samples are often a source of confusion for students. It will be useful to distinguish between unrestricted random samples and stratified random samples. We need also to clarify the exact nature of a nonrandom sample with known probabilities of selection. An *unrestricted random sample* occurs when each sample member of a population is selected from the total population—that total population not having been previously divided into subordinate segments. *A stratified random sample* is one in which the total population is first stratified (divided into segments), and then samples are drawn randomly from each segment of the total population.

Consider Figure 11.2. The unrestricted population depicted on the left in Figure 11.2 contains 221 elements. If these 221 elements constitute the entire population, and if each element that finally becomes a part of our sample has a probability of 1 in 221 of being represented in our sample, the sample is both unrestricted and random. Now consider the stratified population depicted on the right in Figure 11.2. Segment A of the total population contains 190 elements. Segment B contains 110 elements. If

[2] This "scientific" basis is, in effect, our understanding of the properties of a normal distribution. For a discussion of normality in sampling distributions, see Leslie Kish, *Survey Sampling*, New York: John Wiley & Sons, Inc., 1965, especially pp. 14ff.

[3] The term random is used here although it has some unfortunate lay interpretations. To some, random means haphazard; to some, it means probability sampling. We shall intend that it be synonymous with "epsem" sampling (equal *probability of selection method*). For a further discussion, see Kish, *op. cit.*, p. 21.

Figure 11.2 Types of Random Samples

An Unrestricted Population | *A Stratified Population*

An Unrestricted Population								Segment A							Segment B			
1	2	3	4	5	6	7	8	1	2	3	4	5	6	7	1	2	3	4
9	10	11	12	13	14	15	16	8	9	10	11	12	13	14	5	6	7	8
17	18	19	20	21	22	23	24	15	16	17	18	19	20	21	9	10	11	12
25	26	27	28	29	30	31	32	22	23	24	25	26	27	28	13	14	15	16
33	34	35	36	37	38	39	40	29	30	31	32	33	34	35	17	18	19	20
41	42	43	44	45	46	47	48	36	37	38	39	40	41	42	21	22	23	24
49	50	51	52	53	54	55	56	43	44	45	46	47	48	49	25	26	27	28
57	58	59	60	61	62	63	64	50	51	52	53	54	55	56	29	30	31	32
65	66	67	68	69	70	71	72	57	58	59	60	61	62	63	33	34	35	36
73	74	75	76	77	78	79	80	64	65	66	67	68	69	70	37	38	39	40
81	82	83	84	85	86	87	88	71	72	73	74	75	76	77	41	42	43	44
89	90	91	92	93	94	95	96	78	79	80	81	82	83	84	45	46	47	48
97	98	99	100	101	102	103	104	85	86	87	88	89	90	91	49	50	51	52
105	106	107	108	109	110	111	112	92	93	94	95	96	97	98	53	54	55	56
113	114	115	116	117	118	119	120	99	100	101	102	103	104	105	57	58	59	60
121	122	123	124	125	126	127	128	106	107	108	109	110	111	112	61	62	63	64
129	130	131	132	133	134	135	136	113	114	115	116	117	118	119	65	66	67	68
137	138	139	140	141	142	143	144	120	121	122	123	124	125	126	69	70	71	72
145	146	147	148	149	150	151	152	127	128	129	130	131	132	133	73	74	75	76
153	154	155	156	157	158	159	160	134	135	136	137	138	139	140	77	78	79	80
161	162	163	164	165	166	167	168	141	142	143	144	145	146	147	81	82	83	84
169	170	171	172	173	174	175	176	148	149	150	151	152	153	154	85	86	87	88
177	178	179	180	181	182	183	184	155	156	157	158	159	160	161	89	90	91	92
185	186	187	188	189	190	191	192	162	163	164	165	166	167	168	93	94	95	96
193	194	195	196	197	198	199	200	169	170	171	172	173	174	175	97	98	99	100
201	202	203	204	205	206	207	208	176	177	178	179	180	181	182	101	102	103	104
209	210	211	212	213	214	215	216	183	184	185	186	187	188	189	105	106	107	108
217	218	219	220	221	222	223	224	190	191	192	193	194	195	196	109	110	111	112

we wish to take a 25 element sample of the total population, but specify that 63.33 percent of that sample must come from Segment A and 36.66 percent of the sample must come from Segment B, we have stratified our sample in a proportional way. If we further specify that the 16 element sample of Segment A (.6333 × 25) and the 9 element sample of Segment B are to be randomly selected from their respective segments, we have a proportional, stratified, random sample.[4]

Finally, what is the nature of a probabilistic nonrandom sample? It seems almost a contradiction in terms. Figure 11.3 depicts a geographical area in

[4] Some writers refer to this sample as a "quota" sample. See, for example, John P. Alevizos, *Marketing Research: Applications, Procedures and Cases,* Englewood Cliffs, N.J.: Prentice-Hall, Inc., 1959, p. 169. As another writer observes, "stratified sampling is a weighted aggregate of unrestricted samples." See Robert Ferber and others, *Marketing Research,* New York: The Ronald Press Company, 1964, pp. 205–206.

which a total of 10,000 households are located. Further, we wish to measure the opinions of these households with a 10 percent sample. If our sample were entirely random, we would expect each household in (say) the NW quadrant to have a 10 percent chance of being represented in the sample. Indeed, if randomness prevailed, we would expect any household to have a 1 in 10 chance of selection. But suppose that for reasons of cost and convenience, we specify that the sample will be drawn 50 percent from the NE quadrant, 25 percent from the NW quadrant, and 25 percent from the SE quadrant?[5] This latter specification will create a nonrandom sample, but one in which the probabilities are nevertheless known. The probabilities that any one household will be represented in the sample are, respectively: SW, 0; SE, 1/10; NW, 1/10; and NE, 2/10.

Figure 11.3   A Nonrandom, Probabilistic Sample

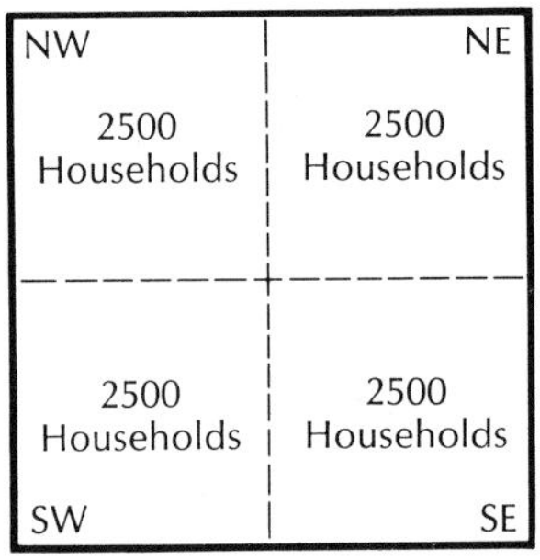

NW	NE
2500 Households	2500 Households
2500 Households	2500 Households
SW	SE

A third vital element in research procedure is identified by the word "validity." Validity is lacking when respondents are either unwilling or unable to answer candidly the questions asked by the research. In short, when validity is lacking, the research does not measure what it purports to. People often view a question asked of them by a researcher as a challenge to their intellectual prowess or perhaps their social awareness. An inability to answer a question may be viewed as a confession of intellectual weakness or of social unawareness. Whatever the specific reasons, some respondents will answer some questions with almost any available answer as a face-saving expedient. Clearly, questions answered in this way lack validity.

A classic instance in which research validity was lacking befell one of the largest automobile manufacturers in the United States. As a prelude to the company's entering the small car market, consumers were asked to articulate their small car preferences. The answers that were received were liberally sprinkled with words like "economy," "inexpensive," "functional"—in short the *expressed* preference was for a Spartan concept. When the car in question was finally introduced, four levels of elegance were offered. Because of the expressed preference for an austere concept, three

---

[5] This type of a sample is also often called a "disproportionate sample."

of the four levels of elegance were in keeping with that concept. Which of the four models was most popular at the cash register? Right! The top of the line sold much better than the others—indeed the most Spartan models were soon discontinued and a new and higher top of the line created.

In retrospect, it may be that the respondents who collectively and unwittingly misled one of the automotive giants were answering questions the way they thought they should answer them rather than with their true feelings. In any event, the research lacked validity.

The research design

The term "research design" refers to the plan through which the needed information is to be developed. And a question that arises both early and often in marketing research involves the proper matching of a particular research design to a particular research problem. The question is all the more difficult because there are so many different research designs that meaningful classification is difficult, if not impossible. The following classification scheme identifies the most frequently encountered research designs, although it should be understood at the outset that the categories are not exhaustive or necessarily mutually exclusive. That is, it is possible to find not only these categories as they are explicitly identified, but virtually any combination of them as well.

1 Research designs developed principally around secondary data
  a. internal data
  b. external data
2 Research designs developed principally around primary data
  a. direct surveys
    (1) pilot or exploratory surveys
  b. observational surveys
  c. experimental surveys
    (1) preexperimental methods
    (2) factorial designs
    (3) Latin-square designs
    (4) field experimentation
    (5) laboratory experimentation

A basic distinction in research design hinges on the nature of the data to be utilized in the research. This distinction recognizes two basic types of data, secondary data and primary data. *Primary data* is "originated by a researcher in view of specific needs."[6] Primary data thus comes into being as a result of original investigative efforts. *Secondary data,* in contrast,

---

[6] Kenneth P. Uhl and Bertram Schoner, *Marketing Research: Information Systems and Decision Making,* New York: John Wiley & Sons, Inc., 1969, p. 390.

is generally originated by others. From the perspective of the researcher using secondary data, the task is one of securing data already extant, rather than creating the required information. Secondary data tends to be general purpose data—trade association statistics, census studies, studies conducted by university bureaus of business and economic research, and so forth. Primary data tends to be more particularized—to be of greatest value in the context of a specific problem. Although this distinction seems clear enough, it is a sometimes disconcerting ambiguity that a single research report may be *both* a primary and a secondary data source. This happens, for example, when a large business organization undertakes a study for its own use (a primary data source), and the results of that study are later released. The data thus released become secondary from the perspective of those who may use it subsequently.

Although it might seem that primary data would always be superior to secondary data (because of its tailor-made nature), this is not always true. Indeed, there are particular types of research problems that would be virtually impossible for an individual firm to resolve with primary data. Two kinds of secondary data are generally recognized: internal and external. *Internal* secondary data includes data that were originally prepared by the researching firm, but which were originally intended for purposes other than those at hand. A time series summary of past sales prepared from income statements of past years is an example of the use of internal secondary data. Note that the data (sales records) were already extant—they did not come into being expressly for the current research usage.

External secondary data is of very great importance in marketing research. Federal, state and local government censuses are extremely useful sources of secondary data. Similarly, professional and trade associations serve as important research sources. Important communications media often produce helpful data: we have already seen that *Sales Management's* "Survey of Buying Power" edition is a useful data source. The list of such sources is, in effect, endless. And a useful precept to follow is to fully explore the availability of secondary data before primary research efforts are undertaken.[7] External secondary sources of data are particularly important in preparing general market surveys, in sales forecasting, and in other circumstances where the scope of the research problem would otherwise point to a costly and extensive survey.

But there are also many circumstances in which available secondary data do not permit the kind of insights that are required. When secondary data are inadequate, surveys are undertaken to develop informational requirements. Surveys are of three basic types: (a) direct surveys, (b) observational surveys and (c) experimental surveys.

Direct surveys involve person-to-person contact between researcher and

---

[7] An extremely complete and useful recitation of external sources of secondary data is in Uhl and Schoner, *op. cit.,* pp. 407–412.

respondent.[8] This person-to-person contact may be by telephone, mail or a face-to-face interview. Direct surveys are the first exposure to a questionnaire for most of us. Sometimes such surveys are highly "structured"—the questions, in both sequence and number, are administered to all respondents in a carefully (indeed, exactly) prescribed manner. A direct survey is said to be "unstructured" when the questioning proceeds more or less casually, with the actual direction of the interrogation being determined in part by the respondent. A distinction is sometimes made between "pilot," or "exploratory," studies and full-scale surveys. A pilot study is often conducted to test a questionnaire or to validate particular questions on the questionnaire that seem capable of various interpretations by respondents. In some instances, these pilot, or exploratory, surveys are simply to educate the researcher in a preliminary way regarding one or more of the issues in the survey.

While the distinctive mark of the direct survey is personal contact, there is an important type of research survey that contemplates virtually no personal contact between researcher and respondent. These no-personal-contact studies are called *observational surveys*. One of the oldest research techniques in fashion analysis, for example, is the fashion count. These fashion counts are employed to provide current market feedback to those interested in diagnosing and anticipating fashion trends. These counts are a form of observational research design. A similar example in which observation may be a valuable research method is the use of traffic counts (either vehicular or pedestrian) to assist in the appraisal of retail locations. But observation can tell us much more than is suggested by either of these examples. As further evidence of the potential value of observational surveys, consider the shopping center arrangement in Figure 11.4.

Figure 11.4 depicts a "community" size shopping center. In order to preserve the anonymity of the business interests involved, the arrangement has been altered in some inconsequential ways. The research problem in this instance was to identify the reasons why Supermarket X fell substantially short of the sales volume projected for it. Several research methods were used in the course of developing an answer to the problem; our interest here, however, is only in the observational methods used.

The first such observational technique was an analysis of originating traffic. Since important residential areas existed to the northwest and to the southeast of the center, it was felt that an analysis of the relative use made of the two entrance/exit provisions of the center might tend to reveal the areas from which the center was pulling customers most effectively and partially explain, in the process, preferred store locations within the center. Originating traffic was determined to be heaviest from

---

[8] Experimental surveys may also involve direct contact between researcher and respondent. However, we shall see momentarily that experimental surveys are distinguished from direct surveys in another and very important regard.

the northwestern residential area. Pedestrian counts within the center at various times throughout the week established the locational superiority of the corner of the center on which a competing supermarket (Y), a drug outlet and a chain variety store were located.

Figure 11.4 The Gothic "L" Shopping Center

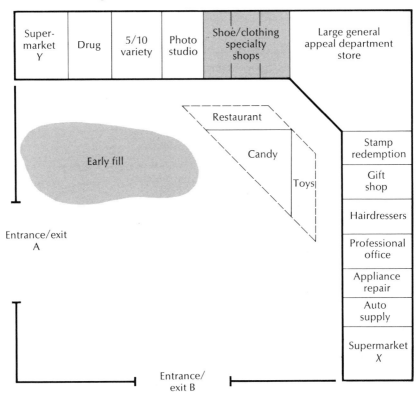

Analysis of parking-fill patterns—another observational technique—identified the point of early-fill to be the shaded area in Figure 11.4. This early-fill area was defined as the portion of the parking area that was the earliest area to fill with cars and which was filled the highest portion of time when the center was open. The location of this early-fill area corroborated the view that the Y arm of the center was drawing more customer traffic than the X arm. Finally, an analysis of customer interchange between stores in the center—still another datum that can be measured with observational methods—indicated that the combination of stores on the Y arm were substantially more compatible than those on the X arm.

Another instance in which observation may represent the dominant feature of the research is in machine forms of television viewer analysis. One such study used the Dynascope—a type of photochronograph—to determine the average amount of time television sets were in use, the average in-home television audience size, and the average no-audience time—the latter being the time a set is on with no viewers present in the room. The Dynascope—taking pictures at preset intervals—is placed at the side of the television set and focused toward the viewing area of the room. A mirror is used to enable the Dynascope to photograph both the audience and the television screen. This latter feature permits a deter-mination of audience size and composition for particular television pro-grams. The data developed by this type of observation must be tabulated from the film in the Dynascope.[9] There are, of course, other observational techniques, but enough has been said to indicate the potential value of the observational survey.

A third major class of research design is the *experimental survey*. There are two essential requirements of a true experimental survey. An experi-mental survey requires subsamples—and the subsamples are normally des-ignated "test group" and "control group." The widely advertised tooth-paste Crest and the research method used to discover whose group had fewer cavities exemplifies the first requirement of an experimental design. But the presence of subsamples alone does not produce an experimental design. A second basic requirement is that the respondents making up the total sample be assigned to the subsamples in a random way. It is this latter provision that assures the integrity of the research. Were it not for this randomness provision, it would be impossible to identify the true cause of variations between the performances of the test group and the control group. A simple illustration will show why this conclusion is warranted.

Suppose that our task is to identify the effectiveness of a special ingre-dient in toothpaste, and we are to use the incidence of cavities as the measure of that effectiveness. Suppose, moreover, that we elect to use a total sample of 1000 grade school students; 500 of these students will compose our test group, and 500 will represent our control group. Our test group will be (say) Denver residents, and our control group will be (say) Omaha residents. The Denverites will brush with a toothpaste that has special ingredients. The Omaha subsample will brush with a toothpaste that does not have the special ingredient. Suppose that after prolonged testing we find an incidence of cavities of 13 percent in the test group, and an incidence of cavities of 29 percent in the control group. What reasonable conclusion may be drawn from the "experiment"?

The cause of the difference in frequency of cavities has not been isolated. Where did we go awry? The glaring shortcoming of the research design is that we failed to assign the subjects to the subsamples (Denver and Omaha) in a random way. We are, as a result, effectively stopped from

[9] See Charles L. Allen, "Photographing the TV Audience," *Journal of Advertising Research,* March 1965, pp. 2–8. The findings of this limited survey are analyzed on pp. 5–7.

attributing any of the measured differences to the special ingredient we set out to test.[10]

There are preexperimental methods—some in rather general use—that do not truly deserve to be called experimental. An example of one of these preexperimental research designs is the simple before-after research format.[11] The simple before-after research design may, for example, endeavor to measure the effect of some selling effort by first observing sales volume before the selling effort has been tried and observing sales volume again after the effort has been spent. This design would normally require the conclusion that any difference in sales volume as measured "pre" and measured "post" is attributable to the controlled environmental factor—namely the sales effort that was present in the "post" environment but not present in the "pre" environment. The preexperimental nature of this research design should be apparent.

The glaring imperfection in the design is the requirement that any difference between "pre" and "post" performances be attributed to the experimental stimulus alone. This before-after design, especially when used in a circumstance in which a large number of other variables are reasonably expected to intervene, is of little real value. Such designs are often used and excused on the presumption that other significant variables were unchanged from the "pre" to the "post" test. It should be noted, however, that when the experimental design is such that other variables can be effectively controlled (as in a laboratory experiment) the before-after format may be quite useful.

While preexperiments are marked by a relative lack of sophistication, there are true experimental research designs that involve extremely intricate conceptual arrangements. An example of this type is the "factorial" design. The factorial design includes as many subsamples as there are combinations of the experimental variables. Table 11.1 summarizes a factorial design that was developed by DuPont "to determine whether or not the market for Teflon cookware could be revived by means of an improved" consumer advertising program.[12]

The factorial design in Table 11.1 is a 3 × 3 design—note that there are as many sample cities (test markets) as there are combinations of the experimental variables. There are three levels of fall advertising—"high" (ten daytime advertisements per week), "low" (five daytime advertisements per week) and "no" advertising. There are three similar levels of following winter advertising. There are, therefore nine subsamples, each receiving some different combination of advertising exposure. Detroit is a high-high

[10] See, for example, Uhl and Schoner, op. cit., p. 182.
[11] This type of preexperimental design is suggested in Seymour Banks, Experimentation in Marketing, New York: McGraw-Hill Book Co., 1965, p. 27. Banks refers to this design as a "one-group pretest-posttest design," and develops an extremely good taxonomy of research designs.
[12] See Charles H. Sevin, Marketing Productivity Analysis, New York: McGraw-Hill Book Co., 1965, pp. 111-113.

Table 11.1 A factorial research design for testing the effectiveness of television advertising

	Fall		
Following Winter	**High Adv.** (10/Wk.)	**Low Adv.** (5/Wk.)	**No Adv.**
High Adv. (10/Wk.)	Detroit Springfield	Dayton	Wichita
Low Adv. (5/Wk.)	Columbus	St. Louis Bangor Youngstown	Rochester
No Adv.	Omaha	Pittsburgh	Philadelphia Grand Rapids

exposure, Columbus a high-low exposure, Omaha a high-no exposure, and so forth.[13]

As a hypothetical research problem, suppose that you wanted to explore, in a systematic way, the impact of various advertising media combinations upon sales. That is, you wanted to identify, in test markets, the impact of radio advertising alone, radio advertising combined with television advertising, television advertising alone, newspapers advertising combined with television advertising, and as many other combinations of media as seemed meaningful given any specified media limitations. This is essentially the nature of a research experiment conducted by the Ford Motor Company. Table 11.2 depicts an experimental design suggested by a Ford study.[14] Note that the numbered cells represent test markets, and that every possible combination of the four media included is represented. Test Market 16, for example, is exposed to newspaper, radio, television and outdoor. Test Market 1, in contrast, receives no advertising exposure. But the factorial design is both complex and costly—working with a large number of subsamples is systematic and thorough, but often very expensive.

A type of research design that can achieve some of the advantages of a factorial design but can reduce the number of required subsamples is the Latin-square design. In order to illustrate the simplification that a Latin-square design can permit, consider the problem of a packaged foods firm that wishes to test the influence of (a) three different package designs (b) in three different groups of stores (c) during three different time periods. As a factorial design, 27 subsamples would be required; the resulting factorial design might be depicted as in Table 11.3.

---

[13] Though it is incidental to our primary concern here, the low-high and the high-high advertising exposures "produced" a higher incidence of purchases of Teflon cookware than the other advertising exposure combinations. See Sevin, *op. cit.*, p. 113.

[14] See Banks, *op. cit.*, pp. 150–151.

Table 11.2 A 2⁴ factorial design of media exposure

| | No newspaper | | | | Newspaper | | | |
| | No radio | | Radio | | No radio | | Radio | |
	No TV	TV	No TV	TV	No TV	TV	No TV	TV
No outdoor	1	2	3	4	5	6	7	8
Outdoor	9	10	11	12	13	14	15	16

Table 11.3

| | Store Group A | | | Store Group B | | | Store Group C | | |
	1st Test Period	2nd Test Period	3rd Test Period	1st Test Period	2nd Test Period	3rd Test Period	1st Test Period	2nd Test Period	3rd Test Period
Package 1	1	2	3	4	5	6	7	8	9
Package 2	10	11	12	13	14	15	16	17	18
Package 3	19	20	21	22	23	24	25	26	27

This same research problem might be approached on a Latin-square basis however, and only nine subsamples would be required. This simplification is effected by systematically rotating one of the variables among the cells corresponding to the other two variables. The Latin-square design for this same problem might appear as in Table 11.4.

Table 11.4

| | Store Group | | |
	A	B	C
1st test period	Package 1	Package 2	Package 3
2nd test period	Package 2	Package 3	Package 1
3rd test period	Package 3	Package 1	Package 2

In addition to the types of experimental designs we have considered thus far, a distinction is often made between *field experiments* and *laboratory experiments*. The field experiments and the test market are virtual synonyms in American business. Test markets may be defined as experiments conducted in carefully selected parts of the market (usually cities or standard metropolitan areas) in order to predict the sales or profit consequences of marketing actions.[15] A test market research design might be used to determine the most effective price for a new product; such a design might be used to test for the ideal promotional expenditure or the optimum number of dealers. Indeed, the test market design might reasonably be used to identify or estimate the ideal *combination* of marketing efforts. As curious as it may seem, the test market is not the best place to test totally new product ideas.

Test markets are expensive—they involve long production runs, distribution to dealers in the selected markets, and substantial commitments in terms of planning alternative marketing strategies.[16] Test markets are best suited for products that you know will sell—the idea is to use the test circumstance to define the *details* of the marketing strategy. Arthur Koponen, Director of Marketing Research for Colgate-Palmolive Company asserts that "there's no excuse for discovering in test market that a product is deficient—there are more economical, sounder ways to do that."[17] And one of the "more economical, sounder ways to do that" is concept testing.

Concept testing is the pretesting of the basic *idea* for a product. Concept testing is based on the notion "that consumers (often) buy ideas rather than physical products," and "it determines individual awareness and appreciation of product characteristics and attributes, it indicates her willingness to buy the product under consideration."[18] Note that concept testing is accomplished without full commitment to a test market design. The Ford Motor Company's very successful Mustang was concept tested—that is, depth interviews over a period of several months identified the

---

[15] This definition is, with minor editing, that suggested by A. Achenbaum in "Management Guide to Test Marketing," *Printers' Ink,* August 27, 1965, p. 27.

[16] Indeed, test markets do not always produce meaningful results. Recent interest has been focused on systematic disturbance, or "static," in test markets wherein a competing firm purposely destroys the normalcy of a market (through his competitive actions) in order to invalidate the findings of the market tester. A case to this point is the Clorox divestiture order. Prior to that divestiture order, Procter and Gamble was alleged to have "disturbed" eastern test markets in order to prevent competitors from sharpening their competitive efforts. See, for the Clorox case, John M. Kuhlman, "The Procter and Gamble Decision," *Quarterly Review of Economics and Business,* Spring 1966, pp. 29–36. See also Richard M. Clewett and others, *Cases in Marketing Strategy,* Revised Edition, Homewood, Ill.: Richard D. Irwin, Inc., 1967, pp. 284–286. For a more complete discussion of some of the pitfalls of test marketing, see David K. Hardin, "A New Approach to Test Marketing," *Journal of Marketing,* October 1966, pp. 28–29.

[17] Achenbaum, *op. cit.,* p. 22.

[18] *Ibid.,* p. 23.

car people said they wanted. Engineering, styling and marketing combined to develop a car that matched that concept—and it sold over 400,000 units in its first year. Similarly, General Foods relies, where possible, upon concept testing. Tang, an orange-flavored, powdered drink costing less than either frozen or bottled juice, was concept tested for consumer reaction to the idea. Indeed, General Foods has indicated that they were not sure whether it should be a soft drink or a breakfast drink. The concept of Tang was tested, and the women interviewed "saw" it as a breakfast drink. Note that concept testing does not *replace* market testing—it precedes it.

Before introduction into 20 test markets, Schlitz Malt Liquor had been extensively pretested for taste, package, and so forth. The purpose of the test markets was to define in a much more precise way the optimum combination of price and advertising. The following brief passage suggests something about the nature of the Malt Liquor test market design.

Of the 20, (test markets) 16 were used with varying weights on advertising and pricing. Four were used as control markets with comparable advertising and pricing strategy. To the greatest extent possible, the test areas were similar in terms of their economies and trading area characteristics.[19]

"Laboratory" experiments most often take the form of corporate consumer jury testing facilities or "auditorium" (or theater) techniques for pretesting. "Pretesting" experiments are conducted in order to identify the competitive actions that consumer groups respond to most enthusiastically before such actions are used generally. Laboratory techniques are normally designed to test for some end result other than sales or profits. That is, laboratory experiments typically focus on the expressed preferences of consumers rather than upon their actual buying actions as did the field experiment.[20]

One laboratory technique for testing the effectiveness of various advertisements is known as the Schwerin Theater system. This system "consists essentially of asking each of several hundred respondents to select, from a brand list for (a particular) product field, that brand which the respondent would prefer to receive a supply of if successful in a lottery; after exposure to the test commercial (interspersed in a group of several other commercials and in a TV filmed program) each respondent is again asked to select

---

[19] *Ibid.,* p. 24.

[20] There are, however, laboratory experiments that endeavor to simulate a complete purchase situation. See, for example, Raymond Marquardt and others, "Measuring the Utility Added by Branding and Grading," *Journal of Marketing Research,* February 1965, pp. 45–50. For a different experimental approach, see Lee K. Anderson and others, "The Consumer and His Alternatives: An Experimental Approach," *Journal of Marketing Research,* February 1966, pp. 62–67.

the brand now preferred if successful in another lottery."[21] The Schwerin system then examines the percentage of respondents who had preferred the brand in question before exposure to the commercial and the percentage of the same respondents who preferred the brand after exposure to the test commercial. The more "effective" the commercial, the greater the increase in incidence of preference for the brand in question.

Auditorium samples are often brought into representative proportions by a post-selection technique. At the beginning of a test session, participants may be asked to fill out a questionnaire that summarizes data about their socioeconomic characteristics. With the use of these "background cards," people that are over-represented in the auditorium sample are identified, and the data pertinent to their brand preferences are eliminated from the results of the experiment. This post-selection technique thus permits the determination of the actual sample after the experiment has been conducted.[22]

The range of questions and issues that may be dealt with in laboratory research is by no means limited to shifts in brand preferences. Burke Marketing Research, Inc., of Cincinnati has a studio in which it obtains information concerning 12 different aspects of commercials. Gallop and Robinson Incorporated has a "Mirror of America" auditorium for laboratory research of diverse kinds. Laboratory research may use sophisticated measurement devices. The legibility of different advertisements may be tested with intricate ocular equipment—outdoor advertisements may be pretested with a mock-up automobile. The driver's job, in this instance, is to keep his "car" on the road—"the posters going by are just part of the passing scene. After he has completed his drive, he is asked to recall what he saw."[23]

Some special problems in marketing research

The degree of intellectual challenge in an area of study is often reflected in the current problems facing that discipline. There are two areas in marketing research that often present difficult problems and that also stand in the way, generally, of a more precise fulfillment of consumer preferences. These two areas are: (a) the precise measurement of essentially qualitative phenomena and (b) the identification of the sources and the measurement of the extent of bias in research procedure.

[21] J. E. Fothergill and A. S. C. Ehrenberg, "On the Schwerin Analysis of Advertising Effectiveness," *Journal of Marketing Research,* August 1965, pp. 298–306. See also Robert D. Buzzell and others, "Television Commercial Test Scores and Short-Term Changes in Market Shares," *Journal of Marketing Research,* August 1965, pp. 307–313.
[22] For a description of the post-selection sampling technique, see Ferber and others, *Marketing Research,* pp. 331–333.
[23] For an excellent discussion of laboratory tests, see D. L. Lucas and S. H. Britt, *Measuring Advertising Effectiveness,* New York: McGraw-Hill Book Co., 1963, especially Chap. 7.

The first of these two problems is exemplified by the need to measure accurately such dimensions as corporate or brand images. Consumer attitudes and perceptions are often relevant along a semantic scale of some kind—a fact that makes their precise measurement difficult at best. Problems with bias are present in every research effort—and we are just beginning to be able to classify types of bias. Consider, for example, a research effort undertaken by the Green Giant Company. The problem was to test two types of canned peas, both packed by the Green Giant Company, with three different research designs. A "side-by-side" test format was defined as one in which the sample housewife received two cans of peas and was asked to serve both at the same meal. An evaluation was to follow. A "staggered" format was defined as one in which the sample housewife received two cans of peas and was asked to serve them several days apart. Again an evaluation followed. Finally, a "monadic" test was used. This monadic test placed just one can of peas in the hands of each housewife, but two separate groups of housewives were used. The results with one test panel were then contrasted with the results of the others. To make an otherwise long story succinct, the *results* of the three methods were different. The problem of evaluating the meaning of the three research methods became a problem of estimating the kind and amount of bias present in each and believing the one that seemed least affected.[24] But we are getting ahead of our point. Let us consider, more systematically, each of these two basic problem areas in marketing research.

ATTITUDE MEASUREMENT

It is often very helpful for a business enterprise to measure the attitudes that any or all of several audiences may have about it. A firm may reasonably want to know how its customers, its noncustomers, its distributors and dealers, its stockholders, or even the general public may feel about it. Knowledge of any of these several "images" may be the first step to a more logical allocation of promotional and public relations activities. Image measurement may reveal corporate issues about which the public is misinformed. Image measurement may suggest aspects of the corporate personality that need to be encouraged.[25] Whatever the specific motive may be, the measurement of attitudes toward the business is a task that faces an increasing number of organizations. And attitudes are usually *qualitative* phenomena. That is, dealing as they often do with human perceptions and levels of affection, attitudes are not readily measureable with the same objective precision as other concepts. This *qualitative* char-

[24] See Roger Bengston and Henry Brenner, "Product Test Results Using Three Different Methodologies," *Journal of Marketing Research,* November 1964, pp. 49–52.

[25] Attitude measurements have been used to predict market share. See, for example, Henry Assael and George S. Day, "Attitudes and Awareness as Predictors of Market Share," *Journal of Advertising Research,* December 1968, pp. 3–10.

acteristic of attitudes suggests that different methods of research are required. And a body of special research techniques has evolved to meet the problem.

Attitude measurements are often accomplished with *scaling devices* of some kind.[26] An illustration will serve to define the nature of one of these scaling devices. The "semantic differential" is a means of measuring connotative meaning that utilizes (a) bipolar adjectives (or adjectival phrases) and permits (b) "evaluative" or "activity" judgments to be expressed on (c) an equal-interval ordinal scale.[27] In spite of the complexity of the jargon, the idea is a simple one. Note the scale below:

Dull ——— : ——— : ——— : ——— : ——— : ——— : ——— Exciting

The adjectives at either end of the scale are bipolar—that is, they express opposite views along some semantic continuum or spectrum. These adjectives are also "evaluative"; they suggest some state of being. And finally, the scale is an equal-interval (seven intervals in this case) *ordinal* scale. If we wanted to make the scale cardinal, and continuous, we might depict it as follows:

Dull ——————————————————— Exciting
    0   .25   .5   .75   1

If we wanted to scale an adjectival phrase rather than single adjectives, we might use a scale anchored as follows:

Dependable products ——— : ——— : ——— : ——— : ——— : ——— : ——— : Undependable products

It is a relatively simple matter to extend these scales into coordinated packages of scales that focus on some common group of attitudes that we wish to measure.[28] The following such group centers, for example, on some physical characteristics of a store.[29]

[26] Although attitudes can also reasonably be inferred from word-association or similar associative techniques. Word association tests are the subject of a subsequent section of the present chapter.

[27] This composite definition is assembled from three sources: William A. Mindak, "Fitting the Semantic Differential to the Marketing Problem," *Journal of Marketing*, April 1961, pp. 28–33; Theodore Clevenger, Jr., and others, "Measurement of Corporate Images by the Semantic Differentive," *Journal of Marketing Research*, February 1965, pp. 80–82; and James H. Myers and W. Gregory Warner, "Semantic Properties of Selected Evaluation Adjectives," *Journal of Marketing Research*, November 1968, pp. 409–412. The basic reference work on the semantic differential is C. E. Osgood and others, *Measurement of Meaning*, Urbana, Ill.: University of Illinois Press, 1957. This latter reference provides both the theoretical considerations relevant to the research technique and examples of applications.

[28] Most attitudinal measurement work to date has been with "unidimensional scales." That is, a single linear continuum has been used most frequently. There is, however, increasing interest in "multidimensional scaling." See, for example, Paul E. Green and Frank J. Carmone, "Multidimensional Scaling: An Introduction and Comparison of Nonmetric Unfolding Techniques," *Journal of Marketing Research*, August 1969, pp. 330–341.

[29] This group of scales is shown in Robert F. Kelly and Ronald Stephenson, "The Semantic Differential: An Information Source for Designing Retail Patronage Appeals," *Journal of Marketing*, October 1967, p. 45.

Dirty	___ : ___ : ___ : ___ : ___ : ___ : ___ :	Clean
Unattractive decor	___ : ___ : ___ : ___ : ___ : ___ : ___ :	Attractive decor
Merchandise easy to find	___ : ___ : ___ : ___ : ___ : ___ : ___ :	Merchandise difficult to find
Wide aisles	___ : ___ : ___ : ___ : ___ : ___ : ___ :	Narrow aisles
Slow checkout	___ : ___ : ___ : ___ : ___ : ___ : ___ :	Fast checkout

Perhaps we may wish to measure attitudes toward several brands of beer. In that event, we might use a package of scaling spectra as follows.[30]

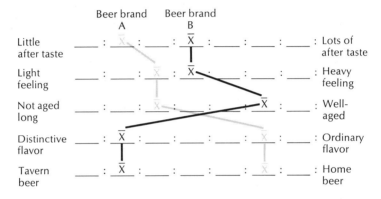

But this latter scale takes the semantic differential one step further. Attitude "profiles" for Brands A and B are summarized on the grouping. Note that these profiles are developed from a mean, or average, response along each of the five semantic dimensions. That is, the average respondent felt that Brand A ranked well down on the "aftertaste" scale. In contrast, the mean judgment for Brand B on the same scale was in the center of the "aftertaste" scale. These five mean "scores" for each brand constitute a kind of overall image—and similar measurements at different points in time might be used to estimate changes in those images. It should also be apparent that we can easily assign numerical values to each of the intervals on the scale and represent these profiles as a series of numbers.

If, for example, the intervals were numbered 1 through 7 reading left to right, then Brand B is a "4" in terms of aftertaste and Brand A is a "2" in terms of the same attribute. This last adjustment permits a more precise measurement and articulation of otherwise subjective and elusive connotative meanings.

But there are techniques for attitudinal measurement other than the

[30] This group of scaling continua are, with some editorial modification, those suggested in Mindak, op. cit., p. 31.

semantic differential.[31] A mock-up of a new automobile design may be evaluated in terms of (say) its "impressiveness" with either of the following scaling methods:

The proposed 1974 model of the Chevrolet is impressive:

( )	( )	( )	( )	( )
extremely	very	somewhat	only slightly	not at all

or alternatively:

The proposed 1974 model of the Chevrolet is impressive:

( )	( )	( )	( )	( )
NO!	no	indifferent	yes	YES!

BIAS IN MARKETING RESEARCH

Bias is one of the truly perplexing problems in marketing research. We will think of bias as any difference between the sample results and "true" results. True results would be those that we would discover if no error of any kind were present in our research design. Bias is usually recognized as being traceable to one of five basic sources:

1 *Measurement error.* This source of bias is introduced by respondents who, for one or more reasons, do not report true values. Respondents may not know true values; they may not care to divulge them.

2 *Nonresponse error.* In sampling the views of a group of selected sample members, it is not unusual to encounter some who refuse to cooperate and some who cannot be contacted at all. These two problems—refusals and not-at-homes—constitute nonresponse error. To the extent that refusal and not-at-home respondents hold different attitudes from other sample members, these different attitudes tend to be understated in the sample results.

3 *Frame errors.* This source of error develops when the sample population is not like the total population from which it was drawn. This error is produced by a lack of "representativeness," as we have used that term earlier.

4 *Random sampling error.* This type of bias is defined as error that occurs even when sampling procedures are random. Any sample, because it employs less than the entire population, will reflect some variation from true values. The amount of this bias can be estimated statistically.

[31] See, for example, C. J. Bartlett and others, "A Comparison of Six Different Scaling Techniques," *Journal of Social Psychology,* May 1960, pp. 343–348. This article discusses (a) a "magnetic board" technique, (b) paired comparisons, (c) ranking, (d) graphic, (e) Likert and (f) equal interval scales. Other scaling devices that have achieved extensive usage include those of Likert and Thurstone. Indeed, a classic work comparing these two scales is Rensis Likert, "A Technique for the Measurement of Attitudes," *Archives of Psychology,* June 1932. The basic statement of the Thurstone scale is in L. L. Thurstone and E. J. Chase, *The Measurement of Attitude,* Chicago: University of Chicago Press, 1929.

5 *Sampling process errors.* This type of bias arises when sample results are weighted on the basis of outdated or inaccurate data.[32]

Of these five sources of bias, measurement error is perhaps the most perplexing. Measurement error may be introduced by the interviewer-respondent relationship, or it may be introduced by the wording of the questions that are asked.[33] Measurement bias includes errors in recording and errors that result from an inability of the interviewer to achieve rapport with the respondent. Recording errors include both the "innocent" types of omission or commission and the not-so-innocent problem of falsification of questionnaire responses. The expectations of the interviewer may produce an innocent kind of recording error. One study, for example, found that interviewers "often record the answer they expect to hear rather than the one actually given."[34]

The not-so-innocent type of interviewer error—referred to as the cheater problem—is well documented in the literature of marketing research.[35] Gross interviewer cheating may be minimized through the use of survey audits or "tandem interviews." Inadvertent recording errors may be discovered and corrected in interview sessions between the interviewer and the survey management.[36] But the problems of interviewer-respondent rapport and prejudicial wording of questions are less easily controlled.[37] It is recognized

[32] See these classes of error discussed in "A Search for the Rationale of Non-Probability Sample "Design," Charles S. Mayer and Rex V. Brown, Proceedings of the 1965 Fall Conference, American Marketing Association, at pp. 305–307.

[33] See R. Ferber and H. Woler, "Detection and Correction of Interviewer Bias," *Public Opinion Quarterly*, Spring 1952, pp. 107–127.

[34] See H. L. Smith and H. Hyman, "The Biasing Effect of Interviewer Expectations on Survey Results," *Public Opinion Quarterly*, Fall 1950, pp. 491–506.

[35] The "classic" article is L. P. Crespi, "The Cheater Problem in Polling," *Public Opinion Quarterly*, Winter 1945–46. More recently, see E. P. Clarkson, "A Symposium on Interviewing Problems: The Problem of Honesty," *International Journal of Opinion and Attitude Research*, Spring 1950, pp. 84–90. See also L. Andrews, "Court Decree on the 'Cheater Problem,' "*Journal of Marketing*, October 1953, pp. 167–169. This latter article describes a court case in which the interviewer had not done valid work.

[36] See, for example, Paul F. Carroll, Jr., "How Can Supervisors in the Field Be More Helpful to Interviewing Services," in Robert S. Hancock, editor, *Dynamic Marketing in a Changing World*, Chicago: American Marketing Association, 1960, pp. 408–409. See also William Ash, "Description of a Pilot Study to Test the Accuracy of Interviewer Recording," in Robert M. Kaplan, editor, *The Marketing Concept in Action*, Chicago: American Marketing Association, 1964, pp. 541–548.

[37] An early study of the influence of interviewers and interviews on the respondent is in L. P. Crespi, "The Interview Effect in Polling," *Public Opinion Quarterly*, Spring 1948, pp. 99–111. More recently, see J. J. Feldman and others, "A Field Study of Interviewer Effects on the Quality of Survey Data," *Public Opinion Quarterly*, Winter 1951-52, pp. 734–761. Another article of interest on this issue is R. H. Hanson and E. S. Marks, "Influence of the Interviewer on the Accuracy of Survey Results," *Journal of the American Statistical Association*, September 1958, pp. 635–55. A very recent article describes the application of paired comparison analysis to quality control of interviewing. See Purnell H. Benson, "A Paired Comparison Approach to Evaluating Interviewer Performance," *Journal of Marketing Research*, February 1969, pp. 66–70.

that the age, the sex and the expected income characteristics of the interviewer can influence interviewing performance. In general, the most effective interviewers are perceived as neutral—but neutral on the respondent's
side. This apparent contradiction in terms suggests that the best (most
candid) responses are produced when the interviewer is perceived as a
person without an ax to grind. The interviewer should, however, adopt
a style and manner that leads the interviewee to believe that he is not
indifferent.[38] Indeed, this problem of achieving a candid relationship with
the respondent has given rise to a special body of research methods.
Particularly where emotional issues are present, it is difficult to develop
a candid relationship between interviewer and respondent. And in order
to meet this need, *projective techniques* are often used. An example will
make the nature of these projective techniques clear.

Mason Haire, a well-known name in behavioral research, argues that
there is a need for special research methods when: (a) snob appeal of
a product is of vital importance, (b) the respondent is influenced by
motives that are to some extent socially unacceptable, (c) the respondent
is not fully aware of or able to articulate his motives and (d) the respondent
believes that a stereotypical answer will avoid further, and possibly uncom-
fortable, questioning. In all these instances the respondent may feel some
sense of advantage in a less-than-truthful answer.[39] But what, exactly, is
a projective technique?

In general, a projective test is one that presents the respondent with
an ambiguous situation—a situation that "does not quite make sense"—and
requires that the respondent explain or clarify the situation. "The theory
is that in order to make (the situation) make sense he will have to add
to it—to fill out the picture—and in so doing he projects part of himself
(his own views) into it."[40] One of the classic examples of the successful
use of a projective technique in marketing research involved the instant
coffee, Nescafé. This Nescafé study proceeded in two stages: First, a conventional study (nonprojective) was undertaken to ascertain the opinions
of housewives about instant coffee. Most of those who disliked instant
coffee said that they did not like it because of the flavor. Suspicion that
this was an explanation that was more convenient than candid prompted
a second kind of research design. This second stage of the research was
projective. It began by presenting housewives with two shopping lists.

Each sample housewife was shown one of these shopping lists. Note
that the lists are virtually the same except for the Nescafé instant coffee
on List I and the Maxwell House ground coffee on List II. Each housewife
was instructed to study her list carefully and to characterize the women
who bought the groceries. Respondents were asked to write a brief descrip-

[38] See L. A. Dexter, "Role Relationships and Conceptions of Neutrality in Interviewing,"
American Journal of Sociology, September 1956, pp. 153–157.
[39] See Mason Haire, "Projective Techniques in Marketing Research," *Journal of Marketing,*
April 1950, pp. 649–656.
[40] *Ibid.,* p. 650.

tion of the shopper's likely personality and character. The results of this projective stage of the study are summarized in the following points.

1 Almost 50 percent of the respondents described the List I shopper as lazy. Only 4 percent thought the List II shopper lazy.
2 Almost 50 percent of the respondents characterized the List I shopper as a poor planner—unable to organize and schedule her day effectively. Only 12 percent saw this character flaw in the List II shopper.
3 Twelve percent of the respondents saw spendthrift traits in the List I shopper. None described the List II shopper as a spendthrift.

These shopping lists are reproduced below:

Shopping List I	Shopping List II
Pound and a half of hamburger	Pound and a half of hamburger
2 loaves of Wonder bread	2 loaves of Wonder bread
bunch of carrots	bunch of carrots
1 can Rumsford's Baking Powder	1 can Rumsford's Baking Powder
Nescafé instant coffee	1 lb. Maxwell House Coffee (Drip Grind)
2 cans Del Monte peaches	2 cans Del Monte Peaches
5 lbs. potatoes	5 lbs. potatoes

Note that at the time of this Nescafé study instant coffee was not yet an accepted convenience—and the results of the survey indicate some hostility toward the type of person who would use it. But, more to our essential point here, observe the candor of the projective responses and the comparative superficiality of the responses to the conventional survey.

In another study, a direct comparison between the results of a conventional (nonprojective) survey and its projective equivalent was possible. In the nonprojective form, the respondent was told to assume that he needed some aspirin and went to a drug store to buy some. The respondent was further told that he had a choice between a well-known brand (100 tablets, 67¢) and another brand (100 tablets, 27¢). Finally, the respondent was asked to make and explain his decision. In projective form, a "thematic apperception" format was used.[41] This technique often utilizes a cartoon drawing with one or more characters whose actions or thoughts are to be interpreted or explained by the survey respondent. In this particular study, the cartoon pictured a man behind a counter in a drug store and a female stick character talking to the druggist. The druggist's balloon

[41] A good general reference on TAT is W. E. Henry, *The Analysis of Fantasy: The Thematic Apperception Technique in the Study of Personality*, New York: John Wiley & Sons, Inc., 1956. For a more recent reference, see J. Zubin and others, *An Experimental Approach to Projective Techniques*, New York: John Wiley & Sons, Inc., 1965. For application of TAT and the picture frustration test to marketing problems, see M. Zober, "Some Projective Techniques Applied to Marketing Research," *Journal of Marketing*, January 1956, pp. 262–268.

says "This widely known brand of aspirin gives you 100 tablets for 67¢, and this brand gives you 100 tablets for 27¢. Which would you like?" The customer's balloon is empty. Note the projective nature of the cartoon test. The respondent is asked to make a decision in behalf of the customer—not directly in her own behalf. And how do the results of the two tests compare?

	Prefer 67¢	Prefer 27¢	No choice
Cartoon respondents	48%	30%	22%
Verbal respondents	74%	18%	8%

The man who conducted this aspirin study believes that "the cartoon responses on brand choice may have provided more accurate evidence because the housewife was under less implied pressure to show that she was concerned with aspirin quality." For whatever the reasons, the two methods produced results that are statistically different.[42]

Projective techniques include, in addition to the thematic apperception test (TAT), several other general formats. The most common of these are (a) the sentence completion test and (b) free and controlled word association tests.[43] Sentence completion tests, as the name suggests, present an incomplete statement to the respondent and, in the process of completing the statement, a candid view is assumed to result. Sentence completion tests are not *necessarily* projective.[44] Association tests present the respondent with a word or phrase and require that he respond with the first word or thought that the cue word suggests to him. Association tests are a systematic modification of the children's game of matching words. These tests are called "free" association tests if the respondent may respond with any thought or word within the universe of his vocabulary. The test is "controlled" if the respondent is provided with a list of words or ideas from which to match his cue. Thus, if the cue is *fast,* and the respondent were asked to indicate the first thought that this word brings to mind, the test is "free." If the cue is *fast* and he is asked to identify the one automobile from a list of five brands provided which seems best associated with the cue, the test is "controlled." Consider the following partial summary of a student study of campus bookstores.

[42] See Lucas and Britt, *op. cit.,* pp. 148–149.
[43] The sentence completion test, TAT, and "association" tests are frequently encountered in marketing research. There are many other projective tests, and a survey of the journal literature of psychology indicates that the most frequently encountered tests ranked as follows: (1) Rorschach, (2) TAT, (3) human figure drawings, (4) Bender-Gestalt, (5) sentence completion, (6) word association, (7) Rosenzweig D-F, (8) house-tree-person, (9) Szondi, and (10) Blacky pictures. See David A. Crenshaw and others, "Projective Methods in Research," *Journal of Projective Techniques and Personality Assessment,* February 1968, pp. 3–9.
[44] For a description of the sentence completion test used by Johnson Wax, see Lucas and Britt, *op. cit.,* pp. 134–135.

Table 11.5 Controlled word association test—campus bookstores

CUE	N (in percents)	C (in percents)	U (in percents)
profitable	84	6	10
swindle	42	30	28
confusion	19	30	51
dreary	3	40	57
place to buy	68	13	19
place to sell (used books)	65	14	21

The bookstores in this study are designated N, C and U. The cues are indicated at the left. Of the student sample, 84 percent associated the cue "profitable" with Store N. Only 3 percent of the sample associated the cue "dreary" with Store N, and so forth. Although the data above are not complete, the insight that such a test can provide should be apparent.

Mathematical models in marketing research

The use of mathematics and, more particularly, the use of quantitative models in business has been a major trend in the last ten years.[45] Students often view mathematical models as a kind of twentieth century form of harassment—intended to put the finishing touches on their already shaky academic performance. It seems clear, however, that to the extent that the complexities of business problems can be represented in quantitative form, models can provide a meaningful form of assistance in the resolution of those problems. The great promise of the model is that it can reflect explicitly the intricacies and interrelationships of a phenomenon too complex for the normal intellect to assimilate readily. When the interrelationships among the relevant variables influencing a particular form of behavior can be identified in a quantifiable form, it is but a short step to the computerization of the model. In a sense, then, the model holds the potential of dealing more effectively with extremely complex phenomena than does the cerebral process of man. All of which is not to say that the computer is smarter than man; clearly that cannot be so. But the computer forces us to order the elements in a complex problem in a more systematic way. In what ways are the mathematical model and the computer of possible assistance in the field of marketing research?

Many mathematical techniques with applications in the field of business belong to the general body of method referred to as operations research.[46] An "OR man" is one trained in the application of mathematical techniques

[45] For a discussion of this issue, see Peter Langhoff, editor, *Models, Measurement and Marketing*, Englewood Cliffs, N.J.: Prentice-Hall, Inc., 1965, particularly pp. 41–54.
[46] See Herbert Solow, "Operations Research Is in Business," in Donald F. Mulvihill, editor, *Guide to the Quantitative Age*, New York: Holt, Rinehart and Winston, Inc., 1966, pp. 184–197. The major elements in the OR "tool kit" are discussed briefly on pp. 188–190.

to practical problems. This body of method—operations research—uses several types of general models, several of which are relevant in the field of marketing research.[47] Illustrative of these models are (a) "allocation" models and (b) "queueing" models.

Allocation models have two distinguishing traits: First, limited resources are available. These limited resources may be dollars, personnel, dealers, or any other productive resource. Second, the allocation model permits these resources to be combined in alternative ways. That is, the allocation problem requires combinational experimentation. The purpose of the allocation model is to determine the best combination of the specified and limited resources given some maximum permissible total expenditure. We might want to know what the best, or optimum, combination of advertising and selling within a store is. We could spend our entire budget on advertising, or, alternatively, we could spend our entire budget on sales salaries and sales training. Indeed, we could spend our budget in any combination of ways between advertising and personal selling. We could, in other words, *allocate* our budget between advertising and personal sales efforts in an extremely large number of ways. Our task is to identify the best allocational combination of those that are possible. But in order to judge this "best" allocational combination, we need some means of evaluating the goodness of each combination of resources. Allocation models, then, deal with specified but limited resources, capable of combination in many ways, subject to some set of constraints; such models seek to identify the most effective combination of resources.

One of the basic techniques of operations research that is useful in solving allocation problems is *linear programming*.[48] The following simplified problem will indicate how linear programming can provide valuable assistance in marketing research. Assume that you are told that you have a maximum of $25,000 to spend on advertising in one year. Assume further that you are asked to maximize the number of company executives reached in the audiences of ten different monthly business periodicals. Table 11.6 summarizes some of the information that you are able to obtain.

On the basis of the data in Table 11.6, how do you believe the $25,000 should be allocated among Periodicals A through J? If you are tempted to spend it all in Periodical G, you would find that impossible to do. These periodicals are all monthly, and the most you could spend with G would be approximately $9000. The best solution is to buy 5½ pages in D, 12 pages in E, and 12 pages in G.[49]

[47] See the excellent summary article, Philip Kotler, "Operations Research in Marketing," *Harvard Business Review,* January-February 1967. See also the more explicit piece, Philip Kotler, "The Use of Mathematical Models in Marketing," *Journal of Marketing,* October 1963, pp. 31–41.
[48] An excellent discussion of linear programming may be seen in James E. Howell and Daniel Teichrow, *Mathematical Analysis for Business Decisions,* Homewood, Ill.: Richard D. Irwin, Inc., 1963, pp. 257–280. This discussion proceeds systematically from a simple example to a three-element problem.
[49] This problem is adapted from James F. Engel and others, *Promotional Strategy,* Homewood, Ill.: Richard D. Irwin, Inc., 1967, pp. 232–233.

If your complaint is that the problem is too simple, that it can indeed be resolved intuitively, you are right. But we can, by increasing the number of restrictions on the way that the $25,000 is to be spent, develop a more realistic problem—and one that most assuredly cannot be resolved intuitively. The media allocation model we have just considered has only two constraints—the maximum expenditure constraint and the 12 insertions-per-year constraint. If the problem had been defined as finding the optimum allocation of $4,000,000 among 20 national weekly magazines to female readers in households earning over $15,000 annually residing in standard metropolitan areas of over one million population, then the plot begins to thicken, and the computer would be a most welcomed ally.[50]

Table 11.6 Media Audience Data

Periodical	Executives reached	Cost per page	Executives reached per dollar spent
A	—	$475	—
B	12,000	792	15.15
C	24,000	730	32.87
D	44,000	890	49.44
E	52,000	918	56.55
F	8,000	456	17.54
G	44,000	756	58.20
H	—	700	—
I	16,000	680	23.53
J	23,000	575	40.00

Queueing models (sometimes called "waiting line," "bottleneck" or "logjam" models) represent a second type of OR model with potential in the solution of marketing problems. The distinctive characteristics of the queueing model are: (a) an arrival pattern, (b) service times and (c) a queueing discipline. Arrival patterns may be thought of as a kind of frequency distribution of the usage through time of some service. The words "usage through time" are especially important, for the arrival pattern describes the demand pattern for some particular service. Demand patterns may be rectangular, skewed, multimodel or normal. Figure 11.5 depicts each of these arrival patterns.

[50] A more challenging allocation problem is described in Engel and others, *op. cit.*, pp. 234–238.

Note that the characteristic of the rectangular pattern of arrival is constancy. The number of units of service demanded are the same in each unit of time. This might be the arrival pattern that would be approximated where auto licenses are sold by month, day and hour, and are scheduled by the surname of the licensee. The skewed arrival pattern, in contrast, places distinctly different demands upon those performing the service at different points in time. The skewed-left circumstance might approximate the customer arrival pattern in an automobile garage, for example. Note also that the so-called normal arrival pattern is not normal in any but a statistical sense. That is, this normal arrival pattern is an approximation of the normal bell-shaped distribution.

Figure 11.5 Arrival Patterns

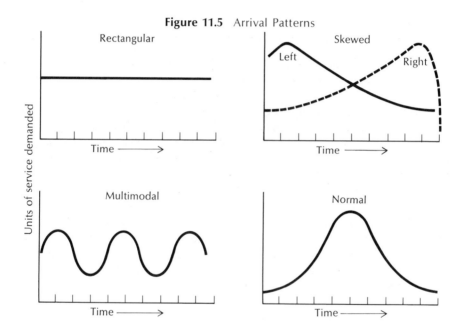

"Service time" is the time required to render the service being demanded. Service time may be the average time required to check out of a supermarket; it may be the average time required to purchase a theater ticket; it may be the time required, on the average, to receive a welfare check. "Queueing discipline" identifies the priority with which demand is accommodated. First come, first served is a queueing discipline; age before beauty is a queueing discipline. A queueing problem that will serve to both illustrate these three components of the model and better define the mathematics of queueing is the checkstand model. The checkstand model seeks to identify the optimum number of checkout lanes in a supermarket. Consider the following hypothetical data.

	Hourly Customer Count	Average Sale	Total Hourly Sales	Hourly Checkstand Capacity	Hourly Checkstand Requirements
9-10 am	600	$5.00	$3,000	$400	8
10-11 am	650	6.00	3900	400	10
11-12 am	650	6.00	3900	400	10
12-1 pm	700	5.00	3500	400	9
1-2 pm	600	7.00	4200	400	11
2-3 pm	750	8.00	6000	400	15
3-4 pm	800	9.00	7200	400	18
4-5 pm	850	8.00	6800	400	17
5-6 pm	800	8.00	6400	400	16
6-7 pm	600	6.00	3600	400	9

Each of the requisite elements of a queueing problem is represented in these data. The arrival pattern is reflected in the hourly customer count. That frequency distribution is skewed-right. The average service time is reflected in the hourly checkstand capacity column. Note that this latter column holds a constant $400 per hour capacity. This figure assumes two experienced check-out personnel—it would be lower if only one person were utilized per check-out lane. The queueing discipline is a loose first come, first served. That is, the *tendency* would be for the first customers in to be the first out—though in any particular case there could be some variation.

We should note that the peak hours demand an extremely large number of checkstands—or some temporary modification in the way the check-out function is accomplished. For example, express lanes might be used to siphon off the small order customers, or we might alter the checkstand capacity upward by adding a third team member in the check-out lane. This latter option often utilizes a checker, a changemaker and a bagger. The task for marketing research is to develop the data required to make these kinds of calculations.[51]

SUMMARY

The purpose of the present chapter has been to identify some of the basic analytical concepts and some of the problems that represent the field of marketing research. Toward this general end, we considered some of the basic statistical concepts employed in marketing research, including the ideas of representativeness, validity and randomness. We identified unrestricted random samples, stratified random samples, and the case where randomness is missing but sampling probabilities are known.

[51] For a complete discussion of these checkstand problems, see Edward M. Harwell, *Checkout Management*, New York: Chain Store Publishing Corp., 1963, pp. 178-186.

We examined the nature of research designs. We observed that research designs may be developed around secondary or primary data. For purposes of exposition, we divided secondary data research designs into those utilizing internal data and those using external data. Research designs that use primary data sources are of three basic types: (a) direct surveys, (b) observational surveys and (c) experimental surveys. Experimental surveys were further divided into those that are preexperimental, and those that involve factorial designs, Latin-square designs, field experiments, and laboratory experiments.

Two special problems in marketing research were of particular interest to us. We were interested in the measurement techniques used with qualitative phenomena, such as corporate images, and in the special problem of research bias. Attitudes are measurable with any of several scaling devices. We examined the semantic differential at length. Bias in marketing research is usually traceable to one or more of five sources: (a) measurement error, (b) nonresponse error, (c) frame error, (d) random sampling error and (e) sampling process errors. Our special concern was with measurement error. And in our discussion of measurement error we explored a special group of research techniques called projective techniques.

Finally, we examined briefly the use of mathematical models in marketing research. More specifically, we considered two kinds of models—allocation models and queueing models.

REVIEW QUESTIONS

1 Carefully define and indicate the relevance of each of the following concepts to the study of marketing:
   a. Marketing research
   b. Market analysis
   c. Statistical representativeness
   d. Statistical validity
   e. Random samples
   f. A research design
   g. Direct surveys
   h. Observational surveys
   i. Experimental surveys
   j. Pilot surveys
   k. Early-fill points in shopping center appraisal
   l. A factorial research design

2 Distinguish carefully between each element in the following pairs of terms·
   a. Advertising allocation studies *and* consumer allocation studies
   b. Research designs using secondary data sources *and* research designs using primary data sources
   c. A preexperimental research design *and* an experimental research design
   d. Test marketing *and* concept testing
   e. Pretesting *and* post-selection of samples

3 Under what conditions is it possible for data to be both secondary and primary?

4 Specifically, how does a factorial research design differ from a Latin-square research design?

5 What is auditorium research? For what types of research questions do you believe it is best suited?

6 If you wanted to measure your own image among acquaintances, specifically how would you do it? If you were asked to use some type of scaling device, what dimensions of your personality would you scale?

7 What is an attitude profile? How can such a profile be helpful in measuring the effectiveness of advertising?

8 What are the major sources of bias in marketing research? Which of these types of bias is the most difficult to estimate accurately?

9 Specifically, what research conditions suggest the possible use of projective methods of measurement?

10 What is linear programming? To what particular types of research problems is it well suited?

11 What is queueing theory? To what particular types of research problems is it well suited?

SUGGESTED SUPPLEMENTARY READINGS IN MARKETING RESEARCH

Adler, Lee, and Irving Crespi, editors, *Attitude Research at Sea,* Chicago: American Marketing Association, 1966.

Alevizos, John P., *Marketing Research: Applications Procedures and Cases,* Englewood Cliffs, N.J.: Prentice-Hall, Inc., 1959.

Alexis, Marcus, Robert J. Holloway, and Robert S. Hancock, *Empirical Foundations of Marketing,* Chicago: Markham Publishing Company, 1969.

Banks, Seymour, *Experimentation in Marketing,* New York: McGraw-Hill Book Co., 1965.

Barksdale, Hiram C., and William M. Weilbacker, *Marketing Research: Selected Reading with Analytical Commentaries,* New York: The Ronald Press Company, 1966.

Bogart, Leo, *Current Controversies in Marketing Research,* Chicago: Markham Publishing Company, 1969.

Brown, Lyndon O., *Marketing and Distribution Research,* New York: The Ronald Press Company, 1955.

Buzzell, Robert D., Donald F. Cox and Rex V. Brown, *Marketing Research and Information Systems,* New York: McGraw-Hill Book Co., 1969.

Cox, Keith K., editor, *Readings in Modern Research,* New York: Appleton-Century-Crofts, 1967.

_____ and Ben M. Enis, *Experiments for Marketing Decisions,* Scranton, Pa.: International Textbook Company, 1969.

Drake, Jerry E., and Frank I. Millar, *Marketing Research: Intelligence and Management,* Scranton, Pa.: International Textbook Company, 1969.

Ferber, Robert, Donald F. Blankertz and Sidney Hollander, Jr., *Marketing Research,* New York: The Ronald Press Company, 1964.

Festinger, Leon, and Daniel Katz, *Research Methods in the Behavioral Sciences,* New York: The Dryden Press, 1953.

Green, Paul E., Patrick J. Robinson, and Peter T. Fitzroy, *Experiments on the Value of Information in Simulated Marketing Environments,* Boston: Allyn and Bacon, Inc., 1967.

_____ and Donald S. Tull, *Research for Marketing Decisions,* Englewood Cliffs, N.J.: Prentice-Hall, Inc., 1966.

Heidingsfield, Myron S., and Frank H. Eby, Jr., *Marketing and Business Research,* New York: Holt, Rinehart and Winston, Inc., 1962.

Holmes, Parker M., *Marketing Research: Principles and Readings,* Second Edition, Cincinnati: South-Western Publishing Company, 1966.

Journal of Marketing Research, Chicago: American Marketing Association (quarterly)

King, Robert L., editor, *Conferences, '55/'65,* Chicago: American Marketing Association, 1966 (especially Chap. 4).

Kish, Leslie, *Survey Samplings,* New York: John Wiley & Sons, Inc., 1965.

Myers, James H., and Richard R. Mead, *The Management of Marketing Research,* Scranton, Pa.: International Textbook Company, 1969.

Sudman, Seymour, *Reducing the Cost of Surveys,* Chicago: Aldine Publishing Company, 1968.

Uhl, Kenneth P., and Bertram Schoner, *Marketing Research,* New York: John Wiley & Sons, Inc., 1969.

Wales, Hugh G., and Robert Ferber, *A Basic Bibliography on Marketing Research,* Chicago: American Marketing Association, 1963.

Wasson, Chester R., *The Strategy of Marketing Research,* New York: Appleton-Century-Crofts, 1964.

Webb, Eugene J., Donald T. Campbell, Richard D. Swartz and Lee Sechrest, *Unobtrusive Measures: Nonreactive Research in the Social Sciences,* Chicago: Rand McNally & Company, 1966.

Part IV

**THE GENERAL
STRATEGY OF
MARKETING
BEHAVIOR**

The purpose of the chapters that constitute Part Four is to develop an understanding of the nature of competitive activities in a socioeconomic environment that we will describe with the term *mixed affluence*. Toward this general end, Part Four will include an examination of five basic issues:

1 The role of competition in general, and the conventional wisdom about what competition should be.
2 The role of competition with products and services in conditions of mixed affluence.
3 The role of competition with promotion in conditions of mixed affluence.

4 The role of price competition in conditions of mixed affluence.

5 The role of competition with distribution in conditions of mixed affluence.

The foregoing list of issues represents the task of Part Four. The major premise of Part Four is that specific, identifiable preconditions dictate, more or less exactly, the nature of competition in any particular socioeconomic system, and that a meaningful understanding of competition must proceed from an examination of these preconditions. In a sense, Part Four presents an argument. It is an argument about what the *natural* character of competition is. It is an argument about modern competition that is not often enough encountered.

Chapter 12

COMPETITION IN MIXED AFFLUENCE

Whether competition is weak or strong is not just an academic issue. The effectiveness of competition should be an immediate concern of every citizen. And it should be of special interest to students of our business enterprise system. The strength of the competition in our business system influences us all, and often in very profound ways. If competition is weak, our incomes are effectively reduced. That is, when competitive vigor is lacking, we tend to pay too much for what we receive, and a given level of earnings cannot provide the level of satisfaction that it otherwise might. Students of business administration should have a special interest in the strength of competition in our business system. For if competition today is weak and uninspired, it is almost sure that the ground rules for the conduct of business enterprise will be altered. In this case, the ground rules are manifest in public sentiment and, ultimately, in regulation of some form. We have seen in earlier chapters that statutory regulation of business is already extensive and complex. But the existing body of state and federal law, complex as it is now, is not necessarily complete.

The student with an interest in marketing is, perhaps more than any other, obliged to refine his thinking about matters of competition. Marketing is, often unavoidably, the area of corporate organization through which the competitive thrust of the firm is determined. How competitive activities are conducted is, by and large, a responsibility of corporate marketing. And even where the nature of competitive efforts are determined collectively by several areas of corporate organization, marketing is often likely to bear an inordinate share of the blame for actions that prove either ineffective or imprudent. Indeed, we shall see that it is a truth of these times that some condemnation of marketing is actually an expression of dissatisfaction with the general vigor of competition.[1] It

[1] See D. Beryl Manischewitz, "Government Attitudes and the Marketing Image," in William D. Stevens, editor, *The Social Responsibilities of Marketing*, Chicago: American Marketing Association, 1961, pp. 41-52.

follows that social responsibility in competition is a goal the achievement of which is decided in large measure by marketing practitioners.

The task of the present chapter is to examine the nature of competition. This task is approached in three basic steps. First, what might be called the traditional view of competition is defined. And there is, unquestionably, a great deal of tradition associated with our perspective of competition. Second, the preconditions that give rise to particular types of competition are identified and discussed. These preconditions will include three "states of nature": (a) the scarcity state, (b) the mixed affluence state, and (c) the state of affluence. Finally, the dimensions of modern competition are identified. This latter section will center on four types of competition: (a) ecological competition, (b) the marketing mix, (c) vertical competition and (d) innovistic competition.

The traditional view of competition

One of the most difficult tasks we face today is to think objectively about issues that are fraught with tradition. Tradition has been defined as "an inherited pattern of thought or action,"[2] and if the "pattern of thought" goes unchallenged long enough, it may acquire the stature of a basic truth. And so it probably is with competition. The tradition of competition traces to the field of economics: It is the discipline of economics that has established the basic frame of reference for studying competition. Although there is by no means total agreement among economists about the basic concepts of competition, there are some features of their thinking that occur regularly enough to be thought of as mainstream thinking.[3] Competition in general is a contest between rivals for some valued article—money or real goods and services. In an economic context, the "rivals" are sellers, and the "valued article" is the patronage of some buyers. Competition is thus viewed as having three distinct components: (a) sellers, (b) buyers and (c) goods or services exchanged. For the economist, the strength, or vigor, of competition results from the interaction of the conditions confronting these three basic components. But we need to be more specific. Consider first the conditions of what has been called *classical competition.*

[2] See, for example, *Webster's Seventh New Collegiate Dictionary*, Springfield, Mass.: G. & C. Merriam Company, 1965.
[3] This lack of agreement is suggested in Dale L. Cramer and William L. Hueser, "Variations in the Definitions of Degrees of Competition," *The American Journal of Economics and Sociology*, July 1960, pp. 383-397. Cramer and Hueser identify pure competition, perfect competition, imperfect competition, workable competition, cutthroat competition, free competition, destructive competition, monopoly, aligopoly, duopoly, and many other "degrees" of competitive vigor. See also, Temporary National Economic Commission, Monograph 21, reprinted in *Managerial Economics*, edited by Joel Dean, Englewood Cliffs, N.J.: Prentice-Hall Inc., 1951. In this monograph, Professor Wilcox undertakes a similar listing of competitive concepts in use by economists.

Classical competition was a point of analytical departure—a state of affairs that was admittedly unreal, but nonetheless valuable because it bared the essential analytical elements of competition. Classical competition developed two basic models—*pure competition* and *pure monopoly.* These models were, respectively, the best and the worst. They were the conditions that produced the strongest and the least vigorous competition. Pure competition contemplated a state of affairs in which: (a) there was a very large number of sellers (each, therefore, having very little influence on the total market), (b) the goods or services purveyed by each seller was the same in every way as those sold by every other seller, and (c) each buyer was informed about the offers being made by all sellers and was perfectly mobile.[4] These conditions were thought of as an essentially unattainable goal, but conditions that could produce an efficient allocation of economic resources among alternative ends. Pure competition posited a condition in which no seller could charge a higher price for a similar amount of goods or services than any other. Pure competition assumed away the need to advertise—the presumed condition of perfect information effectively eliminated the need for mass, or even person-to-person, communications. As the nomenclature suggests, the purely competitive model was the best of all economic worlds. Note especially that the principal thrust of competition (the mechanism through which competition was exerted) had to be price.

The worst of all competitive worlds was embodied in the monopoly model. Pure monopoly featured one seller of a product or service for which there were no close substitutes. It is often implied in the monopoly model that the product or service is needed in a psychological sense—that is, it cannot be easily done without. This latter condition makes the position of the monopolist all the more ominous. For if there is but one seller, *and* there are no effective substitutes *and* the product or service is necessary, the seller enjoys a position that is conducive to gross exploitation of buyers. Pure monopoly is thus the antithesis of pure competition—it is a kind of summary of all things that should be avoided in planning an economic system. The monopolist could price at exorbitant levels; he could lower the quality of his product to the point of undependability; and he could do these things with assurance that his customers would not (could not) take their business elsewhere. It bears repeating that both pure competition and pure monopoly represent unreal, oversimplified, approximations of the real world. They are perhaps most useful as a pedagogical device—though they are often taken as inaccurate descriptions of a world about which their creators knew very little. But there is a second

---

[4] One factor that has restricted the value of the idea of competition is a failure to distinguish between competitive behavior and competitive (or market) structure. See this issue discussed in Paul J. McNulty, "Economic Theory and the Meaning of Competition," *The Quarterly Journal of Economics,* November 1968, pp. 639-656.

chapter, as it were, to the tradition of competition, and this second chapter is often identified by the phrase "neoclassical competition."

Neoclassical competition, in effect, recognizes the degrees of competition that exist between the "pure" ends of the classical scale.[5] That is, pure competition and pure monopoly are polar opposites, and there are intermediate positions that embody some good and some bad. The neoclassical concept of competition has also been called "imperfect competition" and "monopolistic competition." These terms both suggest that there is likely to be some "imperfect" or "monopolistic" element in the competitive behavior of a firm, and, indeed, both these terms tend to emphasize a lack of market purity. The truly significant difference between the classical and neoclassical view of competition lies in the nature of the products in which sellers deal. While the classical view assumed that demand was for homogeneous products, there is the suggestion in the neoclassical view that buyers seek differentiation in products—that demand is not for homogeneous product offerings, but for choice and selection. This demand for distinctive product offerings marks a significant change in the economists' concept of competition. For, while competition could only focus on price in the classical view, the neoclassical view permits competitive efforts to focus upon the product itself and upon its promotion. Figure 12.1 summarizes what we have said thus far.

Figure 12.1 Concepts of Competition

Pure Competition	Imperfect or monopolistic competition	Monopoly
Many sellers	Many to few sellers	One seller
Homogeneous products	Some product differences	No substitutes
Only price competition	Competition with price, product, promotion, and distribution	No price or product competition

We should emphasize several points about this traditional scale of competition; lay attitudes toward competition, as well as those of some legislators, are often identifiable in terms of this or a similar scale. We have observed that the science of economics formally recognizes the middle ground rather than the poles of this traditional scale as being a more accurate representation of the kind of competition that characterizes our business system. But, having thus recognized that fact, the discipline

[5] The definitive statement of neoclassical theory may be seen in either Joan Robinson's *The Economics of Imperfect Competition,* or in Edward Chamberlin's *The Theory of Monopolistic Competition.*

of economics often continues to focus inordinately on the extremities of the scale. Even more specifically, while the science of economics admits to the existence of nonprice competition, it continues to emphasize the price aspects of competition.

There are several possible reasons for this reluctance on the part of economists to deal more rigorously with the nonprice aspects of competition. First, the discipline of economics has what is fairly called a deep intellectual commitment to price competition. Virtually all the analytical concepts in the discipline of economics are price oriented. Value theory is, essentially, price theory. And to abandon the analytical focus on price competition altogether would effectively sterilize the field of microeconomics: to deemphasize price would seriously weaken the science. Moreover, economics was born a "dismal science"—a science dedicated to resolving the problem of scarcity and human deprivation. This heritage of scarcity and of excessive preoccupation with price competition is, to an extent, to be expected. Second, nonprice forms of competition are essentially qualitative phenomena. Nonprice forms of competition are not as easily and conveniently measured as price (what are the nonprice differences between a Cadillac and a Lincoln Continental?), and they are not, therefore, easily woven into the traditional fabric of economic theory.[6] Moreover, and this is a point that deserves special emphasis, nonprice competition may be viewed by economists as a second-best, cautious form of rivalry—one that is relatively ineffective.[7]

For whatever combination of reasons, the traditional view of competition dwells at inordinate length on price competition; the nonprice forms of competition are recognized, but very little else. One result is that the student of economics is often confused—unable to reconcile the real world and the competitive environment that he has studied. When time has erased the details of his exposure, the student tends to remember those aspects of the exposure that were introduced in the first instance as pedagogical simplifications—the "pure" models. He often tends to be strongly pro price competition and anti everything bearing the alleged imperfection of nonprice competition. The result, in turn, is often that the absence of evidence of strong price competition is taken as unassailable

---

[6] Typical coverage of competition under "imperfect" conditions may be seen in the recent book by Heinz Kohler, *Scarcity Challenged: An Introduction to Economics,* New York: Holt, Rinehart and Winston, Inc., 1968. This work devotes 36 pages to imperfect competition. Virtually all the discussion is given to pricing in imperfect competition and in total no more than three paragraphs is given to nonprice forms of competition. The book is about 625 pages in length.

[7] This argument is a trap. Some critics argue that nonprice competition is weak and ineffectual, while others argue that advertising (perhaps the most obvious form of nonprice competition) tends to produce an undesirable concentration of power and monopoly. These two views would seem to be mutually exclusive. The reader is directed to Jules Backman, *Advertising and Competition,* New York: New York University Press, 1967, p. 155.

evidence that no competition at all exists. To make the matter quite blunt, a study of competition in which there is virtually no meaningful consideration given to nonprice forms of rivalry is necessarily and substantially incomplete. An appreciation and understanding of modern competition must include both price and nonprice considerations.

The preconditions of competition

In a responsible system of business enterprise, the forms of commercial rivalry that evolve are determined in part by the socioeconomic needs and requirements of the economy. Competition thus both determines and is determined by prevailing socioeconomic conditions. Consider, for example, an economy in which the level, or standard, of living of the total population is distributed as depicted in Figure 12.2.[8]

Figure 12.2 The Scarcity State

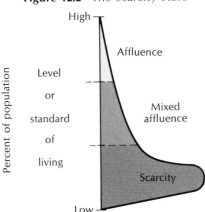

Note that the majority of the population is characterized by a level of living that is relatively low. The economic system depicted in Figure 12.2 is one dominated by scarcity—it is one in which the physical needs of food and shelter are most pressing. A responsible system of business enterprise should respond to this state of affairs in a way that reflects this condition of scarcity. More specifically, the variety of products offered would be limited; the emphasis of production would be upon commodities. Because the emphasis is upon commodities, competition tends to emphasize low price. The system of business enterprise would act irresponsibly if it did not concern itself primarily with the efficient production of commodities. A potato in every pot is, in effect, the charge given the business

[8] Although the "level of living" and the "standard of living" are not always treated as synonyms, we shall do so here. Some students of economics use the term "standard of living" to identify aspirations, and the term "level of living" to identify actual accomplishments.

system. Note carefully that the traditional economic view of competition (defined in the previous section) was born in an environment of scarcity.

Now consider the hypothetical economic system depicted in Figure 12.3. We have depicted in Figure 12.3 an economic system in which the level, or standard, of living is, on the average, very high.

Figure 12.3 The Affluent State

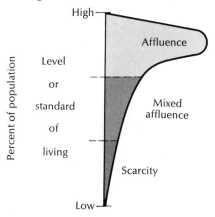

This condition of general affluence is one in which physical needs of the population are not at all pressing. Figure 12.3 depicts a condition in which the social-psychological needs are of greatest immediate concern. Nor should it be inferred that these social-psychological needs are any less deserving than were the physical needs of the economic system shot-through with scarcity. The responsive and responsible business enterprise system would, if confronted by this state of affluence, logically respond in a distinctive way. The role of price competition should be less dominant than in the scarcity state; the human desire for differentiation, for individual self-expression, should be answered. It would be as improper to fail to answer this demand as it would be to fail to answer the demands of the populace of the scarcity state for low-priced commodities. Note that it is not being suggested that exploitive pricing should be used by the business system; it is being suggested that, to the extent that differentiation and individual self-expression can be served only at higher costs (and prices), higher prices are required. In effect, the charge given the business system in the affluent state is to cater to individual self-expression at the optimum cost level. But the third case, the case of mixed affluence raises more difficult problems for the responsible business system.

Consider Figure 12.4. This condition of mixed affluence is one in which a relatively large proportion of the total population enjoys a comfortable level of living and a relatively large proportion of the total population is confronted by a low level of living. The cues to which the business enterprise system must respond are thus "mixed." The state of mixed affluence is complicated because there exist elements in the total population that do not have proper food and shelter and still other elements that are primarily concerned with what we have called social-psychological requirements. To put it another way, for every vocal expression that prices should be lower, there is another that believes that quality should be higher or that the need for individual expression is not adequately attended. The business system may logically react to either or both of these expressions—indeed, that is what the system should do. But we should take special note of one point: In either the state of affluence or the state of mixed affluence we can logically expect some businesses to endeavor to compete most aggressively with means other than price. There is no a priori reason to expect all competition to be price competition. Indeed, we shall see later that, to some consumers, price competition may have a curious negative effect. But with this brief note of introduction let us explore the dimensions of modern competition more completely.

Figure 12.4 The State of Mixed Affluence

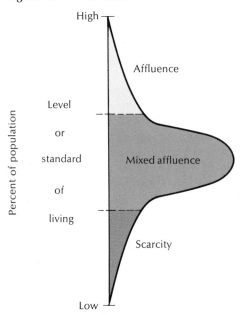

The dimensions of modern competition[9]

We have argued that the marketing system within a responsible business enterprise system should behave in a manner dictated in part by the

[9] An extremely good general statement of the character of modern competitive means is in Richard H. Holton, "The Role of Competition and Monopoly in Distribution: The Experience in the United States," in Lee E. Preston, editor, *Social Issues in Marketing,* Glenview, Ill.: Scott, Foresman and Company, 1968, pp. 137–167. The bibliography at the end of this article is excellent.

basic socioeconomic conditions that exist. We have argued that there is no form of competition that is necessarily best, except in the context of a specified socioeconomic environment. Thus, price competition is most desirable in a condition of scarcity, nonprice competition most desirable in a condition of abundance. But we need to refine this general proposition. In the discussion that follows, we will explore four basic concepts: (a) ecological competition, (b) competition with the marketing mix, (c) vertical competition and (d) innovistic competition.

ECOLOGICAL COMPETITION

The term "ecological competition" sounds much more elegant than it actually is. This term identifies competition in which the individual firm attempts to survive by making a continuous adjustment to its changing environment.[10] The idea is akin to the Darwinian proposition that the "fittest" survive by blending well into their environment. Thus, a business firm is roughly analogous to a moth, for example, which is able to survive and perpetuate the species because he can lose himself on the bark of a tree. The business firm adjusts to its environment by changing its manner of operation (including products, services, prices, promotion, location, and so on) as changes in the market dictate. Thus, ecological competition emphasizes a very important element of competition that was not explicitly identified in the earlier concepts of competition that we have considered. An ecological view of competition recognizes that markets are not static—that a firm must continually seek to redefine its niche. This is an important point, for many firms have been destroyed or irreparably weakened because they have failed to recognize the transient nature of most markets.[11]

Retailers have, on occasion, overcommitted themselves to one line of merchandise only to see it replaced by new product concepts. Many manufacturers have been surprised to see lines of products that once were "bread-and-butter" items decline to the point where they make only an insignificant contribution to company profits. This kind of shortsightedness has been called "marketing myopia," and there is evidence that many once important industries have seen their influence decline because they believed that their markets would remain essentially unchanged. As one writer puts it, "the history of every dead and dying "growth" industry shows a self-deceiving cycle of bountiful expansion and undetected

---

[10] The idea of ecological competition is an outgrowth of J. M. Clark's "economics of differential advantage." The integration of the concept into marketing literature has been effected primarily through the efforts of Wroe Alderson. Much of the ensuing discussion is adapted from Alderson's *Marketing Behavior and Executive Action: A Functionalist Approach to Marketing Theory*, Homewood, Ill.: Richard D. Irwin, Inc., 1957, particularly Chap. 4.

[11] See Theodore Levitt's widely reprinted article "Marketing Myopia," *Harvard Business Review*, July-August 1960, pp. 45–56. Levitt's basic theme is expanded in *Innovation in Marketing*, New York: McGraw-Hill Book Co., 1962.

decay."[12] It is probable that the railroads, the petroleum industry, the movie-making industry, and many others have suffered in varying degrees from this myopic affliction. As strange as it may sound, the forward-looking firms must engage in the *creative destruction* of their present product or service lines. They must, in a sense, destroy their own source of livelihood. They must, themselves, develop the kinds of products and services that will appeal to the markets of tomorrow. As Levitt argues the case, the petroleum companies:

. . . have no choice about working on an efficient long-lasting fuel (or some way of delivering present fuels without bothering the motorist). For their own good, the oil firms will have to destroy their own highly profitable assets. No amount of wishful thinking can save them from the necessity of engaging in this form of creative destruction.[13]

But an ecological concept of competition is distinctive in still other ways. Ecological competition is characterized by *segmentation* and by a *bilateral search* that culminates in a matching process. When we say that segmentation is a part of the ecological concept of competition, we mean that the firm normally defines its niche as something less than the total market. Thus, Volkswagen's market segment has been the economy, workmanship, subcompact, part of the total automobile market. Since we have introduced the concept of segmentation earlier, there is no need to expand the idea here. But the notion of a bilateral search procedure—a search procedure that culminates in a matching process—is an altogether new idea and deserves elaboration. The ecological concept of competition assumes that markets comprise heterogeneous want patterns. An extreme example would treat every human being as a distinctive, virtually unique demand pattern. Or, as the man responsible for the ecological concept of competition expresses it, "in the perfectly heterogeneous market, each small segment of demand can be satisfied by just one unique segment of supply."[14] But not only is demand assumed to be heterogeneous, supply is differentiated as well. A condition of both heterogeneous supply and heterogeneous demand involves a state of affairs in which a firm (supplier with a unique capacity to serve) and a buyer (consumer with a unique demand pattern) search in an endless process for the best match. This bilateral search procedure was not required in the classical concept of competition because, after all, both demand and supply were homogeneous—it was a matter of no concern to the buyer which particular seller

---

[12] Levitt, *op. cit.,* p. 48.

[13] Levitt, "Marketing Myopia"; reprinted in T. L. Berg and Abe Shuchman, *Product Strategy and Management,* New York: Holt, Rinehart and Winston, Inc., 1963, p. 21.

[14] Wroe Alderson, "Marketing Systems in the Ecological Framework," a paper delivered to the Marketing Theory Symposium University of Illinois, October 1963; reprinted in Harvey W. Huegy, editor, *The Conceptual Framework for a Science of Marketing,* University of Illinois Bulletin, October 1963, pp. 29–43. (The quotation is on p. 36.)

he bought from. This search procedure is bilateral—rather than unilateral—because both the buyer and the seller, in effect, seek each other. It is not a one-way chase in which the buyer or prospect is the pursued and the seller the pursuer.

Because ecological competition is characterized by bilateral search, communications plays an extremely important role. That is, the very fact that the buyer is seeking "his" seller and the seller "his" buyer, implies communications. For it is in the process of communicating his individuality and his particular skills in serving that the seller is most likely to "find" his market segment. Moreover, and this is an important point, we can fully expect such communications as will flow from prospective seller to prospective buyer to involve any conceivable item of information—including information on price, physical characteristics of the product or service, sociopsychological dimensions of the product or service, or any other item of information that may more precisely identify the nature of the offering. This idea of bilateral search may be better visualized with the aid of a schematic arrangement. To this end, assume that each of the triangles in Figure 12.5 represents a seller of a distinctive product or service. The distinction of the product or service may be physical or sociopsychological. Assume further that each circle in Figure 12.5 represents a buyer who has a differentiated demand pattern; that is, each buyer would find his satisfactions maximized where the product or service he bought was tailored to his particular needs, whether those needs were sociopsychological or physical. We might now depict the ecological concept of a market as follows:

Figure 12.5 Bilateral Search Procedure

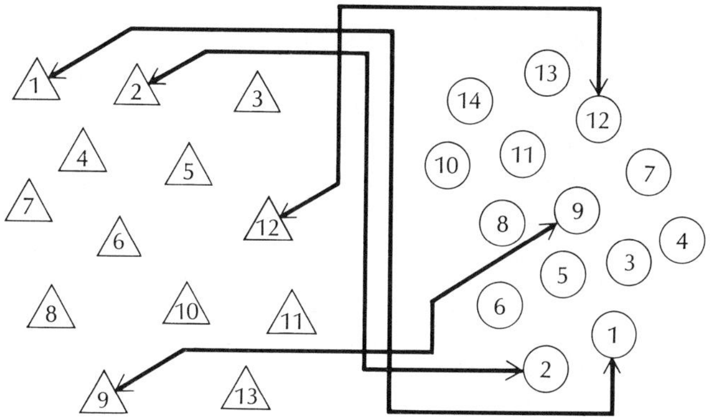

Figure 12.5 directs our attention to the necessity to communicate and to inform in order to locate the buyer whose particular preferences best fit the particular offering of each seller. It makes little difference whether we now visualize each symbol in this "market" as being a single household and a single seller or make each buyer symbol the equivalent of, say,

10,000 buyers and each seller symbol equal to, say, 100 sellers. In any event, the necessity for search and communications is evident, and, as we shall see, this communications process is an extremely important part of modern competition. How would you interpret the fact that there is no matching number 14 on the seller side in Figure 12.5?

There is one other trait of ecological competition that we should note. In the traditional view of competition, it was apparent that when a new firm appeared it preempted the market it served from other sellers. There was, in the classical view of competition, room for some given number of sellers, and that was that. When too few sellers existed, "excess" profits would attract new firms and such excess profits would be eliminated. Similarly, if too many firms existed, losses would drive some operators to other pursuits, and balance, or equilibrium, would be achieved through a resulting decrease in the number of sellers. But an ecological concept of competition suggests a quite different perspective regarding competitive opportunity. The ecological concept of competition suggests that opportunity "proliferates," or, as the notion was originally expressed:

> . . . to say that opportunity proliferates is to say that there is opportunity for the entry and survival of new firms precisely because of the success of existing firms. The firms already in the field help to determine the character of opportunity for the newcomer as well as make opportunity available.[15]

Market opportunity may arise: (a) when the pioneering firm encourages emulation through abuse of having been the first in the field, or (b) when the pioneering firm, by virtue of having declared itself to a particular market segment, must leave some other segments essentially unserved or served with a compromise product that does not reflect the precise preferences of such segments.

Before we continue our consideration of modern competition, let us briefly recapitulate what we have said about the ecological concept of competition. The character of ecological competition is effectively identified by four ideas. Ecological competition presumes a *transient market condition*—it is this changing nature of markets that necessitates a continual redefinition of the firm's basic market objectives. Ecological competition is characterized by *segmentation*—by the definition of specific market subgroups rather than general markets. Further, the ecological concept of competition acknowledges a heavy dependence upon communications—communications that result in a *matching* of heterogeneous components of demand with heterogeneous elements of supply. Finally, this ecological view of competition integrates the important notion of *opportunity proliferation*. With these basic ideas now identified, we are in a position to identify the combinations of competitive efforts developed by firms operating in an ecological system of competition.

---

[15] Alderson, *Marketing Behavior and Executive Action*, pp. 115–116.

THE MARKETING MIX

An extremely important element in developing a full understanding of modern competition is suggested by the term "marketing mix."[16] In general terms, the marketing mix is *the combination of competitive efforts exerted by a firm to accomplish some sales or profit goal.* The word "combination" is important in this definition. The firm normally has at its disposal several competitive elements that it can manipulate or control. Thus, for example, a particular firm may charge a very low price and not advertise at all; and that combination of efforts represents a very simple type of marketing mix. Another firm may advertise aggressively and charge a relatively high price; that combination of efforts is another simple type of marketing mix. Or, the marketing mix may involve a more elaborate combination of efforts. A cigarette company may elect to: (a) emphasize television and radio advertising, (b) distribute through high quality tobacco shops, (c) charge a premium price, (d) sell in 60 millimeter lengths, and (e) feature an air-tight plastic package. This "mix" is more realistic in the sense that most firms confront a relatively large number of controllable competitive variables. Indeed, the precise number of controllable variables thought to make up the elements of the marketing mix varies widely. Some writers suggest as few as four, others suggest much more extensive lists.

One of the first people to articulate the idea of the marketing mix, Professor Neil H. Borden, identifies 12 more or less basic elements in the marketing mix. These elements are the product, price, brand, channels of distribution, personal selling efforts, advertising, special promotions, packaging, display, servicing, physical handling, and fact finding and analysis. It should be apparent that one could well subdivide many of these elements into other essentially independent elements. One might also augment the Borden list with elements that are omitted—company organization, for example. But our concern here is not to list in a definitive way the possible components of the marketing mix. For our purposes, we will think of five basic elements as representing the backbone of the marketing mix, and we will recognize that any of these five basic elements might reasonably be viewed as several subordinate but independent elements. We will define the marketing mix more specifically as the combination of competitive efforts exerted by a firm to accomplish some sales or profit goal—those competitive efforts including: (a) variations in the products or services being offered, (b) variations in the price of the products or services being offered, (c) variations in the system(s) of distribution utilized, (d) variations in the type of promotional blends utilized and (e) variations in the marketing organization that the firm uses.

[16] The origin of the term "marketing mix" is described in Neil H. Borden, "The Concept of the Marketing Mix." This article, originally published in the *Journal of Advertising Research,* has recently been reprinted in Ben M. Enis and Keith K. Cox, editors, *Marketing Classics: A Selection of Influential Articles,* Boston: Allyn and Bacon, Inc., 1969, pp. 365-376.

In order to sharpen this concept of the marketing mix, consider the following hypothetical summary of competitive efforts exerted by three soap manufacturers.

Firm	Product	Price	Distribution	Promotion	Organization
A	Mild detergent action	Above competition	Through drug and department stores	Magazine advertising, little personal selling done	Geographical limits on responsibility
B	Average detergent action	Same as majority of competitors	Through supermarkets and drug stores	All media, saturation campaigns, some display work with dealers	Total brand man responsibility
C	Harsh detergent action	Below competition	Through industrial supply outlets	Direct mail and selected business periodicals	Responsibility vested in product committee

Note that these three soap manufacturers place varying emphasis on each of the five basic elements of the competitive mix. The marketing mix is, in one important respect, a kind of competitive fingerprint—it would be rare to find any two mixes that are exactly the same. Indeed, when all the controllable elements actually confronting the marketing management of a firm are considered, it would be virtually impossible to find any two firms with exactly the same competitive mix. But there are some marketing mixes that occur often enough and in a form similar enough to represent prototype mixes. That is, in spite of the fact that marketing mixes of close competitors are rarely exactly alike, there are some basic patterns into which marketing mixes tend to fall. These prototype mixes are identified in a subsequent chapter. For now we need to consider several other aspects of the marketing mix concept.

To this point in our discussion we have described some of the types of variation that one may encounter in marketing mixes. It remains for us to examine the much more important questions of: (a) how particular marketing mixes evolve and (b) why particular types of marketing mixes are preferable to others.

To answer the first of these questions, it will be useful to view each of the five basic elements of the marketing mix as *subjective reaction ratios*. What, then, is a subjective reaction ratio? We can perhaps best identify this idea by first observing that the best possible marketing mix would be one to which buyer prospects were most responsive—positively responsive rather than negatively responsive. The notion that there are combinations of competitive efforts to which prospects are unresponsive (or negatively responsive) and combinations of competitive efforts to which they are positively responsive is fundamental to the concept of a reaction ratio.

Each of the five major elements in the marketing mix has some cost or expense associated with its manipulation. That is, the decision to change price costs something—the cost of re-marking for retailers or the cost of changing inventory records or whatever. Similarly, the decision to promote more aggressively has some identifiable cost associated with it. The cost of implementing new distributors or dealers is likewise associated with changes in channels of distribution. And so it is with all major competitive efforts. But each such manipulation of a basic competitive element is also capable, as we have seen, of effecting a response from the market to which it is directed. Thus, there is both a *cost* and a *response* associated with each major element in the marketing mix. We may represent this cost/response relationship as follows: [17]

$$\frac{\Delta R_a}{\Delta C_a} = \text{the reaction ratio for competitive element } a$$

The numerator in this ratio is the change in revenue attributable to a purposeful change in competitive element a—let us assume that a is a change in product quality. The denominator is the change in cost attributable to the same purposeful change in competitive element a—namely the change in product quality. Note that it is the cost of *implementing* the change that we are concerned with here, not the cost of the product after the change in quality has been made. This ratio might assume virtually any value, either negative or positive. If the value of the reaction ratio were very large and positive, it would indicate a high level of responsiveness on the part of the market to such a change. If the value of the ratio were very low or negative, it would indicate either an indifference to the change or, worse, a kind of repugnance to the change.

The plot, however, is thickened by two further matters. First, there is a reaction ratio for each of the major elements in the mix; and second, these ratios are judgmental in nature. We need to examine each of these points in order. Consider, now, the set of reaction ratios below:

1. $\dfrac{\Delta R_a}{\Delta C_a}$ = Reaction ratio for a change in product

2. $\dfrac{\Delta R_b}{\Delta C_b}$ = Reaction ratio for a change in price

[17] This ratio may be thought of as *net* revenues over *total* cost.

3. $\dfrac{\Delta R_c}{\Delta C_c}$ = Reaction ratio for a change in distribution

4. $\dfrac{\Delta R_d}{\Delta C_d}$ = Reaction ratio for a change in promotion

5. $\dfrac{\Delta R_e}{\Delta C_e}$ = Reaction ratio for a change in organization

The process through which the best marketing mix is developed involves a judgmental evaluation of the probable value of each of these five basic reaction ratios. The evaluation is largely judgmental because there is no effective way to measure the exact market response that each competitive change will produce. It is, in other words, the numerator in each of these ratios that must be subjectively estimated. The denominator is more easily, though not necessarily precisely, measured. But we can introduce some numbers into the summary of these reaction ratios, and in so doing illustrate its nature even more clearly.

Estimated Reaction Ratio—Product Change:	1.6
Estimated Reaction Ratio—Price Change:	1.2
Estimated Reaction Ratio—Distribution Change:	.7
Estimated Reaction Ratio—Promotion Change:	1.3
Estimated Reaction Ratio—Organization Change:	1.6

Suppose that a particular marketing executive has a budget of $100,000 to spend. In what way would he allocate his budget among the five competitive elements constituting the marketing mix? Observe the ratio values for each of the five mix ingredients in the data above. Two mix elements are perceived as incapable of returning revenues above costs of implementation. Indeed, a change in distribution is not viewed as capable of breaking even. Note that product change, price change and promotion change are all subjectively viewed as actions capable of producing revenues in excess of costs of implementation. The marketing mix actually developed will tend to depend upon the cost of implementing each competitive change. That is, the budget would be spent first on the action thought capable of producing the largest response, then to the next most effective action, and so forth until the budget was exhausted.

We might think of these reaction ratios as a kind of subjective "payoff." And in general, this subjective payoff would be thought largest for innovative changes in the product, distribution, promotion and so forth. Innovative changes would involve a substantially different level of product performance, a new distribution mode, a radically different price or method of pricing (such as leasing, for example), and so on for each of the basic competitive elements. An important part of competition with the marketing mix is this quest for high payoff competitive actions. Note that this form of competition uses the market as a true sounding board—a lack of market response identifies the unwanted change; a good market response identifies the change desired by the market. But we have not yet fully explored the second basic question about the marketing mix. Why are some types of marketing mixes preferred to others? That is, why is the reaction ratio, or payoff, often thought better for some competitive actions than for others?

In addition to the cost and revenue characteristics of each element in the marketing mix, each element embodies several other dimensions that can influence its relative attractiveness in use. These additional dimensions include: (a) the temporal, or longevity, dimension, (b) the creative-distinctiveness dimension and (c) the likelihood-of-reprisal dimension.

Any competitive action either may be of lasting benefit or may yield its benefits only over a very short span of time. That is, a payoff is not just an instantaneous event—it is an expected payoff *over a period of time*. And the length of time during which a particular payoff ratio is expected to prevail is often an important part of the strategy of developing a mix. In general, a ratio that is expected to prevail over a relatively long period is to be preferred to one that could change on very short notice.

But competitive actions vary, as well, in terms of their creative distinctiveness. In general, the less the creative element is present in a particular competitive action, the easier it is for competitors to neutralize such an act through emulation. In addition, competitive actions vary in terms of the likelihood that they will induce neutralizing retaliatory actions. Some competitive actions almost beg for retaliation from competitors; others do not.[18] Each of these three factors plays a role in the development of a marketing mix.

Mix element	Temporal dimension	Creative distinctiveness	Liklihood of reprisal
Price	may be instantly neutralized	virtually none	very high
Promotion	can enjoy long payoff	yes, can be unique	high
Distribution	can enjoy long payoff	yes	low
Product	can enjoy long payoff	can be unique	relatively high
Organization	can enjoy long payoff	yes	low

[18] An interesting description of retaliatory type of competitive action is in Ralph Cassidy, Jr., "The New York Department Store Price War 1951: A Microeconomic Analysis," *Journal of Marketing*, July 1957, pp. 3–11.

The most desirable marketing mix would be one that was not easily neutralized through emulation—and this requirement argues for a mix that emphasizes some competitive elements and deemphasizes others. Consider the summary matrix on page 301.

This summary matrix suggests generally that nonprice forms of competition hold the promise of longer payoffs, embody the greatest opportunity for creative distinction and are probably somewhat less likely to precipitate reprisal. Note that all the nonprice forms of competition can enjoy a long payoff and that an aggressive use of price can be instantly neutralized. While it is very difficult to use price in a creative or distinctive way, promotion, distribution, product and organization all hold the potential of distinctiveness.

Consider the Benson & Hedges 100mm campaign of several years ago. As an example of a creative and distinctive use of distribution, consider the dealership network of General Motors or of Volkswagen of America. There are few that would argue that the distribution teams assembled by those two firms are not an extremely valuable element in the marketing programs of the two companies. There are other automobile manufacturers that would pay dearly for similar distribution systems. Consider the distinctiveness of the Polaroid-Land camera. Indeed, our patent laws favor the use of the product as an important element of distinction in the marketing mix.

An effective internal organization likewise holds the potential of distinctiveness. In the field of retailing, Sears-Roebuck has in the past had no peer in terms of its ability to develop good middle and upper-level management. Price competition, in part because it is so easily neutralized, seems to invite retaliatory efforts by competitors.[19] In contrast, the nonprice elements seem less of an open invitation to reprisal.

In a recent study of the marketing mixes used for 485 "successful" products, nonprice elements of competition were viewed as clearly superior to price. In this particular study, sales effort, including sales management, personal selling, advertising and "other promotional programs" were ranked most important. Competitive efforts that centered on changes in the product ranked next. Pricing ranked third, and distribution was, relatively speaking, the least important element. It is interesting to note that the major executives associated with these successful products felt that nonprice strategy was most important because of the need to communicate complexities in products and because "consumers in the wealthier nations of the world are not primarily concerned about price."[20]

---

[19] See John S. McGee, "Predatory Price Cutting," in Donald S. Watson, *Price Theory in Action,* Boston: Houghton Mifflin Company, 1965, pp. 196–202.
[20] See Jon G. Udell, "The Perceived Importance of the Elements of Strategy," *Journal of Marketing,* January 1968, pp. 34–40.

Vertical competition

The kinds of competition we have emphasized thus far have been essentially horizontal—that is, they have contemplated a kind of rivalry between firms at the same level of distribution. But modern competition also embodies some distinctly vertical aspects. Vertical competition may be defined as rivalry or conflicts between manufacturer and wholesaler, wholesaler and retailer, or manufacturer and retailer.[21] It is a curious omission that the traditional view of competition did not give explicit recognition to these vertical forms of competition, for they are often an extremely effective dimension of competition.

There are firms that have retailing as their primary activity but which perform some manufacturing activities as well. Conversely, there are firms that are primarily manufacturing enterprises that perform some retailing activities. Many petroleum companies find themselves not only in the manufacturing or refining business but in the service station business as well. Large retail firms, such as Sears-Roebuck, Montgomery Ward and A&P, find themselves manufacturing some items of merchandise to be distributed through their stores. This phenomenon suggests that the performance of particular economic activities is not irretrievably the property of any special type of economic enterprise. When economic activities are performed inefficiently, or at best in a lackluster way, such activities may be forfeited on a competitive basis to institutions operating principally at some other level of distribution that can perform them with greater enthusiasm. Thus, a large retail organization may tacitly or overtly threaten a marginally efficient supplier to shape up or expect new competition.

This basic notion—that competition may exert its influence vertically in the performance of dissimilar distributive functions—has been widely popularized in the phrase "countervailing power."[22] The role of the Great Atlantic and Pacific Tea Company (A&P) as a countervailing power illustrates the concept. The following quotation is taken from a report of the Justice Department:

Occasionally, A&P used the tactic of suggesting to suppliers of manufactured goods that it would manufacture these products itself, if price reductions were not forthcoming. Thus, in 1939, when negotiating a contract with the Ralston-Purina Company on flake cereals, A&P received an additional price preference of 10¢ per case and agreed not to enter the flake cereal business for five years.

[21] See Joseph C. Palamountain, Jr., "Distribution: Its Economic Conflicts," in Bruce E. Mallen, editor, *The Marketing Channel: A Conceptual Viewpoint,* New York: John Wiley & Sons, Inc., 1967, p. 116. See also, Bruce Mallen, "Conflict and Cooperation in Marketing Channels," in L. George Smith, editor, *Reflections on Progress in Marketing,* Chicago: American Marketing Association, 1965, pp. 68-71.

[22] The idea of "countervailing power" as introduced in John K. Galbraith's *American Capitalism: The Concept of Countervailing Power,* Boston: Houghton Mifflin Company, 1952.

At the time, A&P felt that the three available suppliers of flake cereals were realizing unwarranted profits.[23]

The notion of countervailing power has been offered as the partial salvation of American capitalism. It has been offered as *the* answer to the Marxist argument that capitalism, containing as it did, the seed of its own demise, would ultimately flounder in revolutionary turmoil. With what is perhaps excessive brevity, the notion of countervailing power asserts that large sellers—the villain of the Marxist argument—are held effectively in check by large buyers. Thus, the large buying enterprise (wholesalers and retailers) intervene, in a sense, to protect the final consumer from the exploitive proclivities of the large manufacturing firm.[24]

Innovistic competition

Thus far we have considered ecological competition, competition with the marketing mix, and we have briefly identified a kind of competition that is vertical in the sense that the combatants occupy different stages, or levels, of distribution. There is one further important dimension of competition, and it is identified by the term *innovistic competition*. The distinctive characteristic of innovistic competition is that it begins with a change in technology—it often has its origin in "new ways of organizing things, new sales-cost relationships, new methods of selling."[25] Sometimes the origin of an innovistic wave of competition is in technical fields that are seemingly far removed from an application in the field of business. Regardless of the precise nature of the technical advance that precipitates a wave of innovative competition, the advance produces two important effects. First, a recombination of productive factors results; and second, a new economic institution develops. It is significant that the new institution normally incorporates sufficiently compelling features to serve as a real threat to the continued existence of forerunner institutions. But this whole process sounds a bit obscure when described in general terms. What does this all mean in more concrete terms?

Consider for a moment the field of retailing. There was a time when the American retailing system was highly centralized. That is, virtually all retailing was done from central or downtown locations; little or no retail volume was done in outlying or peripheral areas. We have seen, in the

[23] Kenneth R. Davis, *Marketing Management,* New York: The Ronald Press Company, 1961, p. 734.
[24] The veracity of Galbraith's thesis of countervailing power is tried in *American Economic Review,* Papers and Proceedings of the Sixty-Sixth Annual Meeting of the American Economic Association, James W. Bell and Gertrude Trait, editors, American Economic Association, Washington, D. C., 1953.
[25] Perry Bliss, "Schumpeter, the Big Disturbance and Retailing," *Social Forces,* October 1960, p. 72.

last 30 years, a decline in the importance of the central business district—including the demise of many retail operations. Indeed the competitive pressures on downtown retailers have been unprecedented. What forces have produced this need for the utilization of survival tactics? Are these powerful competitive forces the "mix" kind of competition we have described earlier? Are these forces the "vertical" kind of competition we have just identified?

An answer is that the forces that have so crimped the style of the downtown area as a retailing institution are largely of an innovistic character. There are two basic factors that have permitted a successful decentralization of the downtown business district. These factors are: (a) customer mobility and (b) customer willingness to accept self-service forms of retailing. And both these factors are, in turn, initially enabled and later assisted by technical advancement. Economically feasible means of personal transportation, for example, is a prerequisite of customer mobility. And the private automobile freed Americans from a reliance upon public transportation facilities that tended to focus on the downtown area. Thus, the mass produced auto represents, in a circuitous but nonetheless logical way, a technical element that has resulted in more vigorous retail competition. Similarly, self-service forms of retailing owe their success, at least in part, to the existence of mass communications media—for it is necessary to presell customers outside the store if there is relatively little or no in-store sales effort. It has been the resulting low-margin, outlying retailing institution that has given the more traditional forms of retailing their most anxious moments. It is, in other words, the K-Marts, the Target Stores, in short, the low-margin, high-stock-turnover stores that represent the competition that counts today. It is the embodiment of new technology in economic institutions such as retailing that can completely rearrange the competitive environment.

An example from another area will sharpen this notion of innovistic competition. We recognize the mix type of competition when we say that General Motors competes with Chrysler, Ford and American Motors. We recognize the vertical aspects of competition when Sears shows more than a casual interest in developing an "urban" car. We recognize the innovistic character of competition when Bill Lear, or someone like him, sets out to develop an external combustion (steam) engine for personal automotive applications. Consider for a moment the competitive impact of a successful steam engine for use in private forms of transportation. "Successful" would mean, in this instance: (a) economical, (b) smogless, (c) desirable performance characteristics and (d) available. Depending, of course, upon how quickly other automotive producers could get into the steamer business, such a development could most certainly represent a jugular vein type of competition. Indeed the *threat* of such a development might reasonably have a substantive effect upon the vigor of competition.

SUMMARY

The purpose of Chapter 12 has been to examine the nature of competition. For purposes of exposition, we developed our discussion around three basic points. First, we considered competition from a traditional point of view. This traditional perspective led us to a discussion of the classical definition of competition, the neoclassical view of competition, and gave us some insights into why the discipline of economics emphasizes some aspects of competition and deemphasizes some others. It was argued that the exact nature of competition is logically different depending upon the socioeconomic preconditions that exist. That is, the scarcity state will logically produce one kind of competitive emphasis; the affluence state will logically produce some other kind of competition. A central part of our argument was that the state that we called mixed affluence is one in which the business system will reasonably react with many different kinds of competition. In some instances price will play an important role in competitive actions; in some instances price will be subordinated to nonprice forms of competition.

We explored four particular types, or concepts, of competition that represent the salient dimensions of modern competition. More specifically, we identified an ecological dimension of competition, competition with something called the marketing mix, vertical competition, and innovistic competition. Ecological competition is characterized by: (a) transient markets, (b) segmentation, (c) a bilateral search procedure and (d) a proliferation of opportunity. Thus the ecological view of competition provides an obvious reason for the tendency of many firms today to place great importance upon promotion as a competitive action.

Competition with the marketing mix was characterized as a search for the most effective combination of competitive actions. This mix was defined as involving product development, price changes, distribution, promotion and marketing organization. Vertical competition was defined as competition between firms occupying different stages of distribution. "Countervailing power" is a phrase that has been used to identify this vertical type of competition.

Finally, competition of an innovistic type was discussed. This innovistic dimension of competition was defined as beginning with a change in technology. Innovistic competition involves a recombination of productive factors and the development of new and more efficient forms of economic institutions. Innovistic competition is competition that is capable of effecting complete change in the nature of our economic institutions.

REVIEW QUESTIONS

1 Carefully define and indicate the relevance of each of the following concepts to the study of marketing:
   a. Classical competition
   b. Neoclassical competition

c. Mixed affluence
d. Marketing myopia
e. The bilateral search procedure of ecological competition
f. Subjective reaction ratios
g. Vertical competition
h. Countervailing power
2 Distinguish carefully between each element in the following pairs of terms:
a. Pure competition *and* pure monopoly
b. The nature of competition in general conditions of scarcity *and* the nature of competition in general conditions of affluence
c. Innovistic competition *and* vertical competition
3 What possible reasons underlie the preoccupation of economists with price competition? Why is it logical that economists would show less interest in nonprice forms of competition?
4 What is meant by the notion that a forward-looking firm must engage in the creative destruction of its present product or service line?
5 How does the assumption that both supply and demand are homogeneous rather than heterogeneous influence the nature of the competition that would result?
6 Discuss the role of the temporal dimension, creative distinctiveness, and the likelihood of retaliation as factors in developing the marketing mix.

DISCUSSION QUESTIONS
7 Suppose that you are given the task of measuring the strength, or vigor, of competition in the United States today. What methods would you employ to develop such measures?
8 In what lines of business (industries, if you prefer) is competition apparently most vigorous? In what industries is competition apparently least vigorous?
9 In what specific ways are the benefits of nonprice competition felt? Do these benefits seem less important or more important than the benefits that are felt from price forms of competition? Why?

Chapter 13

THE GENERAL STRATEGY OF MARKETING

We have seen that both nonprice and price forms of competition are entirely natural. We have noted that in a circumstance of mixed affluence competition may logically and properly feature nonprice elements. We have likewise noted that competition between similar firms with the marketing mix components is not the only, or necessarily the most influential, kind of competition. We have observed that vertical competition and innovistic competition play a most important role in modern commercial rivalry. In the present chapter, we turn our attention to a more careful scrutiny of the nonprice aspects of the marketing mix. More specifically, our concern here is with a more careful definition of the relationships that exist between: (a) the product or service, (b) the distribution network and (c) the promotional plan. This relationship is an important one—for there is a logic, a rationale, a kind of *general* marketing strategy, that relates these three elements of the marketing mix. And a failure to recognize the logic of this relationship can result in very costly economic waste.

The product

Every product or service may be viewed as both a problem in distribution and a problem in promotion. That is, for every kind of product or service there is some most logical plan of distribution and some most logical plan of promotion. In a sense then, given a particular product or service the challenge of marketing is often to identify the most logical plans of distribution and promotion.[1] Each alternative plan of distribution and each

[1] This statement should not be taken to imply that the job of marketing begins after the product is a completed concept. That is not true at all—marketing should and does have a significant role in product development. See, for example, S. C. Johnson and Conrad Jones, "How to Organize for New Products," in T. L. Berg and Abe Shuchman, New York: Holt, Rinehart and Winston, Inc., 1963, pp. 357-374.

alternative plan of promotion involves some cost of implementation. And insofar as illogical plans of distribution or promotion are utilized, economic waste results. Few would think it proper, for example, to see pianos distributed through shops as numerous as supermarkets. Few would think it correct to see candy bars sold by technically oriented sales engineers well versed in the nutritional sciences. A socially responsible marketing system is both aware of and dedicated to the fulfillment of this obligation to achieve distribution and promotion at the lowest cost consistent with market preferences.

The product or service is, then, a signal for a particular kind of marketing mix. And in order that we can develop an understandable statement of the relationship between the product or service and the proper plans of distribution and promotion, it behooves us to consider more carefully: (a) what products really are and (b) what basic classes of products we recognize.

There are essentially three views of what products are: (a) the physical concept, (b) the embodiment-of-satisfactions concept, and (c) the vector-amoeba concept. The physical concept of a product is perhaps the most obvious way to view the product—it is perhaps also the least insightful perspective. The physical concept of a product defines the product as a measurable set of specifications—specifications that include nuts, bolts, dimensions and definable aesthetic properties. To some, this is the practical view of a product, it does not recognize any of the intangibles that may be thought of as a part of the product. In a sense, the physical concept of the product is a thing devoid of any emotional entanglements—it tends to view all products of the same genre as adequate substitutes. This physical view of the product is likely to treat the package as though it is not a part of the product.

A systematic contrast to this physical concept is represented by the "embodiment-of-satisfactions" concept of the product. This perspective focuses on what the product can do rather than what it is in a physical sense. And what the product can do includes: (a) its functional performance, (b) its social performance and (c) its psychological performance.

The functional performance of a product relates to the adequacy of its utilitarian properties—in the case of an automobile, does it start easily? does it accelerate properly? is it comfortable? is it serviceable? and so forth. Thus, the embodiment-of-satisfactions concept defines the product in terms of something akin to the tasks that it will accomplish. Note carefully that these tasks often include both social and psychological performance. This view of the product admits to some intangibles—indeed, it often holds that intangibles are a significant part of the product. If the physical concept of the product was essentially free of emotional dimensions, the embodiment-of-satisfactions concept pulls these dimensions forcibly front and center. But what is meant by social and psychological performance?

Social performance includes acceptance—acceptance by the right people. And if this sounds like snobbery, it probably is. But snobbery is not the exclusive domain of the wealthy and the near-wealthy. Far from it. A product may have snob value (acceptance) in one group and not in another. Indeed the consumer type who refuses steadfastly to believe that there are differences between brands—the person who buys the lowest price habitually—often unwittingly succumbs to a special kind of snobbery. In effect, he says "in my group, we don't believe in snob value"—and his philosophy thus acquires snob value. A particular brand may be acceptable if it does not apparently concern itself with acceptability.

Psychological performance relates to the *self* as we have developed that idea earlier, and to such affective matters as self-enhancement, pride of ownership, and similar phenomena. Two cautions relate to the idea that products perform in a social and in a psychological dimension. First, there are some types of products for which performance other than in a functional sense is not especially meaningful. Food staples, potatoes, lettuce, and some hardware items such as nails, rivets, and similar products have little or no psychological or social performance dimensions. The types of products that are likely to embody functional, social and psychological dimensions are, typically, conspicious to a degree. They are often seen, and they are indeed sometimes *displayed*. The second caution about the idea of social and psychological performance relates to the separability of these two ideas. These dimensions of product performance are not easily separated—indeed they are discussed here as separate classes largely for reasons of expositional convenience.

A third concept of the product is suggested by the term vector-amoeba. Consider Figure 13.1. This vector-amoeba concept of a product defines the product in terms of "a range of values on each of several dimensions."[2] Note that the axes in Figure 13.1 are labeled "sudsiness" and "harshness," and the range of each runs from 0 to 10 on a graduated scale. It is possible to define products in terms of their specific position within the quadrant formed by the X and Y axes. Thus, for example, the amoeba-like area labeled A might embody the characteristics of a highly detergent, foaming cleaner suitable for, say, industrial rug cleaning. The amoeba-like area designated D might suggest a foaming product with more lubricating properties than cleaning properties—say, a shaving lather. The area labeled B might delineate the limits, or boundaries, of acceptability in terms of sudsiness or harshness for general purpose household cleaners. In a similar way, the area labeled C might identify the normal boundaries for industrial all-purpose cleaners. Although we have developed our example here in terms of detergents/cleaners, the notion that products may be defined

[2] See Leon E. Richardz, *A Game Theoretic Formulation of Vertical Market Structures*, Working Paper No. 45. Berkeley: Institute of Business and Economic Research, University of California, October 1968, p. 6.

by ranges of values is by no means limited to this context. Indeed, there is no reason to limit our interest to just two variables—we might, in other words, define the product in terms of three or more dimensions. Our reason for not doing so here is only that the artwork is substantially more complex.

Figure 13.1   Vector Amoeba

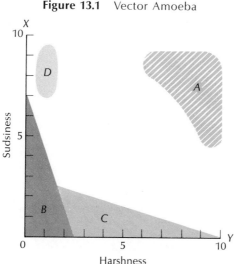

THE BASIC PRODUCT TYPES

The most meaningful classification of products begins with a consideration of buyer behavior. That is, if we wish to develop a taxonomy of product types that we can later relate to particular distribution and promotional plans, it is reasonable that buyer behavior should influence that taxonomy. The *best* plans of distribution and of promotion should, by definition, accommodate buyer preferences. Because buyer behavior plays such a central role, we will begin our discussion of product classes by introducing an analytical device called a "shopping matrix."[3] Consider Figure 13.2.

This shopping matrix summarizes two aspects of consumer or buyer behavior: it reflects both the number of different brands considered prior to a purchase and the number of stores visited prior to a purchase. This device permits us to identify a wide range of buyer actions, and to relate those actions to particular types of products. Indeed, we shall see in a moment that we can define products by the types of shopping patterns that they normally produce. But before we do that, let us make sure that we understand how one of these shopping matrices is interpreted. Figure 13.3 summarizes the shopping patterns for ten different purchases of each

[3] This very insightful concept is described in William P. Dommermuth, "The Shopping Matrix and Marketing Strategy," *Journal of Marketing Research,* May 1965, pp. 128–132.

of three different products by an entirely hypothetical buyer. Note, first, the pattern of buyer behavior suggested by the X's. Each X denotes a purchase pattern. There were, for example three purchases made of this product in which five brands were considered and in which only one store was visited. The most curious aspect of the pattern of X's is that the buyer apparently does not explore the offerings of other stores and that there is little evidence that he is strongly committed to any one brand. Notice that this particular matrix does not tell what brand was actually purchased—it only reveals the number of different brands considered.[4]

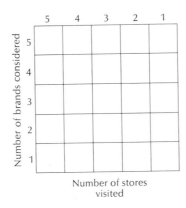

Figure 13.2   The Shopping Matrix

Consider now the pattern of Y's. Note that they are concentrated in the northwest corner of the matrix. This product, whatever it is, clearly elicits a different type of shopping behavior. Note, in this latter connection, that on four occasions, five different stores were shopped and five different brands were considered. On four other occasions, our Y buyer explored the offerings of five different stores and examined four different brands. Finally, note the pattern of buyer behavior suggested by the Z's. Observe that whatever this latter product is, *no* brand shopping is done, although a relatively large number of stores are consulted. Obviously, many other purchase patterns are possible. But these will serve for the moment to illustrate the nature of the shopping matrix.

The foregoing illustrative discussion of the shopping matrix patterns for different types of products suggests a fundamental characteristic of consumer, or buyer, behavior. This fundamental characteristic is that we tend to routinize some purchases and tend not to routinize others. Note that the pattern of X's in the shopping matrix is more routine than the other two patterns. At least the buyer always bought from one store. The only nonroutine element in the pattern of X's lies in the fact that several brands were considered. The greatest degree of purchase routinization would

---

[4] This information could, however, be incorporated with the shopping matrix.

occur if all ten X's were in the 1 × 1 cell of the matrix in Figure 13.3. The least degree of routinization would occur when all the X's appear in the 5 × 5 cell. Consider, for a moment, your own shopping behavior. When you buy cigarettes or a candy bar, you buy without expending much search effort. You might even tend to buy in terms of locational convenience. But if you are about to buy a car, you may search in a very thorough way—you treat the auto purchase as nonroutine, you treat the cigarette and candy purchases as routine.

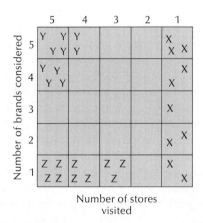

Figure 13.3 The Shopping Matrix and Buyer Behavior

Clearly then there are products that demand a full search (brand, interstore and intrastore comparisons); there are products that demand a casual search (intrastore only); and there are products that are purchased with little or no conscious consideration given to comparison or search (after an initial exploratory shopping phase is complete).[5] This last case we will call the *no search* case, although the term is slightly misleading. A housewife might, as an illustration of our no search case, shop several supermarkets in a new neighborhood to identify "her" store and, having completed this exploratory phase, fall thereafter into a routine, or habitual, use of one particular store. The ideas of casual search and no search purchase procedures serve to introduce the first of the three basic types of products we will consider: the convenience good.

THE CONVENIENCE GOOD   The idea of the *convenience good* may be defined in three different, but mutually consistent, ways. First, convenience goods are characterized by what we have called a high probability of routinization. Buyers tend to use habitual solutions when the need arises for one of these products. The word "convenience" suggests that

[5] The idea of degrees of search is suggested in the excellent article by Louis P. Bucklin, "The Concept of Mass in Intra-Urban Shopping," *Journal of Marketing*, October 1967, pp 37–42. The terms used here are, however, slightly different from those suggested by Bucklin.

the preference of the buyer is for an easy, quick solution to a need. Second, we can define the convenience good in terms of the shopping matrix. In this view, the convenience good is one that tends to produce a shopping pattern in which most purchase events involve visits to only one store. Search is limited to the casual (intrastore) type, or it does not occur at all. Note especially that the behavior of a buyer relative to convenience goods does not necessarily suggest strong brand loyalty. The buyer may, in fact, be indifferent to brand—she may buy any of several brands that are regularly stocked (such as breakfast cereals). The distinction to remember is that the buyer does not engage in anything like a full search. Finally, we can define convenience goods in terms of their economic and use characteristics. In this perspective, convenience goods are distinguished by: (a) their relatively low unit price (to consumers), (b) their relatively great frequency of purchase and (c) a general inability to draw meaningful inferences about the user's taste from the brand selected. Each of these characteristics deserves some clarification.

Obviously, products vary in terms of their unit price. There are items the prices of which represent a substantial percentage of the monthly earnings of an average household. And there are items that are so low in unit price that they have only a negligible impact upon the household budget. Convenience goods tend toward the lower end of this unit-price scale. Indeed, it is believed that one of the reasons that the purchase procedures for convenience goods become highly routinized is that such expenditures, viewed singly, are of little harm to the bank balance.

Products vary also in terms of the frequency with which they are purchased. There are products that yield the services embodied in them over a lifetime—homes, fine cameras and watches exemplify this type of product. There are also products that exist at the opposite end of this spectrum—they are highly perishable in the sense that they yield the services embodied in them over a very short span of time. Convenience goods include the types of products requiring most frequent replenishment of stocks. Bakery and dairy items are, in fact, so perishable that the purchase procedure is sometimes fully routinized—the products are delivered to the house. In this instance, search effort by the buyer is at an absolute minimum. It is interesting to note that anything the consumer can do to impede the perishability of a product may serve to remove the product from the convenience good category. Thus, hamburger or ground beef may require frequent purchase for the household with limited freezer facilities; the purchase procedure would tend to be routinized. But the household with a large freezer may buy a quarter of a beef at each purchase, and may precede such a purchase with a fairly elaborate search for the best buy.

But there is one other identifying characteristic of the convenience good. The convenience good tends not to reflect the buyer's or user's personal taste. This is a fairly subtle point, but one that adds a significant dimension of understanding to the convenience good concept. The literature of the social sciences has long recognized that certain types of consumer products are selected or rejected because they either are or are not in basic agreement with the buyer's perception of his own personality. We have discussed this concept of the self and self-perception before. There are some products—usually those that embody a significant degree of style differentiation—from which it is possible to infer something about the tastes and values of the buyer or user. Thus the convertible automobile is equated, rightly or wrongly, with the "swinging" personality. High fashion wearing apparel is suggestive of sophistication. There are other products that are relatively sterile in the sense that one cannot infer user values either from the basic product or perhaps even from the particular brand. Convenience goods tend to be of this latter genre. Thus, flour, sugar, canned goods, candy, and similar products do little to enlighten us regarding the personal idiosyncrasies of the buyer.

THE SHOPPING GOOD   The term *shopping good* is used to identify the type of product that is, in every respect, the opposite of the convenience good. The shopping good is a product that requires a full search before purchase. That means, it will be recalled, that brand comparisons, interstore comparisons and intrastore comparisons are normally a part of the purchase procedure. The purchase of a shopping good tends to be nonroutine—the prospective buyer must make himself informed anew on virtually every occasion requiring purchase. In terms of the shopping matrix (Figure 13.3), the shopping good is one that is characterized by a northwestern solution—that is, the appropriate shopping pattern would tend to emphasize the northwestern quadrant of the matrix. A large number of store offerings and a large number of brands or styles would be considered. The greater search normally expended for the shopping good can be explained in two different ways.

The first of these explanations is called the *funds-for-search* theory. The shopping good, again in direct contrast to the convenience good, tends to have a higher unit selling price. It is a product the purchase of which has a substantially greater impact upon the household budget than the convenience good. Because it sells for a higher price, a careful prepurchase search holds the promise of greater savings. It is this promise of savings that, in effect, funds (or finances) a more elaborate and (from the buyer's point of view) a more costly search procedure. A 10 percent saving on a $300 dishwasher, would "fund a search," or compensate an effort valued at $30. A fund of that size might very well justify an interurban shopping trip. Note, in contrast, that a 10 percent saving potential on a convenience good (having, as it does, a lower unit price) would "fund" only a meager search if any at all.

A second explanation of the full search character of the purchase procedure for shopping goods is suggested by the phrase *search-for-information* theory.[6] This theory recognizes that the purchase of a shopping good is normally less frequent than the purchase of convenience goods, and it recognizes that the shopping good is much more likely to embody style distinctions that reflect the user/buyer's personal taste. Because the purchase of shopping goods normally occurs less frequently, the likelihood that the universe of product alternatives will have changed between purchases is high. This makes sense. If one buys a product every few days, there is little reason to believe that the universe of products available will have changed significantly in the time interval between purchases. One will come to act as though there has been no significant change and repeat the purchase procedure used previously. On the other hand, if one buys a product only, say, once each year, there is less reason to believe that the universe of product choice available at the time of the last purchase will exist in unchanged form. The uncertainty thus introduced by the passage of time dictates that the buyer reeducate himself regarding the product universe now extant—in other words, full search now seems appropriate.

Because the shopping good is much more likely to embody a distinctive element—because such goods tend to display the taste of the buyer—a more elaborate search for information is needed. The purchase of shopping goods often requires a very subtle matching of the product with the tastes and personality of the buyer. Both because the item is relatively more costly and because it can, if selected in error, reflect adversely on the buyer, a greater degree of assurance is required. Such assurance is acquired through search, and the search is thought to terminate when additional search efforts on the part of the buyer reveal no addition to the universe of product choice. This reasoning suggests a diminishing marginal increase in information as the search procedure progresses. Thus, the first wave of search produces relevant new information and compels a second wave of search. The second wave of search is also productive in the sense that it yields new information, but it represents a less profound educational experience than the first wave of search. The productive second wave of search leads to another, and so on until the marginal increment of information is so small that the value gleaned from it is felt to be minimal. Search then terminates.

The concepts of convenience goods and shopping goods are well established in the literature of marketing.[7] And they are useful concepts. But there is a real danger that the ideas may be used in a way not fully

[6] See Richard H. Holton, "The Distinction Between Convenience Goods, Shopping Goods, and Specialty Goods," *Journal of Marketing,* July 1958, pp. 53–56. Although the terminology used is not precisely the same, this approach is the principal thrust of Holton's argument.

[7] The original statement of these concepts may be seen in Melvin T. Copeland, "Relation of Consumer's Buying Habits to Marketing Methods," *Harvard Business Review,* April 1923, pp. 282–289.

intended. Specifically, there are two interpretive amendments that we should be explicit about. First, the concepts of convenience goods and shopping goods are not discrete, or insular, classes. They are, rather, positions at the poles of a continuum. That is, they are the extreme positions on a spectrum of values. Consider Figure 13.4.

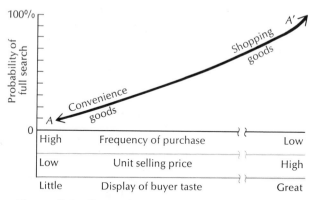

Figure 13.4 Convenience Goods—Shopping Goods

Note in Figure 13.4 that there is no effective discontinuity between the shopping goods end and the convenience good end of the line AA'. This suggests that there are *ambiguous* products that are not clearly one or another of these two basic types of products. That is, there may be some products that embody some of the characteristics of shopping goods and some of the characteristics of convenience goods. And second, this suggests that products may shift along line AA' during their life cycle. That is, a product that once may have been accorded the purchase procedures normally associated with shopping goods may, in time, come to be purchased in a highly routinized manner. Products can shift along this continuum for any number of reasons. Higher consumer income may expel some products from the full search category. Production efficiencies may reduce costs and prices to the point that products may be purchased as convenience goods. Portable radios have, for example, moved from a position near the A' end of the curve to somewhere near the midpoint of the curve. Paper house dresses may dictate essentially convenience good purchase procedures by buyers.

THE SPECIALTY GOOD   There is one further type of product in which we have an interest. This product is the *specialty good*. And this third basic type of product will enable us to recognize a product dimension not readily accessible from the convenience-shopping spectrum. We will define the specialty good as a *branded product characterized by a low cumulative switching-out rate as competing brands are made relatively more attractive*. A relatively low cumulative switching-out rate implies a strong, or loyal, tie between the buyer and the brand. Consider Figure 13.5.

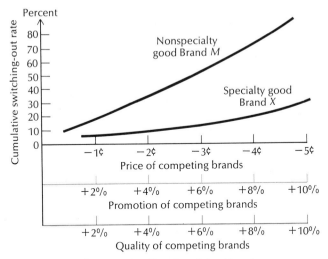

Figure 13.5 The Specialty Good

Figure 13.5 distinguishes the specialty good from nonspecialty brands, and it does so in terms of three different variables. The first horizontal axis relates a declining price for competing brands to the switching-out rate for brand X and for Brand M. Note the general insensitivity of the Brand X buyer to the lowered price of competing brands. In contrast, note the rapidly rising cumulative switching-out rate for a nonspecialty brand given the declining price of competing brands. Observe also the relative insensitivity of Brand X buyers to increased promotion and to increases in the quality of competing brands. Specialty good status clearly implies a hard core of satisfied buyers or users. Buyers who would "rather fight than switch," those who would "walk a mile for a Camel," view their respective brands as a specialty good.

Our reason for giving the specialty good separate treatment is that the relationship of the specialty good to the convenience good-shopping good continuum is not always clear. Students are not quite clear whether a convenience good can be a specialty good; whether a shopping good can achieve specialty status; or, indeed, if a specialty good is neither a convenience good nor a shopping good. What, then, is the relationship between the specialty good concept and the convenience good-shopping good continuum? It is the general *product* characteristics that determine whether a product is a convenience good or a shopping good. Thus, cigarettes are, in general, convenience goods. But if a *brand* of cigarettes achieves specialty status, search behavior may be induced. A buyer, or group of buyers, *may* be forced to engage in a brand search if he views the product as a specialty good but does not find it widely distributed—that is, does not find it available conveniently. In the same way, an automobile is, intrinsically, a shopping good—there are very few people who would or could treat it as a convenience good. Yet if a particular brand of automobile becomes a specialty good in the mind of a buyer or group of buyers, concern with other brands is necessarily reduced. And such shopping as is then done, may be done on a price or dealership basis, not on a brand basis. That is, for the man who views a Ford as a no-substitute brand, the only shopping he can do is for price or service among Ford dealers. Thus, specialty status can be achieved by any kind of product—and such status need not interfere conceptually with the basic convenience good-shopping good spectrum.

The distribution network

In Chapter 5 we introduced the concept of the channel of distribution. The discussion at that time was limited to a definitional statement so that we could examine the exact nature of business expansion more systematically. We noted in Chapter 5 that we would find it necessary, at a later time, to develop a more precise understanding of this "channel" idea. The time for that refinement is now here. The channel of distribution may be thought of as a legal path, a physical path or an institutional path. The channel of distribution viewed as a legal path would trace the sequence of specialized market institutions having *title* to the products they sell—it would omit those types of institutions that do not take legal title to the goods they sell. The channel of distribution viewed as a physical path would be described by the sequence of institutions that take actual possession of the products they sell—it would omit those institutional specialists that do not take possession of the goods they sell.[8] The channel of distribution viewed as an institutional path would include all market specialists who directly influence the transfer of title. This latter definition is the one that we shall use here.

Our principal need at the moment is to introduce the notion of channel length. The length of a channel is indicated by *the number of institutional specialists that intervene between manufacturer and final consumer.* Consider the representation of several channels of distribution in Figure 13.6.

Four channels are depicted in Figure 13.6. Channel A is called a direct channel—it involves direct sales contact between the manufacturer and the final consumer. Channels B, C and D are all indirect from the perspective of the final consumer. But our real concern with Figure 13.6 relates to the fact that these four channels are characterized by different length.

[8] There are more nontitled and nonpossession institutions than one might think. These and other institutional hybrids are identified and discussed in Chapter 15.

Figure 13.6 Channel Length

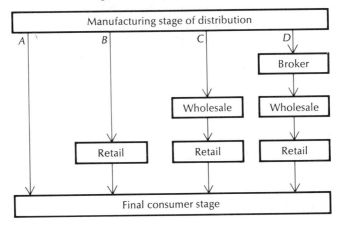

More specifically, Channel A is the shortest channel, Channel D is the longest. Note carefully that length, as that term is used in this context, is not measured in physical distance. That is, a manufacturer who sells directly to consumers in another state nonetheless sells through a shorter channel than a manufacturer who sells to a retailer located in the same city and who, in turn, sells to final consumers. Length is indicated by the number of market intermediaries utilized in a particular channel of distribution. And the longer the channel, the greater the amount of *distribution leverage* the manufacturer has. This idea of distribution leverage requires elaboration. Consider the two channels of distribution in Figure 13.7.

Figure 13.7 Distribution Leverage

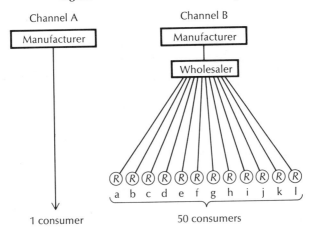

Note that the direct channel, Channel A, produces a one to one contact basis between manufacturer and consumer. Note, in contrast, that one contact for the manufacturer in Channel B produces about 600 final consumer contacts. That is, one contact (between manufacturer and wholesaler) produces 12 contacts with retail stores, and if each store, in turn contacts 50 customers, about 600 final consumer contacts result from the original contact. The distribution leverage in Channel A is unity; the distribution leverage in Channel B is about 600. It is a most important part of our argument to recognize that the longer the channel, the greater the distribution leverage tends to be. A manufacturer who distributes through brokers-wholesalers-retailers to final consumers (as in Channel D in Figure 13.6) may enjoy distribution leverage of well into the thousands. We need now to identify the idea of a promotional blend, and we will then be ready to assemble the components of a general strategy of competition in mixed affluence.

The promotional blend

The term "promotion" is a general term that is understood to include three types of sales activity: (a) mass, impersonal selling efforts (advertising); (b) face-to-face, or personal, sales situations; and (c) activities other than personal selling and advertising, such as point-of-purchase display (POP), shows and exhibitions, demonstrations, and other nonrecurrent selling efforts. This latter form of sales activity is called "sales promotion." It is useful to consider these three dimensions of promotion as alternative avenues of expenditure for the firm's promotion budget. That is, if a particular firm has a total promotion budget of $1,000,000 that budget may break down as follows: $500,000 to advertising, $400,000 to personal selling and $100,000 to sales promotion. Or, indeed, the $1,000,000 budget may be allocated to these three types of sales activity in virtually any number of other ways. The manner in which the total promotion budget is allocated among the three basic types of sales activity is referred to as either the promotion "mix" or the promotion "blend".[9] We will use the term "blend" here to avoid possible confusion with the "marketing mix" concept. And there are two distinct types of promotion blends that we will recognize. These blends are a "pull" blend and a "push" blend.[10]

A *pull blend* is one in which mass, impersonal sales efforts are given the greatest emphasis. The purpose of the pull blend is to presell final

[9] The latter term is employed, for example, in Edwin H. Lewis, "Sales Promotion Decisions," *Business News Notes,* Minneapolis, Minn., School of Business Administration, University of Minnesota, November 1954.
[10] This dichotomy is widely recognized. See, for example, John S. Wright and Daniel S. Warner, *Advertising,* New York: McGraw-Hill Book Co., 1966, pp. 132–135.

consumers so that they demand the product at the retail level of distribution. To the extent that final consumers are presold through mass, impersonal selling efforts, the retailer (and the wholesaler for that matter) need not provide as much in-store sales effort of his own. The pull blend deemphasizes personal, or face-to-face, sales efforts. The firm using a pull blend would not allocate as much of the total promotional budget to sales salaries, and a relatively large proportion of the budget would be devoted to advertising and sales promotion.

In contrast, a *push blend* emphasizes the personal, or face-to-face, types of sales activity. A firm that employs a push blend of promotion develops a strong sales force—one capable of vigorous sales efforts at both the distributor and the dealer level. The rationale for using the term "push" is that such sales tend to push the product through the channel of distribution. The distinction between push and pull is depicted in Figure 13.8.

Figure 13.8 Push and Pull Promotion

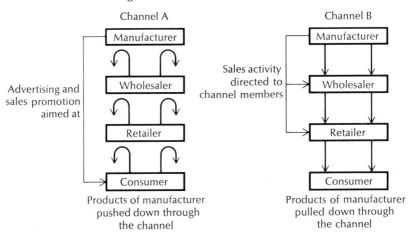

The general strategy of competition in mixed affluence

We have now identified the principal components, or concepts, of a general strategy of modern competition.[11] In brief review, these components are: (a) the convenience good-shopping good continuum, (b) the concepts of channel length and distribution leverage and (c) the notion of push and pull promotional blends. We need now to combine these elements in an analytical form that will permit us, within general limits, to deduce the proper distribution and promotion plans for particular types of prod-

---

[11] This "general strategy" is, in fact, a model of the relationships between product type, distribution plans and promotion plans. At least it is a model in the sense that Lipson uses that term. It is used "to show how the variables or factors in the particular operation will interact." See Harry A. Lipson, "Formal Reasoning and Marketing Strategy," *Journal of Marketing,* October 1962, pp. 1–5.

ucts. It will be recalled that this objective was the principal goal of this chapter. Toward this goal, then, consider Figure 13.9.[12]

Figure 13.9 The General Competitive Strategy

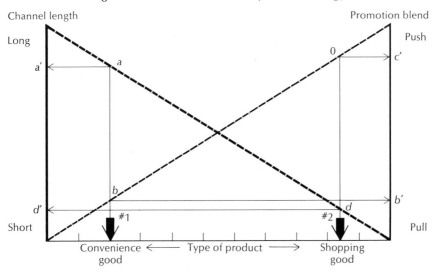

Figure 13.9 (a) accommodates various product types (convenience to shopping); it (b) depicts a range of promotional strategies (push to pull); and it (c) depicts a range of channel lengths. Note that the right vertical identifies the promotional blend and the left vertical identifies channel length. Figure 13.9 is complicated to some extent because it also illustrates the manner in which this diagrammatic representation of the general competitive strategy is interpreted.

Begin at the point labeled #1. This arrowhead represents the position of a product on the horizontal scale. The #1 arrowhead is near the convenience good end of the scale. For a product of this type, the proper channel length is indicated by reading straight up from the product arrowhead to the black diagonal at point a. The correct channel length for the convenience good is given by the point a'—a relatively long channel is recommended. The proper promotional blend for Product 1 is read straight up from the #1 arrowhead to point b on the diagonal, thence to b' on the blend line. Product 1—the convenience good—would normally utilize a pull strategy. A relatively long channel and a pull promotional blend represent a prototype mix for convenience goods.

---

[12] This summary device is suggested by Leo Aspinwalls "Parallel Systems of Promotion and Distribution." This significant article is published in a commemorative collection of four of Professor Aspinwall's marketing theories by the Bureau of Business Research, University of Colorado, Boulder, Colorado, 1961. This work is not page numbered, but the Parallel Systems Theory is the last idea to be treated in the short pamphlet.

Now consider the shopping good prototype mix. Arrowhead #2 is positioned at the shopping good end of the product continuum. What is the proper distribution/promotion mix for this product? Read the channel length straight up from arrowhead #2 on the diagonal and point *d,* thence to *d'.* A relatively short channel is suggested by the model. In order to read the promotion blend for Product 2, read straight up from arrowhead #2 to the diagonal and point *c,* thence to *c'.* A push policy is suggested. This general model of distribution and promotion strategy associates the convenience good with pull promotion and a long channel. The model likewise associates the shopping good with a push blend and a relatively direct (short) channel. We said earlier that there was a logic that related different types of products to different types of distribution and promotion. Just what is that logic?

By its very nature, a convenience good tends to be uncomplicated; there is normally very little of a technical nature about it. This fact suggests that selling appeals for convenience goods can be relatively simple—and impersonal sales methods (notably advertising) can handle the task efficiently and effectively. Mass communications media can deliver, at a very low cost-per-exposure, messages that involve no intricate technical explanations. In short, the mass media are ideally suited for the promotional task presented by most convenience goods. That fact argues, of course, for a pull type of promotional blend. Moreover, the convenience good, as the name implies, requires distribution in as many outlets as feasible. If the good is to be available "conveniently," it must be available through a relatively large number of retail outlets. This fundamental need for distribution through as many outlets as possible is consistent with the long channel of distribution because of the distributive leverage provided by such a channel. It will be recalled that this leverage idea relates the number of manufacturer sales contacts to the number of final consumer contacts. And we demonstrated earlier how a longer channel provides access to a larger number of final consumers.

The prototype shopping good "mix" of a short channel of distribution and a push policy of promotion is also quite logical. Shopping goods tend to be more technical—they often require nonroutine sales appeals. It is often helpful to have a face-to-face sales situation in order that the prospect can raise specific, and perhaps technical, questions as they occur to him. Because the product is basically more complex, the role of personal selling can be relatively greater.[13] This suggests, of course, that the push policy of promotion is more consistent with the sales task than the pull blend. Because the shopping good is a more costly purchase than the convenience good, and because consumers are willing to exert greater search efforts prior to purchase, distribution need not be as ubiquitous

[13] It is well-informed personal sales efforts that are required. Poorly informed personal sales efforts are never needed.

as with the convenience good. Distribution may, in other words, be accomplished through relatively fewer outlets, and no great imposition is thrust upon the final consumer. Note that this restricted type of distribution is perfectly consistent with a shorter channel of distribution because of the reduced distributive leverage normally associated with the more direct channel.

Our description and explanation of the general model of competitive strategy is now complete. But we would be remiss if we did not identify some of the more important faults that are embodied in the model. This brief criticism will center around two basic difficulties with the model. The discussion that follows is developed around: (a) some answers that the model does not give us and (b) some answers that the model gives us that may *seem* to represent unsound advice.

To begin with, the general model does incorporate some unfortunate ambiguities. If a product is not clearly a convenience good or clearly a shopping good—that is, it falls in the ambivalent middle portion of the product spectrum—the model gives virtually no advice at all. At very best, the model says only that the channel should be of intermediate length and the promotional blend should be neither push nor pull but, one must suppose, some of both. And there is another related ambiguity—the model does not tell us the precise ingredients of the promotional blend. We are told that a pull blend is best for a convenience good—but how many parts of advertising effort to how many parts of personal selling effort should we use? The model does not instruct us in sufficient detail: It would be more useful if more precise directions could be deduced from it.

Moreover, the model may *seem* to give bad advice at times. That is, a critic will sometimes say, "I know of a successful product that does not feature a mix such as that suggested by the model." And there are undoubtedly instances in which such deviations may make very good sense. One such instance occurs when the particular strengths of a firm involve skills that run contrary to those suggested by the model. For example, if a convenience good manufacturer possesses, for one reason or another, an excellently trained sales organization or does not have ready access to a good distributor-dealer network, a successful organization may nonetheless be developed. Such an organization will probably not, indeed cannot, realize the full natural advantages of the competitive course of action prescribed by the model. An example of such a circumstance was provided by the Curtiss Candy Company, makers of Baby Ruth candy bars. Curtiss used a driver-sales force to call on retail outlets—they used, in other words, a push blend and a relatively short channel of distribution for a convenience good. And for many years their policy may have seemed to work. In recent years, however, the weaknesses of such a system became apparent, and the driver-sales force was abandoned. Indeed, Curtiss was acquired in 1964 by Standard Brands Inc.

But there is one other instance in which a competitive policy opposite to that suggested by the model may make sense. When a competitive condition exists in which every closely competing firm employs essentially the same marketing mix, there may be advantage in differentiation—even if such differentiation runs counter to the advice of the model to some extent. It is, though, an unfair criticism of the model to say that not all successful firms pay heed to it. The vast majority of convenience goods are promoted and distributed through a mix similar to that suggested by the model. The great majority of shopping goods are distributed through relatively shorter channels of distribution than those used for convenience goods. The promotional task for shopping goods is generally more likely to require personal, face-to-face, sales effort. Thus, while the model may seem to give advice of questionable value, it gives sound economic advice generally.

SUMMARY

Our purpose in Chapter 13 has been to develop greater insight into the nature of modern competition through the identification of a model of the general strategy of marketing activities. This general strategy of marketing activity relates in a systematic way: (a) the product, (b) the promotion of that product and (c) the distribution plan for that product. Our approach to developing this model required first that we explore basic concepts of "the product." Accordingly, we identified three viewpoints of what products are: (a) the physical concept of a product, (b) the embodiment-of-satisfactions concept of the product, and (c) the vector-amoeba concept. We identified three basic types of products—the convenience good, the shopping good and the specialty good.

We defined promotion as including three elements. Those elements were advertising, personal sales efforts and sales promotion. We further defined the promotion blend as a particular mixture of these elements. Special attention was focused on the pull promotion blend and the push promotion blend. We were also particularly interested in channel of distribution length—and we defined this idea as the number of institutional specialists that intervene between manufacturer and final consumer. Long channels comprise many institutions, short channels, few. And greater distribution leverage is a characteristic of long channels.

Our model of general marketing strategy was summarized as two prototype marketing mixes. The convenience good prototype mix combined a pull promotion blend with a relatively long channel of distribution. The shopping good prototype mix combined a push promotion blend with a relatively short channel of distribution. We noted and emphasized that this model of marketing strategy provides logical guidance for planning. The very nature of convenience goods argues for ubiquitous distribution and mass sales techniques. The very nature of shopping goods argues for relatively restricted distribution and more personalized sales efforts.

1 Carefully define and indicate the relevance of each of the following concepts to the study of marketing:
   a. A shopping matrix
   b. A vector-amoeba concept of a product
   c. The convenience good
   d. The specialty good
   e. A direct channel of distribution
   f. A promotional blend
2 Distinguish carefully between each element in the following pairs of terms:
   a. The physical concept of a product *and* the embodiment-of-satisfactions concept of a product
   b. The functional performance of a product *and* the social and psychological performance of a product
   c. Full shopping search *and* casual shopping search
   d. The funds-for-search theory of buyer behavior *and* the search-for-information theory of buyer behavior
   e. The channel of distribution as a legal path *and* the channel of distribution as a physical path
   f. Distribution leverage *and* channel length
   g. A pull promotional blend *and* a push promotional blend
3 What is the general model of competitive strategy? What does this model suggest regarding the promotion of convenience goods? What does it suggest regarding the promotion of shopping goods? What logic can be offered in support of this general model?

DISCUSSION QUESTIONS

4 In what specific ways would you modify the general model of marketing strategy that we developed? That is, how can the model be made more realistic?
5 Explain as carefully as you can the kinds of economic waste that may exist when a push policy of promotion is used for convenience goods. What kinds of waste or inefficiency can result when a pull policy of promotion is used with a complicated shopping good?

Chapter 14

MARKETING CHANNELS
—WHY THEY EVOLVE

It was necessary in Chapter 5 to define, in a preliminary way, the concept of the channel of distribution. Our purpose for that early definition was to assist in the development of the idea of business expansion. It was again necessary, in Chapter 13, to develop the concept of length in channels of distribution. We introduced the concept of channel length in order that we could fully identify the prototype marketing mix for both the convenience good and the shopping good. We should thus have developed a basic understanding of what a channel of distribution is and what one of its basic properties is. But the idea of a channel of distribution deserves a great deal more emphasis than it has been given to this point. The channel of distribution is thought by some students of marketing to be the *natural* focal point for the study of marketing—the channel of distribution is a concept that is uniquely a part of the marketing discipline.

Our task in the present chapter is to identify more systematically than we have thus far the reasons that underlie the natural evolution of marketing channels. We are interested, in other words, in developing a more complete understanding of the forces that give rise to the distribution channel. To this general end, we will consider six different perspectives, or views, of the channel of distribution. Each of these views will highlight a different underlying reason for the channel of distribution. More exactly, we will examine: (a) the channel of distribution as a sequence, or series of activities to be performed; (b) the gap, or separationist, theory of channels of distribution; (c) the channel of distribution as a means of gaining transactional efficiency; (d) the capacity, or pipeline, theory of channels of distribution; (e) the channel of distribution as a set of power relationships; and (f) the vertical marketing system and dealer/distributor responsiveness.

The functional view of distribution channels

The functional view of channels of distribution holds that channels of distribution evolve as a particular kind of specialization and division of labor. The economic process of creating total market value requires, unavoidably, the creation of form, time, place and possession utility.[1] And the functional view of the channel of distribution identifies each of these different utilities, or types of value, as distinct *functions,* or *activities,* that can be divided among any number of different market institutions. At one extreme, the manufacturer may perform all these unavoidable activities; at the other extreme the performance of these activities may be shared among many different, and necessarily more specialized, institutions. Figure 14.1 depicts the channel of distribution when viewed as a set of unavoidable functions or activities.

Figure 14.1   Specialization and Channels of Distribution

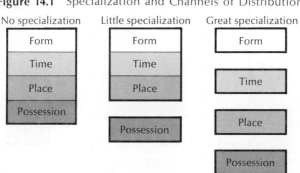

Figure 14.1 depicts three different channels of distribution—each involving a different degree of specialization and division of labor—each reflecting a different arrangement for the performance of the functions or activities that produce final market value. Note that in the "no specialization" case all the basic functions are performed by one firm—a kind of jack-of-all-trades enterprise. In the "little specialization" case, the creation of possession utility has been spun off (farmed out) to a selling specialist. And note that in the "great specialization" case, each of the basic utilities is the responsibility of a separate institution. But while Figure 14.1 is a

---

[1] The "functional" emphasis in marketing has produced a great difference of opinion as to the exact nature of these "unavoidable" functions. Virtually every writer of note has his own list of such functions. One widely adopted textbook identifies eight such functions, and one source indicates that "various writers have listed from 5 to 120 functions." For a good discussion of marketing functions, see P. D. Converse and others, *Elements of Marketing,* Seventh Edition, Englewood Cliffs, N. J.: Prentice-Hall, Inc., 1965, p. 127. See also T. N. Beckman and William R. Davidson, *Marketing,* Eighth Edition, New York: The Ronald Press Company, 1967, pp. 421–428. See, more recently, Edwin H. Lewis, *Marketing Channels: Structure and Strategy,* New York: McGraw-Hill Book Co., 1968, pp. 1-7.

good point of departure for discussing the functional view of channels, it has one fatal shortcoming: It seems to suggest that each basic function is indivisible. That is, Figure 14.1 seems to imply that there is one institution that creates time utility, one institution that specializes in the creation of place utility and one institution for possession utility. Each of the basic functions are, in fact, divisible, and are very often divided among several different intermediaries. Figure 14.2 corrects this conceptual weakness.

Figure 14.2   Shared Function and Channels of Distribution

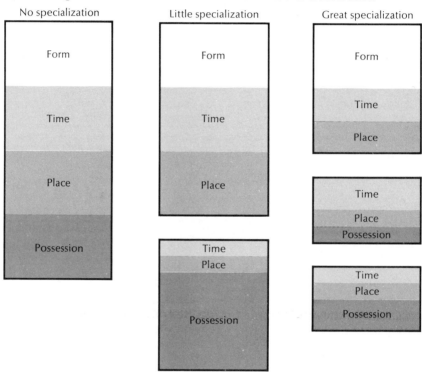

Figure 14.2 again depicts three degrees of specialization—three different channels of distribution. Now, however, the manner in which they are shared is quite different. The "little specialization" case now depicts a sharing of the time and place functions between two different institutions, and, as before, the performance of the possession function is handled by a single member of the channel. The "great specialization" case reflects a sharing of the time and place functions by all channel members, and two of the three channel members share the performance of the possession function.

Note again that the functional view of the channel hinges on the notion that different institutions evolve in order to perform one or more of the basic functions required to create total economic value. The storage specialist may be a warehouse organization, a wholesaler or a retailer. Similarly, institutions evolve to create place value—these institutions may be transportation agencies or other types of enterprise with transportation capabilities. The institutions that evolve for the creation of possession utility may be advertising agencies, sales agencies of various types, or wholesalers and retailers. Each channel member is thus viewed as skilled in the performance of some function or set of functions, and the economic rationale for the channel of distribution is that those functions can probably be performed more efficiently by a specialized organization than by a jack-of-all-distributive-trades.

This functional view of the channel of distribution seems also to imply that the final consumer may become a part of the channel—at least in the sense that some responsibility for functional performance may fall upon the final consumer. Consider, for example, the case of the "bargain" type of retail store in which there are no sales personnel, and the customer is expected to arrange for the delivery and (if necessary) the installation of any item of merchandise he buys. Clearly, some of the responsibility for functional performance has been *offered* to the consumer. The buyer is asked to educate himself regarding the nature and capabilities of the merchandise (possession value), and he must create some of the place value as well. There is a very profound lesson in this notion that channels of distribution may enlist the aid of the final consumer through a shifting or sharing of the required functional performance.

Consider the case wherein a young man buys an electric razor and pays $29.95 for it. His friend buys a razor—same brand, same model, on the same day—but he pays only $24.95 for it. The first temptation is to say that the two young men bought the same thing but paid different prices. But consider the manner in which the functions are shared within the channel before you reach that conclusion. One seller in our example may handle any required replacements of parts immediately from his own stock—the other may require that the customer send the ailing razor to the factory for repair. One seller may provide in-store sales assistance that will assist in the proper use and extended life-expectancy of the razor. The other may, in effect, ask the buyer to educate himself regarding the proper methods of use for the razor. In short, the low price may require that the customer be brought in, in a sense, as a channel member. Our point is not that all price differentials can be accounted for in terms of different sharing arrangements of the basic channel functions; it is only that *some* such price differences can be explained in that way.

The gap theory of channels of distribution

The gap theory of channels of distribution emphasizes the fact that there are fundamental economic differences between an ideal set of conditions for supply and an ideal set of conditions for demand. That is, while ideal economic conditions from the manufacturer's point of view might tend toward extremely long production runs of identical physical products and the resultant low unit costs, ideal conditions from the point of view of the consumer (demand) might be a supply of products and services that would permit a significant degree of individualized self-expression.[2] Clearly, these two ideals are at odds, and particular types of human endeavor are required to resolve the difference. The difference between these ideals represents the "gap" that must be bridged—and the special forms of economic institutions that evolve to reconcile these differences make up the channel of distribution. But a specific example will serve to clarify this whole idea.

Consumer demand is, on any single purchase occasion, limited to relatively small quantities. That is, the level of household and individual consumption is such that purchases of anything in case quantities is rare, and one-at-a-time purchases are more nearly the rule. But production that is geared to one-at-a-time consumption would be prohibitive in cost. One of the most profound reasons for our relatively high level of economic welfare is traceable to mass production and the economies that result from extremely long production runs. Thus, while we as consumers normally want one item at a time, the economic facts of life push in the direction of mass production. This gap in quantities is resolved by successive *breaks in bulk*—breaks that are accomplished by market intermediaries that constitute the distribution channels.

But consider still another aspect of this economic gap. Your personal wardrobe may reasonably comprise several basically different types of clothing. There may be clothes for leisure, clothes for dress and clothes for work. Your preferences for clothing are diverse in the sense that you want a different type of clothing for different occasions. But to clothing manufacturers, specialization may be *the* key to success. That is, there are well-known makers of work clothing, well-known makers of dress clothing and well-known makers of sportswear. Levi Strauss & Company, McGregor, and Botany Industries, Inc., are distinctly different organizations, yet each may contribute something to your wardrobe. This tendency to specialize by style in the production of many items is met by a desire for many different styles by final consumers, and another type of economic gap is the result. This gap in assortments is closed by the actions of market specialists (the channel members) who carry inventories from several and diverse sources.

---

[2] The idea of the "gap" theory is, basically, a notion that Wroe Alderson called economic "discrepancies." Alderson developed the idea of discrepancies in assortments to show one of the types of economic contributions made by marketing specialists. The terms "gap" or "separationist" as used to describe this idea were apparently coined by William McInnis in "A Conceptual Approach to Marketing," in Reavis Cox and others, editors, *Theory in Marketing: Second Series,* Homewood, Ill.: Richard D. Irwin, Inc., 1964. See the Alderson discussion in his *Marketing Behavior and Executive Action,* Homewood, Ill.: Richard D. Irwin, Inc., 1957, pp. 215-216.

And we could, likewise, view time and place as particular types of economic gaps—gaps that are closed by the market specialists who constitute the channel of distribution. But enough has been said to suggest the nature of the gap theory of distribution channels. It is, in some respects, like the functional explanation of channels—it is, in other respects, a unique perspective.

The channel of distribution and transactional efficiency

The word "transaction" identifies an act of economic exchange. And transactions, many thousands of them, are required to fully exchange the specialized units of production of a complex, modern economy among the members of that economy. While no exchange transactions are required in an economic system in which each household is self-sufficient, it follows that the number of exchange transactions must increase as households become more specialized. And it can be demonstrated that the evolution of market specialists—the institutions that constitute channels of distribution—*simplifies the otherwise complex process of exchange by reducing the number of exchange transactions required.* It is this relationship between (a) the degree of economic specialization, (b) the number of exchange transactions and (c) the development of specialized market intermediaries that represents the nucleus of a principle that we will refer to as "transactional efficiency."[3]

To be more specific, the principle of transactional efficiency says that the gain in transactional efficiency—a gain that is traceable to the development of market specialization—is identified by the term $\frac{n-1}{2}$, where n represents the number of specialized producers in an economic system. In order to demonstrate this principle in a definitive way, consider the situation in which there are four households on an island. Each of these households specializes in the production of some commodity—and this commodity is exchanged for the specialties of each of the other households. Figure 14.3 depicts this hypothetical island economy.

In this figure note that Household W specializes in the production of wheat; X specializes in the production of meat; Y in milk; and Z in vegetables. Each of these respective specialties is grown in surplus—the surplus of one household being exchanged for some part of the surplus of each of the others. As a means of understanding this principle of transactional efficiency, count the number of economic transactions that would be required, at a minimum and without a market specialist to effect complete exchange. That is, what is the smallest number of transactions

[3] The idea of economic efficiency in this transactional sense is one of Wroe Alderson's many insightful contributions to the discipline of marketing. See Alderson's original discussion of the idea in "Factors Governing the Development of Marketing Channels," in *Marketing Channels for Manufactured Products,* Richard M. Clewett, editor, Homewood, Illinois: Richard D. Irwin, Inc., 1954, pp. 5-34.

required to put the specialty of each of the four producers into the hands of each of the others when there is no market specialist? Your answer should be six, or in general, $\frac{n(n-1)}{2}$. Again, n will represent the number of specialized producers in the island economy.

Figure 14.3 Transactional Efficiency

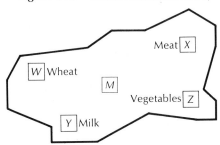

But suppose that a market specialist—the incipient channel of distribution—is added to the island economy. Assume that the market specialist locates at the point designated M in Figure 14.3. If we presume further that the market specialist carries on his shelves stocks of the specialties of each of the producers, we are in a position to deduce the number of transactions required to effect complete exchange with the assistance of the market specialist. Indeed, let us put the question formally. What minimum number of economic transactions is required to effect complete economic exchange in a system comprising four producers and in which a stocked market specialist exists? The answer now is four—or, in general, simply n.

We have now seen that with four producers and no market specialist, six economic transactions are required to effect complete exchange. We have likewise seen that with four producers and a stocked market specialist, four economic transactions are required to effect complete exchange. We stated at the beginning of our numerical illustration that the *gain* in transactional efficiency that is traceable to the market specialist—the incipient distribution channel—is identified by the term $\frac{n-1}{2}$. We can now test the veracity of that original claim. Substituting in the number of producers in our example, the gain in transactional efficiency from the use of a stocked market specialist is:

$T_{w/o}$ = Number of transactions required to effect complete exchange without a market specialist $= \frac{n(n-1)}{2} = 6$

T_w = Number of transactions required to effect complete exchange with the assistance of a stocked market specialist $= n \qquad = 4$

T_g = The gain in transactional efficiency occasioned by the market specialist $= \frac{n-1}{2} = 1.5$

Observe that the 1.5 value of T_g does correctly identify the relationship between $T_{w/o}$ and T_w. That is, 1.5 times the number of transactions is required without the market specialist as is required with the market specialist. And the gain in transactional efficiency offered by the market specialist is a valuable economic contribution—especially when the number of producers in the system is increased to a more realistic level of complexity.

Consider, for example, the transactional character of the island community if it became specialized to the extent that there were 25 producers of different products. What would be the corresponding values of $T_{w/o}$, T_w, and T_g? The answer is as follows:

$$T_{w/o} = \frac{n(n-1)}{2} = \frac{25\,(24)}{2} = 300$$

$$T_w = n \qquad\quad = 25$$

$$T_g = \frac{n-1}{2} \qquad = \frac{25-1}{2} = 12$$

If the calculations are correct, the new and more complex economic system would require 300 transactions to effect complete exchange in the absence of a market specialist. Only 25 transactions would be required where a stocked market specialist stood ready to serve the system. The ratio of gain is identified by the number 12—that is, 12 times the number of transactions is required without the market specialist as is required with such specialization. The following tabular summary reflects the relationship of n, the number of specialized producers, to T_g:

n	T_g
4	2.0
25	12.0
50	24.5
100	49.5
200	99.5
1000	499.5

Note especially that the gain in transactional efficiency with the market specialist is extremely important in economic systems characterized by a great degree of specialization. Consider, for example, the number of transactions that would be required, and the resultant demands upon the time of consumers, if all the purchases made just in the supermarket alone were purchased directly from all the individual suppliers whose products are offered there. The supermarket may have three or four thousand items—and, conservatively, hundreds of suppliers would be represented. The cost to the consumer of dealing directly with producers in a case such as that, if the cost were measured in terms of transactions, would be effectively prohibitive.

Pipeline theory and distribution channels

We noted in one of the early chapters of this book that the channel of distribution may be thought of as a very special kind of pipeline. We observed that the channel of distribution acts in a way that is analogous to the role of the pipeline in the distribution of liquids and gases. It will be useful for us to return to this pipeline concept of the channel, at least briefly. Our concern now, however, is primarily with the idea that channels of distribution have a more or less definable *capacity* to move goods and services to final consumers, and that this channel capacity has a great deal to do with the type of channel that will evolve. Although there is nothing sacred about the nomenclature we will use, we will identify two basic types of channels of distribution: the low margin, high turnover channel is the *high capacity* channel; the high margin, low turnover channel is the *low capacity* channel. The distinction between these two basic types of channels is an extremely important one.

A low margin, high turnover (high capacity) channel of distribution is one in which members of the channel are persuaded philosophically that profits in business are the result of *both* margin (or markups) and stock turnover. That notion sounds simple, but it is at the heart of one of the most profound differences in business philosophy—especially among wholesale and retail organizations. The low margin, high turnover channel comprises organizations that tend to emphasize the rapid movement of merchandise with relatively small margins rather than the reverse. Institutions making up the low margin, high turnover channel of distribution tend to deemphasize *nongoods services*. That is, the high capacity institutions tend to offer relatively fewer services that alter the physical nature of the products being sold. Nongoods services include personal selling, delivery and credit.[4] These and other nongoods services can, when offered in excess, become both the rationale for higher margins in pricing and the reason for a restricted flow of goods and services in the channel of distribution.

The low margin, high turnover channel of distribution is made up largely of institutions the management of which is persuaded that impersonal, mass sales efforts are best adapted to achieve a desirable rate of merchandise movement. In terms that we have used earlier, the low margin, high turnover channel tends to be pull oriented in its promotional philosophy.

The high margin, low turnover (low capacity) channel displays what is almost a completely opposite set of philosophical traits. The low capacity channel tends to be made up of institutions that tend to offer an abundance of the nongoods services—indeed, they often tend to view themselves as a distinctive business enterprise *because of the unique nature of the service bundle that they offer.* These services are "free" to consumers in

[4] Nongoods services are distinguished from "rented goods services" and "owned goods services." See Robert C. Judd, "The Case for Redefining Services," *Journal of Marketing,* January 1964, pp. 58–59.

the sense that no separate charge is made for them: such services are included in the price—the markup, or margin, that is taken "accommodates" the cost of these services. The proportion of sales expense to sales salaries is significantly higher for the high margin, low turnover prototype institution. The emphasis is more nearly on a push policy rather than a pull policy. Expense ratios are relatively high for the high margin, low turnover channel. Such channels are likely to comprise "full service" institutions—institutions providing financing, management services for their accounts, and relatively higher prices than the counterpart high capacity channel.

The high margin, low turnover institution is likely to feature a much more complex organizational structure than its high capacity counterpart. The organizational structure of the high margin, low turnover institution tends to be *vertical;* the organizational structure of the low margin, high turnover institution tends to be *flat.*[5] A vertical organization structure is one that has a relatively large number of executive and supervisory positions. The term "vertical" is used to suggest that a significant number of executive positions exist above the departmental level. There may be an inordinate concern with *general* policy. The flat organization—the trait of the low margin, high turnover institution—tends to have many fewer executive and supervisory positions. Such an organization is "flat" because the number of management positions above the departmental level is relatively small.

In brief summary, then, the low capacity and the high capacity channels may be characterized as follows:

Low Capacity Channel	High Capacity Channel
1 A concern with nongoods services and a belief that patronage depends primarily on such services.	1 A concern with low prices and belief that many nongoods services do not carry their own weight in the sense that they recover their own cost.
2 A preference for a promotional mix that emphasizes the personal sales effort. A tendency to think "push" rather than "pull."	2 A preference for a promotional mix that emphasizes the power of mass selling techniques. The tendency is to think "pull" rather than "push."
3 A tendency to organizational complexity. Organization structure tends to be relatively vertical, with a considerable degree of managerial specialization.	3 A tendency toward organizational simplicity. The organization tends to be relatively flat, with few executive positions.

[5] For a much more complete consideration of the low margin, high turnover institution and the high margin, low turnover institution, see Ronald R. Gist, *Retailing: Concepts and Decisions,* New York: John Wiley & Sons, Inc., 1968, especially Chap. 2.

The channel of distribution as a set of power relationships

There is another perspective regarding the channel of distribution that we can profitably consider. This viewpoint is concerned with what might be called the power relationships of the distribution channel. Perhaps more accurately, this viewpoint is concerned with whether the channel of distribution as it exists today is: (a) a unified and closely integrated "team" of institutions or (b) a loose coalition of institutions, each prompted by the profit motive and each having little basic concern about what goes on before or after them in the distributive sequence. The first of these two views—the "team" concept of the channel—implies a power source within the channel.[6] That is, if the set of institutions we call a channel of distribution tends to think as a coordinated team, some type of channel leadership probably exists, and that leadership is a type of power focus. In contrast, the "loose coalition" view of the channel may imply a lack of an identifiable power focus within the channel. The loose coalition view of the channel presumes a set of institutions that are interdependent but not given to concerted action—not able to act or think as a unified whole.[7]

Although it may have been essentially correct to describe many of the channels of distribution that existed ten to fifteen years ago as being of the loose coalition type, there is impressive evidence that the unified, coordinated channel is playing a substantially more important role today. These evolving and coordinated channels of distribution are called *vertical marketing systems,* and three basic types have been identified. There are: (a) *corporate* vertical marketing systems, (b) *administered* vertical marketing systems and (c) *contractual* vertical marketing systems.[8] These vertical marketing systems are normally characterized by a relatively well defined set of power relationships.

Corporate vertical marketing systems "achieve operating economies—by combining successive stages of production and distribution under a single ownership."[9] The corporate vertical marketing systems represent the dis-

[6] This power source is often identified with the term "control." See, for example Louis W. Stearn's "Channel Control and Inter-Organization Management," in Peter D. Bennett, editor, *Marketing and Economic Development,* Chicago: American Marketing Association, 1965, pp. 655-665. See also, Louis P. Bucklin, "The Focus of Channel Control," in Robert L. King, editor, *Marketing and the New Science of Planning,* Chicago: American Marketing Association, 1968, pp. 142-147. In both these sources, the concept of "control" is defined, more or less, as an ability to influence the policies and practices of other channel members.

[7] This loose coalition view is developed in the widely reprinted article by Phillip McVey, "Are Channels of Distribution What the Textbooks Say?" *Journal of Marketing,* January 1960, pp 61-65.

[8] These basic classes of vertical marketing systems are introduced in Bert C. McCammon, Jr., "The Emergence and Growth of Contractually Integrated Channels in the American Economy," in Bennett, *op. cit.,* pp. 497-499.

[9] From Bert C. McCammon, Jr., "Perspectives in Distribution Programming," a paper presented at the Vertical Marketing Systems Workshop, American Marketing Association, 1968, p. 10.

tribution channel with the most sharply defined internal power relationships. The owning corporation has absolute control, by virtue of ownership, over the actions of the channel members. Examples of corporate vertical marketing systems are easy to find: Sherwin-Williams, a a paint manufacturer, owns over 2000 retail paint stores; Hart, Schaffner & Marx, a dominant force in the men's wear field for many years, owns over 100 retail outlets. No less a power than Sears Roebuck has an "ownership equity" in companies that supply about 30 percent of that company's needs.[10] These corporate systems give to the dominant force in the channel, whether it be a manufacturer or reseller, assurance of customer contact or assurance of supply. That is, the manufacturer that integrates forward by purchase of retail outlets assures himself a place through which to sell his products. The retail organization that integrates backward assures itself a source of supply.[11]

The *administered vertical marketing system* is one in which the dominant force in the channel achieves a position of power because of some "administrative strategy." A particular firm, because of financial strength, management expertise or a particularly strong line of products and brands, can exercise a degree of control over the actions of firms operating in the same channel of distribution. Note that this type of power is much less definitive than that encountered in the corporate system. Indeed, the power encountered in the administered system often seems more in the nature of a call for cooperation from other channel members. The members of a channel of distribution may be put into a mood of cooperation through the use of discounts, sales aids, research expertise, and any of many other concessions and services. The administered vertical marketing system is the first step away from the loose coalition concept of the channel of distribution. We will detail the nature of these administered systems in a section that follows.

Positioned between the administered system and the corporate system is the *contractual vertical marketing system*. Contractual systems fall short of outright common ownership of the institutions within the channel, but they are often characterized by a very well-defined power structure nonetheless. Contractual vertical marketing systems have experienced phenomenal growth in the last 15 years, and generally assume one of three different forms: the franchise, the voluntary organization or the coopera-

---

[10] These figures are from McCammon, "The Emergence and Growth of Contractually Integrated Channels," p. 497.

[11] As of January 1966, "only 19 of the 170 merger complaints issued by the Federal Trade Commission and the Department of Justice could be identified as primarily vertical in form, while an additional 45 concerned acquisitions with both horizontal and vertical or conglomerate and vertical aspects." Thus, about 11 percent of the complaints issued during the first 15 years of the Celler-Kefauver Amendment to the Clayton Act were directed at vertical acquisitions. See Betty Bock, *Mergers and Markets: An Economic Analysis of the First Fifteen Years Under the Merger Act of 1950,* New York: National Industrial Conference Board, 1966, p. 100.

tive. All these contractual vertical marketing systems embody an integration of marketing activities between two or more channel members on a contractual basis. In all instances, the avowed goal of the contractual system is to create a larger and competitively more effective business entity.

The *franchise* has been defined as an arrangement "whereby the franchisor—who has developed a pattern or format for a particular type of business—extends to franchisees the right to conduct such a business provided they follow the established pattern."[12] The focus of power in the franchise system is the franchisor. The franchisor may permit the use of his name, the use of a method of doing business or the resale of his product or service. In return, the franchisee agrees that the conduct of the business will be largely (or exactly) as the franchisor specifies. The franchisee, it should be emphasized, often owns (or is in the process of buying) the physical premises upon which he conducts the business. Thus, the franchisor does not own all the institutions in the channel, as is the case with the corporate system. The franchisor exercises such powers as he may have as a result of a contractual agreement that permits him to do so rather than as a result of his ownership prerogative.

And the franchisor may, himself, occupy virtually any position within the channel—that is he may be essentially a manufacturer (Midas Mufflers); he may be essentially a service specialist (Kelly Girl and Manpower, employment agencies); he may be a retailer franchising other retailers. Indeed, because the universe of franchise agreements is quite complex, we will do well to identify some of the major types of such agreements. An especially useful set of classes identifies: (a) the manufacturer-retailer franchise, (b) the manufacturer-wholesaler franchise and (c) the service sponsor-retailer franchise.[13] This classification emphasizes the vertical nature of these agreements, and it will also provide a convenient means to distinguish among what are otherwise indistinguishable business entities.

The manufacturer-retailer franchise agreement is exemplified by the new passenger car and truck business. Virtually all such cars and trucks are sold through a franchise dealer system. The manufacturer-wholesaler franchise agreement is exemplified by the soft drink industry. Coca-Cola, Pepsi-Cola, Royal Crown Cola and Seven-Up all operate through a system of franchised wholesalers; these soft drink companies are, in effect, manufacturers of soft drink syrups. The service sponsor-retailer franchise agreement is especially visible today. Well-known service sponsors (franchisors) include Avis, Hertz and National (car rental); McDonald's, Chicken Delight, Col. Saunder's Kentucky Fried Chicken, Taco-Tio (prepared foods); Howard

[12] Edwin H. Lewis and Robert S. Hancock, *The Franchise System of Distribution,* Minneapolis: University of Minnesota Press, 1963, p. 8.
[13] See this set of classes elaborated in William P. Hall, "Franchising—New Scope for an Old Technique," *Harvard Business Review,* January-February 1964, pp. 60–72.

Johnson's and Holiday Inn (lodgings and food); Manpower and Kelly Girl (employment agencies); Midas and Aamco (auto transmission repair); and many, many others.[14]

The second type of contractual vertical marketing system, the *voluntary organization*, is exemplified by the Independent Grocers Alliance (IGA). In this case, the voluntary agreement is between a wholesale organization (IGA) and a large number of independently owned retail "members." In effect, IGA is a franchisor (wholesale) and the member stores are franchisees; but there is longstanding convention for identifying this particular type of organization as a "voluntary wholesale arrangement." We will therefore honor that convention. Note that the wholesale enterprise—IGA—represents the power source in this channel. Note also that the contractual agreement may specify the type and amount of purchases the member must place with the organization wholesaler. In return, the members of the voluntary arrangement enjoy the lower prices of the larger buying organization and the management expertise of the power source within the channel.

Finally, there is the *cooperative* form of contractual vertical marketing system, which is easily confused with the voluntary system. The cooperative contractual system involves the common ownership of a wholesale organization by a number of retail businesses, each of which is independent of the other. The cooperative wholesaler is, literally, owned by its customers—and in this instance, those customers are the retail businesses served by it. The source of power is normally the wholesale enterprise, dedicated as it is to the welfare of the member (owner) firms. Coordination of the activities of the owner firms is achieved largely through the actions of the wholesale enterprise.

Of the several types of vertical marketing systems that we have discussed, students seem most regularly to confuse the corporate system, the voluntary system and the cooperative system. Figure 14.4 will assist in distinguishing these three types of vertical marketing systems.

Note in Figure 14.4 that the corporate VMS embodies both vertical and horizontal ownership. The connective lines denote common ownership. Thus, in the corporate VMS depicted, manufacturer, wholesaler and all the retailers are *commonly* owned. Note the total absence of the connective ownership lines in the voluntary VMS; the wholesaler and each of the member retail firms are independently owned. The cooperative VMS is between the corporate system and the voluntary system in terms of ownership characteristics. The cooperative system features common own-

---

[14] Still another type of franchise, the determination of which involves some value judgment, is the "restricted" or "restrictive" franchise. This type is defined as a franchise system in which the number of sellers is "limited below the number that would be observed with (free) entry." See this idea discussed in Bedros Peter Pashigian, *The Distribution of Automobiles, An Economic Analysis of the Franchise System,* Englewood Cliffs, N.J.: Prentice-Hall, Inc., 1961, pp. 14–15.

ership of the wholesale enterprise by independent (of each other) retail firms.

Figure 14.4 Vertical Marketing Systems

Corporate VMS

```
        ┌──────────────┐
        │ Manufacturer │
        └──────┬───────┘
               │
        ┌──────────────┐
        │  Wholesaler  │
        └──────────────┘
```

[R]──[R]──[R]──[R]──[R]──[R]──[R]

Cooperative VMS

```
   ┌────────────┐
   │ Wholesaler │
   └────────────┘
```

[R] [R] [R] [R] [R] [R]

Voluntary VMS

```
   ┌────────────┐
   │ Wholesaler │
   └────────────┘
```

[R] [R] [R] [R] [R] [R]

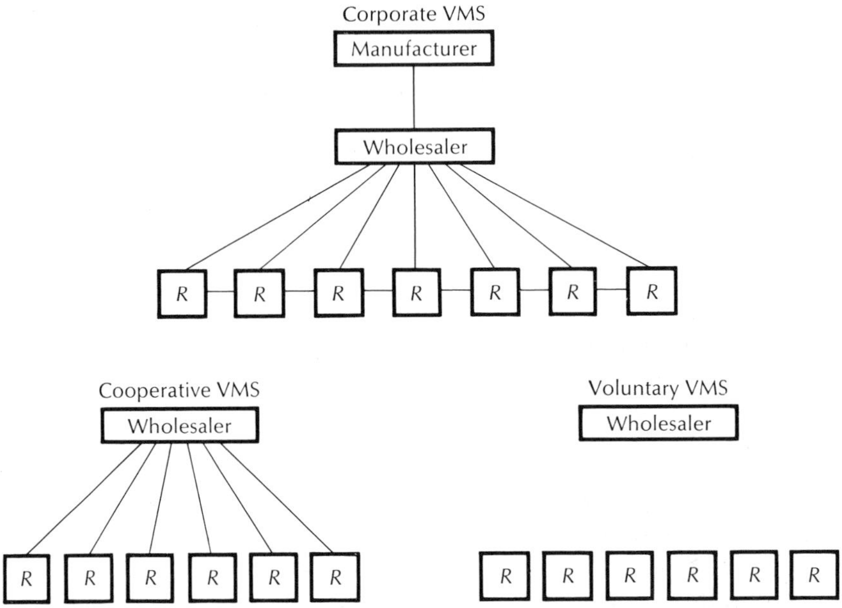

The vertical marketing system and dealer/distributor responsiveness

We have seen that vertical marketing systems are developed in order to achieve a degree of control over the cost and the quality of the activities performed by the various channel members. Often, the manufacturer sits in a position of power at the origin of the channel, controlling, through various means and with varying degrees of precision, the activities of "his" distributor/dealer network. From the point of view of the manufacturer in such a position of power, the channel of distribution may appear as in Figure 14.5.[15]

Observe that from the viewpoint of executive level corporate management, the channel may be defined as three managements: (a) corporate sales management, (b) distributor sales management and (c) dealer sales management. Note also that the first of these three management groups is labeled "responsive," and the others are labeled "nonresponsive." These terms, responsive and nonresponsive, may not be especially well chosen.

[15] This figure is adapted from T. A. Staudt and Donald A. Taylor, *A Managerial Introduction to Marketing*, Englewood Cliffs, N. J.: Prentice-Hall, Inc., 1965, p. 329. Although the figure used here is a simplified version of the Staudt and Taylor "total line organization," it conveys virtually the same thought.

Figure 14.5 Dealer/Distributor Responsiveness

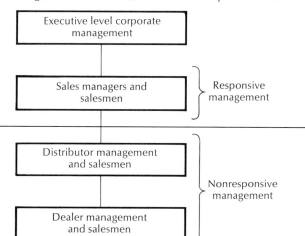

They are not intended to suggest, for example, that distributor and dealer management is totally unresponsive to the wishes of corporate management. The terms suggest, instead, a matter of degree. Corporate management has line control over its own sales management team; the responsiveness of that group is, relatively speaking, assured. Corporate management does not have anything like line control over the distributor/dealer management groups; these latter groups are, relatively speaking, nonresponsive. These distributor/dealer management groups are, effectively, "independent businessmen who are neither employed nor paid by the manufacturer, who generally carry other product lines, and who have other commitments and demands upon their time and resources."[16]

But because these nonresponsive groups have an extremely important role in the success of the manufacturer's product line, he must develop ways to secure their cooperation. The "administered" vertical marketing system is the course of action most often selected. And efforts to create a vertical marketing system administratively may be developed through the use of: (a) monetary incentives, (b) promotional incentives and (c) inventory protection incentives.

Monetary incentives are often used to encourage responsiveness from both distributors and dealers. Perhaps the most obvious of these monetary incentives is the margin, or markup, that the channel member is given. The greater the margin, the greater the responsiveness of the middleman. But monetary incentives also take the form of PM's—a trade term for "push money." These PM's encourage interest in, and special efforts in behalf of, particular products by offering cash bonuses based on the number of units sold.

[16] *Ibid.,* p. 328.

The types of promotional incentives that are used in efforts to achieve a degree of distributor/dealer responsiveness are diverse. These promotional incentives include cooperative advertising, with mat services and point-of-purchase materials being a frequent part of that "cooperation." All manner of dealer/distributor sales training programs are likewise used to induce or encourage channel responsiveness. These sales training programs include special schooling on new products, key-man plans, and the use of missionary salesmen.

Inventory protection incentives are similarly diverse, but extremely liberal cash discount periods (such as future datings) exemplify this type of plan. Another inventory protection scheme is to give distributor/dealers 100 percent return privileges. In effect, the manufacturer assumes the risk of ownership. These inventory protection plans may also attempt to protect the dealer from some of the costs of rapid product obsolescence.[17]

SUMMARY

It has been the purpose of Chapter 14 to examine the reasons why channels of distribution evolve. Our principal task has been to identify concepts and theories that attempt to explain the particular kind of economic activities that specialized marketing institutions perform. Toward this end, we identified: (a) the functional theory of channel development, (b) the gap theory of channel development, (c) the transactional efficiency explanation of channels, (d) the pipeline (or capacity) theory of channel development, and (e) a vertical systems explanation of channel development.

Each of these five basic viewpoints provided a different kind of insight into the channel of distribution. The functional viewpoint emphasized the idea that a channel of distribution is a set of activities to be performed in the promotion and distribution of goods and services. These activities may be shared by several institutions, or they may be performed by a single firm. Indeed, some of these activities may be performed by final consumers. The gap theory emphasized the idea that there is often a substantial difference between ideal conditions for production (supply) and ideal conditions for consumption (demand). The channel of distribution evolves in part in order to resolve these differences.

The principle of transactional efficiency suggests that specialization in distribution tends to reduce the number of exchange transactions required to effect complete exchange in a specialized economic system. The nature of this gain is suggested by the term $\frac{n-1}{2}$, where n represents the number of specialized producers in the economic system. The pipeline theory

---

[17] See, for example, Ralph Westfall and Harper W. Boyd, Jr., *Cases in Marketing Management*, Homewood, Ill.: Richard D. Irwin, Inc., pp. 229-234, which reprints Article II of the Bell and Howell "Declaration of Interdependence." See especially p. 231.

suggests that channels act in a role analogous to water pipes. Channels thus expand (or contract) in total capacity as the quantity of goods or services expands (or contracts).

Finally, the channel of distribution was viewed as a system having more or less well-defined internal power characteristics. It was this latter perspective that led us to the concept of vertical marketing systems. These systems were classified as: (a) corporate systems, (b) administered systems and (c) contractual systems. Contractual vertical marketing systems included franchise systems, voluntary systems and cooperative systems.

REVIEW QUESTIONS

1 Carefully define and indicate the relevance of each of the following concepts to the study of marketing:
  a. The functional view of distribution channels
  b. The gap theory of distribution channels
  c. Breaking bulk
  d. Transactional efficiency
  e. T_g
  f. Channel capacity
  g. Nongoods services
  h. A vertical marketing system
  i. An administered VMS
  j. PM
  k. Mat services

2 Distinguish carefully between each element in the following pairs of terms:
  a. The quantity gap *and* the assortment gap
  b. $T_{w/o}$ *and* T_w
  c. A high capacity channel *and* a low capacity channel
  d. A vertical organizational structure *and* a flat organizational structure
  e. A corporate vertical marketing system *and* an administered vertical marketing system
  f. A voluntary vertical marketing system *and* a cooperative vertical marketing system

3 Specifically, how do manufacturers attempt to create administered vertical marketing systems? That is, what methods do they employ to administer a channel?

4 What is a franchise system of distribution? What are the basic types of franchise agreements?

5 What advantages are there, from a manufacturer's point of view, to creating a vertical marketing system? Answer as completely as you can.

DISCUSSION QUESTIONS

6 Suppose that there were no wholesalers or retailers. How would your behavior as a consumer be changed?

7 As a kind of mini-project, identify the nature of the channels of distribution that connect:
   a. Automobile manufacturers and automobile buyers
   b. Food processors and consumer households
   c. Soft drink bottlers and consumer households
   d. Soft drink bottlers and drug store fountains
   e. Prescription pharmaceutical manufacturers and final consumers.

Chapter 15

DISTRIBUTION CHANNELS: TYPES AND COMPONENTS

In the preceding chapter, we considered several different explanations of why channels of distribution evolve. We identified, in the course of that discussion: (a) the functional explanation of channels, (b) an economic gap explanation of channels, (c) an explanation of channel development that centered upon transactional efficiency, (d) the pipeline, or capacity, explanation and (e) some of the power aspects of channels of distribution. Our task in the present chapter is to develop two further points about channels of distribution. We need, first, to identify some of the specific types of distribution channels that evolve and, second, to define some of the basic types of marketing specialists that make up these channels of distribution.

More specifically, in the discussion that follows, we will examine the concepts of: (a) the fully integrated channel, (b) the intensive channel, (c) the selective channel, (d) the exclusive channel, (e) the multiple channel and (f) the intermittent channel. We will also consider such basic institutional forms as: (a) multiunit organizations, (b) general merchandise outlets, (c) shopping centers and (d) some of the most important forms of wholesalers.

Distribution channels—some basic types

To this point in our discussion of channels, we have thought of a channel of distribution as though it originated with a manufacturing process. We have, primarily as a means of simplification, depicted the channel of distribution as a set of economic institutions beginning with a manufacturer of some kind and culminating at the retail stage of distribution.[1] In fact,

---

[1] See, for example, Figures 15.1, 15.2 and 15.5.

however, a channel of distribution may contain several different manufacturing stages and several different wholesale stages. In one sense, a channel
of distribution must begin with a *raw material* and culminate with sale
to the final consumer. And this fact, that there are often channels of
distribution behind (or preceding) other channels of distribution, is a
potential source of ambiguity. As a means of clarifying this matter, consider
Figure 15.1.

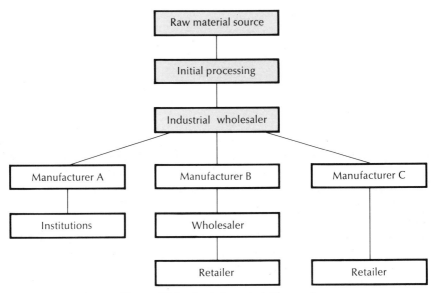

Figure 15.1   An Integrated Channel

Figure 15.1 depicts three different channels of distribution that share,
or have in common, several institutions. Note that the three institutions
labeled "raw material source," "initial processing," and "industrial wholesaler" are a part of each of the three channels that evolve below them.
When a complete set of institutions—running from raw material to final
consumer—is owned by a single business interest, we say that that channel
is *fully integrated*. Examples of fully integrated channels of distribution
are found in the petroleum business, in food distribution, and in many
other instances. It is not uncommon for a petroleum company to own
oil deposits, refining facilities, bulk tank stations (wholesalers) and retail
service stations. It is likewise not uncommon for a large food distributor
(such as A&P) to own coffee plantations, coffee processing plants, and
both wholesale and retail facilities for the distribution of coffee products.

But channels of distribution are also distinguished in terms of the type
of market coverage that they provide. Some channels of distribution provide what might be called ubiquitous, or intensive, coverage; some channels provide what is referred to as exclusive coverage. We introduced the

notion of channel length in Chapter 13, and it will be worthwhile for us to recall that idea. A long channel was defined as one in which there are a large number of intermediaries, or marketing specialists. Channel length refers not to physical distance but to the number of market specialists involved in the distribution and sale of a particular product or related group of products. And the long channel of distribution tends to produce more complete market coverage. It will be recalled that distribution leverage with the long channel is relatively great. Long channels of distribution, therefore, correspond with intensive distribution coverage; and shorter, more direct, channels of distribution correspond generally with what we call exclusive distribution coverage.

An *intensive channel of distribution* provides convenient contact with the largest possible number of potential buyers. The intensive channel of distribution, because it utilizes the services of many wholesale and retail firms, tends to create greater place convenience for the buyer. The intensive channel of distribution goes wherever the prospect might be—at home (supermarket sales), in public places (vending machines), or virtually anywhere else. One estimate is that Coca-Cola is available through no fewer than 1.6 million retail outlets.[2]

The truly *exclusive channel of distribution,* in contrast, places the product in only one outlet in each market. The exclusive channel makes sense when the product has a very specialized use, and the number of prospective buyers is therefore relatively small. Many very expensive, high quality, products are distributed through what are very nearly exclusive channels of distribution. Cameras such as Leica and Hasselblad have been distributed exclusively. Similarly, products that require special dealer (retailer) training are good candidates for restricted, if not exclusive, distribution channels.

Intensive distribution and exclusive distribution represent polar positions—limiting cases—on a spectrum that embodies the number of possible retail outlets that might be used. For many products, the right degree of market exposure lies somewhere between the intensive case and the exclusive case. We recognize therefore, in addition to these two basic types of distribution, a third case—*selective distribution.* Selective distribution is the term used to designate a controlled selection of dealers—and often a purposeful restriction of the number of dealers permitted to sell the product. Selective distribution results, then, in the appointment of several dealers in any given market, the exact number being determined by the market potential. Thus, a manufacturer of men's suits may appoint one dealer for every 100,000 persons in a metropolitan area; an automobile manufacturer may create one dealer for every 60,000 persons. Dealers who are members of a selective group are likely to be chosen on the basis

[2] William R. Davidson, "Innovation in Distribution," in M. S. Moyer and R. E. Vosburgh, editors, *Marketing for Tomorrow—Today,* 1967 June Conference Proceedings, American Marketing Association, p. 35.

of their ability to implement the general policies of the manufacturer whose products they are selling.

Two other types of channels occur frequently enough to merit our brief attention. These additional types are the multiple channel and the intermittent channel. A *multiple channel of distribution* occurs when a given product is distributed through several different combinations of institutions to several different markets or market segments. A manufacturer of hand tools might, for example, use one channel of distribution to provide the requirements of (say) manufacturing businesses and another for the requirements of home owners. Multiple channels may develop along a domestic-international dichotomy. Thus, for example, a firm that sells to both domestic and international markets may serve those two markets through two (or more) different distribution channels. A special form of multiple channel is exemplified by the practice of distributing different brands through different channels although the basic product is essentially the same. Thus, for example the Outboard Marine Corporation, maker of both Johnson and Evinrude products, maintains separate channels for those two brands. One well-known manufacturer of typewriters sells under both a manufacturer's brand and a dealer's brand name—and different channels are employed. General Electric makes both the GE line of home appliances and the Hotpoint line: different channels of distribution are maintained for these two lines.

Some channels of distribution are *intermittent;* that is, they do not function continuously. Consider, for example, the case of July 4th fireworks stands. The distinctly seasonal nature of the demand for these products produces a temporary channel of distribution. Consider, further, the stores that open for the rush of the Christmas season but close when the rush is over. Toy stores in particular afford an example of channel intermittency. Extremely good margins on some toys thus lure some entrepreneurs into the retail business on a two- or three-month basis. Normally, a short-term lease is taken on an otherwise vacant downtown property. These intermittent channels represent a special type of temporary increase in channel capacity. In this instance, the capacity of the channel is temporarily increased and then permitted to return to normal size. The student should note that this adaptation in the capacity of a channel may occur within a store, as well as with the addition of new outlets. The capacity of the channel is altered within the store when the space given to various lines of merchandise is adjusted to meet seasonal variations in demand. Thus, for example, virtually all major department stores provide much more floor space for toys in the pre-Christmas weeks than at other times.

Multiunit organizations as channel elements

Multiunit organizations are an extremely important part of many distribution channels. As we will employ the term here, multiunit organizations are those that include more than one outlet, all of which serve the same stage of distribution. Typically, multiunit organizations have been most influential at the retail level of distribution. And, as the principle of distribution leverage suggested earlier, multiunit organizations are important because they provide efficient contact with a relatively large segment of some market. Types of multiunit organizations that have particular importance in the context of channels of distribution include: (a) chains, (b) common ownership groups and (c) franchise arrangements. Any of these types of multiunit organizations can provide efficient market access for a manufacturer.

The *chain organization* is one that has two or more outlets with the following characteristics:

1 They are commonly owned and controlled.
2 They sell similar lines of merchandise.
3 They are, to an important degree, centrally merchandised.
4 They may incorporate a similar architectural motif.

Several of these characteristics of the chain organization deserve clarification. First, the exact number of units required to constitute a chain is arbitrary.[3] We have elected to use "two or more" in order to provide maximum latitude to the concept. Second, the common ownership and control characteristic is an extremely important requirement. The economic advantage of the chain traces to its collective size—that is, the aggregate size of all the individual units that constitute the chain. The efficiency of the chain organization is, in large measure, a result of the common ownership and centralized control of the activities of the total organization. And when we specify that the chain is, to an important degree, centrally merchandised, we highlight another important attribute of this multiunit organizational type. The "centrally merchandised" requirement means that the true chain takes maximum advantage of its collective size by buying the requirements of the entire organization in one or a few massive orders, thereby securing the advantage of maximum quantity discounts.

The retail organization that is most nearly the prototype chain today is the supermarket organization. Such multiunit organizations as Kroger, A&P and Safeway, meet most of the requirements of a chain that have been specified above. But there are chain-like organizations that present all the external appearances of a chain, but which fail in some significant ways to meet the conditions of our list of prototype requirements. These facsimiles tend to fall into one of two classes: common ownership groups and franchises.

The *common ownership group* embodies all the requirements of a chain except that it is not centrally merchandised. That is, the common ownership

---

[3] The U.S. Bureau of the Census has variously defined the actual number of units constituting a chain at from two or more to over a hundred units.

group comprises several outlets that are commonly owned, selling similar lines of merchandise, but whose merchandise requirements are not purchased centrally. Each unit in the common ownership group enjoys a degree of autonomy within the organization. Multiunit department store organizations exemplify the common ownership group. And it is generally presumed that differences in merchandise preferences among the clientele of the various stores in the group effectively preclude complete centralization of purchasing by the members of a common ownership group.

The *franchise organization* often presents the external appearance of a chain; we have seen, however, that the individual units of a franchise organization are very often independently, not commonly, owned.

Shopping centers as channel elements

The shopping center is an increasingly important element in the distribution plans of large business enterprise. And for many manufacturers, an inability to achieve representation for their products in some types of shopping centers is a potentially significant impediment to growth. There are four types of center, or cluster, institutions that are important today. These basic types of centers are: (a) the central business district, (b) the regional shopping center, (c) the community shopping center and (d) the neighborhood shopping center.

THE CENTRAL BUSINESS DISTRICT

The central business district (CBD) has undergone a gradual relative decline in importance since about 1950. It is important to note that this decline has been relative; while the CBD presently accounts for a greater total dollar volume than in the past, it accounts for a smaller percentage of total retail sales. The central business district is normally defined by the following attributes:

1 It is often situated at or near the point of convergence of the major radial streets in a city.
2 It is often the focus of operations of public conveyences.
3 It is made up of a cluster of stores in which apparel and home furnishings are the most frequent offering.
4 It is, in larger cities, distinguishable as two areas: the core and the frame.

The central business district has been the principal focus for the sale of shopping goods in the United States. The American department store has for many years been the dominant distributive force in the CBD. The CBD core is characterized by very intensive land usage—indeed the core area of the CBD tends to grow vertically rather than horizontally. The primary mode of movement within the CBD core is pedestrian, and the peripheral limits of the core are defined by convenient walking distances.

The CBD core is the natural habitat, as it were, of the department store and the specialty apparel shop.[4] The CBD core "does not exceed one square mile in size and tends to average 30 square blocks."[5]

The central business district frame area, in contrast, is less intensively utilized. Rents are relatively lower, and businesses are more likely to be based on a low margin, high turnover philosophy. Businesses that require substantial area for display or storage of inventories make sense in the frame area or in outlying areas. Census data indicate that the frame area is most important in the distribution of automobiles and auto supplies, lumber, building materials, and hardware.[6]

The dominance of the CBD as a distributive institution was eroded rapidly after World War II. This decline was the result of many interrelated factors. Widespread ownership of private automobiles meant less dependence upon CBD oriented public conveyences. Crowded conditions in the core area made parking very difficult and shopping was often less than pleasurable. High real estate values and rentals in the CBD encouraged prospective retailers to look to other areas for growth potential. Growing consumer interest in the suburbs as a place of residence made the CBD relatively less accessible. And the result of this general challenge of the CBD concept was the beginning of what might properly be called the decentralized era in American retailing. The process of decentralization of American retailing has produced three planned types of outlying shopping centers, which may be distinguished in terms of their size and the nature of the merchandise assortments they offer.

THE REGIONAL SHOPPING CENTER

The largest of the outlying shopping centers is the "regional" center. The regional shopping center serves a market of from 100,000 to 1,000,000 population within a 30-minute driving radius. These regional shopping centers have from 40 to over 100 stores and may contain in excess of one million square feet of gross leasable area.[7] It is a further distinguishing mark that the regional shopping center carries primarily a shopping goods assortment. That is, although regional centers are likely to contain some convenience goods outlets, the great bulk of their sales is of shopping or comparison goods. The generative strength—the customer pulling power— of the regional shopping center is usually developed around one or more

[4] See Louis C. Wagner, "A Realistic Division of Downtown Retailing," *Journal of Marketing,* July 1964, pp. 39–42.
[5] See R. F. Murphy and J. C. Vance, Jr., "A Comparative Study of Nine Central Business Districts," *Economic Geography,* October 1954, pp. 302–330.
[6] See Wagner, *op. cit.,* p. 41.
[7] For a more complete examination of the important types of centers or clusters, see Ronald R. Gist, *Retailing: Concepts and Decisions,* New York: John Wiley & Sons, Inc., 1968, pp. 48–61. See also Frank Meissner, "Planned Shopping Centers," in Ronald R. Gist, editor, *Management Perspectives in Retailing,* New York: John Wiley & Sons, Inc., 1967, pp. 86–93.

full-line department stores. Early regional shopping centers were developed like a wheel around one large generator—as was Detroit's Northland Center. The two generator model subsequently became very popular. This design features two strong department stores at the opposite ends of either a tunnel mall or an eave mall. Figure 15.2 depicts these two versions of the two generator regional shopping center design.

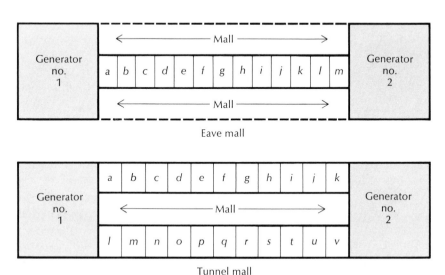

Figure 15.2 Mall Centers

Note that the connecting stem of stores in the eave mall (labeled *a* through *m*) leaves a wide pedestrian mall on both sides of the center under which customers are protected from adverse weather. Note that the tunnel mall design is developed around two connecting stems of specialty shops. This is ideal for the climate-controlled (domed) center. Many of the regional shopping centers built during the 1960's are of the two generator mall type.

During the late 1960's regional centers began to feature three and even four generator designs. Indeed, some of the more recent designs are developed on two or more levels. The Lakewood shopping center in Los Angeles, the Englewood Center in Denver, and the Westroads Center in Omaha exemplify this tendency to more than two generative units and multiple level structures. Figure 15.3 depicts the design prototypes for a three generator and a four generator regional shopping center.

Both the three and four generator centers encourage a peripheral pedestrian traffic pattern. When these centers are properly designed and planned, traffic flows are well balanced in all parts of the inner area. That is, there are no points or areas in which little or no shopper traffic is generated.

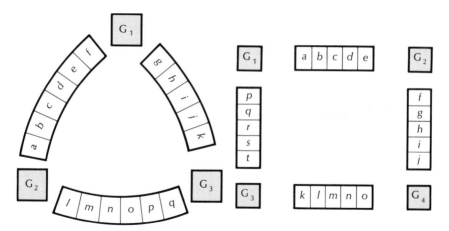

Figure 15.3   Three Generator and Four Generator Malls

Again, the small letters in Figure 15.3 represent complementary specialty shops of various types.

THE COMMUNITY SHOPPING CENTER

The shopping center of intermediate size is called a community shopping center and serves a population of from 20,000 to 100,000. It normally contains from 100,000 to 300,000 square feet of gross leasable area. As a rule of thumb, about 90 percent of the clientele of the community center resides within a radius of 1.5 miles of the center.[8] The major generative unit in a community shopping center is normally either a department store branch or a full-stock variety store. Such operations as J. J. Newberry, W. T. Grant or F. W. Woolworth often dominate the community center. And the merchandise assortments found in these centers represent a mixture of both shopping and convenience goods. The community shopping center most often assumes either an **L** or an **I** configuration. And it is not uncommon to find the shopping goods stores concentrated at the "origin" of the **L** type or near the center of the **I** type. Figure 15.4 will clarify this latter feature of the community shopping center.

Note that the major generator in the **L** type center depicted in Figure 15.4 is normally the primary shopping goods outlet in the community center. It is customary to find the stores immediately adjacent to the generator selling complementary shopping goods. Indeed, as one moves from the middle of the community shopping center toward the ends, one

[8] Recent research has been directed to the more systematic identification of these distances. See, for example, Bernard J. LaLonde, *Differentials in Supermarket Drawing Power*, Marketing and Transportation Paper 11, East Lansing, Mich.: Michigan State University Press, 1962, p. 37.

often moves through a progression from shopping goods to convenience goods. Outlets that develop very heavy traffic, such as supermarkets, may occupy the end positions in these community centers.

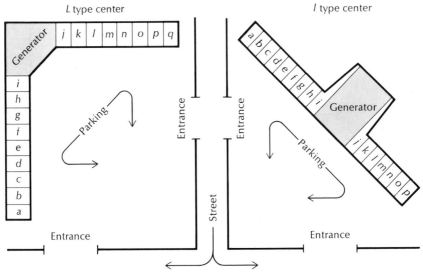

Figure 15.4 Community Shopping Centers

THE NEIGHBORHOOD SHOPPING CENTER

The smallest, and most numerous, shopping centers are those that serve a neighborhood area. These neighborhood centers normally contain from 5 to 15 stores and serve a population of less than 10,000 residents. The neighborhood center enjoys a substantial level of walk-in trade and pulls a clientele from no farther than a 5-minute driving time radius.[9] The neighborhood shopping center specializes in the distribution of convenience goods. Such stores as the supermarket, the small variety store outlet, the drugstore and small service establishments represent the usual composition of the neighborhood shopping center. The service establishments may include dry cleaning establishments, self-service laundries, appliance and shoe repair shops, and so forth. The neighborhood center is frequently an unplanned center—at least in the sense that the developer has no especially well-defined plans for tenancy of the units in the center. That is, the neighborhood center may be a loose coalition of stores that are situated in a strip-like configuration, with little or no thought given to central planning for the center itself.

[9] See Samuel Feinberg, *What Makes Shopping Centers Tick?* New York: Fairchild Publications Inc., 1960, p. 1.

Wholesale organizations as channel elements

To this point in our discussion, most of our interest has been focused on retailing institutions—those that serve final consumers. But wholesale institutions—those serving retailers and other businesses—are an extremely important part of the channels of American distribution.[10] Throughout the discussion that follows we will use the terms wholesaler, jobber and distributor as synonyms. A useful means of distinguishing various types of wholesalers is suggested by the terms "agent wholesaler" and "merchant wholesaler."

Agent wholesalers do not take title to the merchandise they sell. They act in the best interests of their principal (the firm that buys their services), and they are usually paid on a commission basis. The agent wholesaler may sell to manufacturers, to other wholesalers or to retailers. It is useful, initially, to think of the agent wholesaler as a specialized marketing institution that can either provide a manufacturer with selling assistance if the manufacturer has no sales force of his own or supplement the manufacturer's sales force in areas that are not, for one reason or another, readily accessible to him. Agent wholesalers may work continuously for a particular firm, or they may work on an intermittent basis. In the latter instance, they may be called free-lance agents.

Agent wholesalers include: (a) food brokers, (b) manufacturers' agents, (c) selling agents, and (d) some specialized forms of agent wholesalers that have evolved to meet particular selling problems.

The *food broker* is an extremely important part of distribution channels that culminate with the supermarket. A manufacturer (or packer) of food products often uses the food broker as a means of achieving entrée to chain retail organizations. The authority of the food broker is defined by his agreement with his principal—that agreement may empower him to find a buyer (or a seller) for a single sale, or it may contemplate a continuous relationship. Though it is difficult to generalize, it can be said that the basic function of the food broker is to provide information both to and for his principal. The food broker serves as a sales organization for food packers that do not possess such organizations of their own.

The *manufacturers' agent* represents a good example of the manner in which specialized wholesale organizations evolve to meet particular problems in selling and distribution. Consider, for example, the case of a manufacturer of a narrow line of products—say radio and tape-deck equipment. The manufacturer may find that there is sufficient demand for his products in heavily populated areas to warrant the use of his own sales force in those areas. But because the volume potential of his line of products alone will not support a sales force in other, less densely populated areas, he is unable to achieve anything like complete market cover-

[10] It is not always easy to identify a particular outlet as being a retail or a wholesale business. Some reselling operations sell to both final consumers and to other businesses.

age. The manufacturers' agent is an answer to his problem. The manufacturers' agent—because he sells the products of several (noncompeting) manufacturers—can achieve sufficient volume to sustain his operation in areas where that would not be feasible with a smaller product offering.

To be more specific, the manufacturers' agent stands ready to assist a manufacturer with the sale of his product (a) in a defined market or territory, (b) usually on a continuous rather than a free-lance basis, and (c) usually with little or no authority to bargain prices or terms of sale in behalf of his principal. In addition to emphasizing the fact that the manufacturers' agent provides sales efforts for the manufacturer in otherwise inaccessible areas, it is important to note that this type of agent can often provide more aggressive sales assistance than other forms of wholesalers. Because the manufacturers' agent tends to specialize in a relatively more narrow line of products than a full-service wholesaler, he is able to develop a degree of expertise with his products that is not attained when sales attention is divided among a wider product offering.

The *selling agent* (or, sometimes, *sales agent*) is a third important type of agent wholesaler. While the manufacturers' agent sells only a part of the output of his principal, the selling agent sells all or a major portion of the output of a client. The selling agent thus represents more nearly the entire sales organization of his client firm(s). Moreover, the selling agent is not likely to be encumbered with restrictions or limitations as to the markets or territories in which he may sell. Still further, the selling agent is more likely to be empowered by his principal to bargain or negotiate prices and terms of sale. The selling agent is potentially most helpful to a client when: (a) the manufacturing firm is new and does not have knowledge of or access to the proper distributive organizations, (b) the product line of the manufacturer is neither deep nor wide (the product line alone will not support a sales force or (c) the market itself is a new one.

In addition to the types of wholesale agents that we have identified thus far, there are some specialized forms of agent wholesalers who function to solve more particular selling problems. Examples of these include "merchandise brokers," auctions, and commissioned merchants. The so-called merchandise broker is, in effect, a manufacturers' representative—though he serves as a source of central market information for retailers. That is, he is engaged by a buyer, but compensated by a seller.[11] Though we are perhaps most aware of retail auctions—that is, auctions in which the customers are final consumers—wholesale auctions are reasonably important and have shown substantial recent growth.[12] These

---

[11] For a more complete discussion, see, Gist, *Retailing*, pp. 296–297. See also John W. Wingate and Joseph S. Friedlander, *The Management of Retail Buying*, Englewood Cliffs, N.J.: Prentice-Hall, Inc., 1963.

[12] See P. D. Converse and others, *Elements of Marketing*, Seventh Edition, Englewood Cliffs, N.J.: Prentice-Hall, Inc., 1965, pp. 237–238.

auctions serve as agents in the sense that the auction companies do not have title to the goods they sell. These wholesale auctions are important in the livestock markets and the used automobile market. Another special type of agent wholesaler—alas, one that is significantly misnamed—is the commissioned merchant. This form of wholesale institution is significantly misnamed because it is not a merchant at all. The word "merchant" normally signifies an institution having title to the goods it sells—and the commissioned merchant does not have title to what it sells. The commissioned merchant functions primarily in the grain and livestock markets, receiving goods on consignment from producers and usually enjoying some power to negotiate in behalf of its principal.

A second major class of wholesale organizations is the *merchant wholesaler*. The merchant wholesaler has title to the merchandise he resells, and it is customary to divide such wholesalers into two basic classes: the full-service merchant wholesaler and the limited-service, or limited-function, wholesaler. The margin (difference between cost and selling price) of the merchant wholesaler is normally greater than for the agent wholesaler. That greater margin reflects the risk of ownership—a risk not borne by the agent middleman.

Service merchant wholesalers have expenses that average very nearly 15 percent of their net sales. The services they perform include any or all of the following: (a) inventory storage, (b) buying and selling and (c) extension of credit to customers (financing). Specialized forms of the service wholesaler include wagon wholesalers and rack wholesalers. *Wagon wholesalers* deal in perishable goods—goods having a relatively short shelf life—and they normally work a route of stores. The wagon wholesaler thus provides and maintains fresh merchandise to a group of retail stores. The term "wagon" suggests that these wholesalers carry their stocks on a truck and make very frequent delivery. *Rack wholesalers* were extremely important in the introduction of nonfood items of merchandise into supermarkets. The rack wholesalers, in effect, manage space provided for them by the retailer: they place display racks of toys, gloves, records, socks, or whatever, and maintain a full display. They may also have responsibility for pricing the merchandise that they rack. The rack wholesaler has expenses that average very nearly 19 percent of his sales.

Limited-service wholesalers include those that are "cash-and-carry" and curiously, those that do not carry inventories of the merchandise they sell. Cash-and-carry wholesalers, as the term suggests, do not finance their customers. "Drop shippers" are a special type of limited-service merchant wholesaler that do not actually possess the goods that they sell. These drop shippers (or desk jobbers) deal in merchandise that is standardized or graded. This standardization or grading permits the resale of the goods on the basis of accurate description, and physical inspection is not necessary. Products that may be drop-shipped include lumber and agricultural products of various types ranging from grain to fresh vegetables and fruit.

These drop shippers may buy and sell "rolling." That is, a particular drop shipper may buy a quantity of (say) apples loaded and moving from the Pacific Northwest toward the Chicago market. He may locate a Midwest buyer before the shipment arrives at its destination and negotiate the sale of the shipment before its arrival.

SUMMARY

The purpose of Chapter 15 has been to identify some of the most important forms of distribution channels and to examine some of the important components of these channels. Our discussion introduced the concepts of the fully integrated channel, the intensive channel and the exclusive channel. In addition, the concept of the multiple channel and the concept of the intermittent channel were identified.

Multiunit organizations—including chains, common ownership groups and franchise arrangements—were identified as an important type of channel component. Shopping centers—including the central business district—were identified as channel components of increasing importance. These centers include the regional center, the community center and the neighborhood center. Some of the design and size characteristics of these centers were briefly noted.

Finally, some wholesale organizations that may represent particularly important channel components were noted. Agent wholesalers are those that do not have title to the goods they sell. Agent wholesalers include food brokers, manufacturers' agents and selling agents, as well as some more specialized forms. Merchant wholesalers assume the risk of ownership and may be classified as full-service and limited-service institutions. Wagon and rack wholesalers exemplify full-service wholesale organizations. Cash-and-carry wholesalers and drop shippers exemplify limited-service wholesale institutions.

REVIEW QUESTIONS

1 Carefully define and indicate the relevance of each of the following concepts to the study of marketing:
   a. An industrial channel of distribution
   b. A consumer channel of distribution
   c. A fully integrated channel of distribution
   d. Selective distribution
   e. A multiple channel of distribution
   f. An intermittent channel of distribution
   g. A chain organization
   h. A regional shopping center
   i. An eave mall center design
   j. A tunnel mall center design
   k. The community shopping center
   l. Wagon wholesalers
   m. Rack wholesalers
   n. Drop shippers

2 Distinguish carefully between each element in the following pairs of terms:
  a. Intensive distribution *and* exclusive distribution
  b. A chain organization *and* a common ownership group
  c. The central business district core *and* the central business district frame
  d. A regional shopping center *and* a neighborhood shopping center
  e. An **L** type community shopping center *and* an **I** type community shopping center
  f. Agent wholesalers *and* merchant wholesalers
  g. Selling, or sales, agents *and* manufacturers' agents

DISCUSSION QUESTIONS
3 Marketing institutions represent a particular kind of specialization and division of labor. Do you agree or disagree? Why?
4 What type of channel or channels of distribution would be most appropriate for each of the following products: Why?
  a. Automobiles
  b. Clothing
  c. Food
  d. Soft drinks
  e. Pianos
  f. Computers

Chapter 16

THEORIES OF CHANGE IN MARKETING INSTITUTIONS

We have now completed a discussion of several theories that purport to explain the development or evolution of marketing channels (Chapter 14). We have also briefly noted some of the important forms of institutions that serve as the elements in distribution channels (Chapter 15). The present chapter is concerned with one further aspect of distribution channels; namely, the nature of the change that the marketing institutions which constitute such channels may undergo.

An understanding of the forces that produce change in marketing institutions is necessarily an important part of understanding our market system. And an ability to predict the nature of the important marketing institutions of the future would clearly be an extremely valuable skill. This kind of predictive ability would permit, for example, the development of channels of distribution today around institutions that are destined for a more important distributive role at some future date. When particular types of marketing institutions begin to grow less important, all the firms that depend upon those declining institutions—all the firms that are a part of the same channel of distribution—suffer to some degree. And this concern with the changing role of various types of marketing institutions has produced a modest collection of theories that attempt to identify the causes of change in distributive institutions and to describe the nature of such change.

These theories of institutional change fall into two general classes. These classes are: (a) adjustment theory and (b) cycle theory. The remainder of the present chapter is devoted to an examination of these two theoretical approaches to the improvement of our understanding of institutional change in marketing.

Adjustment theory and institutional change in marketing

Adjustment theory attempts to explain changes in marketing institutions as a result of prior changes in the environment in which those institutions function. Adjustment theory thus makes the institutional environment the independent phenomenon and the institutional adjustment, or change, the dependent phenomenon in what is sometimes a complex set of causal relationships. More specifically, the adjustment theory of institutional change identifies specific elements that make up the environment of an institution and attempts to identify the relationship between changes in these environmental elements and changes in the characteristics of the institution itself. But all this may sound much more complicated and obscure than it actually is. Consider, as a means of clarification, Figure 16.1.

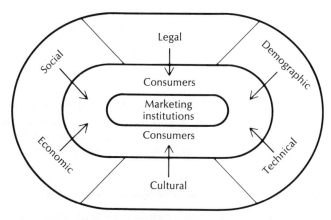

Figure 16.1 Institutional Adjustment Theory

Figure 16.1 identifies more completely the basic notion underlying adjustment theory and change in marketing institutions. Note that the outer band of Figure 16.1 identifies six dimensions of a general environment within which consumers and businesses react. That is, consumers are influenced by their social, legal, demographic, technical, cultural and economic environments. These various environmental elements shape and modify consumer preferences. Thus, for example, a general increase in the real income of consumers (a change in the economic environment) might produce a preference for a type of marketing institution that offers more services—or for one that purveys more elegant merchandise. A change in the social environment—say a general decline in the social role of shopping—may produce a preference for a type of marketing institution that is less personal. The self-service kind of retail operation may be one result. Similarly, a change in technology—say, for example, the perfection of economically feasible means of personal transportaion—may produce new institutional preference patterns among consumers. Consumers may elect to shop in areas not previously thought feasible for retailing.

This kind of reasoning may offer the basis for understanding some important changes in the forms of institutions that constitute marketing channels. The general decentralization of retailing in the United States is, indeed, a special case of adjustment to a changing environment. And one highly regarded study makes a persuasive argument that some institutions enjoy a better growth rate than others because of a superior ability to sense and react to environmental change.[1] We should note the similarity of this adjustment theory to the Darwinian survival-of-the-fittest argument. Darwin's theory of natural selection holds "that a species that most effectively adapts to its environment is most likely to survive and perpetuate its kind." The moth that is virtually indistinguishable from the bark upon which it rests has a relatively high probability of survival. Stated with a slightly different emphasis, of two moths exactly the same in every respect except their coloring, the one least well blended with his environment is the one most likely to become the dinner of some hungry predator and is therefore least likely to pass his color pattern on to succeeding generations. Adjustment theory, as we are most interested in that term, views the marketing institution as an economic species—a species that must adjust in order to survive. The relevant "environment" becomes a social, economic, technical, cultural, legal and demographic complex which shapes and, in turn, is shaped by consumer preferences.

Cycle theory and institutional change in marketing

A second basic approach to understanding institutional change in marketing is suggested by the term *cycle theory*. Cycle theory begins with the premise that, if a rhythm of change is evident in some phenomenon, and if the rhythmic nature of that change can be measured, then (a) factors underlying the change may be identified and (b) the future direction of the cycle can be anticipated or predicted. Most such cycle theories in marketing are, in reality, theories of partial cycles rather than theories of a complete cyclical phenomenon. That is, most cycle theories deal only with the ascension to prominance of some form of institution and its subsequent decline in importance rather than with a repetitive, truly cyclical, wave-like phenomenon. Figure 16.2 will distinguish more clearly between these two types of cycles.

Note that the Type A institutional cycle (the partial cycle) in Figure 16.2 depicts the rise in popularity of some institutional form and its sub-

[1] See Robert Entenberg, *The Changing Competitive Position of Department Stores in the United States by Merchandise Lines*, Pittsburgh, Pa.: University of Pittsburgh Press, 1957. See also Delbert J. Duncan, "Responses of Selected Retail Institutions to Their Changing Environment," in *Marketing and Economic Development*, American Marketing Association Proceedings, 1965, pp. 583–601.

sequent decline in importance. The Type B cycle (the complete cycle) depicts the ultimate return to prominence of an institutional form that has experienced both popularity and decline. In the discussion that follows, we will identify one theory of institutional change that involves a complete cycle, one partial cycle theory of change and one theory of institutional change that combines elements of both a partial and a complete cycle.

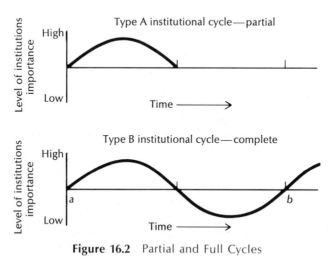

Figure 16.2 Partial and Full Cycles

AN ACCORDIAN THEORY OF INSTITUTIONAL CHANGE IN MARKETING INSTITUTIONS

A very simplistic theory of institutional change is suggested by the term "accordian."[2] The accordian theory asserts that American marketing institutions have been characterized by a complete and repetitive cyclical variation in the nature of the merchandise lines they sell. More specifically, the accordian theory tentatively identifies a complete cycle described alternately by wide merchandise lines and narrow merchandise lines; that is, institutions having general merchandise lines have been displaced by institutions having more specialized lines of merchandise, and these more specialized institutions have, in turn, been displaced by general institutions. Those who see merit in this particular form of cycle theory point to (a) the era of the general store, (b) the subsequent era of the specialty shop and (c) the current trend toward general merchandise retail institutions as evidence in support of the theory.

Note that this accordian theory of institutional change focuses on something called merchandise line width, which may be defined as the number

[2] This theory was developed initially by Edward Brand in *Modern Supermarket Operation,* New York: Fairchild Publications, Inc., 1963, pp. 242-244. The theory was "named" by Stanley Hollander in "Notes on the Retail Accordian," *Journal of Retailing,* Summer 1966, pp. 29-40.

of different generic classes of merchandise carried by the average retail store. The era of the general store was an era in which virtually any human need could be filled in the general store. The general store was not only a source of groceries and clothing, it was a stable, a pub and a post office as well. The width of merchandise lines that characterized the retail industry during that era was great. The era of the specialty shop was, in contrast, an era that required multistop shopping. The era of the specialty shop—quite literally, an era in which the butcher, the baker and the candlestick maker were the retailing norm—was an era characterized by narrow merchandise lines. The accordian theory contends that the recent tendency to diversified merchandise lines in retailing—exemplified by both individual store line-scrambling and the one-stop convenience of clusters or shopping centers—is but another wave of the accordian cycle.

The accordian theory would seem to suggest that the next institutional era will be one in which greater line specialization returns. But note that this theory is essentially descriptive—it does not explicitly identify the causes of cyclical change in the form of retail institutions; it simply points out a symptom of the cycle. The accordian theory is essentially devoid of explanation—and for that reason does not provide particularly satisfying or valuable insight into change in marketing institutions.[3] As we have noted, the real value of institutional theory is in the predictive insight it may give. The accordian cycle theory is perhaps a useful historical summary, but it does not tell us when or where the next wave of the cycle will appear.

THE WHEEL THEORY OF INSTITUTIONAL CHANGE IN MARKETING

Another theory of institutional change in marketing—one that is "partial" in the sense that we have used that term earlier—is called the wheel thesis, or the wheel theory.[4] This theory suggests that innovative marketing institutions undergo an inevitable process of maturation—a process during which they become less and less effective in a competitive sense. To be more specific, the wheel thesis suggests that: (a) a new and innovative form of marketing institution appears, that it (b) gains market acceptance and encourages emulators, and that it (c) gradually trades up the quality of its operation to the point where it is competitively vulnerable to other

[3] Hollander identifies several forces that "promote contraction" (line specialization). These forces include: (a) noneconomic, (b) miscellaneous restraints, (c) capacity, (d) costs and (e) the market. Unfortunately, many of these forces for contraction seem to be forces for expansion as well and do not clarify the essential notion of the accordian theory—namely, why one period of time seems best for contraction and another period of time seems best for line expansion. See Hollander, *op. cit.*, pp. 36–40, 54.

[4] The wheel theory (or thesis) was first identified by Malcolm P. McNair in "Significant Trends and Developments in the Postwar Period," in A. B. Smith, editor, *Competitive Distribution in a Free High-Level Economy and Its Implications for the University*, Pittsburgh, Pa.: University of Pittsburgh Press, 1958, pp. 17–18.

new (and innovative) forms of competition. When the point of vulnerability has been reached, the once innovative institution is mature, and the wheel cycle begins anew with the next institutional innovation. Figure 16.3 will assist in the clarification of this theory.

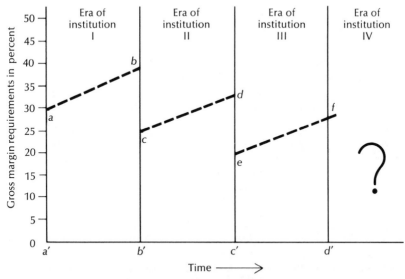

Figure 16.3 The Wheel Theory

Note that the vertical axis in Figure 16.3 represents percentage gross margin requirements—that is, it depicts the minimum percentage of gross margin required for the institution to produce a net profit. For example, point a' on the horizontal axis represents the birthday, as it were, of Institution I. On that day, Institution I has an organizational character that permits it to show a profit with a 30 percent gross margin. But note that as Institution I matures, its minimum gross margin requirement increases—this latter tendency is reflected in the upward slope of dashed line ab. The wheel theory suggests that as this gradual process of growing economically less efficient occurs, the maturing institution grows increasingly vulnerable to the threat of new (and innovative) institutions. At point b in Figure 16.3, for example, Institution I is challenged by innovative Institution II. Note that when Institution II arrives, Institution I requires almost a 40 percent gross margin to turn a profit. And the cycle repeats for Institution II until such time as it, too, becomes vulnerable and is challenged by a third innovator.

But there are several additional points that relate to this theory and which are not entirely obvious. First, it is not accidental or arbitrary that the points a, c and e, when connected with a straight line, produce a generally down-sloping line. The slope of this line a—c—e reflects the tendency for innovative institutions to incorporate new technology—new methods of operation—so that each successive institution is capable of more efficient operation during its incipiency than were predecessor institutions.

Thus, for example, Institution I might have been the large downtown department store in the 1920's—the size of that institution and the large market it served made economies available that could not easily have been realized by smaller predecessor firms. Institution II might have been the multiunit organization—the chain-like organization that could realize even further economies in buying and in selling and could, therefore, operate profitably on a lower gross margin than the downtown department store. Similarly, Institution III might have been a multiunit organization featuring, in addition, self-service. The acceptance of self-service by consumers meant, in effect, that an institution with substantially lower in-store selling expenses could not only survive, but prosper. And Institution IV might be an automated or semiautomated type of store in which check-out procedures and stock handling procedures are much more efficient. Each succeeding institution in this wheel-like pattern is capable initially (before it begins to grow less efficient) of more efficient operation than prior institutional forms.

But why does each innovative form of institution undergo the gradual process of decay depicted by the up-sloping gross margin lines ab, cd, and ef? Thus far the theory only seems to claim that this process of decay is inevitable. What forces work to bring about this institutional decay? And, indeed, what evidence do we have that such decay actually occurs? These two questions clearly require good answers if we are to regard the wheel thesis seriously.

CAUSES OF THE WHEEL PROCESS The tendency of innovative marketing institutions to gain initial access to markets on a low-price, efficiency-of-operation, basis and subsequently to evolve into less efficient forms requiring greater gross margins is explained in terms of two basic forces. First, there is what might be called a secular-growth-in-affluence argument. This argument rests on the premise that our economic system has, during the last 40 years, produced a more or less steady growth in the real income of consumers—and that this progressively greater affluence of consumers logically requires a regular or periodic adjustment in the mode of operation of the economic institutions serving them. Because consumers have been generally more and more affluent, the form of this institutional change very often assumes the form of additional services—services presumably befitting the growing affluence of the market. This alleged tendency to trade up the quality and number of services tends, in turn, to add to the expense structure of the original institutional form and ultimately to drive gross margin requirements up in the pattern suggested in Figure 16.3. Note that this secular-growth-in-affluence argument contains an answer to the critic who believes that our market system should display a greater willingness to use price aggressively as a competitive thrust. This critic is, in effect, told that growing affluence may not demand lower prices but, indeed, higher quality in products and in attendant services. These services may include more elegant store decor, more imposing store fixtures, better locations, more convenient hours, more liberal returns and allowances policies, and so forth.

The second basic force that is thought to underlie the gradual process of institutional decay described by the wheel thesis is suggested by the phrase "comfort of success." This argument presumes that a predictable change in the willingness of management to confront risk occurs as the management of an enterprise begins to know the comfort of success. It says that the entrepreneurial spirit that characterizes a young and lean management group is such that risks are willingly taken—there is little to lose for nonmembers of the establishment. But when success is realized, a special kind of entrepreneurial conservatism is alleged to set in. The bold competitive steps that gained an initial foothold for the innovative institution are increasingly less likely to be taken. The argument presumes that when confronted by several different courses of action, the comfortable management will tend to select that course to which the lower but surer payoff is attached rather than the riskier but higher payoff alternative. This managerial conservatism allegedly produces a lethargic, often overmanned organization; an organization particularly susceptible to a kind of malignant growth in its expense structure.

EMPIRICAL EVIDENCE OF THE WHEEL PROCESS   What objective evidence is there that something like this wheel process of institutional change is actually operative? Available data suggests that the wheel thesis is not just a convenient analytical device. Expense ratios for American department stores, for example, moved up, on the average, 2.4 percent from 1948 to 1955. Variety chains experienced a 4.1 percent increase in their average expense ratios during that same period. In a landmark study, increases in gross margin requirements were identified for department stores, mail-order firms, variety stores and jewelry dealers for the span of time 1890-1947.[5] In addition, recent publications of the supermarket industry show that type of retailing institution to be requiring, on the average, a larger and larger gross margin. Chain Store Age, a publication of and for the supermarket business, reflects an upward trend in supermarket gross margin requirements.[6] Although the evidence is not as systematic as would be desirable, there is some suggestion that discount stores have been trading

[5] See Harold Barger, Distribution's Place in the American Economy Since 1890, Princeton, N.J.: Princeton University Press, 1955.
[6] See, for example, Calvert Hahn, "What Will It Cost to Open a New Supermarket in 1967?" Chain Store Age, Grocery Executives Edition, December 1960, pp. 38-39. See also Wilbur B. England, Operating Results of Food Chains, Harvard Business School Bulletin No. 158, November 1960.

up in recent years through the addition of services and—at the same time—increasing their average expense ratios. The precise status of these discount operations is blurred somewhat because of data collection problems and because of the use of "schedule" pricing by some discount stores.[7]

THE DIALECTIC—A PROCESS OF INSTITUTIONAL CHANGE

A device that can have both descriptive and analytical value in the context of institutional change in marketing is suggested by the term "dialectic process." The dialectic process identifies a means through which the nature of change itself may be observed more systematically. More specifically, the dialectic process asserts that the effective components of change are: (a) a thesis, (b) an antithesis, and (c) a synthesis. The "thesis" in this process of change is an established institution of some kind—it may be an organization; it may be a pattern of thought that has become institutionalized. The "antithesis" is innovative—it may likewise be thought of as real or conceptual. And the "synthesis" is a combination of both the thesis and the antithesis—that is, the synthesis embodies some of the characteristics of the thesis and some of the characteristics of the antithesis. But all this may sound much more complex than it is. Consider Figure 16.4.

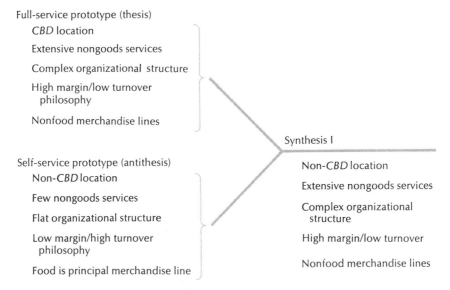

Figure 16.4 The Dialectic Process—Stage One

[7] "Schedule" pricing identifies the practice of offering many nongoods services but not including the cost of those services in the price of the merchandise. The cost of each of these services is added, at the option of the buyer, to the base merchandise price—so that fewer services are bought unwillingly. For a discussion of schedule treatment of services, see Ronald R. Gist, editor, *Management Perspectives in Retailing*, New York: John Wiley & Sons, Inc., 1967, pp. 311–315.

Figure 16.4 depicts the first stage of synthesis of two historically important prototype marketing institutions. These two prototypes—the full-service nonfood retail outlet and the self-service supermarket—play the roles of the thesis and antithesis institutions, respectively. The full-service institution serves analytically as the established institution, the self-service prototype is cast in the role of the innovative, or challenger, institution. Our two prototypes embody what are virtually opposite operating characteristics. Note that these two prototypes differ in terms of location, services, organizational characteristics, merchandising philosophy, and, indeed, in terms of merchandise lines. Synthesis I represents a kind of first order of change—it describes the first wave of emulation of the self-service prototype by the evolving institutional form. Note that Synthesis I is the same as our full-service prototype except for its location. Synthesis I is our full-service prototype with an outlying (non-CBD) location. Figure 16.5 depicts the second stage of synthesis of our prototype institutions.

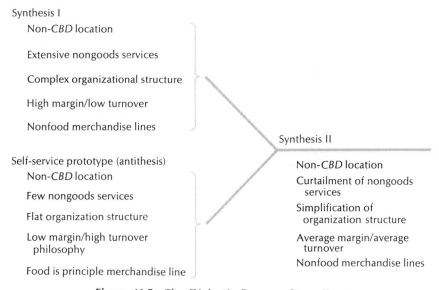

Figure 16.5 The Dialectic Process—Stage Two

The second stage of institutional synthesis produces an intermediate institutional type that we might properly call a discount department store—indeed, the basic character of Synthesis II is not unlike the K-Mart, Target and GEM type of store. Note that the self-service prototype (antithesis) continues to exert the dominant influence in the determination of the character of Synthesis II. That is, at Stage Two, the synthesized institution is more like the antithesis than the thesis. This kind of change process may produce a stable new type of institution—one that itself becomes institutionalized as did the full-service prototype in an earlier era. Synthesis may continue through several other stages. If and when the synthesized institutional form stabilizes, another antithetical prototype may evolve and challenge it, just as the self-service prototype represented an earlier challenge to the original full-service institutional form.

SUMMARY

The purpose of Chapter 16 has been to explore one final aspect of distribution channels. Our principal interest has been to identify various theories that attempt to explain the nature and causes of change in the form of important marketing institutions. We identified two basic types of theory—adjustment theory and cycle theory.

Adjustment theory attempts to gain insight into the likely forms of important future marketing institutions by systematically observing the environment within which such institutions evolve and identifying the elements within that environment that play an important role in the determination of the character of such institutions. We noted that a simple model of this adjustment process would include such environmental factors as social mores, legal constraints, demographic characteristics, technical know-how, cultural values and economic conditions. We also noted the parallel between the analytical method of adjustment theory and the Darwinian survival-of-the-fittest argument.

Cycle theory was divided into two classes: (a) partial and (b) complete. The accordian theory of change in marketing institutions exemplifies the complete type of cycle theory. This theory asserts that there is a historical pattern that suggests that marketing institutions tend to vary cyclically in terms of the widths of the merchandise lines they offer. That is, there is a general store era; there is a specialty store era; and, indeed, we are now into another era of line generalization. This theory is essentially descriptive, although there is no reason why it cannot be modified with further study so that it may acquire some moderate predictive value.

The wheel theory was presented as an example of a partial cycle explanation of change in marketing institutions. The wheel thesis identifies the tendency for innovative institutional forms to gain early acceptance on the basis of low prices and efficient organizational characteristics. As the innovative institution matures, it tends to grow progressively less efficient and it ultimately falls prey to another competitive innovative institution. The wheel theory is supported by some highly respected research efforts and by logic.

Finally, an explanation of institutional change that embodies some aspects of adjustment theory and some aspects of cycle theory was identified. This concluding theory is suggested by the phrase dialectic process. This process traces the development of new institutional forms from a thesis institution and an antithesis institution. The dialectic process occurs in steps or stages—and each such stage provides a slightly different synthesis of the thesis and the antithesis. It was noted that stable new institutional forms may be the result of this dialectic process.

1 Carefully define and indicate the relevance of each of the following concepts to the study of marketing:
   a. Adjustment theory
   b. Institutional environment
   c. Cycle theory
   d. The accordian theory of institutional change
   e. The wheel theory of institutional change
   f. A thesis institution
   g. An antithesis institution
   h. A synthesis institution
   i. A high-margin, low-turnover institution
   j. A low-margin, high-turnover institution.
2 Distinguish carefully between each element in the following pairs of terms:
   a. Darwin's theory of natural selection *and* adjustment theory
   b. A partial institutional cycle *and* a complete institutional cycle
   c. Wide merchandise lines *and* narrow merchandise lines
   d. The dialectic process of institutional change *and* the wheel theory of institutional change
   e. The full-service prototype institution *and* the self-service prototype institution.
3 Explain as carefully as you can the relationship between the minimum gross margin requirements of a marketing institution and the economic efficiency of that institution.
4 Referring to Figure 16.3, explain the forces that produce: (a) the upward slope in dashed line segments *ab, cb,* and *ef* and (b) the down-sloping line that would result from connecting points *a, c,* and *e.*

5 What factors do you believe play an important causal role in the current tendency toward generalized merchandise lines in retailing? Why?
6 What institutional form do you believe will represent the most serious competitive threat to:
   a. The supermarket?
   b. The department store?
   c. The service station?
   d. The drive-in bank?
7 What factor or factors stand in the way of a successful fully automated retail store?

SUGGESTED SUPPLEMENTARY READINGS IN CHANNELS OF DISTRIBUTION

Applebaum, William, and others, *Guide to Store Location Research,* Reading, Mass.: Addison-Wesley Publishing Company, Inc., 1968.

Baligh, Helmy H., and Leon Richartz, *Vertical Market Structures,* Boston: Allyn and Bacon, Inc., 1967.

Berry, Brian J. L., and Allen Pred, *Central Place Studies,* Philadelphia: Regional Science Research Institute, 1961.

Dalrymple, Douglas J., and Donald L. Thompson, *Retailing: An Economic View,* New York: The Free Press, 1969.

Entenberg, Robert D., *Effective Retail and Market Distribution,* Cleveland: The World Publishing Company, 1966.

Gist, Ronald R., editor, *Management Perspectives in Retailing,* New York: John Wiley & Sons, Inc., 1967.

_____, *Retailing: Concepts and Decisions,* New York: John Wiley & Sons, Inc., 1968.

Goeldner, Charles R., *Automatic Merchandising,* Chicago: American Marketing Association, 1963.

Hollander, Stanley, *The Rise and Fall of a Buying Club,* East Lansing, Mich.: Michigan State University Press, 1959.

Lewis, Edwin H., *Marketing Channels,* New York: McGraw-Hill Book Company, 1968.

Mallen, Bruce E., *The Marketing Channel,* New York: John Wiley & Sons, Inc., 1967.

Rachman, David J., *Retail Strategy and Structure,* Englewood Cliffs, N.J.: Prentice-Hall, Inc., 1969.

Simmons, James, *The Changing Pattern of Retail Location,* Chicago: University of Chicago Press, 1964.

Wingate, J. W., and J. S. Friedlander, *The Management of Retail Buying,* Englewood Cliffs, N.J.: Prentice-Hall, Inc., 1963.

_____, Elmer O. Schaller, and Irving Goldenthal, *Problems in Retail Merchandising,* Englewood Cliffs, N.J.: Prentice-Hall, Inc., 1961.

Chapter 17

LOGISTICS AND PHYSICAL DISTRIBUTION

In earlier chapters we have emphasized the importance of a careful and continuous appraisal of market opportunity to the success of business. We have taken the position that a careful appraisal of market opportunity is necessarily a pivotal element in the determination of an efficient market system. But an appreciation of how much market opportunity exists is not enough—it is necessary also to be able to deliver what is demanded by a market or market segment to the proper place and at the proper time. The preferences of a market may be correctly appraised, but unless the timing and placement of the items representing those preferences is also correct, such knowledge is of relatively little value.

In order to illustrate the nature of this idea, it will be useful to think of markets and market segments as being served by flows—flows of goods and services having both a *rate-of-movement* dimension and a *size dimension*.[1] It should be emphasized that while a particular flow of goods or services may embody the preferences of target markets, it may move at a rate that does not coincide with the timing of demand, and it may involve quantities that are not in basic agreement with the level of demand. Consider Figure 17.1.

The data series in Figure 17.1 labeled GS represents the level of flow of some good or service through an average year. This pattern of flow is achieved (controlled) through the coordination of: (a) production, (b) inventories (storage) and (c) transportation. If the bold line labeled EE' represents the level of production, then January and February represent months when inventories are being depleted (GS is less than D and EE')

---

[1] See J. L. Heskett, "Ferment in Marketing's Oldest Area," *Journal of Marketing*, October 1962, pp. 40–45. These two dimensions correspond conceptually to what Heskett has called "movement control," and "demand-supply coordination."

and July represents a month in which inventories in storage are accumulating (EE' is greater than D and GS). The basic task of logistics and physical distribution is to adjust these goods and services flows to demand through the systematic control of production rates, inventories (storage) and transportation. And the problem is not normally an easy one to resolve. It is obviously possible for production to confront unexpected interruptions; clearly there is less than complete understanding of the behavior of demand; and it is a normal state of affairs to have less than full control over the rate of flow of goods and services. This extreme uncertainty, influencing as it does each of the major components in the problem, makes for a challenging and sometimes frustrating task. And it should be apparent that the general efficiency of our market system is influenced to an important degree by the efficiency with which these goods and services flows are accomplished. The product may be right, the price may be right, and promotion may be right; but failure can nonetheless result from mistakes of a logistical nature.

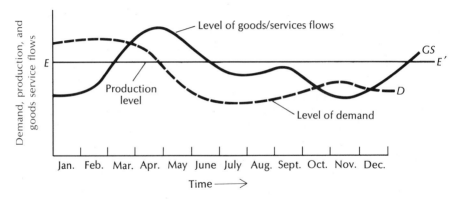

Figure 17.1 Goods and Services Flows

In the discussion that follows, we will consider the nature of the task of logistics, or physical distribution systems, in considerable detail. The terms "logistics" and "physical distribution" are used herein as synonyms. They will both be understood to suggest activities that relate to "the movement and handling of goods from the point of production to the point of consumption or use." This definition is suggested by the definitions committee of the American Marketing Association. The following discussion will be developed around two basic sections, one dealing with special problems that relate to inventory, and the other dealing with special problems that relate to transportation.[2]

---

[2] The most important components of the study of physical distribution are: (a) traffic management and transportation, (b) order and materials handling, (c) warehousing and (d) inventory planning and control.

Inventories and market efficiency

We have suggested that economic efficiency is normally improved when the rate of goods and services flows correspond closely to consumer demand. If there were no sources of friction in the process of physical distribution, goods and services could flow to each of us instantaneously upon order—much as we get the service of electricity by flicking a switch or of water by turning on a spigot. Because the demand for electricity and water is virtually continuous, a pipeline or continuous type of distribution is economically feasible. For most other goods and services, something less than continuous distribution is sensible. In any event, some type of storage or inventory system is required in order to absorb irregularities in the rate of consumer demand for these goods and services flows. And these inventories are an important determinant of market efficiency. When inventories are excessive, economic resources are used in less than an optimal manner; when inventories are inadequate, a similar conclusion is warranted.

Because inventories are important to general market efficiency, they are of special interest to us here. The word "store" itself implies an inventory—and few business operations do not in some way confront inventory problems. Even a strictly service institution—one not dealing in tangible or physical products—has, in a sense, an inventory of services embodied in the personnel and hardware that are used to purvey the service it offers. And this embodied inventory of services may be inadequate or excessive—just as a physical inventory may be inadequate or excessive for an enterprise dealing in real goods.

Our concern here is with two special aspects of inventory. First, we are concerned with what we shall call the ordering aspects of inventories—problems of determining the proper order size, the correct frequency of order placement, and similar matters. Second, we are concerned with the physical placement of inventories—that is, the location planning of inventories.

ORDER PLANNING AND INVENTORY CONTROL

A logical point of departure in order planning is to consider the pattern of demand confronting the goods or services being handled. For purposes of illustrating this point, it may be useful to contrast the pattern of demand confronting a staple good with that confronting a fashion good. Figure 17.2 will assist in making this distinction.

Figure 17.2 depicts the demand pattern confronting three different types of products. These three products represent a progression from continuous demand (A) to intermittent demand (B) to discontinuous demand (C). Note that Product A, confronts a demand pattern that is essentially level throughout the year—demand is relatively certain. Note in this connection that the level of next year's demand is depicted with certainty. Product

B confronts a type of discontinuous demand, one in which there is uncertainty regarding the level of next year's demand. Note that for Product B, next fall's demand may approximate any of three different levels—a, b or c. Product C is confronted by one-time demand—it seems to embody a fadishness; what does not sell this fall may never sell.

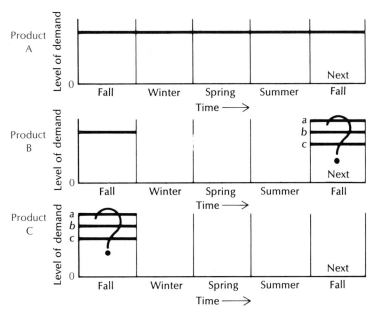

Figure 17.2 Demand Patterns

Product A embodies the demand pattern of a staple—an item that sells regularly and in a reasonably predictable pattern. Order planning and inventory control for a product confronting continuous demand is very different from that for a product that embodies some degree of discontinuity in demand. The pattern of demand confronting Product C is most like that confronting a fashion good—though the demand pattern of Product B is not inconsistent with some types of fashion goods.[3] It is important to note that Products A, B and C also represent a progression of *risk*. There is relatively little risk of ownership suggested by the demand pattern for Product A. There is a distinct risk of ownership suggested in the demand pattern for Product C. Note that any of three levels of demand (a, b or c) may exist this fall for Product C.

---

[3] A very common form of carelessness is to use the notion of fashion as though it were synonymous with style. Thus, one frequently encounters the phrase "in style." Something is fashionable because it enjoys consumer acceptance, and all objects embody style of some kind. Style refers to intrinsic properties of design, aesthetics or color. The phrase "in style," when it is used to convey the idea of fashionableness, is an inaccurate use of the term.

Order and reorder planning for products confronting a continuous type of demand pattern may be developed around some form of *automatic replenishment plan.* That is, procedures that might properly be described as automatic buying may be developed when demand approximates a continuous pattern. These automatic buying plans may be either symmetrical or asymmetrical. Both these types of automatic buying plans are depicted in Figure 17.3.

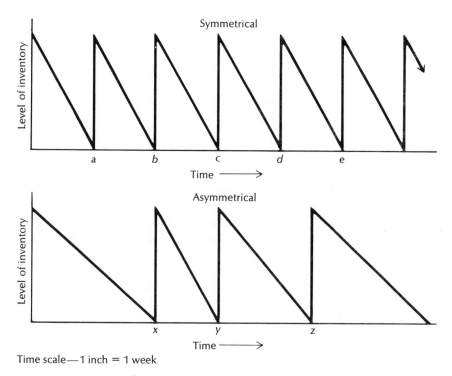

Time scale—1 inch = 1 week

Figure 17.3 Automatic Buying Plans

The symmetrical automatic buying plan is one in which inventories are replenished at regular intervals. In Figure 17.3 new stocks are received every week. The asymmetrical automatic buying plan involves a replenishment of inventories at irregular time intervals.[4] Note that the rate of movement of inventory items through the selling organization is constant in the case of the symmetrical plan. Both the symmetrical plan and the asymmetrical plan may involve a threshold reorder point.

The notion of a *threshold reorder point* deserves elaboration. If no time were consumed in replenishing stocks, then a seller could wait until his

---

[4] The asymmetrical plan that is depicted in Figure 17.3 reflects a constant order size. Asymmetry could also be achieved with regular purchase intervals but various reorder sizes.

last item of inventory was sold and instantaneously replenish his inventory. If delivery of new orders were truly instantaneous, the seller could maintain very little inventory (or none?) and still meet the demands of his customers. If delivery of replenishment orders requires some time to accomplish, then orders must be placed before stocks are totally exhausted. Consider the relationships depicted in Figure 17.4.

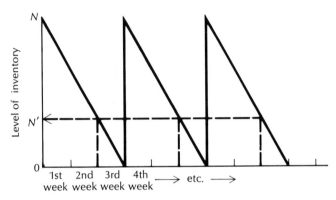

Figure 17.4 Reorder Planning

Figure 17.4 depicts a situation in which an inventory of N is sold regularly in a three-week period. The smooth slope of the declining inventory curve indicates that there is no variation in the rate of sale of the inventory items. In this very simple case, inventory reorders are placed at the number of delivery days required before the point at which inventory would be exhausted. If, for example one week is required from order placement to order receipt, then reorder would occur at the end of the second week, at the end of the fifth week, at the end of the eighth week, and so on. The threshold reorder point is reached when inventories fall to the level N'. But if there are significant variations in the rate of sale of the inventory items, the determination of the inventory replenishment point would be slightly different. This latter case is depicted in Figure 17.5.

In Figure 17.5, an inventory N is sold at various rates. The rate of sale labeled a is the most rapid rate; the rate of sale labeled d is the slowest rate (rate c is very nearly the same as d). And when rates of sale vary unpredictably, the determination of the inventory reorder point is somewhat more complicated. The complication stems from the fact that we cannot depend upon selling some predictable number of inventory items from the time that an order is placed to the time that that order is received. If the rate of sale after the reorder is placed is greater than anticipated, we may very well find our stocks completely exhausted before delivery of the new order is taken. Conversely, if the rate of sale is less than that anticipated, we may find excessive inventories on hand after delivery of the new order is taken. How is this dilemma resolved?

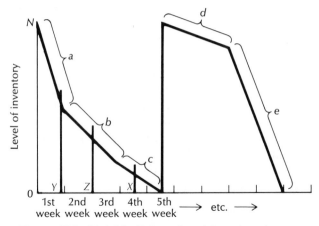

Figure 17.5 Variable Demand and Reorder Planning

At least three courses of action can be identified. A *pessimistic reorder strategy* would presume that the least rapid historical rate of sale would occur after the order placement and before delivery. An *optimistic reorder strategy* would presume that the most rapid historical rate of sale would occur after the order placement and before delivery. And an *averaging reorder strategy* would presume that an average historical rate of sale would occur after the order placement and before delivery. In Figure 17.5, the pessimistic reorder strategy corresponding to a one-week order-delivery period is depicted by the reorder point labeled X. The optimistic reorder strategy corresponding to a one-week order-delivery period is depicted by the reorder point labeled Y. The averaging reorder strategy corresponding to a one-week order-delivery period is depicted by the reorder point labeled Z.

ECONOMIC ORDER QUANTITY CALCULATIONS We have not yet given much thought to one important aspect of inventory planning. Just what amount is the *right* amount of inventory? Clearly, too much inventory can result in excessive costs. Just as clearly, too little inventory can produce a loss of sales. A sales organization that sells 1000 units of some product each year may buy one order of 1000; it may buy 1000 orders of 1 each; or it may order in quantities anywhere between these two extremes. Economic order quantity calculations help to resolve this inventory problem. As a point of departure, it will be useful to break the economic order question into components so that we can grapple more efficiently with the problem. Toward this end, consider Figure 17.6.

Figure 17.6 summarizes the behavior of two basic types of costs as the size of an order is varied. Though some oversimplification is involved, we will presume that inventory costs (not including the cost of the merchandise itself) are made up primarily of (a) carrying costs and (b) procurement costs. These two types of costs include the costs of acquiring, handling and storing an inventory. Carrying costs include costs of interest charges on funds committed to inventory; costs of storage; and costs of inventory devaluation during storage, whether caused by physical damage or market changes.[5] Procurement costs include costs of buying, costs associated with invoicing procedures, costs of receiving and checking incoming merchandise, and costs of making payment and other clerical routines. Unit, or average, procurement costs tend to decline as the order size increases: unit, or average, carrying costs tend to increase as the order size increases. The behavior of these two types of costs is depicted in Figure 17.6. Note also that the unit (or average) of inventory costs is simply the sum of unit carrying and unit procurement costs.

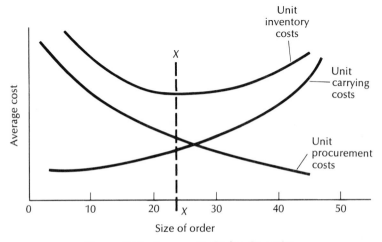

Figure 17.6 Economic Order Quantity

The *economic order quantity* is defined as the order size that corresponds to the lowest total of unit carrying costs plus unit procurement costs. The vertical dashed line in Figure 17.6 crosses the "unit inventory costs" line at its low point. The vertical dashed line indicates that an order size of about 24 units is the economic order quantity in our example.

INVENTORIES, SPACE AND ECONOMIC EFFICIENCY

Another aspect of physical distribution—one that has an important relationship to the cost and efficiency of our market system—is the geography of inventory placements. We have seen that manufacturers of all kinds often conduct their businesses at a great distance from the markets and market segments that they serve. An unavoidable question when physical

---

[5] An extremely good source in this matter is John F. Magee, *Production Planning and Inventory Control,* New York: McGraw-Hill Book Co., 1958. See especially pp. 44 and 45.

distance intervenes between the producer and the consumer is, "Where should inventory accumulation take place?" And in general, there are two answers to the question. In some instances, inventory accumulation is centralized; in some cases inventory accumulation is decentralized. But how does the centralized system of inventory accumulation differ from the decentralized system? Consider Figure 17.7.

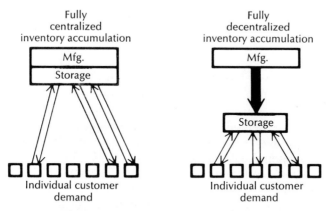

Figure 17.7 Inventory Accumulation

Note: The reader should not conclude that the two systems of inventory accumulation depicted are the only such systems. Indeed, as depicted, these two systems are not even the most common. The systems depicted represent polar opposites. Most commonly, there is some storage facility at the point of manufacture even with the decentralized system. Likewise, there may well be some storage (retail stores, for example) near the consumer level even with the centralized system.

Figure 17.7 suggests the essential difference between a centralized and a decentralized system of inventory accumulation. An important economic consequence of the *centralized system* of inventory accumulation is that *small quantities* of inventory tend to move relatively *long distances*. An example of the centralized system is found in mail-order retailing—in which case the individual customer places an individual order, and the order may be filled from a manufacturer's inventory. Mail-order specialty houses (like Sunset House) often operate on this type of drop-ship basis. Note, in contrast, that an important economic consequence of the *decentralized system* of inventory accumulation is that *large quantities* of inventory tend to move relatively *long distances*. The decentralized system of inventory accumulation tends to place important storage points near the market(s) being served. The relatively small order of the individual final consumer moves a relatively *short* distance. In effect, the use of a decentralized system of inventory accumulation is a special case of economic postponement—a concept we will explore more fully in a later chapter. In this case, the event being postponed is the breaking of bulk. The great economic advantage of decentralized inventory accumulation systems is that unit costs of transportation are substantially lower when large quantities of merchandise are moved for relatively long distances. We shall see in the following section how much of an advantage in lower costs of transportation a decentralized inventory accumulation system may produce.

Decentralized inventory accumulation points are an important part of the overall marketing plan of an extremely large number of businesses. Businesses may use warehouses—either owned or public—or distribution centers. Distribution centers may be thought of as convenient points for order assembly, as well as storage facilities. Many large firms, both manufacturers and retailers, have turned to the distribution center concept as a means of gaining efficiency in the process of physical distribution. These distribution centers are often equipped with modern order-picking systems, including conveyor belt order delivery. Continuous information concerning the status of particular items of inventory may be available as a part of a computerized perpetual system of inventory. J. C. Penney, Sears Roebuck, Brandeis, Pillsbury, and countless other organizations are developing their long-range corporate objectives around these highly efficient distribution centers. These centers have done to traditional warehousing what the self-service supermarket has done to American retailing. In some instances, when several distribution centers are developed by a single firm, a centralized system of perpetual inventories is kept simultaneously for all the centers. Thus, a centralized computer inventory system is used as an important part of a decentralized inventory accumulation system.

Transportation and our marketing system

It has been suggested that physical distribution is an extremely costly part of our nation's total marketing bill. Physical distribution costs have been estimated at between 10 and 30 percent of sales for many kinds of business. Physical distribution costs in the food industry often exceed 25 percent of sales.[6] The sheer magnitude of physical distribution costs makes them an important focal point for efforts to increase distributive efficiency. To the extent that the physical distribution of our nation's output can be effected more efficiently, we pay too much. Thus, it is a social issue whether or not those persons engaged in physical distribution work at the greatest level of efficiency known. In the discussion that follows, we will consider transportation and its influence upon our physical distribution system. More specifically, we will be concerned with two questions. First, what is the relationship between transportation costs and storage costs? And second, what specialized forms of transportation agencies and arrange-

[6] See, for example, Richard E. Snyder, "Physical Distribution Costs," *Distribution Age*, December 1965, pp. 35–42.

ments can, when correctly utilized, serve either to improve the quality of transportation service or to reduce its cost?

TRANSPORTATION AND STORAGE—RECIPROCAL COSTS?

In the introductory comments of this chapter, we noted that it was a useful simplification to think of goods and services flows from points of manufacture to points of consumption. We observed that the essential task of physical distribution was to regulate these flows so that they were in reasonable agreement with the characteristics of consumer demand. The two basic ingredients in physical distribution have been identified as movement (transportation) and storage. The task of physical distribution is thus to employ movement and storage in a manner well suited to the characteristics of demand. The point that we wish to emphasize here is that these two basic ingredients of physical distribution are, to some extent, reciprocals. That is, as expenditures for one increase, the required expenditures for the other tend to decrease.[7] But we should illustrate this relationship more completely.

Suppose that a particular firm has manufacturing facilities located in the north-central area of the United States. Suppose, moreover, that this firm sells in West Coast markets through its own dealer organization. To be more specific, our example firm ships by rail to four warehouses located at Seattle, San Francisco, Los Angeles and San Diego. Dealer requirements are met from these warehouses. To be even more specific, let us assume that the total cost of physical distribution (including a fair share of overhead) is allocated between transportation and warehousing as depicted in Figure 17.8.

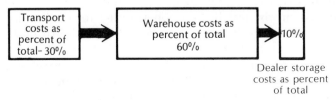

Figure 17.8   Physical Distribution Systems

Figure 17.8 indicates that 30 percent of the total expenditure for physical distribution for our example firm is spent for transportation; warehousing accounts for 60 percent of the total expenditure for physical distribution;

[7] Reciprocals are any two numbers which, when multiplied, produce unity. Thus, 5 and .2 are reciprocals; 10 and .1 are reciprocals; 4 and .25 are reciprocals. The reader should note that the use of the term "reciprocals" in the context of transportation and storage does not suggest an exact mathematical relationship. It suggests, rather, that transportation and storage costs tend to have an inverse relationship.

storage costs at the dealer level account for the remaining 10 percent of total physical distribution costs. The principal form of transportation used by our hypothetical firm is rail. Now, suppose that we were to consider the use of air transport in place of rail. What influences would this proposed modification in our manufacturer's physical distribution system have?

The most obvious answer is that air transport would cost a great deal more than rail. And the very nearsighted may abandon further consideration of air transportation at that point. But the total impact, that is, the impact upon the total physical distribution system, of a switch from rail to air will be felt reciprocally on storage costs as well as on transportation costs.[8] That is, the speed of air transport will mean that less elaborate storage facilities may now serve to meet demand requirements. Air transport may, in other words, enable the development of a new physical distribution system—one similar to that depicted in Figure 17.9.

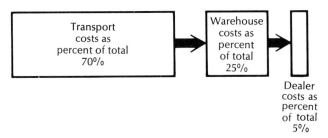

Figure 17.9 Transportation and Storage Costs

Figure 17.9, when contrasted with Figure 17.8, suggests a kind of trade-off effect.[9] Note particularly that Figures 17.8 and 17.9 do not suggest that the total cost of physical distribution is either lowered or increased as a result of the change in transport mode. It may, however, be possible to reduce the total cost of the physical distribution system *and* improve the service given customers as well. The profound lesson suggested by this *physical distribution trade-off effect* is that an undue (myopic) concern with lowering one cost may only serve to increase the cost of some other component in the system. When the various combinations of transport costs and storage costs are known, the best such combination can be identified with linear programming techniques.[10]

[8] It is the impact upon the entire physical distribution system—that is, all the elements depicted in Figure 17.8—that is most meaningful.
[9] For a further discussion of this idea, see J. L. Heskett and others, *Business Logistics: Management of Physical Supply and Distribution,* New York: The Ronald Press Company, 1964, pp. 446–454, 473–474.
[10] *Ibid.,* pp. 148.

A discussion of physical distribution and its relationship to the society that it serves would necessarily be less than complete if some attention were not given to the means through which specialized transportation facilities and services can be employed to meet more nearly the requirements of business. In a general sense, the greater the precision with which a transportation system meets the needs of the business community, the more precisely is the transportation system serving the needs of society. We might fairly conclude that a responsive transportation system is a responsible transportation system. How does our system of transportation meet the special requirements of the business community? There are at least three aspects of the transportation business that tend to reflect a special concern for business and its needs. These three aspects are: (a) rate structures, (b) accumulation privileges and (c) processing privileges.

The elements that serve as a basis for the *rate structure* of the transportation business in the United States are quantity and type of material. The principal distinction in terms of quantity is rail carloads (60,000–100,000 pounds) or truckloads (15,000 pounds or more) as distinct from less-than-carload lots (LCL) or less-than-truckload lots (LTL). Rate structures invariably favor the carload (CL) or truckload (TL) quantities. And the difference between these two rates is not insignificant. Rates for LCL and LTL are often twice as high as for CL and TL. We shall see presently that the substantial differences between carload and less-than-carload rates provide a special kind of incentive for shippers. And these rate differences are the probable cause for the development of some forms of specialized transportation intermediaries.

But rate structures typically depend also upon the type of material being shipped. Rail rate structures are developed around: (a) class rates, (b) commodity rates and (c) special, or exception, rates. Class rates are relatively high rates. Class rates exist for over 10,000 different types of products. Because class rates are relatively high, less than 5 percent of rail shipments move at these rates. Commodity rates are established or can be established for bulk items, for items that have the potential to be heavy traffic items, and for products moving regularly between two or more geographic locations. The commodity rate is a lower rate (than class) given or negotiated in deference to the promise of a substantial volume of business by the shipper(s). Virtually all the freight moved by the railroads today moves at commodity rates. Special, or exception, rates are "discriminatory" rates that are given to special types of products that would move by alternative and competing modes of transportation were such rates not allowed. These special rates are discriminatory only in the sense that they normally do not cover the full cost of the service rendered—not in the sense that they are not given on equivalent terms to competing shippers of goods of like grade and quality.

The rate structure of the American transportation industry is also characterized by various types of *accumulation privileges*. Accumulation privileges enable a shipper or group of shippers who would, individually, not be able to qualify for quantity rates (CL or TL) to do so. One type of accumulation privilege is known as *pooling*. Pooling occurs when several buyers coordinate orders and shipments so that greatest quantity rates are in effect. Pooled cars are cars that contain a shipment of one product or item—but the contents of the car are ultimately destined for more than one buyer-shipper. Another type of accumulation privilege involves the *mixed car*. A mixed car is one that contains different products or commodities, and the highest rate applicable to any of the items in the mixed car usually applies to the entire car. The saving to the shipper results from the fact that the highest CL rate on the car is nonetheless lower than the sum of the LCL rates that the shipment would otherwise comprise.

A special transportation agency, the *freight forwarder*, also assists in the shipment accumulation process. And in so doing, the freight forwarder purveys a special kind of accumulation privilege. More specifically, the freight forwarder accumulates LCL shipments into CL shipments. The freight forwarder thus pays CL (lower) rates and his clients pay LCL (higher) rates. The reason an LCL shipper would prefer to work with the forwarder is that delivery time is usually reduced by the forwarder; that is, it is a further characteristic of LCL shipments that they move relatively more slowly than CL shipments. Thus, the freight forwarder, by accumulating several LCL shipments into CL volume, also expedites the movement of those shipments.

Still another characteristic of the American transportation rate system is suggested by the term *processing privileges*. In general, processing privileges permit the shipper to effect necessary changes in the products he is shipping without being penalized for any inconvenience that those changes may cause the mover. Consider, for example, the case of "in-transit" privileges. These privileges permit a shipper to move a shipment toward its destination, stop the shipment, effect some change in the products that make up the shipment, and after reloading, move on to the original destination (or any other in the same general direction) for the "balance of the through rate." The value of this in-transit privilege can be demonstrated more forcibly with the assistance of a diagram. Consider Figure 17.10.

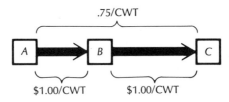

Figure 17.10 In-transit Privileges

Figure 17.10 depicts three cities, A, B, and C. The local rate for a particular product is $1.00/cwt. The through rate for the same product is $.75/cwt. Suppose, for purposes of illustrating the idea of an in-transit privilege, that a firm in City A wishes to move utility poles to Market C. Suppose further that it is necessary to process those poles at City B with some kind of preservative. Without an in-transit privilege it would be necessary to ship the utility poles to B (at the local rate), process the poles, and then ship the poles to C (at the local rate). An in-transit privilege, however, would permit the shipper to ship from A to B, unload, process, reload, and ship to C for "the balance of the through rate." In effect, this privilege permits the shipper to pay as though the shipment had moved from City A to City C without interruption.

SUMMARY

The purpose of Chapter 17 has been to consider the relationship between the efficiency of our market system and physical distribution. We noted that physical distribution deals with activities that relate to "the movement and handling of goods from the point of production to the point of consumption or use." More specifically, our interest was with (a) inventory or storage and (b) transportation.

Our discussion of inventory centered on two points. First, we explored the ordering aspects of inventory. We identified several basic patterns of demand, including continuous demand, discontinuous demand and intermittent demand. We noted that the continuous demand pattern may suggest the use of an automatic buying plan—either symmetrical or asymmetrical. We noted also that economic order quantity calculations assist in the identification of the best inventory plan. Second, we briefly explored the rationale for centralized and for decentralized systems of inventory accumulation.

Our discussion of transportation likewise centered on two points. First, we identified the reciprocal relationship between storage costs and transportation costs. We identified a kind of physical distribution trade-off effect that was apparent when we viewed storage and transportation collectively as a system rather than singularly as independent elements. Second, we briefly considered some of the characteristics of transportation rates and privileges. We distinguished CL and LCL rates; we identified class, commodity and exception rates. Accumulation privileges and processing privileges were shown to be an important part of the rate structure of the transportation industry.

REVIEW QUESTIONS

1 Carefully define and indicate the relevance of each of the following concepts to the study of marketing:
   a. Physical distribution
   b. Logistics

c. Automatic buying plans
d. A threshold reorder point
e. An economic order quantity
f. A decentralized system of inventory accumulation
g. A distribution center
h. The trade-off effect in physical distribution systems
i. Class rates
j. Commodity rates
k. Special (exception) rates
l. Accumulation privileges in transportation rate schedules
m. Processing privileges in transportation rate schedules
n. A freight forwarder
o. In-transit privileges

2 Distinguish carefully between each element in the following pairs of terms:
a. Staple goods *and* fashion goods
b. Symmetrical automatic buying plans *and* asymmetrical automatic buying plans
c. An optimistic reorder strategy *and* a pessimistic reorder strategy
d. Procurement costs *and* carrying costs
e. The principle of postponement *and* inventory accumulation
f. Carload quantities *and* less-than-carload quantities

3 What is the basic task of physical distribution, or logistics?

4 Contrast the problems confronting order planners for products having continuous demand characteristics with those of planners for products having discontinuous demand characteristics.

5 Under what conditions or circumstances does it make sense to utilize a centralized system of inventory accumulation?

6 Explain the tendency for transportation costs to vary reciprocally with storage costs.

DISCUSSION QUESTIONS

7 If your job were to coordinate production levels and physical distribution for an enormous corporation, what kinds of information would you find most helpful? Why?

8 Under what particular circumstances would a decentralized system of inventory accumulation be preferable to a centralized system of inventory accumulation?

Chapter 18

MASS COMMUNICATION, ADVERTISING, AND SOCIETY

We have noted that when distinctive elements of market demand exist, and when a differentiated supply is produced to meet that demand, there is an inescapable need for bringing together, or matching, specific elements of supply with the specific elements of demand that most nearly correspond to them. We have characterized this matching process as a kind of bilateral search procedure. "Bilateral search" suggests that sellers seek out those buyers whose preference patterns are best suited to the sellers' offering, and that buyers seek out the sellers whose offerings are best suited to their preference patterns.[1] When an economic system achieves an extremely high degree of specialization and division of labor, it is virtually inevitable that this bilateral search procedure becomes a very important form of economic activity.[2]

Indeed, specialized institutions normally evolve to fulfill a need for this massive "locator service." And clearly, the most prominent means for accomplishing this matching process in our society is the set of institutions that we refer to collectively as "the mass media." The mass media are, for the foregoing reasons, inextricably a part of our marketing system—and the importance of a well-developed system of mass communications to the success of our market system is difficult to overstate.[3]

Our concern in this chapter, and in the next as well, is with this mass

[1] The buyer-to-seller type of search is explored in Louis P. Bucklin, "The Informative Role of Advertising," *Journal of Advertising Research*, September 1965, pp. 11-15.
[2] Advertising volume in 1969 was estimated at over $19 billion. Estimates are for over a $20 billion volume by 1970. See *Marketing/Communications*, August 1969, p. 68.
[3] Indeed, some students believe that "marketing is almost entirely communications." See, for example, Marion Harper, Jr., "Communications Is the Core of Marketing," in John S. Wright and Daniel S. Warner, editors, *Speaking of Advertising*, New York: McGraw-Hill Book Co., 1963, pp. 187-190.

communications system and its role in our society. More specifically, our concern in these two chapters is with three matters. First, it is necessary that we develop formal definitions of some of the specialized terms that we will find it necessary to deal with. Second, we will consider some existing attitudes toward commercial uses of our system of mass communications—as well as some of the defenses offered in behalf of the commercial use of the mass media. And third, we will examine recent efforts to achieve greater efficiency in the use of the mass media for commercial purposes. The present chapter is developed around the first two of these tasks; Chapter 19 is concerned with the last.

Advertising and the advertising "industry"

As a preliminary means of defining the limits of our discussion, we should note that our system of mass communications media acts principally as a purveyor of information—a purveyor of both commercial and noncommercial information. Both the print media (newspapers, magazines, direct mail) and the transmitted, or broadcast, media (television and radio) normally carry editorial and entertainment content as well as commercial content. And it seems fair to say that the conduct of the mass media regarding both editorial/entertainment policy and commercial policy has been a source of recent widespread controversy. Certainly the effects of crime and violence in the mass media is one issue that centers on the noncommercial practices of the mass media, and there are many others.[4] But as interesting as the noncommercial aspects of the mass media may be, our interest here is with the commercial behavior of the media. Much more particularly, we are concerned with advertising. *Advertising is the impersonal communication of ideas, goods or services to a mass audience by an identified paying sponsor.* The elements in this definition are sufficiently important that we identify them separately. Advertising is the:

1 impersonal
2 communication of ideas, goods or services
3 to a mass audience
4 by an identified
5 paying sponsor.

Two forms of mass communication that are sometimes confused with advertising are publicity, and propaganda. If we eliminated item 5 above— the "paid" requirement—we would have the elements of publicity left. That is, publicity is, technically speaking, advertisement without payment. In a similar manner, if we eliminate the requirement of an identified sponsor (4), the resulting communication is propagandistic.[5] It is important

---

[4] See Joseph T. Klapper, *The Effects of Mass Communication,* New York: The Free Press, 1960, pp. 134ff.
[5] This represents a slightly different connotation of the word than is assumed in E. D. McGarry, "The Propaganda Function in Marketing," *Journal of Marketing,* October 1958, pp. 131–139.

for us to emphasize that advertising may involve the communication of *ideas* or *goods* or *services*. We are all aware that advertising attempts to sell goods and services—we may overlook the more important fact that it often sells ideas. Advertising necessarily involves *persuasive* efforts by a sponsor. Advertising may persuade with information; it may persuade with emotion; more frequently, it endeavors to persuade with some mixture of both. To fail to recognize the persuasive nature of advertising is to omit what is perhaps its most salient characteristic. We should also clarify what is meant by the "impersonal" requirement (1) in the definition above. We do not mean that it is cold, or without compassion. Impersonal in this context simply specifies that the communication does not involve a face-to-face relationship. The relationship is always a medium-to-face relationship, as it were.

TYPES OF ADVERTISING

Advertising assumes numerous and sometimes complex specific forms. Advertising is distinguished in six basic ways. Advertising may be identified according to: (a) the medium it utilizes, (b) the audience to which it is directed, (c) the extent of its geographical coverage, (d) the timing of the response it elicits, (e) the type of demand it attempts to appeal to and (f) the number and type of sponsors of the advertisement.

Perhaps the most common classification of advertising is by the medium used—such a scheme produces the familiar distinctions between television, radio, magazine, outdoor, business periodical, newspaper and direct mail.[6] Indeed, this classification is so common in use that it is mentioned here only for the sake of completeness. But the term "medium" is often misused. We will reserve that term for the general classes of communication just listed. When we wish to speak of a particular television station or newspaper or magazine, we will use the term "vehicle." Thus, magazines represent a communications medium; *Life* is a vehicle within the magazine medium. Television is a medium; station KXYZ is a vehicle.[7]

When advertising is classified according to the audience to which it is directed, attention is normally directed to consumer advertising, trade advertising and industrial advertising. Most of our exposure is to consumer advertising, though trade advertising (to retailers, wholesalers and contractors) and industrial advertising (to manufacturers, assemblers and fabricators) are important as well. When advertising is classified by the extent of its geographical coverage, the resulting taxonomy is usually local, regional and national—or some such similar division.

A type of advertising that is much less frequently encountered—but still of considerable importance—is distinct because of the timing of the market

---

[6] And, sometimes, "specialty" advertising, such as matchbook covers, calendars or ball-point pens.

[7] This useful distinction is suggested by Albert Wesley Frey in *Advertising*, Third Edition, New York: The Ronald Press Company, 1961, p. 234.

response it hopes to elicit. The classification that results from this distinction is: (a) the direct action (or immediate response) advertisement and (b) the indirect action (or delayed response or, sometimes, institutional) advertisement. Most consumer advertisements encourage direct action—indeed many such acts admonish us to hurry lest the last available item be gone (a curious promotional thrust if one reflects on it). But other advertisements do not say "hurry on down" or even imply it. Some advertisements seem to care not at all if we come in today—or even in the near future. These latter advertisements may tell us how long the company has been in business, present some exciting vignette from the company's history, or indicate how dutifully the company plans to serve us in the future. These indirect appeals are the distinctive trait of the institutional advertisement. Such ads rarely feature a specific product—though they may dwell on the completeness of the company's product line. An institutional ad may editorialize—the sponsoring company may take a position on an issue of concern to itself and to its customers. An institutional ad may "clarify a misunderstanding"—it may, for example, correct a misconception about company policy.

Still another distinction is made according to the type of demand being sought from the advertisement. We recognize ads that are directed to the encouragement of primary demand and those that are directed to the stimulation of selective demand. *Primary demand* is demand for a general class of products as opposed to a specific brand of a product. An advertisement that recites the virtues of milk in general (such as might be sponsored by the American Dairy Association) is an ad that features a primary appeal. If you are alert, you may notice this type of advertisement for metal containers, glass containers, poultry products, and diverse other generic classes of products. An advertisement that is directed to the enlargement of *selective demand* endeavors to sell a particular brand of milk, poultry, or whatever. The primary demand advertisement is usually sponsored by a group—normally a trade association or growers association having a common interest in the generic class of products being featured.

There is one final class of advertisements that we should identify. This classification is developed on the basis of the number and type of sponsors of the advertisement. The basic distinction made here is between single-sponsor ads and multiple-sponsor (cooperative) advertisements. Multiple-sponsor advertisements are, themselves, diverse in character. We will recognize plans that involve: (a) horizontal cooperation and (b) vertical cooperation. In both these cases, the distinctive trait of the advertisement is that its cost is defrayed by more than one business entity. The *horizontal cooperative advertisement* is defined as one in which several sponsors, each operating a business at the same stage of distribution, share the cost of an advertisement or a series of advertisements. These horizontal cooperative plans are exemplified by advertisements or ad campaigns sponsored by merchants associations of various types. These merchants associations may be "downtown" groups, shopping center groups, or even groups of franchise retailers—such as Firestone dealers or Western Auto dealers.

An advertisement that involves *vertical cooperation* is one for which the costs are defrayed by several business firms, each operating at a different stage of distribution. Thus, for example, an automobile dealer may place an advertisement with a local vehicle, and upon receipt of a bill, send it to a regional office of the manufacturer. The manufacturer may pay a specified percentage of the total cost, the dealer the remainder. There may be more than two vertical sponsors—that is, the dealer, the distributor and the manufacturer may all share in the cost of advertisements placed by the dealer. This description is purposely quite simple; but the reader should be apprised of the fact that these cooperative advertisement agreements can get complex. Such agreements may specify that only particular media be used, they may specify conditions governing the placement or timing of competing advertisements, they may specify maximum dollar assistance and they may specify elaborate methods of proof that the ads actually ran.

There is one type of advertisement that may seem to be cooperative but is not. There is a type of advertisement in which the product featured in the ad and the sponsor of the advertisement do not seem to agree. The owners of the rights to the Sanforizing process may sponsor an advertisement or series of advertisements featuring (say) Arrow shirts, although these ads do not necessarily involve a cooperative defrayal of costs. The advertisements may simply be *derived-demand ads,* from which the licensers of the Sanforizing process gain in proportion as the final product (Arrow shirts) is sold.

THE ADVERTISING INDUSTRY

The advertising "industry" is composed for the most part, of three principal groups: (a) sponsors, (b) media and (c) advertising agencies or advertising "departments." Of these three basic components, only the agencies and departments should require any special explanation. Agencies are of two basic types: independent and house. An independent agency is a business that is free to compete for and select its clients (accounts). A house agency is owned by its major client. A house agency is, therefore, not completely free to serve other accounts. The advertising department—common in retailing, for example—is an integral part of the organization that it serves. The agency, whether independent or house, serves more as an organizational appendage—*separated* from the firm that utilizes its services, but *coordinated* with the sponsor firm in matters involving mass communications. The advertising agency provides for the client a minimum of: (a) media information, such as the availability of time and space; (b) creative skills, such as campaign planning and "appeal planning; and (c) research capabilities, such as providing brand preference data. The agency may be thought of as a source of communications expertise—it stands ready to conceive, plan and implement the communications requirements of the client accounts that it serves.

The advertising agency, because of its popular identification with Madison Avenue, is, quite literally, thought by some to be the point of origin of every advertisement. Quite the opposite is true. Advertising departments of retail stores and production crews in media organizations create a tremendous volume of advertisements. The majority of newspaper advertising is developed by creative skills within the newspaper organization—and newspapers are the medium in which the greatest advertising expenditure occurs.

The size of the advertising agency is measured in what may seem to be a curious way. While we indicate the size of most business organizations by their sales volume, the size of the ad agency is measured by a "billings" figure. And this billings figure is not the same as the revenues or income of the agency. An agency with billings of $1,000,000 actually enjoys an income of around $150,000. This latter figure assumes that the agency is compensated on a 15 percent commission basis and that it has no supplementary "fee" income. The billings figure is the price of the time or space charged by the media that is placed through the agency. Thus an agency with billings of $1,000,000 buys for its clients time and space priced by the media at $1,000,000. An illustration will clarify this relationship between billings and agency commissions. Consider Figure 18.1.

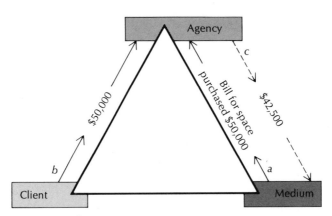

Figure 18.1 Agency Compensation

Note that the agency in Figure 18.1 has purchased, in behalf of its client, space with a gross value of $50,000. For the sake of illustration, let us suppose that the space purchased is a full-page, four-color ad in a nationally distributed, general appeal magazine. Note that the client pays the agency $50,000 and that the agency forwards $42,500 to the vehicle.

If there was no other work placed by the agency, and if there was no "fee basis" income (such as research contracts) for the agency, its billing size would be $50,000. The income of the agency is $7,500—or 15 percent of $50,000. This illustration is perhaps oversimplified, but it indicates the basic relationship that exists between client-medium-agency. One such complicating factor is the giving of cash discounts by the medium.[8]

Criticisms of advertising

A great deal of criticism, both social and economic, has been leveled at advertising. This criticism, in its most systematic form, seems to come from economists, legislators and sociologists.[9] As one critic puts it, "in the face of repeated attacks from educators, Congressional committees and journalists, the advertising fraternity has veered between a posture of a misunderstood and aggrieved innocent and that of a repentant sinner."[10] Our task in the present section is to explore the nature of this criticism in a systematic and, hopefully, objective manner. Specifically, we will examine six recurring criticisms. These criticisms are:

1 That advertising raises consumer prices.
2 That much advertising is in bad taste.
3 That advertising insults consumer intelligence.
4 That advertising appeals mainly to emotions.
5 That advertising is the prime source of social unhappiness and discontent.
6 That advertising encourages the sale of inferior and worthless products.

ADVERTISING AND PRICES

The notion that heavy advertising expenditures raise consumer prices is, superficially, a compelling argument. On occasion, the argument is true; on other occasions it is not. The "logic" of this criticism is simple. It involves what might be called a stacking-up concept of costs. The view often held is that all elements of production costs and marketing costs must be summed and covered (or recovered) in the final selling price. All these costs accumulate in this vertical, or "stacking up," sense, and we end up necessarily paying for each layer of the stack, as it were. The cost of advertising is seen as simply another element in the stack, and its elimination is viewed as tantamount to price relief for us all. We should

---

[8] A brief discussion of the effect of cash discounts in this agency-client-medium relationship may be seen in Otto Klepner, *Advertising Procedure,* Fifth Edition, Englewood Cliffs, N.J.: Prentice-Hall, Inc., 1966, p. 474.
[9] See, for example, Carlston E. Warne, "Advertising—A Critic's View," in J. Howard Westing and Gerald Albaum, editors, *Modern Marketing Thought,* New York: Crowell-Collier and Macmillan, Inc., 1964, pp. 223–229.
[10] *Ibid.,* p. 223.

note that this argument need not be applied only to the individual advertisement or the advertising campaign, but to any promotional effort—trading stamps and "games" included. But in spite of the seeming simplicity and clarity of the logic of this criticism, a categorical statement that advertising raises consumer prices is wrong. Wherein is the logic of the criticism faulty? Consider the Figure 18.2.

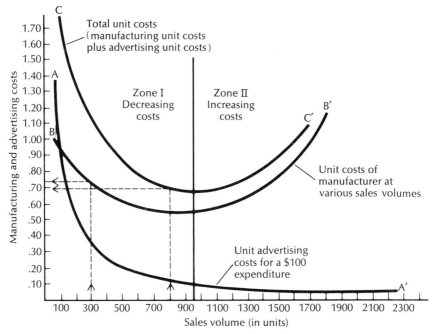

Figure 18.2   Advertising and Prices

Note, to begin with, that costs of two kinds are represented on the vertical axis of Figure 18.2. Note that sales volume (in units) is represented horizontally. The curve labeled AA' represents a $100 advertising expenditure divided by various sales volumes. Thus, unit advertising costs are $1 when sales volume is 100 units; unit advertising costs are $.10 when sales volume is 1000 units; and so on. The curve labeled BB' is the familiar U-shaped manufacturing cost curve. Note that it first falls (economies of scale are involved) and then increases (diseconomies of scale are encountered). Finally, note the curve labeled CC'. This curve is the vertical summation of curves AA' and BB'. The area between BB' and CC' should be the same as the area between AA' and the horizontal axis. At least this latter observation is true if the curves are properly drawn. But where does this lead us, analytically speaking?

As a preliminary use of Figure 18.2, assume that without advertising we can sell 300 units. Observe that manufacturing costs at this volume of sales are about $.75 per unit. (We consulted curve BB' because we assumed there was no advertising). Now suppose that we spend $100 for the advertising of whatever our product is. What unit costs would then be incurred? If sales volume remains unchanged, then unit costs would clearly have to increase—indeed if we continued to sell only 300 units, the total unit costs (read the CC' curve) would rise to about $1.10. But consider the more realistic case in which sales volume increases as a result of the advertising expenditure. What then would be the result. Any increase in sales volume will tend to reduce unit costs below $1.10. If we assume that sales volume increases to 600 units, the total cost per unit is in fact about the same as it was without any advertising. Indeed, if we assume that sales volume increases to 750 units, the total unit cost falls below $.70. It is thus possible, though admittedly not in all circumstances, for advertising to produce lower unit costs and therefore possibly lower consumer prices.

But Figure 18.2 will tell us more. We can reasonably infer from Figure 18.2 the circumstances in which advertising can serve to lower costs as well as the circumstances in which advertising cannot serve to lower costs. We can also identify precisely where the fallacy is in the logic of the stacking-up cost concept. Taking these points in reverse order, the fallacy of the vertical accumulation of costs idea lies in the implicit assumption of constant manufacturing costs per unit of output. That is, the critic who claims categorically that advertising raises consumer prices presumes constant (or increasing) unit costs of manufacture. This presumption runs contrary to the fundamental notion of scale economies. But we are not claiming that all advertising lowers manufacturing costs—that would be as silly as the criticism we are challenging. The charge that advertising increases consumer prices may be true in three particular circumstances: (a) when market saturation exists, (b) when decreasing returns to scale are encountered and (c) when the advertising itself is ineffective. We will examine each of these circumstances briefly.

Market saturation exists when no amount of encouragement will entice new buyers to try a particular product or service. Suppose for example, that every house in the United States were wired electrically and had a serviceable and well-designed washing machine in it. To advertise in the face of that circumstance would be essentially futile—for demand could not be stimulated by the advertising. The advertising costs would tend then to "stack-up"—they could not be defrayed through lower, compensating costs of manufacturing. When market saturation occurs, then a battle between competing firms with a not-to-be-outspent attitude clearly represents an economic waste. This standoff situation could only result in losses to the battling firms or in higher prices to final consumers.[11]

[11] This term is suggested in an address by Professor John K. Galbraith, presented at the American Association of Advertising Agencies, Eastern Annual Conference, New York City, October 10-11, 1967. This address is reprinted and distributed by the 4A's as Papers from the 1967 Region Conventions.

Another instance in which advertising costs can push prices up is when sales volume is extended into Zone II in Figure 18.2. In this instance, the advertising may increase sales volume, but it cannot produce a lower unit cost of manufacturing. When costs of manufacturing increase with increases in sales volume (sometimes called decreasing returns to scale) further advertising expenditures must accumulate in the vertical sense that we have discussed earlier.

Finally, advertising may result in higher prices if it is simply ineffective—if it does not result in increased sales volume even though market saturation has not yet developed. In brief summary, then, there are three instances in which advertising can increase consumer prices; but as long as a market is expandable (unsaturated), as long as lower manufacturing costs per unit are possible, and as long as the advertising produces (or helps to produce) increased sales volume, it is possible for advertising to lower total unit costs, and therefore it is possible to achieve lower consumer prices.

ADVERTISING AND BAD TASTE

The charge that much advertising is in bad taste is much more difficult to grapple with effectively, than the allegation that prices are increased because of advertising. One articulate critic argues that "if the commercials are telling it like it is, as the saying goes, we Americans must smell worse, have more dandruff, and suffer more allergies, colds headaches, sinus trouble, acid indigestion, upset stomach, tension and insomnia than any other people on earth."[12] The variations on this theme are infinite. Stan Freberg puts down the "gastro-intestinal school of advertising" at every opportunity; other critics attack the graphic short courses in internal medicine and curse the incessant drip in the duodenum. But the charge of bad taste runs in nonmedicinal dimensions too. Billboards, it is alleged, mar the otherwise aesthetic magnificence of the landscape. Movie ads are repulsive to the most liberal souls. Ads are noisy, abrasive, often ill-timed and, on occasion, stupid. Clearly, the indictment is severe—it is undeniably true that advertising, at one time or another, irritates almost everyone.[13]

But some such criticism is not entirely justified. Advertising is, basically, an art form. It has been called "creative communications," and there are no hard-and-fast rules for judging art—other than the personal judgment of the critic. This is an important point, and one that is often glossed over. What is witty, cute and clever to one man is inane noise to another. Some students truly enjoy the Freberg humor in advertising; others find him shallow and silly. It should be recalled that to the fans of the Grand

---

[12] Philip H. Love in *Entertainment in the Midlands* (Sunday Supplement), *Omaha World-Herald,* November 24, 1968, p. 11 (NANA).

[13] A good general reference on the malpractices, alleged and real, of the advertising business is E. S. Turner, *The Shocking History of Advertising,* Baltimore: Penguin Books, Inc., 1965.

Ole Opry, the Metropolitan Opera is in singularly bad taste. It should likewise be noted that to Metropolitan Opera fans, the Grand Ole Opry is the result of an unpardonable lapse of standards by the FCC.

Indeed, though they are, as a group, far less vocal than the critics, there are those who are bold enough to praise the creative content of commercials. No less a luminary than Goodman Ace has recently written that TV commercials "lately have been more entertaining than the stuff in between."[14] The critic of art necessarily exercises a value judgment—and it is too often not explicitly identified as such.

But there are other matters that are relevant to the "bad taste" charge. One phenomenon that undoubtedly contributes to charges of bad taste is identified by the term "imperfect segmentation." If we could have the best of all advertising worlds, we would have a system of communications that talked to everyone in the terms that he, individually, found most meaningful and communicative. Yet by the very nature of our system, it is unavoidable that, figuratively speaking, the words and appeals best suited for one man must necessarily fall to some extent upon the ears of another. Our mass communications system does not segment its targets with rifle shot accuracy—it is more in the nature of a full-flare shot pattern. This point is an important one, and yet the argument is rarely encountered. Consider the relationships depicted in Figure 18.3.

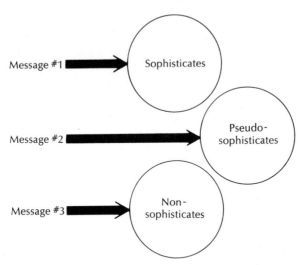

Figure 18.3 Communication Segmentation

If it were possible to pinpoint a communications target as depicted in Figure 18.3, it would be reasonable to expect fewer reports of bad taste and abrasion from advertising. But to the extent that pinpoint accuracy cannot be accomplished, we must logically expect some messages to fall

[14] "Top of My Head," *Saturday Review,* December 7, 1968, p. 8.

on the "wrong" ears. Or, what is the same thing, we will encounter messages so compromised by the "general" nature of the audience that they are very likely to offend with their blandness. It is particularly true of our general media—television and general appeal printed media—that a pinpoint matching of messages and tastes is very nearly impossible. Some very particular vehicles (for example, *New Yorker* and *Fortune*) enjoy, in contrast, a homogeneity in their readership that permits a more precise matching of message and tastes. In general then, the more specialized the communications vehicle, the better the opportunity to match messages and audience taste.

There is one further perimeter of defense for the "bad taste" charge. It is a perfectly human foible to conveniently simplify a complex phenomenon. And one such simplification is to identify all advertising, both good and bad, with "agencies" and Madison Avenue. It is useful, however, as a means of gaining additional insight into the problem of bad taste in advertising to separate the industry into what we will call "professional" and "peripheral" elements.

The peripheral element is certainly not the cause of all poorly conceived advertising, but it is very much involved with particular types of offensive advertising. What is this peripheral element? It comprises advertising and public relations men with relatively little formal education. The sales philosophy of this peripheral group often is to accomplish the sale at any cost—as long as the cost is not money. The use of deceit, trickery and outright fraud to complete the sale is common. The "advertising" that accompanies many movies and some popular fiction is produced by this peripheral element. The creative minds behind this type of advertising often view themselves as "practical" men, and they often pride themselves more on their ability to survive in a complex world than they do on the social responsibility manifest in the advertisements they create. Real estate deals and patent medicines are often sold by these modern-day hucksters.

ADVERTISING AND CONSUMER INTELLIGENCE

Still another charge that is leveled at the commercial aspects of our mass communications system is that much advertising insults the intelligence of the consumer. Brand X gasoline gives us "more economy." More economy than what?—the claim is indefinite. Volvo featured an advertisement several years ago that made the brazen claim that it was the largest-selling compact. The success of VW was sufficiently publicized to make the Volvo claim *seem* like an obvious misstatement of fact.[15] But there is another facet to this charge. Some critics dislike being talked down to—having the most simple ideas explained in a tedious, childlike manner. And the

---

[15] The apparent misstatement of fact actually hinged on definitions. The VW is, according to auto industry jargon, a subcompact. The Volvo claim was, therefore, technically correct.

popular notion that advertising copywriters aim their copy at a hypothetical audience with a sixth-grade education adds fuel to the "Dick and Jane" treatment. Educators in particular seem perturbed by the fact that much advertising may be directed to low levels of formal educational achievement. In addition to the notion of imperfect segmentation—an idea just discussed—there are three explanations of this "insults intelligence" charge.

First, it is entirely possible that there is insufficient intellectual challenge in much current advertising. We may, to some extent, be inattentive because we see little promise of true enlightenment. This is, of course, to admit to the charge.

It is also possible that there is a subtle form of self-flattery involved in this "insults intelligence" allegation. The critic who claims that advertising insults his intelligence is, in effect, saying that he cannot be fooled. And the old declaration, "You can't fool me," is an obvious form of self-praise.

Moreover, there is an explanation of this charge that involves what might be called the "technical definition." In the Volvo case cited above, for example, a careful reading of the copy would reveal that VW is a "subcompact" and therefore not included in the "compact" market. Similarly, headlines often proclaim several winners of automobile economy races. Thus, one brand will claim victory at precisely the same time that another brand will be claiming victory. These seemingly mutually exclusive claims are often explicable in terms of the "technical definition." There are, it turns out, several classes of competition in the economy runs—and given this additional fact, it is entirely possible to have two or more "winners." But the headlines that proclaim victory should, in the interest of fullest disclosure, claim their respective victories by specific class. We will have much more to say about the "sixth-grade copy" charge in the next chapter. We will, at that time, discuss the use of comprehension scores in advertising.

ADVERTISING AND EMOTIONS

Another criticism of advertising that is frequently encountered is that it appeals mainly to emotions. Advertising does not, this argument alleges, maintain the kind of objective, rational thrust that it should. It dwells excessively on matters that are not amenable to precise measurement. It sells, if you will, the sizzle rather than the steak. This criticism is primarily that of the professional economist—who would insist that purely informative communications are the only truly justifiable kind. This view holds that the use of emotional sales appeals interferes with an extremely important aspect of the free allocation of scarce resources among alternative ends. Emotional sales appeals are felt to produce a fogging of the mind—a fogging that presumably prevents rational (self-enlightened) decision making.

But what is an example of an emotional appeal? Consider an aftershave lotion. We might appeal on the basis of price or antiseptic prowess and be using an informational and rational appeal. But should we claim that its use makes one more desirable—a hit with the girls—we have entered the domain of emotion. It is informative to tell the weight-watcher how many pounds she will lose, but it is emotional to suggest that the weight-watcher will be more popular in a svelte condition. The line is certainly not easy to draw—indeed in most instances advertisements carry elements of both rational and emotional appeals.

Is it a justifiable criticism to deplore the use of emotional appeals in advertising? To do so, indeed, is illogical. The human being is at very least a social, mental, economic, moral, physical and religious being. And a sales appeal directed to any or all of these facets of the human being may make good sense. The economist's concept of what is informative and what is not informative is often a strange and unreal thing. As Galbraith himself confesses, "advertising begins under a general handicap in economic theory." [16] As we have argued before, the total performance of a product or service includes performance in more abstract realms as well as functional performance. Just because the value added as a result of performance in these intangible areas is difficult or impossible to measure, there seems little reason to pretend that such value does not exist at all. It is absurd to contemplate mass communications based exclusively on economic appeals.

ADVERTISING AND DISCONTENT

The criticism that advertising is the prime source of unhappiness and discontent is another, recently popular, charge. This argument asserts that, were it not for advertising, we would all be less aware of the material things that are to be had in this world, and that we would therefore feel greater content. This is another criticism founded in economic doctrine. For, "the prime purpose of applied economics was to maximize the satisfactions of the individual." This was accomplished by an allocation of economic resources of labor and capital and the other requisites of production which most efficiently satisfied the wants each person brought to the market. But, and here is the most important provision of the theory:

It was assumed that these wants were original with the individual and expressed in his purchases without inhibition or restraint. If his wants are not his own, if they originate not in his soul but in the creative mind of J. Walter Thompson, B B D & O, and Young and Rubicam, then some of the moral edge is off. For then the allocation of economic resources is not in the service of the individual: it is in the ultimate service of those who persuade him as to what he should have or those who retain those who so persuade him. [17]

[16] Papers from the 1967 Region Conference, American Association of Advertising Agencies, Eastern Annual Conference, New York City, October 10–11, 1967.
[17] *Ibid.,* p. 1.

It follows, does it not, that the least informed, least imaginative individual was the most satisfied. For a want, in order to be legitimate, had to originate with the individual. It was no good for the most informed, most imaginative to pass their thoughts along to those less facile. This is a curious argument—and a kind of insulated soul emerges as the ideal consumer. This person is "clean" in the sense that nothing, but nothing, has fiddled with his preference patterns. He wants what he knows, and he knows what he wants. Anything that interferes with this insulated soul is, more or less, an instrument of the devil. Or is it?

Consider for a moment the infinite number and types of exposures that must regularly soil the "insulated soul." He goes to school and sees a Porsche Targa; but the resulting want is not real—it did not originate within him. It is, moreover, the source of great discontent—for he can never be happy with the car he now owns. He also attends the church of his choice—and while there he is smitten by a silk suit one member of the congregation is wearing. His want patterns have, once again, been assaulted. But even if he does not strive for his intellectual betterment, even if he neglects the spiritual side of his person, he may nonetheless learn of the good things to be had. It is all the more curious that the critic sees the discontent produced by advertising as an undesirable state of being, while those who are persuaded of the merits of advertising see discontent as perhaps its most desirable result. The person who is deeply steeped in the free enterprise system would argue that were it not for occasional discontent nothing very exciting would ever happen. Indeed, every significant invention has necessarily evolved from discontent. The critic of advertising who advances the "unhappiness and discontent" argument holds a view that is fundamentally so different from that of the advertising proponent that continued debate is probably of little real value.

ADVERTISING AND PRODUCT QUALITY

There is one final criticism of advertising that we should examine. This criticism alleges that advertising encourages the sale of inferior and worthless products. A corollary of this argument is that advertising focuses on inconsequential product features—that it attempts to differentiate products in what are often ludicrous ways. It is the very nature of competition in mixed socioeconomic conditions that diverse products will be offered to the market. Whether they are inferior or worthless depends upon one's economic status and upon one's value or preference structure. There are tires with a one-year warranty and there are tires with a 40,000 mile warranty. The former is, relatively speaking, inferior to the latter. Yet a $50 tire is not every man's tire—not even with the relatively high average incomes of today. As long as a market segment expresses a preference for a cheap tire, a responsive enterprise system will answer that demand.

It is no semantic dodge to say that what is worthless to one person is not necessarily worthless to another. Value is determined, in the final analysis, in the mind of the beholder. And the critic who claims a product is worthless, while others continue to buy it and find satisfaction in it, is asking that his values be considered worthy of emulation by those who are "less insightful." It is doubtless true that insignificant product differences sometimes become the focus of advertising. But it is equally true that the quest for meaningful product differentiation is the single most significant economic catalyst. In effect, the quest for differentiation does not bear fruit for all firms, but the fact that virtually all firms pursue, and vigorously, the promise that meaningful product differentiation can bring is the more important point.

Advertising and society

The advertising fraternity is perhaps our principal social whipping boy. Advertising has been accused of causing, either directly or indirectly: (a) an escalating national crime rate, (b) a catastrophic series of summer race riots, (c) declining respect for leadership of every kind and (d) miscellaneous lesser events. Vance Packard charges, for example, that advertising: (a) employs strategies for the manipulation of children, (b) uses sub-threshold effects to slip messages past our conscious guard, (c) deliberately sells products for their status enhancement value, (d) creates illogical, irrational loyalties, (e) exploits our deepest sexual sensitivies and (f) applies the insights of depth selling to politics.[18]

Advertising is at once a scapegoat, an imperfect social institution and a force of imponderable proportions. We have every right to expect such a force to act in a fully responsible manner—we have a responsibility ourselves to understand the inherent imperfections of our commercial mass communications system. We have seen that there are essentially three avenues of challenge to advertising. First, advertising is challenged on an aesthetic front—the "bad taste" argument exemplifies this line of attack. Second, advertising is challenged on the moral front—the charges here range from exploitation of sex to that of "creating" wants. Third, advertising is challenged on the economic front—its effect on prices, its influence on the vigor of competition, in short, its effects on the allocation of scarce resources exemplify this last challenge.

It is difficult to define good taste; it would be impossible to legislate it into being. Good taste is what you and I, and very few others, possess. Yet there are commercial uses of the mass media that are repugnant to the majority concept of good taste. And the advertising industry—to an extent—attempts to regulate itself to ensure against such abuse. Each of the three components of the advertising "industry"—sponsor (client),

---

[18] See Vance Packard, "The Growing Power of Ad Men," in C. H. Sandage and Vernon Fryburger, editors, *The Role of Advertising*, Homewood, Ill.: Richard D. Irwin, Inc., 1960, pp. 271-273.

agency and media—has established the means through which standards of taste may be controlled. Advertising sponsors may be "regulated" by a company code of ethics, as well as by an industrial code developed by an association of firms. Note that these codes are self-imposed and "entered into without compulsion or threat of penalties."[19] At General Foods, all product claims of performance, quality and value must be approved by an advertising policy committee composed of representatives from the advertising, merchandising, products control, public relations and legal departments. Revlon, a large cosmetics advertiser, says, "Any statement we make must bear scientific verification." The Falstaff Brewing Company has a list of advertising guides that include the following provisions:

1 Any appeal to children or minors is avoided, and minors are never referred to on radio, TV, or in print.
2 Tavern and restaurant scenes are always shown in an atmosphere of respectability.
3 The so-called "Cheesecake" or sex angle is never stressed, and even mild kissing scenes are not permitted.
4 Words that imply that our product gives a "lift" or is "zippy" are avoided.[20]

The advertising policy of Purex is especially noteworthy. Purex management believes that:

Advertising in our field has become more and more exaggerated as products tended to level out in performance. To achieve competitive advantage, advertising has sought to magnify unimportant differences, has resorted to the clever, tricky product promise, and has claimed more and more unbelievable benefits.

As a result, consumer belief in the honesty and sincerity of advertising has declined in the past few years, and in our opinion is rapidly becoming a serious problem. Purex management is concerned selfishly, because we realize that without a justifiable confidence in the honesty and sincerity of the advertising message, the value of that message in selling our products is heavily discounted.

Purex has the following rules of advertising conduct.

1 Purex advertising shall not claim or promise by implication any product performance or characteristic which is not fully supported by laboratory research, consumer research or similar factual information.
2 Purex advertising must not make use of the legal but dishonest device of the "hedge" or "weasel," by which displayed promises are legally discounted in fine type.
3 In TV commercials, visual demonstrations will be real ones within the time limits of the commercial.

---

[19] See, for example, *Self-Regulation in Advertising,* Washington: US Department of Commerce, 1964, p. 9.
[20] *Ibid.,* p. 19.

4 Comparative claims for Purex products must be clearly supported by research laboratory or consumer tests vs. competitors products. Such tests are not to be made against inferior brands, but against the best competitive products on the market.

The member agencies of the American Association of Advertising Agencies similarly operate under the provisions of a "creative code." Member agencies will not knowingly produce advertising that contains:

1 False or misleading statements or exaggerations, visual or verbal.
2 Testimonials which do not reflect the real choice of a competent witness.
3 Price claims which are misleading.
4 Comparisons which unfairly disparage a competitive product or service.
5 Claims insufficiently supported, or which distort the true meaning or practicable application of statements made by professional or scientific authority.
6 Statements, suggestions or pictures offensive to public decency.

And, in the matter of good taste, the *AAAA* Code says:

We recognize that there are areas which are subject to honestly different interpretations and judgment. Taste is subjective, and may even vary from time to time as well as from individual to individual. Frequency of seeing or hearing advertising messages will necessarily vary greatly from person to person. However, we agree not to recommend to an advertiser, and to discourage the use of, advertising which is in poor or questionable taste, or which is deliberately irritating through content, presentation or excessive repetition.[21]

It is, of course, possible to argue that these codes and other efforts toward self-regulation within the advertising industry are ineffectual and token reform measures. And that charge has indeed been made. But the professional elements in the advertising fraternity are sincere—they are, as they themselves admit, selfishly concerned—and fully aware of the likely consequence of grossly irresponsible commercial use of the mass media.

As to the alleged moral transgressions of advertising, moral standards are set in a collective way. There is no single, well-defined moral code; there are many such codes. The moral range might run from outright prudishness to the "free everything" philosophy. In one sense, advertising functions within the moral constraints imposed by society—not by those that would be imposed by the most prudish elements within the society. All of which is not to condone some movie advertisements.

But to those who believe that it is morally wrong that advertising must persuade—that it is wrong for advertising to develop new "wants"—there is an even more emphatic answer. For many years critics have distinguished between economic "wants" and economic "needs." To satisfy

[21] *Ibid.,* p. 39.

an economic need has been viewed as a worthy cause, to satisfy a want as much less worthy. The classic statement of the issue is as follows:

The fact that wants can be synthesized by advertising, catalyzed by salesmanship, and shaped by the discreet manipulations of the persuaders shows that they are not very urgent. A man who is hungry need never be told of his need for food. If he is inspired by his appetite, he is immune to the influence of Messrs. Batten, Barton, Durstine and Osborn. The latter are effective only with those who are so far removed from physical wants that they do not already know what they want. In this state alone, men are open to persuasion.[22]

It will be recalled that this "manipulation" of wants becomes a moral question because it allegedly interferes with the process of free choice. It invades the inner sanctum of the mass mind and prevents clear thinking. But advertising "is designed to predispose its readers to a favorable consideration of its sponsor and his product. It is deliberately planned to make its readers and listeners take sides—to affiliate and ally themselves under its banner and to ignore all others."[23] Advertising is not, and never was, a dispassionate, objective and unbiased dissemination of truth. Advertising has, in other words, a distinctive persuasive dimension to it.

And the line between a "need" and a "want" is not always clear. There is impressive evidence that even basic needs may not always be resolved without persuasion. It took nearly two hundred years to introduce the potato into the diets of Europe and North America.[24] The potato was an unacceptable answer to the basic "need" of food even in the face of recurring famine and agrarian conditions not well adapted to other crops. In short, entire populations had to be *persuaded* to accomodate a *need*. And this is not the way man is supposed to act—we are told that only his *wants* require persuasive sales effort. The allegedly evil, or at least amoral, influence of advertising is a convenient fiction—what is a contrived want and what is a need is very much an individual matter. Indeed a list of "needs" today would most surely contain an ample number of what must have been "wants" yesterday. Need is, in summary, necessarily a flexible concept, defined largely by a particular environment at a particular time. The "wants" created by advertising result in what has been called *constructive discontent*; and as one student of the matter sees it, this constructive discontent represents a very important aspect of human progress. "While some excesses as a creation of frivolous obsolescence might be deplored, technological development is so rapid and the desire of people for new things is so great that advertising has become a vital form

---

[22] John Kenneth Galbraith, *The Affluent Society*, Boston: Houghton Mifflin Company, 1958, p. 158.

[23] McGarry, *op. cit.*, p. 132.

[24] See Jean Boddewyn, "Galbraith's Wicked Wants," *Journal of Marketing*, October 1961, p. 15.

of communication and a vital tool for keeping up the pace of continuous progress." [25]

The efficiency of advertising is challenged principally by economists. The argument, as we have seen, is that advertising increases consumer prices, and that advertising is one means of avoiding really vigorous forms of competition; namely, competition with prices. Advertising, it is held, must serve therefore to reduce the level of living of us all. This conclusion follows because higher prices and less vigorous competition must act to give us smaller real incomes than we would otherwise enjoy. The argument suggests, further, that (a) heavy advertising expenditures serve as (b) barriers to entry that, in turn, (c) further encourage economic concentration that (d) produce still higher (monopolistic) prices that (e) produce excessively high profits and renew the chain of events so that the position of the large firm is assured in perpetuity. [26] As is so often the case, the argument is logical, but it does not agree with the evidence that is accumulating. Consider the following points:

1 Few brands, however invincible they may appear, are truly assured of a large future market share. Rinso, Super Suds and Oxydol had 48 percent of the 1948 household detergent market, less than 9 percent in 1960. Camel, Lucky Strike and Chesterfield each lost about 7 percent of the market between 1956 and 1966. The fifth largest brand of dentifrice in 1961 was no longer in the big five in 1965. In ready-to-eat cereals, two of the five best-selling brands in 1961 had been replaced by 1965. Between 1950 and 1964, Coca-Cola lost ten percentage points in market share. [27]
2 Categories of products that are most heavily advertised "have tended to show smaller increases in price than less heavily advertised categories during the post-World War II price inflation." [28]
3 Profit rates are only slightly higher for heavy advertisers. The average return earned by 102 manufacturers with the largest dollar expenditures for advertising was 14.7 percent as compared to 13.8 percent earned by 2298 leading manufacturing companies reported by the First National City Bank of New York. [29]

---

[25] Ernest R. Dichter, "How Advertising Shapes Decision," in Westing and Albaum, op. cit., p. 222.
[26] This chain of logic is identified in Jules Backman, Advertising and Competitition, New York: New York University Press, 1967, p. 155.
[27] These facts are gleaned from a report titled "Advertising in a Competitive Economy," presented by Jules Backman to the American Association of Advertising Agencies Eastern Annual Conference, New York City, October 10–11, 1967.
[28] Backman, Advertising and Competition, pp. 203–211.
[29] Ibid., pp. 212–216, 152.

SUMMARY

Chapter 18 has had two basic purposes. First, we developed some important definitional matters; and, second, we examined some critical attitudes toward the commercial uses of the mass media. More specifically, we defined advertising as the impersonal communication of ideas, goods or services to a mass audience by an identified paying sponsor. We distinguished advertising from both publicity and propaganda. Advertising was classified in terms of (a) the medium it utilizes, (b) the audience it is directed to, (c) its geographical coverage, (d) the timing of its response, (e) the type of demand it attempts to develop and (f) the number and type of its sponsors. The nature of the advertising industry was briefly examined.

Six major criticisms that are frequently brought against the commercial use of our mass communications system were examined. The notion that advertising increases consumer prices is not a valid blanket condemnation—though there are, indeed, instances in which advertising may tend to have that effect. The charge that most advertising is in bad taste was answered in several ways. First, such a charge unavoidably involves the personal judgment of the critic. Second, imperfect segmentation may be the cause of some abrasion in advertising. Third, some abrasive advertisements came from what we called a peripheral element in mass communications.

The charge that advertising insults the intelligence of the consumer was examined briefly. It was noted that this charge may involve a subtle form of self-flattery, and that the technical definition may also produce some "insult to intelligence." The charge that advertising is directed to emotional appeal, and that this type of appeal prevents rational decision making on the part of the consumer, was answered with the argument that any facet of the human character can be a meaningful basis of appeal. Thus, for example, social, mental, economic, moral, physical, religious, and many other appeals are legitimate. Advertising does create discontent through its informational capacity. This latter charge, however, is viewed as a strength, not a weakness, of the commercial use of our mass communications system. Finally, product quality is influenced by advertising. An economic system characterized by mixed affluence is one that will produce low as well as high quality goods and services. What is a "worthless" product is a matter of individual judgment.

REVIEW QUESTIONS

1 Carefully define and indicate the relevance of each of the following concepts to the study of marketing:
   a. Advertising
   b. Primary demand advertising
   c. Selective demand advertising

 d. Cooperative advertisements

 e. Derived-demand advertisements

 f. The advertising industry

 g. The billings size of an advertising agency

 h. A standoff advertising battle

 i. Imperfect communications segmentation

2 Distinguish carefully between each element in the following pairs of terms:

 a. Direct action advertising *and* institutional advertising

 b. An advertising medium *and* an advertising vehicle

 c. Horizontal cooperative advertisements *and* vertical cooperative advertisements

 d. An independent advertising agency *and* a house advertising agency

3 Being as clear and complete as you can, indicate the precise circumstances that must exist in order that advertising expenditures can reduce consumer prices.

DISCUSSION QUESTIONS

4 Develop a list of the characteristics of advertisements that you personally prefer. That is, list the characteristics that you believe tend to produce a good advertisement. When you have done that, compare your list with that of any other class member.

5 Specifically, what steps would you take to improve the level of taste reflected in mass, commercial forms of communication?

6 How is it possible to achieve a greater degree of communications segmentation? What effects would (could) this greater degree of segmentation produce?

Chapter 19

EFFICIENCY IN PROMOTION

Promotion, including advertising, personal selling and sales promotion, is an extremely important part of modern marketing. From a broad, social point of view, promotion in one form or another accounts for the great majority of the total dollars spent for marketing. Because promotion is, in the aggregate, an expensive socioeconomic activity, the efficiency of modern promotional methods is an issue of significance to all consumers. To the extent that promotion can be implemented less expensively than present methods require, we all stand to gain. Our concern in this chapter is with this issue of efficiency in promotion—our task is to examine some of the important modern techniques of promotion, with special emphasis on the influence of these techniques on the efficiency of promotional efforts.

More specifically, we will consider six issues that are subordinate to the general question of efficiency in promotion. These issues are: (a) the use of formal rules, or principles, of persuasion in promotion, (b) the application of formal rules of learning theory in promotion, (c) the use of symbolic means of communications, (d) the matching of promotional messages with particular audiences, (e) the measurement of the effectiveness of promotional efforts and (f) procedures for audience authentication.

Persuasion

Though it is not yet well integrated into the study of marketing, there is a substantial body of knowledge that deals with the process of persuasion. And persuasion is a common denominator in all facets of promotion.[1] Advertising, personal sales efforts and sales promotion all require persuasion; each involves: (a) a persuader, (b) some issue or set of issues to be presented and (c) an audience with opinions and attitudes. Indeed, the purpose of promotion might well be defined in terms of these three components. Promotion is, thus, the presentation of an issue or a set of issues to an audience in order to solidify or change the attitudes or opinions of that audience. Because persuasion is inextricably a part of promotion, any systematic study of promotion must proceed from the body of scientific knowledge dealing with persuasion. But before we examine that body of knowledge, we need to consider one related question.

Is it proper, in an ethical sense, to study and refine a subject matter that might be used exploitively by persons with antisocial purpose? It is clear that an understanding of the process of persuasion is knowledge that could be used in an exploitative way. A man who is perhaps the foremost expert on persuasion today asks the provocative question as follows:

What is the probability that within the lifespan of many of us (that) enough will have been learned about the techniques of persuasion to subvert many of us without our awareness of anything happening? On a different value plane, what is the likelihood that the right research findings in the wrong hands could result in many of us buying products we do not really want, taking our vacations at places we really are not interested in, and generally behaving as consumers the way that someone else wants us to behave? [2]

The history of persuasion is replete with techniques that are apparently potent, that are allegedly manipulative, and, worst of all, that appear to persuade without the conscious participation of the audience being persuaded. Persuasion is, to some, a modern day form of witchcraft. An example of this kind of devious persuasion is suggested by the phrase "subliminal perception." [3] In 1957, rumor had it that a marketing research experiment had isolated a means of persuasion that did not appeal to the conscious human senses. This device was "sub" (below) "liminal" (the threshold of perception) or outside the range of conscious perception. A high-pitched dog whistle is "subliminal" or below the *human* hearing threshold. Similarly, one can speak so softly that the sounds are not audible—such sounds are subliminal. There is a conscious range of reception for all human senses. A weight that is microscopically small, when placed on the palm of a blindfolded subject may not be sensed; that weight is subliminal relative to the sense of feeling.

But the 1957 scare was related to sight—and the method of alleged persuasion was to flash brief commercial messages at high speed (1/3000 of a second) on a movie screen. These messages avoided (were subliminal)

[1] One of the early, candid recognitions of this fact of life is Rex F. Harlow, "Persuasion and Public Relations," *Public Relations Journal,* October 1957, pp. 14–16, 18.
[2] Herbert I. Abelson, *Persuasion,* New York: Springer Publishing Co., Inc., 1959, p. 91.
[3] See Edward L. Brink and William T. Kelley, *The Management of Promotion,* Englewood Cliffs, N.J.: Prentice-Hall, Inc., 1963, pp. 140–143. See also James V. McConnell and others, "The Ethics of Subliminal Influence," *American Psychologist,* May 1958, pp. 237–239.

the consciousness of subjects, but were thought to have inordinate powers to persuade—they were believed to hit, as it were, when the conscious of a person was not on guard. The evidence that was first reported indicated sales of both soft drinks and popcorn in a movie theater could be significantly altered though the use of these subliminal messages.

The psychologist calls this process of perceiving a stimulus that occurs below the level of conciousness "subception.[4] And the possibility that sellers could send messages that were received through this process of subception was received with the same warmth and hospitality as the plague. The hue and cry for protection from such means of persuasion went up long before the alleged powers of the technique were properly documented. And, indeed, in retrospect, subliminal perception as a means of commercial persuasion promised much more than it ever delivered. With a great deal of evidence now in, use of subliminal impressions for advertising purposes not only does not produce the zombie-like result it was supposed to, but it probably does not have even the same persuasive impact as more conventional exposures.[5] The evidence suggests that a subliminal message: (a) cannot cause a person to act against his own best interests, (b) cannot communicate complex or carefully reasoned persuasive messages and (c) will not work at all on many subjects. In short, subliminal advertising, if it did work, would be both relatively ineffective and relatively inefficient.

But the use of subception as a sales technique demonstrates clearly the ethical issues involved in the study of persuasive processes. Do the social sciences have a social responsibility to discontinue the systematic study of the process of persuasion? Is an understanding of persuasion too hot to handle? It is not. And the position on this issue taken here is that as progress is made in sharpening the rules of persuasion, the audiences upon whom such rules are to be used probably grow less susceptible to persuasive influences. The much-feared candy-from-a-baby situation does not seem to be a realistic assessment. Indeed, it is possible that the sophistication of the consumer progresses at a more rapid rate than the general state of the science of persuasion.[6]

[4] See, for example, J. C. Naylor and C. H. Lowshe, "An Analytical Review of the Experimental Basis of Subception," *Journal of Psychology*, July 1958, pp. 75–96.

[5] See J. M. Champions and W. W. Turner, "An Experimental Investigation of Subliminal Perception," *Journal of Applied Psychology*, December 1959, pp. 382–385. This study concludes that subliminal presentations had no effect on recognition of a test trademark. A stronger indictment of the effectiveness of the use of advertising at subliminal levels is in M. L. DeFleur and R. M. Petranoff, "A Televised Test of Subliminal Persuasion," *Public Opinion Quarterly*, Summer 1959, pp. 168–180. A study that indicates some subliminal influence is P. A. Kolers, "Subliminal Stimulation in Problem Solving," *American Journal of Psychology*, September 1957, pp. 437–441.

[6] This is the view argued by Raymond A. Bauer in "Limits of Persuasion," *Harvard Business Review*, September-October 1958, pp. 105–110. See also Harold H. Kassarjian and Thomas S. Robertson, *Perspectives in Consumer Behavior*, Glenview, Ill.: Scott, Foresman and Company, 1968, pp. 86–93.

BASIC RULES OF PERSUASION

Not all the rules of persuasion are devious efforts to manipulate and control the human psyche. Most such rules center around: (a) the manner of presentation of the issues and (b) the character of the persuader. These rules of persuasion have been developed from empirical studies in the fields of psychology and social psychology. These rules represent, collectively, a kind of "how to" foundation for effective persuasion. Consider the following example.

Suppose that we would like to know which is the more effective persuasive tactic: (a) an explicit statement of conclusions or (b) an implicit conclusion (let the audience reach its own conclusion). Suppose further that our concern over this issue relates to an advertisement we are planning. In the advertisement we will compare our product with several competing products in several different dimensions of performance. The demonstration will actually reveal the superiority of our product—but should we let the audience infer such superiority on their own? One rule of persuasion is: *there will probably be more opinion change in the direction you want if you explicitly state your conclusions than if you let the audience draw their own conclusions.*[7]

Another problem in persuasion involves the order of presentation of opposite points of view.[8] When there are essentially two points of view on an issue, the question before the persuader may be whether to present the view that he prefers first or last. Suppose, in order to develop a more realistic illustration, that we wish to persuade housewives that detergents with bleach built in are not as good as detergents that require that bleach be added to the wash water separately. Our problem then becomes: (a) should we present both sides of the argument, and if so, (b) which position should be presented last? The rules of persuasion say: (a) *when it is probable that the audience will hear the other side from someone else, present both sides of the argument;* (b) *when opposite views are presented one after another, the one presented last will probably be more effective.*[9]

But the reader should not get the idea that rules exist to guide every question in persuasion. Indeed, the real intellectual challenge in this area lies in the more precise definition of these rules. Too often, research experiments provide opposite results—no general rule can be relied upon.

Such an instance is the argument about "anticlimax order" and "climax order". A question that often confronts a seller relates to the proper ordering of the sales points he wishes to make. Suppose, as an example, that there are five distinct sales points that could be made about a product.

[7] See Abelson, *op. cit.,* p. 10.
[8] See, for example, A. A. Lumsdaine and I. L. Janis, "Resistance to 'Counter-Propaganda' Produced by a One-Sided Versus a Two-Sided 'Propaganda' Presentation," *Public Opinion Quarterly,* Fall 1953, pp. 311–318.
[9] See, for example, H. Cromwell, "The Relative Effect on Audience Attitude of the First Versus the Second Argumentative Speech of a Series," *Speech Monograph,* Spring 1950, pp. 105–122.

Some of these points are more important than others; there are, if you will, strong benefits and weak benefits. The question for the persuader is should the sales points be presented in weak-to-strong order (climax order) or in strong-to-weak order (anticlimax order)? Which sequence of benefits provides the greatest change in attitude or opinion—or, which is the more persuasive order? Unfortunately, there is no general rule available. There are, apparently, offsetting advantages (or disadvantages) in both the anticlimax and the climax order. There is some indication that the anticlimax order is best when the audience is judged to be uninterested.[10] That is, an uninterested audience that is bombarded with weak arguments is not likely to develop great curiosity about the approaching climax argument. The interested or friendly audience would, according to this guide, be best suited for the climax sequence.

Consider one other question in persuasion and the rules that have evolved to answer that question. We have all seen persuaders who rely primarily upon impressive, logical, carefully reasoned arguments. We have all likewise seen those who rely primarily upon unsupported generalities or illogical and irrelevant argumentation. Indeed, in politics, the victory often seems to go to the glib argument that does not stand up under close critical examination. What are the implications of this phenomenon for selling? Under what circumstances is the glib argument best? The persuasion rule in this case specifies a dependence upon the intellectual ability of the audience. If an audience is bright—possesses learning ability, can analyze critically, and can draw an inference when the opportunity is present—the logical argument is most persuasive. The evidence suggests, conversely, that an audience with less intellectual ability is often most persuaded by glib generalities and "apparent" logic.[11]

Let this brief discussion serve as an indication of the applicability of the rules of persuasion to promotion. And let this introduction to the rules of persuasion serve as a bridge to another body of knowledge that relates closely to promotion. This latter body of understanding is "learning theory."

Promotion and the "rules" of learning theory

Learning theory is the body of interrelated principles that deal with human memory.[12] Learning theory is the basic content of the field of educational

[10] See Abelson, *op. cit.*, p. 9.

[11] *Ibid.*, pp. 58–59.

[12] Several good general references in learning theory are E. R. Hilgard and G. H. Bower, *Theories of Learning*, Third Edition, New York: Appleton-Century-Crofts, 1966; E. R. Guthrie, *The Psychology of Learning*, Revised Edition, New York: Harper & Row, Publishers, 1952; and B. R. Bugelski, *The Psychology of Learning Applied to Teaching*, Indianapolis, Ind.: Bobbs-Merrill, 1964. See also H. E. Krugman, "Application of Learning Theory to T.V. Copytesting," *Public Opinion Quarterly*, Winter 1962, pp. 626–634.

psychology. The notion that learning theory may be relevant and helpful in the field of marketing suggests that the task of the teacher is not altogether different from that of the seller. That is, both the educational context and the sales context have: (a) a disseminator of information, (b) an audience and, in both cases, (c) the disseminator can have a measurable impact on the audience. This close parallel between education and some forms of commercial communication suggests that the laws that govern learning in an educational context may also be useful when applied in a commercial circumstance. The commercial sponsor necessarily has a distinct interest in knowing that his messages do not just hit an audience and glance off—if learning does not result from his promotional expenditures, then the seller is guilty of an inefficient allocation of his budget. To the extent that the use of learning theory produces more effective and memorable exposures to commercial messages, promotion is accomplished more effectively.

The basic concept of the learning theorist is the *learning curve.* The learning curve depicts recall, or more specifically, it depicts the percentage of a particular learning exposure recalled by a subject at various points in time after the exposure.[13] Observe Figure 19.1. Note that the vertical scale is labeled "exposure recall." Note that time is represented on the horizontal scale:

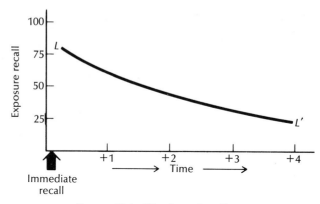

Figure 19.1 The Learning Curve

"+1" identifies exposure plus one time unit—say one day; "+2" denotes exposure plus two time units, and so on. Observe that the curve slopes down to the right, indicating that exposure recall decays, or becomes less vivid, as time passes. The intersection of LL' with the vertical axis indicates

[13] Note that "recall" and "persuasiveness" are two distinctly different things. Rules of persuasion are concerned with *changing* opinion or attitude. Laws of learning are concerned with ability to recall—ability to recall the details of a learning exposure through time, whether or not the subject subscribes to the views expressed in the exposure.

the immediate recall level—the percentage of an exposure absorbed and recalled at the instant of the exposure. This idea of a learning curve is a most versatile one; it has some properties that we need to recognize explicitly.

A most important point to note is that the learning curve is an *empirical* device—we can produce such a curve for any kind of learning exposure, and do so relatively inexpensively. Because this learning curve is a measurable phenomenon, it is possible for us systematically to identify the circumstances under which learning occurs most efficiently.

Consider the set of three learning curves in Figure 19.2. Assume for the sake of illustration, that these three curves summarize the learning results of three independent classroom exposures. Which of the three represents the most lasting recall? Which is the least effective learning exposure? Each of the curves has some attribute that is desirable; two of the curves are very weak in some particular respect. Curve C reflects very good instantaneous recall, but the rate of forgetting is precipitous. Curve B is relatively weak in terms of the level of instantaneous recall, but shows admirable properties of retention. Curve A is a kind of standard; it embodies both high levels of immediate recall and good retention. These three curves are by no means the only possible shapes and positions that may occur, but they serve to demonstrate an important idea about learning. Whether or not learning is efficient or totally ineffective depends upon two factors: (a) the receptivity of the minds doing the learning and (b) the environment of the learning.

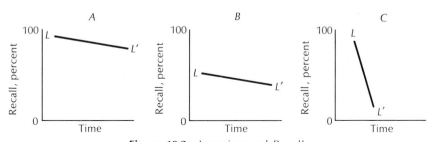

Figure 19.2 Learning and Recall

The "receptivity" of the learner's mind is determined by the interest level and the intellectual capacity of the learner. There is relatively little that the disseminator can do to achieve a significant degree of control over the receptivity of the learner's mind. There are, of course, techniques for getting attention (or of attracting the interest of the learner), but unless some learner interest is there in the first place, such attention is fleeting. But, what we have called the environment of learning—the conditions under which the exposure is made—can, to an important degree, be controlled by the disseminator. And the body of laws or principles that we call learning theory often specifies the best environments for effective learning. Expressed in terms of the learning curve, the laws and principles of learning theory indicate the learning environment that is most likely to produce the ideal learning curve; namely, a curve with relatively high instant recall and good retention.

The average person is exposed to several thousand commercial messages each day—indeed such messages are so ubiquitous that we may seem to have come a long way toward developing a filter within ourselves that reduces our annoyance to tolerable levels. We are, in short, oblivious to much of the commercial material that occurs around us. Because there is so much commercial material seeking to attract our attention, it follows that the most memorable commercial exposure—the commercial message that produces the most lasting learning experience—is in some way differentiated from run-of-the-mill commercials. The laws of learning theory suggest the manner in which such differentiation might be developed.

Consider, for purposes of illustration, the problem of a candy manufacturer. The promotion task confronting this manufacturer was to establish a particular brand of candy as being of high quality without resorting to the use of already overworked superlatives. The message could not say "we use only the best chocolate," "the nuts we use are very fresh," "made with the most rigid quality controls," or any of the other quality claims that we have all heard variously applied to diverse types of products. The message had, in some way, to convey quality without using the word quality. The technique that was used in this instance is one suggested by learning theory. An advertising campaign was ultimately developed that used the simple statement, "Rolls Royce is a car—Almond Rocha is a candy." This manner of conveying the notion of quality utilizes the psychological law of "belonging"—the learning precept that specifies that "ideas or objects that are naturally related and organized into meaningful relationships can be remembered better than those that have no logical connection." [14] The Rolls Royce is a well-established symbol of highest quality—and the verbal association of the candy brand with Rolls Royce says something, by inference, about the quality of the candy. In a sense, most of us have stored in our memory units a mental notation about the high quality of Rolls Royce; the advertiser wanted us to make use of this stored information to "learn" better what brand represents a parallel standard of excellence for candy. To express all this in terms of the learning curve, we are suggesting that this use of the law of belonging would produce higher recall of the exposure, and better retention of the high quality of Almond Rocha, than if a more conventional learning environment had been provided.

But consider another application of learning theory. Suppose that your assignment is to promote a new, young singing star. Suppose further that the young man has a strong voice, a generally attractive appearance and

[14] See Brink and Kelley, op. cit., p. 134.

the name George Dorsey. In preliminary discussions with the young man's manager, there has been some indication that a change to a professional name might make him a more memorable entertainment event. What type of name would you suggest? How about names in the Hollywood tradition—names like Steve Smooth, Ricky Rich and Mike Muscle? The best answer is often one that interrupts tradition, if anything like a "tradition" can fairly be said to exist. In this case a good choice of name might even be Engelbert Humperdinck. Promotion that consciously attempts to avoid me-too kinds of appeals—promotion that is, in a calculated way, "out of step" with sellers of similar products or services, takes advantage of the principal of learning called *incongruity,* or *difference.* Thus, if all ads for men's shirts show carefully groomed, almost anonymous young men as models, it might be very smart to use a model with an eye patch or a hearing aid. If all magazine advertisements are four-color, full-page, use black and white and a partial page.[15]

Our memory plays what may seem to be curious tricks on us—the learning theorist is an expert concerning these tricks. Consider, for example, the way in which our mind recalls a listing or recitation of some kind. More immediately to the point, consider the relationship between how our mind recalls a listing and the most effective promotion strategy. When you are given a listing of numbers or syllables to memorize and to repeat to an interviewer, you tend to recall most accurately the early elements in the list, then the ending elements in the list. The middle portion of the list is, for most people, relatively the most difficult to recall correctly. This tendency is called, in learning theory, the law of *primacy-recency.*

The idea of primacy-recency has some obvious implications for advertising. The law suggests, for example that the best position within a clutter of ads is either early or late but not in the middle. In television, the clutter position is the two- or three-minute period between programs during which several spot ads may be shown in rapid succession. Although the matter is not resolved in a definitive way, it is possible that primacy-recency works to reduce the impact of the "middle" ads in this clutter. Note carefully that this "law" of learning says that, other things being equal, the middle position in a listing is most difficult to recall accurately. It is, in other words, entirely possible that a good ad in the middle of a clutter may be recalled more accurately than a poor ad at either the beginning or the end of the sequence. Note, as well, that the position of an ad within a magazine may relate to recall and the rule of primacy-recency.

Another law of learning, one that is much closer to the daily life of a student, and one that also relates to promotional effectiveness, is called the principle of *distributed effort.* This rule says that learning is more

---

[15] See, for example, the results of a test in D. B. Lucas and S. H. Britt, *Measuring Advertising Effectiveness,* New York: McGraw-Hill Book Co., 1963, pp. 162–163.

effective when learning effort is evenly distributed over time rather than absorbed in intensive bursts or cram sessions. Given similar intellectual capacity, a student who crams may score as high on a given exam as the student who grinds it out on a regular study schedule. But the difference in the two exposures is in the retention of the exposure through time. The cram effort fades faster; the well-distributed effort endures. If exams were given on the same material six months after the first exam, the difference in performance might be quite marked. But how does this all relate to the more effective use of promotion? There is a definite parallel between the "cram" study session and a promotion technique known as "blitzing." A sales blitz is a campaign characterized by short life and great noise—it is a concentrated sales effort as opposed to one that is spread over a longer span of time. The law of distributed effort suggests that blitzing would be least effective when good future recall of the exposure is important. The best use of the blitz would be in those circumstances when the event to be promoted has only current importance.[16]

Still another principle of learning that may explain some types of advertising is the principle of involvement. This principle says that the learning experience is more effective if the learner is actively involved rather than a passive witness. Involvement itself requires cerebral cooperation—and the result of such cooperation is often a much more indelible impression on the learner's psyche. This is the rule of learning that recommends classroom dialogue over classroom monologue; this is also the rule of learning that recommends *participative commercials.* Participative commercials are those that invite the viewer/listener/reader to complete something, sing along, or otherwise become an active part of the commercial message. Thus, commercial contests may be prompted not only by the insights that may be provided by the entrants, but they may also, because they force a contestant to think both long and hard about a particular brand, have lasting promotional value as well. A singing jingle that achieves humming or whistling popularity is well established in the cranial cavities.

Symbolic communications in promotion

To this point in our discussion, we have indicated that the efficiency of promotional activities rests to some extent upon the degree to which formal rules of persuasion and learning are utilized. To the extent that such formal rules are utilized, promotion can be more efficient. But there is a third means through which substantial gains in the efficiency of mass communications may be achieved: through the use of *symbolic communications.* Communication is said to be symbolic when it is: (a) nonver-

---

[16] See S. H. Britt, "How Advertising Can Use Psychology's Rules of Learning," in James V. McNeal, *Readings in Promotion Management,* Des Moines, Iowa: Meredith Publishing Company, 1966, p. 32.

bal and (b) accomplished with some symbol or set of symbols. The old saw that a picture is worth a thousand words is a reference to symbolic communications. And that same old maxim highlights an important attribute of symbolic communications; namely, its efficiency. We communicate symbolically to a much greater extent than would at first be supposed. There are, in fact, some contexts in which entire symbolic languages are used. The orchestra leader and the traffic policeman communicate nonverbally and may deal effectively with reasonably subtle nuances of meaning. These languages are *explicit* symbols. But our lives are influenced, and sometimes profoundly, by *implicit* communications symbols. We interpret and draw inferences about a person's wealth, health, occupation, education, and endless other characteristics from the symbols of his dress, his home and his automobile. These symbols are implicit because they do not constitute a well-defined language—they are subject to a degree of individual interpretation; but they are of no less consequence in the lives of a modern community.[17]

But our principal concern here is with the efficiency of symbolic forms of communications and with the use of this means of communication in the development of commercial messages. Because symbols are very often a shorthand for expressing complex thoughts, they hold the potential for increasing the efficiency of a commercial mass communications system. We might reverse this proposition and use the *frequency of use* of symbolic communications as one indication of the extent to which an economic system avails itself of existing opportunities for increases in efficiency. By this criterion, greater efficiency in communications would be associated with the use of high levels of symbolic communication, and lower efficiency would be marked by a relatively light use of symbolic forms of communication. What, then, is the overt evidence of symbolic communications in our economic system? For now, we will answer the question with one word (although we will find it necessary to refine this answer momentarily). Our one-word answer is *brands*.

The use of brands in promotion is so widespread that it is virtually impossible to imagine what the modern business community would be like without them. By the term "brand" we will mean any *name, term, sign, symbol, design or combination of these things that is used to identify the goods or services of a seller or group of sellers*. The term "brand" is the general, and therefore inclusive, term—but we will identify two, more specific, terms that are understood to be subordinate to the general term. These two subordinate terms are: (a) *marks* and (b) *brand names*. This further distinction is necessary in order to avoid some later possible seman-

[17] This discussion is elaborated in Pierre Martineau, *Motivation in Advertising*, New York: McGraw-Hill Book Co., 1957, pp. 133–135. See also Sidney J. Levy, "Symbolism and Life Style," in Philip R. Cateora and Lee Richardson, editors, *Readings in Marketing: The Qualitative and Quantitative Areas*, New York: Appleton-Century-Crofts, 1967, pp. 196–205.

tic confusion. We will use the term "mark" to suggest a legal concept; it will mean that a particular brand is registered under the provisions of the US Patent Office or some state provision. It is the words, symbols or both and the distinctive style of writing or representing those words and symbols that may be the registered property of a firm—and which may therefore be recognized by the term "mark". In order to assure that a symbolic business property (a brand) is not misappropriated, the means exist through which a firm may register its brand and, upon registration, such a brand achieves the additional status of a mark. Such marks are of four basic types—the trademark, the service mark, the certification mark and the collective mark. Each of these types accommodates a slightly different need.

The *collective mark* is used to identify the goods or services of some group of persons. The collective mark may show, for example, that the workmanship of a particular union is embodied in a particular product. The collective mark may tie the members of a group together under a common symbol—such as "Quality Courts," the collective mark for a group of independently owned motels.

The *certification mark* is a "third-party" mark.[18] The certification mark represents some form of testimony regarding the quality of the good or service, and this mark is awarded by an independent third party. Thus, the Underwriters' Laboratories seal attests to the quality standards of various products; the Good Housekeeping Seal presents objective testimony about the products to which it is affixed. These certification marks can perform a valuable service—as long as the integrity of the mark is maintained.[19] Such marks, in concept, can provide meaningful guidance to consumers not otherwise able to make complex technical comparisons between competing products. It is a form of testimony to the potential usefulness of these certification marks that unscrupulous interests sometimes copy and misappropriate them.

The *service mark* distinguishes the services of one company from those of another—"Greyhound" is a registered service mark. Similarly, many insurance companies own service marks—the umbrella of Travelers and the "good hands" of Allstate are examples.

By far the most frequently encountered legal mark is the *trademark*. The trademark identifies the products of a particular manufacturer—and

---

[18] See Donald A. Taylor, "Certification Marks—Success or Failure," *Journal of Marketing,* July 1958, pp. 39–46.

[19] The Good Housekeeping Seal is awarded after an advertiser submits "representative samples of their product to the Good Housekeeping Institute." If the Institute is satisfied that it is a good product, then "two things can happen (1) the product can be advertised in Good Housekeeping and will be covered by the Consumer's Guaranty—whether the advertiser chooses to use the seal or not, and (2) the product may then also display the seal on its package and wherever it is advertised, subject to the issuance and conditions of a Seal licensing contract."

is usually affixed either to the product or to the package. Coke, Coca-Cola and Tab are all registered trademarks of The Coca-Cola Company. Pepsi, Pepsi-Cola, and Diet Pepsi are all registered trademarks of the Pepsi-Cola Company Division of Pepsico Inc. Often, though not always, a registered trademark is indicated by the symbol ® placed near the trademark in an advertisement. When a trademark is properly registered with the US Patent Office, the protection afforded by such registration remains in force "for twenty years and may be renewed without limit for additional twenty-year periods."[20] Though we will have more to say about the value of legal marks as symbolic forms of communications, we may note now that legal marks of the four types we have just defined are an indispensible part of modern competition.

The term *brand name* is used to identify the part of a brand that can be verbalized—the part that can be written or uttered as a meaningful word. Thus, "Chevrolet" is a brand name—but the trademark includes both "Chevrolet" and the symbol $\overline{}$, the latter not being easily pronounced. Similarly "Coca-Cola" is the brand name, but the distinctive cursive script in which that term is written is part of the legal mark.

Before we proceed, let us summarize briefly what we have said about these three terms—(a) brand, (b) mark and (c) brand name. Brand is the general term—it includes words, terms, designs, symbols and names. Mark represents a legal concept—this term denotes those parts of the brand that are protected by registration procedures. Brand names are those parts of the brand that can be spoken—brand names therefore do not include artistic distinctions not readily produced as a spoken sound.

But the importance of brands as modern means of commercial communications is such that we distinguish many different types.[21] More particularly, we distinguish brands according to: (a) their ownership, (b) the relationship among brands of a single firm, (c) the geographical coverage of the brand, (d) the order of importance of the brands to the firm and (e) the special purposes for which they are created.

BRAND OWNERSHIP

When brands are classified according to ownership, two basic classes emerge. These two classes are manufacturers' brands and distributors' brands. *Manufacturers' brands* are those owned by business enterprises that are engaged primarily in manufacturing. According to this criterion, General Electric, Westinghouse, Chrysler, General Motors, Kodak, and similar brands are manufacturers' brands. *Distributors' brands* are those owned by a business enterprise that is engaged primarily in distribution—in

[20] See Charles A. Holcomb, *Trademarks: Orientation for Advertising People,* New York: American Association of Advertising Agencies, 1964, p. 4.
[21] See Thomas F. Schutte, "The Semantics of Branding," *Journal of Marketing,* April 1969, pp. 5–11. See particularly the "partial list of terms," p. 6.

a wholesaling or retailing business. Kenmore, Airline and Ann Page, are, respectively, distributors' (or dealers') brands for Sears Roebuck, Montgomery Ward, and the Great Atlantic and Pacific Tea Company. This distinction between manufacturers' and distributors' brands is an important one and, often, an ambiguous one. The distinction is important because these two classes of brands represent the point of competitive contact that has been called the "battle of the brands." This competition between distributors' and manufacturers' brands is often the focal point for competition of the vertical type which we discussed in Chapter 12. The distinction between manufacturers' and distributors' brands is often ambiguous in the sense that it is not always possible to define whether a firm is primarily a manufacturing enterprise or primarily a distributive undertaking. In spite of this operational difficulty, the distinction between distributors' and manufacturers' brands is very frequently encountered.

FAMILY AND MULTIPLE BRANDS

When one distinguishes between brands according to the relationship among the brands of a single firm, the *family-brand* concept and the *multiple-brand* concept emerge. There are two forms of brand families. When a firm produces a line of products that are closely related in use or characterized by some trait that is common to all, a single brand may be applied to all the products. Again, General Electric and Westinghouse exemplify this first type of brand family. From an economic point of view, this type of family brand can involve substantial economies. Other things being the same, a product bearing a known brand requires less extensive promotional effort than one which is totally unknown to the average consumer. As the president of Raymond Loewy-William Snaith Inc. phrases it, "once a corporate symbol catches on with the public, a company has a communications device of incalculable worth. A company like Nabisco can go to market with a brand new product, unknown to consumers, and gain acceptance on the basis of its brand. Used in advertising, a brand keeps building up the strength of the product line."[22]

But there is a second basic type of brand family—one that is built on the idea of a recurring single syllable. This monosyllabic family is exemplified by the Eastman Kodak Company's use of "Kod"—as in *Kod*ak, *Kod*achrome, *Kod*acolor, *Kod*el, *Kod*aire, and so forth. The Celanese Corporation's *Cel*afil, *Cel*aspun, and so on; the Borden Company's use of "lac" in Star*lac*, Pronta*lac*, Forti*lac*; and the "tos" of Frito-Lay Inc., as in Fri*tos*, Chee*tos* and Ta*tos*, all further exemplify this brand policy.[23]

---

[22] *Printers Ink*, December 9, 1966, p. 52.
[23] Indeed the courts have recognized the right of a company to a syllable. Frito-Lay was able to prevent a competitor's use of "Prontos" for a food product because, in the words of the court, Frito-Lay had "made a deliberate and insistent effort to create a 'family' of marks characterized by 'tos'."

A brand policy that stands as an opposite to the family concept is the multibrand plan. Multibrand plans, in pure form, assign every individual product a different brand. Consider, for example, the policy of Procter and Gamble. It owns Crest and Gleam—both toothpastes; Jiffy and Big Top—both peanut butters; Prell, Drene, Shasta, and Head and Shoulders—all shampoos; and a list of soaps and detergents that has at one time or another included Tide, Cheer, Oxydol, Duz, Joy, Dreft, Ivory Snow, Ivory Flakes, Salvo, Bold, and on and on. General Foods also employs a multibrand strategy. General Foods owns several well-known brands of coffee, several gelatin products, and a multitude of brands of cooking and baking products. It is important to note that these multibrand plans do not necessarily involve products of different quality—that is, the firm may have several *fully* competitive brands. Why use such a policy? There are some fairly subtle answers to the question.

First, a multibrand policy makes good sense when there is evidence that consumers tend not to develop strong brand loyalty—that is, when consumers brand-hop in a spirit of experimentation. When brand loyalty patterns reflect continuous brand experimentation, the firm with only one brand in the market may be permanently assigned to a minor role. This effect is especially likely where consumers believe that little real product differentiation exists—that any of (say) ten different brands will perform in an acceptable manner. Indeed, where this is the case, brand-shares-of-market (the percentage of a given market claimed by a particular brand) *tend* to be randomly distributed. A random distribution of share-of-market would appear like that in Figure 19.3.

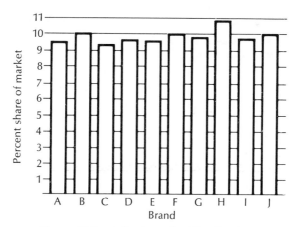

Figure 19.3 A Rectangular Distribution

The distribution of market shares in Figure 19.3 is very nearly "rectangular"—that is, there are no truly dominant brands in the market. And such a brand share distribution may reflect the type of brand experimentation by consumers that could logically produce a multibrand policy.

Suppose, for example, that consumers believe that there are about ten different brands—any one of which is as good as any other. Consumers would (if all brands were equally available) be indifferent as to which brand they bought. Brand share-of-market for each of the accepted brands would tend to be 1/10 of the total market. Rather than be content with 1/10 of the market, it might make better sense to: (a) create a second brand, (b) persuade consumers that the universe of acceptable products is now 11 brands and, as a result, (c) realize a 2/11 share of the total market. This multibrand policy would clearly be the logical course to pursue if increased advertising of existing brands could not appreciably enlarge the market share for any existing brand.

But there are other salient reasons why a firm might pursue a multibrand policy. A multibrand policy might be prompted by market segmentation, by product differentiation or by a desire to create intracompany competition. While all brands of a product may, superficially, appear the same, there may actually be subtle differences. Thus, market segmentation may be an explanation of multiple branding; there may be a shampoo for the dandruff-conscious person, a shampoo for the "naturally dry scalp," and so on. There may be toothpaste for the breath-conscious soul, and toothpaste for the white-smile fanatic. It is also possible to explain a multibrand policy in terms of product differentiation. The reader will recall that product differentiation is a kind of illusory segmentation—it involves the sale of identical products to different groups with different sales appeals. While such a policy seems less than pure, it may produce economies of scale— lower unit costs—and may not be as evil as first suspected. Finally, it is possible that a multibrand policy could be prompted by a desire to develop strong intracompany competition. This notion is rarely encountered—indeed, the traditional theory of competition has no room at all for such an idea. Yet one of the major convenience goods producers in the country—a company that spends over $150,000,000 each year for advertising—uses a multibrand policy avowedly to develop brand rivalry *within* the company. This firm is organized along lines that make a member of management responsible for a brand; if the man's brand flounders, the man suffers. In some product lines, this firm probably feels its most severe competition from within its own organization.

BRANDS AND GEOGRAPHICAL COVERAGE

A third basic way to classify brands is according to geographical coverage. This classification dimension produces, at least, national brands, regional brands and local brands. A point of longstanding confusion is the relationship between national brands and manufacturers' brands. It is perhaps tempting to conclude that manufacturers' brands are also national—at any rate there is evidence in the literature of marketing to indicate that such a relationship is often assumed. Regional or local brands were often assumed to be, essentially, distributors' brands. It is entirely possible that there has been a time in the past when only manufacturers' brands achieved national coverage, but such is clearly not the case today. There are many very successful manufacturers' brands that are not promoted nationally—some brands of beer, for example, enjoy a devoted consumer following but have never been distributed or promoted outside a region of five or six states. Similarly, there are distributors' brands that are household words, not only nationally but internationally. The Sears Kenmore brand enjoys such international status.

BRANDS AND LEVEL OF IMPORTANCE TO SELLER

For the sake of completeness, we should note that brands are also distinguished according to their importance to the owner. The great Atlantic and Pacific Tea Company—one of the largest food chains in the world—recognizes a primary brand, a secondary brand and a tertiary brand. These three brands are, respectively, Ann Page, Sultana and Iona: and they represent a kind of excellent-superior-good scale—intended to accommodate pocketbooks in various states of fill. A variation on this theme is to offer several quality levels, but not to formalize such levels with separate brand nomenclature. The good-better-best triad of mail-order fame is an instance to this latter point.

Another instance of implied difference in levels of importance of brands is in the distinction between house brands and individual brands. A house brand is often the general corporate name—thus Ford is a house brand, and Mustang is an individual brand. In the past, General Foods has emphasized only its individual brands—today the phrase "a product of General Foods" gives that house brand a greater degree of public exposure. Quaker Oats, while having many individual brands, has tied some parts of its product line together with the big Q that is its house mark (it has not, for obvious reasons, used the big Q on Puss-n-Boots cat food). Some firms use the house brand on all their products—DelMonte (the California Packing Company) is a case in point.

SPECIAL PURPOSE BRANDS

Finally, brands may be classified according to some special purposes for which they may be created. Examples of special purpose brands are: (a) experimental, or test, brands and (b) fighting brands.

Experimental, or test, brands may be used when there is some unreasonable level of risk associated with the use of a better known brand. Consider, for example, the plight of a watch manufacturer who has a national reputation for high quality, jewel-movement watches and who is confronted, indeed clobbered, by competition from inexpensive pin-lever movements. Suppose further, only in the interest of intrigue, that pin-lever movements, while serviceable, are still unreliable in the sense that they are affected by extreme humidity. The watch manufacturer thus has mixed emotions about the pin-lever movement: on the one hand, pin-lever sales are eroding the jeweled movement market; on the other, the pin-lever concept is not yet up to the reputation of his brand. If he should market a pin-lever model under his brand, and should pin-lever popularity prove to be a fleeting matter, the reputation of his brand would, at least, have been tarnished. This kind of situation may be resolved with the introduction of an experimental brand.

Such a brand is not readily associated in name with the primary brand—it may or may not be distributed through the same outlets. Should the unreliability of the pin-lever movement prove a fatal shortcoming, the ultimate failure of the experimental brand is in no important way harmful to the primary brand. Should the pin-lever movement prove reliable as further engineering is complete, the experimental brand might gradually be eased into the parent brand—that is, the parent company might first be advertised along with the experimental brand, and ultimately the experimental brand may be shed in favor of the primary brand. This use of the experimental brand is not uncommon—indeed such a technique has actually been used in the watch business; it has also been used in the ball-point pen business. The experimental brand is transient in the sense that it may be replaced with other nomenclature when the experiment is complete.

Another transient use of a brand involves the *fighting brand* or, sometimes, the fighting model. This brand may be used to meet particularly devastating price competition. Suppose, for example, that a competitive brand of vacuum cleaner is being offered at low prices and with trade-ins allowed. The combination of low price and trade-in probably means that there is no profit in the competitor's sale—but the special sales event may serve to clear shelves for new models. Whatever the reasons, the competitor's sale is hurting us. What do we do? We can cut existing models to no profit levels, or we can introduce a fighting brand. This latter strategy may simply involve the sale of a "stripped" model of our vacuum cleaner. The "stripped" brand costs us less, and it permits us to answer the competitor's special sale without disposing of our primary brand at prices below cost.

BRANDS AND GENERIC DEATH

There is one further aspect of brands that we should consider. As odd as it may sound, the brand that is too successful may lose much of its value as a business property. This curious result occurs when a brand name falls into the public domain because of widespread generic usage. Consider the following list of words: aspirin, cellophane, linoleum, thermos, shredded wheat, mimeograph, kerosene, escalator, and cola. Each of these words has a similar business ancestry: each was once a private business property but is now in the public domain. How does a word become public property? The stories of "thermos" and "aspirin" will illustrate the process.

In 1900 the Bayer Company got a patent for a drug called acetylsalicylic acid—Bayer named its version of the drug "Aspirin." A noted patent authority asserts that "less than a year and a half before the patents expired, Bayer realized that by making aspirin the name of the product and not the name of the product's origin, it had fixed it so that when the patent expired Bayer would be bereft of both the patented process and the name."[24] Consumers began calling all acetylsalicylic acid "aspirin," competitors went to court, and Bayer lost its word.

On June 10, 1958, King-Seeley "began waging a five-year tooth-and-nail battle over the words 'thermos bottle.'" The issue was whether Thermos Bottle was still a proper noun spelled with capital letters, or whether the words had become a common noun written "thermos bottle," in lower case. The judgment of the court was that the words were in the public domain—that is, the public had appropriated the words to describe any similar container—not just those manufactured by King-Seeley.

Nor are the Bayer and King-Seeley cases great rarities. In a similar way, DuPont lost its word "cellophane" in a battle with the Waxed Products Company; Nabisco lost its "shredded wheat" in a celebrated court battle with Kellogg; and, in what must be the strangest case of all, the Singer Sewing Machine Company lost and later regained the word "Singer."

And there are many firms who own brands that have been threatened with generic death. Indeed, you may have unwittingly contributed to the lower-case demise of some brands. Are all paper facial tissues "Kleenex"? Are all denim, narrow-cut trousers "Levis"? How about gelatin mixes—are they all "Jello"? Is all transparent tape "Scotch" tape? The list goes on and on. The owners of the words Fiberglas, Formica, Band Aid, Coke, Jeep, and Ping-Pong have all felt the threat of damage to their brand due to widespread generic use.

But suppose that a brand name does become generic—it goes public, so to speak. What are the economic consequences for the firm that formerly owned the name? The answer to this question is not obvious—indeed students often believe, erroneously, that such an event might even be a blessing in the sense that buyers would all use your brand name. Consider the hypothetical result of Kimberly-Clark losing exclusive rights to "Kleenex" (it has not, but suppose it did). Such a loss would mean that every seller of facial tissues could now use the word "kleenex" (note the lower-case form) to describe his tissues. Indeed, it would mean that the only avenue left to differentiate the facial tissues of different sources would be to identify the product by company name. A customer in a store asking

[24] Mylas Martin, "Continuing Battle of Trademarks: Upper vs. Lower Case," New York Herald Tribune-Post Dispatch Special Feature, November 11, 1963.

for "kleenex" could reasonably mean anyone's brand. That customer would have to specify Kimberly-Clark Kleenex in order not to be vague. In effect, then, the popularity of "kleenex" would help sell all brands of facial tissue—and might, on specific instances, encourage the substitution of other brands.

Because brands can become very valuable commercial properties, and because brands can be effectively lost to generic usage, knowledgeable management will exercise great care both in selecting and in protecting its brands. Normal precautions in selecting brands include making sure that brands to be used are free from legal encumbrances—meaning that words, terms, names, and so on, to which other persons or businesses may have prior claims do not make good brands. The Ford Motor Company reportedly paid a substantial price for exclusive use of the name "Maverick." The company "had to buy it from a Canadian manufacturer who used 'Maverick' for a line of auto accessories." [25]

Another, and less costly way, to avoid legal encumbrances is to create a brand distinctiveness by assembling your own brands. This assembly process may include: (a) the use of coined words, (b) the use of arbitrary brands and (c) the use of pictorial brands. Coined words are, when truly distinctive, likely not to have been used for any commercial purpose (indeed, any purpose at all). Coined words include acronyms such as Sunoco, Nabisco, Alcoa; purposely mispelled words such as Arrid and Keen Kutter; and brands such as Yuban and Zerex. Arbitrary brands are often safe from possible legal encumbrances because of the small probability that they would have been used out of context. Successful arbitrary brands include Arrow for men's shirts, Camel for cigarettes and Admiral for appliances. A pictorial brand may be protected both by patent registration and, because of the aesthetic properties of such a brand, by copyright laws as well. Successful pictorial brands include Log Cabin Syrup, RCA's His Master's Voice, Bon Ami, the Campbell Kids, White Owl, Borden's Elsie, and the Green Giant.

Matching the message and the audience

We have observed earlier that: (a) there tends to be imperfect target segmentation in mass communications and (b) advertising is sometimes criticized for talking down to its audience—for making everything painfully obvious. We are now far enough along to explore both these matters somewhat more fully. More specifically, our purpose in the discussion that follows is to examine the processes that can be employed by promotion planners to achieve a reasonable matching of messages and audiences. Our basic position is that, while communications segmentation is imperfect, there exists both the means and the willingness to develop specialized

[25] See Bill Kilpatrick, "Detroit Listening Post," *Popular Mechanics*, February 1969, p. 12.

forms of communication for different audiences. The general efficiency of our commercial mass communications system must necessarily be enhanced because of such specialization. But what are these special processes through which a matching of messages and audiences is achieved?

These special processes are identified, in general, by the elegant term *comprehensibility scoring devices.* And these scoring devices represent the means through which advertising copy (or "canned" sales presentations) can be evaluated in terms of its understandability. The scoring devices proceed from the fundamental notion that some people call a spade a spade—some people call it an instrument of excavation. The comprehensibility score for the latter phrase would clearly be different than for the former. But let us be much more specific. Consider the following copy from a Uniroyal advertisement:

Your front wheels steer the car. Your rear wheels push the car. The way we see it, having different tires specifically designed for both places makes a lot of sense. Which is why we at Uniroyal created a new tire especially for the front of the car and another one especially for the rear of the car. We call these tires the Uniroyal Masters. And now we'd like to tell you a little about them. First of all, what makes our front tire so right for the front of your car? Well to begin with, it has nine tread rows (count them) as opposed to the five tread rows that most of the tires on the road today have. So you always have an enormous amount of biting edges (they're the little slits in the tread rows) in contact with the road. This obviously leads to excellent steering control.

As a means of illustrating a comprehensibility scoring device, this Uniroyal copy will be graded with the Dale-Chall readability formula.[26] This formula requires that we determine each of several characteristics of the copy to be graded and that we proceed through an intricate scoring procedure for converting the copy characteristics into grade equivalents of educational achievement. The procedure is suggested by following scoring format:

1. Number of words in the sample	150.0
2. Number of sentences in the sample	10.0
3. Number of words not on the Dale list	12.0
4. Average sentence length	15.0
5. Dale score ([Line 3 ÷ Line 1] × 100)	8.0
6. Multiply average sentence length by .0496	.7440
7. Multiply Dale score by .1579	1.2632
8. Constant	3.6365
9. Formula raw score (sum of lines 6, 7 and 8)	5.6437

[26] The Dale-Chall formula, a widely used device, is described initially in two articles by Edgar Dale and Jeanne S. Chall. These articles are "A Formula for Predicting Readability," *Educational Research Bulletin,* January 21, 1948, pp. 11–20, and "A Formula for Predicting Readability: Instructions," *Educational Research Bulletin,* February 18, 1948, pp. 37–54.

This raw score of 5.6437 is then converted to a grade level of difficulty with the following conversion table.

Table 19.1 Dale-Chall conversion table

Formula raw score	Grade level
4.9 and below	4th and below
5.0 to 5.9	5th–6th
6.0 to 6.9	7th–8th
7.0 to 7.9	9th–10th
8.0 to 8.9	11th–12th
9.0 to 9.9	13th–15th
10.0 and over	16th and above

Note that the Uniroyal advertisement scores at the lower levels on our conversion table. Note also in the Dale-Chall scoring procedure that average sentence length and something called the "Dale list" serve to determine the ease or difficulty of reading the copy. In general, the larger lines 3 and 4 are (in the Dale-Chall scoring format), the higher the grade requirement for comprehension. The Dale list is a standard list of 3000 words that 80 percent of all fourth-graders comprehend. If we should score copy in which there were no words not on the Dale list, the copy would be very simple—almost monosyllabic. But we should also note that there are several constants used in the scoring process—the value .0496 in Line 6, the value .1579 in Line 7, and the 3.6365 in Line 8 are such constants.

But if we now apply the Dale-Chall formula to another advertisement, we can see more about this scoring procedure. The following copy is from a Voice of Music Stereo ad.

Say you're shopping for a stereo-phono with an FM Stereo radio in it. Ours has the look and the sound that gives you goose bumps. But our name, Voice of Music, doesn't seem as familiar as some of the big name brands. Maybe not, but let us assure you that's exactly why its our policy to look a little better, sound a little better, and cost a little less. Consider our brilliant new "Constellation." New modular design. The base of the handsome changer and panels of the speakers are elegant Rosewood. All quite modern. But nicely understated. Underneath the posh dust cover is our own new VM Supreme record changer. Four speed. Fully automatic. Handles records more gently than you can. And features our new "Cue" tone arm control. When something interrupts your listening, the VM "Cue" control suspends the tone arm over the record, and holds your place. Then whenever you're ready, it lets you lower the tone arm and start playing again where you left off—all automatically.

The Dale-Chall scoring procedure—familiar to us now—is as follows:

1. Number of words in the sample 172.0
2. Number of sentences in the sample 15.0
3. Number of words not on Dale list 33.0
4. Average sentence length 11.4
5. Dale score ([Line 3 ÷ Line 1] × 100) 19.1
6. Multiply average sentence length by .0496 .... .5753
7. Multiply Dale score by .1579 .... 3.0158
8. Constant 3.6365
9. Formula raw score (sum of Lines 6, 7 and 8) 7.2276

Consulting the conversion table, we learn that this copy reflects a ninth to tenth grade level of educational achievement. It is through the use of comprehensibility scoring devices such as the Dale-Chall formula that it is possible to "tailor" a promotional message to a particular audience. And, there are many specific devices for such tailoring—including some that are easier to implement and some that are more difficult to implement than the Dale-Chall formula.

One such technique that is very much easier to apply than the Dale-Chall formula is called the Fog Index.[27] This index uses: (a) average sentence length and (b) the number of words three syllables or longer per 100 words to define the comprehension score. The following example will suffice to illustrate the Fog Index.

	Copy sample daily newspaper	Copy sample college text
Average sentence length	19.3	23.6
Hard words/100	3.0	12.3
Total	22.3	35.9
Fog Index	**8.9**	**14.4**

The Index value of 8.9 for the sample copy from a daily newspaper indicates that about a ninth-grade education is required for ready comprehension. The 14.4 Index value for the college text indicates that it is written for the college sophomore. The Fog Index, though not as precise as the Dale-Chall method, is very simple to use. The sum of average sentence length and hard words per hundred (hard words are defined as words having three or more syllables) provide a total. These totals (22.3 and 35.9 in the example above) when multiplied by .4 are reduced to an approxi-

[27] The Fog Index is described in Robert Gunning, *The Techniques of Clear Writing,* New York: McGraw-Hill Book Co., 1952.

mation of the corresponding grades of educational achievement. Thus, .4 × 22.3 = 8.9; and .4 × 35.9 = 14.4. We should emphasize that techniques like Dale-Chall and the Fog Index, though applied here to printed advertising copy, may be used just as easily in matching spoken lines to the audience to whom it is directed. That is, the talk portions of television ads and the sales monologue used by salesmen are readily evaluated with these comprehension scoring techniques.[28]

MATCHING THE MESSAGE AND THE TASK OF PROMOTION

To the casual observer, all promotion efforts may seem to say "buy! buy! buy!" A more careful scrutiny of promotional activities will reveal that there are very different types of promotion—each with a different task or tasks to perform. This process of matching promotion and a specific task again reflects the level of efficiency of our mass communications system. That is, were there no such special efforts to match the message and the task, the process of communication would necessarily be less efficient.

A convenient means for summarizing some of the basic types of promotional efforts and some of the special tasks to be performed by such promotion is the "hierarchy of promotional effects" depicted in Figure 19.4:

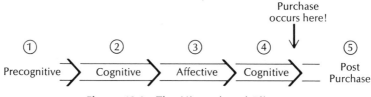

Figure 19.4 The Hierarchy of Effects

Figure 19.4 depicts five mental states. These mental states, beginning with "precognitive" and culminating with "postpurchase" are believed to approximate the sequence of mental states through which a consumer-buyer moves prior to and after a purchase decision.[29] The terms used to identify each of these mental states are, primarily, from the field of psychology. And while the jargon may seem at first unnecessarily obscure, the terms will not prove to be cumbersome. The state described by the term precognitive is one in which buyers (or prospects) are unaware of

[28] For a very complete listing of various scoring devices, see Pompeo Abruzzini, "Measuring Language Difficulty in Advertising Copy," *Journal of Marketing*, April 1967, pp. 22–26.
[29] See Robert J. Lavidge and Gary A. Steiner, "A Model for Predictive Measurements of Advertising Effectiveness," *Journal of Marketing*, October 1961, pp. 59–62. See also Kristian S. Palda, "The Hypothesis of a Hierarchy of Effects," in L. George Smith, editor, *Reflections on Progress in Marketing*, Chicago: American Marketing Association, 1965, pp. 174–179.

the class of products being sold. The promotional task when large numbers of buyers are believed to be precognitive is *pioneering* in the sense that the general characteristics of the product are defined—the promotional theme is generally informative; it dwells on creating an awareness of the product or the brand. The result of successful pioneering promotion is to move large numbers of consumer-buyers into the second mental state, a state of cognition. Product and brand *awareness* exists in this cognitive state (note the similarity between the words "cognition" and "recognition") but product or brand *preference* does not. Promotional efforts that are easily recalled create awareness and are therefore associated with the cognitive mental state. Teaser campaigns, slogans, jingles, and similar devices are thought to be effective in moving buyers from the precognitive to the cognitive mental state.[30]

When a significant number of consumer-buyers exist in the cognitive mental state, the task of promotion is logically different. The fundamental problem in moving from State 2 to Mental State 3 is to develop product or brand *preference*. And, typically, the appeals used in promotion that are intended to achieve buyer preference are different; such promotion is likely to feature argumentative copy—it will likely say "ours is better than theirs," but hopefully in a more creative way than that. Promotion that is intended to effect preference or affection is often promotion built upon *emotion*. The problem is to alter attitudes and feelings, as distinct from awareness. Promotion will appeal with images—status, glamour, success, beauty, and all the rest. Much of the criticism of promotion that we have noted traces directly or indirectly to the problem of creating affection—or, what is often the same thing, to the use of emotional sales appeals. We should note also that promotion of the sort that develops brand or product preferences may not seek to elicit immediate action—it often does not suggest that we hustle right down and part with our purchasing power. Advertisements of the Doyle, Dane, Bernbach agency represent a kind of communication standard for dealing tastefully with the problem of creating affection. That agency masterminds the Volkswagen of America account, the Burlington Mills account, and many others. America's collective affection for the "beetle," "bug," or whatever else one may call it, is a masterpiece in the systematic creation of *feeling* about a particular brand.

When affection exists—in terms of our hierarchy of effects, when significant numbers of consumer-buyers exist in Mental State 3—still another promotion task is confronted. The task now is to move customer-buyers into the conative state. The conative state is a "striving" mental state—the product or brand becomes a positive goal of the buyer. This state is perhaps the least easily defined and identified; it is characterized by unrest and desire to acquire a particular brand or product. A consumer-buyer existing

---

[30] See Lavidge and Steiner, *op. cit.,* p. 61.

in the conative state would express well-defined purchase plans—intentions to buy would be very high in probabilistic terms. The types of promotion that are appropriate in the conative state often provide the motives to induce direct action—these are the ads that urge us to "hurry right down while the supply lasts." Accordingly, the promotional emphasis is likely to be on price deals, trade-ins, "last chance" offers and point-of-purchase inducements to buy.

Finally, and this should surprise you to some extent, the promotion task quite properly continues after a sale has been made. Figure 19.4 depicts a postpurchase mental state. The total promotion task may logically include efforts to reduce something that the psychologist calls postpurchase dissonance. Postpurchase dissonance occurs when we begin to doubt that our decision was wise—we reflect on our purchase and begin to wonder about its wisdom. This very human trait is recognized in the literature of psychology as the "theory of cognitive dissonance," and it has been the subject of a great deal of recent research.[31] The available evidence suggests that buyers seek to reduce postpurchase dissonance by exposing themselves to reassurances that their decision was, in fact, proper. Indeed, there is evidence that new car owners "noticed and read ads" about the cars they had recently purchased more than ads about others cars.[32] This apparent need for reassurance—reassurance to reduce postpurchase dissonance—is another promotion task. And it may be a more important promotional responsibility than is yet fully realized; it is possible that brand loyalty is, in part, determined by postpurchase dissonance, and that "reassurance" promotion may play a significant role in encouraging repeat purchases.

Measuring the effectiveness of promotion

In a very real sense, the integrity of promotional activities rests on how well those activities work. A promotional budget that is spent to accomplish some poorly defined task is more likely to be viewed as an economic waste than a similar expenditure for which the results can be precisely measured. Any social institution upon which a significant portion of our total productive effort is expended should be able to point to its specific accomplishments. Indeed, it is a source of discomfort both to those with

[31] See, for example, Leon Festinger, "Cognitive Dissonance," *Scientific American*, October 1962, pp. 93–102; Harold H. Kassarjian and Joel B. Cohen, "Cognitive Dissonance and Consumer Behavior," *California Management Review*, Fall 1965, pp. 55–64; Stanley Kaish, "Cognitive Dissonance and the Classification of Consumer Goods," *Journal of Marketing*, October 1967, pp. 28–31; Donald Auster, "Attitude Change and Cognitive Dissonance," *Journal of Marketing Research*, November 1965, pp. 401–405; and Sadaomi Oshikawa, "The Theory of Cognitive Dissonance and Experimental Research," *Journal of Marketing Research*, November 1968, pp. 429–430.

[32] See Robert B. Zajonc, "The Concepts of Balance, Congruity, and Dissonance," in Perry Bliss, editor, *Marketing and the Behavioral Sciences*, Second Edition, Boston: Allyn and Bacon, Inc., 1967, p. 104.

paranoiac inclinations in the business of promotion and to outside critics that the specific results of promotional activities have not always been subject to precise measurement. There are those—both practitioners and critics—who feel that promotion will only be accepted as a socioeconomic institution with "full rights and privileges" when the means exist to prove that promotional dollars are productive dollars. It is undoubtedly a source of no little embarrassment that although we have men on the moon we are unable to say in definitive terms what a $5 million expenditure for advertising will accomplish. Our job in this section is to consider two questions that relate to the measurement of the effectiveness of promotional activities. These questions are, why is it so difficult to measure precisely the effectiveness of promotional activities? and how well can we *now* measure promotional effectiveness?

The exact result of a given promotional expenditure is extremely difficult to predict because: (a) the reaction of consumer-buyers to the promotional effort cannot be known in advance, (b) the reactions of competitors cannot be accurately anticipated and (c) fortuitous events that may influence the results of the promotional efforts cannot always be predicted. Consider the hypothetical case of a retailer who contracts to spend $500 with a local newspaper for a special sales event. The ad is run, and the crowds are greater than early estimates—what caused the success of the sale? The advertisement? The excellent prices that were quoted during the sale? Was it a case of the products themselves being superior? Or did it have something to do with the fact that on the day of the sale there were no competing sales of a comparable nature anywhere in the city? Or, indeed, did it have something to do the beautiful weather that prevailed during the sale? Alas, the success of the sale was doubtless due to all these things—and the exact role of any one of the elements is virtually impossible to isolate.

The problem is one familiar to all social scientists—namely, the inability to establish in advance precise cause and effect relationships where a multitude of variables impinge upon a particular event. It is entirely possible that even with poor promotional support a sales event may prove to be a success because everything else falls into proper place. It is likewise possible that an effective promotional effort may be limited in its performance by offsetting factors that work counter to it. Critics of mass promotional techniques would clearly have less to criticize if it were possible to predict accurately the results of a given promotional expenditure—but the complexity of the environment in which that promotional expenditure is usually made largely precludes accurate forecasting.

But to concede that it is virtually impossible to predict the effects of a promotional effort is not to say that we cannot measure, ex post facto, the effects of particular promotional efforts. An ex post facto measurement is one that is made *after* the event has been completed. Clearly an ex post facto measurement of promotional effectiveness is not a good substitute for prediction—but the stature of mass promotional techniques has doubtless been enhanced as a result of some of these ex post facto studies. We are, however, getting ahead of ourselves—we need to consider more systematically the nature of methods used to measure the effectiveness of promotional efforts, beginning with the least complicated and progressing to the more sophisticated. We will, toward this goal, organize the following discussion around three basic types of procedures: (a) audience authentication, (b) laboratory tests of effectiveness and (c) market tests of effectiveness.

AUDIENCE AUTHENTICATION PROCEDURES

Careful audience authentication is a logical first step in the process of measuring promotional effectiveness. The phrase "audience authentication" may be defined as a systematic effort to develop accurate estimates of the number of readers of printed media or the number of listeners/viewers of broadcast media. Audience authentication is a *general* measure of promotional effectiveness—it endeavors to show the numbers of persons influenced by a medium or by a particular communications vehicle. Sometimes, authentication of audiences is done by independent third parties; sometimes it is done by a particular newspaper, magazine, or radio or television station. Authentication procedures almost always distinguish at least three audience concepts; these are: (a) gross potential audiences, (b) net potential audiences and (c) delivered audiences.

Simply as a means of distinguishing these different audience concepts, consider the case of a national, general interest magazine. The *gross potential audience* for such a vehicle would include every person with a good liklihood of exposure—including paid circulation, newsstand sales and, even, pass-along readership.[33] The *net potential audience* would include only those who actually read some part of the magazine in question. The net potential audience concept is still called a "potential" because there is no assurance that they read all of the magazine. *Delivered audiences* include only those persons who were actually exposed to a particular feature in the magazine. That feature might be editorial or commercial.

The term "commercial delivery," or "ad delivery," designates the number of persons actually exposed to some printed advertisement. It is even possible to distinguish various degrees of commercial delivery; the Starch readership reports, in fact, distinguish between the percentage of readers who: (a) recall an ad generally, (b) remember the ad and can associate it with a particular product and (c) read most (51 percent) of the copy in an advertisement. These Starch data are very specialized delivered audience figures.

For broadcast media, the three ideas of gross potential audiences, net

[33] Pass-along readership is important for some magazines. *Reader's Digest,* for example, is a mother-to-daughter, daughter-to-friend kind of vehicle.

potential audiences and delivered audiences are in use—but in slightly different form. The gross potential audience for a particular TV or radio station is defined by the number of operable sets within a station's signal range. The net potential audience is defined by the number of receivers in use. Thus, if the signal range of a particular radio or TV station is defined by a circle with a 5 mile radius, gross audience potential would be defined by the number of operable receivers (radio or TV) within the circle. The net potential audience would be defined by the total number of sets in use; the *program delivery* would be reflected by the number of sets in use tuned to a particular program. The program delivery figure is the familiar "rating" by which TV programs often live or die. In terms of more concrete numbers, the sets-in-use figure is 100 percent; the program delivery is some percentage of that. A 65 percent program delivery would mean that only 35 percent of the sets in use were tuned to some other programs.

But the measurement of broadcast media commercial audiences is slightly different also. With the broadcast media, both a commercial exposure potential and a commercial delivery are recognized. *Commercial exposure potential* is the percentage of sets in use tuned to a particular station at the time commercials are shown. *Commercial delivery* is the number, or proportion, actually exposed to the commercial. This distinction between commercial exposure potential and commercial delivery is a necessary distinction. For it is apparent that TV viewers, especially, may use commercials as an opportunity to conduct business that they may have away from the set. There is, therefore, often a significant difference between commercial exposure potential and commercial delivery.

But these concepts of audience authentication raise some interesting problems in measurement. That is, while all these different audiences are fine to talk about, how are they actually measured? In general, audience authentication procedures for the broadcast media use samples from which the nature of behavior of the total is estimated. Such samples may be telephone samples or diaries—the latter being listener/viewer reports maintained by a representative sample of households. These diaries may be manual or mechanical. The manual diary is simply a log of stations and programs viewed; the mechanical diary—such as the A. C. Neilsen Audiometer—records "precisely when the television or radio is tuned in and channel or station to which it is tuned." The cost of the mechanical diary is often high because of the need to wire into the circuits in the receiver.[34] Samples may be used to estimate both commercial potentials and commercial delivery. A series of telephone calls placed at the time of commercials can estimate both of these audience concepts.

Audience authentication is provided, as we noted briefly, by independent organizations, by media associations and by individual vehicles. The Audit

[34] See D. B. Lucas and S. H. Britt, *Measuring Advertising Effectiveness,* New York: McGraw-Hill Book Co., 1963, p. 245.

Bureau of Circulations (ABC) provides audience authentication for "fully paid" circulations of newspapers, consumer magazines and some business publications. The Business Publication Audit (BPA) provides a similar service, although this organization is composed of members from industry, agencies and publications (media). A specialized authentication service is provided by the Traffic Audit Bureau (TAB). The Traffic Audit Bureau is to outdoor advertising what the ABC is to printed media. The principal responsibility of the TAB is to measure audiences of standardized billboards—and this matter of standardization results in the exclusion of most small and irregularly shaped outdoor signs. TAB counts as billboard audiences the number of persons passing a site upon which a billboard of standard size is erected.

LABORATORY TESTS OF PROMOTIONAL EFFECTIVENESS

Laboratory tests of promotional effectiveness are those that are conducted in an environment other than an actual market. Laboratory tests of effectiveness include the use of consumer panels, the use of ocular equipment and the use of auditorium simulations. Laboratory tests are often used to pretest a particular advertisement or set of coordinated advertisements. Thus, a panel may be shown several ads and later questioned about what they saw—and perhaps about how much of the exposure they can recall. Panels of housewives (presumably representative of general audiences) may, in fact, play a vital role in determining which of several ads are actually used in a full market exposure. Suppose, for example, that an advertising agency is anxious to identify which of several possible copy appeals is best. Suppose moreover, that each of these several copy appeals is to be ranked in terms of the panel's opinion of its desirability, its exclusiveness and its believability. To make our example more specific, assume that the product involved is a kitchen and bathroom cleaner and that the several copy appeals under consideration are: (a) cleansing power, (b) pleasant odor and (c) no sink scum. In order to make our illustration as succinct as possible, we will let the following brief tabulation summarize the opinions of the panel.[35] Note carefully that the values in Table 19.2

Table 19.2 Scaling and Copy Appeals

Copy appeal	Average rating for desirability	Average rating for exclusiveness	Average rating for believability
Cleansing power	.95	.09	.55
Pleasant odor	.80	.76	.67
No sink scum	.61	.34	.25

[35] This illustration is from Lucas and Britt, *op. cit.*, p. 124.

are mean ratings—they represent the average of the panel members' opinions about each of the three copy appeals and each of the three dimensions: desirability, exclusiveness and believability. The value ".95" indicates that on a 0-to-1 scale, the panel ranked cleansing power as highly desirable copy appeal. Note, however, that the cleansing power appeal was thought to be very low in exclusiveness. Thus, while the panel thought cleansing power a good appeal, they also felt that everyone else (competitors) was using it. To be sure that you understand these values, what does a panel rating of .25 for the believability of the "no sink scum" appeal mean? Note that this laboratory procedure for pretesting promotional claims suggests that the best claim—the most effective claim in the opinion of the panel—is the "pleasant odor" theme. This type of laboratory test of effectiveness reflects the concern of professional advertising interests in the use of precise decision criteria in order to assure an acceptable level of efficiency in promotion.

Other laboratory tests that may assist in the search for the most effective forms of promotion include elaborate ocular devices. One such device, the Mackworth Optiscan, "simultaneously photographs both the scene which is exposed to the subjects' view and the specific point within that scene at which the subject happens to be looking at any given moment."[36] In one study using the Optiscan, it was possible to identify the characteristics of particular advertisements that were able to "communicate most effectively."[37] The procedure in this study involved the correlation of the number of subject eye fixations on printed ads and the subjects' ability to answer questions about the content of the advertisements later. Thus, the scanning patterns that produced the most effective learning experience were identified.

Another laboratory pretest device may assist in the identification of the most legible formats and color combinations. Often, especially in outdoor ads and in TV spots, legibility is crucial to the effectiveness of the advertisement. With the use of special equipment that controls the time that subjects are exposed to particular forms of promotion, the most effective visual combination of factors can be developed.[38]

MARKET TESTS OF PROMOTIONAL EFFECTIVENESS

Market tests of promotional effectiveness require: (a) exposure of a promotional effort to a market or part of a market (a test group) and (b) some systematic means of tracing the impact of that promotional effort upon

[36] Donald E. Payne, "Looking Without Learning: Eye Movements When Viewing Print Advertisements," in M. C. Moyer and R. E. Vosburgh, editors, Chicago: American Marketing Association, 1967, p. 78.

[37] Ibid., p. 80.

[38] The tachistoscope is one device used for this purpose. See "Tachistoscopic Tests and Recall and Recognition Techniques," in The Study of Memory, New York: Advertising Research Foundation, 1957.

sales volume or upon awareness or attitudes. Some market tests are of fairly simple design, some are very sophisticated. Beginning with the least complicated, we will consider five specific types of market tests of promotional effectiveness. These tests are: (a) the incremental sales method, (b) the store audit system, (c) an enquiry method, (d) a simple before-after correlation test and (e) a special technique called a playback audit.

The incremental sales method—exemplified by Starch's net ad-produced sales approach—requires that several samples of consumers be questioned.[39] At a minimum, we would want some consumers who had not been exposed to the promotion being tested and some who had. We can then use any differences in the incidence of product ownership (of the product being promoted) between those two groups as evidence of the influence of the promotion. In effect, we assume that a cause and effect relationship exists between the exposure to the promotion and the incidence of product ownership among our sample. But consider the following hypothetical table—it suggests the working of the incremental sales method in greater detail.

Table 19.3 Promotion and Incremental Sales

Sample Type	Sample size	% of total sample	Incidence of owner- ship	Incre- mental sales %	Incre- mental sales— units
Unexposed to test promotion	100	25%	10%	—0—	—0—
Noted	100	25%	12%	2%	2
Saw, remembered product	100	25%	15%	5%	5
Read 51% or more of copy	100	25%	20%	10%	10

The first column identifies four types of consumer samples—persons totally unexposed to the promotion we are testing, those who "noted" the promotion but where unable to be specific about it, those who both saw and remembered some of the important characteristics of the promotion, and those who read most of the copy in the promotion. The second and third columns simply specify the size of each sample group and the proportion of each to the total sample. The column labeled "incidence of ownership" indicates the percent of each sample that own or use

[39] See Daniel Starch, *Measuring Advertising Readership and Results,* New York: McGraw-Hill Book Co., 1966, Pt. II.

the product featured in the test promotion. Note that 10 percent of the unexposed sample own the product. And note that, in our example, the incidence of ownership increases with more complete exposure. This incremental sales approach to testing promotional effectiveness presumes that in the absence of any promotion at all, all subsamples would act like the unexposed portion of the sample. Without promotion we would expect our sample of 400 consumers to own 40 of the products featured in the promotion. We would expect 400 persons—exposed to the test promotion as those in Table 19.3—to own 57 of the featured products. The net ad-produced sales would thus total 17.

The *store audit system* of testing promotional effectiveness requires the use of a field research team. The A. C. Neilsen Company, among others, can provide what is called a "continuous audit" of the movement of particular brands of products through retail stores. This continuous audit is possible with the use of field personnel who sample store shelf inventories both in the morning and in the afternoon to measure the rates of brand sales. When the field personnel maintain something approaching a constant vigil, changes in the rate of brand movement through sample stores can be related to promotional events. That is, continuous feedback on the rate of brand sales may reflect the influence of changes in promotional efforts. It is thus possible to estimate the effects of promotional efforts from changes in the rates of brand sales in retail stores. This type of audit can obviously also tell a firm how effective a promotional effort of a competitor is.

Enquiry tests of promotional effectiveness vary in their specific forms, but all have one common trait: they all invite overt audience reaction. An overt reaction is one that is open to view—it is "apparent" in contrast to (say) a mental or emotional reaction. The most common type of enquiry test uses the coupon—and it is possible to measure the relative effectiveness of several different advertisements by comparing the rate of coupon response to them. Thus, if one particular advertisement consistently produces a greater coupon response than others, it may be a more effective promotional piece than others. But there is one word of warning: good coupon response may be induced to some extent even though the promotional message that purveyed the coupon is not read carefully. Consider the two ad formats depicted in Figure 19.5.

Ad A may produce a much better coupon response but fail in the sense that it exposes the true promotional message to fewer people. The format for Ad A produces an adverse selection—it may encourage responses by persons who have no interest in the product featured in the ad. Indeed, there is no reason to believe that all coupon responses involve a careful perusal of the copy of the ad. Ad B, in contrast, does not make a conspicuous free offer—the offer is buried in the copy. The responses to Ad B are likely to be of a higher quality because respondents had to read the copy more carefully to know of the free offer.

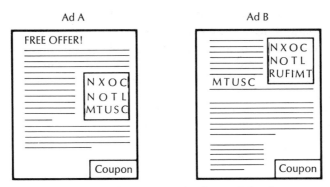

Figure 19.5 Coupons and Adverse Selection

The *before-after correlation test* of promotional effectiveness involves at least two waves of data accumulation. The "before" wave may seek to identify consumer attitudes toward specified products or services—it may seek to identify consumer awareness of product or service features. These "before" measurements become the bench mark against which subsequent measurements are judged. The "after" wave of data accumulation will normally parallel the earlier measurements closely, at least in terms of the questions asked of respondents. The promotion to be tested is sandwiched between the "before" and "after" waves of data accumulation so that the effects of the promotion will show in the "after" but not the "before" data. The test is complete when any differences between the results of the two surveys are analyzed in terms of statistical significance. A good example of this technique is that employed by the Scott Paper Company.

The Scott Paper Company wanted to measure the effects upon purchasing agents of a six-month trade-paper and direct-mail campaign. The procedure included: (a) a measurement of the knowledge and opinions of purchasing agents about the Scott Paper Company before the campaign and (b) a measurement of the knowledge and opinions of purchasing agents about the Company after the campaign. In order to avoid the difficulties of open-end interviewing, the sample of purchasing agents was given rating scales that permitted a precise measurement of their opinions and awareness. These rating scales permitted the quantification of the survey results, and a statistical comparison of the before and after results was simple.[40]

Another example of the before-after correlation test is a study conducted by the Ford Motor Company. The Ford study was, more exactly, a before-during-after test. It was conducted in nine cities that had been "especially weak markets for the company's cars." The promotion to be tested con-

[40] See Harry D. Wolfe and others, *Measuring Advertising Results,* New York: National Industrial Conference Board, 1962, pp. 39–41.

sisted of full-page, two-color, newspaper advertisements in both morning and evening editions. As a control device, interviews were also conducted in nine other markets in which the newspaper advertising was not used. Ford wanted to accomplish three tasks with the promotion. They wanted to (a) increase the number of persons who were aware of their advertising slogan, (b) increase dealership visitation and (c) "predispose more people with car-buying intentions toward the company's car."[41] The Ford management reports that the use of test and control markets and the use of the before-after design "made it possible to isolate changes caused by the campaign."

Finally, there is a type of test of promotional effectiveness that is best suited for the measurement of sales training efforts. A part of the total promotion budget of a firm may reasonably go to training sales personnel, and the *playback audit* represents a means for the measurement of the effectiveness of such training efforts. One supermarket chain uses the playback audit to assure that checker training is effective. In its most simple form, this technique involves a fake shopping visit that actually tests the salesperson's selling effectiveness. Thus, check-out personnel in supermarkets may be "audited" for price call-off; hardware salesmen may be audited for suggestion selling. The makers of Royal typewriters used a type of playback audit technique to "learn whether dealers and their sales clerks were remembering and repeating" a particular sales theme. The company had stressed the rugged construction of its portables in advertising to final consumers and in a direct mail campaign aimed at its dealers and their salesclerks. For a period of one month, company representatives visited dealers and pretended to be interested in buying a typewriter. The visit was really an opportunity to "audit" the effectiveness of promotion directed to dealers.[42]

SUMMARY

Chapter 19 has been concerned, in general, with efforts and activities that tend to increase the efficiency of promotional activities. It has been an important premise of Chapter 19 that a growing scientific basis for promotional activities is evidence of growing professionalism and a more efficient market system. We have explored the nature of this growing scientific basis from six different viewpoints.

First, we were interested in the use of formal rules of persuasion in mass communications. We noted that these rules deal with such questions as implicit versus explicit conclusions, the wisdom of presenting opposing points of view, and climax order and anticlimax order. Second, we considered the relationship between learning theory and promotion. We defined the nature of the memory curve and identified several rules of learning;

[41] *Ibid.*, p. 37.
[42] *Ibid.*, p. 26.

namely: (a) belonging, (b) incongruity or difference, (c) primary-recency, (d) distributed effort and (e) involvement.

Next, we considered the nature of symbolic communications. We distinguished brands, brand names and marks. We noted that there are trademarks, service marks, certification marks and collective marks. We also observed that brands are distinguished by: (a) ownership, (b) the relationship among the brands of a firm, (c) the geographical coverage of the brand, (d) the importance of the brand to the firm and (e) special purposes.

Our fourth area of interest was with efforts to match messages and audiences. We noted that scoring devices such as the Dale-Chall readability formula and the Fog Index can be used to tailor messages to particular audiences. We noted also that the tasks of promotion may be defined as a kind of hierarchy of effects, and that some matching of messages to the tasks suggested by this hierarchy occurs. In this context, we defined pioneering promotion and the theory of cognitive dissonance.

The last two sections of Chapter 19 dealt with efforts to measure the effectiveness of promotion. More specifically, we examined the use of audience authentication procedures, including gross audience potentials, net audience potentials and delivery of audiences. We also noted some laboratory methods of testing promotional effectiveness, as well as some market tests.

REVIEW QUESTIONS
1 Carefully define and indicate the relevance of each of the following concepts to the study of marketing:
   a. Persuasion
   b. Subliminal perception
   c. The rule of persuasion regarding explicit versus implicit conclusions
   d. Psychological learning theory
   e. The learning curve
   f. The psychological law of belonging
   g. The psychological law of incongruity
   h. The psychological law of primacy-recency
   i. The psychological law of distributed effort
   j. The psychological principle of involvement
   k. An experimental brand
2 Distinguish carefully between each element in the following pairs of terms:
   a. Persuasion *and* subception
   b. Brand names *and* legal marks
   c. Service marks *and* certification marks
   d. Collective marks *and* brands
   e. A family brand policy *and* a multiple brand policy
   f. A house brand *and* an individual brand
   g. Pioneering promotion *and* reminder promotion
3 What is the anticlimax order versus climax order argument in the area of persuasion rules?

4 Your text describes two types of brand families. What are these two basic types, and what is the rationale for their use?

5 What, exactly, is a comprehensibility scoring device? In what way is it used, and how does its use relate to the efficiency of mass communications?

6 What is the Dale-Chall readability formula? Using this system, grade two short pieces of copy—one from your text, one from a newspaper advertisement.

7 What is meant by the phrase "hierarchy of promotional effects"? What kind of message is a precognitive message? An affective message?

8 What is the theory of cognitive dissonance? What does this theory suggest about when promotion might be used?

9 Why is it inherently so difficult to predict or measure the precise influence of given promotional expenditure?

10 What is the difference between gross potential audiences, net potential audiences and delivered audiences?

11 What is a laboratory test of promotional effectiveness?

12 What are some market tests of promotional effectiveness? Why are these tests related to the general efficiency of our market system?

SUGGESTED SUPPLEMENTARY READINGS IN PROMOTION

Abelson, Herbert I., *Persuasion: How Opinions and Attitudes Are Changed,* New York: Springer Publishing Co., Inc., 1959.

Backman, Jules, *Advertising and Competition,* New York: New York University Press, 1967.

Baker, Samm Sinclair, *The Permissible Lie,* Cleveland: The World Publishing Company, 1968.

Bauer, Raymond A., and Stephen A. Greyser, *Advertising in America: The Consumer View,* Cambridge, Mass.: Harvard University Press, 1968.

Bearden, James H., *Personal Selling,* New York: John Wiley & Sons, Inc., 1967.

Berelson, Bernard, and Morris Janowitz, editors, *Public Opinion and Communication,* Second Edition, New York: The Free Press, 1966.

Bogart, Leo, editor, *Psychology in Media Strategy,* Chicago: American Marketing Association, 1966.

———, *Strategy in Advertising,* New York: Harcourt, Brace and World, Inc., 1967.

Borden, Neil H., and Martin V. Marshall, *Advertising Management,* Homewood, Ill.: Richard D. Irwin, Inc., 1959.

Boyd, Harper W., Jr., and Sidney J. Levy, *Promotion: A Behavioral View,* Englewood Cliffs, N.J.: Prentice-Hall, Inc., 1967.

———, and Joseph W. Newman, *Advertising Management,* Homewood, Ill.: Richard D. Irwin, Inc., 1965.

Brink, Edward L., and William T. Kelley, *The Management of Promotion,* Englewood Cliffs, N.J.: Prentice-Hall, Inc., 1963.

Cook, Victor S., and Thomas F. Schutte, *Brand Policy Determination,* Boston: Allyn and Bacon, Inc., 1967.

Crane, Edgar, *Marketing Communications,* New York: John Wiley & Sons, Inc., 1965.

Crawford, John W., *Advertising: Communications for Management,* Boston: Allyn and Bacon, Inc., 1960.

Dirkson, Charles J., and Arthur Krueger, *Advertising Principles and Problems,* Homewood, Ill.: Richard D. Irwin, Inc., 1964.

Durkee, Burton R., *How to Make Advertising Work,* New York: McGraw-Hill Book Company, 1967.

Dygert, Warren B., *Advertising Principles and Practice,* Totowa, N.J.: Littlefield, Adams & Company, 1949.

Engel, James F., Hugh G. Wales, and Martin R. Warshaw, *Promotional Strategy,* Homewood, Ill.: Richard D. Irwin, Inc., 1967.

Essentials of Outdoor Advertising, New York: Outdoor Advertising Committee, Association of National Advertisers, 1952.

Fox, Harold W., *The Economics of Trading Stamps,* Washington: Public Affairs Press, 1968.

Frey, Albert W., *Advertising,* Third Edition, New York: The Ronald Press Company, 1961.

Grissy, W. J. E., and Robert M. Kaplan, *Salesmanship: The Personal Force in Marketing,* New York: John Wiley & Sons, Inc., 1969.

Groner, Alex, *Advertising: The Case for Competition,* New York: Association of National Advertisers, 1967.

King, Robert L., editor, *Conferences, '55/'65,* Chicago: American Marketing Association, 1966, (especially Chap. VI).

Kirkpatrick, C. A., *Advertising: Mass Communication in Marketing,* Second Edition, Boston: Houghton Mifflin Company, 1964.

Klapper, Joseph T., *The Effects of Mass Communication,* New York: The Free Press, 1960.

Kleppner, Otto, *Advertising Procedure,* Fifth Edition, Englewood Cliffs, N.J.: Prentice-Hall, Inc., 1966.

Lucas, Darrell Blaine, and Steuart H. Britt, *Measuring Advertising Effectiveness,* New York: McGraw-Hill Book Company, 1963.

Lyon, David G., *Off Madison Avenue,* New York: G. P. Putnam's Sons, 1966.

Mandell, Maurice I., *Advertising,* Englewood Cliffs, N.J.: Prentice-Hall, Inc., 1968.

Marketing Science Institute, *Promotional Decisions Using Mathematical Models,* Boston: Allyn and Bacon, Inc., 1967.

Martineau, Pierre, *Motivation in Advertising,* New York: McGraw-Hill Book Company, 1957.

McClure, Leslie W., and Paul C. Fulton, *Advertising in the Printed Media,* New York: Crowell-Collier and Macmillan, Inc., 1964.

McNeal, James U., editor, *Readings in Promotion Management,* New York: Appleton-Century-Crofts, 1966.

Miracle, Gordon E, *Management of International Advertising,* Ann Arbor, Mich.: University of Michigan Press, 1966.

Pederson, Carlton A., and Milburn D. Wright, *Salesmanship: Principles and Methods,* Fourth Edition, Homewood, Ill.: Richard D. Irwin, Inc., 1966.

Perspectives in Advertising Management, New York: Association of National Advertisers, 1969.

Robinson, Patrick J., and David J. Luck, *Promotional Decision Making: Practice and Theory,* New York: McGraw-Hill Book Company, 1964.

Ross, Billy I., *Advertising Education,* Lubbock, Tex.: Texas Tech Press, 1965.

Sandage, C. H., and Vernon Fryburger, *Advertising Theory and Practice,* Homewood, Ill.: Richard D. Irwin, Inc., 1967.

_____, *The Role of Advertising,* Homewood, Ill.: Richard D. Irwin, Inc., 1960.

Seehafer, Gene F., and Jack W. Laemmar, *Marketing and Advertising,* New York: McGraw-Hill Book Company, 1959.

Starch, Daniel, *Measuring Advertising Readership and Results,* New York: McGraw-Hill Book Company, 1966.

Stroh, Thomas F., *Salesmanship: Personal Communications and Persuasion in Marketing,* Homewood, Ill.: Richard D. Irwin, Inc., 1966.

Taplin, Walter, *Advertising,* Boston: Little, Brown & Company, 1963.

Thompson, *Selling: A Behavioral Science Approach,* New York: McGraw-Hill Book Company, 1966.

Thompson, Willard M., *Salesmanship: Concepts, Management, and Strategy,* New York: John Wiley & Sons, Inc., 1963.

Tillman, Rollie, and C. A. Kirkpatrick, *Promotion: Persuasive Communication in Marketing,* Homewood, Ill.: Richard D. Irwin, Inc., 1968.

Wales, Hugh G., and Robert Ferber, *A Basic Bibliography on Marketing Research,* Chicago: American Marketing Association, 1963, Chaps. XII, XIII, XIX.

Whitney, Robert A., Thomas Hubin, and John D. Murphy, *The New Psychology of Persuasion and Motivation in Selling,* Englewood Cliffs, N.J.: Prentice-Hall, Inc., 1965.

Wolfe, Harry D., James K. Brown, and G. Clark Thompson, *Measuring Advertising Results,* New York: National Industrial Conference Board, 1962.

Wright, John S., and Daniel S. Warner, *Speaking of Advertising,* New York: McGraw-Hill Book Company, 1963.

Zacher, Robert V., *Advertising Techniques and Management,* Homewood, Ill.: Richard D. Irwin, Inc., 1967.

Chapter 20
PRODUCTS AND SOCIETY

It is a point that sometimes evades critics of our business enterprise system that every person who is gainfully employed provides either tangible products or intangible services for his fellow man. Products and services are the culmination of all economic activity. And some very important social issues are related to the types and number of products and services provided within our economic system. Our interest in the present chapter is, in general, with the changing nature of the products and services that constitute the output of our system. More specifically, we will focus our attention on five issues that relate to this general area. We will be concerned: (a) with the transient composition of our cultural inventory of products and services, (b) with the role of the individual firm in effecting changes in that cultural inventory, (c) with the economic principle of postponement, (d) with the economic role of the package and (e) with the economic role of the product/service warranty.

Our cultural inventory

The combination of products and services used by any society or group has been called that society's "cultural inventory."[1] This cultural inventory represents and embodies the consumption requirements of a particular society or group. And the particular composition of this cultural inventory often provides great insight into the value systems of those groups for whom it represents an acquisitive requirement. There are societies for which the cultural inventory is quite literally "a jug of wine, a loaf of bread—and thou." There are social systems in which the cultural inventory

[1] This term is suggested by Wroe Alderson in *Marketing Behavior and Executive Action: A Functionalist Approach to Marketing Theory*, Homewood, Ill.: Richard D. Irwin, Inc., 1957, p. 267.

is a thing of great complexity and a thing that requires a great deal of effort to acquire and maintain. Our present cultural inventory is perhaps the most complex ever known to any society. And it is this complex cultural inventory—this materialistic representation of our societal values—that is the focus of much recent controversy. Youth communes and similar drop-out phenomena are often avowedly the result of society's having exalted the material things in life and diminished the human things. The concept of the cultural inventory is obviously of considerable importance in each of our lives today—indeed, our success is often informally judged by our ability to acquire this inventory of goods and services. It behooves us to consider this inventory carefully. More specifically, we are concerned in this section with two questions: (a) how does this inventory of consumption requirements originate and (b) how are changes in this inventory effected?

Our cultural inventory of products and services is the result of three distinct forces. These forces are: (a) what people want, (b) what our technical skills can produce and (c) what business or government can provide. Any one of these three forces can deny a particular product or service access to our cultural inventory. Consumers may want an automotive fuel that eliminates the frequent service station stops—and business may be anxious to provide such a fuel to consumers—but without the technical "permission" to provide such a fuel, it cannot be realized. This notion that three forces working together provide our consumption requirements is an important one—for it is often concluded that our market system of enterprise is ineffective if it does not give us precisely what we, as consumers, want. This charge would be true only if the other two prerequisites were met and we still did not find our requirements provided for. But there is another characteristic of the cultural inventory that is of fundamental importance. This consumption inventory is not static; it is in a perpetual state of change. Indeed it may be helpful to think about the cultural inventory as the substance delivered on a kind of *conveyor belt effect*. Figure 20.1 depicts this idea.

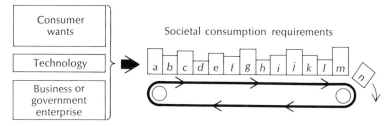

Figure 20.1 The Conveyor Belt Effect

The cultural inventory depicted in Figure 20.1 is transient—it is endlessly redefined by original additions from the triad of forces we have just identified; it is altered perpetually by a discarding process.[2] And although this conveyor belt effect may at first seem to be a dangerous oversimplification, it leads us logically to an extremely profound lesson. This lesson is that no item in the inventory, however firmly it may seem to be established, is necessarily and forever a part of that inventory. And if consumer wants, technology, and business or government enterprise originate additions to this cultural consumption package, what forces produce the demise of elements within the inventory? Our answer is that these same three forces also effect the death of specific components in the inventory. That is, any specific item in the cultural inventory can be eliminated by consumers, by technology or by business or government enterprise—or by any combination of these forces.

Products and services obviously lose favor with consumers and are thus eliminated from the inventory. Products and services are likewise eliminated because of technical reasons—technical obsolescence has killed hundreds of products and services that once may have seemed a permanent part of our culture. And, finally, business and government enterprise may effect the demise of specific components of our cultural inventory. This latter form of change occurs primarily when the incentives that originally prompted the provision of the inventory components no longer exist. In the case of business enterprise, this means that a particular item in the inventory is no longer profitable; in the case of government enterprise, it may mean that the skills required to provide the service are no longer available.

But change in our cultural inventory is not always easily effected. Indeed, there is often a systematized resistance to such change. There is resistance to additions to the inventory; there is resistance to deletions from the inventory. Our concern for now is with the nature of resistance to additions to the cultural inventory; we will consider the nature of resistance to deletions from the inventory in the next section. Resistance to additions to the cultural inventory moves through a more or less well-defined cycle. This *resistance cycle* has five stages, though each of them is not always clearly distinctive. These stages are as follows:

Stage I: In this stage the new product or service is a "wild idea"—it is for crackpots and visionaries to espouse. It is a period during which it is "clear" to all thinking persons that the idea, whatever it is, should not be taken seriously.

Stage II: In this stage the innovation has articulate proponents. Factions, pro and con, are crystallized. The innovation is an emerging force to be reckoned with—it is no longer a plaything for the lunatic fringe.

[2] One source estimates that, in terms of scientific developments, "we are as far removed from the 19th Century as from prehistoric time." This observation suggests what has been called the law of technical acceleration. See Eugene J. Kelley, *Marketing: Strategy and Functions,* Englewood Cliffs, N.J.: Prentice-Hall, Inc., 1965, p. 77.

Stage III: This is a *showdown stage.* It occurs in those instances in which the innovation represents a threat to an existing element in the cultural inventory. Organized resistance is greatest at this stage.

Stage IV: This is a *toehold stage*—the idea, whether product or service, is a probationary part of the consumption inventory. This is a critical stage, however, because any notable failure may negate any progress the innovation has made.

Stage V: During this stage, the innovation enjoys full rights of membership. It is accepted and proven. This is the stage of *full acceptance,* and the resistance cycle is complete.[3]

Virtually every innovative modification in our cultural inventory has had to struggle through the resistance cycle outlined above. It is particularly important that we note that such resistance occurs even with nontrivial innovations—that is, resistance attends even those kinds of change that prove, in retrospect, to have been "needed." We emphasize this point in order to further quiet the criticism that really necessary change will occur without having to be sold. It will be recalled that one criticism that has been leveled at our market system is that it wastes scarce economic resources on frivolous or unnecessary products and services; and that such pioneering sales efforts would not be necessary if the products and services being sold were, in fact, worthy in the first place. Resistance to change is a part of human nature—it is not a phenomenon that attends only the "unworthy" proposals for changes in our way of life.

The product life cycle

We observed earlier that there is also a resistance to change of the sort that involves a deletion of some item from our cultural inventory. In order to develop this idea fully, we need to explore the idea of a product or service life cycle.

Just as the cultural inventory of products and services is a transient package—one characterized by perpetual change in composition—so is the product or service mix of the individual firm. But before we can explore this parallel carefully we need to define two basic concepts—the idea of the product or service mix and the product life cycle.

The *product or service mix* of a firm is the combination of products and services offered by that firm. And, in order to communicate more precisely such differences in the product or service mix as we may encounter, we use the related concepts of product line width, product line depth and product line consistency. *Product line width* is indicated by the number of different classes of products offered by a particular firm.

[3] This type of cycle, with slight modification, is suggested in Goodwin Watson, "Resistance to Change," in Warren G. Bennis and others, editors, *The Planning of Change,* Second Edition, New York: Holt, Rinehart and Winston, Inc., 1969, pp. 488-496.

The greater the number of different classes of products, the greater the product line width. Thus for example, the firm that sells cigarettes, razor blades, men's toiletries, chewing gum, and assorted industrial products (as Philip Morris Incorporated does) has a relatively wide product line.[4] The firm that sells only one basic product line has limited width.

We use the term *product line depth* to designate the number of styles or brands offered by a firm within any one product class. The greater the number of styles or brands in any product class, the greater the line depth. Thus, for example, the line depth of the Chevrolet Division of General Motors—sedans, convertibles, station wagons, sports cars and economy cars—is great. The product line depth of an automobile manufacturer such as Avante, Incorporated—a firm that produces only one model—is shallow. Note that there is no suggestion that deep and wide product lines are good and that shallow and narrow product lines are bad. This is not the case at all. Indeed, there are some extremely well-managed and profitable firms that represent all possible combinations of line width and line depth.

Finally, we need to define the dimension of the product or service mix that we call *consistency*. We say that a product or service mix has consistency if the same or similar skills are required in the manufacture or distribution of each of the classes of products constituting the line. An inconsistent product line is one that comprises products that are totally unrelated in terms of manufacturing processes or in terms of the channels of distribution required.

But in addition to width, depth and consistency, the product or service mix has an *age* dimension. That is, the product or service mix of any firm is definable in terms of its average stage of maturation. And the stage of maturation of a product or service is defined with the assistance of the concept that we have called the *product life cycle*. This product life cycle is depicted in Figure 20.2.[5]

Figure 20.2 identifies the stages through which a product innovation proceeds from its birth until its demise. These stages represent a maturation process that corresponds with the period of time that a particular product or service innovation is a part of what we have called our cultural inventory. That is, the product or service innovation becomes a part of our consumption requirements at the beginning of the cycle and is discarded at the end of Period IV. This product life cycle is thus compatible with the

[4] Concerning Philip Morris's diversification, see Ross R. Millhiser and F. Harrison Poole, "Diversification as a Marketing Strategy," in Frederick E. Webster, Jr., editor, *New Directions in Marketing,* Chicago: American Marketing Association, 1965, pp. 108–115.

[5] The idea of the product life cycle was apparently developed by Jay W. Forrester in his widely reprinted article, "Advertising: A Problem in Industrial Dynamics," *Harvard Business Review,* March-April 1959, pp. 100–110. This particular representation of the product life cycle is a simplified version of the cycle of product acceptance developed in Chapter 7.

conveyor belt effect that we noted earlier, except that it gives us a more detailed account of what is happening to the innovation during its ride on the conveyor belt.

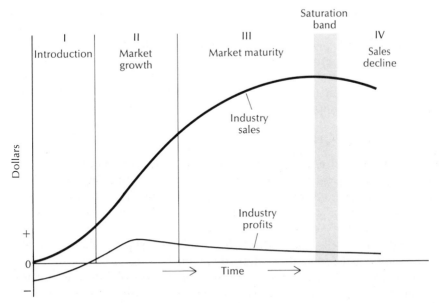

Figure 20.2 The Product Life Cycle

We should also note that the product life cycle is a representation of the effective life of a *class* of products, not of the life cycle of a particular *brand*. This is an important point, for students often tend to confuse the basic nature of what is depicted on the life cycle. The cycle may represent automobiles, but not a particular brand of automobile. The cycle may represent television, but not a particular brand of television. As we begin to explore the subtleties of this life cycle, the reasons for calling it a life cycle for a basic product class rather than a brand life cycle will become apparent.

We should also observe that Figure 20.2 depicts flexible chronological time on the horizontal axis, rather than sharply defined clock time. The practical implication of this limitation is that the time actually required from the introduction of an innovation to the decline of that innovation varies for different types of products. For some innovations, the life expectancy may be several decades; for others, a combination of factors may work to shorten the cycle. In order to accommodate various lengths of life cycles, we simply represent the time axis as flexible, chronological time. The vertical scale depicts dollars—both sales dollars and profit dollars. No special effort has been made to picture profits at a correct proportion to sales. Finally, note that the vertical scale provides both positive and negative values—the industry profit line is, for example, negative during the early part of the introductory stage of the innovation.[6]

While this product life cycle is an industry curve, it is also suggestive of the kind of competition that the individual firm encounters during each of the cycle stages. That is, the marketing mix—a concept that we have encountered earlier—is normally different during the various stages of the product life cycle. And it is this shift in competitive emphasis throughout the life cycle that provides the basis for understanding the process through which the product is ultimately discarded from the cultural inventory. There are four competitive mixes associated with the product life cycle.

STAGE I: INTRODUCTION

During the stage of introduction, there is only one seller of the new and innovative product—the "industry" comprises but one firm. Figure 20.2 indicates that losses are normally a part of this introduction process. Educational efforts are required to develop generic demand—advertising will focus on the advantages of using the generic product rather than some other basic class of product. Heavy pioneering promotional expenditures produce the deficit position depicted in Stage I of the cycle. The price of the innovative product during the period of introduction is at premium levels and normally is not aggressively used in competition in this stage. Distribution is not extensive in the stage of introduction. That is, the innovation is not yet in the hands of mass distributors—it is more frequently handled by specialty distributors who can and will treat it as a special and novel sales opportunity. To briefly summarize then, the Stage I marketing mix is: (a) heavy pioneering or generic promotion, (b) little or no agressive use of price as a competitive weapon and (c) limited distribution.

STAGE II: MARKET GROWTH

During the introductory stage of the cycle, other firms have been watching with more than a little curiosity. As it becomes apparent that the product innovation is earning a hold in the market, these firms stand ready to offer their own version of the innovation. This period of market growth is, for this reason, often called the *emulative period.* Note that what was, in Stage I, a one-firm industry now becomes a multifirm industry. And because several firms now constitute the innovative industry, competition is focused on differences between competing brands. The principal thrust of competition during the period of market growth is for selective rather than generic demand. And the differences between competing brands are

---

[6] This life-cycle analysis presumes that the innovative product is not the exclusive legal property of the innovating firm—that patent rights or other exlusive rights do not preclude emulation.

greater during this period of market growth than they will ever be again. Stage II is, in a very real sense, a stage of experimentation during which the several firms constituting the industry are in continuous quest for the most appealing combination of aesthetic and engineering properties for their products.

Because of these marked differences between brands, the marketing mix of each of the firms emphasizes promotion—and since there are real differences between competing brands, it is no problem to develop meaningful promotional appeals around these points of difference. And because meaningful promotional appeals are available, price still plays a minor role as a competitive enticement. We should note also that industry profits are relatively high—note in Figure 20.2 that industry profits peak during Stage II. This period of market growth is the state of affairs preferred by every profit motivated firm—it will be, in retrospect, the "good old days" for this product from the point of view of the selling firms.

Note carefully that Figure 20.2 indicates that industry profits begin to decline even before the period of market growth has ended. This latter point in the product life cycle is a most significant point. In the later part of the market growth stage, the experimentation that we described earlier—the quest for the most appealing aesthetic and engineering combination of properties—begins to decline in vigor. And this is for a very good reason. As individual brand experimentation proceeds, the results of that experimentation begin to indicate what the most appealing aesthetic and engineering properties of the product are. And once this evidence is available, *real* product differences between brands begin to lessen. That is, as the results of brand experimentation on the part of the various firms in the market become known, the "best" product can be developed. And since research of consumer preferences conducted by the firms constituting the industry tends to point to a similar list of product specifications, differences between brands are gradually eliminated. And when real differences between competing brands begin to disappear the basic thrust of competition will necessarily change.

STAGE III: MARKET MATURITY

The stage of market maturity is a period of mass acceptance and mass distribution of what was, originally, our product innovation. And the market maturity stage is characterized by efforts to postpone the most severe forms of price competition through a *renewal* of the life cycle. We have already noted that competing brands tend to be more and more alike as the maturity stage approaches. We have observed also that when differences between brands are slight, the opportunity to promote any given brand intelligently must decline. When the opportunity to develop distinctive brand appeals is diminished, price competition is very often the result. This rule of competitive priorities means, in effect, that the individual firm can seek new forms of product distinctiveness or face competition in the form of lower prices.

Efforts to renew the product life cycle take the form of a quest for new means of creating brand distinctiveness. And since real differences between brands are limited, a period of "silly-millimeter" promotion may ensue. The market maturity stage is, for this reason, the nemesis of the creative advertising man—it is a period of great, and sometimes ulcerating, search for brand distinctiveness where such distinctiveness may not exist. This effort to renew the product life cycle often involves the use of a strategy that we will call *partial obsolescence.*

The strategy of partial obsolescence may involve either: (a) a systematic release of functional product improvements—with the release timed to coincide with periods of most difficult price competition or (b) a systematic modification in the styling of the product. These two forms of life-cycle renewal are referred to, respectively, as partial *functional obsolescence* and *style obsolescence.* Note that we identify both types of renewal as *partial*—this is to suggest the tendency for such improvements to be relatively minor. Either or both of these renewal procedures is thought capable of bringing back the much more desirable state of competitive affairs that prevailed in the earlier period of market growth. And both the practice of partial functional obsolescence—especially when product improvements are held until needed—and style obsolescence have been the subject of some criticism. Both constitute a form of planned obsolescence.[7]

Planned obsolescence is apparently a paradoxical term—it suggests an intentional shortening of the life of a product; but the motivation for it, as we have seen, may be to extend the life cycle of the product. The answer to the paradox is, of course, that planned obsolescence does shorten the life of one version of the product, but it tends to extend the period of nonprice competition for the general class of products. Thus, a manufacturer of refrigerators delays or softens the use of price competition by introducing such modifications as split doors in one year, freezer below the next, freezer above the next, pastel shades the next, and so forth. The automobile producer features fins in one year, a wide C-post the next, and belt-line hop-up the next. All of which: (a) hastens the aging process of each previous model and (b) permits a degree of nonprice competition that would otherwise not be possible. As one critic puts it: The more important the functional or style change can be made to seem, the closer to "obsolete" the old units become, and the more willing customers will be to replace what they have. And it is further alleged that planned obsolescence sometimes depends upon social pressure in

[7] For a discussion of obsolescence, see Gerald B. Tallman, "Planned Obsolescence: The Setting—The Issues Involved," in Thomas L. Berg and Abe Shuchman, editors, *Product Strategy and Management,* New York: Holt, Rinehart and Winston, Inc., 1963, pp. 54–63. See also Martin Mayer, "Planned Obsolescence: Rx for Tired Markets," in S. George Walters and others, editors, *Readings in Marketing,* Cincinnati: South-Western Publishing Company, 1962, pp. 209-219.

order to be most effective. Thus, "upper income elements of the market have been encouraged to believe that they are socially declassed if they are seen driving an old automobile."[8] Proponents of planned obsolescence suggest that an unavoidable part of progress is rapid obsolescence, and that "planned obsolescence is a sound policy for the economy because it stimulates consumption and raises the level of the gross national product."[9]

STAGE IV: SALES DECLINE

Finally, the product life cycle enters a saturation stage wherein virtually every possible prospect for the product has his quota. The resulting condition is one in which only replacement sales can be made. This saturation band, and the sales decline stage that follows, are characterized by increasingly feeble attempts to differentiate the various brands being offered. Unavoidably, price becomes a more important competitive vehicle—unavoidably profits decline even further. The product in this saturation, sales decline stage may become a leader item—it may be sold "stripped" as a traffic builder. Promotion is now often of the "reminder" type—it tends to talk only about price. Distribution is ubiquitous: every mass dealer possible has the product in some form. In short, the fat is out of the fry—the product holds less and less profit potential. And the life cycle of the product is in the closing stages.

The age of the product/service mix

We have now defined the dimensions of the product/service mix: We have seen that it has width, depth and consistency. We have also seen that a product has an age dimension. But we have not yet considered carefully the idea that the product mix for any single company or firm has a definable *age composition*. Because there is a life cycle process for every type of product, it is possible to define the product/service mix of any company in terms of its average age. And the average age of the product/service mix provides the motivation for much of the behavior of the firm. Some companies would thus have young product/service mixes; some would have mature product/service mixes; and some would have product/service mixes that exceed the proper age for retirement. Clearly, both the growth potential and the stability of a company is influenced by the age composition of its product/service mix. A relatively young mix may show great promise for the future but few current profits; a relatively mature mix may show good current profits but an unsure future. The ideal product/service mix is one that includes both youthful and mature products. Consider, as a means of illustrating this point, Figure 20.3.

[8] Mayer, *op. cit.,* p. 210.
[9] Mark E. Stern, *Marketing Planning,* New York: McGraw-Hill Book Co., 1966, pp. 48–49.

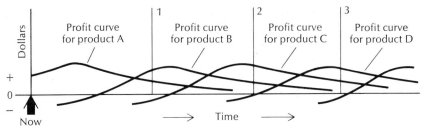

Figure 20.3 Age of the Product Mix

Figure 20.3 depicts the profit curves for four products that are either maturing at different rates or were introduced at different times so that their life cycle age is noncoincident. The profit peak for Product A will occur at the same time that the losses during introduction occur for Product B. Product B is achieving a good profit at the time that losses during the introduction of Product C will occur. This set of profit curves produces stable earnings through time and produces an average age for the mix that is rarely older than late market growth. Make sure that this last statement is clear. Consider, for example, the average age of the product mix for the firm having the products represented in Figure 20.3 at the point in time labeled 1. At that time, Product A is "mature," Product B is "growth," and product C is "introduction." The average life cycle age at point 1 is therefore "growth." Consider the future point labeled 2. Product A is "late mature" to "saturation," Product B is "early mature," Product C is "growth," and Product D is "introduction." The average life cycle age is approximately "market growth."[10]

The principle of postponement

We noted in an early chapter that one of the reasons that our marketing system incurs a relatively high cost is that is often caters to the specialized preference patterns or unique demand characteristics of individuals or, at least, to small segments of the market. We noted at that time that we could substantially reduce the aggregate cost of our market system by asking less of it—in effect we could reduce marketing costs by catering less precisely to the individual's preferences. We could, for example, make shoes in only three sizes—small, medium and large—all in some average width. Clearly such a simplification would reduce not only the marketing costs involved but probably also the production costs. We return now to this general subject and examine more carefully the relationship between efficiency in marketing and the product or products being distributed. More specifically, our concern in this section is with something called the principle of postponement.

[10] This life cycle mix is discussed in Donald K. Clifford, Jr., "Leverage in the Product Life Cycle," in J. Howard Westing and Gerald Albaum, editors, *Modern Marketing Thought*, Second Edition, New York: Crowell-Collier and Macmillan, Inc., 1969, pp. 247-253.

The idea of economic *postponement* implies that changes in the physical form of a product—changes that tailor the product more precisely to the individual demand of consumers—can be delayed or postponed.[11] The principle of postponement suggests that there may be economic advantage in such a delay of differentiation.[12] But let us explore this idea from the point of view of a manufacturer wishing to provide monogrammed dress shirts to final consumers. Suppose that our hypothetical manufacturer wishes to provide three initials on the pocket of each of the shirts bought by one of his dealer's customers. One possibility would be to make a study of the frequency with which all three-initial combinations occur in the United States, and supply each dealer with a stock of shirts that are premonogrammed to reflect that frequency distribution. This solution to the problem would produce a special form of haberdashers' roulette: it would, in effect, attempt to anticipate the initials of buyers. And we should note that such an answer to the problem would probably increase the dealer's costs rather substantially. For the dealer would now be required to carry stocks in sufficient numbers to provide a reasonable likelihood that customers would be able to find the initial combinations they sought. As a second possibility, we might provide only two initials—such a reduction would result in a tremendous simplification in the total number of initial combinations we would be required to offer, and it would clearly trim dealer stock requirements. But such a solution does not meet with the degree of personalization that the manufacturer wishes.

Still another possibility is to *postpone* the process of monogramming until the shirts are purchased by final consumers. This course of action would mean that dealers would carry only the normal size and color assortments, and that differentiation through monogramming would occur only after a customer had purchased a shirt. In this case, the customer's demand is catered to in a precise way (his exact initials) and yet the dealers have not been required to bloat their stocks to accommodate the personalized treatment. The economic savings through postponement may include not only the costs associated with larger dealer stocks but also lower unit manufacturer costs of production.

Consider, for example, the parallel situation in the automobile business. How many different automobiles would a new car dealer be required to stock if he was to meet the exact demands of his customers? If we are quite precise in our answer, we would have to say that the dealer

[11] The discussion here is concerned only with physical changes in the product. The notion of "postponement," as originally developed, included not only changes in the physical product, but also other means of differentiation, including the location of the product. See this original discussion in Wroe Alderson's *Marketing Behavior and Executive Actions*, Homewood, Ill.: Richard D. Irwin, Inc., 1957, pp. 423–427.

[12] The idea of postponement has not been as completely developed as is possible. For some interesting applications and refinements of the idea, see Louis P. Bucklin, "Postponement, Speculation and the Structure of Distribution," *Journal of Marketing Research*, February 1965, p. 26–31.

would require each color of each basic model and every possible combination of extra or optional equipment for each one. And clearly such a stock of cars would not only blanket miles of terrain, but it would also be extremely costly to finance and insure. Again, the answer is postponement of differentiation—the dealer carries a basic stock of popular colors and models and tailors the basic automobile to the exact preferences of the consumer by adding the desired options.

For many kinds of products—such as our monogrammed shirts and automobiles—the preferences of the consumer are virtually unique. This is particularly true when there are many different size, color or performance features. The challenge to the business system in these instances is to devise ways of economically filling these unique demand requirements. And the notion of postponing the differentiation of a product until the latest possible point in its movement to final consumers may: (a) avoid some of the costs of risk, financing and insurance for dealers and distributors; and (b) still permit long production runs (and the realization of economies therefrom) for the manufacturer. The reader should note that it is not being suggested that the product differentiation (for example, monogramming) can be accomplished any less expensively by the dealer than by the manufacturer. The potential gain from postponement is rather in the smaller inventories required of dealers and from the economies of scale permitted by longer manufacturing runs.

The product and the package

Except in the case of some bulk-sale situations, the package is very often a part of what we buy.[13] And it is a condition of great concern to some people that packaging may, in some cases, cost more than the product being purveyed. It is particularly true that in those instances where the processes of manufacturing the product are thoroughly and highly automated (as for cigarettes, cereal, detergents, crackers) the package may cost more than the ingredients that it contains. One source estimates that "in 1966, United States manufacturers spent an estimated $15 billion for packaging materials—or nearly as much as the $17 billion spent for advertising." Indeed, this same source indicates that if all packaging forms were combined, the annual investment would exceed $26 billion.[14] But the role of the package is an important one. It may: (a) protect the product, (b) adapt the product to production-line speeds, (c) promote the product, (d) increase the density of the product, (e) facilitate the use of the product

[13] A concise historical perspective of the role of packaging may be seen in William C. Simms, "A History of Packaging," in Robert M. Kaplan, editor, The Marketing Concept in Action, Chicago: American Marketing Association, 1964, pp. 334-348.
[14] Dik Warren Twedt, "How Much Value Can Be Added Through Packaging?" Journal of Marketing, January 1968, pp. 58-59.

and (f) provide some reuse value for the consumer.[15] Some of the foregoing list of package functions are perfectly obvious and do not require clarification or illustration. The protection function, the reuse-value function (for example, cottage cheese containers for leftovers) and the facilitate-use function (for example, the collapsible salt spout) are reasonably obvious services that may be provided by the package. But other items in this list of package functions involve ideas that are not at all obvious. Consider the apparently simple observation that the package promotes. Consider also the following data.[16]

Table 20.1 Planned and unplanned purchases

	1945	1949	1954	1959
Specifically planned and purchased	48.2%	33.4%	29.2%	30.5%
Generally planned and purchased	11.0	26.7	21.0	15.9
Substituted	2.6	1.5	1.8	2.7
Unplanned	38.2	38.4	48.0	50.9

The data in Table 20.1 are summarized from a continuing study sponsored by E. I. duPont de Nemours & Company. They are of special interest to us here because they reflect the extent to which in-store promotion, including packaging, influences the American supermarket shopper. The row labeled "Specifically planned and purchased" indicates the percentage of total supermarket purchases that were planned in detail—in recent years only about one-third of supermarket purchases are "specificallly planned." All other supermarket purchases are planned only generally or not at all. A purchase that is planned only in a general way is one for which no specific brand decision has been made. And the basic point suggested by these data is that today over two-thirds of all supermarket purchases are potentially influenced by in-store promotion. The role of the package is necessarily more important in these conditions than it would be if impulse or unplanned buying were less frequent.

To be more specific, we may identify four different types of impulse buying. First, there is the "pure" impulse purchase; this is the "lark purchase"—it is a novelty or escape-from-it-all purchase. Second, there is the "reminder" impulse purchase—the shopper has not planned this purchase,

[15] This list is suggested by William R. Mason in "A Theory of Packaging in the Marketing Mix," *Business Horizons,* Summer 1958, p. 91–95.
[16] See these data in "Latest Facts About Today's Shoppers in Supermarkets," dated annually, copyright by E. I. duPont de Nemours & Company.

but the sight of the product is a reminder that stocks at home are depleted. The third kind of impulse purchase occurs when the buyer sees a product for the first time and visualizes a need for it. And finally, there is an intriguing kind of buyer behavior suggested by the term "planned impulse" buying. And this practice of planned impulse buying is an important reason for the current popularity of the package as a promotional means. Planned impulse buying occurs when the shopper begins the shopping trip with the expectation of making some purchases that will depend upon price specials, coupon offers, and similar "specials." Thus, for example, a housewife may plan to spend a total of $30 on a particular trip and only (say) $25 will be planned definitely. The remainder will be spent contingent upon the availability of special offers.

These four types of unplanned, or impulse, buying behavior represent, when considered together, an imposing argument for taking in-store promotion seriously; and they account for much of the sales clamor that greets the customer in the typical supermarket. Another study, one conducted by *Progressive Grocer,* indicated that 112 of 308 shoppers interviewed waited until they were in the store and "that their ideas for meals shaped up as they shopped." The evidence is impressive that the point-of-purchase is a critical point in the purchase decision.

A second function of the package that may require some clarification is the notion that the package should, when feasible, increase product density. *Product density* may be defined as the ratio of the space occupied by the product alone to the space occupied by both the product and the package. Consider, for example, Figure 20.4.

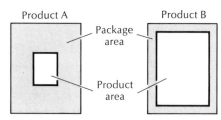

Figure 20.4 Product Density

If the total area for Product A (product plus package) is taken as 100, then the area of the product alone may be on the order of 25. The product density is .25, or 25/100. If the total area of Product B (product plus package) is taken as 100, then the area of the product alone may be approximately 90. The ratio of product density for product B would be .9, or 90/100. The idea of product density is a challenge for the packaging engineer—the task is simultaneously to protect the product and to maximize the product density.

But there is a second form of product density that is also of concern to us. We will call this second type of density "shelf-space" density. And we will define shelf-space density as the ratio of the area of product plus package to the shelf space required to accommodate the product plus the package. Consider, for example, the following two plastic detergent containers:

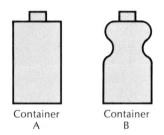

Container
A

Container
B

Figure 20.5 Shelf-space Density

The test of shelf-space density is in placing a number of packages tightly side by side and examining the efficiency with which the shelf space is thus utilized. The shelf-space density of Container A in Figure 20.5 would approach 1 (unity). That is, the total shelf space required would be about the same as that of the product and the package. There would be little unproductive space of any kind. But consider Container B; the shelf-space density of this container would be considerably less than unity. The saddle-back bottle would, in effect, use space that is neither package nor product. Be sure that this distinction between product density and shelf-space density is clear—for they are entirely different ideas. That is, the product density for Containers A and B in Figure 20.5 may both be very high—they may both be thin-wall containers with virtually 100 percent fill. But the configuration of Container B results in a less efficient utilization of shelf space than does that of Container A.

The notion that both product density and shelf-space density should be maximized, given the prior obligation of the package to adequately protect its contents, may lead to some curious results. First, there is one shape that must win the test of shelf-space density. That shape is the rectangle. And it is a curious twist of fate that the inherent efficiency of the rectangle as a container shape may work to its detriment at the point of purchase. We noted in an earlier chapter that the most efficient package in terms of product density and shelf-space density may not be the most effective sales device. This turn of events follows because the rectangle with a similar amount of product in it will often appear smaller in size than the package with artistic embellishments. Thus, while the conscientious firm may wish to use the package that is most efficient from the standpoint of space utilization, it may be forced to do otherwise. It would appear that the *perceived* size—what the buyer believes a package to contain—is the most important single determinant of packaging practices today.

There is one final function of the package that deserves clarification. Some packages facilitate production-line handling; some do not. When possible, the package should contribute to efficient handling procedures. As a means of illustrating this point, consider the "tray-pack system" and the "white-spot system." the tray-pack system is effected by using a perforated shipping carton as a miniature pallet—the contents of the shipping carton need not be emptied on the shelf. Rather, the lower portion of the shipping carton is slid onto the shelf as a single unit. This seemingly small convenience reduces the handling required by shelf stockers considerably and produces a more efficient stocking procedure. The white-spot system is a packaging practice that is also related to handling efficiency. It is the practice of some packers to provide a package that leaves a small white spot clear for the retailer's price. When the retailer prices such merchandise, it is possible to get a legible price marking; and if the white spot is correctly placed, the price-marker may be able to mark hundreds of items in a matter of minutes.[17]

The product and the warranty

We have seen earlier that consumer behavior may be viewed as a special form of risk taking. The buyer confronts risk when he buys a new product, when he buys a new brand, when he buys a product that has been modified (a "new," improved version), and when he buys from a dealer with whom he has had no previous dealings. The kind of risk confronted is, in general, risk that the product will not perform as it should. The general purpose of the warranty is to reduce risk. The warranty is treated here as though it were an intangible part of the product that the buyer acquires.

A warranty is some form of obligation that is assumed by the seller. And, curiously enough, a warranty need not be written or spoken in order that a seller incur such an obligation. Warranties are sometimes *implied;* sometimes they are *express.* A warranty is express when the seller assumes the obligation in express words. A warranty is implied when it does not appear in so many words but is made a part of the sales transaction by custom, statute or by the court.[18] Sellers today normally give, by implication, a warranty of title, a warranty of correspondence, a warranty of merchantability and, on occasion, a warranty of fitness-for-known-purpose. The *warranty of title* assures the buyer that the item of merchandise being sold to him is, in fact, within the seller's rights to sell. The *warranty of correspondence* is an implied warranty that the goods to be delivered correspond substantially with the goods contracted for. The warranty of

---

[17] See Curt Kornblau, "Packaging and Super Markets: The Package in the Market Place," in Ronald R. Gist, editor, *Management Perspectives in Retailing,* New York: John Wiley & Sons, Inc., 1967, pp. 253–258.

[18] See Dow Votaw, *Legal Aspects of Business Administration,* Englewood Cliffs, N.J.: Prentice-Hall, Inc., 1965, pp. 387–388.

correspondence is especially important in transactions in which the buyer buys by sample or by description (catalog order, for example). The *warranty of merchantability* assures the general fitness of the goods for purposes to which they are normally put. The *warranty of fitness-for-known-purpose* arises when the buyer makes it known to the seller, before purchase, that he intends to use the product in a particular manner. If the seller completes the sale with knowledge of this particular use and the product proves ineffectual for the purpose, the buyer may have legal recourse.

Express warranties appear in such diverse forms that a meaningful classification is difficult. One such classification, however, distinguishes the protective warranty from the promotional warranty. And this distinction is one that provides helpful insight into the use of express warranties as a part of the modern parcel of competitive weapons. The most apparent weakness of this classification is the implication that all express warranties fall clearly into one of these two classes—and that is not always the case. The *protective warranty* is, as curious as it may seem, a form of protection for the seller. The protective warranty, while expressly defining the circumstances against which the buyer will find protection, serves primarily to guard the seller against unreasonable claims of purchasers.[19] The protective warranty will normally emphasize three basic limitations of seller's or manufacturer's responsibility: (a) defects in material and workmanship in (b) normal use for (c) some reasonable period of time. *Promotional warranties* are usually dramatic blanket expressions of assurance to the prospective buyer. They may be "unconditional guarantees of satisfaction" (as many of the mail-order firms use); they may be "double your money back guarantees"; or they may be replacement warranties. A replacement warranty will provide the buyer with a new unit at any time he is dissatisfied with the performance of the product.[20]

The protective warranty and the promotional warranty are normally used in different circumstances. The protective warranty is most commonly used with the durable good. It is especially common with the product that is complex enough that it will reasonably require service in its later years. This is not to suggest that the protective warranty is an unfair escape hatch created for the benefit of the manufacturer or brand owner; the provisions of the protective warranty may, in fact, be very liberal from the buyer's point of view. The statement of the limits of the seller's responsibility in the protective warranty protects the seller from unreasonable claims—it does not necessarily, force the buyer to waive his right to reasonable service from the product. Some consumers abuse, often flagrantly, their role as the "little man"—they are, in short, unreasonable in the demands they place upon the seller.

[19] See in Jon G. Udell and Evan E. Anderson, "The Product Warranty as an Element of Competitive Strategy," *Journal of Marketing,* October 1968, p. 1.
[20] See D. Maynard Phelps and J. Howard Westing, *Marketing Management,* Third Edition, Homewood, Ill.: Richard D. Irwin, Inc., 1968, pp. 239-241.

The promotional warranty, on the other hand, tends to be associated with the relatively inexpensive product—sometimes one that is quickly consumed—or with a product that is virtually foolproof. A well-known manufacturer of cigarette lighters, for example, offers a lifetime free service policy—and the product is not only foolproof, it borders on indestructibility.

The use of the express warranty as a competitive weapon is, for some manufacturers, a "damned if we do, damned if we don't" matter. If they do offer a liberal warranty, they invite the abuse of themselves and their dealers; if they don't, they are accused of avoiding their responsibility as an enterprise dedicated to serving the public. For most firms, the best answer is to provide an express warranty but not to make it the subject of great promotional efforts. The result is either the "quiet" warranty or the warranty that is so ambiguous that it makes little in the way of effective promises.

SUMMARY

The general purpose of Chapter 20 has been to examine the relationship between products, services and our society. Toward this end, we have developed several basic analytical concepts. First, we introduced the idea that a transient cultural inventory of products and services is a most important part of our economic system. This cultural inventory may be thought of as being on a massive conveyor belt—one that regularly adds new products or services, and which regularly disposes of older product or service concepts. A resistance cycle was identified that works to interfere with both additions to the cultural inventory and deletions from that inventory.

The product life cycle represents an analytical device that traces a new product or service concept from its incipiency to its demise. This product life cycle traces the process of maturation of an innovation through four stages, or steps. These stages are introduction, market growth, market maturity and sales decline. A business firm may be characterized by the age-composition of the product/service mix that it offers. That product/service mix embodies a width dimension, a depth dimension and a consistency dimension.

In an economic system characterized by some significant degree of affluence, the products offered must satisfy the individualized tastes of the society. The principle of postponement was identified as a means through which the economic advantages of mass production could be realized and individualized self-expression catered to.

The package is an important part of a product. The ideas of impulse purchases, product density and shelf-space density were introduced. Impulse purchases include four different types of consumer actions—all of which suggest that point-of-purchase promotion plays an extremely important role today.

Finally, the warranty was considered. Four implied warranties were identified. These were: (a) the title warranty, (b) the correspondence warranty, (c) the merchantability warranty and (d) the fitness-for-known-purpose warranty. Two types of express warranties were examined: the protective warranty and the promotional warranty.

REVIEW QUESTIONS

1 Carefully define and indicate the relevance of each of the following concepts to the study of marketing:
   a. A cultural inventory
   b. The conveyor belt effect
   c. A cycle of resistance to change
   d. Product line width
   e. Product line depth
   f. Product line consistency
   g. The product life cycle
   h. The emulative stage of the product life cycle
   i. Postponement of product differentiation

2 Distinguish carefully between each element in the following pairs of terms:
   a. The market growth stage of the product life cycle *and* the market maturity stage of the product life cycle
   b. Functional obsolescence *and* style obsolescence
   c. The age of the product *and* the age-composition of the product mix
   d. Product density *and* shelf-space density
   e. Pure impulse buying *and* planned impulse buying
   f. An express warranty *and* an implied warranty
   g. A warranty of correspondence *and* a warranty of merchantability
   h. A protective warranty *and* a promotional warranty

3 Carefully describe the nature of competition during each of the several stages of the product life cycle.

4 Provide examples of retail stores that:
   a. Have wide product (or merchandise) lines
   b. Have deep product (or merchandise) lines

DISCUSSION QUESTIONS

5 Analyze the effects of men's stretch socks on dealer inventories, and upon the costs of risk bearing, financing and insuring.

6 In about 1965 or 1966 a major supplier of facial tissues "removed the air" from its package—that is, they compressed the tissues much more completely. What is the possible result of this action (a) from the standpoint of economic efficiency and (b) from the standpoint of competitive strategy?

SUGGESTED SUPPLEMENTARY READINGS
IN PRODUCT AND SERVICE PLANNING

Berg, Thomas L., and Abe Shuchman, *Product Strategy and Management,* New York: Holt, Rinehart and Winston, Inc., 1963.

Buzzell, R. D., W. J. Salmon, and Richard R. Vancil, *Product Profitability Measurement and Merchandising Decisions,* Boston: School of Business Administration, Harvard University, 1965.

Eastlack, J. O., Jr., editor, *New Product Development,* Chicago: American Marketing Association, 1968.

Karger, Delmar W., *The New Product: How to Find, Test, Develop, Cost, Price, Protect, Advertise and Sell New Products,* New York: The Industrial Press, 1960.

King, Robert L., editor, *Conferences, '55/'65,* Chicago: American Marketing Association, 1966.

Pessemier, Edgar A., *New Product Decisions: An Analytical Approach,* New York: McGraw-Hill Book Company, 1966.

Reynolds, William H., *Products and Markets,* New York: Appleton-Century-Crofts, 1969.

Chapter 21
THEORIES OF PRICING

Long tradition holds that prices are an important economic regulator. That is, relatively high prices are believed to attract productive resources and thus prevent their use in other ways. Conversely, relatively low prices are thought to tend to divert resources into other uses. And there is no quarrel with this traditional view. Yet we have seen that price in an ecological system of competition is only one among several possible dimensions upon which competition may focus. And we have indicated that there is often very good reason for developing the principal thrust of competition around nonprice dimensions. We have likewise noted that the relative deemphasis afforded price competition is a source of real concern to some observers. Prices are controversial: they affect us all. We have all heard higher prices explained as a wage-cost spiral—though we seem never to be the beneficiary of such a spiral.

In recent years we have heard that unfair prices are a cause of social disorder. Ghetto prices seem, in some instances, exploitively higher than those elsewhere.[1] Ghetto businessmen answer that it often costs more to do business in economically deprived areas. We are told, for example, that losses from theft, damage and bad debts all exceed the level of similar losses encountered in more affluent market areas. These higher costs require higher prices—we are told. Yet the argument is not fully quieted. Those who control prices control something as profoundly important as rates of taxation and our own pay raises. Any intelligent person should be concerned with the mechanisms through which prices are determined. In this and the next chapter, we turn our attention to a systematic consideration of the issue of prices in our market system.

[1] An especially strong position on this issue is argued in Frederick D. Sturdivant, "Better Deal for Ghetto Shoppers," *Harvard Business Review,* March-April 1968, pp. 130-139. A more moderate preliminary exploration of the problem is described in Charles S. Goodman, "Do the Poor Pay More?" *Journal of Marketing,* January 1968, pp. 18-24.

More specifically, our concern in the present chapter is threefold. First, we will provide some preliminary vocabulary requirements—there are several specialized terms that we will find necessary in subsequent discussions. Second, we will consider the rule of competitive priorities—an idea that we have mentioned previously but have not considered with proper care. Third, we will examine the most frequently encountered explanations of prices. We will, toward this latter goal, examine the role of historical cost and opportunity cost in pricing; we will examine briefly the traditional supply and demand explanation of pricing; and we will examine several explanations of pricing behavior that are miscellaneous but not unimportant. We will assume an essentially critical point of view regarding the traditional, or supply and demand, explanation of pricing; and, where possible, we will suggest modifications to that theory that will bring it closer to realism.

Some preliminary definitions

Before we undertake an examination of pricing theory, we will find it helpful to define some of the special language we will have to use. Specifically, we will distinguish between the tactical use of price and the strategic use of price as a competitive weapon. We will also find it necessary to distinguish between price level and price structure. And we will find unavoidable the use of the terms margin and stock turnover.

When we say that price plays a relatively unimportant role in ecological competition, we really mean that it is used infrequently as a strategic form of competition. The fact is that price is quite often used in a tactical situation. What do these terms mean? A *strategic* form of competition is the main thrust of a competitive mix. The firm that uses price as a long-run, regular market appeal is using price in a strategic sense. The firm that uses price strategically will not be undersold—and may aggressively claim just that. A *tactical* use of price is essentially defensive. If a firm uses price when it is needed to meet unexpected competitive situations—to stave off what is believed to be a short-lived competitive challenge—price is being used as a tactical weapon. This is an important distinction because, while the strategic use of price is not at all common, the use of price as a tactical matter is virtually unavoidable.

When we use the term *price level*, we will refer to the price we, as consumers, see ticketed on merchandise. The price level is a single number—the amount for which we write a check for a cash purchase. It is entirely visible and necessarily has meaning in some context of "high to low." We tend to classify stores by their price level—some have high price images, some exude generally low price images. Much of the exposure that beginning students in economics get to pricing is concerned with the level of prices. But there is another dimension to prices—one that is rarely visible to us as final consumers, and one that may require more actual time in determination than price levels. This second, and less apparent, aspect of prices is called structure. *Price structure* deals with three aspects of price. These three aspects of price are: (a) when payment is to be made—that is, the temporal aspects of price, (b) where and when title is to be taken by the buyer and (c) the nature of the discounts to be allowed the buyer. Our concern in the present chapter is primarily with price levels—we will examine the structural dimensions of prices in the next chapter.

Another term that we will find it necessary to use is *margin*: we will mean by that term the difference between cost and selling price. An item of merchandise that sells for $5 and which costs a reseller $3 carries a margin of $2, or 40 percent of selling price. The $2 margin may also be expressed as a percentage of cost—in this latter context the margin is called a *markup on cost*—and it amounts to 66⅔ per cent. The term margin may be used to designate either the diffe ence between cost and selling price for an individual item or for an aggregate—such as the overall departmental gross margin for a particular department in a retail store. In a subsequent chapter we will explore these and related matters much more fully, for now this brief definition will suffice.

Finally, we will find it useful in the discussion that follows to have a good working understanding of the term *stock turnover*. This term refers to the rate of movement of merchandise, or stocks, through time. Stock turnover is usually expressed in terms of a one-year time period. Thus, a stock turnover rate of 26 would mean that the average inventory of a store or other business is sold 26 times each year, or once every two weeks. A stock turnover of 10 means that the average inventory of a store or other business is sold ten times annually. There are three basic measures of stock turnover—though only two of them are in widespread use. These three measures are:

(a) $\dfrac{\text{Net sales in dollars}}{\text{Average inventory in selling prices}} = \text{Stock turnover}$

(b) $\dfrac{\text{Cost of goods sold in dollars}}{\text{Average inventory in cost values}} = \text{Stock turnover}$

(c) $\dfrac{\text{Net sales in units}}{\text{Average inventory in units}} = \text{Stock turnover}$

A brief example will both illustrate the manner in which these stock turnover ratios are calculated and reveal the relationship between them. Assume that a business achieved net sales of $100,000 in a given year. Assume, moreover, that the business sells only one item—a patented panoramic nondistorting rearview mirror. The mirror is sold for $10, and a margin of 30 percent is realized on it. An average of 2000 mirrors is held in inventory by the firm. What is the stock turnover rate for the business as measured by each of the three stock turnover ratios?

(a) $$\frac{\$100,000}{\$\ 20,000} = 5$$

(b) $$\frac{\$\ 70,000}{\$\ 14,000} = 5$$

(c) $$\frac{\$\ 10,000}{\$\ \ 2,000} = 5$$

Observe that the three calculations above correspond to the three ratios previously identified. That is, the (a) calculation is made in terms of selling price values; the (b) calculation is made in terms of cost values; and the (c) calculation is made in terms of units. Note also that the three ratios yield exactly the same answers—namely, a stock turnover rate of 5. Think through what would happen to the stock turnover rates if we were able to reduce the inventories carried by the business. To be more specific, what would be the new stock turnover rate if we, hereafter, maintained an average inventory of 1500 units? Your answer should be that the stock turnover rate would then be 6.66.

The rule of competitive priorities

Discussions of the marketing mix often treat price as if it were like other elements in the mix—namely, another independent variable to be used to best advantage. Indeed, in our earlier definitional encounters with the marketing mix, we simplified matters by maintaining such a view. But price is not like other competitive elements—and it is different in some significant ways. Our central point in this section is that price is very often a dependent phenomenon—dependent in at least two ways.

First, price is dependent upon the other elements that constitute the competitive mix—that is, "changes in the other components are likely to affect price."[2] A change in distribution, a change in the product or a change in promotion is very likely to influence costs—and possibly price as well. But price is dependent in still another way. Price is dependent in the sense that it is often used strategically as a competitive weapon only after other competitive means prove ineffective. This idea, that price is last in line as a competitive weapon, is the heart of the *rule of competitive priorities*. This rule is represented graphically in Figure 21.1.

Figure 21.1 suggests that the probability that a firm will use price strategically depends upon whether the opportunity to use promotion is good or poor. When the opportunity to use promotion is good, there is a low probability that price will play an important role. Conversely, when the opportunity to use promotion is poor, the likelihood that price will become an important element in the competitive mix is higher. What, then, deter-

[2] This idea is developed in John Fayerweather, *International Marketing*, Englewood Cliffs, N.J.: Prentice-Hall, Inc., 1965, p. 102.

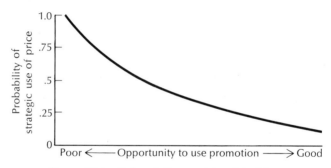

Figure 21.1   Rule of Competitive Priorities

mines the level of opportunity to use promotion? The opportunity to use promotion is determined, in large measure, by four basic conditions. These conditions are: (a) that the product have qualities not easily judged by consumers, (b) that the brand be demonstrably different from other products of the same general class, (c) that primary demand (the demand for the general class of product) be increasing and (d) that the funds required for promotion be regularly available.[3] Our rule of competitive priorities says, then, that when the funds required for promotion are available and any of the other conditions outlined above are present, promotion will tend to precede price in terms of its strategic importance in the marketing mix. Price can, and does, occupy a prominent tactical role. In the gasoline "wars," for example, the periodic emphasis on price is essentially a tactical action.

Some general theories of price

There are two basic explanations of price.[4] These two explanations emphasize, respectively: (a) the collective effects of buyers and sellers and (b) the individual efforts of sellers. We use the term *market prices* to identify prices established by the collective and impersonal forces of many buyers and sellers. Market prices may exist for commodities and other essentially undifferentiated products. The price for a share of IBM stock is a market price; the price for a bushel of number two hard red winter wheat is a market price. It is important to emphasize that market prices are impersonal; they presumably result from the independent actions of many buyers and sellers. Such a price has traditionally been viewed as a "good" price—a price produced, as it were, by all persons in the market, not by any individual acting from motives of avarice or greed.

We use the term *administered,* or *judgment* prices to identify prices established by the individual seller. The great majority of goods and services

[3] This list of conditions is, in amended form, a list suggested by Neil H. Borden and Martin V. Marshall in *Advertising Management: Text and Cases,* Homewood, Ill.: Richard D. Irwin, Inc., 1959, pp. 162–165.
[4] Price in the "level" sense, as opposed to the "structure" of prices.

in the United States are sold at prices that are administered.[5] There are two special points about administered prices that we should make. First, administered prices are administered in varying degrees. Some nonmarket prices are set almost solely by executive or administrative action, others are set by a combination of administrative and market forces. Stated in another way, pure market prices and purely administered prices are actually polar positions—the great majority of prices are established by the combined forces of both the market and the seller's judgment. As one nears the "administered" pole, the role of the individual seller is enhanced; as one nears the "market" pole, the role of the seller is diminished.

The second special point about administered prices we need to make is that price "administration" is not the same thing as price "fixing." Price fixing necessarily involves collusion—that is, several parties agree to set and maintain prices at a particular point. Horizontal price fixing is illegal per se. Vertical price fixing is permitted by law under some circumstances.[6] But an administered price is the decision of one firm acting in what it believes to be its own best interest—there is no overt act of collusion. And, indeed, many administered prices cannot be made to stick. That is, executive judgment may prove wrong. Sometimes prices are set at too high levels, and the forces of the market bring them down to proper levels; sometimes the price is "administered" too low, and the market forces it up. Early experimentation with the price of Polaroid color film suggested, in fact, that the market price would have been above the administered price.

If the nature of the administered price is not yet clear, consider the plight of a man who has exclusive distribution rights for a precision Swedish camera. The camera has never been sold before anywhere. It is ultramodern and made of extremely high quality materials—it is unlike any other camera. At what price should it be sold? Clearly, pricing the precision camera presents a different problem from, say, pricing a share of IBM stock. A price always exists for the share of stock—we have, in that case, the continuous judgment of the market to guide us. But what market guidance does the distributor get about the precision Swedish camera? Certainly there is no continuous market feedback (such as the stock market provides) that could help price the camera. He must, unavoidably, exercise his own judgment about what values may be perceived in the camera. When product differences exist, some degree of administrative judgment in pricing is required.

And how are judgments regarding prices made? That is, what process or procedure is used in the administration of prices? We will consider three explanations: (a) the cost theory of prices, (b) the supply and demand theory of prices, and (c) some explanations of administered prices that,

[5] See Robert F. Lanzillotti, "Why Corporations Find it Necessary to 'Administer' Prices," *Challenge*, January 1960, pp. 45–49.
[6] See the discussion of resale price maintenance in Chapter 5.

although they do not represent fully developed theories, attempt to explain the price making procedure in special circumstances.[7]

THE COST THEORY OF PRICE

In the theory of price, there are two important types of cost. These two types of cost are, in the order that we will consider them: (a) historical cost and (b) opportunity cost.

Historical costs are perhaps the most popular explanation of the administered pricing process. At least, historical costs are usually given some causal role—though such costs may be supplemented by other forces.[8] Historical costs are accounting costs as opposed to conceptual costs. Historical costs are exemplified by payments made to employees, payments made to suppliers for merchandise or services rendered, payments made for plant and equipment, and similar out-of-pocket expenditures. An example of a conceptual cost would be the cost that a firm might have to pay for the services of a lawyer who, in fact, provides his service free. Thus, a historical cost is real in the sense that an outlay of cash is normally required for it. Historical costs provide an understandable explanation of price determination. There are four types of historical cost explanations of price that concern us here. There is: (a) the simple cost-plus explanation, (b) the uniform percentage gross margin explanation, (c) the variable percentage gross margin explanation and (d) the dollar margin explanation.

COST-PLUS PRICING   A cost-plus explanation of prices is familiar to us all. Indeed the popular "wage-price spiral," an explanation of increases in the general price level, provides an introduction to a cost-plus explanation of individual prices. Government contracts and building contracts sometimes emphasize the term cost-plus. And the use of costs as an explanation of prices undoubtedly has a degree of social sanction. After all, who can feel altogether put out with a man who prices at a level to cover his costs? Certainly an emphasis on costs tends to provide a built-in rationale for price increases. One of the most widely publicized studies of industrial pricing found that pricing to cover "full average costs" was the most frequent explanation of industrial pricing procedures.[9]

A special form of cost-plus pricing is the *sum-of-margins* method. This technique involves the building up of prices from the manufacturer, to the wholesaler, to the retailer, to the consumer. Thus, the retail price of a particular item might be the manufacturer's costs plus his gross margin plus the wholesaler's gross margin plus the retailer's gross margin. This

[7] A useful summary of the influence of cost and other factors in pricing in four industries may be seen in Albert A. Fitzpatrick, *Pricing Methods of Industry,* Boulder, Colo.: Pruett Press, Inc., 1964. See especially the tabular summaries on pp. 68, 72, 73.

[8] *Ibid.,* p. 72.

[9] See R. L. Hall and C. J. Hitch, "Price Theory and Business Behavior," *Oxford Economic Papers,* No. 2, May 1939, pp. 12–45.

resulting chain of gross margins represents, in effect the sum of manufacturing and distribution, and promotional costs.

UNIFORM PERCENTAGE GROSS MARGIN PRICING   Another special form of cost-plus pricing is identified by the term *uniform percentage gross margin* pricing.[10] This pricing technique has been widely used in retailing. When the uniform percentage gross margin method is used, the price policy of a particular department may be described with a single term such as "35 percent" or "40 percent" or perhaps "20 percent." These percentage terms specify the amount of markup, or margin, taken by a department expressed as a percentage of selling prices. Thus a uniform departmental price policy of "35 percent" means that all items in the department are marked up so that 65 percent of the selling price is merchandise cost, and 35 percent of the selling price is gross margin. The popularity of this method of pricing traces in part to its simplicity, in part to its convenience. It is common practice, for example, to calculate expense ratios for the various departments within a store. Thus, a particular department may have an expense ratio of 30 percent. This means that the expenses of running the department—including direct expenses and a provision for its share of overhead, but excluding the cost of merchandise sold—averages 30 percent. A convenient way to designate a price policy for that department would be to add a profit margin to the expense ratio and use the resulting figure as a uniform percentage gross margin for the department. Thus, a 30 percent departmental expense ratio and a 5 percent target rate of profit would produce a uniform percentage gross margin pricing policy of 35 percent.

VARIABLE PERCENTAGE GROSS MARGIN PRICING   A modification of the uniform percentage gross margin approach (but still a form of cost-plus pricing) is the *variable percentage gross margin* technique. An obvious fault of the uniform percentage gross margin method is that it does not give proper attention to the nuances of demand. That is, competitive circumstances would rarely, if ever, dictate similar margins on all items of merchandise. Such circumstances would more nearly suggest different margins—relatively low margins for some items and relatively higher margins for others. The variable percentage gross margin pricing method recognizes that the strength of competition varies widely between items of merchandise. A variable percentage gross margin price policy may recognize any number of different margin classes—an example would be 20-30-40. This triad of margins suggests that some items in a department are marked at a 20 percent gross margin, some others at a 30 percent margin, and still a third group is marked at 40 percent.

[10] See Roger Dickenson, "Markup in Department Store Management," *Journal of Marketing,* January 1967, pp. 32–34.

It is a normal part of this pricing method to estimate the relative sales volume to be achieved in each margin class so that an overall departmental target margin may be achieved. If, for example, we expected 50 percent of departmental sales volume to occur in the 20 percent margin class, 30 percent of departmental sales volume to occur in the 30 percent margin class, and 20 percent of departmental sales volume to occur in the 40 percent margin class, we would anticipate an overall, or departmental, target gross margin of 27 percent. This calculation is made as follows:

Margin class		Percent of sales		Gross margin
20%	×	50%	=	10%
30	×	30	=	9
40	×	20	=	8
Totals		100%		27%

DOLLAR MARGIN PRICING   Dollar margin pricing is still another approach to pricing that embodies some cost-plus overtones but is also, to a degree, demand oriented. Dollar margin pricing explicitly considers the probable volume of sales achieved at each of several prices under consideration. The goal of covering estimated expenses with *each* item sold (a characteristic of the uniform percentage gross margin method) is abandoned with dollar margin pricing. The goal with the dollar margin approach is to move all the merchandise in order to cover total merchandise costs by some dollar amount. The distinction between these two pricing methods is perhaps not easy to understand, but the difference is not trivial. The dollar margin method recognizes that no profits can be determined until all the items in an order of merchandise are sold. Indeed, it is often patently silly to talk about profits on a single item sold—especially if the rest of the items in the inventory do not sell. It is of special significance that the dollar margin method requires that an estimate of total sales volume at different prices be developed. The dollar margin method is "cost-plus" only inasmuch as the pricing procedure may be described as (say) cost plus $10 per unit. The manner of arriving at the amount of the dollar margin involves an understanding and consideration of price elasticities.

As a means of illustrating the dollar margin approach to pricing, consider the following hypothetical example. A large retail store receives 100 rotary power lawn mowers. We are given the following additional information about these lawn mowers and the retail store:

Lawnmower cost to the store (per unit): $70

Expense ratio for garden equipment generally: 24%

Estimated demand schedule:
100 mowers @ $75 in 1½ weeks
100 mowers @ $80 in 4 weeks
100 mowers @ $90 in 7 weeks
100 mowers @ $95 in 10 weeks

The data above indicate that the total merchandise cost to the store on the order of lawn mowers was $7000. If the store used the uniform percentage gross margin approach, the mowers would carry a margin of 24 percent plus a predetermined profit margin. If that profit margin were, for example, 6 percent, then the selling price would be $100. But if the concern of the store management is with demand, and with how quickly the merchandise will move at different prices, a dollar margin of $5 per unit is estimated to recover the cost of the original order plus $500 in about 1½ weeks. Similarly, a dollar margin of $10 per unit will return $1000 over the original investment in four weeks. The relevant question when the dollar margin approach to pricing is used is not just what can we realize on each unit, but how fast will the merchandise turn over? We may well make a better total profit if we reinvest the $7500 in some other line of merchandise at the end of the 1½ weeks and turn it over quickly, again with a low margin. The dollar margin approach emphasizes the rate of movement of merchandise—stock turnover—for profits are clearly related not only to margins but to rates of sale as well.

Pricing with opportunity cost

To this point in our discussion of pricing methods, we have been concerned with techniques that utilize historical cost as a basis for determining prices. Another cost concept—one that is sometimes very helpful in pricing decisions—is *opportunity cost*. Opportunity cost recognizes that there are almost always alternative ways to accomplish any task and that the "price" of these alternatives may provide some guidance in pricing.

Consider, for example, the inventor who became intrigued with the downtime problem of an automatic wrapping machine. The wrapping machine in question tended to overheat and, because the areas needing lubrication were not readily accessible, the machine was stopped periodically for cooling. This overheating problem alone produced about a 10 percent downtime. When operating properly, the wrapping machine could earn its owner about $100 in an eight-hour workday. The inventor developed a system for manually dispensing oil through a series of neoprene tubes from a centralized oil and pressure source. The system looked like a small rubber box, with a plunger on top and neoprene tubing leading to the points in need of lubrication. Altogether, the parts in the oil dispensing system cost about $4. What price should the oil dispensing system sell for?

If we use the opportunity cost approach, we ask ourselves first what the alternative costs for the prospective buyer are. The owner of the wrapping machine now "solves" his downtime problem by letting the machine cool itself—the cost to the owner is about $10 per workday. And, when viewed as an opportunity cost, the value of the oil dispenser system is reflected in the cost of this alternative way of solving the problem. It might be argued that the value of the oil dispenser is therefore approximated by $10 for each day in the life expectancy of the dispenser.

It is apparent that the opportunity cost approach will often suggest a price that is completely unrelated to historical cost. Measured strictly in terms of its contribution, the inexpensive oil dispenser may easily be worth several hundred dollars. Since the dispenser system does not seem to be unique in any patentable way, however, it is doubtful that its inventor could sell it for that much for an extended period of time.

There is one well-known piece of office copying equipment that was priced at over ten times its estimated historical cost.[11] And this price may make good sense in an opportunity cost sense. That is, this particular copying machine may correctly be thought of as a replacement for some specific number of typists—typists whose services would be required in place of the copying machine. The typists' salaries are thus the opportunity cost of the copying machine.

But price cannot be satisfactorily explained in terms of costs alone. Both historical cost and opportunity cost often play an important role in pricing, but there are other factors that must be given at least as much attention as cost. More specifically, there are explanations of the pricing process that consider the influence of both cost and demand simultaneously.

The economic theory of price

The most meticulously reasoned explanation of price making is the supply and demand explanation that has been a part of value theory in economics since the work of the English economist Alfred Marshall. The essence of Marshall's explanation has, for more than half a century, provided the principal concepts for the economic theory of pricing. The economic theory of prices develops the concepts and interrelationships between costs and revenues into a finely honed exercise in logic. The graphical representation of these cost and revenue functions can humble even the most assertive college sophomore. Figure 21.2 summarizes the basic concepts in the economic theory of price.

[11] One of the most popular office copying machines (Xerox) had an early estimated cost of about $2,500. The selling price was, initially, $29,500. This situation is described in Ralph Westfall and Harper W. Boyd, Jr., *Cases in Marketing Management*, Homewood, Ill.: Richard D. Irwin, Inc., 1961, pp. 252–254.

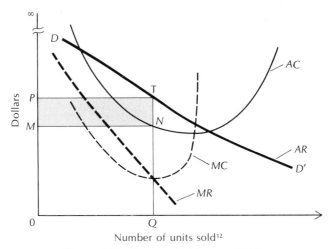

Figure 21.2 Economic Theory of Price

Figure 21.2 depicts: (a) revenue data, (b) cost data, (c) the profit maximizing price, (d) the ideal sales volume in units, (e) profits per unit sold at the profit maximizing price and (f) total profits earned at the profit maximizing price. It is important to note that *given* the revenue and cost curves that are depicted in Figure 21.2, and the assumption that the pricing decision maker seeks to maximize profits, the conclusions suggested by the theory are inescapable. That is, it can be demonstrated that price OP and quantity OQ will produce the maximum level of profits. The unit, or average, profit earned is PM; the average cost is OM. This explanatory apparatus is actuated by the proposition that total profits (the area in rectangle PMTN) are greatest at the point where marginal costs are just equal to marginal revenue.[13]

And the truth of this proposition can be demonstrated quite easily. Select any other price on the vertical scale and determine the amount demanded that corresponds to it. Now connect the AC corresponding to the amount demanded to the vertical scale with a straight horizontal line. The area of the resulting profit rectangle will always be less than the area of PMTN. It should be emphasized that this economic explanation of pricing explicitly includes a consideration of both costs and revenues (or supply and demand) and represents, therefore, a more complete explanation of the pricing process than the earlier methods examined. But there are some disconcerting aspects to this supply-demand explanation of pricing.

---

[12] This general approach to pricing was developed originally for the manufacturing enterprise. The horizontal axis here could, as easily, read "number of units produced."

[13] To be quite precise, the optimum quantity is determined by the point on the horizontal scale directly below the intersection of marginal cost and marginal revenue. The profit maximizing price is determined by the length of the line segment QT or, read directly on the dollar axis, OP.

SOME PROBLEMS WITH THE ECONOMIC THEORY OF PRICES

The logic that is embodied in the economic theory of pricing is impressive—indeed it may be *too* logical to represent a realistic explanation of the pricing process. We noted that the integrity of the economic theory of prices rests: (a) upon the validity of the profit maximizing assumption and (b) upon the accuracy and availability of the cost and revenue curves that are an integral part of that pricing theory. In the brief critique of the economic theory of prices that follows, these two foundation stones of the theory are examined.

Figure 21.2 not only depicts cost and revenue functions with admirable precision, but it presumes some basic behavioral laws, or tendencies. Thus, the demand curve DD' in Figure 21.2 slopes down to the right, and, in doing that, it embodies the *economic law of demand*.[14] The cost curve AC is dish-shaped, reflecting the traditional notion of economies of scale at lower levels of activity and diseconomies at higher levels of output. Each of these three points: (a) the precision with which cost and revenue curves are represented, (b) the slope of the demand curve, and (c) the dish-shape of the average cost curve, invite some form of question.

The general precision with which cost and revenue curves are depicted presumes that such costs and revenues can, in fact, be precisely measured. Yet we know that for some products—particularly by-products and products requiring an allocation of overhead or indirect expenses—cost estimates are, to an important degree, arbitrary. And it is, after all, the precise representation of the cost and revenue curves that permits a *point determination* of price. If the theory were completely candid about these cost and revenue curves, it would depict them as "fat" curves—a modification that would enhance their realism. "Fat" curves do not produce point solutions; fat cost and revenue curves yield, instead, a range of acceptable prices and a range of proper quantities. Consider Figure 21.3.

Note that when the ambiguities of imperfect information are introduced in the economic theory of prices, the points of intersection between marginal cost and marginal revenue curves are blurred. Imperfect information similarly produces a "fat" demand curve. Figure 21.3 suggests that we may know the *general area* in which marginal cost and marginal revenue equate, we may know *roughly* what the demand will be at different prices; but we don't know these things with point precision. And because our information is less than perfect, the guidance given us by the model is less than perfect. The set of estimated and imperfect cost and revenue curves in Figure 21.3 suggests that the optimum quantity to sell is some-

[14] While beginning students are likely to feel that a demand curve is of little real value in pricing because of the difficulty of estimating the curve, there are practical ways to do just that. Three ways that are used include the questionnaire method, experimentation, and the statistical method. See, for example, Edward A. Ide, "How to Use Marketing Analysis in Price Determination," in *Summer Proceedings of the American Marketing Association,* 1957, pp. 198–214.

where between OQ and OQ'. The right price to charge is somewhere between OP and OP'. We can no longer say the price should be (for example) $4.39; we are able to suggest only that it should be somewhere between $4.25 and $4.50.

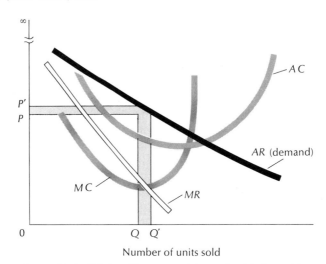

Figure 21.3 Pricing Theory and Imperfect Information

The slope of the demand curve that is generally depicted is likewise not necessarily an accurate representation of a realistic demand schedule. The representation of the demand curve sloping down to the right embodies what has been called the "law of demand." This law says, in effect, that more of something will be sold at a lower price than at a higher price. And causality is implied—that is, the lower price is presumed to prompt the greater quantity sold. While this proposition may seem accurate, there is increasing evidence that the law of demand is no law at all. Or at least, if the law has any validity, the exact circumstances in which it is operable need to be much more carefully defined. General disenchantment with the law of demand stems from the fact that some types of products appear to sell better (in larger quantities) at higher prices than at lower prices. Bag-Boy—one of the leading brands of golf-cart—was introduced with limited success at a competitive price; when the price was increased, it increased its share of market. But we will return to this issue in the next chapter in the section dealing with price-quality associations. For now, suffice it to say that a high volume of sales is not necessarily associated with low prices.

Another point of criticism about the economic theory of pricing that should be recognized is related to the shape of the average cost curve. If there is no unique low point on the average cost curve—that is, if it stays essentially flat for a broad range of outputs, and the demand curve is flattened (elastic)—then the marginal cost curve and the marginal revenue curve converge by imperceptible stages, and indeed may run as tangents over broad ranges of output. In this latter case, there is no unique point of equation—and there is no unique price solution. We should always remember that the shape of the marginal revenue curve and that of the marginal cost curve are derived mathematically from the average revenue curve and the average cost curve, respectively. It is a pedagogical convenience of critical importance that the average cost curve is depicted as a deep dish although it might also, on occasion, be extremely shallow.

The special problem of conjectural interdependence

We have seen that the traditional, or economic, theory of pricing presumes that information about costs and revenues are available and accurate. We have suggested that a dimension of realism is added when cost and revenue information is less than perfect. But there is a special type of problem in pricing that is virtually assumed away by the economic theory of pricing. This problem is suggested by the term *conjectural interdependence*.[15]

Conjectural interdependence identifies a condition in logic that precludes any conclusive reasoning. Consider the following analogy from the annals of crime fiction. Sherlock Holmes is aboard a train somewhere in Europe in pursuit of his arch foe, Dr. Moriarty. Holmes sees Moriarty and Moriarty sees Holmes (two cars away) as the aisles of the cars are cleared of passengers for an instant. What course of action will Holmes use in efforts to confront Moriarty? What evasive course of action will Moriarty use? The problem is *conjectural* because we cannot be sure what either party will do, and *interdependent* because the strategy of one party may be based on the assumed strategy of the other. Thus, Holmes may reason that he should stay where he is because Moriarty will think that he (Holmes) will move toward the car in which Moriarty was seen and therefore Moriarty will move the other direction (toward Holmes) in disguise. But, Moriarty may be reasoning that Holmes will not yield to the temptation to pursue directly—Holmes will, instead, and in disguise, gravitate toward the opposite end of the train. There is no logical solution to the problem, and the best we can do is bet that Moriarty will narrowly elude Holmes—an outcome for which there is ample precedent.

Under some competitive circumstances, the selection of a price by one seller is interdependent in a conjectural way with the price that a competitor may charge. More specifically, in an oligopolistic condition—one in which just a few sellers dominate the market—it may be effectively impossible to change your own price without inducing competitors to alter theirs also. But the supply-demand explanation of price avoids this difficulty

[15] The phrase "conjectural interdependence" is associated most closely with William Fellner. And a good definitional discussion of conjectural interdependence may be seen in Fellner's *Competition Among the Few,* New York: Alfred A. Knopf, 1949, p. 14.

altogether. By the very fact of depicting a demand curve as a down-sloping function, the presumption is that a firm may lower its price and increase the quantity of a product it sells. But suppose that competitors also lower their price—is the advantage not neutralized? And if the slope of the demand curve already anticipates the price reactions of competitors, the basic difficulty of the problem—the problem of conjectural interdependence—has been neatly and simply assumed away. At any rate, the basic interdependence of price decisions in oligopoly requires something more than the supply-demand analytical apparatus depicted in Figure 21.2.

There are two ways that we can modify the economic theory to correct for this deficiency. First, we can incorporate an assumption about leadership into the theory, and second, we can incorporate a simple probabilistic means of anticipating competitive response to price changes.[16] As the term suggests, *leadership models* of pricing presume some form of leader-follower heirarchy within the set of competing firms. Some firms may be assumed capable of leading prices upward—some may be assumed capable of leading prices only in a downward direction. In effect, the identification of the leader-follower components indicates how various competitors will react to a price change. The general leadership model is depicted in Figure 21.4.

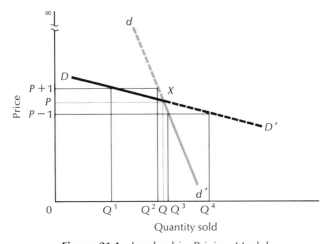

Figure 21.4 Leadership Pricing Model

Figure 21.4 represents a set of conditions that might confront a follower firm in oligopoly—a firm contemplating the possible effects of a change in the price of its product. The present price is OP, the present quantity sold is OQ. Note that two demand curves confront the firm: DD' is

[16] Another approach to the problem of conjectural interdependence is suggested in William M. Morganroth, "Price Determinants in an Oligopoly," in William S. Decker, editor, *Emerging Concepts in Marketing,* Chicago: American Marketing Association, 1963, pp. 359-362.

relatively elastic, *dd'* is relatively inelastic.[17] The letter *x* marks the intersection of these two demand curves. The reason for representing part of these curves with a solid line and part of them with a broken line will soon become apparent. But consider first the thoughts that the hypothetical firm might have regarding a planned price reduction. Should the firm reduce its price from OP to OP−1, the quantity it would sell could be either OQ³ or OQ⁴. If the new quantity sold was OQ³, total revenues would be lower than they are now (at OP × OQ). If the new quantity sold was OQ⁴, total revenues would be increased. Which of these two possibilities, then, seems most likely to occur? That is, will a price reduction to OP−1 produce a new volume at OQ³ or OQ⁴?

This general leadership pricing model assumes that *any* firm can be a leader with a price decrease; therefore the other firms will follow—neutralizing, in part, the effectiveness of the price cut—and quantity OQ³ will most likely prevail after the price reduction. Note that OQ⁴ would occur only if the other firms in the competitive set did not lower their prices.[5] Thus, in the mind of the conservative firm, a price cut will be met by competitors, and the slight resulting increase in quantity sold will not serve to increase total revenue.

But what about the case of a planned price increase? Consider the reasoning of the firm when a price increase from OP to OP+1 is contemplated. Again, there are two possible outcomes of this price increase. The quantity sold could either decrease to OQ¹ or to OQ². And which of these two new, and lower, quantities is most likely to occur? Since the firm is a follower firm, its ability to lead prices in an upward direction is suspect. It is therefore most likely that quantity OQ¹ will represent the sales volume after the planned price reduction. And observe that quantity OQ¹ and price OP+1 produce a much smaller level of total revenue than do OQ and OQ. In effect then, the follower firm in an oligopolistic situation expects its price reductions to be neutralized by offsetting actions of competitors, and it expects its price increases to be ignored by competitors. In either event, the firm will give up some sales volume.

This general leadership model suggests a demand curve that is elastic above the existing price (section D*x*) and inelastic below the prevailing price (section *xd'*). And this curve (D*xd'*) is called a kinked demand curve. We illustrated the *dx* and *x*D' portions of the two demand curves with broken lines in order to emphasize that these parts of the curves are expected by the follower firm to be inoperative.

But there is still another way that we can include the means for anticipating competitive response into our pricing procedure. This second method involves the development of a *conjectural coefficient*. A conjectural coefficient expresses a historical relationship between the price ac-

---

[17] The student is assumed to have a working familiarity with the concept of elasticity. If, however, review of the idea is in order, Chapter 23 includes some illustrative review problems involving price elasticity.

tions of two competing firms. These conjectural coefficients may be *simple* or *judgmental.* Consider the following data:

Table 21.1 Price reaction coefficient

Time of change	Price action Firm A	Price reaction Firm B	Price reaction Firm C
t − 5	+ 10%	+ 10%	−0−
t − 4	− 10%	− 5%	− 10%
t − 3	+ 20%	+ 10%	+ 10%
t − 2	+ 5%	−0−	−0−
t − 1	− 10%	− 10%	− 10%

Table 21.1 summarizes the price actions of Firm A on five past occasions. At time t−5, Firm A increased its price 10 percent; at time t−4 Firm A decreased its price by 10 percent, and so on. Table 21.1 also indicates the reactions of Firms B and C to each of A's price changes. Firm B matched the 10 percent t−5 price increase of Firm A—Firm C ignored it. It is from data such as these that we can develop conjectural coefficients.

A simple form of conjectural coefficient is suggested by the following ratio:

$$\text{Expected } t+1 \text{ price reaction of Firm B} = \frac{\dfrac{\%\Delta B}{\%\Delta A}_{t-5} + \dfrac{\%\Delta B}{\%\Delta A}_{t-4} + \dfrac{\%\Delta B}{\%\Delta A}_{t-3} + \dfrac{\%\Delta B}{\%\Delta A}_{t-2} + \dfrac{\%\Delta B}{\%\Delta A}_{t-1}}{5}$$

As imposing as this ratio appears, it is only a simple arithmetic average of the relationship between price actions of Firm A and price reactions of Firm B. Consider the first element in the numerator of the ratio. This element reads "the percentage change (%Δ) in the price of B over the percentage change (%Δ) in the price of A in time period t−5, and so on for the other historical time periods. Using the data in Table 21.1, this ratio becomes:

$$\text{Expected } t+1 \text{ price reaction of Firm B} = \frac{\dfrac{+10\%}{+10\%} + \dfrac{-5\%}{-10\%} + \dfrac{+10\%}{+20\%} + \dfrac{-0-}{+5\%} + \dfrac{-10\%}{-10\%}}{5}$$

$$= \frac{1 + .5 + .5 + 0 + 1}{5} = .6$$

The conjectural coefficient for price changes and for Firms A and B—based on five equally weighted past observations—is .6. Which means that we can, as an average, expect Firm B to change price in the same direction as Firm A, but only with a 60 percent reaction. If we believed that conditions were essentially the same now as when the elements in the ratio above were obtained, we would expect (and forecast) Firm B to follow a 5 percent price increase by Firm A with a 3 percent increase.

But we may want to refine this conjectural coefficient judgmentally. It may be the judgment of the management of Firm A that the conjectural coefficient should not be a simple arithmetic average of past responses. In order to illustrate one of these *judgmental coefficients,* consider the data in Table 21.1 that relates the price actions of Firm A with the price reactions of Firm C. Note that on two of three occasions when Firm A increased its prices Firm C did not react at all. On the one occasion when firm C followed Firm A with a price increase, it did so only to the extent of 50 percent. Note also that Firm C is consistent in meeting the price decreases of Firm A. Because of this pattern, we might develop two separate coefficients—one for price increases, one for price reductions. We would then have:

$$
\begin{aligned}
\text{Expected } t + 1 \text{ price} \\
\text{reaction of Firm C} \\
\text{to Firm A price} \\
\text{increase}
\end{aligned}
\quad
\begin{aligned}
&= \frac{\dfrac{0}{+10\%} + \dfrac{+10\%}{+20\%} + \dfrac{0}{+5\%}}{3} \\[2mm]
&= \frac{0 + .5 + 0}{3} \\[2mm]
&= .16667
\end{aligned}
$$

This coefficient tells us that given a price increase of (say) 10 percent now, we would expect Firm C to increase its price, but by only 1.6667 percent. And our coefficient for price reductions would be:

$$
\begin{aligned}
\text{Expected } t + 1 \text{ price} \\
\text{reaction of Firm C} \\
\text{to Firm A price} \\
\text{reduction}
\end{aligned}
\quad
\begin{aligned}
&= \frac{\dfrac{-10\%}{-10\%} + \dfrac{-10\%}{-10\%}}{2} \\[2mm]
&= \frac{1 + 1}{2} \\[2mm]
&= 1
\end{aligned}
$$

This latter coefficient suggests that if conditions are essentially the same in period $t+1$ as they were in the past, we may expect Firm C to meet, on proportional terms, the price reductions of Firm A.

We may also want to use varying weights for the elements in these conjectural coefficients. That is, we may believe that the most recent historical observations are most reliable; we may therefore reduce the effective weight of the earliest observations in the series. We may use the data that relates Firms A and B to illustrate this idea of a *weighted conjectural coefficient.* Observe the ratio at the top of p. 492:

$$\begin{aligned}
\text{Expected t + I price} \\
\text{reaction of Firm B} \\
\text{to Firm A price} \\
\text{change}
\end{aligned} = \frac{\frac{10\%}{10\%}(0) + \frac{5\%}{10\%}(1) + \frac{10\%}{20\%}(2) + \frac{0}{5\%}(3) + \frac{10\%}{10\%}(4)}{10}$$

$$= \frac{0 + .5 + 1 + 0 + 4}{10}$$

$$= \frac{5.5}{10}$$

$$= .55$$

The economic theory of prices and profit maximization

We have noted that a key assumption underlying the economic theory of prices is profit maximization. The economist calls this assumption "the postulate of rationality"—the inference being that for a business to act in a non-profit-maximizing way is irrational. And there is no quarrel with this general assumption. But there are circumstances when the pricing of individual products may not be *directly* prompted by the profit maximization motive. Two of these instances are: (a) in the pricing of highly complementary products and (b) in the pricing of traffic building items.

Complementary products are those that are related in use. Left shoes and right shoes are perfect complements—it is virtually impossible to buy one without the other. And where products are strong complements, a special kind of pricing policy may be called for. Consider the case of cameras and film. There was a time in the history of the home photography industry when it made very good sense to absorb losses on cameras so that the potential for film sales was enhanced. This rule is especially true if the product in the complementary pair that is purchased most frequently carries a good profit. Another case to this point is the razor and razor blade combination. It may once have made very good economic sense to almost give safety razors away because the profit potential and the sales volume for the complementary product (the blade) was very good. But note carefully that this special case is not truly a denial of the profit maximization rule. Indeed, it is a concern with maximizing profits on the components in the complementary set viewed as a *single product* that prompts the "loss" price on one of the products.

There is also the case of the traffic building product—the sacrificial lure. This product is priced at less than profit-maximizing levels—indeed, the term "loss leader" is commonly employed to describe it. And at first this practice may seem like a pricing circumstance in which less than maximum profits are sought: marginal revenue seems to be less than marginal cost. But upon more careful consideration, the rule of profit maximization is not seriously challenged by the practice of using price leaders. The answer to this apparent contradiction is that the true marginal revenue from the loss leader is "the change in total receipts of the firm" rather than the change in receipts from the sale of the sacrificial product or line.[18] Thus, as long as the loss on the price leader is less than the increment to profits occasioned by the use of the price leader, the firm may be acting in a profit maximizing manner.

Some other forms of administered pricing

We have explored briefly the role of historical and opportunity cost in pricing. We have examined, critically, the supply-demand explanation of the pricing process. Both cost pricing and supply-demand, or marginal, pricing are, of course, forms of administered prices. But there are some other administered pricing practices, both alleged and real, that we would be remiss to omit. These additional forms of administered pricing include: (a) the skim-penetration cycle in pricing, (b) the stayout pricing tactic and the extinction price, (c) unit oriented pricing and (d) pricing by convention.

On occasion there are pricing problems that defy ready solution. A particular style of dress may be so different that it does not warrant the same price as others in its cost class. A new household appliance may be unlike anything else available—it may embody special aesthetic appeals. When these one-of-a-kind items occur, a special approach to pricing may be helpful. When an item is clearly different and the right price is not apparent, the *skim-penetration pricing cycle* may be used. This approach to pricing is, in effect, an experimental search for the right price—and it may result in a market determined price. The method starts with a high price (skim price) and moves the price downward by steps until the right price is evident. The idea is that when one is unsure about what price to charge, it is advantageous to err with too high an initial price and move systematically down. This procedure is thought better than starting the price experiment at too low a price and subsequently increasing the price. In a sense, the pricing procedure with the skim-penetration cycle results in a price determined in part by buyers (and abstainers). It is therefore a self-administered price rather than wholly execu-tive-administered.

The inherent difficulty of assessing the value of fashion merchandise has resulted in a kind of mechanical application of the skim-penetration cycle by some fashion retailers. This version of the skim-penetration experiment is developed around *price lines*. Price lines are simply customary classes of prices—such as the $29.95 line, the $24.95 line, the $19.95 line, and so forth. There may be five or six such lines. A new line of merchandise may automatically be "started" at the top price line and moved into the

---

[18] See George Stigler, *The Theory of Price,* New York: Crowell-Collier and Macmillan, Inc., 1946, p. 314n.

next lower price class on a rigid timetable. Thus, a new style of coat may be started at $49.95; at the end of two weeks, those that have not been sold may be moved to $39.95. When another two weeks have passed, the coats remaining may be moved down to the next step.

The *stayout price* and the *extinction price* are of special interest to us because they demonstrate how difficult it is to determine the motivations that underlie the aggressive use of price as a competitive weapon. We have discussed the allegation by critics that price is not used by American business to the extent that it should be. That argument was that nonprice forms of competition are soft; that they do not really serve the consumer, they serve the seller. But there is evidence that the firm that uses price aggressively may not be the public benefactor that economic theorists have so often presumed. Indeed, the same critics who have elaborated the weaknesses of nonprice forms of competition have, on occasion, had to concede that some kinds of price competition may be prompted by devious motives.[19] Stayout pricing is the term used to identify the pricing policy—usually tactical—of lowering prices when it appears that a threat of competition may be developing. The lower "stayout" prices promise lower profits, and the developing competition is discouraged from entry.

Clearly, to the extent that such a tactic could be effectively implemented, it would not work to the long-run interests of the public. The fascination of such a policy is that it is virtually impossible to tell if the low price is a philanthropic act or greed in disguise. Extinction pricing has been discussed before.[20] But it is worth noting that it is another pricing policy that is ambiguous in terms of the motives that may prompt its use. A firm may price at very low levels wishing to pass the resulting bargain values along to its customers; a firm may price at low levels wishing to use its superior financial resources to inflict great damage on weak competitors.

Unit oriented pricing has the goal of achieving some specified unit volume of sales. An automobile dealer may have a unit goal of 100 cars in July. The principal emphasis in this pricing scheme is on the number of units sold rather than expressly on profits or dollar sales volume.[21] When unit maximization is the goal of the firm, there are special analytical devices that may assist in the determination of the unit-maximizing price. More specifically, it is possible to develop a system in which subjective proba-

---

[19] See a case involving A&P in Kenneth R. Davis, *Marketing Management,* New York: The Ronald Press Company, 1961, pp. 731–738. This case contains extensive quotations from a consent decree issued by the Justice Department and signed by A&P. A central point in the consent decree centered on A&P's aggressive use of price and the ulterior motives that might prompt such pricing. See especially the discussion of "market development" procedures on p. 734.

[20] See Chapter 5.

[21] See Robert A. Lynn, "Unit Volume as a Goal for Pricing," *Journal of Marketing,* October 1968, pp. 34–39.

bilities are used to assist in the price decision. Consider, as an example, Figure 21.5.

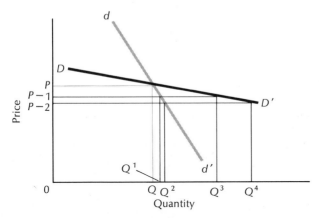

Figure 21.5 Unit Oriented Pricing

Figure 21.5 is not entirely new to us: it depicts a state of affairs in which a firm is contemplating the possible effects of a planned price reduction. In this case, however, the firm is in quest of a price that will maximize *unit* volume. Note that OP and OQ represent the current price and current volume, respectively. Two prices, both lower than the prevailing price, are contemplated. There are two possible responses to each price—one when competitors meet the new price and one when competitors ignore the new price. Should we reduce the price to OP−1, for example, we would realize volume OQ¹ if competition also cuts price; we would realize volume OQ³ if they do not. Similarly, if we lower the price to OP−2 we may enjoy a volume of OQ² if competition meets the new price, and we may enjoy a volume of OQ⁴ if they do not. These four possible volume increases represent the following percentage increases over the quantity currently sold:

Quantity	Increase over present volume
OQ^1	8%
OQ^2	10%
OQ^3	60%
OQ^4	100%

Using these data, and the pricing executive's judgment about which of these outcomes is most likely, we can identify the best price to use.

Suppose, toward this end, that it is the judgment of the pricing executive that the following probabilities prevail:

New price	Probability that competition will match	Probability that competition will not match
OP − 1	.3	.7
OP − 2	.6	.4

And combining these subjective probabilities with the earlier estimates of changes in quantities sold, we may construct the following payoff matrix.

Expected payoff at Price OP−1:

$$1.08 \times .3 = .324$$
$$1.60 \times .7 = 1.120$$
$$\overline{1.444}$$

Expected payoff at Price OP−2:

$$1.10 \times .6 = .660$$
$$2.00 \times .4 = .800$$
$$\overline{1.460}$$

And, although the victory is not a landslide by any means, the price alternative with the greatest expected volume increase is OP−2. Price OP−1 will produce an expected volume 1.444 times the present volume; Price OP−2 will produce an expected volume 1.460 times the present volume.[22]

In addition to the pricing situations we have thus far discussed, there is the circumstance in which there is virtually no pricing decision to make. There are, in some instances, strong *conventions* for particular prices. Thus candy bars are priced at coinage prices, cigarettes are often priced for coinage convenience, and so forth. But there are customary differentials in prices also. These differentials, in effect, make the pricing decision

[22] The use of decision theory in marketing is discussed in Robert D. Buzzell and Charles C. Slater "Decision Theory and Marketing Management," *Journal of Marketing*, July 1962, pp. 7–16. See also Paul E. Green, "Bayesian Decision Theory in Pricing Strategy," *Journal of Marketing*, January 1963, pp. 5–14.

automatic. In the petroleum business, for example, $.02 per gallon is considered the "normal" or "proper" differential between retail prices for national brand and private or "off brand" gasoline. It is claimed, as well, that there are traditional differences between wire prices in the steel industry and in nail and barbed wire prices.[23] But the convention of prices goes even further than that. There is some evidence that particular trade groups prefer particular prices to others. One study indicates, for example, that 49 cents and 35 cents are extremely popular prices in the grocery trade, and the price of 50 cents is extremely popular in the drug trade.[24]

SUMMARY

Chapter 21 has been concerned with an examination of the manner in which prices are established. This question is an important social issue—for prices influence the purchasing power embodied in the incomes of all of us. More specifically, we discussed three aspects of price determination. First, we developed some preliminary definitions that were prerequisites to subsequent discussion. We distinguished between the tactical and the strategic use of price as a competitive weapon; we distinguished between price levels and price structure; and we defined the term margin and the concept of *stock turnover.*

Second, we identified the rule of competitive priorities. This rule suggests the order of priorities given different forms of competition by American business and that the strategic use of price depends upon the opportunity to promote: When promotional opportunity is good, the probability of the strategic use of price is relatively low.

Third, we explored some explanations of pricing. We identified the concepts of market prices and administered prices. We developed several explanations of pricing that depend upon a historical cost basis. More particularly, we considered simple cost-plus pricing, uniform percentage gross margin pricing, sum-of-margins pricing, variable percentage gross margin pricing and dollar-margin pricing. We distinguished historical cost pricing from opportunity cost pricing procedures.

We identified, briefly, and criticized, at length, the economic theory of prices. Specifically, we challenged the assumption of perfect information, the validity of the so-called law of demand, and the avoidance by conventional theory of the problem of conjectural interdependence. We offered two answers to the problem of conjectural interdependence—the leadership model and the historical conjectural coefficient.

Finally, we identified some specialized forms of administered pricing. These special cases included: (a) the skim-penetration cycle, (b) the stayout pricing tactic, (c) unit oriented pricing and (d) pricing by convention.

[23] See Stanley C. Hollander, "Customary Prices," *Business Topics,* Summer 1966, p. 51.
[24] *Ibid.,* p. 48.

1 Carefully define and indicate the relevance of each of the following concepts to the study of marketing:
   a. Stock turnover rate
   b. The rule of competitive priorities
   c. Uniform percentage gross margin pricing
   d. Sum-of-margins pricing
   e. Dollar gross margin pricing
   f. The economic law of demand
   g. Conjectural interdependence
   h. Leadership pricing models
   i. A conjectural coefficient
   j. The skim-penetration pricing cycle
   k. Price lines

2 Distinguish carefully between each element in the following pairs of terms:
   a. A tactical use of price *and* a strategic use of price
   b. Price level *and* price structure
   c. Markup on cost *and* markup on selling price
   d. Administered prices *and* market prices
   e. Vertical price fixing *and* horizontal price fixing
   f. Historical cost *and* opportunity cost
   g. Stayout prices *and* extinction prices

3 What is meant by the term unit oriented probabilistic pricing?

4 What is the difference between classical (economic) competition and neoclassical economic competition?

DISCUSSION QUESTIONS

5 Develop a systematic criticism of the rule of competitive priorities. That is, are there exceptions to this rule? If so, where or when?

6 What conditions or circumstances would make it possible for one firm in an industry to lead the others in terms of the prices they all charge?

Chapter 22

PRICE: PERCEPTIONS AND STRUCTURE

There are three aspects of price that remain for us to consider. First, there is the general area that we will call "price perceptions". Price perceptions include the psychological aspects of prices—the inferences buyers may draw from prices and price changes. Second, we are concerned in the present chapter with discount structure of prices—the nature of prices quoted by manufacturers to wholesalers or retailers, and prices quoted by wholesalers to retailers. We shall see that the structure of discounts is often an intricate problem in pricing that we, as final consumers, rarely encounter. And third, we are concerned in this chapter with the temporal and spatial dimensions of prices. Prices often reflect an acknowledgement that time is money and the use of time in pricing is often very effective. Similarly, there are important spatial dimensions to prices.

Price perceptions

A good general working definition of *perception* is the receipt of stimuli through the senses (sight, hearing, smell, touch or taste) *and* the giving of meaning to those stimuli.[1] Thus, when we use the term *price perceptions*, we refer to the way people view and interpret prices of different kinds. One person may thus perceive a very high price as, for example, a reflection of the insatiable greed of big business—another person may perceive the same very high price as a reflection of high product quality. An extremely important part of the general process of perception is the meaning that a person associates with the sensual stimuli. And our interest in the discus-

[1] Perception is "the complex process by which people select, organize and interpret sensory stimulation into a meaningful and coherent picture of the world." See Bernard Berelson and Gary A. Steiner, *Human Behavior: An Inventory of Scientific Findings,* New York: Harcourt, Brace & World, Inc., 1964, p. 88.

sion that follows will center on three aspects of price perceptions. These special areas of interest are: (a) the price-quality association, (b) the perception of price changes and (c) the perception of odd versus even prices.

PRICE-QUALITY ASSOCIATION

It is infinitely more difficult to be an intelligent buyer today than it was in the past. The sheer number of products and services available has multiplied many times in the last two decades. And the technical nature of many products quite literally requires training in chemistry and engineering to fully appreciate. The universe of products from which consumers today are asked to make intelligent decisions includes hundreds of synthetic fibers and blends of fibers—not just cotton and wool. The variety of "plastics" available—each with slightly different durability characteristics—is a universe that, by itself, is bewildering. The consumer today is asked to make decisions in the context of an extremely complex set of alternatives. And it is for this reason that the average consumer may turn increasingly to forms of simplified quality indexes.[2] These indexes or guides to quality may be a company name or brand, the number of years the company has been in business, the size of the company or, perhaps curiously, price. And our concern here is with the use of price as a quality index.

There is a growing body of evidence that consumers use price as one of several gauges of quality—that is, when other means of judgment about quality are unavailable or ineffective, high prices may be presumed to reflect high quality, and low prices, low quality. This tendency to relate price and quality is called the *price-quality association*. Consider, for example, an experiment in which some research subjects made 24 "purchase trials" over seven months among three brands of beer that were identical except for price and brand. The details of the experiment are suggested in the following quotation:

. . . for each of the three brands, subjects were shown the prices in two ways. First, the price per six-pack was on a card because this is how most consumers see beer prices in stores. Second, because the beer was being given away, some realism was added to the selection process by taping a nickel to each bottle of the least expensive Brand P ($0.99 per six-pack), and two cents to each bottle of the medium-priced Brand L ($1.20 per six-pack). Nothing was added to the most expensive Brand M ($1.30 per six-pack).[3]

It is important to note that the brand names were, by intent, neutral letters—consonants thought incapable of suggesting quality differences.

[2] This argument is developed in Tibor Scitovsky, "Some Consequences of the Habit of Judging Quality by Price," in Perry Bliss, editor, *Marketing and the Behavioral Sciences: Selected Readings*, Boston: Allyn and Bacon, Inc., 1963, pp. 477–485.
[3] J. Douglass McConnell, "The Price-Quality Relationship in an Experimental Setting," *Journal of Marketing Research*, August 1968, pp. 300–303.

This precaution was necessary in order to be sure that such differences in quality as might be perceived were, in fact, attributable to price differences. This experiment suggested that the relationship between price and imputed quality is direct, but not linear. That is, chi-square values suggested that the quality perceptions of the beers was significant at the .005 level. Similarly, the "t" test of differences indicated that the high-priced and the low-priced brands were perceived as being of different qualities (.99 level of confidence) and the high-priced and the medium-priced brands were perceived as being of different quality (.94 level of confidence).[4]

But apparently not all types of products are price-quality associated. Another experiment suggested that the price-quality association is strongest when consumers believe there are significant differences between competing brands. For example, a group of consumers placed cooking sherry and moth flakes in the "all alike" category, in contrast, floor wax and razor blades were placed in the "considerable difference" category. And, when given a chance to "shop" for these four products (priced at different levels and branded only with letters such as "A," "B," and so on) 57 percent of the subjects selected the higher priced floor wax, 30 percent selected the higher priced razor blades, 24 percent the higher priced moth flakes, and 21 percent the higher priced cooking sherry. "The difference between the extremes is significant at better than the 1 percent level."[5] Certainly, all the evidence is not in, but it seems clear that higher price is, in the minds of many consumers, an indicator of higher quality. It would seem reasonable to assume that such a relationship would be strongest when: (a) the product is difficult to evaluate before actual use, (b) the risk associated with the use of the product is high and (c) status is an important part of the rationale for the purchase.

David Brinkley, the NBC news analyst, was the tongue-in-cheek moderator of a short-lived, weekly exposé of America's foibles. One segment of one of his shows was devoted to the poodle parlor—a place of enterprise where madame's dog could be coiffured. Brinkley related the story of a poodle parlor operator who opened his business at a price of $5 per hour for his services. That price did not produce adequate levels of business so he raised his price—a move hardly in the tradition of classical economics. But the result of the price increase was a slight increase in business. Heartened by the results of his experiment, he raised his price again—and again. At $20 per hour (so the story went) the demand for his services required that he take on an assistant. This anecdote suggests, possibly, the price-quality association for status products (or, in this case, services).

A low price may reasonably be perceived as low quality when great risk is associated with the product or service. Consider, for example, the

[4] Ibid., p. 301.
[5] See Harold J. Leavitt, "A Note on Some Experimental Findings About the Meaning of Price," Journal of Business, July 1954, pp. 205–210.

incongruity of a brain surgeon charging "family rates." Likewise, there must be some level of insurance premium below which the prospect doubts the ability or willingness of the company to meet its claims. For the same reason, cosmetics and drugs may also be "quality suspect" when they are priced below certain levels.

PRICE CHANGES AND WEBER'S PSYCHOLOGICAL LAW OF PERCEPTION

Another special case involving consumer perceptions of price relates to the way price changes are viewed. There is some evidence, for example, that some price changes are subliminal—that is, they are not noticed.[6] The original price charged and the new price may be perceived as effectively the same price. This issue is pertinent in the taking of markdowns and, conceivably, in the determination of initial price levels. "Markdowns" occur when a price is reduced to some level below its original selling price. If an item of merchandise is priced initially at $1, and subsequently marked down to $.80, then the markdown is $.20, or 25 percent. And there is a great potential for waste in the improper taking of markdowns: If the price reduction is too small, it is unnoticed; if it is too large, it represents an unnecessary loss of revenue. The best price reduction is one that the buyer sees (perceives) as a different price but which is not excessively low. And the means for determining this ideal price reduction is suggested by a law from the field of psychology—Weber's law of perception.

Weber's law of perception says that "the size of the least detectable change in intensity of a stimulus is a function of the initial intensity: the stronger the initial stimulus, the greater the difference needs to be."[7] In order to be more precise in the statement and implementation of this proposition, we may represent Weber's Law as the following ratio:

$$\frac{\Delta I}{I} = k$$

In this ratio, I represents the intensity of the initial stimulus, ΔI represents the just noticeable change in intensity of the stimulus, and k represents a constant for a particular type of stimulus. This ΔI is also called a "Jnd"—a just noticeable difference. But an example will clarify all this strange jargon. Suppose that we have a current price of $95 for a man's suit. Suppose further that we are concerned with knowing the price to which this suit should be reduced in order to move it. Note that we may price it too low—in which case the change in price would be noticeable, but sacrificial. We may price it not low enough—subliminally—and the price change will go entirely unnoticed. In effect, we want to mark the suit down by the "Jnd"—the just noticeable difference in price.

[6] Thus, a slight price change may go unnoticed or fail to register as a conscious perception. In this sense, such a change in price is "subliminal."
[7] Berelson and Steiner, op. cit., p. 95.

Psychologists have systematically developed "Weber ratios" for virtually all the human senses. The value of k for visual brightness, for example, is .016; the value of k for lifted weights is .019; the value of k for smell is about .104; and the value of k for taste is .200.[8] In the context of the suit problem, the intensity of the initial stimulus (I) is $95, the "just noticeable difference" (ΔI) is unknown, and k is unknown. Research is thus needed to define k for different classes of products and for different price levels within those classes. And the experimental processes used in the identification of k are not unduly complex. Again, in terms of the suit problem, suppose that we had first marked the suit down to $85.50. And suppose further that the suit did not move at that price—we could conclude, therefore, that k is at least greater than .10. If, through further systematic experimentation, we found that $14.75 was the just noticeable price change, k would be defined as .15. Figure 22.1 identifies graphically the elements in this markdown problem.

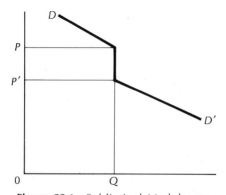

Figure 22.1 Subliminal Markdowns

If price OP represents the current price of $95, then all prices decrease between OP and OP' are subliminal. The just noticeable change in price must be just less than OP'. Anything below that is more reduction than is needed; anything above it is ineffective.

ODD-EVEN PRICING AND CUSTOMER PERCEPTIONS

One final aspect of price that is also believed to be subject to perceptual bias is suggested by the term "odd-even pricing." In a study of pricing practices of the leading food chains in the top 23 "A" metropolitan areas (areas that account for 40 percent of retail food sales), an overwhelming preference for odd prices was revealed. More specifically, of 30,878

[8]With brightness measured in photons, lifted weights in grams, smell in olfacties, and taste in moles per liter concentration. See S. S. Stevens, "Sensation and Psychological Measurement," in E. G. Boring and others, editors, *Foundations of Psychology,* New York: John Wiley & Sons, Inc., 1948, p. 268.

"brand-price occurrences," 64 percent of the prices ended in the digit "9," 19 percent ended in the digit "7," and 9 percent ended in the digit "5." Thus, 92 percent of the prices in that study ended in odd numbers.[9] This phenomenon is so widespread that the use of the terminal digit "9" in pricing has been called the "9 fixation." What accounts for the popularity of odd terminal numbers in pricing?

There are several (not necessarily compatible) explanations of what appears to be a great preference for odd numbers in pricing. The notion has been advanced, for example, that odd prices are, in part, a result of the growth of sales taxes as an important source of state revenues. Odd prices then came about, it is alleged, as a convenience to the customer: the odd price plus the tax combined to an even denomination of currency and made payment simple. Another explanation—one that runs completely counter to the sales tax explanation—is developed around the idea that odd prices reduce the opportunity of sales personnel to pocket the proceeds of a sale themselves. In this view, the odd price serves to increase the need to make change, and presumably forces the salesperson to use the cash register. Still another "explanation" is that there is no explanation at all—one writer suggests that the preference for odd prices may result from "pluralistic ignorance" among retail pricers.[10] This explanation implies that everyone assumes that everyone else knows why odd numbers are best and that no one wishes to counter such a firmly entrenched pricing practice.

But our principal concern here is with the psychological explanation of odd prices. And one such explanation supposes that odd prices are somehow perceived as better values—that some odd prices appear to be marked down from some higher price. Thus, it is alleged that "$5.99 connotes a price-appeal store, perhaps a chain store specializing in low-priced women's wear."[11] And, such prices as $5.95 and $5.75 are "not quite the same." Both of these prices seem "correct" for a different kind of store. A second psychological explanation of prices suggests that there are critical points in pricing, and to be ever so slightly off these points produces a disproportionate reduction in sales volume. One writer suggests that these critical points may be at $1, $5, and $10.[12] This line of argument asserts that to establish a price that is perceived as being below these points is advantageous. This perspective seems to presume a type of item-budget theory of consumer behavior—the consumer mentally allots no more than (say) $5 for a purchase. A price ever so slightly above that

[9] See Dik Warren Twedt, "Does the '9 Fixation' in Retail Pricing Really Promote Sales?", *Journal of Marketing*, October 1965, pp. 54-55.

[10] *Ibid.*, p. 55.

[11] Robert A. Lynn, *Price Policies and Marketing Management*, Homewood, Ill.: Richard D. Irwin, Inc., 1967, p. 226.

[12] See Edward R. Hawkins, "Price Policies and Theory," *Journal of Marketing*, January 1954, p. 235.

point would sell virtually nothing, even though it may be only pennies away from an acceptable price.

Both these psychological explanations of odd pricing suggest a very strange kind of demand curve. If, for example, buyers see some prices as "marked down," and other lower prices as not reduced, it is conceivable that a saw-toothed demand curve could exist. Figure 22.2 depicts this type of curve.

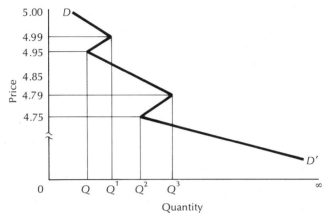

Figure 22.2 Saw-toothed Demand

That consumers actually perceive certain prices in the manner suggested by this demand curve has never been established in a definitive way. It is clear, however, that many retailers presume that some prices are interpreted by consumers in this manner.

The discount structure of prices

We have noted briefly that prices have both a "level" and a "structural" dimension. And one important aspect of the structure of prices is defined by the series, or "chain," of discounts that may be used to quote a price. Because we are so accustomed to thinking of price as a single number, it is often a surprise to students to learn that prices may also be expressed as a series of numbers. Thus, "40, 10, 3, and 2/10, net 30" is a price; and "30, 10, 5 and 2/10 EOM" is another price. As final consumers, we rarely see these kinds of prices, but they are important nonetheless. And these prices convey very special and precise specifications—that is, they communicate very precisely the nature of the offer being made.

Our task in the present section is to identify and analyze the major discount elements in pricing. Toward this goal, we will examine: (a) the idea of a list price, (b) the idea of a flexible price policy, (c) the trade-position discount, (d) the special function discount, (e) the quantity discount, (f) the promotional discount and (g) the cash discount.

The term "list price" has two different meanings, depending upon the context in which it is used. List price is often used to designate the approximate, or suggested, retail price of a product. Thus, a manufacturer may suggest a list price of $12.75 as a means of providing general pricing guidance for his dealers. Note that the list price is not necessarily the actual retail price—the dealer may elect to sell under list or, on occasion, over list. But the term *list price* also identifies the price from which all quoted discounts are calculated. Thus, if an item of merchandise carries a list price of $8, and a particular dealer is quoted a discount series of "40, 10, and 2" then the price that the dealer pays is: $8.00 − .40($8.00) = $4.80; $4.80 − .10($4.80) = $4.32; and $4.32 − .02($4.32) = $4.23. Note that the list price of $8 serves as the starting point for the application of the chain discount, and that each discount element in the chain is applied against a successively smaller number. Note, also that the $4.23 is not the same answer one would get through a simple summation of the elements in the chain discount. That is, $8.00 − .52($8.00) ≠ $4.23. We will have more to say about chain discounts and the arithmetic of such chains in Chapter 23.

One other idea that we will need to distinguish for subsequent discussion is that of the flexible price policy. By far the easiest price policy for the seller to implement is the *one-price policy.* The one-price policy offers the same price to all customers, regardless of what kind of buying organization they represent, or how much they buy. Thus, a manufacturer that practices the one-price policy may sell to any class of customer (other manufacturers, institutional buyers, wholesalers, or retailers) at one price. Such a price is perfectly legal, though it may not work in the best interests of the manufacturer. You and I confront a one-price policy in most retail stores—most particularly in those in which there is no "bargaining" permitted. The one-price policy in this respect is a take-it-or-leave-it price. The opposite of the one price policy is the variable-price policy. And the *variable-price policy* involves the giving of different prices to customers of different types or to customers buying in different quantities. Thus, for example, a manufacturer may sell at a different unit price to retailers than to wholesalers; he may sell at a different unit price to other manufacturers than he does to wholesalers; and he may sell to wholesalers ordering in larger quantities at a lower price than to other wholesalers. The means through which a variable price policy is implemented is called a *discount structure,* and this discount structure is the subject of the discussion that follows.

The first type of discount with which we are concerned is the *trade-position discount.* The trade-position discount is given on the basis of the position in the trade channel occupied by the buyer. Thus, wholesalers get one trade-position discount, retailers customarily get another. And these trade-position discounts can have a profound influence upon the strength of competition. Consider, for example, the situation depicted in Figure 22.3.

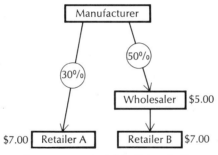

Figure 22.3 Variable Price Policy

Figure 22.3 depicts a situation in which a manufacturer practices what we have called a variable price policy. This manufacturer grants a 30 percent trade position discount to retailers—he grants a 50 percent trade-position discount to wholesalers. If we assume that the unit list price on an item is $10, Retailer A would pay $7 per unit if he bought directly from the manufacturer. If we also assume that the wholesaler takes a $2 margin (20 percent of list), Retailer B will also pay $7 per unit. The situation we have depicted is balanced in the sense that the costs of merchandise to the competing buyers are the same.

But it is most difficult to achieve and maintain this type of balance. The manufacturer may, unwittingly, by the granting of an excessive trade-position discount to the wholesaler, do great damage to the direct channel. Conversely, the trade-position discount given to the direct channel may involve inequities that tend to favor that channel. The ideal trade-position discount is one that correctly reflects the activities actually performed by the various types of middlemen. One noted student of the subject observes, in this connection, that trade-position discount "structures should be established by the seller only after careful analysis of the functions that he would like distributors to perform for him, the discounts offered by competitors, the need to attract more or fewer distributors, (and) the costs of selling to different kinds of distributors."[13] It should be noted that trade-position discounts that were initiated many years ago usually will not properly reflect the work distribution within the channel of distribution. That is, the retailer or wholesaler may be performing less or more selling activity than in the past. As the work load shifts within the channel, inequities creep into the trade-position discount structure.

A second type of discount is the *special function discount*. This discount is granted to channel members as compensation for activities they may perform above the normal call of duty. That is, the trade-position discount treats all retailers identically in the sense that they get the same trade-position discount. But there are clearly cases in which some retailers do more work for a particular manufacturer than other retailers. Consider, for exam-

[13] Donald V. Harper, *Price Policy and Procedure*, New York: Harcourt, Brace & World, Inc., 1966, p. 288.

ple, the automobile dealer who acts as a parts depot for other dealers in the area. This special dealer carries extremely deep parts stocks, thus saving other dealers the expense of doing so. Or, consider the large retail film dealer who maintains stocks of film for himself and for extremely small film dealers—service stations, small grocery outlets, and the like. Clearly, these "retailers" are not all the same. Thus, while the same basic trade-position discount may be given to all customers of the same basic type, it makes sense to provide a special discount for special activities that may be performed. We should note, however, that the special function discount could easily be discriminatory. That is, unless the special function discount is carefully administered, those dealers who do not receive the discount could be injured. Such a discount must accurately reflect the cost of performing the special function—if the discount is less than that, the large special dealer may be hurt; if it is more than that, the small (nonspecial) dealer may be harmed.

Another important type of discount is the *quantity discount.* The quantity discount varies directly with the size of the order(s) placed by the buyer. A quantity discount schedule summarizes the discount that applies to each of several order sizes. The following quantity discount schedule is illustrative:

Units purchased	Discount
1– 50	1%
51– 500	1½%
501– 1,500	2%
1,501– 4,000	3%
4,001–10,000	4%
Over 10,000 units	5%

Because quantity discounts obviously attempt to encourage larger purchases, they can be an important means of encouraging the movement of merchandise within the channel of distribution. And quantity discounts assume varied forms. A quantity discount schedule may be based upon units (as the schedule above is) or it may be based upon dollars. The quantity discount schedule may also be noncumulative or cumulative.

A *cumulative* quantity discount schedule is based not upon the size of any single order but upon the sum of the value (in units or dollars) of all orders placed within some specified period of time. A cumulative quantity discount schedule might specify, for example, that the total dollar value of all orders placed in a given month be used to determine the amount of the discount. We should note that cumulative quantity discounts have lost some favor in recent years because of their legal vulnerability. We saw in an earlier chapter that illegal price discrimination can result when different prices charged to competing buyers cannot be supported with cost data. And a cumulative quantity discount schedule does not necessarily bear a close correspondence to the costs of serving different customers. This point may deserve clarification. The following cumulative quantity discount schedule summarizes the purchase, or order, patterns of two different firms.

Cumulative purchase quantity discount		Order pattern Firm A	Order pattern Firm B
$1–$500	1%	2 @ $250	1 @ $7,000
$501–$2,000	2%	4 @ $1,000	
$2,001–$5,000	3%	1 @ $2,500	
$5,001–$10,000	4%		
over $10,000	5%		

Note that Firm A placed a total of seven orders during the time period for which data are summarized. Two of these orders were very small orders—indeed only one was over $1000. Firm B, on the other hand, placed only one order. We might reasonably expect the cost of doing business with Firm A to be greater than the cost of doing business with Firm B. Such costs as packing, delivery, order processing and collection tend to vary directly with order size.[14] And yet the cumulative quantity discount "earned" by both the firms above would be 4 percent. While there are instances in which a cumulative quantity discount schedule will not produce inequity of the sort described here, such a schedule may only serve to invite challenge by regulatory authorities. The great advantage of the cumulative quantity discount schedule is that it can encourage a concentration of purchases from one source. And undoubtedly the reason for its use in the past has been to encourage such patronage rather than to inflict harm through discrimination. Indeed, the cumulative quantity discount may *tend* to aid the small firm.

Still another type of discount is the *promotional discount.* The promotional discount is intended to encourage the use of special promotional efforts by dealers and distributors. The type of promotional discount that is a part of the price discount structure is the *implicit* promotional allowance—it does not result in a reimbursement of dealers and distributors for extra promotional efforts expended. These implicit promotional allowances, or discounts, are quoted as a part of the chain discount and thus

---

[14] See D. Maynard Phelps and J. Howard Westing, *Marketing Management,* Third Edition, Homewood, Ill.: Richard D. Irwin, Inc., 1968, p. 366.

serve to lower the price paid by the buyer, but they do not explicitly provide the money for such promotional efforts. There are, of course, cooperative advertising plans that are *explicit*—indeed, we discussed those plans briefly in an earlier chapter. Promotional discounts must be given to competing buyers on "proportionately equal terms," which is to say that such discounts must correspond in amount to the volume of business done with the firm receiving the promotional allowance. Promotional allowances may be tied to units purchased or to dollars of volume, as long as they are administered uniformly and proportionately to all competing buyers.

One final type of discount that is an important part of the discount structure of prices is the *cash discount*. While the cash discount is normally cited as a form of encouragement to prompt payment, it may also be an important form of *trade credit*. And because the cash discount has this dual character, we will discuss at this time only the means through which the cash discount may be used to hasten payment; the use of the cash discount as a form of granting trade credit will be considered in the next section of the present chapter. A cash discount has three identifiable elements: (a) a rate of discount, (b) an indication of some period of time during which the cash discount may be taken and (c) an indication of some time limit for payment of the total bill without a reduction in the remittance for the cash discount. A simple example will serve to illustrate these components of the cash discount. Consider the following chain discount quotation:

40, 10, 5, and 2/10 net 30

There are four distinct elements in this chain. The "40" is the trade-position discount—it would presumably have a different value for different types of customers. The "10" is the quantity discount—and, as we have seen, it is determined by order size. The "5" is the promotional allowance, or discount. And "2/10 net 30" is the cash discount—it specifies *when* as well as *how much* is to be paid.

In order to make our example more realistic, let us assume that the list price on the item of merchandise for which this chain discount is quoted is $1000. If we subtract the first three components of the chain discount from the list price, we are left with $513, an amount that we will refer to as the *invoice amount*. The invoice amount is defined as list price minus all discounts except the cash discount. Thus we are left with an invoice amount of $513 less "2/10 net 30," or $513 less an additional 2 percent for prompt payment. But what, exactly, is prompt payment?

To get an answer to this question we need to consider the detail of the cash discount. We said earlier that a cash discount has three components: the discount rate, the cash discount payment period and the total invoice payment period. The elements in our cash discount are as follows:

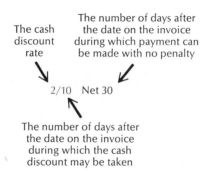

The cash discount rate — The number of days after the date on the invoice during which payment can be made with no penalty

2/10   Net 30

The number of days after the date on the invoice during which the cash discount may be taken

This cash discount directs the buyer to: (a) pay $513.00 less 2 percent within 10 days after the invoice date or (b) pay the full invoice amount of $513 on or before 30 days after the date of the invoice. Thus, the buyer may pay $502.74 promptly (within 10 days) or $513 more slowly (within 30 days). The cash discount thus offers an additional discount of $10.26 to the buyer who responds quickly to the indebtedness evidenced by the invoice. We may summarize the proposition being offered by the cash discount element in the chain of discounts as follows:

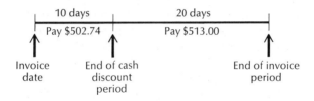

The temporal and spatial structure of prices

The foregoing discussion suggests that price quotations may be distinctive in a temporal sense; thus, the price quotation "40, 10, 5, and 2/11 net 30" is better than the quotation we have just dissected because it permits one additional day during which to take the 2 percent cash discount. Note that the amount of the price is the same in either case—it is different only in the dimension of time. But time is often money, and a price concession may well be made in terms of time units. Indeed, the role of time in pricing is a profound one for all of us, not just as it relates to the members of a trade channel. The volume of installment credit extended to consumers is adequate testimony to the influence time-pricing has on all of our lives. But, in addition to time, there is often a *spatial* dimension to pricing. This spatial dimension of prices indicates where the buyer takes title (or the seller relinquishes title) to the goods involved in the transaction. Our task in the present section of this chapter is to explore these temporal and spatial dimensions of price.

FORWARD DATINGS AND CONSUMER CREDIT PLANS

Two important means through which time becomes a part of price are forward datings and various credit plans. A *forward dating* is a provision in a price quotation that results in an extension of trade credit over a significant period of time. Some forms of cash discounts, for example, do not encourage even reasonably prompt payment by the buyer; some forms of cash discounts actually define a relatively long period of time before payment of any kind is due. These "cash discounts" regardless of their name, are, effectively, forward datings. They enable a buyer to generate the revenue required to pay his debt from the sale of the merchandise on which the debt is owed. Examples of these cash discount quotations that provide an extremely liberal cash discount period include "EOM" datings and "extra" datings. And while our principal concern is with the role of time in the discount quotation, it will be helpful to demonstrate each of these types of datings with a numerical example.

Consider first the cash discount "2/10 EOM." In order to expedite the discussion that follows, we will presume a list price of $1000, and a chain discount of 40, 10 and 5, excluding the cash discount. The invoice amount is, in other words, $513, as it was before. If we replace the original cash discount of "2/10 net 30" with this new term, "2/10 EOM," what is the influence of this change in discount on the price being offered the buyer? There is no change in the amount to be paid—but there is a profound change in the time given before payment is due. The letters "EOM" stand for end of month. And the statement 2/10 EOM means that the cash discount may be taken up to 10 days after the end of the month in which the invoice is dated. Thus, for example, an invoice dated May 2 and specifying a 2/10 EOM cash discount grants the buyer the remainder of the month of May and 10 days into June before it is necessary to forego the cash discount. Rather than an encouragement to prompt payment, this cash discount represents a significant use of time to alter the structure of price.

The "extra" dating is another device that is used as a cash discount but is often, in effect, a forward dating. An extra dating, for example "2/10 60X" extends the cash discount period for the number of days "extra." The 2/10 60X statement actually provides a total of 70 days after the date of the invoice during which the buyer may deduct an additional 2 percent from the invoice amount. Thus, for example, an invoice dated May 2 for an amount of $513 and specifying a cash discount of 2/10 60X permits the buyer to pay $502.74 at any time before July 12. (29 days in May, 30 in June and 11 in July). Note that this extra dating provides almost 20 percent of a year during which the buyer may exercise his discount option. Again, rather than an encouragement to prompt payment, this dating is an extremely liberal granting of time as a part of the price quotation.

Still another important use of time in pricing is in *consumer credit plans.* Credit includes four basic components—trust, risk, economic exchange and futurity.[15] And "futurity" is nothing but an elegant word for time. The very heart of a credit agreement is that payment will be made at some *future time.* Such payment may be in a single, or lump, sum or it may be periodically amortized. And time payments are so inextricably a part of America today that time is often understood as a part of the price being offered. Thus, a price of $3800 for a new car is not viewed as requiring savings—it is simply understood that that price can be extended in time. The relevant question to the buyer/prospect is not whether he has $3800 or even a significant part of it, but whether the time-price can be matched conveniently to his monthly income. And the use of credit is an extremely important part of pricing. There are clearly many lines of business in which it would be virtual suicide not to offer credit or at least not to make credit conveniently available. Particularly in the sale of durable goods is credit an unavoidable structural addition to price.

Open-account credit is a form of short-term credit of 30 to 45 days duration extended by department stores and other retail outlets as a convenience to customers whose ability to pay is not open to serious question. Normally, there is no service or interest charge made on the open account—it is paid off each month. But note that from the point of view of the buyer, the price offer being made by the store is very much like some of the trade credit arrangements we have discussed. Thus a buyer may see a price of $395.95 for a couch—but if the buyer has open-account credit he will see the price as $395.95 *plus* some period of time before payment is due. Depending upon when the purchase is made and when the buyer is billed, the price may be, for example, $395.95 payable in 35 days. Time is implicitly a part of the price.

With other forms of credit the role of time is much more explicit. Revolving credit plans normally give time a much more explicit role in the price quotation. Revolving credit is a multiple-payment plan "that permits a customer to have some prescribed maximum level of indebtedness at all times."[16] A $30 monthly payment and an eight-month revolving plan would fix the customer's maximum level of indebtedness at $240. From the customer's viewpoint, any purchase (so long as it does not produce a total indebtedness of more than $240) is a commitment to make a payment of $30 each month. Thus, the revolving credit plan produces a very special type of time structure. And the more attractive the time structure of the price, the less attention is apparently given to the level of the price. That is, there seems to be a special type of trade-off between price level and the time structure of prices. A seller might opt to offer a very low cash price (level) and no time convenience—a seller

[15] See *Credit Management Handbook,* Homewood, Ill.: Richard D. Irwin, Inc., 1958, p. 6.
[16] Ronald R. Gist, *Retailing: Concepts and Decisions,* New York: John Wiley & Sons, Inc., 1968, p. 425.

may opt to offer a liberal time structure but not a particularly low cash price. At present, buyers seem collectively more attracted to time structure adjustments than to level adjustments.

THE SPATIAL STRUCTURE OF PRICES

In addition to the time structure of prices, prices may have a distinctive spatial dimension. Our discussions of price to this point have not given proper attention to transportation costs—and since such costs may influence the price quotation, they need to be considered. A price that is quoted without transportation costs—costs that the buyer may have to pay—may be a different price than a price quotation on which the seller agrees to absorb such costs. The disposition of transportation costs, then, is often a third, and important, aspect of pricing. And there are three pricing methods that relate to the disposition of transportation costs: (a) FOB pricing, (b) zone pricing and (c) basing point pricing.

FOB pricing is a system of pricing that identifies: (a) the responsibility for paying transportation charges and (b) the point in transit where title is transferred from seller to buyer. Both the cost of transportation and the point in transit where legal title is exchanged are subject to negotiation in the same sense that price levels and price discounts are. Thus, an extremely strong buyer may negotiate a price that provides that the seller pay transportation charges. Similarly a strong buyer may negotiate a price in which the title passes to him only after the merchandise is actually delivered to him. If the title is passed to the buyer before delivery is complete—that is, at any point in transit before the buyer receives the goods—the buyer must bear the responsibility for any claims made against the common carrier. The buyer must also bear the responsibility for damages not covered by the liability of the common carrier if he has title to the goods at the time such damage occurs. Because both transportation charges and the point of title transfer can be significant elements in pricing, special means have evolved to identify the various combinations of responsibility that are possible.

Literally, "FOB" means *free on board* at some named point. Thus, "FOB origin" is the shipping term that is used when the buyer's order is placed into the hands (on board) of a common carrier at the point of origin (seller's place of business) and, at that point: (a) title is passed to the buyer and, (b) transportation charges are the responsibility of the buyer.[17] Note, again, that this shipping arrangement means that the buyer both bears the cost of transportation from the origin to destination, and, because he has title during transit, must initiate and pursue any litigation resulting from damage of merchandise in transit. A much more liberal shipping term from the perspective of the buyer is "FOB destination." In this in-

[17] FOB mill, FOB factory and FOB origin are generally equivalent, although they may have slight technical differences due to trade practices. See Harper, *op. cit.*, p. 204.

stance, the merchandise in the buyer's order is free on board at destination (buyer's place of business) and title remains with the seller until destination is reached. Transportation charges are the responsibility of the seller, and any claims against the common carrier must be handled by the seller.

There are some FOB terms that produce partial responsibility for the seller and partial responsibility for the buyer. The term "FOB origin—freight prepaid" gives the buyer immediate title to the merchandise in the order, but assigns the responsibility for paying transportation charges to the seller. Thus, the cost of transportation falls on one party to the exchange, and the inconvenience of handling damage claims may fall upon the other. The term "FOB destination—charges reversed" will result in a different combination of responsibility. This term will give the buyer responsibility for transportation charges but delay passing title until delivery at destination.

In addition to FOB pricing systems, there are *zone pricing* systems. While an "FOB origin" system produces a state of affairs in which every buyer pays a transportation charge that reflects his distance from the seller, zone systems are less cumbersome to administer. In a zone system of pricing, the buyer pays a transportation charge that is the same for everyone in the same zone. Figure 22.4 indicates the nature of a zone system of pricing.

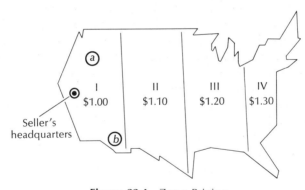

Figure 22.4 Zone Pricing

Figure 22.4 depicts a zone pricing system for a firm with headquarters on the West Coast. Note that any buyer residing in Zone I pays a transportation charge of $1 per case of (say) bond paper; a buyer residing in Zone II pays $1.10 per case; and so forth. There are two important points that we should make about zone pricing systems. These two points deal with: (a) the equity of such systems and (b) the legality of such systems.

Zone systems of pricing normally embody an unavoidable inequity. And this inequity stems from the fact that two buyers within any single zone, but at different distances from the seller, may not pay the amount of transportation cost they actually incur. Consider Firm *a* and firm *b* in Zone I. Firm *a* is very near the seller; Firm *b* is not. Yet both pay the same transportation charges. It should be clear that Firm *a* pays more transportation costs than it actually incurs, Firm *b* pays less. We say that Firm *a* pays some "phantom freight," and Firm *b* has some "freight absorbed." This inequity in the zone system of pricing points up the fact that zone charges are an *averaging device*.

The second point that we should make about zone pricing systems is that they are perfectly legal if they do not produce a discriminatory circumstance. And a condition of discrimination is effectively avoided where the zones are defined so that sellers in contiguous zones do not serve a common market. For this reason, good price zone boundaries often meander in and through desolate areas.

Zone pricing systems are a move in the direction of uniform "delivered" prices.[18] Uniform delivered prices are, as the name suggests, the same to all geographical areas. In effect, uniform delivered prices represent the case of a single price zone. And the averaging inequity that is a necessary part of any zone system of pricing is potentially magnified in the case of the uniform delivered price system. Because the potential for inequity is great with the one-zone price system, it is usually employed in connection with products for which transportation costs are relatively insignificant. Uniform delivered prices are often called "postage stamp" prices to point out that a six-cent stamp will send a letter anywhere in the United States— near or far—in the same sense that the uniform transportation charge will transport the merchandise in question anywhere in the United States.

One final system of pricing that is related to transportation costs is called *basing point pricing*. Basing point pricing systems charge the buyer transportation from the basing point to the buyer's location whether or not the order actually moves on that route. This seems a strange method of pricing, but there is a rationale for such a system. Basing point pricing systems originated as a means of extending the geographical perimeters of a market. Consider, as a means of illustrating this point, Figure 22.5.

Suppose that a seller whose factory is located in city A wishes to extend his market into city X.[19] Suppose, moreover, that FOB origin pricing will not permit this desired extension. That is, the transportation costs that the buyer located in the X area would have to pay on orders coming from A would be prohibitive. This is, of course, the classic shortcoming of the "FOB origin" pricing system. It is said to produce natural geo-

[18] Actually, the term "FOB—destination" represents a form of delivered pricing system. That is, the transportation charge may be included in the purchase price so that no separate charge is made.

[19] This is very nearly the circumstance that prompted the use of a "Pittsburgh Plus" single basing point pricing system by the steel industry. Because of Federal Trade Commission opposition to that system, the steel industry later turned to a multiple basing point system of pricing.

graphical monopolies. What kind of pricing system would effectively open the X area for the seller located in area A? An answer is a pricing system developed around an intermediate geographical point called a *basing point*. Consider, for example, the point designated BP in Figure 22.5. If the seller located at A charged all buyers—regardless of their location—transportation from BP, even though their orders were shipped from A, the effect would be to reduce the charge that would have to be made on distant buyers. Thus, X buyers would have to pay transportation charges from BP to X under the basing point system. This then, is the essence of basing point pricing—though the system can be much more complex when multiple basing points are used.[20]

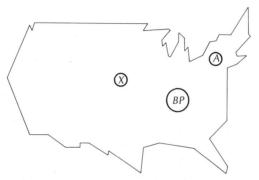

Figure 22.5 Basing Point Pricing

What are the effects of basing point pricing? It should be apparent that the ability of a seller located in A to effectively overcome the higher transportation charges required to serve a distant market area is provided by the excessive transportation charges levied against buyers residing near A. These buyers are charged transportation from BP to A when their orders actually move less than that distance. This excess of transportation charge over actual transportation costs incurred is "phantom freight." But note that the real beneficiary of basing point pricing is the buyer in the most distant market. In our example, a buyer located in X should pay transportation charges from A to X—such a buyer pays, instead, transportation charges from BP to X. In this latter case, freight is "absorbed" by the seller—that is, the transportation charges the seller collects are less than those actually incurred.

Basing point pricing systems are not illegal per se. If such plans involve collusion or result in price discrimination, however, they may be judged in violation of the Clayton Act. In cases since World War II, basing point pricing systems used in the cement industry, the rigid steel conduit industry and the corn products industry have been found to violate the

[20]A lucid discussion of multiple basing point systems may be seen in Martin L. Bell, *Marketing: Concepts and Strategy*, Boston: Houghton Mifflin Company, 1966, pp. 567–568.

intent to our antitrust laws.[21] Moreover, the practice of collecting phantom freight is likely to destroy a basing point pricing system from within.[22] That is, the firms who are asked to pay more than their actual share of transportation may represent the seed of discontent that will lead to modification or abandonment of the basing point concept.

SUMMARY

Chapter 22 has been directed to two basic purposes. First, we have examined several pricing phenomena that involve buyer perceptions of prices. These price perceptions were defined as the way people view and interpret prices of different kinds. Our examination of price perceptions led us to the conclusion that quality inferences are often drawn from price levels. This price-quality association tends to refute the very traditional economic law of demand. We also noted that Weber's psychological law of perception has some applicability in the context of pricing. We noted that price changes, like any other sensory event, may be subliminal; that is, price changes may not be perceived as significantly different from earlier prices. Weber's law provided the analytical vehicle through which the potential waste of subliminal markdowns could be reduced or avoided.

We discussed odd-even pricing and briefly explored some of the theories that attempt to explain this ubiquitous phenomenon. We were particularly interested in explanations of odd-pricing that presume the existence of some perceptual bias on the part of consumers. We concluded that a special kind of saw-toothed demand schedule may be presumed to exist when odd prices are used extensively.

The second general task of Chapter 22 was to examine the structural characteristics of prices. Accordingly, we considered: (a) the nature of various price discounts, (b) the time or temporal character of price quotations and (c) the spatial character of price quotations. We developed the concepts of list prices, flexibility in price policy, and such important discount forms as trade-position, quantity, special function, promotion and cash discounts. Cash discounts were examined as a means of demonstrating the time character of some price quotations. Consumer credit plans served further to define the use of time in price quotations.

Finally, the notion that there is a spatial dimension to prices led us to examine the practices of FOB pricing, zone pricing and basing point pricing. More specifically, we identified the concepts of FOB origin, FOB destination, and FOB quotations with reversed charges. We noted that zone pricing systems embody a cost averaging characteristic that is a potential source of inequity. Basing point pricing systems were viewed as an effort to extend the geographical limits of the markets of particular

---

[21] See Kenneth R. Davis, *Marketing Management,* Second Edition, New York: The Ronald Press Company, 1966, p. 754.
[22] See John A. Howard, *Marketing Management: Analysis and Planning,* Revised Edition, Homewood, Ill.: Richard D. Irwin, Inc., 1963, p. 383.

sellers. These basing point pricing systems are not illegal per se, although they may be if they involve collusion or if they result in price discrimination.

REVIEW QUESTIONS
1 Carefully define and indicate the relevance of each of the following concepts to the study of marketing:
   a. Price perception
   b. The price-quality association
   c. Weber's law of perception
   d. A "Jnd"
   e. Price structure
   f. List price
   g. A trade-position discount
   h. A one-piece policy
   i. A variable-price policy
   j. An invoice amount
   k. Forward datings
   l. Revolving credit plans
   m. Open-account credit
   n. FOB pricing
   o. Zone pricing
2 Distinguish carefully between each element in the following pairs of terms:
   a. A special function discount *and* a quantity discount
   b. A cash discount *and* a promotional discount
   c. A cumulative quantity discount schedule *and* a noncumulative quantity discount schedule
   d. An implicit promotional discount and an explicit promotional discount.
3 Does the so-called law of demand agree or disagree with the evidence called the price-quality association? Explain your answer.
4 Does the phenomenon we have called the price-quality association seem to be most clearly defined for particular types of products? If so, which classes?
5 Suggest as many "reasons" for using odd prices as you can. Which of these several reasons is most plausible?
6 What is basing point pricing? Why is it likely to be illegal?
7 What is the effective difference between "FOB origin" pricing and "FOB destination" pricing? If you were a buyer, which term would you prefer?
8 What is phantom freight? Under precisely what circumstance does it arise?

Chapter 23

SOME SPECIAL PROBLEMS IN PRICING

In the two preceding chapters, we examined some issues in pricing that were essentially nonmathematical. There were, however, several instances in which we might properly have introduced some mathematical relationships. This chapter is the result of postponing a discussion of some of these basic mathematical relationships in pricing. More specifically, this chapter develops the procedures for the solution of eight types of problems that relate to pricing. These eight types of problems are: (a) conversion problems, (b) effective total discount problems, (c) channel pricing problems, (d) pricing to target margins, (e) product profitability problems (a special type of problem integrating margins and stock turnover), (f) break-even analysis, (g) elasticity calculations and (h) discount calculations.

Conversion problems

We noted earlier that a markup may be expressed either as a percentage of selling price or as a percentage of cost. And this fact is at the source of a special problem in pricing because it may be necessary to compare markups when they are expressed on different bases. And a "conversion" problem in pricing is one that requires converting from one markup base to another in order to develop a solution. Some conversion problems may be quite obvious—but it may not always be perfectly clear that a base conversion is necessary to effect a solution. In its most obvious form, a conversion problem provides products with two markup bases and requires their comparison. Consider, for example, the circumstance wherein one supplier sells a product that will yield a margin (markup on selling price) of 40 percent and a competing supplier can provide the same product at a cost that will yield a markup on cost of 50 percent. Assuming that the product from both sources sells for the same retail price, which source provides the best margin? Clearly, what we need to do in order to resolve this problem is reduce these two markup percentages to a comparable base. We may convert the cost markup to a selling price basis, or we may convert the selling price markup to a cost basis. Whichever route we choose, we must go through this conversion process.

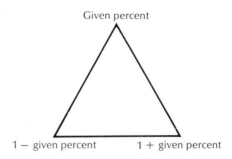

Figure 23.1 The Conversion Triangle

How is this conversion performed? A useful device with these conversion problems is the triangular summary suggested in Figure 23.1. By filling in the particular elements of our problem, we can *systematically* solve these conversion problems. Suppose, for example, that we elect to convert the 50 percent markup on cost in our problem to its equivalent expressed as a percentage of selling price. The numbers in our conversion triangle now become:

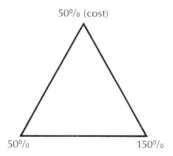

Note that the 50 percent markup on cost that we wish to convert to selling price is in the position of the "given" percentage. The left angle is 1 minus the given percentage, or 50 percent; the right angle is 1 plus the given percentage, or 150 percent. The actual conversion is always made by *dividing one of the two lower angle values into the given percentage.* In this particular case, we will divide 150 percent into the given percentage because that is the only division that will yield a quotient that is smaller than the given percentage. And when we convert from a markup on cost to an equivalent markup on selling price, we know that the selling price markup we seek has to be smaller than the given markup on cost. In the case of our problem, the markup on selling price that is equivalent to a markup on cost of 50 percent is $50 \div 150$, or 33⅓ percent. We would therefore realize a larger margin from the supplier offering a 40 percent (selling price) markup than from the source offering a 50 percent (cost) markup.

But let us return to a point that is of central importance and may not be entirely clear. Why is it necessarily true that in converting a markup on cost to an equivalent markup on selling price the latter percentage will be smaller than the former? Consider the following summary of the relationship between cost, markup and selling price:

Observe that the line length labeled "markup" is necessarily a smaller portion of the line length labeled "selling price" than it would be of the line length labeled "cost." Any portion of "cost" would always be a lesser portion of selling price. Therefore, we can use this rule that markups on cost are always larger than equivalent markups on selling price.

One more simple conversion problem will serve to review what we have said. Suppose that competing suppliers offer a similar item of merchandise that carries from one source a markup of 25 percent of cost and from the other a markup of 20 percent on selling price. Which is the better margin? Our triangular summary would appear as follows:

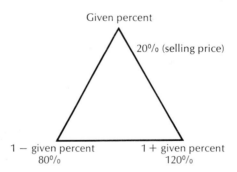

In this illustration, however, note that we have treated the selling price markup as our "given" percentage. This means that we are seeking the equivalent of a 20 percent selling price markup expressed as a percentage of cost. Our rule is that we will make the conversion by dividing one of the two lower angle values into the given percentage. But in this case we must select a divisor that, when divided into the given percentage, will produce a *larger* equivalent percentage. We must therefore divide 80 percent into 20 percent, and our answer is 25 percent. This means that both suppliers in this problem offer the same markup: 25 percent of cost is the same as a 20 percent markup on selling price. So our triangle will work in converting from cost to selling price and in converting from selling price to cost.

We claimed earlier that conversion problems are sometimes not perfectly obvious. Consider the following data. The markup on an item is quoted as 40 percent of cost. The selling price of the item is $200. What is the cost of the item? If your temptation is to determine 40 percent of the $200 and subtract that amount from $200, that would involve an unnatural mixing of cost values (the markup) and selling price values. The problem can, however, be solved with conversion. If we first convert the 40 percent cost markup to its selling price equivalent, we are then in a position to work directly with the $200 selling price and determine cost. The triangular scheme would now appear as follows:

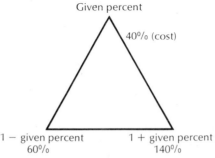

Given percent

40% (cost)

1 − given percent
60%

1 + given percent
140%

Since we are converting from cost to selling price, we seek a lower markup percentage than our given of 40 percent. And the 140 percent angle value will provide a divisor that will give us a quotient lower than 40 percent. To be more specific, $40 \div 140$ gives us an equivalent (selling price) markup of 28.57 percent. Our dollar cost would then be $100\% - 28.57\% = 71.43\%$; $71.43\% \times \$200 = \$142.86$. We thus have a dollar markup of $57.14, and it can be shown that $57.14 is 40 percent of our calculated cost figure—namely, $142.86.

The effective total discount

We have seen that prices are often quoted as a chain, or series, of discounts. This "chain" is deducted from a specified "list" price. It is often helpful to be able to appraise these chain discounts in terms of *effective total discounts*. An effective total discount is what the chain would be if quoted as a *single* discount from list price. A simple example will illustrate this idea. Assume that competing suppliers offer discounts from the same list price of (a) 30, 10, 5, 2 and (b) 35, 5, 5, 2. Which of these chains represents the larger effective total discount, and what is the effective total discount for both offers?

The chain discount from source (a) taking all discounts results in a payment of 58.653 percent of list price. The effective total discount of that chain is, then, 41.347 percent. That is, a chain discount of 30, 10, 5, and 2 results in a total discount of 41.347 percent. Note that the effective total discount is not simply the sum of the elements in the chain. The effective total discount is defined as one minus the product of the complements of each of the elements in the chain. Our 41.347 percent is derived as follows:

$$1 - (.7 \times .9 \times .95 \times .98) = .41347, \text{ or } 41.347\%$$

Note that the .7, .9, .95 and .98 in the statement above correspond to the four elements in the chain discount—they are simply complements. Note also that in calculating the effective total discount of a chain it makes no difference in which order the elements of the chain are considered. This is not to say that the order of the discounts is inconsequential when determining the amount of a specific discount—such as the quantity discount, the promotional discount, and so forth. If the amount of a specific discount element is sought, then one must take the discounts in order. What is the effective total discount corresponding to our second (b) chain? It is, again, defined as $1 - (.65 \times .95 \times .95 \times .98)$. This second source then offers an effective total discount of 42.51075 percent off list price.

Channel pricing problems

A third type of pricing problem, one students often find a traumatic experience, is the channel pricing problem. This class of problem may be a *build-up* type or it may be a *demand-backward* variety. A build-up channel pricing problem begins with a estimate of manufacturer's cost and, by adding intermediate margins, develops a retail price. Consider, for example, a manufacturer of chromed wire wheels. Let us suppose that these wheels cost him $15 each. Suppose, moreover, that the wheels are to be distributed though (a) wholesalers who require a margin of 15 percent of their own selling price and (b) retailers who require a margin of 30 percent of their own selling price. If the manufacturer aspires to a margin of 25 percent of his selling price, what is the approximate retail price of each wheel? This build-up problem may be viewed as a sequence of calculations as below:

Manufacturer's Cost	$15.00
Manufacturer's Markup (25% of selling price)	5.00
Wholesaler's Cost	$20.00
Wholesaler's Markup (15% of selling price)	3.53
Retailer's Cost	$23.53
Retailer's Markup (30% of selling price)	10.08
Retail Selling Price	$33.61

Note that the markup percentages cannot be applied directly against the corresponding cost figure. The $20.00 wholesaler's cost (also the manufacturer's selling price) is derived as follows:

Manufacturer's Cost	Markup
$15	25%

Manufacturer's Selling Price?

If the manufacturer's selling price is considered 100 percent, then the cost portion of selling price ($15.00) is 75 percent. And $15 ÷ .75 equals $20. Similarly, the $23.53 is $20 ÷ .85, and the final selling price, $33.61, is $23.53 ÷ .70.

The demand-backward type of channel pricing problem begins with a retail price and works back through intermediate margins to either a feasible cost estimate or, if costs are known, to a margin estimate. It tells a manufacturer what cost constraints he will have to meet given intermediate margins and a particular retail price. Or, if his costs are given, what margin he can realize. Consider the case of a radio manufacturer who has developed an assembly technique for small transistor radios that he believes might introduce a good profit margin. With this lower cost, he can manufacture such radios for $2.60. Such radios sell customarily at around $5.95. Now, given a retail margin of 35 percent and a wholesale margin of 12 percent, what margin could the manufacturer realize on each radio? This demand-backward channel pricing problem is, in effect, a series of calculations as follows:

Retail Selling Price	$5.95
Retailer's Margin (35% of Selling Price)	− 2.08
Wholesaler's Selling Price	$3.87
Wholesaler's Margin (12% of Selling Price)	− .46
Manufacturer's Selling Price	$3.41
Manufacturer's Cost	− 2.60
Manufacturer's Margin	$ .81

Pricing to target margins

A very practical pricing problem is one which requires the development of a price to meet estimated expenses and target profits. Suppose, for example, that a used car cost a dealer $600. Suppose further that the average expense ratio for this dealer is 15 percent—meaning that expenses average

15 percent of net sales. Suppose still further that this dealer prices *initially* at a level that would yield a profit of 16 percent before taxes. At what price should the used car be offered if average expenses and target profits are to be covered and achieved? This kind of problem is conveniently viewed as having the following components:

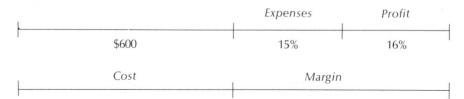

Without being told, we may infer that the target markup is 31 percent, and that the cost of $600. is 69 per cent of the price at which the car should be offered. It therefore follows that the selling price should be $600 ÷ .69, or about $869.55.

Consider another similar problem. Assume that experience indicates that the expenses associated with the sale of a particular appliance is $24. The cost of the appliance is $100. What selling price should be placed on the item in order to achieve a target rate of profit before taxes of 10 percent of selling price? This problem may be divided into the following components:

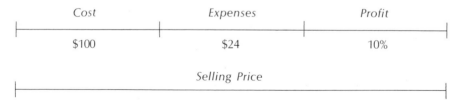

And the problem is resolved by presuming, once again, that the unknown selling price is 100 percent and that costs plus expenses are therefore 90 percent. It follows that $124 ÷ .90 is the desired selling price. And that price is $137.77.

Product profitability problems

A very useful exercise—one that includes virtually all the pricing concepts we have encountered—is a profitability problem. Assume that a retailer is considering the addition of a new product line to his present line of merchandise. In an effort to be as systematic as possible about the procedure he uses to determine which of several lines he should add, he has gleaned the following data.

Product X	
Beginning Inventory Requirements (at selling price values)	$10,000
Estimated Inventory Requirements	
with Mature Line (at selling price values)	$15,000
Estimated Annual Stock Turnover	5
Estimated Total Expenses	10%
Gross Margin (markup on selling price)	40%

Product Y	
Beginning Inventory Requirements	
(at selling price values)	$ 8,000
Estimated Inventory Requirements	
with Mature Line* (at selling price values)	$16,000
Estimated Annual Stock Turnover	6
Estimated Total Expenses	12%
Gross Margin (markup on selling price)	35%

These two product lines seem to be the best of some 10 or 12 lines the retailer has considered. Note that both product lines require a larger "mature" inventory than initial inventory. This results from a gradual build-up of depth in those parts of the inventory that prove especially well suited to a particular market. We will assume that the inventory "matures" by the end of one year—so that the estimated mature inventory is, in effect, an ending inventory requirement for the first year. The problem now is to determine the more profitable of these two product lines for the retailer. And in making this determination, we are asked to present our comparisons in the form of profit or loss statements for each of the product lines under consideration.

Consider Product X first. How can we determine (a) net sales, (b) cost of goods sold, (c) gross margin, (d) total expenses and (e) net profits before taxes from the information we have? We may deduce net sales from what we know about stock turnover and inventory requirements. Indeed, stock turnover is defined as:

$$ST = \frac{\text{Net sales in dollars}}{\text{Average inventory at selling prices}}$$

And we know both the value of stock turnover and the average inventory at selling prices. Stock turnover is given as 5; average inventory at selling prices is defined as beginning inventory plus ending inventory divided by 2. Therefore, the average inventory at selling prices is ($10,000 + $15,000) ÷ 2, or $12,500. And net sales is:

$$5 = \frac{\text{Net sales}}{\$12,500}$$

$$\text{Net sales} = 5 \times \$12,500$$
$$\text{Net sales} = \$62,500$$

Having deduced the value of net sales, we may now calculate the other elements of the profit or loss statement.

Net Sales	$62,500
Cost of Goods Sold	37,500
Gross Margin	$25,000
Expenses	6,250
Net Profits before Taxes	$18,750

Cost of goods sold is .6 × $62,500, or $37,500; gross margin is the difference between net sales and cost of goods sold—or $25,000. Total expenses are $6,250, and estimated net profits before taxes for Product X are $18,750.

And a similar analysis of the data for Product Y would reveal the following profit and loss summary.

Net Sales	$72,000
Cost of Goods Sold	46,800
Gross Margin	$25,200
Expenses	8,640
Net Profits before Taxes	$16,560

Break-even analysis

Break-even analysis is a simple analytical device that may be of assistance in reaching pricing decisions. Break-even calculations may be developed in terms of dollars or units. Dollar break-even analysis will identify the dollar volume of sales required to just cover fixed and variable costs. Unit break-even analysis will identify the number of units of a product one must sell in order to just cover fixed and variable costs. Break-even calculations—whether dollar or unit—are influenced by the price decision. Consider the representation of costs and revenues in Figure 23.2.

There are essentially three kinds of information summarized in Figure 23.2. The horizontal cost line represents total fixed costs—in this example, these costs aggregate $200 regardless of the number of units sold. Total variable costs are depicted as being about $35 per unit of the product, and no economies result from greater volume. Make sure that you can see why these last two conclusions are warranted. The total cost line is simply the vertical summation of total fixed costs and total variable costs. The third element depicted in Figure 23.2 is price—and in fact we have two prices in our summary. Which of these two prices is the higher? How do you read the price from the line labeled "Revenue, Price I"? Your answers to these questions should be (a) that Price I is higher, and (b) that price is read by the *slope* of either revenue line. Thus, for example, Price I is about $100; Price II is about $60. An imaginary line immediately above "1" on the units sold axis will verify this statement.

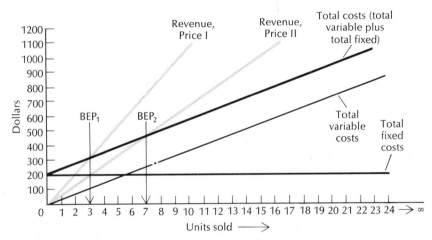

Figure 23.2 Break-even Analysis

Note that this information about fixed costs, variable costs and price permits us to estimate the units of sales required to break even. The break-even point with Price I is about three units. The break-even point with Price II is about seven units. And while this example is highly simplified, break-even analysis can provide meaningful assistance in pricing. Note that break-even analysis does not automatically disclose the best price. The best price is determined, as always, by the exercise of some judgment. But break-even analysis requires a systematic identification of costs—both fixed and variable—and indicates precisely what sales volume (dollars or units) is required at any price being considered. Break-even analysis thus assimilates complex cost and revenue relationships so that judgment may be focused on a more manageable universe of data.

The basis for a true understanding of break-even analysis lies in understanding the distinction between variable costs and fixed costs. Any time that the selling price of an item exceeds the variable costs represented in that item, and the fixed costs associated with that item can be defined, it is possible to define the point at which that item will just start to generate a profit. The selling price of an item may be viewed as having two important components—the first part goes to recover variable costs, the second part goes first to cover total fixed costs, and having done that, to develop a profit fund. This second part of selling price we will call *contribution to fixed costs or profit*. If the variable costs associated with a product selling for $4 are $3, then the contribution to fixed costs or profit is $1. If a product selling for $5 has a variable cost ratio of 70 percent, then the contribution to fixed costs or profit may be expressed as either 30 percent (of selling price being understood) or $1.50. And in addition to the graphical representation of break-even analysis depicted in Figure 23.2, we can define the break-even point as a ratio. The unit break-even point is defined as:

$$BEP_{units} = \frac{\text{Total fixed costs}}{\text{Contribution to fixed costs or profit}}$$

The dollar break-even point is defined as:

$$BEP_{dollars} = 1 - \frac{\dfrac{\text{Total fixed costs}}{\text{Unit selling price}}}{\text{Variable cost per unit}}$$

The following "brain twister" will serve to indicate the relationship between these two break-even formulas. Assume that total cost at a sales volume of zero units is $5,000. Assume, moreover, that total cost at a volume of 500 units is $10,000. Finally, assume that total revenue at a sales volume of 1500 units is $22,500. Given these data, we can determine (a) the sales price per unit, (b) the variable cost per unit, (c) the amount of total fixed costs, (d) the break-even point in units and (e) the break-even point in dollars.

First, total fixed costs must be $5,000. Variable costs must be $10 per unit. And selling price per unit is, necessarily, $15. The element of selling price that we have called contribution to fixed costs or profit per unit is $5, or the difference between unit selling price and unit variable costs. Thus, of every unit sold, $15 in revenue is received; $10 of that goes to defray variable costs, the remaining $5 goes first to cover fixed costs, and when that is completed, to profits. Our formula for unit break-even tells us that:

$$BEP_{units} = \frac{\text{Total fixed costs}}{\text{Contribution to fixed costs or profit}}$$

$$= \frac{\$5,000}{\$5}$$

$$= \$1,000$$

Thus, sensibly, we must sell 1000 units, each of which contributes $5 to the defrayal of fixed costs, in order to just offset $5,000 in total fixed costs. The first unit above 1000 will contribute $5 to profits. And our dollar break-even formula tells us that:

$$BEP_{dollars} = 1 - \frac{\dfrac{\text{Total fixed costs}}{\text{Unit selling price}}}{\text{Variable cost per unit}}$$

$$= \frac{\$5,000}{1 - 66\frac{2}{3}\%}$$

$$= \frac{5000}{\frac{1}{3}}$$

$$= \$15,000$$

Thus, the example is internally consistent—that is, 1000 units @ the $15 selling price give us a dollar break-even point of $15,000 and our formula solution agrees.

But we can also relate these two formula solutions to the graphic solution. Figure 23.3 embodies the same data as this illustrative problem. Figure 23.3 indicates a dollar break-even point (read the vertical axis) of $15,000. The unit break-even point is 1000 (read the horizontal scale). Note that profits or losses are reflected by the wedge-like area between the total revenue line and the total cost line. Where TR is over TC, profits exist; where TC is over TR, losses are incurred.

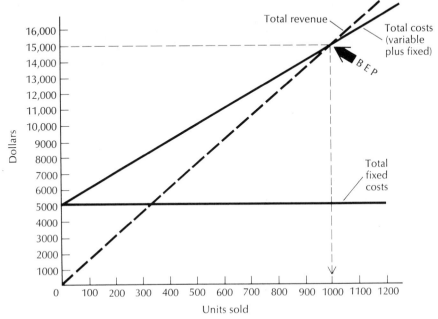

Figure 23.3 Break-even Analysis

Elasticity calculations

Price elasticity measures the degree of sensitivity between a change in price and a change in the quantity sold. Should a slight price change elicit a great change in quantity sold, the relationship is said to be elastic. When the quantity sold is unchanged as a result of prior price changes, the relationship is said to be inelastic. But in order to avoid ambiguities, we normally define the degree of sensitivity between a change in price and a change in the quantity sold as a coefficient—we can then define the exact relationship that may exist between changes in price and quantity sold as a number. And we may use particular values of these coefficients to distinguish an elastic relationship from an inelastic relationship. This coefficient of price elasticity is defined as the percentage change in quantity sold divided by the percentage change in price. Or, expressed in a formula, the coefficient of price elasticity is:

$$\text{Price elasticity} = \frac{\dfrac{\text{Old quantity} - \text{New quantity*}}{\text{Old quantity sold}}}{\dfrac{\text{Old price} - \text{New price*}}{\text{Old price}}}$$

The coefficient of price elasticity is thus a "ratio of ratios"—it results from a ratio in the denominator and another ratio in the numerator. And when the value of this coefficient of price elasticity is greater than unity, we say that the relationship is elastic; when the value of the coefficient is less than unity, we say that the relationship is inelastic. When the value of this ratio is unity, we refer to that circumstance as *unit* elasticity.

It is customary to depict a highly elastic demand schedule as one that is essentially horizontal. A demand schedule that is very inelastic is depicted as being essentially vertical. The student may thus conclude, erroneously, that the slope of the demand schedule alone determines elasticity. Consider the demand schedules represented in Figure 23.4.

The two demand curves AA' and BB' are of identical slope. Yet the proximity of the AA' curve to the vertical scale means that the elasticity of the schedule is different from that of BB'. Consider, as a means of demonstrating this point, the result of lowering price from $2 to $1.50. On demand schedule AA', such a reduction in price increases the quantity sold by a very sizeable percentage. To be more specific, a 25 percent reduction in price increases the quantity sold by more than 25 percent. Observe that the same 25 percent reduction in price on schedule BB' produces a very small relative (percentage) change in the quantity sold. Schedule BB' is inelastic; schedule AA' is elastic—and the cause of such difference is in the position of the curves relative to the origin of the price-quantity quadrant.

*Disregard the algebraic sign.

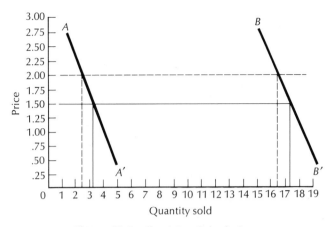

Figure 23.4 Elasticity Calculations

In effect, the slope and the proximity of the demand curve to the origin of the price-quantity quadrant reflect the interest of the market in price changes. An inelastic curve suggests a lack of market interest in price changes; an elastic demand schedule reflects a concern on the part of the market for slight price differences. The demand curve thus represents a kind of response curve. And there is no reason whatever to limit our discussion of elasticity to price elasticity. We may properly have just as much concern for say, promotional elasticity or product quality elasticity or, indeed, for the responsiveness of the market to any competitive actions. When we broaden the concept of elasticity to include nonprice variables as well as price, we are confronted with some of the most important questions in business today. Consider, for example, the promotional response curve in Figure 23.5.

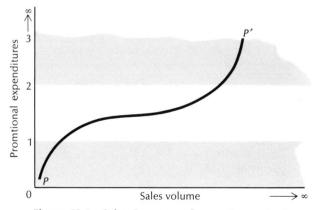

Figure 23.5 Sales Response Curve (Promotion)

Note that there are two fundamentally different types of response zones on the vertical scale in Figure 23.5. The zone 0-1 on the promotional expenditures scale is essentially one of little promotional response. That is, a given increase in promotional expenditures produces a less than proportionate increase in the sales volume. The lower portion of zone 1-2 is promotional unit elasticity—the responsiveness of the sales volume is about proportionate relative to an increase in promotional expenditures. The middle portion of zone 1-2 is characterized by an extremely elastic section of response curve. The zone labeled 2-3 depicts an insensitive relationship between an increase in promotional expenditures and the resulting increase in sales volume. We can easily formalize this idea of promotional elasticity with a mathematical definition of the idea. Note in the following formula that the independent variable is in the denominator of the ratio, and that the dependent variable is represented in the numerator.

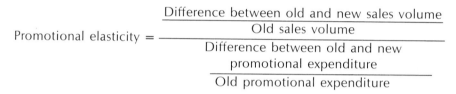

$$\text{Promotional elasticity} = \frac{\dfrac{\text{Difference between old and new sales volume}}{\text{Old sales volume}}}{\dfrac{\text{Difference between old and new promotional expenditure}}{\text{Old promotional expenditure}}}$$

We might further extend the idea of a market response curve to include changes in product quality. Product quality response curves might, for example, be depicted as in Figure 23.6.

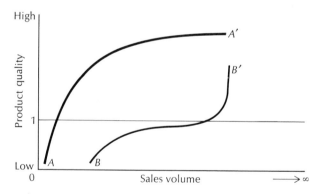

Figure 23.6 Sales Response Curve (Product Quality)

Note that the curve AA' represents one basic type of product, BB' represents another. The response curve for AA' suggests that medium to high quality is a prerequisite to market acceptance. An increase in product quality from the lowest possible levels to 1 on the vertical scale produces a disproportionately small increase in sales volume. But observe that for product BB', an increase in quality from the lowest levels to 1 more than doubles the quantity sold. To test your understanding of what we are suggesting here, develop a formula that would reflect product quality elasticity.

Discount calculations

Earlier in this chapter, we developed the idea of the effective total discount. The purpose of this concept was to enable a direct comparison of the total effect of two or more chain discounts. There are some other facets of discount calculations that are worth our brief consideration. More specifically, our concern in the present section is with the mechanics of determining discount amounts.

The following problem is illustrative. Suppose that a retailer is given a chain discount of 25, 10, 8, and 2/10 net 30. The list price is $200. Determine the following:

1 The amount of the invoice.
2 The amount of the trade-position discount.
3 The amount of the quantity discount.
4 The amount of the promotional discount.
5 The amount of the cash discount—if earned.
6 The amount the retailer should remit to his supplier if he qualifies for the cash discount.

In order to resolve these problems we must first establish ground rules to identify each element in the chain discount. We will, primarily for reasons of convenience, assume that the chain discount is always quoted in order of (a) trade-position, (b) quantity, (c) promotion and (d) cash. Thus, the "25" in the chain above is the trade-position discount; the "10" is a quantity discount; the "8" is a promotional allowance; and the "2/10 net 30" is the cash discount term. Since the amount of the invoice is defined as "list less all discounts except the cash discount," we may determine the amount of the invoice as follows:

$$\text{Invoice amount} = \$200 - (.75 \times .90 \times .92 \times \$200)$$
$$\text{Invoice amount} = \$124.20$$

The remaining elements in the problem are resolved as follows:

$$
\begin{aligned}
\text{Trade position discount} &= 25\% \times \$200 = \$50.00 \\
\text{Quantity discount} &= 10\% \times \$150 = \$15.00 \\
\text{Promotional discount} &= 8\% \times \$135 = \$10.80 \\
\text{Cash discount} &= 2\% \times \$124.20 = \$2.49 \\
\text{Retailer's remittance} &= \$121.71
\end{aligned}
$$

1 If the markup on a particular item is $4 and the markup is also 40% on cost, what is the selling price?

2 If the retail price on an item of merchandise is $.75 and the markup on cost is 40%, what is the amount of the markup in cents?

3 If a markup of 90% of selling price is taken, what is the equivalent markup expressed as a percentage of cost?

4 What is the maximum possible markup on selling prices? Under what circumstances might this maximum be realized? What is the maximum possible markup on cost? Why?

5 What are the effective total discounts for each of the following chain discount quotations:
   a. 37, 10, 3, 3/10 net 30
   b. 30, 13, 2, 2/10 net 30
   c. 40, 5, 4, 3/15 net 30

6 A manufacturer quotes a chain discount of 37, 17, and 4 to his distributors. If we are told that the distributors' cost is $115, what is the list price?

7 If a manufacturer has total unit costs of $40 and if the manufacturer takes a markup of 50% of cost, the wholesaler takes a markup of 20% of his selling prices, and the retailer takes a markup of 40% of his selling prices, what is the retail price?

8 If an item costs a retailer $50 and he wishes to price the item with a markup of 40% of selling price, what price should he use?

9 If the cost of a stove to a retailer is $100 and the estimated expenses associated with the sale of the stove are 33% of selling price, what price is required in order to obtain a target margin of 7% before taxes?

10 Suppose that the cost of an item is $2. Suppose further that expenses are 15% of selling price, and that target profits are 10% of selling price. Determine (a) selling price, (b) the markup percentage on sales, (c) markup percentage on cost.

11 Using the product profitability problems discussed in the text as a guide, determine the most profitable product from the data below:

a. Product X

Beginning Inventory Requirements	$20,000 (at selling price)
Mature Inventory Requirements*	15,000 (at cost value)
Markup	40% (on selling prices)
Stock turnover (estimated)	7
Expenses (estimated)	15% (on selling prices)

b. Product Y

Beginning Inventory Requirements	$17,000 (at cost values)
Mature Inventory Requirements*	32,000 (at selling prices)
Markup	50% (on cost)
Stock turnover (estimated)	5
Expenses (estimated)	20% (on selling prices)

12 Assume the following data:
   a. Total cost at a volume of zero units, $12,000
   b. Total cost at a volume of 500 units, $20,000

*Assume that mature inventory requirements are reached at the end of the first year.

c. Total revenue at a sales volume of 1500 units, $45,000

Determine each of the following:

a. Selling price per unit
b. Variable cost per unit
c. Total fixed costs
d. Break-even point in units
e. Break-even point in dollars

13 If total fixed costs are $20,000 and variable costs are 80% of selling price, what is the dollar break-even point?

14 Can the unit break-even point be calculated in Problem 13 above? Why or why not?

15 If list price is $440, and a supplier quotes a chain discount of 30, 8, 3, 3/10, 30X, what is:

a. The invoice amount
b. The trade position discount amount
c. The quantity discount amount
d. The promotional discount amount
e. The cash discount amount
f. The proper remittance to the supplier if all discounts are taken?

SUGGESTED SUPPLEMENTARY READINGS IN PRICING

Albaum, Gerald, *Price Formulation,* Tucson: Division of Economic and Business Research, College of Business and Public Administration, University of Arizona, 1965.

Berry, J. L., *Geography of Marketing Centers and Retail Distribution.* Englewood Cliffs, N.J.: Prentice-Hall, Inc., 1967.

Dalrymple, Douglas J., *Merchandising Decision Models for Department Stores,* East Lansing, Mich.: Michigan State University Press, 1966.

Eiteman, Wilfred J., *Price Determination in Oligopolistic and Monopolistic Situations,* Michigan Business Reports No. 33, Ann Arbor: Bureau of Business Research, School of Business Administration, University of Michigan, 1960.

Fitzpatrick, Albert Arthur, *Pricing Methods of Industry,* Boulder, Colo.: Pruett Press, Inc., 1964.

Harper, Donald V., *Price Policy and Procedure,* New York: Harcourt, Brace and World, Inc., 1966.

Hollander, Stanley C., *Discount Selling, Retail Price Cutting and Resale Price Controls,* Chicago: American Marketing Association, 1956.

———, *Restraints Upon Retail Competition,* East Lansing, Mich.: Bureau of Business and Economic Research, School of Business Administration, Michigan State University.

———, *Retail Price Policies,* East Lansing, Mich.: Bureau of Business and Economic Research, School of Business Administration, Michigan State University.

King, Robert L., editor, *Conferences, '55/'65,* Chicago: American Marketing Association, 1966, pp. 85–86.

LaLonde, Bernard J., *Differentials in Supermarket Drawing Power,* East Lansing, Mich.: Michigan State University Press, 1962.

Lynn, Robert A., *Price Policies and Marketing Management,* Homewood, Ill.: Richard D. Irwin, Inc., 1967.

Nelson, Paul E., and Lee E. Preston, *Price Merchandising in Food Retailing: A Case Study,* Berkeley, Calif.: Institute of Business and Economic Research, University of California.

Oxenfeldt, Alfred R., *Pricing for Marketing Executives,* Belmont, Calif.: Wadsworth Publishing Company, Inc., 1961.

Stigler, George J., *The Theory of Price,* New York: Crowell-Collier and Macmillan, Inc., 1947. (This work represents a classic statement of price theory.)

Watson, Donald Stevenson, editor, *Price Theory in Action,* Boston: Houghton Mifflin Company, 1965.

Indexes

Author Index

Winick, C., 164
Wingate, J.W., 358
Woler, H., 270
Wolfe, H.D., 446
Wright, J.S., 321, 391

Zajonc, R.B., 438
Zaltman, G., 164
Zober, M., 272
Zubin, J., 272

Subject Index

Net potential audiences, 440
Newlywed stage, 176
Nondiscretionary pattern of allocation, 167
Noneconomic irrelevant appeals, 48
Nongoods services, 336
Nonprice competition, 302
Nonprobabilistic explanations of brand loyalty, 202
Nonresponse error, 269
Non-signer clause, 121
North-Hatt occupational prestige scale, 183

Observational survey, 257
Occupational profiles, cities, 196
Odd-even pricing, 503
One-step flow of influence, 219
Open-account credit, 513
Operations research, 274
Ophthalmographic equipment, 4
Opinion Research Corporation, 214
Opportunity proliferation, 296
Optimistic reorder strategy, 381
Order planning, 377
"Overprivileged" consumers, 198

Parking-fill patterns, 258
Partial obsolescence, 460
Payoff ratio, 301
Pedestrian counts, 258
Perception of risk, 208
Persuasion, 413
Pessimistic reorder strategy, 381
Photochronograph, 258
Physical distribution systems, 376, 385
Physical distribution trade-off effect, 386
Physical product, 309
Pilot of exploratory surveys, 255
Pipeline theory, 336
Place utility, 9

Planned-impulse buying, 466
Planned obsolescence, 34, 157, 460
Planned and unplanned purchases, 465
Playback audit, 447
PM's, 343
Point-of-purchase display, 111
Pooling, 388
Possession utility, 9
Post Office Department, 96
Post purchase dissonance, 438
Post-selection technique, 265
Power relationships, 338
"Pre" and "post" tests, 260
Preexperimental methods, 255, 260
Present oriented, 147
Pretesting, 263
Preticketing, 85
Price discrimination, 135
Price discrimination, defined, 125
Price fixing, 135
Price level, 474
Price lines, 493
Price perceptions, 499
Price-quality association, 500
Price reaction coefficient, 490
Price structure, 474
Pricing-target margins, 525
Pricing theory and imperfect information, 486
Pricing with opportunity cost, 482
Primary data, 255
Primary demand, 394
Principle of distributed effort, 421
Principle of incongruity or difference, 421
Principle of kitsch culture, 18
Principles of involvement, 422
Printer's Ink Statutes, 98
Probabilistic brand-switching matrix, 154
Probabilistic explanations of brand loyalty, 203
Probabilistic nonrandom sample, 253